AUSTRALIAN POLITICAL INSTITUTIONS

AUSTRALIAN
POLITICAL INSTITUTIONS

9

SINGLETON AITKIN JINKS WARHURST

Copyright © Pearson Education Australia (a division of Pearson Australia Group Pty Ltd) 2009
Pearson Education Australia
Unit 4, Level 3
14 Aquatic Drive
Frenchs Forest NSW 2086

www.pearsoned.com.au

The *Copyright Act 1968* of Australia allows a maximum of one chapter or 10% of this book, whichever is the greater, to be copied by any educational institution for its educational purposes provided that that educational institution (or the body that administers it) has given a remuneration notice to Copyright Agency Limited (CAL) under the Act. For details of the CAL licence for educational institutions contact: Copyright Agency Limited, telephone: (02) 9394 7600, email: info@copyright.com.au

All rights reserved. Except under the conditions described in the *Copyright Act 1968* of Australia and subsequent amendments, no part of this publication may be reproduced, stored in a retrieval system or transmitted in any form or by any means, electronic, mechanical, photocopying, recording or otherwise, without the prior permission of the copyright owner.

Senior Acquisitions Editor: Karen Hutchings
Acquisitions Editor: Joanne Stanley
Project Editors: Bernadette Chang and Kathryn Munro
Associate Editor: Imogen Smith
Production Coordinator: Barbara Honor
Copy Editor: Emma Driver
Proofreader: Robyn Flemming
Copyright and Pictures Editor: Emma Gaulton
Indexer: Lisa Knowles
Cover design by Natalie Bowra
Cover photograph from iStockphoto
Typeset by Laserwords Private Limited, India

Printed in China (SWTC/05)

5 13 12 11

National Library of Australia
Cataloguing-in-Publication Data

Author:	Singleton, Gwynneth, 1943-
Title:	Australian political institutions / Singleton ... [et al.]
Edition:	9th ed.
ISBN:	9781442504080 (pbk.)
Notes:	Includes index.
Subjects:	Australia. Parliament.
	Constitutional law — Australia.
	Australia — Politics and government.

Dewey Number: 320.0994

Every effort has been made to trace and acknowledge copyright. However, should any infringement have occurred, the publishers tender their apologies and invite copyright owners to contact them.

An imprint of Pearson Education Australia
(a division of Pearson Australia Group Pty Ltd)

CONTENTS

Preface to the first edition — xi
Preface to the ninth edition — xiii
About the authors — xv
Acknowledgments — xvii

CHAPTER 1 Politics and democracy — 1

Why study politics? — 2
What is politics? — 3
The state and society — 5
Political ideologies and the state — 6
Representative and responsible government — 7
Comparative analysis of modern liberal democracies — 11
An institutional approach to understanding the Australian political system — 12
Questions for discussion — 13
Further reading — 14
Useful websites — 14

CHAPTER 2 The political culture of Australia's political institutions — 17

The institutions of Australia's system of government — 18
Politics and the economy — 26
Pressures for change — 28
Political culture from a comparative perspective — 34
Questions for discussion — 41
Further reading — 41
Useful websites — 41

CHAPTER 3 The Australian Constitution — 43

The function of a constitution — 44
The Australian Constitution: the path to federation — 46

The making of the Australian Constitution	49
Provisions of the Constitution	54
Influences on the Constitution since federation	63
Judicial interpretation: the High Court	64
Cooperation between governments	71
Formal amendment of the Constitution	72
Constitutional reform and the political agenda	78
The republic and constitutional change	80
Questions for discussion	85
Further reading	85
Useful websites	86

CHAPTER 4 The federal system 87

The principles of federalism	88
Reasons for choosing a federal system	90
The role of the states in the Australian federal system	94
The role of the Commonwealth	100
The territories	103
Local government	106
The politics of Australian federalism	109
Federalism and 'efficiency'	112
Federalism and policy making	113
Federalism and responsible government	117
Political parties and federalism	119
Financial control by the Commonwealth	121
The future of Australian federalism	130
Questions for discussion	132
Further reading	132
Useful websites	133

CHAPTER 5 The Australian Parliament 135

Origins of parliament	136
Parliament and the modern state	137
Functions of parliament	141
Problems with parliamentary government	143
Australia's parliamentary system	146
The Australian parliament	147
Parliament House	149
The representative function of members of the Australian parliament	151
Procedures in the House of Representatives	152
The legislating function	156

The Senate and money bills	162
Investigating expenditure function	163
The 'scrutiny' function of parliament	164
The Senate as a house of review	171
Questions for discussion	176
Further reading	176
Useful websites	177

CHAPTER 6 Executive government: cabinet and prime minister — 179

The executive	180
Cabinet	182
The prime minister	186
Government in Australia	188
Selection of ministers and cabinet	193
Ministers' careers	195
Ministerial office	198
Ministers, cabinet and Westminster conventions	201
The power of the prime minister	212
Desirable qualities of a prime minister	219
Questions for discussion	222
Further reading	222
Useful websites	223

CHAPTER 7 The public service — 225

Public administration and bureaucracy	226
The origins of modern bureaucracy	231
Bureaucracy in the modern state	233
The development of public administration and bureaucracy in Australia	237
The Australian Public Service (APS)	241
Staffing the APS	248
Financing the APS	254
Treasury and economic management	254
Policy and administration	255
The policy process: coordination and control	258
Accountability and administrative review	260
Non-departmental organisations	265
Questions for discussion	267
Further reading	267
Useful websites	268

CHAPTER 8 Elections and voting behaviour — 271

- The importance of elections — 272
- Types of electoral systems — 275
- The Australian electoral system — 280
- The development of the Commonwealth electoral system — 287
- Redistributions — 289
- 'Fairness' — 291
- Public funding and disclosure — 292
- Electronic voting (e-voting) — 293
- Voting behaviour — 294
- A note on voting methods: counting the votes — 304
- Questions for discussion — 310
- Further reading — 310
- Useful websites — 311

CHAPTER 9 Political parties and party systems — 313

- The nature of political parties — 314
- Ideology — 317
- Organisation — 319
- Policy making — 321
- Party discipline — 322
- Party systems — 323
- The party system in Australia — 327
- Australia's two-party system in retrospect — 337
- Changes to the Australian party system — 339
- Questions for discussion — 341
- Further reading — 342
- Useful websites — 343

CHAPTER 10 Australia's major parties — 345

- The Australian Labor Party — 346
- The Liberal Party of Australia — 356
- Policy differentiation in the 'catch-all' context — 365
- Questions for discussion — 368
- Further reading — 368
- Useful websites — 369

CHAPTER 11 Minor parties and independents in Australia — 371

- Minor parties — 372
- Minor parties with representation in Australian parliaments — 376
- Significant minor parties not represented in Australian parliaments — 390

Independents in the Australian parliament	396
Questions for discussion	401
Further reading	401
Useful websites	402

CHAPTER 12 Interest groups — 405

Why are interest groups important?	406
What is an interest group?	406
Types of interest groups	407
Interest group strategies	409
Groups and government	412
Insiders and outsiders	416
Policy networks	420
Social movements	422
Groups and democracy	425
Questions for discussion	426
Further reading	426
Useful websites	427

CHAPTER 13 Political communication — 429

The mass media	431
Politics in the Australian media	437
The parliamentary press gallery	441
Political advertising	443
Political polling	445
Technology and political communication	447
E-government	452
E-democracy	454
Questions for discussion	455
Further reading	455
Useful websites	457

Appendix: The Australian Constitution	459
Index	483

PREFACE TO THE FIRST EDITION

This book is intended to do several things:

- It sets out the essential facts about the main institutions of Australian politics and government.
- It provides enough history to place the political institutions in perspective.
- It summarises many of the talking points surrounding political institutions. (Are ministers 'responsible' to parliament? How different are the Liberal and Labor parties?)
- It indicates the main problems and possible changes in the processes of government.

We thought of writing this book because we found most texts on Australian politics either too sketchy or too detailed. The sketchy ones need supplementary reading lists to fill them out; the detailed ones, too, take up class time in organising their material and summarising their arguments.

The teaching problem is obvious: too much basic instruction and part of the class dozes off; too much assumed knowledge and the rest of the class is lost. We have tried to strike a balance. Students should use this book to complete their basic study and leave class time for analysis and argument. General readers will be able to fill in gaps in their knowledge.

The need, then, is to provide a maximum of information as briefly as possible. We have tried to do this by moving away from the practice, common in senior and tertiary books, of presenting chapter after chapter of long paragraphs and unbroken text. We have arranged the material under numerous headings and subheadings and have displayed sets of facts, as well as points for discussion, in a layout designed to catch the eye. This is not intended as a treatise, but as a book for learning and teaching.

We have often been asked: Why bother about books (or school or university courses, for that matter) on political institutions? Should people not concern themselves with the great issues of the day—the plight of Aborigines and other minorities, unemployment, 'big' government? Of course they should. But if these issues are to be dealt with effectively, Australians need to know about the machinery of government which is expected to tackle them. Most Australians learn little of their nation's politics and political history at school. There have been some steps forward in recent years, notably in Victoria, but it will be some time before most of those gaining the vote have much idea of what that means. In the meantime, the bombast, empty rhetoric and search for scapegoats that so often pass for political debate in this country will usually go unchallenged.

However, what if one sees the vote as a useless symbol? If the political rituals of Western capitalism seem to be disguising inequality and repression, why bother with it at all? Well, revolutionaries have often been the most careful students of the systems they have sought to topple. For the reformers, an intelligent discussion of how things might be improved is impossible in the absence of knowledge about the way the system actually works and why it works that way. As for conservatives—it would be nice to think they know what they are defending.

We thank the many politics students at Macquarie University who have made all kinds of constructive criticism over the years. Allie Buckby and Cathy Charlton provided reams of clean typing. Complaints and suggestions should be directed to us.

Don Aitkin

Brian Jinks
Sydney 1979

PREFACE TO THE NINTH EDITION

The ninth edition of *Australian Political Institutions* is a political text designed primarily for first-year university students who have limited knowledge of the Australian federal political system. The aim is to provide students with an information base about the structure and organisation of Australia's federal political institutions, together with a basic understanding of key issues that arise from their operation.

This concept was begun by the original authors, Don Aitkin and Brian Jinks, and has been maintained through all editions of the book.

This edition takes a new direction by introducing a comparative approach not used previously. Examples from Britain, the USA, Germany and Malaysia illustrate how the essential elements of a liberal democracy, such as constitutions, legislatures, executive government, electoral systems and political parties, have been formulated, or are operated, in different ways from the Australian system. Britain and the USA are important because of the influence of their respective systems on the structure and operation of the Australian political system. Germany and Malaysia were chosen because they are both federal systems, but with different political cultures that have impacted on the way they operate.

There is also greater emphasis on introducing students to theoretical concepts related to the study of politics and political institutions, and these are explained in a straightforward way. Chapter 1, for example, includes discussion about state and society and significant political ideologies that have defined ideas about the authority of the state over its citizens, and an explanation of the principles of liberal democracy, including representative and responsible government. Chapter 8 on the electoral system includes a section on voting behaviour and Chapter 9 contains a theoretical explanation about the nature and classification of parties, and the significant ideologies that underpin their beliefs and ideas.

Any political system is subject to continuing change, which makes any textbook such as this a snapshot in time. For this reason, website addresses have been provided where appropriate to enable students to research up-to-the-minute information.

Gwynneth Singleton
Adjunct Associate Professor in Politics, University of Canberra, 2008

ABOUT THE AUTHORS

Dr Gwynneth Singleton is Adjunct Associate Professor in Politics, University of Canberra. She is the editor of several books on Australian politics, including *The Howard Government: Australian Government Administration 1996–1998* (University of New South Wales Press, Sydney), and most recently author of 'The Senate a Paper Tiger?', in C. Aulich and R. Wettenhall (eds), *Howard's Fourth Government: Australian Commonwealth Administration 2004–2007* (University of New South Wales Press,  Sydney, 2008) and 'Jon Stanhope—What You See is What You Get', in J. Wanna and P. Williams (eds), *Yes, Premier: Labor Leaders in Australia's States and Territories* (University of New South Wales Press, Sydney, 2005).

Don Aitkin is Emeritus Professor, University of Canberra.

Brian Jinks is a former Senior Lecturer in Management at Macquarie University.

John Warhurst is the Professor of Political Science, Faculty of Arts, Australian National University, specialising in the study of interest groups, political parties, political lobbying and elections.

ACKNOWLEDGMENTS

The authors and publisher would like to thank the following academics for their invaluable feedback and suggestions during the development of the current and previous editions: Jeff Archer, University of New England; Robyn Hollander, Griffith University; Doug Hunt, James Cook University; Robert Imre, University of Notre Dame; Ros Irwin, Southern Cross University; Andrew Jakubowicz, University of Technology, Sydney; Jim Jose, University of Newcastle; Greg Melleuish, University of Wollongong; Penny Rossiter, University of Western Sydney; Harry Savelsberg, University of South Australia; Ariadne Vromen, University of Sydney; Ian Ward and Rae Wear, University of Queensland; Virginia Watson, University of Technology, Sydney; Suzanne Mutton, University of South Australia; Peter Gale, University of South Australia.

POLITICS AND DEMOCRACY

THIS CHAPTER EXPLAINS:

- why it is important to study politics, and its significance for understanding how government works;
- what is politics?
- politics and power in a political system;
- the state and society;
- political ideologies and the state;
- representative and responsible government;
- a comparative analysis of modern liberal democracies; and
- why this book uses an institutional approach to understand the Australian political system.

WHY STUDY POLITICS?

People today lead busy lives. Many have to manage the pressures of work, family responsibilities, study and leisure time. Sitting in front of the television is a popular form of light entertainment, but many students do not watch serious current affairs or news programs on a regular basis, nor do they read newspapers or listen to radio current affairs, apart from the short news bulletins on the hour that interrupt the flow of music. For many, the computer has become their access point for entertainment, news and political dialogue, including websites such as YouTube, MySpace and other chat rooms. Even so, political interest may be awakened only when something sensational occurs, such as an economic crisis, a scandal associated with a ministerial sacking, debate about whether Australia should become a republic, or an occasion such as the one that occurred in February 2008, when the Australian parliament supported a motion moved by the Rudd government to say 'sorry' for the hurt occasioned Australia's Indigenous people by the removal of their children in the past.

We mainly think of our own political activity in terms of electing a new government. This is important, but our participation in the political system as individuals and citizens is more widespread and constant than the act of voting for members of parliament.

As individuals we have a range of interests and activities that bring us into contact with the world of politics on a regular basis, either directly or indirectly. For example, people's increasing concern about the effects of climate change has raised political awareness about the issue and generated debate about what citizens and governments should do to alleviate the problem. Many people belong to sporting clubs, and the act of voting for club office-bearers constitutes political activity within the organisation. Members of the club participate indirectly in the political system when that executive acts on their behalf to acquire better facilities or funding from government. Many students attending university belong to the student union. Some may participate directly in elections for student representatives on the union, either as candidates or as electors. Indirect participation in the political system occurs when the student union negotiates on behalf of its collective membership with government on issues such as student fees or government funding for universities.

Political decisions affect our daily lives in many ways. For example, pay and conditions at the workplace are protected by government industrial relations laws. The safety standards of the car you drive are regulated by government. The fees and charges you pay for university study are affected by government policy. The taxes you pay on your income or through the purchase of goods and services, such as petrol, alcohol and cosmetics, or the charges to transfer ownership of a block of land, are determined by the level of government that has responsibility for the particular issue.

The political role of a student union

'Currently, the Federal Government is responsible for overseeing the development and structure of the higher education sector in this country. Through government legislation and policy things like funding and student fees are determined.

The UQ union, through the National Union of Students, strives to ensure that decision-makers in Federal government give consideration to the student perspective.'

(*Source*: University of Queensland Student Union n.d., 'About Your Union', http://www.uqu.uq.edu.au)

> **The Australian government introduces a new tax system**
> In July 2000, the Howard government implemented 'A New Tax System' incorporating changes to income tax rates and the introduction of a 10 per cent tax on goods and services (GST).

It is in our best interests as individuals, and our responsibility as citizens, to know how the Australian political system works, and to do this we need to understand the political process that drives it. This means we need to know about politics and the role it plays in determining a system of government and making it work. In Australia we are governed by a system commonly called a liberal democracy. What does this mean and how does it work? What are the alternatives? How does our system compare with other liberal democratic states?

WHAT IS POLITICS?

> **Politics** has been explained as
> - the process of deciding who gets what, when and how.
> (Source: Lasswell, H.D. 1936, *Politics: Who Gets What, When, How*, McGraw-Hill, New York)
> - 'the use of power to reconcile conflicts over the distribution of goods and values . . . typically done through the institutions of government'.
> (Source: Isaak, A.C. 1981, *Scope and Methods of Political Science*, The Dorsey Press, Homewood, Illinois, p. 23)

A political system creates the framework within which the competing demands of individuals can be resolved in a harmonious and peaceful manner. Without such a system, people are more likely to resort to violence and aggression to sort out their differences, or, as the political philosopher Thomas Hobbes famously wrote in his treatise, *The Leviathan*:

> during the time men live without a common power to keep them all in awe, they are in that condition which is called war; and such a war, as is of every man, against every man ... and which is worst of all, continual fear, and danger of violent death; and the life of man, solitary, poor, nasty, brutish and short.
> (Source: Cited by Parker, N. 1985, 'Hobbes: *The Leviathan*', in Held, D. et al (eds), *State and Societies*, 2nd ed., Blackwell, Oxford, pp. 68–9)

The situation that Hobbes described in 1651 is no different today. As a society we look to the political system and its rules and regulations to provide a secure framework for our lives, and to help resolve the conflicts that arise from time to time. As individuals we have a broad range of interests related to our activities at home, work and play. Our neighbours, friends and colleagues at work, similarly, have their own sets of interests. The problem arises when those interests come into conflict. For example, some of us want money spent on sealing the road that goes past our house, but others want the available money spent in their own neighbourhood. Some people want the government to spend more money on health and education, but others in the community think that is the responsibility of the individual. Some businesses want the government to give them financial assistance, other businesses want the money spent on their industries, while others do not think it is the responsibility of government to fund private business activity at all. Some people might be happy to pay extra taxes to the government to fund a comprehensive welfare system and public education, but their friends would rather keep the money and spend it according to their own needs. No one wants to pay large amounts of tax, which means that there are limited resources available to government and not everybody's demands can be met.

So, how does society go about resolving these differences? How do we decide how the scarce resources available to government will be allocated? This is the function of the political system, and of the power allocated to governments within that system to make laws for the whole community.

Politics and power

> 'Max Weber argues that "politics" means striving to share power or striving to influence the distribution of power, either among states or among groups within a state.'
> (Source: Isaak, C.A. 1981, *Scope and Methods of Political Science*, The Dorsey Press, Homewood, Illinois, p. 18)

Political power, according to Lasswell as we saw above, is a significant factor in determining who gets what, when and how in any political system. In simple terms, the use of power is the exercise of control by one person over another, or by governments taking decisions that are binding on the citizens of the state. This includes the capacity not to make decisions—in other words, the determination not to proceed with a certain policy or activity. Power is also exercised by those who influence the decision-takers in government. This includes groups or individuals who lobby governments successfully, or who are consulted by governments and, as a result, have a substantive say in government policy. The influence of interest groups is explained in Chapter 12.

> **Four types of political power**
> - *Coercion*: control of citizens by force or the threat of force.
> - *Authority*: the right of designated persons and institutions to make and implement decisions.
> - *Influence*: the exercise of direct or indirect influence over the decision-takers in government.
> - *Manipulation*: shaping the political opinions, values and behaviour of others without them being aware of it.
>
> (Source: Birch, A.H. 1993, *The Concepts and Theories of Modern Democracy*, Routledge, London, pp. 139–40)

Political power in a community can be wielded in different ways. In feudal societies, the monarch and the aristocracy reign supreme. In tribal societies, the tribal chieftains make the rules. In most contemporary societies, political authority lies with the state—with governments that make and implement the laws for the political communities for which they are responsible.

THE STATE AND SOCIETY

The contemporary world is divided into states. These states have the power to make laws that structure the way we live.

> A **state** is a legal entity possessing sovereign independence, having unfettered control over its own territory, defining its own citizenship rules and equal in international law to all other states. Seen from the inside, a state manifests itself in a collection of public institutions, legislative, executive, administrative and judicial having the power to govern the territory and all its inhabitants.
> (*Source*: Birch, A.H. 1993, *The Concepts and Theories of Modern Democracy*, Routledge, London, p. 14)

The definition of a sovereign state outlined by Birch should not be confused with territorial sub-governments that in Australia and the United States are called 'states', or in other countries such as Canada where they are called 'provinces'. (We will examine the relationship between Australia's central government and sub-governments in Chapter 4.)

States run their own affairs through a system of government that manages society with laws and regulations. For example, the government can levy taxes and determine how that money is spent. It can decide to go to war.

> **The power of the Australian government to make decisions on behalf of the people**
> 'The Government has decided to commit Australian forces to action to disarm Iraq because we believe it is right, it is lawful and it's in Australia's national interest.'
> (Source: Prime Minister John Howard 2003, 'Address to the Nation', 20 March 2003, transcript: http://australianpolitics.com/news/2003/03/03-03-20c.shtml)

> **Authority** is the exercise of power by a government that is deemed legitimate by the citizens of the state; in other words, citizens accept that the government has the legitimate power to make decisions on their behalf and they agree to be bound by those decisions.

Except in those instances where the state is controlled by a coercive administration using fear, intimidation or military power, the authority for the government to make the rules comes from the consent of its citizens. This imparts legitimacy to the laws the government makes.

> 'A government must have the consent of its citizens, based on legitimacy, in order to resolve social conflicts, to defend the territory against external enemies, and to maintain essential services for its citizens. Without legitimacy, it has to use coercion to maintain its authority.'
> (*Source*: Jackson, R.J. & Jackson, D. 1997, *Comparative Government: An Introduction to Political Science*, 2nd ed., Prentice Hall/Allyn & Bacon, Toronto, p. 13)

The type of government and the institutions that support it can vary between states. How the political system and its institutional framework is structured, and the relationship between its different elements, is a function of political ideology.

POLITICAL IDEOLOGIES AND THE STATE

> An **ideology** 'is concerned with ideas, values and principles which guide the political behaviour of the people who believe in that ideology'.
> (*Source*: Jaensch, D. 1997, *The Politics of Australia*, 2nd ed., Macmillan Education, Melbourne, p. 31)
>
> '**Ideologies** are belief systems which help to structure how the world is understood and explained. **Political ideologies** are sets of ideas which provide the basis for some kind of political action.'
> (*Source*: Heywood, A. 1992, *Political Ideologies: An Introduction*, Macmillan, London, p. 2)

Political ideologies influence the way power is distributed and exercised in a political system.

> 'What is the relationship between state and society? What is the most desirable form this relationship might take? What does and should the state do? Whose interests does and should the state represent?'
> (*Source*: Held, D. 1985, 'Introduction: Central Perspectives on the Modern State', in Held, D. et al (eds), *States and Societies*, Basil Blackwell/The Open University, Oxford, p. 2)

There are different ideas about what authority the state should have over its citizens, and what the state and its institutions should do as part of that process. Political ideology has played a significant role in trying to find a solution to these issues. Political philosopher Thomas Hobbes, as we saw above, was concerned that without some form of political authority, anarchy would prevail, that is, there would be no law and order to control the actions of citizens. It was his view that the answer lay with people surrendering their rights to a single authority with absolute power, 'an all-powerful Leviathan'. This view has been associated with absolute control by a monarchy.

> **Absolute monarchy** is a despotic political system in which power is concentrated in the hands of a monarchy that controls the institutions of government and the law, and determines policy. Power may be transferred from one group to another by hereditary succession, a palace coup undertaken by a group seeking to wrest power from the incumbents, or a war between contending rivals. Contemporary examples can be found in some Arab Gulf states such as Saudi Arabia.

We can also find the practical political expression of these ideas in authoritarian regimes. However, these regimes normally do not exist with the consent of the people. They are more likely to be imposed upon the citizens through violence and force.

> **Authoritarianism** is characterised by a strong central authority that demands obedience from the people and permits no dissent from government policy and decisions. Opposition parties (where they exist) and dissidents are suppressed, usually with violence. North Korea is a contemporary example of an authoritarian state.

Communist regimes started life from the perspective that power should reside with the people, but developed into authoritarian forms of government. Communist ideology, based on political ideology espoused by Karl Marx, takes the view that conflict in society stems from the different and competing interests of the capitalist and working classes. The bourgeoisie—that is, the capitalists who control the means of production—exploit the proletariat, or working class, whose labour is used to produce the goods. According to Marx, the way to resolve this problem was through a socialist revolution to replace state authority (the state is considered to act as the agent of capital) with a political system based on collective decision making controlled by the people themselves.

> The four basic elements of Marxist ideology can be summarised as follows:
> 1. Capitalism is unjust and doomed.
> 2. Capitalism has internal contradictions which provide economic depression.
> 3. Capitalism should be abolished and replaced with the collective ownership of the means of production.
> 4. The Communist Party, the instrument of the working class, will provide the means to carry out the overthrow of capitalism, which will lead to the new society and the withering away of the state.
>
> (Source: Jackson, R.J. & Jackson, D. 1997, *Comparative Government: An Introduction to Political Science*, 2nd ed., Prentice Hall/Allyn & Bacon, Toronto, p. 174)

This conception of collective authority, however, was corrupted in its implementation by the political leadership of communist parties, such as in the former Soviet Union. In this case, the party took control of the political system and its institutions and the people they governed, repressing dissent with state-sanctioned violence.

REPRESENTATIVE AND RESPONSIBLE GOVERNMENT

Political philosopher John Locke (1632–1704) considered a supreme authority necessary to prevent anarchy in society, but it was his view that the authority delegated to this body should be limited to the preservation of 'life, liberty and estate (property)', and that the governing body had to be subordinate to the people.

> According to Locke, 'the state exists to safeguard the rights and liberties of citizens who are ultimately the best judges of their own interests; and … accordingly the state must be restricted in scope and constrained in practice in order to ensure the maximum possible freedom of every citizen'.
> (Source: Held, D. 1985, 'Introduction: Central Perspectives on the Modern State', in Held, D. et al (eds), *States and Societies*, Basil Blackwell/The Open University, Oxford, p. 13)

Locke's view that sovereignty must remain with the people provides the foundation for the system of liberal democracy that Australia and many other states have adopted as their preferred form of government. Indeed, many citizens in countries with restrictive political systems strive to achieve a democratic form of government, at the expense sometimes of their liberty or their lives.

Principles of democracy

Democracy is regularly defined as 'government by the people'. It incorporates the concepts of popular participation and majority control of the political agenda and policy process. In a democracy, power and authority rest with the citizens, rather than a ruling elite.

> **Democracy** is characterised by the following institutions:
> - a constitution which limits the powers and defines the formal operation of government;
> - free and fair elections of public officials;
> - the right to vote and stand for election;
> - a free press;
> - freedom of association and freedom of speech; and
> - equality before the law.
>
> (*Sources*: For discussion on the elements of democracy see, for example, Tansey, S.D. 1995, *Politics: The Basics*, Routledge, London; or Birch, A.H. 2001, *The Concepts and Theories of Modern Democracy*, 2nd ed., Routledge, London.)
>
> Democracy relies on basic principles in order to operate effectively:
> - 'the right of equality of participation;
> - the principle of "majority rule";
> - the concepts of "minority rights", representation, responsibility; and
> - the rule of law'.
>
> (*Source*: Jaensch, D. 1994, *Parliament, Parties and People*, 2nd ed., Longman Cheshire, Melbourne, pp. 14–15)

The term *democracy* comes from the Greek *demos*, meaning citizens, and *kratos*, power or rule. Athenian citizens came together to debate and vote on the laws to regulate and administer their state, and the Athenian system of citizen participation in the decision-making process is widely regarded as an example of direct democracy.

> **Direct democracy** is the direct participation of each citizen in decision-making.

The principle of majority rule derives from the need to reach agreement on what is to be done. If it did not apply, it would be impossible to make laws for society as a whole. The question of what constitutes a majority may vary according to the particular system in place. For example, laws might be decided on a majority vote of 50 per cent plus 1, or a two-thirds majority might be required to pass a resolution. Regardless of how the majority is determined, it means there is a minority of citizens who disagreed with the policy or law that is introduced, and whose interests are not being met. Under a democratic system, these people would accept the majority verdict.

> A referendum was held in 1999 to determine whether Australia would become a republic. The referendum required a majority of electors plus a majority of states to pass, but those requirements were not met and the resolution failed. Those in favour of the republic accepted the fact that the majority decision had gone against them.

Practical difficulties in operating a system that involves the direct personal participation by each citizen in the decision-making process mean that most democracies operate as a form of representative democracy, where citizens elect some of their number to take decisions on their behalf. Even the Athenian system incorporated elements of representative democracy. Only male citizens over 20 years of age could participate, which meant in practical terms that they took decisions on behalf of the rest of the population, including men who did not qualify, women and slaves. There were also representative institutions, in the form of an elected council of 500 with the responsibility for organising and proposing public decisions, and an elected committee of 50 to advise the council.

> **Representative democracy**
> The basis of democracy is the notion that power and authority is vested in the people. A common definition of democracy is 'government by the people for the people'. Each citizen has the right to vote for representatives in parliament in regular and fair elections. Governments are formed by a majority of those who hold seats in the parliament. That majority may be made up of members of a particular political party, a coalition of two or more political parties, or a combination of political parties and independent members not aligned to any particular party.

There have been criticisms that representative democracy cannot function effectively as government by the people, because the representatives form an elite group which citizens may not be able to influence. Also, minority interests may be ignored by the governing majority. These problems are overcome to some extent by the concept of responsible government, which functions as a derivative of representative democracy in that those who are elected to make the decisions are responsible and accountable to the electors for their actions.

> '**Responsible government** is the term used to describe a political system where the executive government, the Cabinet and Ministry, is drawn from, and is accountable to, the legislative branch.'
> (Source: australianpolitics.com 2008, 'Key Terms: Responsible Government', http://australianpolitics.com/democracy/terms/responsible-government.shtml)

This takes a practical form when the elected representatives have to satisfy the electors that they have done a good job in representing their interests in order to be re-elected. For example, Australian governments are judged on their record in office when seeking re-election. Sometimes, as with the Howard government in 2004, they are returned, but on other occasions the judgement will go against the party in power and the Opposition will win the election, as occurred in 2007.

The rule of law

> 'The **rule of law** means that everyone, including government, has to obey or be subject to the law. It means that people know what the law is, or at least can find out. It means that law is applied by courts, which are independent from outside influence, including government.'
> (*Source*: Saunders, C. 1998, *It's Your Constitution*, The Federation Press, Sydney, p. 126)

The principle of the rule of law means that every citizen is subject to the laws enacted by government. The concept also embodies the notion that citizens must accept the legitimacy of the laws passed by the legislature and agree to abide by them. It protects citizens from the abuse of power by those in government, who are also bound to work within the rules and laws of the country.

Liberal democracy

> 'A **liberal democracy** is a political system in which *democratically* based institutions of governance exist alongside *liberal* conceptions about the rights of individuals and about market-based mechanisms for economic production and distribution.'
> (*Source*: Parkin, A. 2002, 'Liberal Democracy', in Summers, J., Woodward, D. & Parkin, A. (eds), *Government, Politics, Power and Policy in Australia*, 7th ed., Longman, Sydney, p. 297)

Citizens' rights need to be entrenched in order to prevent a system of representative democracy deteriorating into a form of elite domination. This can be achieved by incorporating the principles of liberalism within the rules or constitution of the political system.

There are two strands of thought identified with the principles of liberal democracy: the democratic right of citizens to participate in the governing process and their responsibilities to work within that system, plus the need to protect the individual rights of the citizen from abuse of power by the state. Liberalism encompasses notions about the separation of powers within a state so that no one person or group becomes too powerful. It is associated with concepts of the predominant rights of the individual, minimal government, and a market economy free from government intervention and regulation. It is possible, however, to find societies that meet the political conditions of a liberal democracy, but might fall short of the ideal of a free market economy. For example, some countries adopt liberal democratic principles as the basis for their systems of government, yet maintain a protected and regulated economic system.

The rules that determine the relationship between the citizen and the state and the institutions of government are usually defined within a constitution. The constitution serves to protect the democratic rights of the citizens by limiting the scope of government. It also establishes the institutional framework within which the political system will operate—in particular, the type of legislature and its functions, the powers of the state and the role of the judiciary.

> A **constitution** is a 'set of rules that allocates duties, powers and functions to the various institutions of government and defines the relationship between individuals and the state'.
> (*Source*: Heywood, A. 1994, *Political Ideas and Concepts: An Introduction*, Macmillan, Basingstoke, UK, p. 97)

COMPARATIVE ANALYSIS OF MODERN LIBERAL DEMOCRACIES

The purpose of this book is to provide you with an understanding of the structures and functions of the Australian liberal democratic political system. As citizens we may assume that our form of government is the 'natural' way of constructing a liberal democracy. However, we will also illustrate throughout the text how some other countries have gone about establishing their own forms of liberal democratic government, using a similar institutional framework of a constitution, a legislature, an executive, a judiciary and an electoral process whereby citizens elect their representatives.

> '**Comparative politics** involves the systematic study and comparison of the world's political systems. It seeks to explain differences between as well as similarities among countries. It is particularly interested in exploring patterns, processes and regularities among political systems.'
> (*Source*: Wiarda, H.J. 1993, *Introduction to Comparative Politics: Concepts and Processes*, Wadsworth Publishing Company, Belmont, California, p. 12)

Why would we want to make this comparison? Identifying similarities and differences in the political systems of other countries that have been identified as liberal democracies will provide you with an understanding of the variety of ways in which this type of political system can be structured, how it can function, and the power relationships between state and society that develop from those frameworks and processes.

> 'Widespread public knowledge about one's own government and those of foreign countries is an important aspect of the democratic ethos.'
> (*Source*: Jackson, R.J. & Jackson, D. 1997, *Comparative Government: An Introduction to Political Science*, 2nd ed., Prentice Hall/Allyn & Bacon, Toronto, p. 71)

This will not only help you gain a practical perspective on how the principles of liberal democracy operate, it will also provide the basis for you to compare these experiences with the Australian political system, and to think about whether there are things that we could do better. For example, as you will see from Chapter 8, there are two different types of electoral systems used to elect the Australian House of Representatives and the Senate. Other countries, such as the United States and Germany, elect their parliaments using different systems. Can we learn anything from this that will improve our own electoral system?

> 'The fact that there are regularities among political systems hints that there are limits to change. That political systems differ argues that there are opportunities for change.'
> (*Source*: Dahl, R.A. 1984, *Modern Political Analysis*, 4th ed., Prentice Hall, Upper Saddle River, New Jersey, p. 62)

As we work our way through the various elements of the Australian political system discussed in this book, we will be providing examples of the British political system because, as you will see in Chapter 3, this was the system, commonly called the 'Westminster system', that the people who drafted the Australian Constitution used as a model for our organisational and political form of responsible government. We will also be looking at the American system of government because, as you will see from Chapter 4, the founding fathers of the Australian Constitution looked to America's federal structure as a model for the development of Australian federalism. It is also interesting because the institutional framework of the executive and the legislature, and the relationship between them, is constructed differently from the Australian system. The German system of government will be examined because it is also federal in nature; unlike Australia, however, it has a multi-party system of government. These countries are functioning liberal democracies, but there are variations in the way they manage the political process to try to achieve that objective. We will also be using examples from Malaysia, which has a constitution that constructs that country's political institutions in a similar way to Australia's. It is also a federal system. There are, however, significant differences in the political culture and processes through which this system operates.

We should bear in mind, however, that there are limitations to using comparative examples from different countries to draw generalised conclusions about matters such as how a constitution should be formatted, or whether there should be one or two houses of parliament. Each country has its own political and social culture that has contributed to its political system and the institutions that support it. The historical background of Australia as a former colony of Britain is different, for example, to the development of post-war Germany or the establishment of a communist state in China.

There are other issues we should be aware of. It may not always be easy to obtain the information we need to examine a society where political information is not freely available. A language barrier may create problems for researchers in gaining access to information on a particular country, so they have to rely on what others have written and the potential bias that might impart to the findings. The questions that are asked, and how they are structured, may also influence the outcomes of research and analysis. The political institutions and processes in one country may be underpinned by a set of norms or conventions that are not written down, such as the conventions derived from the Westminster system that support the Australian system of responsible government, while others have a formal, legal constitution. Do political practices that are particular to one country make it difficult to draw generalisations or to develop a set of common principles about what should constitute a system of liberal democracy? Or do they reveal the richness and diversity in how these theoretical principles have been adapted to suit the needs of a particular state? We need to keep these issues in mind when we are looking at how other countries have developed their constitutions, their legislatures, their judicial systems and their electoral systems.

AN INSTITUTIONAL APPROACH TO UNDERSTANDING THE AUSTRALIAN POLITICAL SYSTEM

'Institutions are important because they *shape* or *influence* the behaviour, power and policy preferences of political actors.'
(Source: Bell, S. 2002, 'Institutionalism', in Summers, J., Woodward, D. & Parkin, A., *Government, Politics, Power and Policy in Australia*, 7th ed., Longman, Sydney, p. 365)

The formal allocation of power within a political system can be established by examining the political institutions of a state and the way in which they operate. However, such an approach, if it is purely descriptive, does not adequately inform us where the real power lies within society. As we have seen above, many states have political institutions with the same names—constitutions, legislatures, and so on—but the fact of their establishment does not give us any indication of the nature of the power relationship between the state and society. The locus of political power can only be ascertained by analysing the relationships between political institutions and the citizens they have been set up to serve: in other words, by making an assessment about whether their functions support the principles of responsible government.

The purpose of this text is to provide students with an understanding of the institutional basis of Australian federal government in the context of Australia as a liberal democracy. The formal institutions of government established within the Australian Constitution are the core functionaries in the operations of the Commonwealth government. These include the governor-general, the judiciary, the legislature (or parliament), and the executive (including the prime minister and cabinet, and the bureaucracy that supports them).

In the following chapters, we will first look at the history and political culture that underpins this institutional framework so that we can understand how and why the system exists in its current form. We will then examine the way in which each of these institutions is structured and operates in the context of the principles of responsible government.

In Australia, we elect representatives to the Australian parliament to make decisions on our behalf, so it is important that we understand how our electoral systems work, and that we examine them to find out if they meet the fair and equal requirements of political participation in a liberal democracy. We will also look at the ways in which other significant groups within society—political parties, interest groups and the media—influence the decisions of government.

QUESTIONS FOR DISCUSSION

1. Why is it important that we understand what is 'politics'? Discuss this question in the context of your own experiences and expectations as a citizen.
2. What is the function of a political system, and what are its objectives?
3. What is political power? Is conflict between different groups within society inevitable?
4. What is political ideology? What is its function in determining the structure of government in a state, and the relationship between the state and society? Discuss this question in the context of forms of government that have developed from different ideologies, and provide examples from contemporary states.
5. What are the characteristics of democracy, and how should they be implemented within a political system? Do you think they are achievable? If so, why? If not, why not?
6. Why do we associate liberal democracies with an institutional framework that includes a constitution, a legislature, an executive, a judiciary and an electoral system? What is the function of each of these institutions in achieving a liberal democratic political system?
7. Is it useful to compare the way the political systems of different states are structured and operate?

FURTHER READING

General texts
Heywood, A. 2002, *Politics*, Palgrave Macmillan, Basingstoke, UK. An introduction to theories of politics, the machinery of government and political interaction.

Lasswell, H. 1936, *Who Gets What, When, How?*, McGraw-Hill, New York. A classic discussion of the theory of politics.

Political ideology
Heywood, A. 2007, *Political Ideologies: An Introduction*, Macmillan, London.

Democracy
Arblaster, A. 1987, *Democracy*, Open University Press, Milton Keynes, UK. Discussion of the principles and critiques of democracy.

Birch, A.H. 2007, *Concepts and Theories of Modern Democracy*, Routledge, London. An introduction to the concepts of democracy, political representation and participation, and political power.

Parkin, A. 2002, 'Liberal Democracy', in Summers, J., Woodward, D. & Parkin, A. (eds), *Government, Politics, Power and Policy in Australia*, 7th edn, Longman, Sydney. An introduction to the concepts of democracy and the liberal tradition, with Australian case studies.

Comparative politics
Blondel, J. 1969, *An Introduction to Comparative Government*, Weidenfeld & Nicolson, London.

Sodaro, M.J. 2008, *Comparative Politics: A Global Introduction*, McGraw-Hill, New York.

Wiarda, H.J. 2007, *Comparative Politics: Approaches and Issues*, Rowman & Littlefield, Lanham, Maryland.

USEFUL WEBSITES

 http://australianpolitics.com

australianpolitics.com

This site provides basic information on politics and the principles of liberal democracy, including:

— What is politics?
http://australianpolitics.com/democracy/what-is-politics.shtml

— Liberal democracy:
http://australianpolitics.com/democracy/liberal-democracy.shtml

— Representative government:
http://australianpolitics.com/democracy/terms/representative-government.shtml

— Responsible government:
http://australianpolitics.com/democracy/terms/responsible-government.shtml

THE POLITICAL CULTURE OF AUSTRALIA'S POLITICAL INSTITUTIONS

THIS CHAPTER EXPLAINS:

- the institutions of Australia's system of government;
- the liberal democratic context of Australia's political institutions;
- the scope of government;
- the significance of political parties to Australia's system of government;
- the function of ideology and partisanship in Australia's political system;
- social and ethnic influences on Australian politics;
- politics and the economy;
- pressures for change, including globalisation, climate change, representation of Australia's Indigenous people, reconciliation with Australia's Indigenous people and the issue of an Australian republic; and
- political culture and the institutions of government from a comparative perspective.

THE INSTITUTIONS OF AUSTRALIA'S SYSTEM OF GOVERNMENT

Australia's political institutions operate within the context of the country's political culture. The political culture is the beliefs and values within society that develop norms, or an understanding, about the way the political system should be structured and what it should do.

> '**Political culture** refers to the broad pattern of values and attitudes that individuals and societies hold towards political objects, including political institutions.'
> (*Source:* Jackson, R.J. & Jackson, D. 1997, *Comparative Government: An Introduction to Political Science*, 2nd ed., Prentice Hall/Allyn & Bacon, Toronto, p. 106)

The Australian federation evolved from a society whose values were rooted in a strong attachment to the 'mother' country, Britain, and its political traditions. Australia's self-governing colonies, not long emerged from the fetters of British colonialism, were determined to maintain their autonomy over all but the restricted powers granted to the Commonwealth government. This belief on the part of the states remains a significant factor in Australia's modern federalism. The attachments to Britain are much weaker, but the values that sustained the development of the Australian Constitution within that framework remain substantially unchanged, despite the multicultural nature of Australian society, and the pressures for change discussed in this chapter.

The liberal democratic context of Australian political institutions

The Australian federal system of government sits firmly within the tradition of liberal democracy. It has a written constitution which defines the powers of the federal government and the institutions of government; citizens aged 18 years and over vote to elect their representatives to the Australian parliament; the rule of law is accepted by citizens and those that govern; and individuals generally have access to basic rights and liberties, including the freedom to participate personally in political activity, or to seek to influence government through membership of groups or as individuals.

Because Australians regard their system as a democracy, they want to make sure that those small groups of elected men and women, to whom they have given the authority to make decisions on their behalf about the allocation of resources, do not abuse their political power. The Australian political system, for that reason, includes a range of institutions, based on the British Westminster tradition, that are intended to make our parliamentary representatives accountable and responsible for their actions to the people who elected them.

> **Responsible cabinet government**
> 'The essence of responsible government in the Westminster model' is that 'Cabinet is collectively responsible to parliament, and that individual ministers within the Cabinet are individually responsible to parliament for their own actions as ministers and for the actions of their departments'.
> (*Source:* Jaensch, D. 1997, *The Politics of Australia*, 2nd ed., Macmillan Education, Melbourne, p. 145)

The other significant aspect of our political system is the federal system of government provided for by the Australian Constitution, embodying a division of sovereignty and responsibilities between the Commonwealth and the states, drawn from elements of the American federal system.

The influence of the Westminster tradition on our political institutions, in particular, is the reason why it is important that we know something about the history and political culture from which they emerged.

Australian politics, while similar to British or American politics in some respects, cannot be understood by reference to general statements about Western democracies alone. Americans, for example, think that a real democracy is a republic. The British think that their system is a real democracy, although formally it is a monarchy. Australians think that they have a democracy, although formally their system is also monarchical, with the monarch resident in the United Kingdom.

The British monarchy is a venerable institution, and it has survived — adapted — in a more or less unbroken line since 1066. Americans date their political system from 1776, the year of their Declaration of Independence against Britain. As Britain was then ruled by its king, assisted by advisers, the Americans saw themselves as having broken away from the system of the monarchy. Their new constitution stressed that each citizen was equal, that rulers had to be elected, and that there had to be restraints on those who exercised power.

In Australia, by contrast, there was no rebellion. Self-government was given to the colonists in the mid-19th century, almost before there was a sustained move to seek it.

The progress of self-government in Australia

1855	New South Wales
	Victoria
	Tasmania
1856	South Australia
1859	Queensland
1890	Western Australia
1901	The Commonwealth of Australia

British traditions, which the colonists brought with them, were adapted where necessary to local circumstances. There was no need to fashion something self-consciously different. Consequently, Australians have no day marking their independence. Instead, Australia Day commemorates the landing of the first settlers at Sydney Cove, a reminder of our colonial heritage. While Australia's national anthem, *Advance Australia Fair*, projects a conscious national sentiment, the positioning of the Union Jack on the Australian flag is a symbol of our British heritage.

The origins of white settlement in Australia have had more profound effects on Australian political culture than attitudes to the monarchy. White Australia began as a gaol, and the form of government was centralised and autocratic for more than half a century. As late as 1810 the governor of New South Wales was personally authorising and paying for the building of roads in the colony. In the development of America, by contrast, local government came first, as settlers moved out into the wilderness and took up land to farm; their towns were small and their communities were self-governing for a very long time. This was never possible in Australia. The inland did not lend itself to small farming and was taken up by pastoralists and their flocks. Most of the population clustered in the coastal settlements; from the very beginning the urban proportion was high. Because of the huge size of the continent and its sparse rural population, local communities were rarely able to provide the facilities they needed. This meant that from the very beginning it was the colonial governments that were called on to plan and provide the basic infrastructure for development.

The scope of government

These circumstances helped bring about two complementary traits in Australian political culture. The first was an acceptance of the need for government involvement in a wide range of matters. Australians accepted that government had an important role, particularly in relation to the delivery of such services as social welfare, health and education.

The second trait followed from the first. Australians saw government in *instrumental* terms: that is, it was there to do things for the people, to provide services, to provide a safety net for the disadvantaged, and so on. This perspective has important consequences for their attitude to politics. Politics is an instrumental activity in which people engage in order to get something out of it. Because Australians did not have to fight for their independence, they do not much prize the possibility of taking part in decisions. They received that independence early, before the great European debates of the late 19th century about democratic suffrage, so they do not feel that taking part in politics is an important part of being a full citizen in a democracy. For many, voting can be a chore, party membership a waste of time, involvement in political activity freakish—unless, of course, there is something in it for them. To say this is not to make lofty judgements about behaviour, but to recognise that the political values of a people flow from their experience and from the experience of their ancestors of what politics and governments are for. In this, every society will have a different tale to tell.

These two traits were well established at the end of the 19th century, and were important preconditions for the growth of government in the 20th and present centuries. By and large, the technical revolution of the early 20th century (mostly in transport and communications) made it possible for governments to govern large groups of people more completely, and this revolution occurred at the time ordinary people in most Western societies were winning a share of power through the extension of the right to vote. One result was the establishment of party systems, which reduced the complexity of political issues to simple choices that made sense to the majority of citizens. Another was the extension of the public service aspect of government.

The growth of government in Australia
1890
- Sir Henry Parkes' Free Trade Ministry in New South Wales consisted of Parkes as premier and colonial secretary plus nine others. Their departmental responsibilities were Vice President of the Executive Council, Attorney-General, Treasury, Postmaster-General, Public Instruction, Justice, Mines, Lands and Public Works.

> **2008**
> - The NSW Iemma government included 22 ministers.
> - The Rudd federal ministry comprised 20 cabinet ministers, 10 outer ministers and 12 parliamentary secretaries. Many of these ministers have administrative responsibilities, such as education, that overlap those of state governments (see Chapter 4).

The reason for this increase in the size of government was an acceptance that problems in public affairs could be resolved by establishing a settled policy and a group of public servants to administer it. Those who seek to change those policies do so by making demands of government. This is done usually through membership of political parties or through the collective efforts of interest groups who lobby the government and the bureaucracy.

Political parties and Australian government

Political parties as a form of political participation and representation traditionally have been an integral part of the Australian political system, for a number of reasons. First, since the modern party system began in 1910—when the Labor and Liberal parties for the first time faced each other and won every seat in the 1910 elections between them, reducing all other contenders to 5 per cent of the vote—the party system has been as much a part of our heritage as is federation itself.

Second, the historical trend has been for the great majority of Australian electors to vote for a political party, rather than for independent candidates. Most of this support has been divided between the Australian Labor Party and the Liberal and National parties, with the result that party politics has been relatively stable.

Third, most Australians grow up into their preference (the tendency has been for Labor parents to bring up Labor children, and so on), which means it has been very difficult for new political parties to get established and maintain long-term support. Two of the three to have lasted for more than 10 years, the National Party (1919) and the Democratic Labor Party (1955), did so by hiving off substantial sections from the existing parties. The Australian Democrats (1977) was created by a former Liberal minister, but also numbers among its members those who have had no formal attachment to either of the major political parties. The stranglehold of the Labor and Liberal parties on government was one reason for the resignation of former Australian Democrats leader, Cheryl Kernot, from that party in 1997 to join the Australian Labor Party, where she considered she would have more opportunity to make a substantive impact on policy.

If the parties did not exist, we should have to establish them, for they are the principal bridge between citizens and their government, and no other institution can do their job of aggregating and articulating the interests of a broad sweep of the population. They do it by simplifying a myriad number of policy choices into one, and by doing so in an ideological way. That is, they portray politics and government in ways that are appealing and sensible to their supporters.

The Australian Labor Party, for example, pictures politics as an arena for ensuring that all members of society have access to political and economic power within the framework of a mixed capitalist economy, with a safety net for the disadvantaged. The party's stated goal is to establish a just, egalitarian society in which ordinary people will have a better life. All of the party's history, its successes and failures, can be interpreted in that context. This interpretation is one of the functions of its politicians, and especially of the party leaders.

But the Australian Labor Party is not in any way special. The Nationals, to take another example, present a different picture to their supporters. Here a minority party battles against an urban-dominated governmental system in the interests of those who produce a considerable amount of the wealth on which Australia depends, fighting for their share of government funding for regional and country roads, schools, cultural facilities, communications, and so on. Many Australians who live in cities might think this is a highly coloured account of politics and government, but the Nationals are not addressing them—they are looking to serve the needs of their constituents and supporters who live in rural Australia.

Ideology and partisanship

> **Ideologies** 'are guides to political action. They give us ideals to believe in, goals to strive for and tell us for what causes to fight'.
> (*Source*: Adams, I. 1993, *Political Ideology Today*, Manchester University Press, Manchester, p. 6)

Ideology is an important part of Australian politics, and not solely with respect to political parties. The shared beliefs of Australians about what 'ought' to be the case in politics and society define the boundaries of Australia's liberal democratic system within which the parties compete for power. For example, it is apparent that Australians share a belief in the virtues of private property, at least as it applies to houses, cars and other individual possessions. They accept that public life is governed by rules, and that rules have to be obeyed if they cannot be avoided. The result of the 1975 election, held after the dismissal of the Whitlam government by the governor-general in controversial circumstances, was accepted without demur by virtually everyone, even by those who argued passionately that the elections ought not to have been held at all. Of course, people's beliefs and attitudes are themselves the consequences of past politics, at least in part. The past has a profound capacity to affect the present.

The almost complete partisan commitment of the Australian electorate has had some important effects on parliamentary politics. It has led, for example, to very high levels of party discipline in and out of parliament. There is nowhere for an errant Labor or Liberal politician to go if, for any reason, he or she comes to disagree fundamentally with the party, apart from an uncertain future with a minor party or as an independent. The alternatives generally are to like it or lump it, and to lump it means resignation and retirement. It is unusual for such politicians to hold their seats when they have lost party endorsement.

Partisanship also means rhetoric and unwillingness to compromise, at least publicly. Australian parliaments are not places of extensive rational discussion of alternatives in public policy and nor are most political arguments among Australian citizens. The doctrine of 'my party right or wrong' is strongly held by the majority of voters. Given the context, as it has been sketched here, it could hardly be otherwise.

Partisanship, finally, is inextricably linked to attitudes to government. Governments are there to do things, certainly, but there is always the danger that they will do things in the interests of one's opponents, if that party is in power. Australia's system of party government, which delivers the policy-making power to the party that gains an electoral majority, often means that minorities are inadequately represented. There is little recognition that government is difficult at the best of times, that there is always a large gap between society's wants and the resources available to meet them, and that a good politician is a very valuable, hard-working person. Australians take their governments seriously, and obey them, if rather grudgingly.

A Morgan Poll conducted in April 2008 found that 23 per cent of respondents considered politicians had a high standard of ethics and honesty.
(*Source*: Roy Morgan Research 2008, 'Nurses Most Ethical (Again)', Finding no. 4283, http://www.roymorgan.com/news/polls/2008/4283)

Politicians generally do not enjoy a great measure of respect, but the local MP is thought to do a 'decent job'. MPs are rarely thought to embody the notion of disinterested public service; they too must be out for themselves. The latter sentiment is most commonly expressed whenever a parliament agrees to raise the salaries of MPs—which have not been especially high, in fact, in the context of corporate wages and salaries in Australia.

Social and ethnic influences on Australian politics

The characteristics of Australian politics come from the particular historical mix of settlers, rather than from the original inhabitants. The Australian Indigenous population make up around 2 per cent of the estimated Australian population. For a long time they were the forgotten people of Australia (see Figure 2.1), but they are now making a mark on Australian

FIGURE 2.1
Puzzled

Jook: 'Are there no aboriginals in the district?'
Hopetoun: 'Only a dozen or so left, not worth troubling about. The march of civilisation has—er—'
Jook: 'Quite so! But, I say, how do these other people fit in with the White Australia policy?'
(*Source*: *The Bulletin*, 11 May 1901, reproduced by permission from *The Bulletin*, www.acpsyndication.com)

politics, particularly since the High Court's *Mabo* and *Wik* decisions relating to the recognition of the rights of Australia's Indigenous peoples to native title.

Unlike Canada, Australia has no profound ethnic or linguistic division generally. Unlike Great Britain, Australia has no ancient division between nobles and commoners. Unlike Northern Ireland, Australia has no deep religious schism, although some citizens became concerned about the practice of the Muslim faith in Australia after the terrorist attacks perpetrated by Islamic fundamentalists on the World Trade Center in New York on 11 September 2001 and the Bali bombings in 2002.

In the 19th century, there were overlapping divisions between those of convict birth and free settlers, between the Irish and the English, between Catholics and Protestants, between landowners and land-seekers; but time and change have softened the edges of these differences. When the United States modified its open immigration system in the 1920s, for example, it gave the Irish an almost perpetual ticket to American citizenship, and thereafter Irish emigrants went to the United States. In consequence, sectarianism in Australia became less important as the Irish in Australia became Irish-Australians, then just Australians. Post-war immigration from Catholic Europe blurred the link between Catholicism and Irish ancestry, while affluence and time reduced the probability that Catholics would be found in disproportionate numbers among the poor. Australia in the 21st century has become a multicultural society, the sectarian issue displaced by a stirring debate about the trend towards more Asian immigration that has occurred since the 1970s.

At the time of Federation, the White Australia policy represented a political response to concerns that Chinese immigration into Australia would upset the predominantly European Anglo-Saxon base of society (bearing in mind that Indigenous people were marginalised from the social and political life of the Australian community). Australia in the 21st century has become a much more multicultural society, as you will see from Table 2.1, which shows the top 15 countries of birth of Australia's overseas-born population at the 2006 census. It is interesting to note that, despite the fact that migrants to Australia now come from a wide range of countries, a large number of the overseas-born people resident in Australia came from England and New Zealand.

The year ended 30 June 2006 saw the highest number of permanent arrivals since 1988–89. The top 10 countries of origin for permanent arrivals in Australia in 2005–06 are listed in Table 2.2, in which it can be seen that people from the United Kingdom and New Zealand dominate the new arrivals.

> 'Recent figures reveal more than 40,000 Kiwis [New Zealanders] arrived in Australia in the past year . . . the lure of a better lifestyle, more career opportunities — and the promise of more money — were factors in the decision to relocate . . .'
>
> One recent arrival explained the differences that attracted him to move from Auckland to Sydney: 'It's fairly similar in terms of the set up but it's just probably a more global city and there's four times as many people here. The weather's a bit nicer, and there's probably just as many nice beaches . . . and better things to do.'
> (*Source*: Hannan, E. 2007, '40,000 Kiwis make smart move', *The Weekend Australian*, 8 December 2007, p. 4)

The relatively homogeneous character of Australian society, its settled nature for more than a century, and the relative ease with which it has accepted large immigrant groups

TABLE 2.1

Overseas-born Australian residents: top 15 countries of birth, 2006 Australian census

Country of birth	Proportion of all overseas born in 2006 (per cent)
England	19.4
New Zealand	8.8
China (excludes SARs and Taiwan Province)	4.7
Italy	4.5
Vietnam	3.6
India	3.3
Scotland	2.9
Philippines	2.7
Greece	2.5
Germany	2.4
South Africa	2.4
Malaysia	2.1
Netherlands	1.8
Lebanon	1.7
Hong Kong (SAR of China)	1.6

(*Source*: ABS 2007, '2006 Census of Population and Housing: Media Releases and Fact Sheets, 2006', no. 70/2007, Cat. no. 2914.0.55.002, ABS, Canberra)

TABLE 2.2

Top 10 countries of origin of permanent arrivals into Australia 2005–06

Country of origin	Ranking
United Kingdom	1
New Zealand	2
India	3
China	4
Philippines	5
South Africa	6
Sudan	7
Malaysia	8
Singapore	9
Vietnam	10

(*Source*: ABS 2007, 'Migration, Australia, 2005–06', Cat. no. 3412.0, ABS, Canberra, pp. 17–18)

since the Second World War all point to another important aspect of Australian politics. In Australia, politics is mostly about money or, more accurately, about the distribution of resources. This helps to account for the passive, somewhat disinterested way in which many Australians regard politics and government, and for why there is relatively little political violence. Most political disputes in Australia can be settled by some kind of financial compensation or its equivalent in government services or other desired things. This is not the case in societies where there are serious divisions over race, language, or religion, because the 'either . . . or' nature of these divisions does not lend itself to incremental adjustments. Such societies have a perpetual problem about the legitimacy of the system of government—the regime—which affects the whole business of politics, the extent to which laws are obeyed, and the temperature at which politics is carried on.

> 'There is no place within our community for those who would traffic, for whatever purpose, in division based on a person's religion, their place of birth, the colour of their skin or their ethnic makeup. There is no place in Australia for any semblance of racial or ethnic intolerance.'
> (*Source:* Prime Minister John Howard 1998, address to the Federation of Ethnic Communities Council National Conference, Sydney, 20 November 1998)

Australia is not like this: the regime is legitimate for all but a handful, and the questions with which politics are concerned are questions of national housekeeping and shares in the purse. It makes for dull and often pragmatic politics, individual freedom and personal safety. Most of those who live in polities beset with problems of legitimacy would gladly trade the oratory and violence of their own society for the coolness and relative calm of Australian politics.

POLITICS AND THE ECONOMY

In Australia, economic questions tend to dominate the agenda of politics, and much of the time of governments and parliaments has been taken up with defining the proper role and behaviour of the private sector and with encouraging private economic activity.

Some of the reasons have been sketched already. In the beginning, the central government had the responsibility of ensuring that there was adequate food in the new colony. Then it had the responsibility of deciding on what terms the huge land resources of Australia should be taken up. Once the gold rushes had swollen the Australian population, it had to undo what had been done (encouraging extensive pastoral occupation) in order to stimulate agriculture, thereby settling some of the new immigrants and providing more food for the colony. At the same time, it began to link the countryside to the city with a system of state-owned railways, the privately owned railway companies having failed to prosper, and a state-owned telegraph system, services for which all communities clamoured and competed.

By the end of the 19th century the economy had reached a level of complexity that presented governments with some difficult choices. On the one hand, Australia had some natural advantages: wool could be grown more cheaply in Australia than anywhere in the world, despite the distances to market, and wheat and dairy products could compete on even terms with equivalent products from anywhere. On the face of it, a wise government would control the economy so that primary producers would always retain their natural advantages—that is, keep domestic costs as low as possible and allow the importation of anything the producers needed (machinery, implements, wire, and so on).

However, these industries had two important drawbacks. They were not heavy employers of labour; indeed, mechanisation was already reducing the total workforce. Also, there was little room for further development in them, because all the useful land had already been taken up. In the cities, there were hundreds of thousands of people who needed employment, and the most useful way to provide it was to encourage local entrepreneurs to set up factories for products that could find a ready sale. As Australia had no natural advantage in the manufacture of, say, shoes or barbed wire, many such infant industries would need the 'protection' of a tariff—a tax on imports that would raise their local price and so render locally made products more attractive to consumers.

Free trade and protection

These two approaches to government control of the economy, termed *free trade* and *protection* in the late 19th century, were incompatible, and the choice between them was not an easy one. Federation in 1901 pushed the problem up to the federal level, and protection won, partly because the weight of numbers in the cities put the primary producers at a disadvantage. When the Australian Labor Party began to argue that improved wages and conditions could be provided under the umbrella of protection, and manufacturers agreed, the success of protection as the basis for the economy was assured.

However, protection did raise farmers' costs, and it was necessary to compensate them in some way, because primary producers were well organised politically, and their party, the Country Party, held the balance of power in the federal parliament for most years after 1919. Slowly, therefore, rural producers were drawn into the ambit of government policy making and provided with bounties, subsidies and advantages of many kinds.

None of this passed without comment. The extent of government control over the economy has been debated incessantly in Australia since the 1880s. The debate has been couched in a mixture of principle, passion and special pleading that has changed very little since then. The principles at stake have been private enterprise, or social justice, or equity, or national development, depending on the case. The special pleading has been carried on by importers, exporters, workers or farmers. The passion has been recognition that in such debate some kind of general agreement is necessary before changes are made to the status quo.

The economic debate since the 1970s has turned government opinion away from support for protection on the basis that Australia's manufacturing industry would stagnate and decline behind its wall of tariff protection, and many tariffs have been reduced as a result. The federal government's approach is also focused on negotiating free trade agreements with its trading partners.

> **Free trade agreements (FTAs)**
> 'Australia's trade policy seeks to maximize trade benefits for all Australians by securing market gains through multilateral, regional, and bilateral approaches. FTAs with individual countries or regional groupings are an important part of this strategy.'
> (*Source*: Department of Agriculture, Fisheries and Forestry (DAFF) 2008, 'Free Trade Agreements (FTAs)', DAFF, Canberra, http://www.daff.gov.au/market-access-trade/fta)

The acceptance that Australian industry must become internationally competitive has been a significant factor in stimulating change in the manner in which Australian government operates.

PRESSURES FOR CHANGE

There is a basic truth that successful institutions outlive their founders. The political institutions that are the object of our attention have lasted until now because they maintained their relevance in addressing the political problems of the day. But changes to the political and ideological context in which these institutions operate, particularly since the mid-1980s, have brought into fashion new ideas about how things should be done, including less emphasis on government providing assistance to industry, tariff reductions, a reduction in the size and role of bureaucracy, scrutiny of the structure of the federal system, and debate about whether Australia should replace the constitutional monarchy with a republic led by an Australian head of state.

Globalisation

The essential reason behind these initiatives was the political and economic imperatives of having to deal with the increasing internationalisation of Australia's economy. The manner in which this was handled had a strong basis in the ideology of economic liberalism—in particular, a preference for the concepts of open competition through free trade and the primacy of the private sector in generating economic activity. This has resulted in a melding of the political and economic threads of liberal democracy (discussed earlier) within the Australian political system. The impact on the way in which government operates in dealing with economic matters has been substantial. This process of reform is discussed further in Chapter 7.

There have been questions whether the structure of the federal system that was established in 1901 remains suitable for today's global marketplace. It has been suggested, for example, that the historic lines on the map that determine the geographic boundaries of the political authority of the states should be replaced by a two-tier system of government, incorporating a national government and regional authorities defined by population and economic activity. The former Howard Coalition government initially preferred moving more Commonwealth functions into the jurisdiction of state governments, but it adopted a national approach to its industrial relations Work Choices legislation, despite the protests of state governments, and expressed an interest in bringing hospitals under the control of the Commonwealth using its control of federal financial arrangements. The Rudd government has expressed a preference for working closely with the states in a form of cooperative federalism to achieve change (see Chapter 4).

Climate change

Economic globalisation has not been the sole reason behind policy responses that have focused attention on the constitutional power of the federal government to make policies in the national interest—for example, through the ratification of international conventions and treaties under the external affairs power (s. 51(xxix) of the Constitution) or intervention in activities where the states have jurisdiction in a cooperative or coercive manner (see Chapter 4). Pressure on the Australian government to do something about climate change has become a political issue. The Howard government refused to ratify the Kyoto Treaty dealing with the greenhouse gas effects of climate change because the prime minister did not consider it to be in Australia's economic interests to do so (*The Age*, 5 September 2002).

> 'I want to ensure that any decision is made very carefully in a way that takes full account of jobs and investment in Australia, of climate change action by others and of global technology developments.'
> (*Source*: Prime Minister John Howard 2007, cited in 'Climate not main challenge, PM', *Sydney Morning Herald*, 23 April 2007, http://www.smh.com.au/news/national/climate-not-main-challenge-pm/2007/04/23/1177180540877.html)

However, Howard did respond to concerns about the low level of the Murray River, and the lack of water for irrigation caused by the drought, by establishing a National Plan for Water Security to take over the management of the resources of the Murray–Darling River Basin from the states.

Political polling in the period leading up to the November 2007 federal election indicated the environment was a significant election issue (e.g. Newspoll results, 17 October 2007). Howard, as a result, posted a short video on YouTube to explain his attitudes to climate change, presumably aiming to reach a younger cohort of voters.

> 'We do not have to sacrifice our economic prosperity to tackle the problem . . . We'll do it in a practical and balanced way in full knowledge of the economic consequences for our nation.'
> (*Source*: Prime Minister John Howard 2007, 'Prime Minister John Howard, Climate Change Announcement', YouTube, posted 16 July 2007, http://au.youtube.com/watch?v=e5jtiJPlv4Y)

Howard's continuing refusal to ratify Kyoto, compared to the Labor Party's promise to do so, may have been a contributing factor to the Coalition's election loss. The Rudd Labor government ratified Kyoto, and the Opposition Coalition, under its then new leader Brendan Nelson, endorsed that action.

Australia's Indigenous people

Constitutional recognition: the 1967 referendum

The Constitutional Alteration (Aboriginals) 1967 referendum was one of the few successful referendums since Federation. (Chapter 3 explains the requirements for amendment of the Constitution.) It made two changes to the Constitution. (You will find the full text of the Constitution as an appendix to this book.) First, it amended s. 51(xxvi) to enable the Commonwealth parliament to make special laws in respect of Australian's Indigenous Aboriginal people. If used in combination with s. 109, this means that Commonwealth legislation in relation to Aboriginal affairs will prevail over state legislation. The 1967 referendum also repealed s. 127 of the Constitution which was discriminatory against the Indigenous Aboriginal people. Section 51(xxix), the external affairs power, has also been used to extend the scope of Commonwealth power over Indigenous issues, based on Australia's ratification of international treaties and conventions such as the International Labour Organization (ILO) Convention against discrimination on the basis of race, colour, sex, religion, political opinion, national extraction or social origin.

> 'No federal power has a greater validity than the power to make special laws for Aborigines.'
> (Source: Whitlam, G. 1985, *The Whitlam Government 1972–1975*, Viking, Melbourne, p. 463. Reproduced with permission.)

Successive Australian governments since 1967 have used those powers to varying degrees, depending on their political agendas and priorities, to legislate a diverse range of policies and services for Indigenous people. High Court judgments, including *Mabo* and *Wik*, have also been significant (see Chapter 3).

Representative institutions

Since the 1967 constitutional referendum, a series of bodies have been established for the political representation of Australia's Indigenous people at the federal level. The Coalition government in power at the time established the Council for Aboriginal Affairs (CAA) with three non-Indigenous members appointed by the government to advise the government. The Whitlam Labor government (1972–75) replaced this with another advisory body, the National Aboriginal Consultative Council (NACC), whose 41 delegates were elected by Aboriginal people.

> 'I want to tell you of a most important election that is taking place tomorrow. Nothing like it has been held before. All Aboriginal people in Australia are eligible to vote. You will be voting to elect the members of the National Aboriginal Consultative Committee. This Committee—the NACC—will have a significant role to play in advancing the cause of Aborigine and Torres Strait Island Australians.'
> (Source: Whitlam, G. 1985, *The Whitlam Government: 1972–1975*, Viking, Melbourne, p. 468. Reproduced with permission.)

In 1978, the Fraser government established the National Aboriginal Conference (NAC) to advise the Commonwealth minister. The NAC was abolished by the Hawke Labor government in 1985 and replaced with the Aboriginal and Torres Strait Islander Commission (ATSIC), a policy-making and administrative body elected by Indigenous people which provided representation and promoted debate on Indigenous political issues, and which was responsible for providing a number of services. In 2005 the Howard government abolished ATSIC because it believed there was no justification for a separate political body and that the Indigenous population should be represented within the mainstream Australian political system. The various programs administered by ATSIC were transferred to the Commonwealth government departments responsible for those functions.

Following the abolition of ATSIC, the Howard government established the National Indigenous Council, whose members were appointed by the government, to provide advice on improving outcomes for Indigenous Australians. The Rudd Labor government decided not to continue with the Council when its term expired on 31 December 2007. It will be replaced with a new representative body, after discussions with Indigenous people.

In September 2007, Aboriginal leaders formed a national representative body, the National Aboriginal Alliance (NAA), to counter what they considered to be government dominance of the Indigenous policy agenda.

> 'They came from land councils, legal services, Stolen Generations organisations, health and housing bodies, the national youth forum, media organisations, bush communities and town camps . . . The NAA has rejected discriminatory elements of the Commonwealth's emergency intervention, called for the immediate removal of business managers from Aboriginal communities and the restoration of the permit system. It also urged Canberra to restore integrity to the Racial Discrimination Act 1975 and called on Aboriginal people to actively but peacefully resist the intervention.'
> (*Source*: Ravens, T. 2007, 'New national Aboriginal body to counter govt policy', *National Indigenous Times*, no. 138, 20 September 2007, http://www.nit.com.au/News/story.aspx?id=12801)

Reconciliation: saying 'sorry' for the Stolen Generations

Reconciliation with the Indigenous people of Australia has become a significant political issue in recent years. In 1997, the *Bringing Them Home* report was released, detailing the forcible removal of Indigenous children from their families in the past. This became the catalyst for a call for an apology for these actions; that is, the need for the federal government to say 'sorry' for what happened. This was rejected by Prime Minister John Howard, whose persistent refusal was based on his reasoning that the current generation should not have to say 'sorry' for what had been perpetrated by other people in the past.

> Speaking to a gathering at Parliament House in Canberra 10 years after the *Bringing Them Home* report was released, the former chairwoman of ATSIC, Lowitja O'Donohue, said: 'We can forgive but we can't forget. But it's important that we move on. And for some, until they hear the word "sorry" they won't move on.'
> (*Source*: ABC News Online, 'Aboriginal leader blasts Stolen Generation "shame job"', 24 May 2007, http://www.abc.net.au/news/stories/2007/05/24/1932665.htm)

During the November 2007 election campaign, Howard promised to hold a constitutional referendum to recognise Indigenous Australians in a preamble to the Constitution, a symbolic approach to reconciliation based on 'equity rather than apologies' (*The Australian*, 12 October 2007).

> 'Mr Howard admitted reconciliation was an area "I have struggled with during the entire time I have been Prime Minister". He said he felt uncomfortable with the idea of guilt and shame for non-Indigenous Australians "based on a repudiation of the Australia I grew up in" and a rights agenda that led to welfare dependency and a sense of separateness. But he said the time was right "to take a permanent, decisive step towards completing some unfinished business of this nation".'
>
> (*Source*: Shanahan, D. 2007, 'Howard's "new reconciliation"', *The Australian*, 12 October 2007, p. 1)

The Rudd Labor government's historic 'sorry' day

Prime Minister Kevin Rudd moved an historic motion on 13 February 2008 on behalf of the Australian parliament to say 'sorry' to the Stolen Generations. The motion was passed with the support of the federal Opposition.

> 'To the Stolen Generation, I say the following: as Prime Minister of Australia, I am sorry. On behalf of the Government of Australia, I am sorry. On behalf of the Parliament of Australia, I am sorry. And I offer you this apology without qualification.'
>
> (*Source*: Prime Minister Kevin Rudd 2008, 'Apology to Australia's Indigenous Peoples', House of Representatives, Parliament House, Canberra, 13 February 2008, transcript: http://www.pm.gov.au/media/Speech/2008/speech_0073.cfm)

Practical reconciliation

The Howard government's policy was to approach Indigenous policies (1996–2007) from the perspectives of 'practical reconciliation' and mutual obligation.

> 'True reconciliation is, in our view, to be best found within practical means to improve the well-being and happiness of Indigenous Australians and raising standards to levels enjoyed and expected by all of us.'
>
> (*Source*: Prime Minister John Howard 2000, 'Reconciliation in Australia Today', address to the Menzies Research Centre, Melbourne, 13 December 2000, http://www.mrcltd.org.au/research/indigenous-reports/Reconciliation_in_Australia_Today.pdf)

In November 2004, the government introduced 'contracts' under which Indigenous communities would agree to implement certain standards of behaviour in return for Commonwealth funding for services. For example, this might take the form of a requirement that children wash their faces each day, in return for Commonwealth health care, education, dole money and services (*The Australian*, 11 November 2004).

> 'Palm Island became the third community in Queensland to sign on to Commonwealth welfare reforms aimed at introducing private home ownership in the community. The agreement includes extra funding for new housing in exchange for improved behaviour and increased school attendance for children.'
>
> (*Source*: Murphy, P. 2007, 'See this through, Brough told', *The Australian*, 12 October 2007)

In 2007, the Howard government took a highly interventionist policy response to a report that revealed sexual abuse of Indigenous children in the Northern Territory. This included medical checks for Indigenous children, alcohol restrictions on Northern Territory Aboriginal land, linking welfare payments to school attendance, quarantining a proportion of welfare payments for the purchase of food and other essentials, removing the permit system for entry to Aboriginal land in the larger townships and the road corridors that connect them, increased policing, improved housing, a ban on the possession of X-rated pornography and audits of all publicly funded computers to identify illegal material, and the acquisition of townships prescribed by the Australian government through five-year leases. Section 122 of the Constitution, which gives the Commonwealth the power to make laws for the government of any territory, provided the basis for this intervention.

> 'The Howard government decided that it was now time to intervene and declare an emergency situation and use the territories power available under the Constitution to make laws for the Northern Territory.'
> (Source: Mal Brough, Minister for Families, Community Services and Indigenous Affairs 2007, second reading speech, Northern Territory Emergency Response Bill 2007, *House of Representative Debates*, 7 August 2007, p. 10)

The response to these policies was mixed. Women in the remote Northern Territory community of Hermannsburg, 100 kilometres west of Alice Springs, supported the aims of the federal intervention ('Indigenous women support NT intervention aims', National Indigenous Radio Service, 26 October 2007). Others were critical, particularly of the plans for compulsory acquisition of land and removal of the permit system.

> 'The Commonwealth Government must respect the permit system and the rights of Indigenous people to their land.'
> (Source: Syd Stirling, Member for Nhulunbuy, Northern Territory Government, 'Indigenous Communities Have Spoken: Territory Government Must Fight to Save Permit System', media release, 9 July 2007)
>
> 'This punitive approach will only have a short term impact—it doesn't address the underlying issues. Worse, you are taking control away from our communities. When you take people's rights away you also take away their ability to act on their responsibilities. Such paternalism reinforces dependency and isn't dependency the problem?'
> (Source: Muriel Blamblett, Chairperson of the Secretariat of National Aboriginal and Islander Child Care Inc (SNAICC), 'We would like to believe you, Prime Minister', *SNAICC News*, July 2007, p. 6)

Commonwealth intervention has continued under the Rudd government.

An Australian republic?

The internationalisation of Australia's economy, particularly the development of closer trading links with Asia and Southeast Asia, together with the growing multicultural make-up of Australian society, brought into question the relevance of Australia's continuing as a constitutional monarchy, with a queen located in Britain as its head of state. The momentum for change accelerated in February 1998, when a constitutional convention held at Old Parliament House in Canberra, made up of a mixture of delegates elected by the voters and nominees of the government, voted in favour of Australia becoming a republic with an Australian head of state.

A referendum was held on 6 November 1999 to put the question to the Australian people. Voters were asked to decide on two questions: whether Australians wanted to insert a preamble into the Constitution, and whether the Constitution should be altered 'to establish the Commonwealth of Australia as a republic with the Queen and Governor-General being replaced by a President appointed by a two-thirds majority of the members of the Commonwealth Parliament'. Further discussion about the referendum can be found in Chapter 3. Both questions were solidly defeated.

The result of the referendum means that the institutional framework of Australian government, for the time being, will not change. However, the republic debate is likely to remain on the political agenda, even though there is no majority support at the present time for Australia to become a republic.

Results of a Newspoll survey, 19–21 January 2007:

1. Should Australia become a republic?

Total in favour	45 per cent
Total against	36 per cent
Uncommitted	19 per cent

2. If Prince Charles does become king, would you then be in favour or against Australia becoming a republic?

Total in favour	62 per cent
Total against	22 per cent
Uncommitted	16 per cent

(Source: Newspoll and *The Australian* 2007, http://www.newspoll.com.au)

If Australia does become a republic, the institutions discussed in this book will continue to provide the organisational framework for Australia's system of responsible government, so it is important that we understand their structure and organisation in detail.

POLITICAL CULTURE FROM A COMPARATIVE PERSPECTIVE

We have seen in this chapter how Australia's political culture, based on the principles of liberal democracy, provides the context and the reasons for the institutional structure of Australia's political system—that is, a constitution, legislature, executive, judiciary, political parties and interest groups. It is useful to examine the political culture of other political systems with similar structures, as it allows us to ascertain the impact this has had on the establishment and operation of these political institutions.

Britain

> 'It has often been said that politics in Britain are influenced by the evolutionary adaptability of its political institutions, the notable continuity of its history, the concept of Parliamentary sovereignty, the unitary nature of the state, the underlying cohesion of the society, and the degree of political agreement on fundamental issues.'
> (Source: Forman, N.F. & Baldwin, N.D.J. 2007, *Mastering British Politics*, 5th ed., Palgrave Macmillan, Basingstoke, UK, p. 3)

The British system of government is structured within a constitutional monarchy and a parliamentary democracy. This framework was shaped over the centuries by the history and traditions of the society from which it developed. Beliefs in liberal democracy were a guiding principle for the relationship between citizens and the state.

The system evolved as the power of the monarchy was gradually whittled away, and parliament—that is, the legislature—assumed the legitimate decision-making power over the state that it has today. The ideas of political theorist John Locke, which were identified with the development of ideas of popular sovereignty based on liberal democratic thought, and the associated principles of responsible and representative government as discussed in Chapter 1, were influential in this movement towards curbing the absolute power of the British monarchy. The constitutional settlement of 1688, after King James II was driven from the throne, imposed limitations on the power of the monarchy. This was followed, in 1689, by a Bill of Rights, which declared that the monarch could not make or suspend laws without the consent of parliament, thus setting the foundations for the United Kingdom to function as a constitutional monarchy.

> A **constitutional monarchy** is a political system in which the monarch has mainly advisory and ceremonial responsibilities, and where the political power lies with the parliament.

The parliament consists of two houses. The House of Lords evolved from the medieval courts, and from the Great Council made up of the nobility and senior clergy, which provided advice to the monarch. The House of Commons was established in the late 13th century, and was made up of representatives from the counties, towns and cities—hence the term 'Commons', which differentiates it from the house of the nobility. The system at that time was not democratic in terms of the principles of representative government outlined in Chapter 1, because ministers were chosen or dismissed by the monarch, the nobility maintained its influence through the House of Lords, and property requirements restricted the elected representatives of the House of Commons to people with wealth. Since the 18th century, and particularly following the adoption of universal suffrage in 1928, the political power of forming government has come to be located in the House of Commons. The powers of the House of Lords have been restricted and, as we saw above, the monarch no longer has any real political power in the political system.

The rule of law, a fundamental principle of a liberal democratic political system (see Chapter 1), is maintained by the independence of the judiciary from the parliament. Parliament makes the laws, but the judiciary interprets them and is responsible for their enforcement.

These are the principal institutions of representative, responsible government within Britain: the constitutional monarchy, the legislature and the judiciary. They are supported by other political institutions: the executive of prime minister and cabinet and the bureaucracy, political parties and interest groups, and the media.

In recent times, British society has become much more multicultural in terms of race and ethnicity, some legislative powers have been devolved to regional parliaments in Scotland and Wales, and the country has become a member of the European Union. Nevertheless, a political culture based in history, tradition and the principles of liberal democracy that underpinned the evolution of its institutional framework continues to provide the core foundation for the modern system of representative and responsible government that exists today.

United States

Historical influences were significant to the development of the political institutions of the United States. People who settled in America were generally independent-minded; they sought a new life away from European religious and political constraints, and, in some cases, from persecution. As a reaction to the despotic rule of King George III, England's colonies in America fought the War of Independence in 1776, and gained their autonomy from England as self-governing states. In 1787 these states established a national form of government within the framework of the Constitution of the United States of America.

The structure and organisation of the federal system of government, where power is divided between the states and the central government, and the political institutions established by the Constitution, reflect the desire of the states to retain their sovereignty. The system is also a reaction against the absolute power of monarchy, and reflects a determination to ensure that no one person, or group, will control the political system. The values and beliefs that underpinned this framework were a limited role for government (associated with the tenets of classical liberalism and the works of John Locke), a strong belief in free market capitalism and individual self-reliance.

> There is much debate about how a **republic** might be constituted and function. The term used here in the American context means a democratic state where sovereign power lies with the citizens and their elected representatives, and not with a monarchy.

The Constitution of the United States of America established a presidential republic which includes a federation of states and a federal, or national, government made up of an executive branch headed by a president, a legislature in the form of a Congress that is comprised of a House of Representatives and a Senate, and a judiciary (the Supreme Court). Separate elections for the president and the two houses of Congress provide the basis for representative government. The principles of limited government were instituted with a system of checks and balances embodied in a separation of powers between the executive (presidential branch), the legislature (Congress), the two houses of the Congress, and the judiciary.

> 'It is this combination of federalism and the separation of powers that gives to the United States its particular characteristics as a system of limited government, in which no single part of the system has the power to dictate to the others.'
> (*Source*: Vile, M.J.C. 2007, *Politics in the USA*, 6th ed., Routledge, London, p. 3)

Informal political institutions, such as the political parties, interest groups and the media, play important roles in facilitating citizen participation in the political process.

The United States has developed into a modern multicultural society that embodies a number of cultural and religious backgrounds, and there are wide disparities in income and wealth within its population. However, its political culture remains embedded within the principles of liberal democracy and the separation of powers that underpin its constitutional arrangements.

Federal Republic of Germany

The current institutional framework of the Federal Republic of Germany was established in 1949 by the Basic Law (constitution). It was forged within the political culture and context of the 1945 defeat of Hitler's fascist Third Reich in the Second World War, the influence of the Western occupying powers, and the prewar constitution of the Weimar Republic that had been in place between 1919 and 1933, when it was displaced by the Third Reich. The Basic Law of 1949 was drafted as a repudiation of fascist control of the state, and of its attendant ideology—that Caucasian or Aryan Germans were the 'master race'. The principles that underpin the Basic Law are, as a result, based on liberal democratic principles of human rights and freedoms that are stipulated in the constitution, and on representative parliamentary government that is democratically elected and responsible to the people.

The institutional framework includes a federation made up of a central federal government and 16 states. There is a president and a legislature in the form of two houses of parliament: the Bundestag, which is directly elected by the people and where the government is located (the Chancellor and the cabinet), and the Bundesrat, which represents the states. The rule of law is upheld by an independent judiciary, and the German Federal Constitutional Court oversees the constitution and the legality of government laws.

The Basic Law, and its liberal democratic principles and institutions, continue to form the basis of German government following the unification of communist East Germany and the West German Federal Republic of Germany in 1990.

> In the Federal Republic of Germany, 'the people exercise government power in elections and have the last word in monitoring the activities of key government institutions. These are the five "constitutional bodies", i.e. the Bundestag and Bundesrat with responsibility for legislation (constituting the legislative branch of government), the Federal Constitutional Court with responsibility for supreme court decisions (constituting the judicial branch of government), and finally the Federal President and the Federal Cabinet with responsibility for executive tasks (constituting the executive branch of government). The Cabinet is responsible for the conduct of government business.'
> (*Source*: The Press and Information Office of the Federal Government [Germany] 2008, 'Structure and Tasks', http://www.bundesregierung.de/nn_6404/Webs/Breg/EN/Federal-Government/FunctionAndConstitutionalBasis/function-and-constitutional-basis.html)

Federation of Malaysia

The political structure of the Federation of Malaysia has its genesis in its British colonial past. The British governed four of the states of the Malay peninsula, as crown colonies known as the Federated Malay States. Other states under British influence, but less direct control, were known as the Unfederated Malay States. British colonial rule was interrupted by the Japanese occupation during the Second World War. In the immediate post-war period, in the context of Britain's policy of colonial self-rule, steps were taken to develop a constitutional framework for an independent Malaya.

The Malayan Emergency, which involved an armed struggle to overcome a communist insurrection, delayed the independence of the Federated States of Malaya from Britain until 1957. The constitution was drafted in London by an independent Constitutional Commission, whose members included constitutional experts from Britain and other Commonwealth countries (including Australia). Advice was provided from representatives of Malay rulers. In 1963, the Unfederated States of Malaya joined the federation, which then became known as the Federation of Malaysia. Singapore, which was included at this time, was expelled in 1965 for political reasons.

It is not surprising, when we look at this historical record, that the institutions of the federal government established by the Constitution of the Federation of Malaysia reflects this British heritage and the development of political unity through federation. The Federation is made up of 13 states and one federal territory. The system of government is a constitutional monarchy, based around the principles of limited responsible, representative government, and of equality before the law. The Malaysian head of state is a king, elected every five years by the sultans from within their own ranks, and whose power is nominal and ceremonial. There are two houses in the legislature: the House of Representatives, the elected lower house, and the Senate, a non-elected upper house. Executive government resides with the prime minister and cabinet in the House of Representatives. The judicial system is based on English common law, and judicial legislative review is the responsibility of the Supreme Court.

The political frameworks established by the United Kingdom, Australia, the United States, the Federal Republic of Germany and the Federation of Malaysia, as described above, bear a striking resemblance in structure—and, in some cases, even use the same names (see Table 2.3). The political culture of liberal democracy is also similar, with either direct or indirect influence from the British experience.

There are differences, as you can see from Table 2.3, in the way these systems have been constructed. Some are federal systems, some are constitutional monarchies, and others are republics. The principles of liberal democracy and representative, responsible, parliamentary government underpin their institutional frameworks, but there are differences in the power relationships between the various institutions of the state and the manner in which they operate. These differences will become evident as we examine the structure and operations of the Australian political institutional framework and our comparative examples in the following chapters.

TABLE 2.3
Political institutions: United Kingdom, Australia, United States, Federal Republic of Germany and Federation of Malaysia

	United Kingdom	Australia	United States	Federal Republic of Germany	Federation of Malaysia
Political culture: history	Limitations on the monarch developed into representative, responsible, parliamentary government	Self-governing British colonies; desire for central government led to adoption of constitutional monarchy with federal system and Westminster-style representative, responsible, parliamentary national government	British colonies, War of Independence created opposition to monarchy; desire for a federal union led to adoption of a republic with a federal system and representative, responsible, parliamentary government	Post World War II defeat and Western leaders' influence on constitution led to adoption of a republic with a federal system and representative, responsible, parliamentary government	British colonies formed into a federation by Britain; post World War II self-government and independence; federal system and constitutional monarchy with representative, responsible, parliamentary government
Political culture: values	Liberal democratic principles, e.g. Locke	Liberal democratic principles adopted from British system	Liberal democratic principles with some influence from British system, rights and freedoms	Liberal democratic principles, equal rights and freedoms, under influence of occupying Western democracies	British influence in drafting constitution; hence, liberal democratic principles adopted from British system
System of government	Constitutional monarchy	Constitutional monarchy/federation	Republic/federation	Republic/federation	Constitutional monarchy/federation
Head of state	Hereditary monarch (Queen of England)	Hereditary monarch (Queen of England and Australia)	President (directly elected for a 4-year term; can be re-elected for a further 4 years only)	President (elected for a 5-year term by members of the Bundestag and members of the 16 federal states)	King (elected for a 5-year term by the sultans of the Federation)

(continued)

TABLE 2.3 (continued)
Political institutions: United Kingdom, Australia, United States, Federal Republic of Germany and Federation of Malaysia

	United Kingdom	Australia	United States	Federal Republic of Germany	Federation of Malaysia
Legislature	• House of Commons • House of Lords	• House of Representatives • Senate	Congress comprising: • House of Representatives • Senate	• Bundestag • Bundesrat	• House of Representatives • Senate
Executive	Prime minister and cabinet formed by majority party in the House of Commons	Prime minister and cabinet formed by majority party in the House of Representatives	President	Chancellor and cabinet formed by governing party in the Bundestag	Prime minister and cabinet formed by majority party in the House of Representatives
Judiciary	There is no formal separation of powers, rather the Executive and the Legislature are intertwined and together are able to override the Judiciary. This position is derived from the traditional idea dating from the seventeenth century that Parliament can do anything it wishes: it can make, amend or repeal any law, with the consequence that primary legislation passed by Parliament overrides any decisions made by the Courts and not even the highest Court in the land (the Law Lords, 12 of whom will constitute a separate Supreme Court from October 2009) can strike down an Act of Parliament as unconstitutional.[*]	High Court	Supreme Court	Federal Constitutional Court	Supreme Court

*(Source: Forman, F.N. & Baldwin, N.D.J. 2007, *Mastering British Politics*, 7th ed., Palgrave Macmillan, Basingstoke, UK, pp. 393–4)

QUESTIONS FOR DISCUSSION

1. Why would we call the institutional arrangements of Australia (and the other countries discussed in this chapter) 'liberal democracies'?
2. What values were important in the way in which these institutions were established?
3. How does this chapter illustrate the benefits and problems associated with comparative analysis?

FURTHER READING

Ahmad, Z.H. 1987, *Government and Politics of Malaysia*, Oxford University Press, Singapore.

Forman, F.N. & Baldwin, N.D.J. 2007, *Mastering British Politics*, 5th ed., Palgrave Macmillan, Basingstoke, UK.

Gomez, E.T. 2007, *Politics in Malaysia: The Malay Dimension*, Routledge, London.

Green, S. & Paterson, W.E. 2005, *Governance in Contemporary Germany: The Semi-sovereign State Revisited*, Cambridge University Press, New York.

Maddox, G. 2005, 'Australian Democracy', in *Australian Democracy in Theory and Practice*, 5th ed., Pearson Education, Sydney.

Meny, Y. & Knapp, A. 1998, *Government and Politics in Western Europe: Britain, France, Italy, Germany*, Oxford University Press, Oxford.

Parkin, A. 2006, 'Understanding Liberal-Democratic Politics', in Parkin, A., Summers, J. & Woodward, D. (eds), *Government, Politics, Power and Policy in Australia*, 8th ed., Pearson Education, Sydney.

Vile, M.J.C. 2007, *Politics in the USA*, 6th ed., Routledge, London.

USEFUL WEBSITES

Australia

 http://www.australia.gov.au
Australian Government
Entry point for institutions of the Australian government.

 http://www.pm.gov.au
Prime Minister of Australia
The prime minister's website, where you can access media releases and speeches, including the 'Sorry' motion to parliament, 13 February 2008.

 http://www.aph.gov.au
Parliament of Australia
See 'Parliament: An Overview' at http://www.aph.gov.au/parl.htm for details of Australia's federal parliamentary system.

http://www.facsia.gov.au
Department of Families, Housing, Community Services and Indigenous Affairs
The department is responsible for coordinating a whole-of-government approach to programs and services for Indigenous Australians.

Other countries

 http://www.direct.gov.uk
Directgov
Follow the link 'Government, citizens and rights' for information about the political institutions of the government of the United Kingdom.

 http://australianpolitics.com/usa/overview
Overview of the United States Political System
This site provides a comprehensive overview of the US political system.

 http://www.bundestag.de
German Bundestag
Information site about the parliament of the Federal Republic of Germany with a link to the full text of the Basic Law (constitution).

 http://www.commonlii.org/my/legis/const/1957
Constitution of Malaysia
Full text of the constitution of the Federation of Malaysia.

3

THE AUSTRALIAN CONSTITUTION

THIS CHAPTER EXPLAINS:

- the function of a constitution;
- influences that determine the format of a constitution, and forms of amendment used by different countries;
- the path to Australian federation;
- the making of the Australian Constitution;
- provisions of the Constitution, including the role of the governor-general;
- influences on the Constitution since Federation;
- judicial interpretation and the High Court;
- cooperation between governments;
- how the Australian Constitution can be amended;
- constitutional reform and the political agenda; and
- the republic and constitutional change.

THE FUNCTION OF A CONSTITUTION

The concept of a constitution derives from the principles of liberal democracy, which consider a formal separation of powers within government to be essential to the protection of individual freedom. The purpose is to put in place a system of checks and balances on the arbitral power of the government.

> A **constitution** in a liberal democracy places a legal limit on what a government can do and establishes the fundamental institutions of the political system.

A constitution is a social contract between the people and the government that sets out the rules by which government must operate. It usually takes the form of a written document, such as the Australian and American constitutions, but as we saw in Chapter 2, the situation in Britain is different. Its constitutional principles evolved from a set of traditions, customs and understandings from which developed a set of accepted practices, or *conventions*, about the exercise of political power and the relationships between the institutions of government.

> A **convention** is an established practice or 'working rule' that is not part of the law.

Basic components of the British constitution

The basic components are:
- statute law (Acts of parliament);
- conventions (established custom and practice);
- common law (case law);
- European Union law; and
- works of authority.

These are underpinned by the principles of:
- the sovereignty of parliament;
- the rule of law (the rights of individuals);
- constitutional monarchy;
- unitary-union state; and
- membership of the European Union.

(Source: Forman, F.N. & Baldwin, N.D.J. 2007, *Mastering British Politics*, 5th ed., Palgrave Macmillan, Basingstoke, UK, p. 25)

Influences on how a constitution is framed

The format of any particular constitution will be determined by the values and wishes of the people who frame it. As we saw in Chapter 2 (Table 2.3), the constitutional arrangements adopted by Britain, the United States, the Federal Republic of Germany and Malaysia were the product of political cultures derived from historical experience. The Australian Constitution similarly drew life from the values and ideas about government of the colonial politicians who drafted it, and from historical experience. They looked to two existing constitutional systems—the imperial motherland (Britain) and the United States—for the form and substance of the contract, and adopted the practices, or conventions, of the British Westminster system.

Constitutions as a function of independence

When the British acquired colonies—first in North America, the West Indies and India, then throughout Asia, Africa and the Pacific—they took with them the skeleton of their government. In some colonies the governor had considerable power, but colonists were gradually allowed such representation in the Legislative Council as the home government considered appropriate. However, many colonists demanded full control over their own affairs and began campaigns, which occasionally ended in war, in order to achieve it. On gaining their independence, colonists drafted constitutions that were intended to correct the faults they perceived in the colonial system of government. The oldest and best known of these written constitutions established the government of the United States, and eventually included three other important features:

- a broad statement of the nation's aims;
- a bill of rights listing the freedoms of individual citizens; and
- a provision for a supreme court to interpret the constitution according to changing circumstances.

> 'We the People of the United States in Order to form a more perfect Union, establish Justice, insure domestic Tranquility, provide for the common defence, promote the General Welfare, and secure the Blessings of Liberty to ourselves and our Posterity, do ordain and establish this Constitution for the United States of America.'
> (Source: The Constitution of the United States of America, cited in Vile, M.J.C. 2007, Politics in the USA, 6th ed., Routledge, New York, p. 286)

These features were later copied by some other countries. For example, the constitution of the Federal Republic of Germany includes principles establishing basic rights and freedoms. The United States Constitution includes a bill of rights.

Constitutions that marked a successful struggle for independence, and particularly those that incorporated a statement of principles, were taken to reflect the spirit of the new nations and their peoples. In one sense they signified a new beginning and were interpreted as such by later generations.

Amendment procedures

As constitutions are seen as providing the foundations of government, they are usually given special status in law. That is, they are not amended in the same way as ordinary statutes, which can be changed by a majority vote of the legislature. The drafters of constitutions believe that constant minor changes will weaken the systems of government they are devising. They also assume that their constitutions will prove of value to the people and should therefore be preserved.

TABLE 3.1

A comparison of procedures for constitutional amendment

Country	Process of constitutional amendment
Britain	Changes to the law and accepted practice
Australia	Referendum passed by a majority of electors plus a majority of states
United States	Amendments proposed by a two-thirds vote of each house of Congress or by a national convention called by Congress at the request of two-thirds of the states Ratified when the proposal is agreed to by the legislatures of three-quarters of the states or by conventions in three-quarters of the states
Federal Republic of Germany	Approval by two-thirds of the members of the Bundestag and two-thirds of the votes of the Bundesrat
Federation of Malaysia	Vote of not less than two-thirds of the total members of each house of parliament

Consequently, constitutions often require special forms of assent before they can be amended. In some instances a large majority of legislators, perhaps two-thirds of those eligible, have to vote in favour of change before it becomes law. Table 3.1 illustrates the different procedures that have been adopted for amending the constitutions of the countries included in our study.

> A **referendum** is a vote by electors to approve a change to the constitution.

Because these special provisions are included in the document, a constitution usually retains much of the same wording for many years, particularly if people see the document as having significance for their way of life. A good case and very persuasive argument will then be needed to convince citizens that proposed changes will be of benefit to them. Judicial interpretation or funding arrangements can also impact on how a constitution operates in practice and these may not necessarily comply with the original intent of its creators.

THE AUSTRALIAN CONSTITUTION: THE PATH TO FEDERATION

Constitutions for the Australian colonies

As the white population of the Australian colonies grew, the free settlers began to demand a larger role in their own government.

The Australian colonies did not have to fight for freedom and independence. The British government had encountered too much opposition from settlers in North America

> 'The drive towards democratic self-government had two components: getting rid of rule from London, and extending the basis of political authority in Australia.'
> (Source: Sawer, G. 1988, *The Australian Constitution*, AGPS, Canberra, p. 2)

to invite more confrontations. The British authorities were ready to make concessions, and as we saw in Chapter 2, between 1855 and 1860 all the colonies except Western Australia, which had to wait until 1890, gained responsible government. This meant that the colonial legislatures had almost complete authority to determine their separate affairs, including the power to amend their own constitutions.

This simple and rapid transfer of power to the Australian colonies meant that:

- because the colonial constitutions were granted rather than won, they held little of the significance for Australians that Americans saw in their constitution; and
- the Australian colonists saw no need to reject aspects of the British system of government, such as the monarch being recognised as head of state, that the Americans had considered oppressive and repugnant.

Consequently, the constitutions of the Australian colonies set out in written form the oldest and most basic features of British government, including the power of the monarch to appoint and dismiss ministers and to give final assent to legislation.

In fact, by the middle of the 19th century it had become accepted practice that the monarch would take direct action almost entirely on the advice of the government of the day. Power over day-to-day decisions had by then devolved to the cabinet, comprising ministers of the government, with the prime minister at its head. Despite these changes, which had been recognised as conventions of government, it was still accepted that, in law, ultimate authority rested with the Crown in parliament, and so written constitutions for the British colonies were drawn up with that in mind, vesting the power of the Crown with the representative of the monarch in the colony, the governor.

> 'The colonists of New South Wales may make what they please out of the colony. They may adopt whatever system of law, of police, of government, of taxation that they like . . . on themselves entirely rests the duty of directing the course of Government.'
> (Source: *Sydney Morning Herald*, 22 May 1856, cited in Crowley, F. 1980, *Colonial Australia 1841–1874*, vol. 2, Nelson, Melbourne, pp. 336–7)

When the colonial parliaments were granted responsible government, they recognised the role of cabinet and the premier, but neither was mentioned in their written constitutions. They copied many other practices from the English parliament. The foundations of colonial government were therefore based on the initial grant of power from Great Britain (the written constitution), with a number of conventions that drew on the traditional workings of the English parliament but were not written into the constitution itself.

Foundations for nationhood

The self-governing Australian colonies had many things in common, in addition to their similar constitutions. Their white populations comprised much the same cross-section of people from the British Isles; each wished to open up the hinterlands and hasten economic development; all needed better transport, more schools and hospitals, and improved communications; and each had much of its population concentrated in a coastal city separated by hundreds of miles from its neighbours' capitals. In each colony the government was drawn mainly from a prosperous group of farmers, graziers and professional men.

Despite these similarities, the colonies continued to develop separate identities and interests. Victoria had the strongest manufacturing industry and wished to protect it with tariffs; New South Wales sought free markets for agricultural produce; South Australia was aware that it was the only colony founded wholly by free settlers; and Western Australia was so remote from the eastern seaboard that it saw few useful links there, until the Kalgoorlie gold rush of the 1890s brought an influx of people with less parochial views.

So long as the colonies remained apart, each tended to develop the trappings of separate nations. Colonial boundaries served as customs barriers that hindered trade, and each colony had to face the problems of establishing defence forces, postal systems, and other complex and expensive agencies.

By the 1880s, some politicians were arguing that a single government was needed to provide a full range of services for an Australian nation. For some years the colonies had remained separated by poor transport and communications, as well as by political rivalries and competing economic interests. It was not until the 1870s that the cities and larger towns were linked by telegraph; nor until the late 1880s that railways were completed between Sydney, Melbourne, Brisbane and Adelaide. From that time the technological foundations of nationhood were available for those who wanted to build on them. It remained for colonial leaders to weigh the benefits of joining with their neighbours against the costs of adjusting their own interests to meet the demands of others. Other factors assisted those wanting to bring the colonies together, including:

- defence—fears that a major power (at various times, Germany, Russia, France and Japan) would threaten Australia's security by establishing colonies near its shores;
- immigration—demands for a united policy excluding cheap labour, which might undermine the conditions that had been won by Australian workers (the beginnings of the 'White Australia' policy); and
- nationalism—feelings that Australia needed to establish its own identity and take pride in it.

Proposals for political action to achieve a federal union were put forward by Sir Henry Parkes in a speech at the School of Arts in Tenterfield in 1889.

> 'The first movement worthy of the noble object of bringing all Australians under one National Government arose from my initiation in October 1889.'
> (Source: Parkes, H. 1892, *Fifty Years in the Making of Australian History*, vol. 2, Longmans, Green and Co., London, p. 337)

In 1891, after discussions between the governments of the colonies, a National Constitutional Convention met in Sydney.

Federalism and the division of powers

The politicians from the colonial parliaments who attended the 1891 Constitutional Convention wanted to establish a national government, at the same time protecting the interests of the separate colonies and preserving as much as possible of their own power bases. It was neither feasible nor thought desirable to set up a single government for the whole continent, in line with the *unitary* system of Great Britain.

Most delegates to the convention wanted to retain the British system of parliamentary government that they had adopted in their own colonies, but they also sought an arrangement in which the constituent parts of the nation would not come to be dominated by its central government. For this they looked to the *federal* system of government that had emerged in Switzerland, Canada and, in particular, the United States.

Federalism involved a division of powers between the national (federal) government and the states (in Switzerland, cantons; in Canada, provinces). Such a division had to be recorded in a detailed, written constitution. There were two main alternatives in determining how power should be divided:

- to give certain limited powers to a weak central government while allowing state governments to retain a high level of autonomy (*confederation*); and
- to divide powers between the national government and state governments in such a way that each had authority in its own sphere (*federalism*).

There was no real doubt that Australia would adopt the federal model. The Australian colonies wanted to create a national government with genuine powers; at the same time they wanted to restrict those powers, so as not to encroach on their own responsibilities. The focus of the framers of the Australian Constitution, therefore, was twofold: the British tradition of parliamentary government, and the American system of federalism.

THE MAKING OF THE AUSTRALIAN CONSTITUTION

Framing the Australian Constitution involved several constitutional conventions with representative delegates from the colonies, and popular referendums within the colonies to endorse their findings:

- 1891—first Australian Constitutional Convention, comprising representatives of the governments of the six Australian colonies and New Zealand; failed to produce agreement among the colonies, mainly because its delegates were more concerned to preserve the powers of their colonial governments than to develop a federal system.
- 1893 and 1896—meetings of those community leaders interested in federation.
- 1897 and 1898—second Australian Constitutional Convention, responsible for producing a draft constitution. Elected representatives, apart from Western Australia, whose delegates were chosen by the Western Australian parliament. The delegations, in fact, comprised mostly colonial politicians. Queensland, which could not agree on how

the colony should be represented, and New Zealand, did not take part. New Zealand went on to form a separate nation, with a unitary government. This second convention included a number of younger politicians who were more strongly committed to federation, and so agreement was reached on a draft constitution.
- 1898—referendums to approve the draft constitution in New South Wales, Victoria, South Australia and Tasmania were passed but failed to receive the requisite majority in New South Wales.
- 1899—referendums in New South Wales, Victoria, South Australia, Tasmania and Queensland produced a narrow majority in favour of federation, with a relatively small percentage of citizens exercising their voluntary vote.
- 9 July 1900—draft constitution passed into law by the British parliament.
- 31 July 1900—Western Australia voted to join the federation.
- 1 January 1901—Commonwealth of Australia, involving six states in the Australian federation, came into force.

Drafting the Constitution

The Australian Constitution reflects the time in which it was drawn up and the interests of the white, male, upper- and middle-class colonial politicians who drafted it. There were no women or Aborigines included among the delegates. Neither was the working class included, with the exception of one Labor delegate to the 1897 Convention.

> Only 16 of the 46 delegates who attended the Sydney Convention of 1891 were born in Australia. They were tall, and 'the superficial characteristic most in common . . . was the amount of hair on their faces'.
> (Source: La Nauze, J.A. 1972, *The Making of the Australian Constitution*, Melbourne University Press, Melbourne, p. 30)

At the end of the 19th century, these influential Australians saw government as having fairly narrow concerns:
- to provide some social services, such as schools and hospitals, to supplement those established by churches and private organisations;
- to expand the facilities—roads, harbours, railways—needed by farmers and merchants to develop the country's economy;
- to raise a certain minimum of money, partly through taxes but often in the form of loans, to finance these services; and
- to provide for the defence and security of the citizens.

Those who attended the constitutional conventions gave different emphases to the general concerns of government, and to the functions of the proposed federal government in particular:
- Some, who had liberal views for that time, wanted to see government with the power to bring about reforms, and in doing so give wide representation to the people.
- Others, who were mostly wealthy, wanted to protect their position by limiting the numbers of voters (restricting the *franchise*) and limiting the powers of governments that might wish to interfere with property.

- Representatives of the smaller and poorer colonies wanted to protect them from the possible dominance of New South Wales and Victoria, whose large populations would give them as many representatives in a democratically elected assembly as the other four colonies combined.

Nevertheless, delegates to the constitutional conventions had much in common:

- All agreed that governments should have modest powers and should be frugal.
- With one exception, they were members of colonial parliaments and saw a duty to protect the interests of their separate colonies.
- The great majority had backgrounds in the professions (mainly law), commerce and the pastoral industry; they scarcely represented the interests of the workers, whose industrial and political strength was only beginning to be exercised through the trade unions and the colonial Labor parties. There was only one Labor representative, and Labor was generally ambivalent about federalism.

The constitution that was drafted by these delegates reflected their essential conservatism—a satisfaction with the patterns of government they knew. Most were content to make no more than essential adjustments to those patterns in order to permit federation.

Social occasions for delegates to the 1891 Constitutional Convention included 'the inevitable banquet', held in the Sydney Town Hall, where the 'assembled statesmen' partook of 'schnapper, braised sweetbreads, fried chicken, lamb cutlets, Salmi de Canard Sauvage and other delicacies', and a band provided musical entertainment.
(*Source*: La Nauze, J.A. 1972, *The Making of the Australian Constitution*, Melbourne University Press, Melbourne, p. 33)

Problems of drafting

The drafting of the constitution nevertheless presented difficulties:

- It was necessary to preserve links with the British Crown, while establishing truly responsible government.
- Delegates to the conventions had to balance the population and wealth of Victoria and New South Wales against the interests of the less powerful and populous states.
- It was essential to provide the federal government with sufficient powers to allow it to function effectively, while preserving the identity of the states.

It was not sufficient that the delegates reach agreement among themselves on these problems. The solutions had to be written in such a way that their meaning would be clear to the citizens in the colonies and to later generations. This led to long discussions on the major problems involving the structure of the federal government, and also on related questions concerning the detailed provisions of the constitution. Agreement was not easy, and delegates had to reach compromises on many points.

In deciding on the structure of the federal government, the delegates were guided by the difficulties they had experienced in their colonies or had read about in other countries.

The Crown and responsible government

The role of the Crown might have been thought to present the greatest problem, for how could conventions that had evolved in Britain over centuries, and which had never been set down fully in laws there, be reduced to writing in Australia? How much detailed wording would be required, for example, to describe the role of the prime minister and its relationship to the monarch or the monarch's representative? What were the true functions of cabinet, and how could these be explained in law? These problems were overcome in the simplest way. Although they received attention during convention debates, they were ignored in the final document. The drafters of the federal constitution merely followed the colonial model:

- wording the document as if the monarch or the monarch's representative (the governor-general) took an active part in everyday government (for example, s. 5 provides: 'The Governor-General may appoint such times for holding the sessions of Parliament as he thinks fit', whereas in practice the government of the day determines the exact dates for meetings); and
- assuming that conventions relating to such things as the powers and functions of cabinet would be accepted as a matter of tradition and general knowledge.

This practice had generally proved satisfactory in the colonies, but its continued effectiveness depended on politicians agreeing to observe the conventions. This would prove particularly difficult if certain conventions came into conflict with each other. Such a conflict was made possible at the national level, where parts of the Westminster and federal systems were grafted on to each other in the final structure of government.

Parliament in a federal system

It was generally accepted that at the national level, as in the colonies, Australia would follow the parliamentary system of government. This meant that a majority of cabinet members and the prime minister would sit in a democratically elected lower house, which would necessarily be the centre of government power. In Britain, decisions of the House of Commons could be reviewed to a limited extent by the House of Lords, but by the 1890s the power of the Lords had been considerably reduced. In the Australian colonies there were legislative councils (upper houses) comprising more conservative politicians, usually elected on a restricted franchise, which could review decisions of the legislative assemblies (lower houses); but even there the power of government was centred in the lower houses.

The Australian Constitution had to establish an orthodox lower house, while ensuring that government as a whole would not be dominated by the representatives of the more populous states, who would comprise the majority of the lower house's members. This meant that the Westminster model, with its unitary government and hereditary House of Lords, could not be followed.

A familiar example was the federal constitution of the United States, where the strong representation of populous states in the lower house was offset by providing all states with *equal representation in the Senate*.

This precedent was followed in Australia, but under the parliamentary system a further step was necessary: the Senate had to be given virtually equal powers with the lower house (House of Representatives) in order to provide the smaller states with at least the potential to influence government actions. This made it possible for the two houses, and the conventions governing their conduct, to come into conflict (with the serious consequences discussed later).

State and federal powers

It was clear that the federal government should be given complete control over certain aspects of policy—for example, defence, customs and currency—as one of the main motives for federation was to achieve a common approach to such matters. However, there was much disagreement about the additional powers the federal government might require. Relatively few were granted, and then only grudgingly, as a consequence of yet more compromises between those delegates in favour of a stronger federal government and others concerned with protecting states' rights. These included powers over such matters as taxation, marriage and divorce, railways, and conciliation and arbitration.

Remaining powers, which at that time appeared most important to the Australian people, rested with the states. The three kinds of powers are often termed:

- those exercised only by the federal government—*exclusive* powers;
- those shared by state and federal governments—*concurrent* powers; and
- the remainder exercised by the states—*residual* powers.

FIGURE 3.1
Arrival of the new baby

Nurse Barton: 'He aint much to look at now. But wait till he grows!'
(*Source: The Bulletin*, 14 July 1900, reproduced by permission from *The Bulletin*, www.acpsyndication.com)

In order to overcome conflict between federal and state legislation in areas over which the governments exercised concurrent powers, the Constitution provided, in s. 109, that federal laws, and indeed the federal constitution itself, should 'prevail'. Other disagreements and uncertainties could be referred to the High Court. Federation was an accomplishment, in view of the rivalries and suspicions among the people who eventually agreed to it.

> The rivalry between New South Wales and Victoria is illustrated by the statement by the Victorian premier at the 1883 Intercolonial Convention that 'he had found Sydney asleep' and 'had awakened the slumberers and led them to do their federal duty'. A New South Wales parliamentary delegate replied 'amid the cheers of the Assembly, that New South Wales was as far above Victoria as Heaven was above the earth'.
> (*Source*: Deakin, A. 1963, *The Federal Story*, 2nd ed., Melbourne University Press, Melbourne, p. 16)

PROVISIONS OF THE CONSTITUTION

The Australian Constitution is not hard to read if one has even a slight acquaintance with 'legal' language. Even without that, it requires only careful attention to the wording to follow the meaning of each section. Clearly, one must read the Constitution itself (see the appendix to this book) in order to appreciate its detailed provisions.

The Australian Constitution comprises eight chapters. Of these chapters, four have posed no problems; two have been the subject of major legal challenge; and two contain provisions that have either led to disagreement or produced results different from those anticipated when the Constitution was drafted.

Non-problematic chapters

The following four chapters in the Constitution have posed few problems:

- *Chapter 5: The States.* The former colonies become states of the Commonwealth of Australia.
- *Chapter 6: New States.* New states may be admitted to the Commonwealth (but so far none has been).
- *Chapter 7: Miscellaneous.* This provides for the location of the national capital and for the appointment of the governor-general's deputies.
- *Chapter 8: Alteration of the Constitution.* The Constitution may be amended by referendum. (Amendment has proved difficult, but the referendum process itself is clear enough.)

Chapters that have been the subject of major legal challenge

The two chapters of the Constitution which have been the subject of major legal challenge are as follows:

- *Chapter 3: The Judicature.* This chapter establishes the federal judicature (the system of courts and judges), especially the High Court (s. 71). The High Court hears appeals from other jurisdictions (including, in many cases, the states), and decides matters relating to the Constitution itself. Its chief justice and justices are appointed until the age of 70 (referendum 1977), and may be removed only by a vote of both houses of parliament for 'proved misbehaviour or incapacity' (s. 72(ii)). This has not occurred, although the question was raised during the public discussion of allegations made against Mr Justice Lionel Murphy in the mid-1980s. The Commonwealth government has also set up (s. 77) the Federal Court of Australia (which deals with bankruptcy, matters relating to trade practices, and a range of appeals), the Family Court of Australia, as well as courts for the Australian Capital Territory and the Northern Territory. From 1976 to 1994, the Federal Court of Australia dealt with industrial matters under federal law, but in 1994 these functions were transferred to the Industrial Relations Court of Australia. In 1996, the Industrial Relations Court was abolished and its jurisdiction transferred back to the Federal Court. Other matters arising under federal laws are heard in the first instance by state courts, which were granted these powers by the federal parliament (see s. 77).

- *Chapter 4: Finance and Trade.* This chapter allows the federal government to decide how much of the money raised by the Commonwealth is returned to the states (under s. 87, which set a fixed proportion of three-quarters to the states and one-quarter to the Commonwealth for the first 10 years of federation *only*). It also:
  — sets out other financial arrangements, which seek to ensure that all states are treated fairly by the Commonwealth government;
  — gives the Commonwealth sole power over customs and excise;
  — provides for free trade within Australia (s. 92);
  — allows the federal government to grant additional money to the states under any conditions it sees fit (s. 96); and
  — permits the Commonwealth to take over states' debts, and allows the Commonwealth and the states to make agreements for the borrowing of money (s. 105, added following a referendum in 1928).

There have been serious disagreements between state governments and the federal government over several of these provisions, following which High Court decisions have generally permitted the federal government to increase its control over finance. Section 92 was intended to ensure that there would be no customs barrier between the states, but until 1988 it was usually interpreted by the High Court in such a manner as to limit federal government control of companies that trade between the states. This includes almost all the larger corporations. (These developments are discussed further later in this chapter.)

Problematic chapters

Chapters 1 and 2 contain provisions that have led to disagreements and others that have produced results different from those anticipated when the Constitution was drafted.

Chapter 1: The Parliament

By far the longest in the Constitution, *Chapter 1: The Parliament* contains almost half of the total number of sections (60 out of 128). It is divided into five parts:

- *Part I — General.* This part relates mainly to the office of governor-general and to the sitting of parliament. Note that s. 2 states that the monarch appoints the governor-general, but by convention such decisions are made only on the advice of the government of the day.

- *Part II—The Senate.* This part mainly concerns the election, term in office and replacement of senators, and the business of the upper house.
- *Part III—The House of Representatives.* This part provides for the direct election of members for a maximum term of three years for the House, and for certain procedures in the conduct of business of the House. Note that the House of Representatives has 'as nearly as practicable' twice as many members as the Senate (s. 24). This is known as the 'nexus' provision.
- *Part IV—Both houses of parliament.* This part of the chapter sets out the qualifications for senators and members of the House of Representatives (MHR, or sometimes MP), and for their disqualification in certain circumstances; provides for payment of members; allows parliament to establish its own rules of procedure; and establishes parliamentary privilege (essentially, freedom of speech on the floor of either house and protection from unwarranted attack on the functioning of parliament).
- *Part V—Powers of the parliament.* The provisions in this part of the chapter have caused trouble, mainly because they allocate power, the distribution of which is one of the main concerns of politics. Distribution here takes place on two levels:

    1. between the federal government and the state governments; and
    2. between the House of Representatives and the Senate.

    The controversial elements of Part V are discussed in more detail below.

The distribution of power between the federal government and the state governments

Specific powers are allocated to the federal government under s. 51. These are set out in 40 subsections, and include:

- the exclusive Commonwealth powers; and
- those shared concurrently with the state governments.

By implication, matters not mentioned in s. 51 or elsewhere in the Constitution comprise the states' *residual* powers. The extent of federal power is a matter for interpretation. For example, does the defence power (s. 51(vi)) allow the federal government to impose wide-ranging economic controls over the nation in carrying on a war? (The High Court ruled in 1916 that it does.) However, at a time when war has not actually been declared, can the Commonwealth, say, outlaw the Communist Party? (The High Court ruled in 1951 that it could not.) A great many arguments have arisen over the powers granted by this and other subsections of s. 51 and they will continue to be brought before the High Court for determination.

The distribution of power between the House of Representatives and the Senate

Section 53 provides that the Senate may neither introduce nor amend laws that raise money or impose taxes for the ordinary annual services of the government, commonly called 'supply'. Such powers are therefore reserved for the House of Representatives.

Section 54 provides that a 'law which appropriates revenue or moneys for the annual services of the Government shall deal only with such appropriation'. The purpose of this section is to prevent appropriations for other purposes being included in an appropriation bill for the annual services of the government.

> For a comprehensive explanation of the meaning of ss. 53 and 54, and a discussion of what is meant by 'supply', see Evans, H. (ed.) 2004, *Odgers' Senate Practice*, 11th ed., Department of the Senate, Canberra, p. 275; Constitutional Centenary Foundation 1997, *The Australian Constitution*, Constitutional Centenary Foundation, Melbourne, pp. 60–2.

Section 53 also prescribes that in all other legislation 'the Senate shall have equal powers with the House of Representatives'. That includes the power to defer or reject laws (including, in the view of most constitutional experts, money bills). The Senate, which was established as a key feature of the federal system, clearly needed substantial powers in order to protect states' interests. This was originally intended as its main function. However, a most difficult situation would arise if the Senate failed to pass the legislation that each year provides the money for the conduct of government. That proved to be the case for the Whitlam Labor government when it was 'refused supply' by the Senate in 1975, and as a consequence of this and other events, Gough Whitlam's commission as prime minister was withdrawn by the governor-general and a new election was held. (See the following discussion relating to Chapter 2 of the Constitution.)

The drafters of the Constitution realised that there would have to be a method of resolving deadlocks between the House of Representatives and the Senate. This is known as the *double dissolution*. It is provided for in s. 57, as follows:

- If the Senate fails to pass a bill in a form considered by the House of Representatives as satisfactory, that bill may be returned to the Senate. (There is a requirement that three months elapse between the first and second presentations.)
- If the Senate again fails to pass the bill after the three-month interval, parliament may be dissolved and a new election held for the House of Representatives and all senators (the double dissolution).
- If, after that election, the Senate still fails to pass the bill, a joint sitting of both houses may be held to consider the legislation.
- If the joint sitting votes in favour of the bill, then the bill becomes law.

Section 57 implies that:

- a double dissolution places matters in the hands of the voters, who will re-elect a government if they want its bills to become law;
- a political party may gain enough seats in the House of Representatives to form a government, but may still lack a majority in the Senate. This occurred in 1974, when the Whitlam government was returned to office after a double dissolution, but with only 29 of the 60 Senate places; and
- the re-elected government will have a large enough majority in the House of Representatives to make up for its deficit in the Senate.

At the first and only joint sitting following the double dissolution election of 1974, the Whitlam government had the numbers and so the bills that led to the double dissolution were passed (see Table 3.2).

However, the provisions of s. 57 may not be sufficient to overcome the difficulties arising from the Senate's failure to grant supply, as two other possibilities can arise:

- The government may not wish to have a double dissolution and election, if it is at all likely that it would lose.
- The government may be running out of money and unlikely to obtain more.

This was the situation in November 1975 when the governor-general withdrew the prime minister's commission and ordered a double dissolution. (The subsequent election produced a Liberal–National Country Party government with a very large majority.)

TABLE 3.2
Votes by party: joint sitting of the House of Representatives and the Senate, 1974

	Members of the House of Representatives	Senators	Total
Government (ALP)	66	29	95
Opposition (Liberal–National)	61	29	90
Others	—	2	2

Chapter 2: The role of the governor-general

The other contentious chapter in the Constitution is *Chapter 2: The Executive Government*. This chapter provides for the governor-general and the Executive Council. It makes no direct reference to the conventions of responsible government under which decisions are made by the cabinet and prime minister and are then ratified by the governor-general in council (that is, with the advice of the Executive Council—a formality, as executive councillors are in fact government ministers). Rather, the chapter reads as if the governor-general:

- exercises power directly (s. 61);
- appoints (and dismisses) executive councillors, whose duty it is to advise him or her (ss. 62, 63);
- establishes departments of the public service and appoints and dismisses the ministers (termed 'officers' in the Constitution) who are responsible for them (s. 64); and
- is commander-in-chief of the armed forces (s. 68).

Section 64 also prevents a minister from holding office for longer than three months *unless* he or she is elected to parliament. This guarantees one of the conventions of the Westminster system, under which ministers are drawn from within parliament.

The founding fathers drew on the British model when they developed the Australian Constitution within the framework of a constitutional monarchy.

> 'In a **constitutional monarchy**, the acts done by the monarch or in the name of the monarch are done in accordance with the constitution and on the advice of ministers, not by the self-will of the monarch.'
> (*Source*: Hasluck, P. 1979, *The Office of Governor-General*, Melbourne University Press, Melbourne, p. 8)

Because the Queen lived in the United Kingdom and for practical reasons could not perform the functions of a head of state on a day-to-day basis, those responsibilities were assigned in the Constitution to the governor-general to act as the Queen's representative.

Appointment of the governor-general

The governor-general is appointed by the Queen acting on the advice of the prime minister. In 2008, on the recommendation of the Rudd government, Quentin Bryce became the first woman to be appointed governor-general of Australia.

> 'A Governor-General appointed by the Queen shall be Her Majesty's representative in the Commonwealth, and shall have and may exercise in the Commonwealth during the Queen's pleasure, but subject to this Constitution, such powers and functions of the Queen as Her Majesty may be pleased to assign to him.'
> (Source: The Australian Constitution, s. 2)

The governor-general, as the Queen's representative in Australia, performs constitutional, ceremonial and non-ceremonial functions as set out below.

Constitutional duties of the governor-general

The governor-general's constitutional duties are as follows:

- dissolving parliament and issuing writs for new elections;
- giving assent to laws when they have been passed by the two houses of parliament—the Senate and the House of Representatives;
- acting on the advice of ministers through the Executive Council to issue regulations and proclamations under existing laws; appointing federal judges, ambassadors and high commissioners to overseas countries and other senior government officials; issuing Royal Commissions of Inquiry; exercising the prerogative of mercy; and
- authorising many other executive decisions by ministers, such as raising government loans or approving treaties with foreign governments.

> The governor-general is the commander-in-chief of the Australian Defence Force, although in practice he or she acts only on the advice of ministers and cabinet. Subject to cabinet, the minister for defence is responsible for Australia's defence policy.
> (Source: Governor-General of Australia 2008, 'Governor-General's Role', http://www.gg.gov.au, copyright Commonwealth of Australia, reproduced by permission)

Ceremonial duties of the governor-general

The governor-general's ceremonial duties are as follows:

- opening parliament;
- swearing in prime ministers and ministers;
- receiving the credentials of foreign diplomats;
- holding investitures;
- reviewing military parades;

- receiving and entertaining foreign heads of state and heads of government; and
- representing Australia on state and official visits to foreign countries made at the invitation of foreign governments and with the advice and approval of the Australian government.

Non-ceremonial duties of the governor-general

The governor-general's non-ceremonial duties are as follows:

- speaking at, and opening, national and international conferences;
- presenting awards at major public gatherings, ranging from exhibitions and sports meetings to university graduations, or at meetings of learned societies and professional institutes;
- attending functions held by all kinds of community organisations, and particularly those of which the governor-general is patron or principal office-bearer;
- making official visits to the states and territories or to regions or localities;
- receiving 'courtesy calls' by office-bearers and other representatives of national, regional and, occasionally, international organisations; and
- giving dinners, lunches and receptions for invited guests from all sections of the Australian community.

(*Source*: Smith, D. *1997, The Role of the Governor-General, Our Australian Head of State*, Australians for a Constitutional Monarchy, Sydney, pp. 12–13)

The republican debate in recent years has brought out differences of opinion about the role of the Queen as Australia's head of state. Sir David Smith, former official secretary to a number of Australian governors-general and a member of the organisation Australians for a Constitutional Monarchy, has argued that the Queen is our sovereign and the governor-general is our constitutional head of state. He also points out that Australians have held the office of governor-general since 1965.

The Final Report of the Constitutional Commission in 1988, on the other hand, states that, because of the role in government assigned to the monarch by the Constitution, 'In the Commonwealth of Australia, the Head of State is, and always has been, the person who, for the time being, is also the King or Queen of Australia'. The constitutional powers exercised by the Queen are the power to appoint and dismiss the governor-general (s. 2); the power to appoint and dismiss administrators (s. 4); and the power to authorise the governor-general to appoint deputies (s. 126).

The 'reserve' powers

If you were to read the Australian Constitution without any knowledge of how the system actually works, it would appear that the governor-general exercises a significant amount of power in the political system, including what are called the *reserve powers*. In particular, these are the powers to:

- appoint and dismiss ministers, including the prime minister (although that specific office is not included in the Constitution);
- dissolve the House of Representatives; and
- simultaneously dissolve the House of Representatives and the Senate (that is, to force a double dissolution in the case of a deadlock between the houses).

> 'Sometimes a Governor-General may make a decision without or even against advice. When this happens, he or she is said to be exercising "reserve" powers.'
> (Source: Saunders, C. 1998, *It's Your Constitution*, Federation Press, Sydney, p. 97)

In practice, however, the exercise of the 'reserve' powers is limited by the conventions of the Constitution, discussed earlier in this chapter. Under those conventions, the governor-general is expected to exercise those powers on the advice of his or her ministers.

There is some debate, however, about the level of discretion that the governor-general can bring to bear when making these decisions. It has been suggested, for example, that there are four possible scenarios under which the governor-general might dismiss the prime minister:

- 'The governor-general has an absolute uncontrolled power of dismissal.
- The governor-general has the power to dismiss a prime minister who is acting against the law and the constitution.
- The governor-general has an ultimate discretionary power of dismissal which should be exercised in exceptional circumstances when the fundamental principles of the constitution are being subverted.
- A governor-general can dismiss a prime minister as a means of resolving a supply deadlock.'

(Source: Cooray, L.J.M. 1979, *Conventions, the Australian Constitution and the Future*, Legal Books, Sydney, pp. 51–2)

Former governor-general Sir Paul Hasluck has argued that the governor-general has a responsibility 'to make sure that all actions of the government are constitutionally correct and lawful'. He suggests that although it is unlikely, in theory the governor-general could return to parliament any bill that contains errors in the text or is clearly in contravention of the Constitution. The first could be remedied easily by redrafting. The second, however, could place the governor-general in conflict with the government of the day, and might spark off a constitutional crisis. He similarly argues that in the case of the dissolution of parliament, it is the responsibility of the governor-general to be sure that the necessary legislative measures have been put in place and, in the case of an early election, 'to make the judgement whether the dissolution is needed to serve the purposes of good government'.
(Source: Hasluck, P. 1979, *The Office of Governor-General*, Melbourne University Press, Melbourne, pp. 13–17)

In practice, however, the governor-general agrees to the prime minister's request.

> 'If the power exists it is confined to emergency situations in which the ordinary operations of government are insufficient to solve the problem.'
> (Source: Sawer, G. 1977, *Federation under Strain*, Melbourne University Press, Melbourne, p. 153)
>
> 'Whether it is proper to force a dissolution depends on the circumstances and about these there may be disagreement. Indeed any exercise of the power will probably produce argument and disagreement, precisely because it is a discretionary power.'
> (Source: Kerr, J. 1978, *Matters for Judgement: An Autobiography*, Macmillan, Melbourne, p. 217)

The dismissal of the Whitlam government

Former governor-general Sir John Kerr, acting without the advice of the prime minister, used the reserve powers on 11 November 1975 to dismiss the Whitlam government, appoint a caretaker government, dissolve the parliament and call a federal election. He argued that he was acting to uphold the Constitution, whereas Prime Minister Gough Whitlam considered Sir John Kerr had acted contrary to the conventions of the Westminster system, which held that the governor-general should act only on the advice of the government of the day.

> 'Mr Whitlam and his colleagues should, I thought, be dismissed because they insisted, contrary to the customary procedures of constitutional government, on governing without parliamentary supply, failing to resign or advise an election.'
> (Source: Kerr, J. 1978, *Matters for Judgement*, Macmillan, Melbourne, p. 336)
>
> 'The crisis of October–November 1975 was essentially a political crisis, capable of solution by political means.'
> (Source: Whitlam, E.G. 1979, *The Truth of the Matter*, Penguin, Ringwood, Victoria, p. 1, reproduced with permission)

According to Sir Paul Hasluck, the fact that the power was used is evidence that it exists and its use is subject to the discretion of the office-holder at the time. This is certainly true, but a governor-general would have to have sound reasons to dismiss a government without overstepping the accepted bounds of the position. The difficulty arises in determining at what point convention or the provisions of the Constitution should prevail.

The reserve powers of the Constitution exist to be used in the exceptional circumstances of a constitutional crisis, but the decision to use them is made in a political context—and, it could be argued, is therefore political. There has been a lot of debate about the timing of the governor-general's intervention in 1975, with supporters of the Whitlam government and others arguing that Kerr acted too soon because a political solution was still possible. Kerr argued that he considered the political process had failed and that there was a substantial risk that the government would be governing without supply. The use of the reserve powers in 1975 is a contentious issue and will remain so until the conditions for their use are codified in the Constitution.

> 'The point at issue in the public controversy . . . is not whether the Governor-General had the power but whether he was justified by the facts as he saw and interpreted them, and if he were justified by the facts whether he was wise to use the power.'
> (Source: Hasluck, P. 1979, *The Office of the Governor-General*, Melbourne University Press, Melbourne, p. 2)

Dismissal of a governor-general

No governor-general has been dismissed from office. The conditions under which a governor-general should be dismissed became an issue in 2003 following a public controversy about allegations that the governor-general, Dr Peter Hollingworth, when he was archbishop of Brisbane, had covered up child sex abuse in the Anglican Church. Dr Hollingworth strongly disputed the allegations, but public pressure grew for his removal as governor-general.

Under s. 2 of the Constitution, it is the responsibility of the Queen to appoint or dismiss a governor-general, but in practical terms, as we know, the Queen acts on the advice of the Australian prime minister. Prime Minister John Howard refused to dismiss the governor-general, but Dr Hollingworth's position became politically untenable as community support for his retention fell away. On 25 May 2003, the governor-general bowed to public pressure and resigned:

> It is with deep regret and after much thought that I have today advised the Prime Minister that I wish to resign from the office of governor-general of the Commonwealth of Australia. I have asked him to put the necessary arrangements in place to advise Her Majesty the Queen. Despite the misplaced and unwarranted allegations made against me as Governor-General, it is clear that continuing public controversy has the potential to undermine and diminish my capacity to uphold the importance, dignity and integrity of this high office [that] I have been privileged and proud to occupy. I cannot allow that to occur.
> (*Source*: *The Australian*, 27 May 2003)

> For information about the functions of the governor-general, see 'Frequently Asked Questions about the Office of Governor-General', Research Note No. 10, 2003–04, Department of the Parliamentary Library, Canberra, http://www.aph.gov.au/library/pubs/rn/2003-04/04rn10.htm.

The Australian Constitution presents complex problems and is a source of continuing disagreement. Many of these difficulties were foreseen when the Constitution was being drafted, but remained unsolved in order that there could be agreement on the larger issue of federation itself. Despite its shortcomings, the Constitution is accepted by Australians as the legitimate source of national political power. Even in the upheaval of late 1975, discussion centred on action taken under the Constitution and not on things that might be done in defiance of it. The Constitution provides the foundations for many of the major political institutions in Australia, and so any discussion of the situation as it is (or as it should be) proceeds with that fact in mind. The form and structure of those institutions and their constitutional underpinnings are integral to the debate about whether Australia should become a republic (discussed later in this chapter).

INFLUENCES ON THE CONSTITUTION SINCE FEDERATION

Those who drafted the Australian Constitution could not have foreseen the great technological and social changes, nor the crises of war and depression, that would occur in the 20th century. They could hardly be blamed for that. Yet, they were designing a system of government that would be used in future decades very different from their own. Today, governments raise and spend vast sums of money, legislate to control a great range of activities, and provide aid for numerous disadvantaged people. The passage of years since Federation has seen the original conception of the federal relationship with its limited role for the federal government undermined by a significant centralisation of power with the Commonwealth. The factors that have brought about this increasing role for the federal government are closely related to each other:

- Members of parliament, once elected, desire to use the powers available to them: federal politicians, no matter what their state backgrounds, usually develop a national point of view (strongly influenced by party attitudes) and, in advancing their own careers, extend the interests of the Commonwealth government.
- Successive federal governments have responded to many demands which necessarily involved an extension of their role: for improved social services, for tariff protection against imported goods, for bounties on Australian produce, for railways that state governments could not afford. The more such demands were met, the more likely it became that others would be made. Since the 1990s, federal governments have sought to devolve some of these operations to the private sector, but demands for government assistance and intervention in new policy areas such as environmental protection and regulation of privatised functions will ensure a continuing, and possibly more regulatory, role for government so long as it accepts responsibility for oversight of these matters.
- New technology has appeared: changes in living patterns and problems created by these developments have required government intervention. Innovations such as the aeroplane, radio, television and wireless broadband have led to the creation of new federal bodies.
- The federal government's increased financial resources brought about by its taking over the collection of income tax from the states, and a greater use of specific purpose grants utilising s. 96 of the Constitution, have added to the economic powers conferred on it by the Constitution (over currency exchange rates, excise, tariffs and international trade). It became the obvious agency for economic management, and the only level of government with the resources to meet some demands. (See Chapter 4 for detailed discussion of federal–state financial relations.) The internationalisation of the Australian economy and the country's involvement with multilateral trading arrangements have also placed greater emphasis on the federal government as the manager of economic change.

The discussion of the changing balance of federal power in the Commonwealth's favour has so far listed the steps involved and the main reasons why the federal government gained its predominance. It is now necessary to consider how this came about, particularly as the Constitution was intended to preserve a balance of powers. The Constitution provided several methods of altering the relationship between the Commonwealth and the states. The first to be considered, and the most far-reaching, has been judicial interpretation of the Constitution's wording.

JUDICIAL INTERPRETATION: THE HIGH COURT

Role of the High Court

'The High Court is the highest court in the Australian judicial system. It was established in 1901 by Section 71 of the Constitution. The functions of the High Court are to interpret and apply the law of Australia; to decide cases of special federal significance including challenges to the constitutional validity of laws and to hear appeals, by special leave, from Federal, State and Territory courts.

The seat of the High Court is in Canberra, where it is located in its own building within the Parliamentary Triangle.'

(*Source*: High Court of Australia 2008, 'About the Court', http://www.hcourt.gov.au/about_01.html)

FIGURE 3.2
The High Court

(*Source*: Courtesy of the High Court of Australia)

The Constitution gave the High Court the power to interpret the Constitution, and this role has been strengthened in recent years with the abolition of all right of appeal to the Privy Council in London. Appeals to the Privy Council from the High Court were abolished in 1975 and from state Supreme Courts in 1986. In fact, constitutional cases are a minority of those that come before the High Court (the rest are appeals from other jurisdictions), but they are of great political significance.

Constitutional cases generally arise from disagreements about the powers of the federal government or state governments (or, on occasion, all of them) to act on certain matters—trade, arbitration, prices and banking, for example. The High Court's attitude to such matters can affect subsequent actions, as its decisions are binding on all lower courts and set *precedents* that are usually followed in later years by the High Court itself.

Constitutional authorities often see the High Court's rulings as falling into four periods. In the first period the court tended to contain federal powers; in the second, it gave broader interpretations of them; in the third, it maintained the Commonwealth's role without adding significantly to it; and in the current, fourth, period it is once again giving a broader interpretation of federal powers.

Phase 1: 1903–20

The majority of High Court justices during this period took a narrow view of the Constitution's provisions, and so their judgments tended to restrict, rather than enlarge, Commonwealth powers. The first three justices had been among the delegates who had drafted the Constitution. The restrictions were expressed in two ways:

1   The Commonwealth government and state governments were prevented from intruding into each other's affairs. (The court held, for example, that federal arbitration could not apply to state government employees.) This was termed the doctrine of 'implied

immunity of instrumentalities'—that is, it was not spelled out in the Constitution, but was consistent with the founding fathers' goal of *coordinate* federalism.
2 The federal government was prevented from legislating on matters that encroached on state responsibilities. This was known as the doctrine of 'implied prohibitions', and drew on the intentions of the Constitution's drafters to preserve the powers of the states.

These limits were imposed during the crucial period of federalism, when the Commonwealth was ready to adopt new approaches to economic and social questions. It is impossible to say whether the early High Court judgments helped to render later governments less adventurous than they might have otherwise been; but innovation became a more complex matter, with extensive litigation likely to follow government initiatives. The High Court interpreted the defence power very widely during the First World War, but at this distance the main significance of that example is that it stands in such contrast to the others.

Phase 2: 1920–42

In 1906 the High Court had been enlarged by the appointment of two more justices, both of whom had supported a wider role for the national government while delegates to the 1897–98 Constitutional Convention. The new appointees opposed the narrow interpretations of their colleagues, but it was some years before the original appointees left the court and those with broad constitutional views formed the majority of justices. The major change came in the *Engineers Case* of 1920, when the High Court abandoned the doctrines of implied immunity and implied prohibitions. The 1920 case and two later decisions allowed a considerable expansion of federal powers, particularly in financial matters.

> **1920**—*Engineers Case* (*Amalgamated Society of Engineers v Adelaide Steamship Co. Ltd*, Commonwealth Law Reports, vol. 28, p. 129, usually written 28 CLR 129). The court ruled that the federal arbitration power (s. 51(xxxv)) could be extended to awards covering an instrumentality of the Western Australian government. In that decision the new majority view prevailed that the Constitution should be interpreted as it was written and not in the light of 'implied prohibitions'. This is much the way in which ordinary statutes are interpreted—that is, giving the words their normal meaning rather than some sense that the drafters might have wished to apply. Normal construction of the Constitution allowed the Commonwealth to exercise powers that had previously been denied it.
>
> **1932**—*Garnishee Case* (*New South Wales v Commonwealth* 46 CLR 155). This case arose from the circumstances of the Great Depression, when the NSW government refused to pay interest on loans, on the grounds that the money could be better used for other purposes. The High Court ruled that the Commonwealth could 'attach' the revenue of a state in enforcing a law made under the Constitution. (The interest accrued as a result of the financial agreement of 1927, drawn up under the provisions of s. 105A.)
>
> **1942**—*Uniform Tax Case* (*South Australia v Commonwealth* 65 CLR 373). The Australian war effort entailed vastly increased spending by the federal government, which introduced four Acts effectively giving it a monopoly over income taxation for the duration of the war. The states objected to their exclusion from the income tax field, but the High Court ruled against

> them. The ruling on three of the Acts applied not only for the duration of the war, but to peacetime as well; the 'duration only' ruling applied to the Commonwealth's acquisition of state taxation departments, but as there might be no tax for the states to collect in peacetime there was little point in their having a staff to perform a function that no longer existed. The *Uniform Tax Case* marked the point at which the Commonwealth gained clear predominance. From 1942 the states had to rely on the federal government to return to them an adequate proportion of the income tax paid by their citizens. (The financial aspects of federalism are discussed further in Chapter 4.)

Phase 3: 1943–83

The High Court generally maintained the principle of broad interpretation set out in the *Engineers Case*, but there were no major extensions of federal power. It could be said that this was a period of 'give and take' on the part of the High Court. In 1947, the federal government's attempts to impose stricter controls on banking were rebuffed (*State Banking Case—City of Melbourne v Commonwealth* 74 CLR 31), as were efforts in 1951 to ban the Communist Party (*Australian Communist Party v Commonwealth* 83 CLR 1). On the other hand, the court upheld the federal government's power over income taxation in a second *Uniform Tax Case* of 1957 (99 CLR 575).

In 1971 the High Court handed down a ruling of great potential significance when it recognised the Commonwealth's power to regulate the activities of corporations (s. 51(xx)), particularly in respect of monopoly practices and restriction of trade (*Concrete Pipes Case—Strickland v Rocla Concrete Pipes Pty Ltd* 124 CLR 468). The judgment perhaps extends to other corporate activities, such as the prices companies charge and the wages they pay. This would amount to granting the Commonwealth power over prices and incomes, one of the instruments of economic management that it has so far lacked. However, as the federal government has not as yet acted in this field, the extent of this power has not been further tested in the courts. In the *Koowarta* and *Dams* cases in the early 1980s, both discussed in Chapter 4, the court gave great weight to the external affairs power as a means whereby the Commonwealth can regulate the *internal* affairs of Australia.

The question of High Court interpretation became an issue in the 1970s, when the court construed the words of taxation laws very legalistically. In doing so, the court made it possible for tax consultants to devise schemes within the strict interpretation of the law but against the government's intentions, which allowed their clients to avoid paying substantial amounts of income tax. The government responded in 1981 by making detailed amendments to the taxation laws and by enacting legislation aimed at requiring courts to give preference in their interpretations to the construction that would promote the purpose underlying the Act. At about the same time, the High Court declared, in effect, that it was already taking notice of the intentions of the legislature. This occurred not long after a new chief justice was appointed to the High Court.

Phase 4: Since 1983

Developments in the 1980s and 1990s suggest that this period will come to be regarded as a new phase, during which judicial interpretation further expanded the powers of the Commonwealth and established new directions in other fields.

The period begins with the decision in the *Tasmanian Dams Case* in July 1983 (*Commonwealth v Tasmania* 158 CLR 1), which confirmed earlier decisions that on the basis of the external affairs power the Commonwealth could act on otherwise domestic matters. In this case, the legislation tested was the *World Heritage Properties Conservation Act 1983*, which was based on implementation of the International Convention for the Protection of the World Cultural and Natural Heritage in the case of the wilderness area in southwest Tasmania. In 1988, a somewhat new court, on which two recent Hawke government appointees were sitting, extended this ruling to include areas, also in southwest Tasmania, which were only in the process of being declared of World Heritage status (*Richardson v The Forestry Commission and others* (1987–88) 164 CLR 261).

Later in that year, the High Court reversed all previous interpretations of s. 92 which guaranteed absolutely free trade, commerce and intercourse among the states. Traditionally, the court, as in the *Botany Case* of the 1940s, had interpreted this section to prevent government regulation, including nationalisation, of private firms. In *Cole v Whitfield and another* (1988) 62 ALJR 303, a case which involved attempted government regulation of the size of crayfish that may be sold in Tasmania, the court ruled that s. 92 did not prevent such regulations, even when an element of interstate trade was involved.

The finding by the High Court in 1992, overturning the government's proposed ban on political advertising by the federal government on the basis that freedom of communication in relation to public affairs and political discussion is indispensable to the efficacy of the system of representative government provided for by the Constitution (*Australian Capital Television Pty Ltd v The Commonwealth (No. 2)* (1992) 66 ALJR 695), raised questions as to whether the High Court had moved from judicial interpretation to lawmaker.

The 1992 *Mabo Case*, which overrode the established common law doctrine of *terra nullius* and recognised the existence of native title, evoked similar questions. *Mabo* was followed by the *Wik Case* in 1996, in which the court decided that the right to a pastoral lease did not automatically extinguish native title and that the issue should be determined by examining the specific circumstances of each lease.

These decisions represented a further inroad into the authority of the states because the combined force of the external affairs power and s. 109 of the Constitution means that any law made by the Commonwealth to implement the judgment would prevail over state law. The Keating Labor government, in this instance, legislated to protect native title, thus preventing the states from acting to undermine the High Court decision.

External affairs power
Section 51(xxix) used in conjunction with s. 109 of the Constitution is one means whereby the Commonwealth can become involved in areas of state responsibility.

2006: The High Court decision on Work Choices

In November 2006, a High Court challenge by the states and Australian trade unions to the federal government's Work Choices legislation was dismissed in a majority decision of 5–2. The states had argued that the *Workplace Relations Amendment (Work Choices) Act 2005* was constitutionally invalid because it established a national industrial relations scheme using s. 51(xx) of the Constitution, which allowed the Commonwealth to make laws 'with respect to . . . Foreign corporations, and trading or financial corporations formed within the limits of the Commonwealth'.

The Work Choices decision is significant because it extends the power of the Commonwealth over policy areas that previously came within the jurisdiction of state governments. There is the potential for the decision to permit the Commonwealth to regulate almost all the activities of corporations within Australia, such as education, health, water, climate change, urban planning, sport and agriculture. The two dissenting judges to the ruling, Justice Kirby and Justice Callinan, expressed concerns about the potential of the decision to facilitate a possible federal takeover of state responsibilities.
(Sources: *The Australian*, 15 November 2006; Solomon, D. 2007, *Pillars of Power*, The Federation Press, Sydney, p. 45)

> 'The framers of the 1901 constitution never anticipated that the corporations power would be used in this way.'
> (Source: Professor George Williams, cited in *Canberra Times*, 14 November 2006)
>
> 'In a single bound, the court has disposed of both Australia's unique system of setting wages and conditions and our federal structure . . . the states stand to lose the last vestiges of an independence that has been steadily eroded by the commonwealth's growing financial muscle, together with the shift in formal powers sanctioned by successive High Court judgments. It means the federal government will have another means to impose its authority on the states: the threat that it will take over a state responsibility if governments do not co-operate.'
> (Source: Steketee, M. 2006, 'Don't fear centralised power grab', *The Australian*, 16 November 2006)
>
> 'After the High Court's Work Choices decision, the states should be in absolutely no doubt that this is a shipwreck of Titanic proportions. Not since the 1920s has the court struck such a devastating blow against Australian federalism.'
> (Source: Professor Greg Craven 2006, 'Work Choices Shipwreck', *Perspective*, ABC Radio National, 6 December 2006, http://www.abc.net.au/rn/perspective/stories/2006/1803817.htm)

Judicial interpretation of the Constitution has been most important in allowing the Commonwealth to extend its activities without formal constitutional change. Yet this extension should be considered in relative terms: by comparison, the US Supreme Court has taken into account changing social circumstances when ruling on federal powers in that country. This is a notion that lies far beyond the *literalist* interpretations favoured by the Australian High Court since 1920. In this context, the High Court appears conservative; the justices have relied on the constitution's wording, and so the sense of the document remains, even if the intentions of its drafters have occasionally been disregarded.

The High Court as a political institution

> 'The High Court's proper function under the Constitution necessarily involves it in deciding on the distribution of political power and the legal propriety of the exercise of that power. It is itself enmeshed in the political process.'
> (Source: Solomon, D. 1999, *The Political High Court*, Allen & Unwin, Sydney, p. 9)

The principles of liberal democracy, as we saw in Chapter 1, incorporate the notion of separation of powers, which means that the High Court should be separate and independent of the political institutions of government—in Australia's case, the parliament and cabinet. There are a range of arguments, put forward by David Solomon, however, to suggest that the High Court does perform a political function and does exercise political power. For example:

- 'The authority of the High Court in constitutional matters diminishes the prospective power of Commonwealth and state parliaments and governments.'
- 'Governments cannot ignore High Court decisions.'
- High Court decisions cannot be overruled by parliament, but 'only by changing the constitution'.
- The decisions of the High Court have a political impact on political institutions as well as on the nature of the power relationship between the Commonwealth and the states.

(*Source*: Solomon, D. 1999, *The Political High Court*, Allen & Unwin, Sydney, pp. 6, 8)

The High Court and Australian democracy

If the High Court is regarded as part of the political process, then this has implications for Australia's system of representative democracy, which places the function of policy-maker with the *elected* representatives in the parliament, not the *unelected* officials of the High Court. High Court judges are neither responsible nor accountable to the people for their decisions.

High Court judges, under the provisions of the Constitution, are appointed by the governor-general in council. In practice, this means the prime minister advises the governor-general on whom the government wishes to appoint. Judges sit on the High Court until they are 70 years of age, so if a person is appointed at the age of 50, for example, he or she will continue to sit on the court for 20 years without having to account politically for his or her decisions.

Appointment by the government of the day also raises the question about political bias in the selection of judges and the ideological standing of the High Court. Governments are likely to appoint someone who identifies closely with their own philosophy or sense of values. Because that person holds a continuing position until retirement, those values might be out of step with contemporary community views or the views of successive governments. Judges are also chosen from a group of barristers, who are likely to be conservative, so it could be argued that the High Court as a result constitutes a conservative elite that does not reflect the interests of the broader community.

Haig Patapan identifies a number of functions of the High Court. These include:

- 'umpire' or keeper of rules and taking no part in politics;
- 'renovator' in bringing laws up to date with community values and expectations;
- 'facilitator' and support for a parliament in determining specialist legal questions;
- 'guardian' or 'protector' in upholding the Constitution and fundamental rights and freedoms and protecting the weak and vulnerable; and

- 'adversary' as an active political contender for political power and authority.

(*Source*: Patapan, H. 2000, *Judging Democracy: The New Politics of the High Court of Australia*, Cambridge University Press, Melbourne, p. 183)

If the High Court, by becoming more 'activist' and taking on the function of lawmaker, is seen as an 'adversary' to the parliament, then clearly that undermines the fundamental principle of representative democracy that the laws should be made by the elected representatives of the people who are held accountable and responsible through a process of regular election. On the other hand, if the High Court is 'activist' in keeping the political executive under scrutiny and within the rule of law, then it could be seen to be upholding the principles of the separation of powers associated with the concept of liberal democracy.

COOPERATION BETWEEN GOVERNMENTS

As the federal government's activities and powers came to overlap those of the state governments and vice versa, it became necessary for these governments to work more closely with each other in the nature of *cooperative* federalism, rather than the *coordinate* arrangement envisaged by the founding fathers. (These concepts are explained in Chapter 4.)

The Constitution provides avenues for such cooperation and, in those cases where full agreement has been reached between the Commonwealth and the states, this has amounted to effective amendment of the provisions of the Constitution. The main avenues are:

- The states may legislate to refer matters to the federal government under s. 51(xxxvii). This has occurred in few cases, mainly in wartime and in respect to such developments as civil aviation. More recently, the Victorian government referred its industrial relations power to the Commonwealth. The reverse is not the case, as the federal government may not refer matters to the states. A referendum in 1984 to make this possible failed to pass.
- The Commonwealth and the states may agree on the management of state governments' debts under ss. 105 and 105A (after that was added by referendum in 1928). Such agreements increased state governments' dependence on the federal government and played an important part in changing the federal 'balance'.
- The Commonwealth may make grants to the states under s. 96 and impose conditions on the way in which the money is spent. The states may find it difficult to refuse such grants, given their regular requests for extra money, but they have often given only grudging 'cooperation' in reporting to the Commonwealth and in allowing the federal government to check on the spending of these amounts.

Even though there have been some instances of Commonwealth heavy-handed 'persuasion' or coercion to get the states to cooperate, there are areas where the Commonwealth and state governments do work together at ministerial and bureaucratic levels to produce mutually agreed policies.

FORMAL AMENDMENT OF THE CONSTITUTION

> **Referendums**
>
> Section 128 of the constitution provides that any proposed law for the alteration of the constitution must be passed by an absolute majority in both houses of the Commonwealth parliament. If passed by both houses, it is submitted to a referendum at least two months, but less than six months, after it has been passed by parliament. In certain circumstances, a proposed amendment can be submitted to a referendum if it is passed on two separate occasions by only one house of parliament.
>
> At the referendum, the proposed amendment must be approved by a double majority:
> - a national majority of all electors who are qualified to vote for the election of members of the House of Representatives; and
> - a majority of electors voting in a majority of the states (that is, at least four of the six states).
>
> (*Source*: Australian Electoral Commission (AEC) 2008, 'Constitutional Referendums', AEC, Canberra, http://www.aec.gov.au/pdf/education/resources/referendums.pdf)

While judicial interpretation and cooperative arrangements have led to a substantial change in the relationship between the federal and state governments, usually in favour of the former, the formal amendment process by referendum set out in s. 128 of the Constitution has produced few significant changes.

- Number of referendum polls: 19
- Number of referendum questions: 44
- Number approved (by majority of voters in a majority of states—at least 4 of 6): 8

(Details of these referendums are set out in Table 3.3.)

This low figure for successful referendums is even less impressive than it first appears to be, as most have been of little importance:

1906   Technical alterations to s. 13, involving the method of calculating senators' terms.

1910   Minor change to s. 105, which had previously restricted the Commonwealth's power to take over states' debts to those existing at Federation. (Eight words were deleted to remove this limitation.)

1928   Insertion of s. 105A, which enlarged the Commonwealth's powers in relation to states' debts.

1946   Insertion of s. 51(xxiiiA), which allowed the Commonwealth to provide a wider range of social service benefits.

1967   Deletion of s. 127, thus allowing Aborigines to be counted in the national census, and alteration of s. 51(xxvi) to allow the Commonwealth to make 'special laws' relating to Aborigines (as well as people of other races).

1977   Expansion of s. 72 to ensure that future Federal Court justices (including members of the High Court) retire at no more than 70 years of age.

TABLE 3.3
Constitutional referendums, 1906–99

Subject	Date of referendum	Government party	States with majority vote in favour	Per cent voting 'Yes'	Per cent turnout
Senate elections	12 Dec 1906	Non-Labor	All	82.7*	50.2
Finance	13 Apr 1910	Labor	Q, WA, T	49.0	62.2
State debts	13 Apr 1910	Labor	All except NSW	55.0*	62.2
Legislative powers	26 Apr 1911	Labor	WA	39.4	53.3
Monopolies	26 Apr 1911	Labor	WA	39.9	53.3
Trade and commerce	31 May 1913	Labor	Q, SA, WA	49.4	73.7
Corporations	31 May 1913	Labor	Q, SA, WA	49.3	73.7
Industrial matters	31 May 1913	Labor	Q, SA, WA	49.3	73.7
Railway disputes	31 May 1913	Labor	Q, SA, WA	49.1	73.7
Trusts	31 May 1913	Labor	Q, SA, WA	49.8	73.7
Nationalisation of monopolies	31 May 1913	Labor	Q, SA, WA	49.3	73.7
Legislative powers	13 Dec 1919	Non-Labor	V, Q, WA	49.7	71.3
Nationalisation of monopolies	13 Dec 1919	Non-Labor	V, Q, WA	48.6	71.3
Industry and commerce	4 Sep 1926	Non-Labor	NSW, Q	43.5	91.1
Essential services	4 Sep 1926	Non-Labor	NSW, Q	42.8	91.1
State debts	17 Nov 1928	Non-Labor	All	74.3*	93.6
Aviation	6 Mar 1937	Non-Labor	V, Q	53.6	94.1
Marketing	6 Mar 1937	Non-Labor	None	36.3	94.1
Postwar reconstruction and democratic rights	19 Aug 1944	Labor	SA, WA	47.0	96.5
Social services	28 Sep 1946	Labor	All	54.4*	94.0
Organised marketing of primary products	28 Sep 1946	Labor	NSW, V, WA	50.6	94.0
Industrial employment	28 Sep 1946	Labor	NSW, V, WA	50.3	94.0
Rents and prices	29 May 1948	Labor	None	40.7	93.6

(continued)

TABLE 3.3 (continued)
Constitutional referendums, 1906–99

Subject	Date of referendum	Government party	States with majority vote in favour	Per cent voting 'Yes'	Per cent turnout
Powers to deal with Communists and Communism	22 Sep 1951	Non-Labor	Q, WA, T	49.4	95.6
Parliament	27 May 1967	Non-Labor	NSW	40.3	93.8
Aborigines	27 May 1967	Non-Labor	All	90.8*	93.8
Prices	8 Dec 1973	Labor	None	43.8	93.4
Incomes	8 Dec 1973	Labor	None	34.4	93.4
Simultaneous elections	18 May 1974	Labor	NSW	48.3	95.5
Mode of altering the Constitution	18 May 1974	Labor	NSW	48.0	95.5
Democratic elections	18 May 1974	Labor	NSW	47.2	95.5
Local government bodies	18 May 1974	Labor	NSW	46.9	95.5
Simultaneous elections	21 May 1977	Non-Labor	NSW, V, SA	62.2	92.3
Senate vacancies	21 May 1977	Non-Labor	All	73.3*	92.3
Territory franchise for referendum	21 May 1977	Non-Labor	All	77.7*	92.3
Retiring age for judges	21 May 1977	Non-Labor	All	80.1*	92.3
Terms of senators	1 Dec 1984	Labor	NSW, V	50.7	92.4
Interchange of powers	1 Dec 1984	Labor	None	47.1	92.4
Parliamentary terms	3 Sep 1988	Labor	None	32.8	92.1
Fair elections	3 Sep 1988	Labor	None	37.4	92.1
Local government	3 Sep 1988	Labor	None	33.5	92.1
Rights and freedoms	3 Sep 1988	Labor	None	30.4	92.1
Preamble	6 Nov 1999	Non-Labor	None	39.34	95.1
Republic	6 Nov 1999	Non-Labor	None	45.13	95.1

* Referendum carried

(Source: Commonwealth of Australia, *Commonwealth Parliamentary Papers*. Copyright Commonwealth of Australia, reproduced by permission)

1977 Additions to s. 128 to allow people of territories that elect members to the House of Representatives (Australian Capital Territory and Northern Territory) to vote at referendums.

1977 Amendment to s. 15 to ensure that, as far as practicable, a casual vacancy in the Senate is filled by a person of the same political party as the senator chosen by the people and for the balance of the term.

Four of the eight successful referendums involved little more than minor adjustments to the Constitution—those of 1906, 1910 and the latter two of 1977. Two others—those of 1928 and 1946—amounted to ratification of actions that were already being taken. The 1977 vote on casual Senate vacancies could perhaps be viewed as limiting the freedom of state parliaments to fill casual vacancies. It is also the only section of the Constitution that refers to the existence of political parties in the parliament. A convention had evolved that appointees should be from the same party as the senators they replaced, but that had been ignored twice in 1975, changing the party balance in the Senate and contributing to the refusal of supply to the Whitlam government later in that year. Yet the very fact that the referendum was proposed in this form suggests that the nation was unable to deal with the major constitutional issue underlying it—that is, the relationship between the Senate and the House of Representatives on the question of supply. The 1967 amendment has greater significance. It has facilitated the Commonwealth government's implementation of the *Mabo* decision on land rights for Aboriginal people at the national level, despite protests and disagreement from some states—in particular, Western Australia.

More can be learned about the Australian attitude towards the Constitution, and particularly the extension of federal power by formal amendment, through an examination of referendum proposals that were *not* approved. Of the 36 unsuccessful questions, 18 concerned:

- trade and marketing;
- corporations (including monopolies);
- prices and incomes; and
- employment and industrial relations.

The remaining 18 concerned the following:

- parliamentary and electoral adjustments (8);
- financial matters (2);
- the Communist Party (1);
- air navigation (1);
- essential services (1);
- interchange of powers (1);
- local government (1);
- rights and freedoms (1);
- preamble to the Constitution (1); and
- the proposal to become a republic (1).

Australian voters have been most reluctant to grant the federal government further control over the nation's economic activities, even though that has been proposed by both Labor and conservative parties (more often and more recently in the case of Labor).

Voters have also rejected seemingly minor extensions of Commonwealth power. More significantly, they rejected the proposal to change the Australian political system from a constitutional monarchy to a republic.

There will be further attempts to amend the Constitution, and their outcomes will depend to a large extent on an understanding of the factors that have contributed to the many failures of the past.

Referendum problems

The reluctance of voters to approve constitutional amendments has been accounted for in several ways. These explanations are related to each other, but to aid discussion they can be divided into three main groups: procedural problems, voters' attitudes and party disagreements.

Procedural problems

The formal requirement of s. 128 that a *majority of voters in a majority of states* must support an alteration to the Constitution seems an obvious difficulty. As there are six states, a majority must in fact be a two-thirds majority, which is never easy to obtain. However, that has rarely been a factor in the rejection of referendums. Of the 36 failed proposals:

- 5 gained a majority of votes throughout Australia, but not in a majority of states (3 in three states, 2 in two states);
- 10 were rejected by the majority of voters throughout Australia, although gaining support in three states;
- 3 were rejected, gaining support in only two states;
- 11 were rejected, gaining support in only one state; and
- 11 were rejected in all states.

The *number of questions* asked at referendums can confuse issues in the minds of voters. At 14 of the 18 referendum polls, voters have been asked to consider multiple questions. Yet, on occasion (1910, 1946, 1967 and 1977), certain proposals have been approved and others rejected, which indicates that people are capable of discriminating between questions posed in a suitable way.

There have been some *extraordinarily complex questions* (notably on 'economic' powers in 1911, 1913, 1926 and 1944). No politician would have made a free choice in favour of measures with such unpredictable consequences; nor did the people.

Compulsory voting has sometimes been blamed for bringing uninterested voters to the polls, but there is little convincing evidence that this has contributed to the 'No' vote. In any event, 13 questions were proposed before voting was made compulsory in 1924, and only two of those passed.

Voters' attitudes

It has been claimed that:

- The people have a *federal sense*—that is, they wish to maintain the identity and powers of their states. Voters seem to respond to emotional appeals based on these grounds. Yet it could be argued that voters are fairly objective: they will accept federal proposals that offer them tangible relief or other benefit (state debt and loans, 1928; social services, 1946); why approve others?

- People in *smaller states* tend to reject referendums, while those in larger states accept them. Smaller states are sometimes pictured as having an unreasonable fear of central control. But note:

	Yes	No
	(out of 44 questions)	
Western Australia	23	21
Queensland	21	23
New South Wales	18	26
South Australia	16	28
Victoria	15	29
Tasmania	10	34

  There is no obvious voting pattern related to population or 'strength'; if anything, it might be argued that smaller states are *more* likely to vote 'Yes'. Only Tasmania supports the hypothesis that it is the smaller states that reject referendums.
- Australians are *opposed to 'big governments'*, and so deny the Commonwealth additional powers. There is something to be said in favour of this argument, although voters have rarely objected to the federal government expanding its role through High Court decisions or the use of the specific purpose grants under s. 96. Referendums, however, provide a more direct avenue for expressing opinion.
- Voters *distrust politicians*, and some reject referendums for that reason. This is mainly conjecture, but there may be some truth in it. Certainly there is a lot of anecdotal evidence to this effect. On the other hand, the opposition to referendum proposals is often led by politicians, usually by the Opposition at the federal level for party political purposes or at the state level resisting what they perceive to be Commonwealth encroachment on their powers.

Party disagreements

Referendum proposals are often identified with the contest between the main political parties. If one party supports a referendum, the other usually opposes it, if only because it wants to deny its opponent first use of the new power. The Liberal Party historically has had a stronger attachment to the concept of decentralisation of power at the state level, and was likely to oppose a referendum that sought to give more power to the Commonwealth at the expense of the states. When there is more than one question, it is easier for an Opposition to oppose them all than to advise its supporters to split their vote. Once the community has divided on party lines, it is very difficult to secure the necessary majorities. Even in circumstances where the leaders of both major parties have supported proposals, campaigns by small parties or by factions within the major party groups have secured a 'No' vote. An example of the former was the Democratic Labor Party's campaign against the 'nexus' proposal of 1967; of the latter, the opposition by Coalition senators and non-Labor state premiers to the 'simultaneous elections' referendum in 1977.

Politicians seem to be in a 'no win' situation with referendums. If a major party opposes a question, many voters assume that there is something wrong with the proposal, and reject it. If major parties agree on a question, some voters conclude that it must be deceptive in order to produce such unusual behaviour from politicians, and they still reject it.

The problem of party rivalry is heightened when referendum polls are held at the same time as federal elections:

- Number of referendum polls at election times: 7
- Number of referendum questions: 20
- Number approved: 3

(Note that one approval was in 1906, before the party system emerged.)

Discussion of referendum failures has centred on the attitudes of voters, rather than on the actions of politicians, who under the provisions of the Constitution necessarily take the initiative in constitutional change. There are several points to note:

- Until recently, the Constitution has not been presented by governments or accepted by the public as a document in need of regular revision.
- As a consequence, referendums have been relatively infrequent, being unusual events rather than part of the regular political calendar.
- Nor have referendums often been put forward as truly major decisions requiring long discussion; too often governments have presented them hurriedly, apparently for motives of political expediency rather than out of a desire for long-term reform.
- Consequently, cases have sometimes been poorly prepared, allowing opponents to use 'scare' tactics and giving the electorate too little time to evaluate arguments.
- Party leaders have rarely campaigned effectively in support of referendum proposals— either because referendums become caught up in the campaign for a general election or because, in the short time available, immediate issues can arise and disturb their attention.

The chances of achieving successful referendums would be improved if Australia's political leaders could reach agreement on the need for constitutional change and what form it should take. Two government-sponsored initiatives in the 1970s and 1980s that resulted in referendums illustrate how a lack of agreement between the major parties contributed to failure. Three referendum questions put to the people in 1977 on which there was common ground were successful, but a fourth proposal relating to simultaneous elections on which the parties remained divided failed to pass. All 1988 referendum proposals lacked bipartisan support and failed to pass. The referendum on the republic was different, in that some members of both parties were in favour while others were opposed.

CONSTITUTIONAL REFORM AND THE POLITICAL AGENDA

Constitutional Convention, 1973

In September 1973 a constitutional convention was held in Sydney to discuss future developments of constitutional reform. It was an initiative mainly of the states, particularly Victoria, and was attended by Commonwealth, state and local government delegates. All delegates were members of legislatures or of local government assemblies. (That is, there was no *direct* representation of the people, nor any specific consultation with them.)

The convention agreed to do little more than discuss matters further. Several questions were referred to four standing committees, which were to report to future meetings. However, the usual tensions between the Commonwealth and the states were heightened by antagonism towards the Whitlam Labor government among non-Labor state governments, and for a time it seemed that the full convention would not meet again. Following the 1975 election, a meeting was convened in Hobart in October 1976, under the Liberal prime minister, Malcolm Fraser. The Hobart meeting again revealed hostilities among members of the rival parties, but it recommended that state powers relating to defamation and aspects of family law be referred to the Commonwealth, and proposed referendums setting a retiring age for federal judges and allowing residents of territories to vote at referendums (these were passed in May 1977). Party rivalry relaxed sufficiently to allow the contentious question of the Senate's power over supply to be referred to one of the convention's standing committees.

A further meeting in Perth in July 1978 produced fewer results, and it became clear that such questions as the Senate's power over supply were still creating divisions along strict party lines.

Another constitutional convention was held in Adelaide in April 1983 just after the election of the Hawke Labor government and this became a full-blown party-political affair, as most of the proposals for change had a Labor origin while the Liberal and National parties held an effective floor majority at the convention. A Labor proposal for a fixed three-year term for the House of Representatives was defeated, although another Labor initiative for simultaneous elections was carried by the convention. Two questions were put to a referendum at the same time as the December 1984 elections. Both were lost, although one achieved a popular majority. The constitutional convention experiment fizzled to a dull and profitless end, and the Hawke government looked around for an alternative.

Constitutional Commission, 1985

In December 1985, the government established a constitutional commission. The commission comprised six (later five, after the resignation of Justice Toohey in December 1986) distinguished members whose combined talents covered political life, government service and academic legal expertise. The commission was assisted in its work by five advisory committees—on the Australian Judicial System; Distribution of Powers; Executive Government; Individual and Democratic Rights; and Trade and National Economic Management—whose 37 members were drawn from almost every field of Australian life.

The commission was asked to report by 30 June 1988 on 'the revision of the Australian Constitution' to:

- adequately reflect Australia's status as an independent nation and a federal parliamentary democracy;
- provide the most suitable framework for the economic, social and political development of Australia as a federation;
- recognise an appropriate division of responsibilities between the Commonwealth, the states, self-governing territories and local government; and
- ensure that democratic rights were guaranteed.

The commission was urged to consult widely, to engage in stimulating public discussion and to conduct public education. It was to hold public hearings and to publish draft reports to encourage further response to its ideas. Its advisory committees did all this energetically and admirably in the context of widespread public apathy and ignorance. They found, for example, that only a bare majority of Australians (only 30 per cent of 18–24-year-olds) even knew of the existence of the Constitution.

The Final Report was handed to the government in August 1988, although it was not publicly released until after the subsequent referendums. The recommendations were extensive, including the preamble and covering clauses, democratic rights and parliamentary elections, the parliament, executive government of the Commonwealth, new states, constitutional recognition of local government, rights and freedoms, distribution of powers, and expended and outmoded provisions.

All of this was just advice, of course, and it was then over to the attorney-general and the government. The initial response was narrow and limited. The Hawke government passed legislation related to four of the recommendations (though not in the same form) relating to (a) one vote, one value, (b) the extension of parliamentary tenure from three to four years and the relationship between the two houses of parliament, (c) constitutional recognition of local government, and (d) constitutional rights and freedoms. The proposals were put to referendum in September 1988. They failed to gain bipartisan support (although the Opposition was divided over several of the questions) and were totally rejected by the electorate.

THE REPUBLIC AND CONSTITUTIONAL CHANGE

The successful development of Australia into a modern industrial democratic state, even though the Constitution, written over 100 years ago, has undergone little substantive change, is one reason for arguing that the document remains a satisfactory base for Australia's political system. In more colloquial terms it could be argued, 'if it ain't broke, don't fix it'.

Nevertheless, there has been increasing pressure for Australia to change from its current status of a constitutional monarchy to a republic with an Australian head of state. These pressures derive from two separate but related factors: nationalism and the imperatives of globalisation. The first fuels the desire to formalise our status as an independent nation, while the second provides a practical reason for doing so. An Australian head of state, by formally breaking the residual and symbolic colonial ties to Britain and affirming a separate and unique national identity, would enhance Australia's efforts to become more closely linked with Asia and thus improve the opportunities for trade.

> A **republic** is a state where all those who hold public office gain their authority from the people.

Republic Advisory Committee, 1993

In 1993, Labor prime minister Paul Keating established a committee to look at how an Australian republic could be achieved. The Republic Advisory Committee was asked to produce an options paper describing the minimum constitutional changes necessary to achieve a viable 'Federal Republic of Australia', while maintaining the effect of current conventions and principles of government. The committee was asked to look at:

1. the removal of all references to the monarch in the Constitution;
2. in light of this, the need for and creation of a new office of head of state, and consideration of what the office might be called;
3. the provisions for the appointment and termination of appointment of the head of state, including the method of selection and appointment, for example:
   - selection and appointment by the government of the day,
   - selection by the government and endorsement by both houses of parliament,
   - appointment by an 'electoral college' comprising representatives of various parliaments,

- appointment following election by the federal parliament, and
- popular election;

4 how the powers of the new head of state and their exercise could be made subject to the same conventions and principles that applied to the powers of the governor-general;
5 the nature of the amendments to the *Commonwealth of Australia Constitution Act* required to implement the options;
6 the implications for the states; and
7 other aspects that arose in the committee's deliberations and consultations, providing they were relevant to the overall objective in the opening paragraph above.

The committee was directed to analyse the main possibilities and the main arguments for and against them, but not to make recommendations.
(*Source*: *Issue Paper,* Republic Advisory Committee, May 1993. Copyright Commonwealth of Australia, reproduced by permission)

The committee was chaired by Malcolm Turnbull, a strong advocate for the republic. It also included representatives from the legal profession, a historian, the media (SBS), the Aboriginal community, a former Liberal state premier and a former Labor federal minister, one representative of the federal Opposition, and two representatives of the states and territories. There was public consultation through meetings in capital cities and regional centres, and private meetings with government and community leaders. Both written and oral submissions were received. (A free-call telephone line was established for this purpose.)

The committee canvassed the following options:

◉ *Does Australia need a head of state?* The office of head of state is optional, but it would be a major departure from our system of government not to have one and there was merit in having a national figure, above day-to-day politics, to represent the nation as a whole.

FIGURE 3.3
Howard to draft inspirational preamble

(*Source*: Cartoon by Nicholson from *The Australian*. www.nicholsoncartoons.com.au)

- *A new office of head of state.* The functions and duties would remain similar to those currently undertaken by the governor-general, being mainly ceremonial, with a term of office from four to seven years. Suggested titles were 'President', 'Governor-General' and 'Head of State'. The holder of the office should be a widely respected, eminent person, able to act in a politically impartial way.
- *Appointment procedures*:
  - appointment by parliament: a joint sitting of both houses, with a requirement for a large enough majority to require bipartisan support; or
  - popular election: although this could result in the person being a member of one or other of the major political parties. To avoid conflict with the elected government, the constitution should be amended to define and delimit the powers of the head of state; or
  - appointment by electoral college made up of representatives of state, territory and Commonwealth parliaments.
- *Removal of head of state.* The method selected should reflect the method of appointment.
- *Powers of the head of state.* Provision should be made for incorporating the existing conventions or codifying the rules, which currently depend on convention in such a way 'that preserves the essential elements of Australian democracy and maintains the present balance between the Government and the head of state'.
- *Constitutional amendment required to achieve a republic*:
  - terminating the Queen's role as head of state and establishing a new office of head of state if it is decided to create one;
  - dealing with appointment and removal of the new head of state and other matters relevant to the new office;
  - dealing with the powers of the new head of state;
  - dealing with the position of the states and their links with the Crown; and
  - making consequential changes, mostly removing the references to the Queen and replacing the references to the governor-general with references to the new head of state, and inserting transitional provisions.

(*Source*: Report of the Republic Advisory Committee 1993, *An Australian Republic: The Options— An Overview,* AGPS, Canberra. Copyright Commonwealth of Australia, reproduced by permission)

In June 1995, Prime Minister Keating responded with his government's 'minimalist' position on the issue to replace the governor-general with a president:

- the president to be an Australian citizen;
- the title to be 'President of the Commonwealth of Australia';
- the term of office to be five years, non-renewable;
- the change to take place no later than 2001;
- the president to be nominated by the prime minister, and chosen by a two-thirds vote of both houses of the federal parliament at a joint sitting;
- no serving federal, state or territory politician to be able to run for president until five years after they have left parliament;
- the president to have the same powers and functions as currently held by the governor-general. The 'reserve powers' to be assumed by the president, but not codified in the Constitution;

- no court challenges to the use of the 'reserve powers' allowed;
- the president able to be removed by a two-thirds vote of both houses of the federal parliament at a joint sitting;
- all references to the Queen, Crown and governor-general to be removed from the Constitution;
- the states to be free to keep their own ties to the Crown; and
- changes to be ratified by constitutional referendum in either 1998 or 1999.

The recommendations of the Republic Advisory Committee and the response by the Labor government were not acted on because Labor lost the 1996 election. The incoming Coalition prime minister, John Howard, instead established a constitutional convention to allow supporters and opponents to debate whether Australia should become a republic.

Constitutional Convention, 1998

The 1998 Constitutional Convention met to consider whether Australia should become a republic and, if so, how and when that would happen. There were 152 delegates, half elected by Australian voters and half appointed by the government. They represented a broad cross-section of the community and included supporters for retaining the monarchy and others who wanted Australia to become a republic with an Australian head of state. Prime Minister Howard promised that he would hold a referendum in 1999 if agreement could be reached on a model for a republic.

The question of whether Australia should be a republic had majority support, but opinion was divided over how the president should be selected. The pro-republicans insisted that the president be directly elected by the people; while others, including delegates from the Australian Republican Movement, preferred selection by a two-thirds majority of both houses of parliament. After vigorous debate on the floor of the Chamber, intense lobbying in the corridors and a round of votes on four different models of selection, the convention finally agreed on the Australian Republican Movement parliamentary election model.

At the subsequent referendum, held on 6 November 1999, electors were asked to vote on two questions, one relating to the republic and the other to the insertion of a preamble into the Constitution.

The republic question
'To alter the Constitution to establish the Commonwealth of Australia as a republic with the Queen and Governor-General being replaced by a President appointed by a two-thirds majority of the members of the Commonwealth Parliament.'

The preamble question
'To alter the Constitution to insert a preamble.'

Draft preamble
The following preamble was proposed by Prime Minister Howard to introduce the Constitution.
'With hope in God, the Commonwealth of Australia is constituted by the equal sovereignty of all its citizens.

> ...he Australian nation is woven together of people from many ancestries and arrivals . . .
> ...ice time immemorial our land has been inhabited by Aborigines and Torres Strait Islanders, who are honoured for their ancient and continuing cultures.
>
> In every generation immigrants have brought great enrichment to our nation's life.
>
> Australians are free to be proud of their country and heritage, free to realise themselves as individuals, and free to pursue their hopes and ideals. We value excellence as well as fairness, independence as dearly as mateship.
>
> Australia's democratic and federal system of government exists under law to preserve and protect all Australians in an equal dignity which may never be infringed by prejudice or fashion or ideology nor invoked against achievement.
>
> In this spirit we, the Australian people, commit ourselves to this Constitution.'
>
> (*Source*: Parliamentary Library 1999, 'Constitutional Alteration (Preamble) 1999', *Bills Digest*, no. 32 (1999–2000), http://www.aph.gov.au/library/Pubs/bd/1999-2000/2000bd032.htm)

Proponents for the 'Yes' case for the preamble argued that it would:

- enable the Australian people to highlight the values and aspirations that unite us in support of our constitution;
- contribute importantly to the process of national reconciliation between Indigenous and non-Indigenous Australians; and
- recognise at the end of our first century of federation the enduring priorities and influences that uniquely shape Australia's sense of nationhood.

Those in favour of voting 'No' argued that it was:

- premature until Australia became a republic;
- a rush job which needed more work and much more publication;
- a politician's preamble on which the people had not had a say;
- part of a political game between the major parties; and
- a deliberate and unnecessary diversion from the republic issue.

(*Source*: Australian Electoral Commission (AEC) 1999, 'Official Referendum Pamphlet', AEC, Canberra)

Electors also argued that there should be debate about the preamble's legal effect and that the proposed content was defective, in that it was far more likely to divide, rather than unite, Australians.

The two referendums put to the people on 6 November 1999 did not reach the required majorities. The preamble question, in particular, was not popular.

Results of the 1999 referendum

Republic question national results:

Yes	45.13 per cent
No	54.87 per cent

Preamble question national results:

Yes	39.34 per cent
No	60.66 per cent

Differences among republicans over the issue of a directly elected president versus the parliamentary selection model created a division among them that contributed to the majority 'No' vote. Many voters who were in favour of a republic voted 'No', because they disagreed with the model proposed in the referendum question.

The question of whether Australia should become a republic has not been a significant political issue since the referendum, mainly because the previous prime minister, John Howard, did not support the concept. Kevin Rudd, who became prime minister in November 2007, is in favour of an Australian republic, but the issue is not an immediate priority for his government.

> 'I am a life long republican . . . it is absolutely clear in the Australian Labor Party platform, that is where we intend to go . . . But we have other fish to fry right now in terms of the priorities back home . . . But let me tell you, once a republican, always a republican, these questions are a matter of time and due process.'
> (*Source*: Prime Minister Kevin Rudd 2008, 'Joint Press Conference with British Prime Minister, Gordon Brown, Number 10 Downing Street, London', 7 April 2008, http://www.pm.gov.au/media/Interview/2008/interview_0172.cfm)

QUESTIONS FOR DISCUSSION

1. Do you think the Constitution, as it stands, is appropriate for Australia in the 21st century?
2. What aspects of the Constitution would you like to see changed, and why?
3. The founding fathers gave the Senate nearly equal powers with the House of Representatives. Do you think this is a good idea?
4. The founding fathers made it difficult to amend the constitutional arrangements they put in place. Do you think it should be easier to amend the Constitution?
5. What are the 'reserve' powers, and should they be codified in the Constitution?
6. What do you think are the most persuasive arguments for Australia becoming a republic, and how would this be achieved?

FURTHER READING

Explaining the Constitution

Cook, I. 2004, *Government and Democracy in Australia*, Oxford University Press, Melbourne. Chapter 4 provides a useful discussion of the role of the governor-general.

Galligan, B. & Roberts, W. (eds) 2007, *The Oxford Companion to Australian Politics*, Oxford University Press, Sydney.

Irving, H. 2004, *Five Things to Know About the Australian Constitution*, Cambridge University Press, Melbourne. A discussion of what the Constitution really means.

Parkin, A. & Summers, J. 2006, 'The Constitutional Framework', in Parkin, A., Summers, J. & Woodward, D. (eds), *Government, Politics, Power and Policy in Australia*, 7th ed., Longman, Sydney. This chapter discusses the relationship between the formal Constitution and the conventions and understandings that make up the 'constitutional' arrangements of the Australian system.

Quick, J. & Garran, R.R. 1976, *The Annotated Constitution of the Australian Commonwealth*, Angus & Robertson, Sydney. This is a classic work on the Constitution.

Saunders, C. 1998, *It's Your Constitution*, Federation Press, Sydney. This book provides a clear and easily understandable explanation of the Constitution and its significance to government in Australia.

Solomon, D. 2007, *Pillars of Power*, The Federation Press, Sydney.

Judicial interpretation

The following books provide an excellent discussion and analysis of the role of the High Court in the political system:

Patapan, H. 2000, *Judging Democracy: The New Politics of the High Court of Australia*, Cambridge University Press, Melbourne.

Solomon, D. 1999, *The Political High Court*, Allen & Unwin, Sydney. Examines arguments about the political role of the High Court and how responsive the court should be to political pressure and public opinion.

The republican debate

Hudson, W. & Carter, D. 1993, *The Republican Debate*, UNSW Press, Sydney. This book presents the arguments for and against a republic.

McKenna, M. 1996, *The Captive Republic*, Cambridge University Press, Melbourne. The idea of Australia becoming a republic is not new. In this comprehensive book, Mark McKenna examines the history of republicanism in Australia from 1788 to 1996.

The Republic Advisory Committee 1993, *An Australian Republic: The Options—The Report*, vol. 1, AGPS, Canberra. The report sets out the minimum constitutional changes necessary to achieve a republic.

Winterton, G. 1986, *Monarchy to Republic: Australian Republican Government*, Oxford University Press, Melbourne. An analysis of the issues relating to an Australian republic.

USEFUL WEBSITES

http://australianpolitics.com
australianpolitics.com
This site has a section related to the Constitution.

http://democraticaudit.anu.edu.au
Democratic Audit of Australia
This site contains articles on a wide range of topics related to the Australian political system.

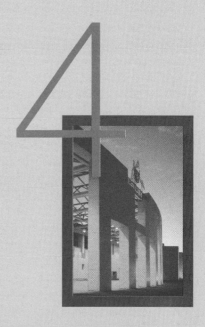

THE FEDERAL SYSTEM

THIS CHAPTER EXPLAINS:

- the principles of federalism;
- reasons for choosing a federal system;
- different forms of federalism, including comparative analysis;
- the states, the Commonwealth, the territories and local government in the Australian federal system;
- the politics of Australian federalism;
- Australian federalism and 'efficiency', policy making and responsible government;
- political parties and federalism;
- federal–state financial relations; and
- the future of Australian federalism.

The Australian system of government is built upon the principles of federalism, so we need to understand how a federal system functions. The founding fathers determined that federalism was the most appropriate way to build our political system so that power is shared between the national government, and the states and territories. It provides the central government with some powers, and at the same time allows the states to maintain a degree of autonomy over their own jurisdictions.

All of us work and live within a state or territory jurisdiction, but we look to the Australian government to provide a range of services. We pay tax to the Australian government and most of us also pay some form of levy or charges to our state or territory government—for example, property rates or driving licence fees. How that money is collected and the way in which it is spent is highly significant to us as private citizens and/or people involved in business. It is important that we understand who has the power to make decisions within our federal system so that we know who to ask when we want improvements made or who to hold accountable for problems and mistakes.

Who has the power in our federal system to determine who gets what, when and how? As we have seen, the Constitution sets out the powers of the Commonwealth, but we cannot take what is written there at face value because the location of power has shifted since Federation. For that reason, we need to understand why this has occurred and the politics of federalism.

How efficient is our federal system in delivering the goods and services we expect from government? Some people have questioned whether a federal system is suitable for Australia as we face the challenges of trading and operating in the global economy. But before we can make a judgement about any of this, we need to understand why some countries decided to adopt a federal system, what is actually meant by 'federalism', and how it is supposed to operate.

THE PRINCIPLES OF FEDERALISM

Federalism is based on the principle that sovereignty is divided between national and territorial governments. Each level of government retains a degree of autonomy that gives it the powers to make laws in relation to certain policy areas.

The powers assigned to the central or territorial government are specified in the Constitution. There are various way in which these powers are allocated.

Confederation:
- 'that form of association between states in which the general government is dependent upon the regional governments'

(*Source*: Wheare, K.C. 1951, *Federal Government*, 2nd ed., Oxford University Press, Oxford, p. 31)

- 'several unitary governments linked together without any agreement to cede final authority to the central organization'

(*Source*: Jackson, R.J. & Jackson, D. 1997, *Comparative Government: An Introduction to Political Science*, 2nd ed., Prentice Hall/Allyn & Bacon, Toronto, p. 221)

Coordinate federalism: separate and discrete spheres of jurisdiction.
Cooperative federalism: mutual agreement and collaborative joint action.

Powers that are not prescribed in the Constitution are called *residual powers,* and these may lie with either the federal or state governments. The way powers are divided between the two spheres of government is determined by the constitutional arrangements within the particular federal system. (See the examples outlined in Table 4.1; it is interesting to note the similarities in the way these systems have been organised.) In some types of federal system, the national government has a lot of power; in others, the power of the national government is limited. Some constitutional arrangements provide for some powers to be shared by the national and territorial governments; these are known as *concurrent powers.*

> Powers that are shared are called **concurrent powers**.

The fact that these powers are set out in the various constitutions does not mean that there are no disagreements between the two spheres of government about who should be doing what. The wording of a constitution may be vague or ambiguous, or it may have been interpreted in different ways over time. These difficulties may be resolved either by cooperation between the national and territorial governments or by determination of a body, such

TABLE 4.1

A comparison of the distribution of power in federal systems

Country	Distribution of power
Australia	Section 51 of the Constitution sets out the powers of the Commonwealth. The residual powers lie with the states. Section 109 provides that if a state law is inconsistent with the federal law, the federal law shall prevail.
United States	Section 8 of the US Constitution sets out the powers of the Congress, i.e. the federal government. Amendment X provides that the residual powers lie with the states: 'If state laws offend against the Constitution or conflict with valid federal laws, then the Supreme Court will declare the state laws to be unconstitutional' (Vile, M.J.C. 2007, *Politics in the USA*, 6th ed., Routledge, New York, p. 5).
Federal Republic of Germany	Articles 32 and 75 of the Basic Law (constitution) set out the legislative powers of the federal government. Articles 74 and 74a set out the subjects of concurrent legislation. The residual powers lie with the Lander (states). Article 31 provides that federal law shall take precedence over Lander law.
Federation of Malaysia	Part VI, Section 74 and lists included in the Ninth Schedule to the Constitution set out the laws which the federal and state governments have power to enact. List 1 sets out the powers of the federal government, List 2 sets out the powers of the states, and the concurrent powers are set out in List 3. Section 75 states that if any state law is inconsistent with a federal law, the federal law shall prevail.

as a court, with the power to arbitrate on these issues. The level of government that has most control over federal–state finances can also be a significant factor in determining where the real power lies within the system.

REASONS FOR CHOOSING A FEDERAL SYSTEM

There are two main reasons for establishing a federal, rather than a unitary, system of government:

- the desire for a political arrangement of convenience, where existing interests and tensions make power sharing imperative if the various groups involved are to come together at all; and
- the need to preserve the special character and rights of diverse people who might otherwise be kept separate by differences in language, race, religion or economic status.

The first of these factors, in particular, was influential in the establishment of federations in the United States, the Federal Republic of Germany, the Federation of Malaysia, and Australia.

The United States

Britain's American colonies, each with its own economic, social and religious interests, formed an alliance in 1781, under the Articles of Confederation, to conduct a war of independence against Britain. Under the Articles, the central government was subordinate to the states. After the war, the newly independent states found this form of association to be inadequate to meet the defence requirements of the nation, and the Articles were replaced by the US Constitution of 1787. The founding fathers who drafted this constitution wanted to create a central government that would have the strength to defend the country against attack and have a common currency across all states, but they also realised that this would only be achieved if the states maintained their political autonomy. To resolve the problem, they created a federation as a *coordinate form of federalism*, which designated some powers to the central government and left the residual powers to the states.

Federal Republic of Germany

The roots of German federalism lie in its history of regional government. Between 1814 and 1866, the German empire was made up of a collection of independent states joined together in a grouping called the German Confederation. In 1867 the prime minister of Prussia, Otto von Bismarck, was instrumental in uniting the states of the German empire under the umbrella of the North German Confederation, which became known as the *Deutsche Reich* after the southern states joined in 1871. Some of the reasons for unity were the desire of business for tariff reform, a reduction in road and river tolls, and a common currency. Unification was only achievable because, under the *confederation*, the states retained their political autonomy, maintaining responsibility for the implementation of most policy decisions (see Lehmbruch in the 'Further reading' list).

The Weimar Constitution was introduced in 1919, after Germany had been defeated in the First World War and revolutionary unrest had forced the abdication of the emperor. The constitution replaced the empire with a republic, with universal suffrage and an elected parliament. It also established a *coordinate form of federalism,* with the powers of the central government (Reich) prescribed in the document and the residual powers lying with the Lander (states), which were also required to have elected parliaments. The Weimar Republic, as it was known, became subsumed within the Nazi regime; in 1949, after Germany's defeat in the Second World War, it was replaced by a new constitution, the Basic Law.

The constitutional system of representative government established by the Basic Law was influenced by the three Western occupying powers and replaced the fascist Nazi regime with a democratic political system. The Basic Law contains a list of citizen rights and freedoms. It maintains the federal framework of the Weimar Republic by establishing a *coordinate system of federalism* operating through a central government and 16 federal states. The policy issues that are the responsibility of each level of government are spelled out in the constitution. The states also have a say in federal legislation through their representation in the states' house of parliament, the Bundesrat.

Federation of Malaysia

There were several significant factors in the unification of Malaysia within a federation. The federal framework established by the British to manage their dealings with the Malay states had set a precedent. There was popular support for nationalism in the aftermath of the Second World War, and a need for a united front against the communist insurgency in the 1950s. Furthermore, there were racial issues involving the power relationship between the Chinese and Malay citizens of the Malay states.

Britain concluded treaties with the Malay states, which became crown colonies governed by the Colonial Office in London and managed by resident administrators. This arrangement, which lasted from 1895 to 1946, was termed the Federated Malay States by the British, but was a federation in name only as the colonies had no political autonomy or independence from British rule. In 1946, when Britain returned to its former colonies after the Second World War, it brought the Malay states together under the auspices of the Malayan Union, but retained full political control. Britain's wish to grant independence to its colonies, and opposition from the Malay states to the Malayan Union, resulted in protracted negotiations with the Malay rulers, which led to the establishment of the Federation of Malaya in 1948. In the federation, the Malay states achieved political autonomy under British protection.

Against a background of a strong nationalist movement, and the need to work together against the communist revolutionary emergency of the 1950s, the federal constitution for a fully self-governing and independent Federation of Malaya, as a form of *coordinate federalism,* was negotiated with the British by the Malay rulers and the major political parties, and came into effect in 1957. Racial issues were also a factor, as the Malays wanted to ensure they had political ascendancy over the Chinese citizens of the Malay states in any constitutional arrangement. In 1963, Singapore, Sabah and Sarawak were incorporated into the grouping, which became known as the Federation of Malaysia. Singapore was expelled from the Federation in 1965.

Australia

The first factor outlined above—the desire to preserve existing interests—was also a major reason for the establishment of Australian federalism. The federal system of government was the preferred option of the founding fathers because it would preserve many of the discrete and distinct responsibilities previously held by the existing colonies, while at the same time putting in place a national government to take care of such issues as defence and foreign affairs. The federation also was established at a time when it was difficult to argue for options other than federalism. A few years later, in an age of improved communications and international crises (culminating in the First World War), it would have been easier to argue for a unitary system of government for the country.

The second factor has less relevance to the Australian situation. Indeed, assumptions about the homogeneous nature of the community provide little cultural or economic justification for federalism:

- Cross-sections of the population in each state in the Commonwealth reveal much the same combination of cultural and economic qualities, with variations in particular factors (percentages of Protestants, average income level, and so on) being no greater than in the different regions of a *unitary* nation, such as the United Kingdom.
- Variations *within* a state are often greater than those between certain regions of *different* states.

Matters are not so simple, however. There are striking geographical and climatic differences in Australia, and these are reflected in the people's way of life and political attitudes. City and country dwellers, for example, have different needs. There can be important economic differences, too. Since the late 20th century the economic interests of Western Australia and Queensland, which depend on mining, have often been different to those of New South Wales, Victoria and South Australia, with more diverse economic interests, including the rural sector, manufacturing and commercial financial activities. Moreover, the postwar immigration program has added a great many ethnic groups to the population, a large proportion of which are clustered on the eastern seaboard, particularly in the cities of Sydney and Melbourne. This makes Australia much less homogeneous than previously and enhances the differences that support the federal structure.

Apparent similarities often veil genuine differences. The focus of much journalism and academic writing is on the activities of the federal government, but state-based media also give prominence to state political issues. Commercial television stations from the same network run different news programs in the various state capitals to take account of state interests as well as national issues. Channel Nine in Melbourne, for example, focuses on events in Victoria, while Channel Nine in Sydney covers the news on what has been happening in New South Wales.

> *National Nine News*, **Channel Nine, 6 pm, Melbourne**, presents national news with a focus on Melbourne, Victoria, as well as international news, and sports and weather reports.
> *National Nine News*, **Channel Nine, 6 pm, Sydney**, presents national news with a focus on Sydney and New South Wales, plus international news, and sport and weather reports.

The same thing happens with sports shows. Melbourne channels are primarily interested in Australian Rules football, while Sydney channels are more focused on Rugby League.

> *The Footy Show*, **Channel Nine, Sydney**, is about Rugby League football.
> *The Footy Show*, **Channel Nine, Melbourne**, is about Australian Rules football.

Several assumptions are made about the uniformity of political institutions that are not supported by the evidence. For example, the party system that functions in Canberra, where the Australian Labor Party confronts a coalition in which Liberals outnumber their Coalition colleagues in the Nationals, is often taken to be 'typical' of Australia as a whole. In fact, only one state follows this pattern—New South Wales. The Nationals have no separate base of power in Tasmania and are very weak in South Australia; it is the junior non-Labor party in Western Australia; it has been the main non-Labor party and governed alone in Queensland (in 2008 the Nationals and the Liberal Party in Queensland joined together to form a new party, the Liberal National Party: http://www.lnp.org.au), while the Liberals in Victoria have governed alone. Certain differences between the states have also been ignored or understated in respect of community attitudes, voting patterns, and political leadership and style.

The federal principle is embedded not only in the nation's political institutions, but is reflected also in the attitudes of its citizens to their national identity. Australians travelling overseas, for example, take pride in their 'Australian' citizenship, whereas those same citizens are likely to identify more with their particular state when it comes to domestic issues, particularly sport. A good example is the way a former Queensland Rugby League player was hailed as a national hero when captaining a successful Australian team overseas, yet booed by a pro-New South Wales crowd when he led his state side on to the ground at the Sydney Football Stadium.

> **Rugby League**: State of Origin is an annual competition between Queensland and New South Wales.
> **Cricket**: Annual competitions are played between state teams.

Athletes participate in the Olympic or Commonwealth games under the Australian flag; when they return, accolades and ceremonial recognition are given by state governments to those athletes who live in their state. For example, a ticker-tape parade down the streets of Sydney takes place for New South Wales-based athletes and a state government function is held in Melbourne for Victorian athletes.

The reluctance of voters to give more power to the Commonwealth at referendums, discussed in Chapter 3, illustrates the significance of the states in relation to the political behaviour of their citizens, a factor which state governments use to their own political advantage. State premiers often campaign strongly against Commonwealth initiatives on the basis that these would disadvantage their particular state. State governments also enter into open and vigorous competition with other states on such issues as attracting investment, bidding for Commonwealth funds, or the right to hold sporting events.

> **State rivalry**
> The South Australian premier said he was 'shattered' when told the Victorian government had persuaded the organisers to move the Formula One Grand Prix from Adelaide to Melbourne. (Source: *The Age*, 18 December 1993)

The strength of this federal culture is reflected in the history of government in Australia in the way the different levels of government function, and in the political relationships between them.

THE ROLE OF THE STATES IN THE AUSTRALIAN FEDERAL SYSTEM

The continuing political importance of the states stems in part from their role in colonial times, which included the following features:

- Each colony formed the only relevant focus of government for the vast majority of its people, for whom events in the other colonies or in London were of little political consequence.
- The constitutions under which the colonies functioned satisfied their influential citizens, and in some respects, such as the granting of adult male suffrage for lower house elections, were even liberal for their era.
- Population was very sparse throughout most of the country, so there was no basis for strong local government and the colonial parliaments remained the focus of political attention.
- The growth of colonial parliaments reinforced the tendency of people to congregate in one major city in each colony (see Figure 4.1), emphasising the separate identity of each and the apparent importance of the colonial authorities.

There seemed to be no obvious reason for this situation to change after Federation. The colonies had given up a few of their functions, but the newly created states retained those that seemed most important at that time. In later years, the Commonwealth gained greater influence and attention through the technological changes, international crises and financial factors outlined in Chapter 3, yet the states continued with their traditional functions, many of which increased in significance.

FIGURE 4.1

Map of Australia, showing the state boundaries

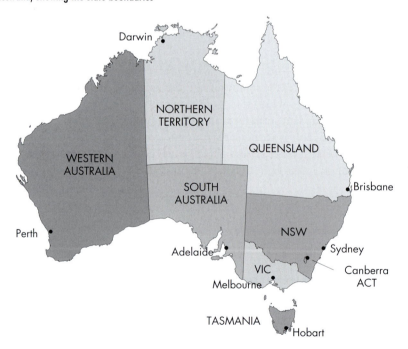

Functions

> The states provide the greatest number of services essential to the community, together with much of the infrastructure for social and economic development.

The extent of state functions can be gauged by glancing through the government listings in the telephone directory for any capital city. For example, the entries for the New South Wales government range from the Department of Aboriginal Affairs, to the Department of Water and Energy, with many others in between. The range of ministerial portfolios listed in Table 4.2 gives a good indication of the type of functions carried out by state governments. Sometimes one minister will be responsible for more than one function.

State governments over the years have established numerous bodies, some of which take the form of statutory organisations, to deal with issues such as rural services, sporting injuries, equal opportunity, building services and environment protection. The wide range of services provided by the states has a great impact on the daily lives of their citizens. A journey by train or bus, a visit to a hospital, concern about a child's schooling, a complaint to the police, a request for advice on farming—all involve state agencies in matters that are vital to the individuals concerned. Today, citizens can find out what is happening in their state, who is responsible, and who to contact by accessing their state or territory government website (see Table 4.3).

The nature of the services they provide presents the states with a number of political and economic problems:

- Increasing Commonwealth government involvement in state matters means that delivering services such as transport, health and education successfully sometimes does not lead to appropriate political credits for the state government.

TABLE 4.2
Typical New South Wales ministerial portfolios

Premier	Education and Training	Public Works and Services
Deputy Premier	Emergency Services	Roads
Minister Assisting the Premier	Energy	Small Business and Regional Development
Vice-President of the Executive Council	Environment	Sport and Recreation
Aboriginal Affairs	Ethnic Affairs	State Development
Aged Services	Fisheries	Tourism
Agriculture/Primary Industries	Gaming and Racing	Transport
Arts	Health	Treasurer
Assistant Minister for State Development	Housing	Urban Affairs and Planning
Attorney-General	Industrial Relations	Women
Community Services	Land and Water Conservation	
Consumer Affairs	Police	
Disability Services	Ports	

TABLE 4.3
Functions of the New South Wales government that can be accessed through the government's website, August 2008

Browse by topic	Life events
Business	Jobs & Careers
Country NSW	Relationships
Culture & Recreation	Having a Baby
Education	Buying Property
Emergency	Moving House
Employment	Retiring
Environment	Caring for Others
Government	Victim Support
Health	Death & Bereavement
Law & Justice	
Property & Housing	
Transport	

(*Source*: NSW Government 2008, 'Browse by topic', http://www.nsw.gov.au, reproduced by permission)

- Nevertheless, these facilities are so important that failures or breakdowns in them bring the public's immediate condemnation of the state government concerned (for example, hospital waiting lists, train delays and rising crime rates).
- Most of the services are labour-intensive, which means that their running costs are relatively high.
- At the same time, they represent massive capital investment, and that presents its own difficulties:
  — Much of it has been met by long-term borrowing, which imposes a burden of interest payments on the states.
  — The cost of renewing or improving key facilities, such as hospitals, railways and urban road systems, is enormous.

State governments in recent years have attempted to reduce government debt by decreasing their direct involvement in the provision of services through the privatisation of some functions, such as state banks and government printing services. Nevertheless, the states still retain responsibility for a great many functions; however, as we will see, the nature of federal–state financial relations means they often lack sufficient funds to provide them adequately.

Finance

The states were effectively precluded from levying income taxes by the *Uniform Tax Case* decision of the High Court in 1942. Since then, their revenue has come from three main sources:

1 *Miscellaneous fees* of four main types: (a) employers' payroll taxes; (b) taxes on property, such as land taxes; (c) gambling taxes; and (d) taxes on the use of goods and the performance of activities, such as motor vehicle registration taxes and fines for traffic

infringements. The various fees and taxes charged by the states make up a limited amount of state government income:

- They do not involve particularly large amounts—for example, in 2006–07 only 15.2 per cent of total tax revenue in Australia was collected by state governments (excluding taxes levied by local government)—while some are quite expensive to collect.

  (*Source*: ABS 2008, 'Taxation Revenue, Australia', Cat. no. 5506.0, 15 April 2008, ABS, Canberra)

- They are unpopular, not only because of their direct cost—for example, the imposition of payroll tax on employers—but also because of the regulation and 'red tape' they represent, particularly for the business sector.
- They tend to be inflationary and regressive—that is, they tend to raise the cost of living and their impact is heaviest on those with lower incomes.

2 *Income from government business undertakings*, such as railways and other forms of public transport that suffer substantial losses, has to be subsidised from state budgets.
3 *Grants from the Commonwealth government*, made up of:
   - *General revenue assistance grants*, which for 2008–09 comprised:
     a goods and services tax (GST) payments;
     b National Competition Policy payments—each state's payments are subject to that state making satisfactory progress with the implementation of specified reform conditions included in the National Competition Policy reform agreement;
     c royalties; and
     d compensation payments.
   - *Specific purpose payments* paid under s. 96 of the Constitution as financial assistance to the states 'on such terms and conditions as the Parliament thinks fit'. This means the Commonwealth government determines how the money is to be spent. For this reason they are called 'tied' grants, and make up a significant proportion of grant money remitted to the states. Specific purpose payments have been used by the Commonwealth government to become actively involved in policy areas that lie outside the powers specified in s. 51 of the Constitution.

     From 1 January 2009, the framework of specific purpose payments comprised:
     a specific purpose payments 'to' the states—the Rudd government introduced a new arrangement of national specific purpose payments commencing 1 January 2009, which will reduce the number of specific purpose payments 'to' the states for particular programs or projects. National specific purpose payments are allocated to particular policy blocks including health care, early childhood development and schools, vocational training and education, disabilities services and affordable housing. The states have to spend the money in the area for which it has been designated, but are free to allocate funds within the sector to meet their own policy requirements;
     b specific purpose payments 'through' the states—that is, payments to state governments to be passed on to other organisations, including payments for non-government schools and general revenue assistance for local governments; and
     c specific purpose payments direct to local government.
   - *National Partnership payments*, another arrangement introduced as part of the Rudd government's new framework for federal financial arrangements. It includes payments

FIGURE 4.2

GST revenue provision to the states, 2008–09 (estimated)

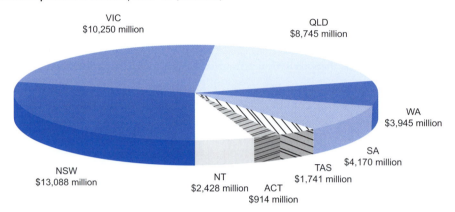

(*Source*: Australian Government 2008, 'Budget 2008–09: Budget Paper No. 3. Part 4: General Revenue Assistance', Australian Government, Canberra, http://www.budget.gov.au/2008-09/content/bp3/html/bp3_overview-01.htm)

FIGURE 4.3

Payments to the states under the new financial framework

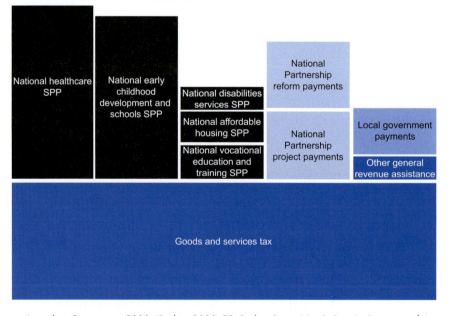

(*Source*: Australian Government 2008, 'Budget 2008–09: Budget Paper No. 3. Part 1: Overview of Australia's Federal Relations', Australian Government, Canberra, http://www.budget.gov.au/2008-09/content/bp3/html/bp3_overview-01.htm, copyright Commonwealth of Australia, reproduced by permission)

for specified projects, to facilitate reforms or to reward the achievement of reform-based performance benchmarks, and financial support for local government.
— *Revenue from the goods and services tax (GST)*—the states have many more functions and responsibilities than they can finance from their own resources, while the Commonwealth collects considerably more money than it can use for its own purposes. This vertical fiscal imbalance is one of the main sources of tension between these levels of government. The states continue to be the main providers of services as opposed to cash benefits, but they do not collect enough money themselves to provide those services. Since 1 July 2000, revenue from the goods and services tax has been remitted to the states by the Commonwealth government using a process of *horizontal fiscal equalisation* to ensure that all state governments, regardless of population size, can provide the same level of services.

GST revenue is not 'tied', and can be spent by the states according to their own priorities. According to the Commonwealth government, the GST is expected to provide the states with a stable and growing source of revenue. Figure 4.2 shows the amounts estimated to be passed to the states from GST revenue in 2008–09.

Figure 4.3 shows how payments are made to the states under the new financial framework that commenced 1 January 2009.

FIGURE 4.4

States whinge—threaten about GST money

(*Source:* Cartoon by Nicholson from *The Australian*. www.nicholsoncartoons.com.au)

> A detailed overview of Commonwealth–state financial relations, including the amounts paid to the states and territories by the Commonwealth, can be found in the Commonwealth Budget 2008–09 documents, Budget Paper No. 3, http://www.budget.gov.au.

> Information about state taxes and budgets can be found in the various state government budget papers, accessed through the state government websites listed at the end of this chapter.

THE ROLE OF THE COMMONWEALTH

Since Federation, Australians have developed a greater sense of national identity (sometimes ascribed to such dramatic events as the Gallipoli landings commemorated on Anzac Day). Australians today look to federal authorities to provide a range of services, such as social welfare benefits, and to manage the national economy.

Functions

At the time of federation, the departments of the Commonwealth public service corresponded with the limited range of the government's activities. There were only seven departments (Attorney-General, Home Affairs, Treasury, Defence, Trade and Customs, External Affairs, and Postmaster-General). The extended range of Commonwealth involvement since that time can be seen in the number and type of ministries that come within the responsibility of the federal government today (see Table 4.4).

This growth reflects not merely the general expansion of government, but also the Commonwealth's intrusion into policy areas, such as health and education, that were largely the responsibility of the states. The federal government still does not have a direct relationship with the community in such matters. In most instances, schools, hospitals and universities operate under state departments or statutes. Other Commonwealth functions, such as international trade, defence, and foreign affairs, are remote from the concerns of most citizens, except in times of crisis.

Since the federal government gained control of income tax it has had a direct relationship with the people in money matters, and that is a very significant area indeed. There are two broad aspects to this, as follows.

Collections by the government

Income tax collected from individuals and companies, and indirect taxes, such as the excise on liquor, cigarettes and petrol, and the GST, have a greater impact on most people than those levied by the states. The mix of Commonwealth government revenues can be found in Table 4.5.

Payments by the government

The Commonwealth has increased its range of payments to citizens over the years, such as pensions for the aged, the family allowance, invalid and widows' pensions, unemployment benefits, and student allowances. How Commonwealth government payments are distributed can be seen in Table 4.6.

TABLE 4.4
Commonwealth government ministries: the Rudd government (as at December 2007)

Cabinet	Outer ministry	Parliamentary secretaries
• Prime Minister	• Home Affairs	• Prime Minister and Cabinet
• Deputy Prime Minister/Education, Employment and Workplace Relations/Social Inclusion	• Competition Policy and Consumer Affairs	• Defence (Procurement)
• Treasurer	• Veterans' Affairs	• Defence
• Immigration and Citizenship	• Housing/Status of Women	• Infrastructure, Transport and Regional Development
• Special Minister of State	• Employment Participation	• Families, Housing, Community Services and Indigenous Affairs
• Trade	• Defence Science and Personnel	• Foreign Affairs
• Foreign Affairs	• Small Business, Independent Contractors and the Service	• Foreign Affairs (Pacific)
• Defence	• Economy/Assisting the Finance Minister on Deregulation	• Social Inclusion and the Voluntary Sector
• Health and Ageing	• Superannuation and Corporate Governance	• Trade
• Families, Housing, Community Services and Indigenous Affairs	• Ageing	• Health and Ageing
• Finance and Deregulation	• Youth/Sport	• Immigration and Citizenship
• Infrastructure/Transport and Regional Development/Local Government		
• Broadband, Communications and the Digital Economy		
• Innovation, Industry, Science and Research		
• Climate Change and Water		
• Environment, Heritage and the Arts		
• Attorney-General		
• Human Services		
• Agriculture, Fisheries and Forestry		
• Resources and Energy/Tourism		

TABLE 4.5

Estimated Australian government tax revenue, 2008–09, by category (not including GST)

Category	$ million
Income tax: individuals and withholding tax	126,700
Fringe benefits tax	4,110
Superannuation funds	9,750
Company tax	73,490
Petroleum resource rent tax	2,920
Sales taxes	48,160
Excise duty	25,180
Customs duty	6,300
Other indirect taxation	2,625

(*Source*: Australian Government 2008, 'Budget 2008–09, Budget Paper No. 1. Statement 5: Revenue — Revenue Estimates by Revenue Head', Australian Government, Canberra, http://www.budget.gov.au/2008-09/content/bp1/html/bp1_bst5-04.htm, copyright Commonwealth of Australia, reproduced by permission)

TABLE 4.6

Commonwealth government expenses by function, 2008–09 (estimated)

Function	$ million
General public services	17,261
Defence	17,896
Public order and safety	3,807
Education	18,764
Health	40,032
Social security and welfare	102,439
Housing and community amenities	3,197
Recreation and culture	2,907
Fuel and energy	5,574
Agriculture, forestry and fishing	3,058
Mining, manufacturing and construction	1,834
Transport and communication	4,727
Other economic affairs	6,770
Other purposes	58,202
Total expenses	292,470

(*Source*: Australian Government 2008, 'Budget 2008–09, Budget Paper No. 1. Statement 6: Expenses and Net Capital Investment — General Government Expenses', Australian Government, Canberra, http://www.budget.gov.au/2008-09/content/bp1/html/bp1_bst6-02.htm, copyright Commonwealth of Australia, reproduced by permission)

It can be argued that the provision of money, rather than services, places the Commonwealth at an advantage over the states in its relations with the electorate. Its tax levies are largely taken for granted and changes in them are so complex, particularly in recent years, that their impact is not immediately clear. On the other hand, its millions of direct social service payments are very tangible, especially to the recipients.

Finance

The relative prosperity of the federal government will be apparent from the discussion so far. Two matters are particularly significant:

1. For many years, Commonwealth expenditure easily kept pace with inflation, as economic growth and the consequent rises in wages placed many workers in categories paying a higher proportion of salaries in income tax. (There were relatively numerous 'steps' in the tax scales.) This is commonly known as 'bracket creep'. Among other things, this meant that the Commonwealth could spend more each year without having to raise its tax rates.
2. The steady increases in income tax collections meant that the Commonwealth improved not only its current revenues but also its loans position. It had built up a very large deficit in financing the war effort during the Second World War, but was able to pay that off by the late 1960s and then lend money to the states, whose debts and consequent interest burdens rose even higher. The disparity between the Commonwealth and the states became so great that in the mid-1970s the federal government decided to take over the states' outstanding debts. Even so, by the mid-1980s, 70 per cent of all government debt in Australia was the responsibility of the states.

The Commonwealth's financial situation since the late 1990s has been one of budget surplus. Commonwealth governments have worked to reduce Commonwealth debt with extensive cuts in government expenditure, and privatisation or part privatisation of Commonwealth assets such as the Commonwealth Bank, Qantas and Telstra.

The nature of the Commonwealth–state relationship, however, has not changed. The Commonwealth remains the dominant partner of the federal system in terms of income generation.

THE TERRITORIES

Section 122 of the Australian Constitution gives the Commonwealth parliament the power to make laws for the government of the territories. Figure 4.5 shows the location of Australia's territories, except for Antarctic/Heard and McDonald Islands.

The degree of local autonomy provided by the various Commonwealth Acts has evolved in response to local demands and conditions. In 1998 these included the following.

The Northern Territory

The Northern Territory (NT) was governed initially by New South Wales, but was transferred to the jurisdiction of South Australia in 1858. The cost of administration and distance from the seat of government encouraged South Australia to pass the administration of the Territory to the new Commonwealth government in 1907 when the Territory came under Commonwealth law, with a local administrator. Demands for a more representative form of government led to the establishment of an advisory Legislative Council in 1947

FIGURE 4.5

Australia's territories

(*Source*: Commonwealth Department of Transport and Regional Services, http://www.dotrs.gov.au/terr/, copyright Commonwealth of Australia, reproduced by permission)

and responsible self-government in 1978, with the administrator performing the function of a state governor. The government is made up of a chief minister and other ministers, who are all members of the Legislative Assembly.

There have been recent unsuccessful moves to advance statehood for the Territory, with a statehood convention and a territorial referendum held in 1998.

The Australian Capital Territory

The Australian Capital Territory (ACT) was created as the seat of government for the national capital. In 1911, the minister for home affairs was made responsible for building the national capital, with administrative control vested in an administrator. Canberra was formally established as the national capital in 1913. In 1920 a Federal Capital Advisory Committee was established to take over the construction and planning of the national capital, and in 1924 the Federal Capital Commission was established to look after the local and national functions of the capital.

Demands for local representation led to the establishment of the first ACT Advisory Council in 1930 to advise the minister on local affairs, but with no formal decision-making powers of its own. Although a 1978 referendum of ACT electors on the question of self-government was defeated, the Commonwealth government legislated in 1988 to establish self-government.

The government currently is made up of a chief minister with four other ministers, who are all members of the Legislative Assembly. The Australian Capital Territory, however, is different because, unlike the states and the Northern Territory, it has no governor or equivalent.

Acts passed by the Legislative Assembly are gazetted by the chief minister. The governor-general has the power to veto any Act for a period of six months after gazettal.

Australia's other territories

The remaining less populous and unpopulated territories are administered in the ways set out in Table 4.7.

TABLE 4.7

Form of government of Australian territories other than the NT and ACT

Territory	Form of government
Norfolk Island	Legislative Assembly established under the *Norfolk Island Act 1979*. Self-government with some federal functions. *Functions of Assembly*: State-type powers similar to the Australian Capital Territory and Northern Territory, but with greater legislative and executive powers and responsibilities, such as immigration, customs and quarantine. *Administrator*: nominal head of the Norfolk Island government. Appointed by the governor-general.
Cocos (Keeling) Islands	Directly administered by the Commonwealth. An *Administrator* appointed by the governor-general oversees Commonwealth responsibilities and functions in the territory. The shire council governs under the applied *Local Government Act 1995 (WA) (CKI)*.
Christmas Island	Directly administered by the Commonwealth. An *administrator* appointed by the governor-general oversees Commonwealth responsibilities and functions in the territory. The shire council governs under the applied *Local Government Act 1995 (WA) (CI)* and exercises the same powers as Western Australian shire councils regarding the provision of a local government framework for administration and provision of services.
Coral Sea Islands	Laws of the ACT apply in this territory, and the Supreme Court of Norfolk Island exercises criminal jurisdiction. Commonwealth laws only apply when they are expressed to extend to the territory. The governor-general may make ordinances for the peace, order and good government of the territory (Uninhabited Commonwealth Territory).
Ashmore and Cartier Islands	Commonwealth laws, laws of the Northern Territory and ordinances made by the governor-general (Uninhabited Commonwealth Territory).
Antarctic/Heard and McDonald Islands	Administered by the Australian Antarctic Division of the Department of the Environment and Water Resources.
Jervis Bay Territory	Acquired by the Commonwealth from NSW in 1915 to give the national capital access to the sea. Jervis Bay is not part of the Australian Capital Territory, but the laws of the ACT apply. The Jervis Bay Administration, located in the territory, is responsible for a range of local and state government-type services.

(Source: Attorney-General's Department 2008, 'Territories of Australia', Attorney-General's Department, Canberra, http://www.ag.gov.au/www/agd/agd.nsf/Page/TerritoriesofAustralia_TerritoriesofAustralia; Department of the Environment and Water Resources (DEWR) 2007, 'Department of the Environment and Water Resources Annual Report 2006–07: Antarctic policy', DEWR, Canberra, http://www.environment.gov.au/about/publications/annual-report/06-07; copyright Commonwealth of Australia, reproduced by permission)

Finance

Both the Australian Capital Territory and the Northern Territory are treated as states for the purposes of Commonwealth grants. Norfolk Island controls its own finances and raises revenue under its own system of laws. The Commonwealth provides funding for a range of operations, including the costs associated with the Administrator's Office, conservation works in the Kingston and Arthur's Vale historic areas, operation of meteorological and ionosphere stations, and a number of other functions.

The provision of Australian government services to Christmas Island and Cocos (Keeling) Islands is the responsibility of the agency supplying the service, for example, customs and quarantine. The shire councils receive funding for general purpose assistance direct from the Commonwealth. The Coral Sea Islands, and Ashmore and Cartier Islands, are uninhabited and attract no specific funding. Heard and McDonald Islands attract no specific funding beyond provision for national and international obligations and research facilities. Government services to the Jervis Bay Territory are funded through the Territories Office of the Commonwealth Attorney-General's Department.

LOCAL GOVERNMENT

> **Local government** is not formally recognised in the Australian Constitution. It exists on the basis of state government legislation and is limited to those functions considered appropriate by those governments.

The founding fathers did not provide for local government in the Australian Constitution. This means that local government does not have an independent place in the Australian political system. This third tier of government was established through legislation by state governments to meet specific needs that are most appropriately delivered at the community level. The factors that led Australians to depend heavily on the colonial governments—penal history, long distances, sparse population, and so on—also limited the role of local authorities. Local authorities perform valuable functions, but they have nothing like the role of similar bodies in the United States or even in the United Kingdom, where local government is closely involved in such matters as education and housing. The number of local government units is declining slowly but steadily as mergers of small local authorities take place.

Functions

Local government is often referred to as the level of government that deals with 'rates and rubbish', but its functions are much broader; as well as garbage collection, they include public works and services, recreation facilities, health and welfare, town planning, and numerous powers to license and inspect community and business activities. Most councils provide information about what they do on their websites.

> 'Wollongong City Council is working for you, to provide a huge range of services to cater for our community's diverse needs. We're also planning for the future, to make sure we also meet the needs of the residents of tomorrow.'

> Services provided by the council include: waste and recycling; community services, including aged and disability, multicultural, youth, family, and respite care; health services; lifeguards; road safety; community safety; and public works, such as roads.
> (*Source*: Wollongong City Council 2008, 'Working with You', http://www.wollongong.nsw.gov.au/community.asp)

These duties are usually delegated to local authorities by the state governments, which retain control of all major works and policies on education, health and numerous other matters. State governments also retain the power to dismiss local authorities; for example, both the Melbourne and Sydney City Councils have been dismissed in the past. The governments of the capital cities have a special importance, even if their sphere of influence and action is little more than the central business district.

Outside the capitals, local government is seen by most of the community as being of less significance, unless a particular decision, related perhaps to a planning issue, provokes a vocal public response. This lack of interest has a further cost: it is all too easy for a council to be dominated by an influential clique, and so charges of corruption have been a regular feature of Australian local government.

In some cases, larger authorities have been set up to supervise certain activities, such as town planning, or to provide services, notably water and electricity, on a scale that a single council would find impossible. There is debate about whether it is appropriate for these functions to be carried out by local authorities or whether they should be privatised. The authorities are restricted to narrow, specialised functions, while still being essentially agents of the state governments.

There is one very large local government body in Australia, the Brisbane City Council, which encompasses the whole of the city and is therefore able to perform all of the functions that in other states must be entrusted to regional or 'county' organisations.

Finance

The bulk of local government finance is either raised by the authorities themselves or has been provided, directly or indirectly, by the Commonwealth in the form of specific purpose payments 'through' the states, as payments to be passed on to local government, including local government general assistance payments. Specific purpose payments are also made direct to local government. General purpose assistance grants provide funds for roads and other general expenditure and are allocated by the treasurer on the basis of population growth and increases in the consumer price index. Distribution of these financial assistance grants is recommended by state local government grants commissions. The primary goal of these grants is for 'horizontal equalisation'.

Another source of revenue is property tax, usually termed 'rates', which is levied on owners within the council area (in contrast to taxes that apply to all users of services and not just owners of assets).

> In 2005–06, rates accounted for 38.6 per cent of total council revenue, while one-third came from user charges.
> (*Source*: Australian Local Government Association 2008, 'About ALGA', http://www.alga.asn.au/about)

Councils also charge for such things as garbage collection, licences (such as the registration of companion animals or permission to build), and the use of their buildings and property, and they receive subsidies to assist them in providing community services. Many councils now have an online facility for making payments.

> 'The City of Melbourne accepts on-line payments from residents, businesses, and visitors for Rates, Parking Infringements and Parking Permit Renewals.'
> (*Source*: City of Melbourne 2008, 'Online Payments Explanation', http://www.melbourne.vic.gov.au)

In recent years, more councils have been establishing business enterprises or adopting a user-pays approach to many of their services, consistent with similar practices in the other spheres of government.

The problem for local councils is how to fund the increasing number of services they are expected to provide when their revenue raising capacity is limited. New South Wales local government is further constrained by the state government's rate-capping system, which controls rate increases. The problem has been exacerbated by *cost shifting* from the Commonwealth and state governments to local government, where functions have been passed down to local government without adequate funding.

> 'Cost shifting describes a situation where the responsibility for or merely the costs of providing a certain service, concession, asset or regulatory function itself are "shifted" from a higher level of government (Commonwealth or State Government) onto local government without the provision of corresponding funding or the conferral of corresponding and adequate revenue raising capacity.'
> (*Source*: Local Government and Shires Association of NSW (LGSA) 2008, 'The Impact of Cost Shifting on Local Government in NSW: A Survey of Councils (Financial Years 2005/06 and 2006/07)', LGSA, Sydney, http://www.lgsa-plus.net.au/resources/documents/lgsa-cost-shifting-survey-200506-and-200607_0508.pdf)
>
> 'The impact of cost shifting has varied from council to council. Cost shifting can take many forms. It might be the transfer of a state or federal asset to councils, such as a regional airport, regional roads or sea walls. Or it might take the form of regulatory functions, previously undertaken by a state which is transferred to local government. Sometimes the responsibility is transferred with funding attached. But the funding is often inadequate or short-lived, leaving local government significantly out of pocket. At the end of the day, it's the community that pays.'
> (*Source*: Australian Local Government Association 2006, 'IGA on Cost Shifting', media release, 12 April 2006, http://www.alga.asn.au/newsroom/media/2006/20060412.php)

A 2003 report by the House of Representatives Standing Committee on Economics, Finance and Public Administration, *Rates and Taxes: A Fair Share for Responsible Local Government*, recommended an inter-governmental agreement be developed to address the issue of cost shifting and its effects on local government. As a result, an historic agreement, was signed in April 2006 by the Commonwealth, state and territory governments and the Australian Local Government Association, called the Inter-governmental Agreement Establishing Principles Guiding Inter-Governmental Relations on Local Government Matters. The agreement provides a framework for the delivery and funding of services carried out by local government, and determines that when a responsibility is devolved to local government, it should be consulted and the financial impact be taken into account (a copy of the agreement can be accessed at http://www.lgpmcouncil.gov.au/publications/charter.aspx).

The Local Government and Shires Association of NSW conducts an annual survey of councils to collect financial data to monitor whether the states and the Commonwealth are complying with the agreement.

Recognition of local government

A further outcome from the 2003 report of the House of Representatives Standing Committee on Economics, Finance and Public Administration was the passage of a resolution through the federal parliament on 17 October 2006 recognising local government as an integral part of Australia's system of government. However, an Opposition amendment to add a clause in support of a referendum to extend constitutional recognition to local government was defeated in both houses. The government voted down the amendment on the basis that it was unlikely to succeed because two previous referendums in 1974 and 1988 on the issue had been defeated. This resolution does not have constitutional status and is therefore purely symbolic. What it does do, however, is give in-principle support to local government's role in the political system, and recognise its contribution to democratic governance in Australia.

> 'The motion acknowledges local government's significance in providing service and as representing and responding to the needs of local communities. The resolution also acknowledges the importance of consulting and cooperating with local government and signifies the importance of all spheres of government working together to address the challenges faced by local communities.'
> (*Source:* Councillor Paul Bell, President of the Australian Local Government Association 2006, 'Milestone for Local Government as Resolution Passes Both Houses', media release, 17 October 2006, http://www.alga.asn.au/newsroom/media/2006/20061017.php)

THE POLITICS OF AUSTRALIAN FEDERALISM

The federal system, in dividing powers, also divided responsibilities among governments. This has made it possible for one government, when under attack, to blame another—or a combination of others—for its shortcomings. The quest for scapegoats takes various forms, including:

- the less populous states claiming that New South Wales and/or Victoria try to dominate their affairs;
- New South Wales and Victoria complaining that their citizens' taxes are subsidising the smaller states;

> 'New South Wales taxpayers will be paying out some $1.5 billion in one year alone to subsidise other States, including Queensland and the Australian Capital Territory.'
> (Source: Michael Egan, NSW Treasurer 2003, *NSW Legislative Council Hansard*, 28 May 2003, p. 1229)
>
> Increases in GST revenue to the states resulted in complaints from New South Wales and Victoria that Queensland and Western Australia 'receive too big a cut of the GST pie'.
> (Source: *The Australian*, 14 January 2005)

- states blaming Canberra for their shortage of money (there is always a shortage of money); and

> 'In recent times a number of decisions by the Commonwealth Government have cost the taxpayers of New South Wales dearly . . . I have often described Federation as a conspiracy against New South Wales and I have to say that the leading conspirator is the Commonwealth Government.'
> (Source: Michael Egan, NSW Treasurer 2003, *NSW Legislative Council Hansard*, 28 May 2003, p. 1229)

- the federal government accusing the states of extravagance and poor management.

> 'They're getting the rivers of GST gold, and if they've got problems with their public hospital systems, they need to spend more of their GST money on the public hospitals . . . they need to lift their game when it comes to public hospitals.'
> (Source: Tony Abbott, Minister for Health 2004, interview with Julia Gillard and Tony Abbott, *Sunrise*, Channel Seven, 7 October 2004)

This process occurs regardless of the political parties in power at the time. It is not uncommon for Commonwealth and state leaders of the same party to be in disagreement, particularly about the amount of Commonwealth funding made available to the states, or on issues such as gun licensing, where the interests of some state governments may be different from those of the Commonwealth, although the electoral disadvantages of doing so may moderate the level and frequency of disagreement.

FIGURE 4.6
Federation is in the air

But where will it land us—in the lion's mouth, or in the happy land of Canaan?
(Source: *The Bulletin*, 23 November 1889, reproduced by permission from *The Bulletin*, www.acpsyndication.com)

The tension is likely to be greater when different parties are in power at each level—for example, between the Queensland government and the Whitlam government in 1974–75, and between the Tasmanian government and the Hawke government in 1983–84. Friction between state governments, even of the same party, is not uncommon: for example, a Tasmanian premier tells the electorate that they are bullied by the mainland states, or the premiers of Victoria and New South Wales criticise each other vigorously in relation to policy matters over which they disagree. Such tactics strengthen the stereotypes that the people in various states of Australia perceive in themselves and in each other, thus enhancing and nurturing the federal culture.

FIGURE 4.7

National Water Plan states squabble

(Source: Cartoon by Nicholson from *The Australian*. www.nicholsoncartoons.com.au)

A further consequence of the federal division of powers and responsibilities is that bargaining within the system has developed its own ritual and set of symbols. This is a common feature of political activity, and needs to be placed in perspective. The basic symbol is federalism itself: the question of making substantial changes to the system (for example, abolishing the Senate) scarcely appears on the political agenda, and the cost of even seeming to tamper with it can be very high, as the Whitlam government discovered. Other symbols include the states themselves, their 'sovereignty' as political units predating Federation, and the Senate as a protector of states' 'rights'. Many of the claims made on behalf of these symbols, particularly state 'sovereignty' and the Senate's role, are empty or misleading, but that need not reduce their political impact: a challenge to any one of them can be presented as a challenge to federalism and to the very Constitution.

The ritual of federalism includes the casting of blame on another jurisdiction, as mentioned earlier. It can be observed on many occasions, including both state and federal elections (see Figure 4.7).

This can create misleading impressions that the relationship between the states and the Commonwealth, and between the states, is one of unending conflict. These are all aspects of the politics of federalism, and are to be expected; but it is important to understand that the theatre of conflict goes hand in hand with ongoing cooperation between the states, and between the states and the Commonwealth, on a large number of issues.

FEDERALISM AND 'EFFICIENCY'

The division of powers between the state governments and the Commonwealth government can make policy making and administration more complex than it might be if just one government made all the important decisions. At least this has generally been assumed by those concerned with 'efficiency' in government—in other words, the achievement of policy goals and outcomes without having to deal with the problems and constraints imposed by the federal system. Under our federal system, there are seven parliaments and public services rather than one, plus the legislative assemblies and public services of the two self-governing territories. This can hardly be helpful in producing clear policies, and seems simply wasteful where it duplicates personnel and functions, particularly since the Commonwealth has moved further into the traditional state areas of health, education, social welfare and resource development.

Criticisms of Australian federalism

Australian federalism has been criticised in terms of:

- overlap and duplication;
- vertical fiscal imbalance;
- inefficiencies when individual states have different rules (for example, education systems); and
- too many tiers of government.

Two defences can be provided against such criticisms:

1. There is in fact little duplication between state governments and the federal government, because the states are concerned mainly with the delivery of services, while the Commonwealth supervises the distribution of money and provides some policy coordination in so doing. Local government, as we have seen, has its own role to play in delivering services to the community. A little duplication may not be a bad thing if it ensures that services actually reach citizens.
2. If services were not provided by the individual states, they would have to be supplied by a single gigantic bureaucracy, which would not necessarily produce economies of scale as it would have to take into account many differences in needs and conditions throughout the country.

Such attitudes often reflect political rhetoric rather than acknowledged facts. Even now, too little is known about the machinery of federalism to make an objective assessment of its 'efficiency', although it seems sensible to assume that too many agencies are involved in providing certain services.

Linked to the defence of federalism, however, is the more general argument that the state governments are 'closer to the people' and are in a better position to understand their needs and to express their demands to the Commonwealth government. In that respect, a federal system is claimed to be more 'democratic' and responsive. Citizens can engage in 'forum shopping' across other levels of government when one avenue proves unfruitful. Whether citizens themselves believe this is another question; it is one of many matters in which attitudes to government have not been surveyed widely and systematically. However, the less tangible benefits, such as the state government's alleged closeness to the electorate, seem to hold more significance for politicians than for ordinary citizens. Of course, many citizens are physically far removed from both Canberra and their state capitals; and Commonwealth administration is just as decentralised as state administration. (For example, the majority of social security officers are located outside Canberra to service the needs of citizens within the community.)

FEDERALISM AND POLICY MAKING

It is less difficult to determine the effect that federalism has had on establishing long-term policies and setting national goals. The politics of the federal process have made it difficult for the Commonwealth to intervene in matters of traditional state concern without being accused of coercion. It has been argued that, as a consequence, governments have been content to do little or nothing about long-term problems such as urban development, energy conservation or human resource planning. The states and the Commonwealth have each blamed the other for lack of planning, assuming that the electorate will be unable to determine responsibility for the inevitable shortcomings.

Such sweeping criticism of federalism is not wholly justified. Both Labor and non-Labor governments in the 1990s looked more to 'market forces' than planning to achieve their policy goals, so the absence of effective strategies for economic management in Australia could reflect party policies as much as failings in the federal system. People tend also to seek rapid solutions to problems and, when they do not appear, to allocate blame indiscriminately—the federal system itself being a handy scapegoat at times. In fact, the states, and the federal government in particular, have used several devices to meet needs that were not envisaged by the architects of federalism—in particular:

- cooperation between governments;
- financial encouragement and coercion; and
- the testing of constitutional provisions in the High Court.

Cooperation between governments

The states and the Commonwealth cooperate in several ways in forming and implementing policies of mutual interest.

Meetings of the prime minister and state and territory leaders at the Council of Australian Governments (COAG) to discuss matters of mutual interest

> 'The Council of Australian Governments (COAG) is the peak intergovernmental forum in Australia. COAG comprises the Prime Minister, State Premiers, Territory Chief Ministers and the President of the Australian Local Government Association (ALGA).'
> (Source: COAG 2008, 'About COAG', http://www.coag.gov.au/about_coag)

The extent to which a prime minister utilises COAG may depend on the nature of the political relationship between a federal government and member state governments at the time. For example, the fact that all state and territory governments were Labor while the Coalition was in power federally meant that Prime Minister Howard was less likely to use COAG as a vehicle for policy reform. On the other hand, Kevin Rudd, the current Labor prime minister, is able to work with a situation where all state and territory governments and the federal government are Labor.

Council for Australian Federation

This council was established on 13 October 2006 by the state premiers and territory chief ministers to create an inter-governmental forum in which a more collaborative, cooperative and effective federal system can be encouraged. On the surface this would appear to be a vehicle for cooperative federalism, but it also enables state and territory ministers to engage as a group to develop agreed policy objectives to enhance their bargaining power in negotiations with the federal government.

Inter-governmental agreements

Inter-governmental agreements are another form of cooperation that may be used in a cooperative, consensual way, such as the cost shifting agreement discussed above. In 2000, for example, the Commonwealth and the states and territories entered into an Intergovernmental Agreement on the Reform of Commonwealth–State Financial Relations in which it was agreed that the revenue from the GST would be paid to the states and territories.

> 'It must be said that the Premiers, Chief Ministers and the Prime Minister set aside political differences to reach this historic agreement which is undoubtedly in the national interest and will forge a stronger federation . . . from a personal perspective, it was wonderful seeing leaders of different political persuasions working together.'
> (Source: Carnell, K., ACT Chief Minister 1999, *ACT Legislative Assembly Hansard*, 20 April 1999, p. 991)

Inter-governmental agreements may also be used as a process to implement any arrangements made necessary as a result of financial coercion by the Commonwealth.

Meetings of Commonwealth, state and territory ministers, and bureaucratic consultation

There is regular communication between Commonwealth and state ministers and between their public service advisers on a great variety of matters, sometimes on an ad hoc basis and on other occasions as a result of agreements reached at higher levels. Many administrative arrangements are required to implement policies such as federal funding for hospitals, housing or roads, to arrange mineral exports, and to study the environmental impact of large construction projects.

> **Ministerial Councils** are formal meetings of Commonwealth, state and territory ministers to consult about cooperative, joint action on policy.
> **Leaders' Forums** are meetings of state and territory ministers (excluding the Commonwealth) to consider issues to be discussed at COAG meetings.

Legislation to implement common rules across all states

The Commonwealth and the states and territories sometimes reach agreement to pass complementary legislation so that there are uniform rules across the nation on a particular policy matter.

Inter-governmental agencies

Agencies such as the Murray Darling Basin Commission are established with the statutory authority to undertake particular tasks.

Most of the activities described above involve 'policy' at various levels, but the processes have sometimes led to long delays, confusion about goals, and tension between those conducting the negotiations. The Commonwealth sometimes uses its financial powers to overcome these problems or to impose its policy preferences on the states.

Financial control and coercion

Specific purpose payments

In addition to the money returned to the states from income tax and GST collections, the Commonwealth, as we have already seen, makes specific purpose payments to the states under s. 96 of the Constitution. These began many years ago, mainly to assist with general needs such as roads and hospitals, with the Commonwealth often supplementing finance provided by the states. The arrangements were extended in the early 1950s to help finance universities, then in the late 1960s to a wider range of educational needs and to assist with the standardisation of railway gauges.

When Labor won office in 1972, it used s. 96 to get involved in welfare and urban development. Subsequently, special purpose payments increased greatly, until by 1975–76 they made up about half of total government grants.

> 'The main constitutional legacy of our federalism was the precedent for wider use of the Australian government's financial powers . . . What had never been attempted before was the use of those grants (s. 96) to achieve far-reaching reforms in education, medical services, hospitals, sewerage, transport and other urban and regional development programs.'
> (Source: Whitlam, E.G. 1985, *The Whitlam Government, 1972–1975*, Viking, Ringwood, Victoria, p. 716, reproduced with permission)

This was a new development in policy making within the federal system, but it met with strong opposition from states where the Coalition parties were in government, and there were misgivings even within Labor states. Further problems were apparent when the Coalition returned to power in Canberra, because the Fraser government was able to dismantle or severely reduce several Labor programs simply by cutting their funds.

Commonwealth governments still use s. 96 grants to direct funds to the states for specific purposes. The difference in the Rudd government's new national specific payments scheme, as we saw above, is the delivery of the bulk of this money in a form that will permit the states to have more say in setting their policy priorities.

General assistance payments/National Partnerships payments

The Commonwealth has also attached conditions to general assistance payments to the states. For example, the Howard government's national competition payments to the states were conditional on the states achieving satisfactory progress on the implementation of agreed reforms. Reform-based performance benchmarks are also an element of the Rudd government's National Partnership payments scheme.

Testing constitutional limitations

Commonwealth governments have sought to have some sections of the Constitution applied in the broadest possible way, often involving complex litigation before the High Court (see Chapter 3), and additional manoeuvres designed to achieve their original goals while observing the court's decisions. At such times, federalism has come to resemble a system not so much of Commonwealth–state cooperation as of confrontation.

The banking system

The most bitter and protracted campaign centred on the control of the nation's banking system. Section 51(xiii) of the Constitution gave the Commonwealth power over 'banks, other than state banking' (intrastate banking), but this meant that it lacked effective control of the money supply and consequently of such important matters as interest rates and the volume of credit. Labor determined in the 1940s to assume responsibility under the defence power for banking policy. There followed a series of challenges to the government's legislation, in which the High Court ruled against the Commonwealth. It was another decade before the Menzies government established a central bank (the Reserve Bank), which finally gave the Commonwealth control of monetary policy. In this instance, a federal government bid for extensive power proved unsuccessful, but some of the original objectives were later achieved by indirect means.

External affairs and finance

When Labor returned to power in 1972, it tried to profit from this example in order to extend its activities. It argued, for instance, that the *external affairs power* gave it control over offshore resources, as well as the authority to legislate to protect human rights (giving effect to international agreements it had signed). The Whitlam government also used the *finance power* granted by s. 81 of the Constitution to grant money to bodies which it set up to perform functions not specifically provided for under the 'powers' section, s. 51. It legislated on such matters as restrictive trade practices, law reform, discrimination and family law, relying on a variety of constitutional provisions and on some ingenious arguments. One of the justifications for legislating on conservation, for example, was that it was said to relate to overseas trade by way of encouraging tourism!

> High Court decisions in the 1980s, notably in *Koowarta* (1982) and the *Dams Case* (1983), have interpreted the Constitution in such a way as to allow the Commonwealth to extend its legislative reach (in these cases, in the fields of Aboriginal affairs and environmental policy) by relying on the external affairs (s. 51(xxix)) and corporations (s. 51(xx)) powers given in the Constitution.

There are limits to the use of this strategy:

- Past experience has shown how circuitous, and even exhausting, the manoeuvring can be.
- Some initiatives have yet to be tested, and others are open to reinterpretation by the High Court.
- State governments have reacted strongly to Commonwealth intrusion into their affairs by this method.
- It is unlikely that the Commonwealth would proceed unless supported by broad public opinion; to do otherwise would risk an electoral backlash.

FEDERALISM AND RESPONSIBLE GOVERNMENT

The tensions and policy limitations of federalism combine with the weaknesses of parliament and the influence of the bureaucracy to pose further problems for the conventions of responsible government in Australia. In some instances, this can mean that no minister in any of the several governments within the country can be made answerable for certain actions, even though they might be approved by all those taking part. For example, agreements concluded by the various ministerial councils cannot be scrutinised effectively by any of the Australian parliaments, as the majority of participants are answerable, in theory at least, only to their own legislature and not to any of the others. Administrative arrangements that flow from agreements between ministers are similarly shielded from close parliamentary investigation.

The fact that little concern has been shown about this situation merely illustrates the lack of awareness, in both the community and its legislatures, of the power that governments in general have acquired under the mantle of federalism. That is, the system presents barriers to coordinated policy making, but once a compromise is achieved it is virtually beyond challenge.

For the most part, the electorate shows concern only when a particular event demonstrates how hard it is to secure accountability within the federal system. A state minister might claim, for example, that the waiting lists in a city hospital result from the shortage of Commonwealth funds.

> 'The failure of the Commonwealth government to provide adequate funding for medical staff and nurse training was stopping the NSW government opening more beds in the public hospital system.'
> (Source: Morris Iemma, NSW Minister for Health 2004, media release, 24 June 2004. This material has been reproduced with the permission of the NSW Department of Health.)

The federal minister responds that the state has not ordered its priorities correctly — and has been wasting money. The voter remains as bewildered as ever by the rhetoric of federalism, feeling that 'someone should do something about hospital waiting lists'.

Aurukun and Mornington Island

The lack of accountability can have pernicious effects, however, as in the case of the Aboriginal communities at Aurukun and Mornington Island, North Queensland.

In 1978 the Queensland government decided to take control of the mission-supervised settlements, possibly because the land was rich in minerals and the residents were opposed to their land being mined. The Indigenous communities appealed for help to the federal government, which by an overwhelming referendum vote in 1967 had been given power to make laws for them (amendment to s. 51(xxvi)). There followed a series of conferences between the two governments and provocative statements by the Queensland authorities, which withdrew funds from the settlements and set up local government authorities in their stead.

When the Indigenous communities continued to oppose the Queensland government's measures, their councils were dismissed and replaced by an administrator, pending fresh elections. In the meantime, the Commonwealth had been urged to use its constitutional powers to acquire the land, but it declined — partly because of the question of compensation to the state, but also because of the aggressive behaviour of the Queensland government and its premier Sir Joh Bjelke-Petersen. Despite Bjelke-Petersen's claim to the contrary, there can be no doubt that the wishes of the Indigenous communities were completely ignored; yet the federal minister took no action to fulfil promises made earlier to the communities.

Several conclusions can be drawn from this case:

- The wishes of an overwhelming majority of the electorate were made clear in the 1967 referendum, which returned a 'Yes' vote of 90 per cent.
- The Commonwealth's legal constitutional power was clear, despite possible difficulties over compensation.
- The federal government was nevertheless politically incapacitated by the opposition from Queensland, which made effective use of the rhetoric of federalism.
- It is not clear to what extent any of the ministers involved was 'responsible' for the situation; certainly, no one was held accountable for it.

This case could be seen as an example of a Commonwealth Liberal/National Party government declining to intervene against an incumbent National Party government in Queensland. The Commonwealth Labor government, however, was not so constrained in overriding objections from the Western Australian Liberal premier to its native title legislation in 1994.

The intrusion of party politics into the relationship between the two tiers of government complicates further the operation of responsible government when the Commonwealth, in operating in what it could justify as the national interest, overrides the wishes of any one state.

Despite these problems, the formal accountability of both state and Commonwealth governments is maintained through the electoral process, where citizens have the opportunity to express their opinions on their actions through the ballot box.

POLITICAL PARTIES AND FEDERALISM

The workings of the federal system have been complicated by party rivalries, and the parties have used the rhetoric of federalism to magnify the differences between them. The Liberal Party and the Nationals in the past found it particularly useful to do this, often presenting themselves as the defenders of the federal 'principle' and of state 'rights', while depicting the Australian Labor Party as 'centralist'.

In practice, there has not been such an obvious difference in the approach to federalism simply on party grounds. Labor has certainly tried more often than its opponents to enhance Commonwealth powers through formal constitutional amendment and the use of existing powers to encroach on state responsibilities, but the party has often been divided in such attempts, usually when state branches or leaders have seen disadvantages for themselves flowing from proposals advanced by their federal colleagues. Moreover, various elements of the labour movement have opposed moves by conservatives to increase Commonwealth powers, particularly over laws related to the workplace. Such things have occurred partly because the ALP is a coalition of groups with differing views and interests; also because the appeal of the federal system varies according to whether it is viewed from one of the state capitals or from Canberra.

Politicians of any persuasion want to protect their own power base, both within their party and by appeal to their electorate, so state Labor leaders, like any others, are bound to have disagreements with their own party when it is in power in Canberra. For example, the Labor premiers of Tasmania, Western Australia and South Australia opposed the Whitlam government's attempts to control offshore resources and mining. Even though federal control was approved Labor policy, the premiers were too jealous of state powers and too concerned for their electoral reputations to observe it in this instance. Likewise, the Labor premier of Western Australia vigorously and successfully opposed the Hawke government's proposal to introduce a national land rights policy for Aborigines, and Labor's Premier Goss of Queensland came into conflict with the Keating Labor government over a development that the Commonwealth government considered posed some threat to the World Heritage values of the Great Barrier Reef off the coast of Queensland.

The location of government is an equally important consideration when assessing the behaviour of the Coalition parties in federal matters. The Liberal Party and the Nationals were in power at the federal level for the majority of the postwar period when the Commonwealth's role grew most notably. The conservatives, therefore, had a great deal of time to act on their federalist beliefs, but generally failed to do so. Prime Minister Menzies, in fact, instigated the Commonwealth's move into state education with grants for school science blocks. As you will see below, the Howard government was more centralist in its approach to Commonwealth-state relations than its Coalition predecessors.

The fact is that any party in power in Canberra finds it attractive, and even necessary, to get involved in issues that involve some intrusion into the policy agenda of state governments:

- For many years there was political gain in proposing a larger role for the Commonwealth government, particularly in welfare matters.
- When viewed from Canberra, many problems—such as globalisation and climate change—seem better dealt with from the national level, rather than from within the states.
- The Commonwealth bureaucracy is a major source of ideas for new schemes that require action at the federal level.

It is therefore not surprising that the Coalition, among other things, opposed the return of effective income-taxing powers to the states, acquired control of Aboriginal affairs, greatly expanded federal support for education, instituted national funding for the arts, prevented the mining of Queensland's Fraser Island, supervised the negotiation of mineral export contracts, and so on.

Labor and federalism

The ALP differs from the conservative parties on federal matters in two main respects:

1. It has tried to do more in the time it has been in power at the federal level.
2. It has been more open about its intentions and much more critical of the states' efforts to deal with major issues.

Federal Labor must be judged on its eight years in office in the 1940s, its three years in the 1970s, and the record of the Hawke and Keating governments of the 1980s and 1990s.

Curtin and Chifley

The Curtin and Chifley governments (1941–49) had ambitious plans for Australian development. During the last years of the Second World War, Labor and its advisers put forward schemes for a National Works Council, regional planning, northern development and a national housing program, among other things, but little came of most of them. There were several reasons for this—including the level of postwar prosperity, which made a number of the tasks seem less urgent, and the vagueness of some of the proposals themselves. Yet a major difficulty was the federal system; and little had changed by the time Labor returned to power in 1972.

Whitlam

The Whitlam government (1972–75) often was repulsed by the main guardians of federalism, the states and the Senate, although the latter was acting out the theatre of party politics resulting from the lack of a government majority in the second chamber.

Hawke and Keating

The Hawke government (1983–91), after its early intervention to prevent the building of the Franklin Dam by the Tasmanian government, tried to avoid conflict with state governments, with Prime Minister Hawke preferring to adopt a consensual approach to intergovernmental relations, particularly on microeconomic reform. Prime Minister Keating (1991–96) was much more willing to override the states with the external affairs power on issues such as industrial relations and native title.

The fact that the approaches of the major parties to federalism have not differed in practice as much as their political rhetoric would suggest is evident from the way the political balance has shifted to the Commonwealth since 1945, particularly through financial control and coercion.

FINANCIAL CONTROL BY THE COMMONWEALTH

The way the relationship has changed between the Commonwealth and the states is best traced through the financial dealings that various Commonwealth governments have had with the states, particularly since the Second World War. (The manner in which the Commonwealth acquired financial dominance was outlined earlier.)

1945–72: Centralisation after the Commonwealth's income tax takeover

Once the federal government gained control of income tax in 1942 it had no desire to return it to the states, even though the original legislation extended to only one year after the war's end. Labor under Chifley passed additional legislation to give permanent effect to the wartime arrangement. The Menzies government undertook to return income-taxing powers to the states, but did not do so. Commonwealth control was reaffirmed in the second *Uniform Tax Case* of 1957.

The Commonwealth increased its tax collections and its activities at a faster rate than the states, forcing the state premiers into the role of supplicant. This ongoing *vertical fiscal imbalance* fostered continuing tension between them. The states were also in conflict with each other for a larger share of the funds provided by the Commonwealth. After many protests from the states at this situation, the federal government in 1959 introduced a new scheme which, it claimed, would end the bitterness and place all states in a better position:

- Each state was guaranteed its percentage of the financial assistance grant.
- Grants were adjusted according to changes in wage levels and population distribution, with a general provision for improving services throughout the country (known as the '*betterment factor*').

This was still not satisfactory from the point of view of the states, as the Commonwealth determined both the amount of the basic grant and the betterment factor. (Moreover, the calculations of population changes tended to disadvantage New South Wales and Victoria.) The basic objection was that the Commonwealth would continue to increase its tax collections at a faster rate than its disbursements to the states, further accentuating the imbalance between finances and functions.

The response of the states was to demand a 'growth tax'—that is, one that would yield greater returns as prices, wages and other costs increased, independent of any action by the Commonwealth. By the early 1970s, federal–state finances became such a vexed issue that Prime Minister Gorton (who, ironically, was considered by his party to be too 'centralist' for a Liberal) agreed to a substantial increase in specific purpose grants and the allocation of all payroll tax to the states.

Nevertheless, there was continuing dissatisfaction, particularly at the lack of progress in improving social services and in dealing with the problems of Australian cities. It was open to the Whitlam government to provide extra money and, in the process, to enlarge the role of the Commonwealth even further.

1972–75: Centralisation by the Whitlam Labor government

Grants to the states

In 1973–74, total Commonwealth payments to the states increased by 50 per cent and by another 30 per cent in 1974–75. Despite this, state objections to the federal government's behaviour grew even stronger.

There were several reasons for this:

- Coalition parties in power in the states were politically hostile to the federal Labor government.
- Section 96 grants (specific purpose payments) grew by more than 60 per cent, untied payments by only 18 per cent. The states saw this as a further restriction on their freedom to act.
- The Commonwealth changed certain categories of existing payments from general to specific purpose, further restricting the states' control of their financial affairs.
- Commissions were established to plan and supervise the spending of specific purpose payments in fields such as education, health and land development, which had until then been mainly under state control.

> 'The most enduring single achievement of my Government was the transformation of education in Australia. The Government achieved a number of notable firsts in education. It established the Australian Schools Commission and Technical and Further Education Commission. It distributed funds to schools on the basis of need. It assumed full financial responsibility for tertiary and technical education. It continued to expand the involvement of the Australian Government in education funding.'
> (Source: Whitlam, E.G. 1985, *The Whitlam Government, 1972–1975*, Viking, Ringwood, Victoria, p. 315, reproduced with permission)

Attempt at constitutional amendment

The Whitlam government proposed a constitutional amendment to allow the Commonwealth to make grants direct to local authorities. It was opposed by the states, which saw the possibility of being bypassed. The referendum was defeated, but not before the episode had further increased federal–state tensions; the state governments saw these manoeuvres as an attempt to centralise power in Canberra. Indeed, certain premiers, notably Joh (later Sir Joh) Bjelke-Petersen of Queensland, contributed materially to the eventual downfall of the Whitlam government.

> 'Newly released state cabinet records show former premier Joh Bjelke-Petersen tried to thwart the federal (Whitlam) government's every move in 1974.'
> (Source: *The Australian*, 7 January 2005)

Labor in the 1970s learned once more that federalism is a powerful force in Australian politics. Certainly, cooperation could not simply be bought.

1975–83: Fraser's 'New Federalism'

Income tax arrangements

Relations between the Whitlam government and most states had become so venomous that the Coalition's accession to power in November 1975 was seen by them as a form of deliverance. Under Malcolm Fraser, the Liberal government introduced two new income tax measures to give the states access to a 'growth' tax: the return of a percentage of income tax collections to the states (in 1976, a figure of 33.6 per cent was agreed on); and Commonwealth legislation to permit a state to levy additional income taxation (a 'surcharge') on its citizens, if it chose, and return part of the initial tax collection to the state's taxpayers (that is, provide a 'rebate'). The Commonwealth would collect the surcharge, or arrange the rebate, as required.

However, the states did not gain any real benefit from these arrangements. Economic activity in Australia was affected by the worldwide economic recession of the mid-1970s which meant that tax collections fell and government expenditure on social services, particularly unemployment benefits, rose. The states' share of income tax collections was, therefore, less than anticipated. The levying of a state surcharge on income tax was not viable because of its potential to politically damage any government that did so.

Grants to the states

The Fraser government provided less finance in specific purpose grants, but failed to make comparable increases in 'untied' general grants. This meant that grants to the states for such things as hospitals and certain programs for the socially disadvantaged declined in real terms (after taking inflation into account).

'New Federalism' dropped from the rhetoric of the Fraser government, and it seems likely that the government was always more interested in reducing government expenditure, as part of its campaign against inflation and 'big government', than it was in restoring the spirit of federalism.

> 'When Fraser took office, Charles Court [premier of WA] and Joh Bjelke-Petersen were of the firm opinion that Fraser's New Federalism meant what it said . . . But they soon found that Whitlam's schemes were not being quickly dismantled, that "big government" was still with them, that the States were not to become paramount. The Department of Prime Minister and Cabinet continued to demand information. The funds for roads, a highly useful source of electoral pork-barrelling, were still being tied by the Commonwealth. So was money for schools, hospitals and public works.'
> (Source: Schneider, R. 1980, *War Without Blood*, Angus & Robertson, Sydney, p. 60)

1983–96: Cooperative and coercive federalism under Hawke and Keating

Economic globalisation and the need to internationalise Australia's economy were significant factors in the Hawke Labor government's 1990 'new federalism' initiatives to encourage microeconomic reform. Prime Minister Hawke's methods were *consensual* and a more *cooperative* style of federalism, but at the same time they further increased the influence of the Commonwealth over the policy agendas of the states. The financial dominance of the Commonwealth, allied with *coercive* use of special purpose grants, also continued.

> 'I was determined, however, to use my fourth term of office to revolutionise the relations between the three levels of government—Federal, State and local—not by referendum but by achieving better co-operation within the framework of the existing Constitution. My goals were to improve our national efficiency and international competitiveness and to improve the delivery and quality of services provided by the different levels of government.'
> (Source: Hawke, R.J.L. 1994, *The Hawke Memoirs*, Heinemann, Melbourne, p. 528)

Cooperative federalism: special premiers' conferences

A number of special premiers' conferences achieved the cooperation of the states in several initiatives: establishing a National Rail Freight Corporation (including completion of a standard gauge railway track to enable uninterrupted rail travel between states for the first time in Australia's history), national food standards and national recognition of qualifications.

Cooperation and financial coercion: grants to the states

Under the Hawke government, the level of specific purpose payments to the states rose to over 50 per cent of total grants. The change of prime ministers in 1991 from Hawke to Keating threatened to halt cooperative federalism in its tracks, as Keating had a more confrontationist approach to the states. However, in 1995 a National Competition Policy was negotiated in COAG. The Commonwealth agreed to maintain the real per-capita level of financial assistance grants to the states on a rolling three-year basis, to make additional general purpose grants to the states in the form of competition payments, and to improve the quality of housing, health and community services using specific purpose payments.

However, these financial arrangements did little to reduce the level of Commonwealth dominance over state finances. Not only did the Commonwealth continue to provide just over 50 per cent of funding to the states in the form of specific purpose payments, but *conditions* attached to the general purpose payments, in the form of performance-based competition payments, tightened the Commonwealth reins over state policy.

What was different under Labor's Hawke–Keating federalism was the consultative processes from which these policies were derived. It took the form of *dual federalism—coordinated* to the extent that the states and the Commonwealth retained separate roles and responsibilities, and *cooperative* in developing policy coordination on a range of issues.

The *coercive elements* attached to the Commonwealth's control over federal–state finances continued unabated, with the high level of specific purpose grants and the attachment of conditions to general purpose payments.

1996–2007: Centralisation and coercive federalism under Howard

> 'All governments use (and change) political frameworks to suit their interests. Nevertheless, federalism had long been an area of marked differences between the parties, with Labor far more centralist than the coalition parties. If Malcolm Fraser had wanted to resuscitate the states as sovereign forces in Australian politics, John Howard allowed and even encouraged a drift towards a unitary state. For the Liberal Party in government, this abandonment even of the rhetoric of federalism marked a clear break with the past.'
> (Source: Stewart, J. 2000, 'The Howard Government and Federalism', in Singleton, G. (ed.), *The Howard Government*, UNSW Press, Sydney, p. 160)

The election of the Howard Coalition government to office in 1996 saw an unprecedented intensification of *centralisation* and *coercive* activity on the part of the Commonwealth in intruding into state policy areas. This induced a conflictual relationship with the states, particularly after 2002 when all states and territories had Labor governments.

Prime Minister Howard's attitude to Australian federalism is evident from the following statement:

> 'I am, first and last, an Australian nationalist. When I think about all this country is and everything it can become, I have very little time for vestiges of state parochialism. This Government's approach to our Federation is quite simple. Our ideal position is that the States should meet their responsibilities and we will meet ours. And our first impulse is to seek state cooperation with States and Territories on national challenges where there is overlapping responsibility. But I have never been one to genuflect uncritically at the altar of States' rights. Our Federation should be about better lives for people, not quiet lives for governments.'
> (*Source:* Prime Minister John Howard 2005, 'Reflections on Federalism', address to the Menzies Research Centre, Melbourne, 11 April 2005, http://www.mrcltd.org.au/research/state-gov.html, copyright Commonwealth of Australia, reproduced by permission)

The following examples show the extent of the Howard government's intervention into state matters, and the range of constitutional and financial measures used to achieve it.

Corporations power: Work Choices

The High Court in November 2006 verified the federal government's use of the corporations power (s. 51(xx)) to pass its Work Choices industrial relations laws. Under s. 109 of the Constitution, once this law had been declared valid by the High Court, it prevailed over the various state industrial relations laws, thus legitimising the national scope of the system, despite the protestations of the states.

External affairs, and interstate trade and commerce powers: Murray–Darling River Basin

Management of the Murray–Darling Basin was a significant issue of contention when the Constitution was being written in the 1890s, and was resolved by the decision that it would remain the responsibility of the states. Nevertheless, disputes over control of these waters remain an issue today, particularly after recent years of drought drastically diminished the river system. According to the Howard government, a national approach was needed to resolve the problem and it sought an agreement with the states to hand over their management of the Murray–Darling Basin to the federal government. Victoria, however, refused to cooperate on the basis that it would disadvantage Victorian irrigators and communities.

> 'The river system doesn't care about the border between Victoria and NSW and I don't care.'
> (Source: Prime Minister John Howard, cited in Coorey, P. & Peatling, S. 2007, 'PM seizes stricken river', Sydney Morning Herald, 25 July 2007)

The Howard government then enacted the *Water Act 2007*, which gave the Murray–Darling Basin authority responsibility for planning the water resources across the whole Basin, including Victoria, using a number of Commonwealth constitutional powers.

> 'This Water Bill relies on a range of powers which are provided to the Commonwealth under the Constitution . . . in relation to external affairs, interstate trade and commerce, corporations and powers to collect information and statistics.'
> (Source: Malcolm Turnbull, Minister for Environment and Water Resources 2007, second reading speech, Water Bill 2007, *House of Representatives Debates*, 8 August 2007, p. 6)
>
> The Commonwealth took responsibility for environmental flows of the river under the *external affairs power*, in the context of Australia 'being signatory to an international treaty on biodiversity and wetlands management'. It used the *interstate trade and commerce power* to 'assume authority for setting extraction caps along the river system and managing water trading'.
> (Source: Coorey, P. & Peatling, S. 2007 'PM seizes stricken river', Sydney Morning Herald, 25 July 2007)

External affairs power: Tamar Valley Pulp mill

In October 2007, a federal minister used the *external affairs power* and s. 109 of the Constitution to intervene in the Tasmanian state government's decision to fast-track the Tamar Valley Pulp Mill. Using its *Environmental Protection and Diversity Conservation Act 1999*, the

Commonwealth imposed a regime of strict environmental controls on the mill; established an Independent Expert Group to assist with the design, implementation, monitoring and approval of the pulp mill; and set a requirement that the owners of the mill report regularly on their compliance with these requirements to an independent auditor agreed by the Commonwealth.

Financial coercion

The Howard government consistently and progressively used its financial strength to *coerce* the states into acceding to prescriptive policies determined by the Commonwealth in areas that previously had been the prerogative of the states:

- Conditions were attached to grants to the states made under the Agreement on National Competition Policy and Related Reforms, such as progress on water reform.
- The states were required to make a fiscal contribution to the Commonwealth to assist its debt reduction, at the same time as they were complaining to the Commonwealth about the inadequacy of federal funding.
- State taxes and charges were abolished in 2005 as part of the Intergovernmental Agreement on the GST, despite the states' vigorous protestations that they could not afford to do so.
- The Regional Partnerships Program was used to fund business development proposals directly, regarded as a *pork-barrelling* exercise because projects were funded in areas most likely to enhance the government's re-election prospects. (For discussion of this issue, see Prasser, S. & Cockfield, G. 2007, 'Rolling out the Regional Pork Barrel: A Threat to Democracy?', Democratic Audit of Australia Discussion Paper 22/07, December, http://democraticaudit.anu.edu.au.)

Financial coercion: education

Education was a major target for extensive and highly prescriptive Commonwealth intervention in state policy. For the first time a four-year funding package for government and non-government schools was tied to a series of specified conditions.

> Education authorities and schools were required to commit to:
> - ensuring national consistency in schooling;
> - plain English report cards;
> - a requirement that schools fly the Australian flag;
> - the availability of information about a school's performance;
> - greater autonomy for school principals;
> - implementation of the National Safe Schools Framework; and
> - a commitment by schools to physical activity, with all primary and junior secondary students to participate in at least two hours of physical education each week.
>
> (*Source*: Brendan Nelson, Minister for Education, Science and Training 2005, '$8.5 billion in federal funding for Australian schools in 2005–06', media release, MINBUD 24/05, 10 May 2005)

In May 2007, future funding for schools was tied to reforms to improve teacher quality and deliver greater accountability to parents, including:

- national teacher training and registration;
- core national standards for curricula;

- external assessments for Year 12 certificates;
- performance-based pay for teachers;
- reporting school and student performance against national benchmarks; and
- a requirement to provide report cards in plain English, with student achievement described using grades A to E, or equivalent.

The prime minister also intended to use the federal government's four-year education funding agreement with the states (due for renegotiation in 2008) to make funding conditional on schools teaching Australian history in line with proposals set out in the 'Prime Minister's Guide to the Teaching of Australian History'.

> 'Once again Mr Howard has taken the view that he should bully the states, bully school communities, and badger people and blackmail school communities using federal taxpayers' money.'
> (Source: John Della Bosca, NSW Education Minister, cited in Kirk, A. 2007, 'History hostilities between PM, states', ABC News, 12 October 2007, http://www.abc.net.au/news/stories/2007/10/12/2057964.htm)

Direct funding: Commonwealth takeover of Mersey Hospital

In August 2007, Prime Minister Howard announced that his government would bypass the state government to keep the Mersey Hospital in Devonport, Tasmania, open by *directly funding* a trust made up of members of the local community to manage the hospital.

> 'It's our opinion that on occasions when clearly the state government concerned has not acted in a way that satisfies local community need that there is a case for the Commonwealth intervening directly.'
> (Source: Prime Minister John Howard 2007, 'Interview with Tim Cox', ABC Radio, Hobart, 1 August 2007)

A formal, binding Heads of Agreement with the Tasmanian government was used to transfer the hospital to the Commonwealth.

We have dealt with the Howard government's record on federal–state relations extensively because this government used a wide range of measures, in particular fiscal coercion, to exert Commonwealth control over areas of state policy. In doing so, the Howard government shifted the balance of Commonwealth–state relations significantly further to the federal government.

2007: A return to a more cooperative approach? The Rudd Labor government

> 'Federal and state Labor Ministers call this the new model of co-operation and say there is a unique opportunity to make it work. If nine leaders of the same political stripe from the commonwealth, states and territories cannot notch up achievements, it will be clear that co-operative federalism has had its last, best shot.'
> (Source: Steketee, M. 2008, 'How PM's red tape will bind recalcitrant states', The Australian, 10 January 2008)

Prime Minister Kevin Rudd's preference is for a cooperative approach to Commonwealth–state relations. This may be more attainable because all federal, state and territory governments are Labor, but success is not guaranteed: state governments will override their party political allegiances to protect the interests of their states in their dealings with the Commonwealth. There is also a history of states fighting among themselves for the same reason. However, the Rudd government has begun its relations with the states in a more cooperative manner, in the context of *coordinate* federalism.

Coordinate federalism through COAG

Service delivery

In December 2007, Prime Minister Rudd convened a meeting of COAG to 'end the blame game' between the states and territories and the Commonwealth. The participants agreed to establish seven working groups, each overseen by a Commonwealth minister, to address ways of overcoming deficiencies in the delivery of services (*The Australian*, 13 December 2007). There was also agreement on funding arrangements based on outputs and outcomes, with payments to the states to be delivered within the framework of the new federal financial system outlined above.

Murray–Darling Basin

The Rudd government within COAG achieved in-principle agreement from the states to place a cap on sustainable water use of the Murray–Darling Basin from 2011, with the states able to ask for reviews, but losing the power of veto (see Steketee, M. 2008, 'Robbing Peter to pay Paul', *The Weekend Australian*, 5–6 April 2008).

Infrastructure

The provision of infrastructure has been a state matter. In February 2008, the Rudd government established Infrastructure Australia as a federal statutory advisory council to develop an action plan, in partnership with the states and territories, to meet Australia's future infrastructure needs.

> 'Nation-building requires not only foresight, but a more nationally coordinated approach to infrastructure reform and investment.'
> (*Source*: Anthony Albanese, Minister for Infrastructure, Transport, Regional Development and Local Government 2008, second reading speech, Infrastructure Australia Bill 2008, *House of Representatives Debates*, 21 February 2008, p. 1093)

Education: consultation and financial coercion

COAG was also the forum for the development of national education policies in a consultative process with the states—more consultative than the heavy-handed fiscal coercion used by Howard. COAG agreed to a productivity and participation agenda from early childhood to adulthood, and the establishment by the Commonwealth of a National Curriculum Board with representatives from the states and territories as well as the Catholic and independent school sectors. The aim of the Board is to develop a national curriculum for all Australian schools by 2010.

A new schools reform plan will be developed by COAG to target disadvantaged school committees, improved teacher quality, greater accountability and more parental engagement. There is also an element of *financial coercion*, however, because the Rudd government will use financial incentives through the National Partnership payments scheme to drive outcomes in the education sector.

The Rudd government's initial strategy of consulting with the states to achieve its national objectives appears to have diminished the heavy-handed dominance of the Howard years, although it is difficult to gauge how much of that cooperation has been achieved as a product of financial coercion.

THE FUTURE OF AUSTRALIAN FEDERALISM

There are a number of issues that raise questions as to whether the existing system of Australian federalism is the best system for governing Australia.

- *Regionalisation* has resulted in the suggestion that it would be more efficient to replace the existing three-tier federal system of Commonwealth, state and local governments, based around less meaningful historic state boundaries, with a two-tier system embodying a national government to deal with national issues and regional governments to deal with policy and the delivery of services at the local level.
- *A more mobile workforce*, moving between states in search of employment, has the potential to water down state loyalties.
- *Privatisation* of public-sector functions could make the jurisdictional differences in responsibility less significant as the role of government becomes more limited.
- *Globalisation* challenges the political autonomy of the nation–state—for example, multinational companies able to move capital, technology and manufacturing from one country or one Australian state to another with great speed make the fact of divided sovereignty less relevant.
- *Internationalisation*, including external pressures on the Australian government to respond to international conventions and standards on matters such as climate change and environmental protection, and membership of multilateral associations, such as APEC and the World Trade Organization, puts pressure on the states to implement policy initiatives agreed by the Commonwealth government in its role as the manager of Australia's external affairs.
- The cumbersome and sometimes slow process of getting the states to agree to implement policies involved with improving Australia's international competitiveness raises questions about the ability of Australia's federal system to produce the rapid response required to deal with *demands of technological change* and the globalised marketplace.
- *The republican issue* raises the question of the role of the states in a republic.

All of these points suggest that some rethinking of the federal compact might be in order as Australia moves through the 21st century. There is no doubt that over the past decade we have seen a strong movement towards centralisation of power within the Commonwealth with the introduction of national policies by the federal government to address some of these issues. Despite the Rudd government's good intentions and promising start towards cooperative partnerships with the states in policy development and delivery, the ongoing success of this process will depend on the extent to which a particular issue or set of objectives jeopardises state interests. Partnerships developed through cooperation will make it more difficult for the states, in the context of state election campaigns, to distance themselves from policy failure by laying the blame with the Commonwealth. There will be ongoing tension between the Commonwealth and the states and territories over the distribution of funds, the strictures imposed on state policy agendas by the Commonwealth's continued use of specific purpose payments, and the conditions attached to other forms of funding. The states continue to squabble among themselves about who gets what from the distribution of GST revenue, with some of the larger states arguing that their greater population justifies a greater share of the revenue cake, and the smaller states insisting that they should not be disadvantaged for equity reasons.

> **'Feral federalism'**
> 'Whether it is an unbuilt freeway, dilapidated railway, needy schools, overcrowded hospitals or inadequate support services for people in trouble, the demand goes up for federal assistance and the finger of blame is swiftly pointed at Canberra. Welcome to feral federalism, where state governments try to fund the infrastructure and services which are their particular political priority but demand Commonwealth help for everything else that needs to be improved.'
> (*Source*: Tony Abbott, Minister for Employment and Workplace Relations 2003, cited in *Weekend Australian*, 28–29 June 2003)

One possible way to resolve this problem would be to rewrite the Constitution in such a way that the division of powers is more clearly and unequivocally stated. The difficulty with doing this, of course, would be to determine how those powers should be divided. Should they return to the intentions of the founding fathers of limited Commonwealth involvement, or should they reflect the situation we have today where the Commonwealth, because of its relative financial strength, has become more intrusive in state affairs? No matter how clear or straightforward the wording, there will always be a question of interpretation to be adjudicated by the High Court or some other mechanism put in place to deal with such disputes. This debate is not without a sense of *déjà vu*, as these arguments have been with us since the birth of Federation.

> - 'The answer is not to junk federalism and turn the states into little more than glorified local councils . . . maybe coming out of the debate about federalism will be a simple recognition that just because something is in the national interest doesn't mean it should be run from Canberra.'
> (*Source*: Mike Nahan, Senior Fellow at the Institute of Public Affairs 2006, cited in *The Australian*, 4 July 2006)
>
> - 'International experience and broader analysis of the principles suggests that the dispersion of power, enhanced democratic accountability and the capacity for effective service delivery makes federalism not only inevitable in a country of Australia's geography, but in fact a progressive concept.'
> (*Source*: Bob McMullan, Shadow Minister for International Development Assistance 2007, 'After the War with the States is Over: Reform in a Post-Howard Era', address to CEDA luncheon, 6 September 2007, http://www.alp.org.au/media/0907/spefsr060.php)

Until there is constitutional change, we have to work within the present federal system. Tensions will arise as the states continue to defend their own power bases and the Commonwealth presses its 'national' agenda. What is encouraging is the degree to which the Commonwealth and the states and territories do work in a cooperative manner on many issues. The need to deal with the challenges of globalisation is a strong incentive to do so.

> 'The continuing discipline of international competitiveness will likely ensure that cooperative efficiency remains a feature of Australian federalism. While the Commonwealth is reluctant to surrender its dominant role, the states retain significant economic jurisdiction and, therefore, are essential partners in intergovernmental policy and management.'
> (Source: Galligan, B. 2002, 'Australian Federalism: A Prospective Assessment', *Publius: The Journal of Federalism*, vol. 32, no. 2, p. 154)

In April 2005, Prime Minister Howard stated that 'in most cases, making our Federation work better will rely on an incremental approach' ('Reflections on Australian Federalism', address to the Menzies Research Centre, Melbourne, 11 April 2005, http://www.mrcltd.org.au/research/state-gov.html). Some progress towards sorting out how that may occur could come from a resolution of the 2020 Summit convened by Prime Minister Rudd in April 2008. The Summit proposed the creation of a Federal Commission 'to review the roles of federal, state and local government, and monitor reform' (*The Australian*, 21 April 2008). The more reform that can be achieved in a cooperative and constructive manner, the more likely it is that the constitutional arrangements laid down by the founding fathers in the 19th century will take Australia through the 21st century, not as a nation divided by state loyalties and jealousies, but as one working together to manage change, while at the same time maintaining the rich diversity of its regional differences.

QUESTIONS FOR DISCUSSION

1. Do you think that a federal system is appropriate for Australia in the 21st century?
2. What could the states do to move the balance of power in the federal system more in their favour, and should they do so?
3. There has been some discussion that it would be more efficient to replace state governments with regional authorities. What are the advantages and disadvantages of this? Could it be done?
4. Why is conflict between the states and the Commonwealth inevitable?
5. How can the federal system deal effectively with globalisation and the internationalisation of the Australian economy?

FURTHER READING

Bennett, S. 2008, 'Specific Purpose Payments and the Australian Federal System', Research Paper No. 17, 2007–08, Parliamentary Library, Canberra, http://www.aph.gov.au/library/pubs/rp/. Explains specific purpose payments, the reasons they are used and their associated problems.

Fenna, A. 2004, *Australian Public Policy*, Pearson, Sydney. Chapter 7, 'Federalism and Public Policy in Australia', is a good introduction to the subject.

Galligan, B. 2002, 'Australian Federalism: A Prospective Assessment', *Publius: The Journal of Federalism*, vol. 32, no. 2, pp. 147–66. This article discusses the challenges posed by globalisation to Australia's federal system.

Galligan, B., Hughes, O. & Walsh, C. (eds) 1991, *Intergovernmental Relations and Public Policy*, Allen & Unwin, Sydney. This is essential reading for anyone interested in Australian federalism. It provides a theoretical and comparative framework for explaining the distinctiveness of the Australian federal system.

Lehmbruch, G. 2000, 'The Institutional Framework: Federalism and Decentralisation in Germany', in Wollmann, H. & Schroter, E. (eds), *Comparing Public Sector Reform in Britain and Germany: Key Traditions and Trends of Modernization*, Ashgate, Aldershot, UK, pp. 85–106.

Painter, M. 1998, *Collaborative Federalism: Economic Reform in Australia in the 1990s*, Cambridge University Press, Melbourne. Argues that the federal system is being reshaped as Commonwealth and state governments cooperate more closely on joint policy making.

Patience, A. 1996, 'The Failure of Federalism', *Arena Magazine*, no. 25. The author argues that substantial political change cannot come about until the federal structure is reformed.

Rudd, K. 2005, 'The Case for Cooperative Federalism', address to the Don Dunstan Foundation: Queensland Chapter, 14 July 2005, http://www.alp.org.au/media/0705/spefa150.php.

Summers, J. 2006, 'The Federal System', in Parkin, A., Summers, J. & Woodward, D. (eds), *Government, Politics, Power and Policy in Australia*, 8th ed., Pearson Education, Sydney. Examines the relationship between the Commonwealth and state governments.

Wanna, J. & Williams, P. (eds) 2005, *Yes, Premier: Labor Leadership in Australia's States and Territories*, UNSW Press, Sydney. This book provides an insight into the administration of Australia's states and territories and the role of state leaders. It is interesting to note the diverse and sometimes competing interests of the individual states and territories, even though they are all governed by Labor governments.

Wilkins, R.B. 2004, 'Federalism: Distance and Devolution', *Australian Journal of Politics and History*, vol. 50, no. 1. This article discusses whether federalism is still relevant for Australia.

Williams, G. 2004, 'Federalism Needs Fixing', On Line Opinion, 9 December 2004, http://www.onlineopinion.com.au. A critique of Australian federalism.

USEFUL WEBSITES

http://www.ag.gov.au/www/agd/agd.nsf/Page/Territoriesof Australia_TerritoriesofAustralia

Attorney-General's Department: Territories of Australia
The website of the department responsible for administering Australian territories.

http://www.budget.gov.au

Australian Government: Budget
Budget Paper No. 3 relates to federal–state financial relations.

- http://www.alga.asn.au/about
  Australian Local Government Association: About ALGA
  This page provides information about the size, functions and funding of local government.

- http://democraticaudit.anu.edu.au
  Democratic Audit of Australia
  Australian National University's Democratic Audit of Australia page. Search for articles in the category 'Constitution/federalism' for discussion and debates on federalism.

Commonwealth, state and territory government websites

- http://www.australia.gov.au
- http://www.nsw.gov.au
- http://www.qld.gov.au
- http://www.sa.gov.au
- http://www.tas.gov.au
- http://www.vic.gov.au
- http://www.wa.gov.au
- http://www.act.gov.au
- http://www.nt.gov.au

THE AUSTRALIAN PARLIAMENT

THIS CHAPTER EXPLAINS:

- the origins of parliament;
- parliament and the modern state;
- the functions of parliament;
- problems with parliamentary government;
- Australia's parliamentary system;
- the representative function of the parliament;
- the procedures of the House of Representatives and the Senate;
- the legislating function;
- the Senate and money bills;
- investigating government expenditure;
- parliament's role in the scrutiny of government activities; and
- the Senate as a house of review.

Why do we need to know how the Australian parliament works? After all, as outlined in Chapter 2, many Australian citizens have a poor regard for our parliament and its members.

Most of us only consider parliament from the perspective of the television news, where we often see our parliamentarians behaving in a rowdy and relatively undisciplined manner at Question Time. But Question Time is the theatre of politics. It is the forum where Opposition and government MPs take the opportunity to score points off each other to try and gain political advantage. Television 30-second news 'bites' don't permit us to see the more substantive work of parliament—the manner in which government legislation is introduced, debated and scrutinised as it makes its way through the parliamentary processes to become law.

Our parliament is important because it is the keystone of our system of representative democracy. We elect the members who sit in the House of Representatives and the Senate. The party holding the majority of seats in the House of Representatives forms the government that makes the policies and frames the laws by which we are governed. The legislating function of parliament is important because it not only passes those laws, it also provides our representatives with the opportunity to debate the merits of what is being proposed and to question what the government is doing. In other words, it has the function of keeping the government accountable to the people.

Because parliament is an integral and core part of our system of democratic government, we will now explain the origins of the parliamentary system, what parliaments do, the different ways in which they can be constituted, and the workings of the Australian parliament.

ORIGINS OF PARLIAMENT

All communities have some form of gathering to discuss problems and decide what action should be taken. The form of gathering, its membership and its discussions vary greatly according to the size of the community and the relative complexity of its life.

In some states, decisions are made by a small elite, such as a monarch, chiefs, military rulers, experts, and their helpers. Other community gatherings involve almost all adult citizens, who engage in direct consultation and decision making—in other words, a form of direct democracy. For example, the citizens of ancient Athens came together to make decisions about the government of their city. In today's more complex society, where this is not usually possible, referendums provide a form of direct democracy.

Power can be wielded by a very small group (an *oligarchy*) or, in some cases, by an absolute ruler (a *dictatorship*). Community views may be expressed by representatives, placed in that role by election, appointment or hereditary office. Some countries, such as Australia, have a system of *representative democracy*, where citizens elect a member of parliament (MP) to represent their interests.

> **Representative democracy** is a system in which citizens elect a member to parliament to represent their interests.

In Britain, from whom Australia has borrowed and adapted many institutions and practices, the modern parliament can be traced back to the council that was summoned regularly to advise the monarch. This gathering was eventually referred to as *parlement* (from the Old French, meaning 'discussion'). The British parliament developed into two houses—the hereditary House of Lords, and the House of Commons representing the medieval towns and boroughs. Parliament's deliberations often resulted in the king approving statutes or laws regulating the life of the country and, most importantly, the granting of money (raised by taxes on the people) to meet the cost of the monarch's government.

There were frequent disputes between the monarchs and their households which were responsible for the actions of government (the *executive*), and the parliament, which demanded greater consultation on the uses of the money it agreed to provide. Over several centuries, power gradually passed from the monarch to the parliament. By the 18th century, senior ministers sat in the Commons (they had formerly been in the Lords), and by the early years of the 19th century ministers required the support of the Commons, not just of the monarch, in order to retain office. In this way, *executive power* came to be centred in parliament (the *legislature*), rather than in a group appointed or elected separately.

> **Legislature**: an institution, either elected or appointed, that has the power to pass laws.

PARLIAMENT AND THE MODERN STATE

Most modern states have a form of parliament, including democratic nations like the ones we have been looking at in this book. So do authoritarian and communist regimes such as:

- Libya: General People's Congress (authoritarian state);
- North Korea: Supreme People's Assembly (communist state); and
- China: National People's Congress (communist state).

In these systems, opposition is suppressed and the parliament is controlled by the ruling group—in Libya by General Qadhafi, and in North Korea and China by the ruling Communist Party. These parliaments exist to 'rubber stamp' the laws drawn up by those who wield the political power.

> **Rubber stamp** is the term that describes a parliament that has no independence from the executive. Its function is to approve the bills put forward by the executive.

A *parliamentary system of government*, by comparison, is one in which the executive is responsible to the parliament and the parliament in turn is responsible to the people.

> 'In all parliamentary systems the legislature holds final decision-making power over lawmaking and the finances of the country.'
> (Source: Jackson, R.J. & Jackson, D. 1997, *Comparative Government: An Introduction to Political Science*, 2nd ed., Prentice Hall/Allyn & Bacon, Toronto, p. 217)

The legislative power of the parliament of any political system is determined by the constitutional arrangements of each country and by political practice. Some countries, such as Britain and Australia (as we saw in Chapter 3), continue to operate as constitutional monarchies and the final assent for legislation lies with the head of state. However, it is a convention that this is purely a procedural act and it is not expected that the head of state will refuse to pass bills into law.

Under the constitutional arrangements for the United States' *presidential system of government*, power is divided so that legislation passed by the parliament (Congress) has to be approved by the president, who can return bills to the parliament for amendment and who also has the power of veto.

> 'In presidential systems a single head of state, often elected, dominates the executive and appoints all members of government such as cabinet ministers and senior public servants.'
> (Source: Jackson R.J. & Jackson D., 1997, *Comparative Government: An Introduction to Political Science*, 2nd ed., Prentice Hall/Allyn & Bacon, Toronto, p. 216)

Parliamentary structure

The way different parliaments are structured is determined by constitutional arrangements and political practice.

One or two chambers?

Some parliamentary systems, such as New Zealand, have *unicameral* legislatures; that is, they only have one house of parliament. Most modern parliaments, like the countries included in our study, are *bicameral*; that is, they have two houses and each may have significant power. In the federal systems that we looked at in Chapter 4, the second chamber was established to represent the interests of the states. In the British system, the second chamber, the House of Lords, is a residual hangover from the monarchical system.

Naming the parliament

Parliaments have been given a range of names by different countries, such as assembly, congress, diet, house of representatives and senate. The British House of Commons and House of Lords, as noted above, have historical roots in the movement from a monarchy to representative government by the people. The federal systems in our study adopted the terms 'House of Representatives' (including Germany's Bundestag) for the popular chamber and 'Senate' (including Germany's Bundesrat) for the house designated as representing the states of the federation.

Seating in the parliament

It may appear to be superficial to discuss the seating arrangements in a parliamentary chamber, but they are based on ideas about how parliament should operate and political practice.

In the British House of Commons, seating is arranged as two blocks of benches facing each other, divided by an aisle, with the speaker's chair at one end. This originates from the past when the chamber was the chapel in the Palace of Westminster prior to being taken over by the Commons as a house of parliament. The seating arrangement has been maintained for historical reasons and supported by the idea that the government and the opposition should face each other directly over the floor of the chamber. A red line is drawn on the carpet in front of each set of benches; the lines are two sword lengths apart. Traditionally, members do not cross these lines during debate. This arrangement gave rise to the modern use of the term 'toe the line'; members who support their party's policies are said to do this. There is not enough seating for all of the 646 MPs in the House of Commons, which has only 427 seats. This means that MPs have to crowd into the chamber when a division is called, with many having to stand.

> Former British prime minister Winston Churchill argued that 'if the House was big enough to contain all its members nine-tenths of its debates would be conducted in the depressing atmosphere of an almost empty or half-empty chamber'. In 1943 an MP said he favoured the existing arrangement because he didn't like turning at a slant to argue with an opposition member.
> (*Source*: Wheare, K.C. 1963, *Legislatures*, Oxford University Press, London, p. 7)

If the governing party has a very large majority, government MPs are crammed to one side, and there are not enough seats for all MPs to take their place in the chamber. It could be argued that this inhibits their democratic right to sit in parliament as elected representatives of their constituents. When the House of Commons was rebuilt in 1950, after being bombed in the Second World War, there was an opportunity for the size of the chamber to be increased, but tradition held and the new chamber replicated the original in size and design.

Most other parliaments (including countries in our study) have adopted a semi-circular arrangement, with seats for all members in the chamber. Members of minor parties and independents sit between the government and the Opposition in what are commonly called the 'cross benches'.

Parliamentary terms

The duration of a parliamentary sitting (commonly called a *term*) varies considerably, as we can see in Table 5.1.

Two-year terms keep a government responsive to the people. However, this does mean a government is always in 'election mode' and as such may be less inclined to take politically unpopular decisions or look to the long term when developing policy. Five years gives a government the opportunity to introduce long-term measures, or policies that may be electorally unpopular, because it has longer for them to take effect. On the other hand, electors have to wait five years (or half a decade) for the opportunity to vote a government out if they are unhappy with what it has been doing.

TABLE 5.1
Parliamentary terms compared

Country/house of parliament	Parliamentary term
Britain: House of Commons	No longer than five years
Australia: House of Representatives	No longer than three years
United States: House of Representatives	Fixed term of two years. Elections are held on the first Tuesday of November in even years
Republic of Germany: Bundestag	No longer than four years
Federation of Malaysia: House of Representatives	No longer than five years

Elected or appointed?

Historically, British parliaments were made up of members appointed by the monarch, or, in Britain's colonies, by the governor, acting on the monarch's behalf. Most modern parliamentary systems are based on the election of members to represent their constituencies, but there are some instances where the appointment process has been retained.

British House of Lords

The membership of the House of Lords is made up of:
- *life peers*, appointed by the Queen on the advice of the prime minister. Since 2000 an advisory body, the Appointments Commission, has made recommendations to the Queen for non-political peers, and vets all nominations for peerages;
- *law lords*, full-time professional judges appointed to hear appeals from the lower courts. These positions will cease when the new supreme court is established in October 2009;
- *Anglican archbishops and bishops*, as representatives of the 'established' Church of the state; and
- *elected hereditary peers*, including office-holders elected by the House; party and cross bench members elected by their party; the Lord Great Chamberlain, who is the Queen's representative; and the Earl Marshall, who is responsible for ceremonies.

(*Source*: UK Parliament: House of Lords 2008, http://www.parliament.uk/lords)

Canadian Senate

Members of the Canadian Senate are appointed by the governor-general on the recommendation of the prime minister.

(*Source*: Parliament of Canada 2008, http://www.parl.gc.ca)

German Bundesrat (Senate)

The Bundesrat is composed of members appointed by the Land (state) governments.

(*Source*: Bundesrat Homepage 2008, http://www.bundesrat.de)

Malaysian Senate

There are two categories of members of the Malaysian Senate: each of the 13 State Legislative Assemblies elects two members (total 26), and the king appoints 44 members on the advice of the prime minister.

(*Source*: Parlimen Malaysia 2008, http://www.parlimen.gov.my)

It could be argued that appointment of parliamentarians undermines the democratic basis of a political system, because we associate representative democracy with parliaments elected by the people. This is particularly the case when the appointed chamber has equal (or nearly equal) powers as the popularly elected house, and has the potential to amend or block government legislation. Problems are likely to develop if the appointees are politically opposed to the party in government, but if the government has a say in the appointments, the members are more likely to endorse government policy.

Power to dissolve parliament

Regular elections are integral to representative parliamentary government. The rules for dissolving a parliament to hold an election vary. In the United States, as we saw in Table 5.1, the dates for the election of Congress and the president are fixed. In other countries the power to dissolve parliament is established by the constitutional arrangements, usually requiring the prime minister to obtain the consent of the head of state. In Britain, for example, the prime minister seeks the agreement of the Queen, who, by convention, accedes to the request. As we saw in Table 5.1, the constitution determines the maximum length of a parliamentary term, but it is often possible for the prime minister, or president, to call an early election. This is usually done at a time when the electoral situation is most favourable to the party in power. When a government is unpopular and likely to lose an election, it is more likely to go the full term.

FUNCTIONS OF PARLIAMENT

> **Functions of parliament**
> Parliament's functions are to:
> - provide a forum where elected members represent the interests of their constituents;
> - provide, test and, in some cases, replace governments and their leader;
> - discuss, amend and pass legislation;
> - supply money for the conduct of government; and
> - question, publicise and investigate the actions of government and the needs of the community.

Legislating

The primary function of a parliament is to pass laws introduced by the executive of the government of the day (sometimes called a *cabinet*: see Chapter 6).

The distribution of legislative power within a parliament varies according to the constitutional and political arrangements that operate within a particular system (see Table 5.2).

The powers of the Australian parliament are discussed in detail below.

Parliamentary debate

Debate is an important function of the parliamentary process in a democracy. Ministers usually introduce a bill into parliament, with a statement about the content and objectives of the legislation, and government and Opposition members 'speak to', or debate,

TABLE 5.2

The legislative process compared

Country	Legislative process
Britain	The government, by convention, is formed from the majority party in the House of Commons, so it usually is able to get its legislation passed in that chamber. The bill then goes to the House of Lords which can only delay legislation. It has the power to initiate non-controversial legislation. Bills that pass both houses are then forwarded to the Queen for her assent. (*Source:* Forman, F.N. & Baldwin, N.D.J. 2007, *Mastering British Politics*, 7th ed., Palgrave Macmillan, Basingstoke, UK, p. 228)
United States	The president initiates policy and submits the executive's bills to Congress. The bills then pass through the House of Representatives and the Senate, both of which have equal power under the Constitution, except that all bills for raising revenue must originate in the House of Representatives. The Congress is more likely to amend a bill if the president represents a different political party. The president can veto legislation passed by Congress. A presidential veto can be overridden if both houses pass the bill again with a two-thirds majority in each house. (*Source:* Vile, M.J.C. 2007, *Politics in the USA*, 6th ed., Routledge, Oxford, pp. 121, 140)
Federal Republic of Germany	The government is formed by the majority party in the Bundestag. Bills must first be introduced into the Bundesrat for comment and then go to the Bundestag. Only bills passed by the Bundestag relating to revenue sharing between the state and federal governments, and imposing responsibilities on the states, require the approval of the Bundesrat. If there is disagreement between the houses, a joint committee of Bundesrat and Bundestag members considers the bill. Amendments are returned to the Bundestag for its approval. A Bundesrat protest vote on bills that do not require its consent can be overturned by a majority vote of the Bundestag. Once a bill has passed both houses, it is forwarded to the president for consent. The president does not have the power of veto. The potential for conflict between the houses is enhanced by the fact that in recent years Opposition parties have had a majority in the Bundesrat. (*Source:* German Bundestag 2008, 'Adoption of Legislation', http://www.bundestag.de/htdocs_e/parliament/function/legislation/passage.html)
Federation of Malaysia	The government is formed by the majority party in the House of Representatives. Bills originate in the House of Representatives. Once passed they are forwarded to the Senate for approval where it is unlikely they will be opposed because the majority of Senate members are appointed on the advice of the prime minister. The bill is then passed to the king for his consent. (*Source*: Parlimen Malaysia 2008, http://www.parlimen.gov.my)

its merits. In a parliament where the government holds the majority, this debate will have no impact on the passage of the bill because the government will use its numbers to pass the legislation regardless of what the Opposition thinks. However, because a government explains what it is doing during the course of the debate, the information is placed on the public record and therefore is subject to the scrutiny of the electorate. In parliaments where a government has to get the support of minor parties and/or independents to pass its legislation, these negotiations usually take place outside the parliamentary chamber, but the process of parliamentary debate provides the forum for them to justify their support for the bill and their reasons also go on the public record.

Question time provides the opportunity for Opposition members to seek information from the government about its policies and to question its performance. It is mostly used by the Opposition for party-political purposes—to probe a government's weaknesses and highlight any mistakes it has made. How well a government handles this situation can have an effect on its electoral prospects.

Parliamentary committees

Many parliaments have established committee systems for detailed consideration of legislation or to investigate and examine a particular policy issue. Their functions vary between parliaments. The British House of Commons has select committees that have no legislative function. Congressional standing committees in the United States, by comparison, do have a significant function in the legislative process. After a bill has been introduced it automatically goes to a congressional committee that has the power to amend the bill before it goes back into the Congress for consideration. The Australian committee system is explained in detail below.

PROBLEMS WITH PARLIAMENTARY GOVERNMENT

There are differences between what parliament should do and what parliament does. The functions discussed above indicate the continuing importance of parliament, but in every instance the procedures that are followed tend to restrict even its traditional powers of discussion. A significant factor has been the development of the modern party system and party politics (see Chapter 9). This has led to the tight party discipline found in many parliaments, where MPs 'toe the party line' in relation to how they vote on bills and on the debating process.

Parliament–executive relations

The parliament is limited in its capacity to act independently of the executive in a system of *parliamentary majority government*. The executive, or *cabinet*, decides government policy and the content of legislation that is put before the parliament. Because the executive is part of the majority party that has formed the government, it has the numbers in the parliament to ensure its enactment. The parliament can pass a *vote of no confidence* in a government, but rarely does, because the party in power will use its majority to defeat such a motion. This situation operates more like a system of party government than parliamentary government.

> 'Party discipline and party unity is always important. I think it goes without saying that if you run an ill disciplined show in Government or Opposition, you lose the respect of the public.'
> (*Source*: Prime Minister John Howard 2002, cited in australianpolitics.com, 'John Howard's Formula for Winning Elections', 10 June 2002, http://australianpolitics.com/news/2002/06/02-06-10.shtml)
>
> 'Because the Australian party system is so inordinately and dysfunctionally disciplined, there is no prospect of the majority in the lower house doing other than closing ranks and supporting a Prime Minister.'
> (*Source*: Costar, B. & Rodan, P. 2002, 'How our constitution allows the Senate to remove prime ministers', On Line Opinion, 21 February 2002, http://www.onlineopinion.com.au/view.asp?article=1756)

The situation is different in parliamentary systems where the upper house, or second chamber, is controlled by opposition parties. This makes it difficult for a government to enact contested legislation and may require negotiation and compromise to succeed. Sometimes the second chamber can block legislation and may force a government to an election, as happened in Australia in 1975 (discussed below).

In the presidential system of the United States, as we have seen above, the separation of powers established by the Constitution vests executive power in the president, who is not a member of Congress. From time to time, conflict does arise over the passage of legislation when the president comes from a different party to the majority parties in the houses of Congress. This can only be overcome through negotiation and compromise, or by a presidential veto.

> 'President Bush said he vetoed legislation that would ban the CIA from using harsh interrogation methods such as waterboarding to break suspected terrorists because it would end practices that have prevented attacks. "The bill Congress sent me would take away one of the most valuable tools in the war on terror. So today I vetoed it".'
>
> There was little prospect of gaining the two-thirds majority necessary in both houses to overturn the presidential veto.
> (Source: msnbc.com 2008, 'Bush vetoes bill banning waterboarding', 8 March 2008, http://msnbc.msn.com/id/23526436)

Power relationships within parliament

Other contests that are a function of party politics also occur within parliament. These include:

- ministers and government backbenchers (often referred to collectively as 'the government') versus the Opposition;
- the government of the day (the prime minister and his or her ministers) versus the rest of parliament (the Opposition plus government backbenchers);
- all backbenchers versus the leaders of all parties;
- the leaders of a single party versus that party's backbenchers (or some of them);
- tension between the lower house and the second chamber; and
- conflict between the government of the day in the second chamber and a majority opposition made up of the formal Opposition party/ies, minor parties and independents, who each bring their own interests to bear on a piece of legislation and vote independently of each other.

> 'You never know with some of the people, the Independents and Democrats, until the bells stop ringing in the Senate, which way they are going to go.'
> (Source: Graham Morris, former adviser to Prime Minister John Howard 1998, 'The Rocky Road Ahead', Sunday, 4 October 1998)

There are also practical limitations on the capacity of a parliament to discharge its wide range of duties, which include the number of members available, the skills they bring to their houses, the advice and assistance they can call on, and the pressure of work in their electorates.

Debate

The number and complexity of matters that come to parliament's attention have greatly increased, which means that there are more bills on a number of wide-ranging and complex issues to debate. This reduces the time available for discussing any one question. Debate is also curtailed because more emphasis is placed on the need for rapid decisions at the expense of a more detailed consideration of affairs. Other problems relating to the management of parliamentary debate include:

- Should the elected representatives be allowed to talk as long as they please? If so, some may make long speeches merely to obstruct other members whose views they oppose or to delay the passage of legislation. (This is called *filibustering*.)
- Should everyone's views be heard? If that occurs often, the parliament would take an extremely long time in coming to decisions.
- Should most of parliament's business be conducted on the floor of the house, or should a good deal of it be divided among committees of members? The latter way allows several matters to be dealt with at once, but means that decisions will be taken by a small group of people rather than by the parliament as a whole.
- Should discussion centre on solving current and future problems, or should much of it concern past actions by the government?

Legislation

There are issues over the management of government legislation in the parliament:

- If the elected government is given full support so that it can deal with problems as rapidly as possible, is it likely to overlook certain questions or to ignore the wishes of parts of the community?
- Should criticisms of government actions be limited to obvious errors and oversights, or should there be a constant campaign on the part of opposition parties aimed at reducing the governing party's chances of re-election?
- Is the government entitled to keep its actions secret, perhaps for electoral reasons or to avoid creating uncertainty among the people? Or, as the government represents them, should citizens be told everything that the government does?

> **Why cabinet secrecy is necessary**
> 'Cabinet secrecy is associated with the principles of collective responsibility that hold that all cabinet ministers should support cabinet decisions, and the practical political advantages that governments achieve from maintaining a united front in public. Cabinet secrecy allows cabinet ministers to engage in full and frank discussion of differing views without the risk of the Cabinet appearing divided, and it ensures that no groups or individuals can benefit from advance knowledge of government policy.'
> (*Source*: australianpolitics.com 2008, 'Cabinet Secrecy—Why?', http://australianpolitics.com/executive/ministry/cabinet-secrecy.shtml)

A general answer to these questions might be that parliament should do each of these things at some time, depending on the circumstances.

The most significant issue relating to the significance of parliament as an institution with real political power, however, remains the tension that develops between those who exercise executive power and those in the parliament who seek to question or challenge it. However, the executive does not necessarily enjoy a monopoly of power. The procedures followed within parliament influence the degree of control that party leaders exert over their backbenchers and, if those leaders are in government, over the parliament as a whole. This is the main reason why much discussion has centred on the workings of parliament. The power exercised by a particular party's leaders will also depend to some extent on the manner in which that party controls those leaders. The factors that contribute to or constrain prime ministerial power are discussed in the next chapter.

We will now look at how the Australian parliamentary system operates in the context of these principles and practices of parliamentary government.

AUSTRALIA'S PARLIAMENTARY SYSTEM

The Australian parliamentary system began with the establishment of colonial Legislative Councils—the first, in New South Wales, was set up in 1824. In the beginning the councils comprised colonial officials appointed to advise the governor, but non-official and elected members were progressively added until responsible government was achieved in most colonies in the 1850s. Colonial legislatures consisted of two houses:

1 *Legislative Councils*—the upper house—remained, with their members nominated by the government or elected on a restricted franchise (that is, only those with a certain amount of property or level of income were allowed to vote).
2 *Legislative Assemblies* (called Houses of Assembly in Tasmania and South Australia) resembled the House of Commons in being the popularly elected chamber and the seat of the executive (cabinet), where the leader of the government was called the premier.

Legislative Councils, although not hereditary chambers (as was the House of Lords until 1958), nevertheless represented the interests of property. It was considered proper for the councils each to act as a 'house of review' to protect that property against the democratic 'excesses' of the Legislative Assembly. There have consequently been regular clashes between lower and upper houses in the states, particularly when Labor governments have been in power and conservative parties have had control of the upper house.

The Queensland Legislative Council was abolished in 1922, and in the other states the councils have become more representative of the whole community. This does not necessarily mean that the tension between the houses has dissipated. In cases where the Opposition has control of the upper house, it can use its power to block government legislation. In recent years, minor parties holding the balance of power in the upper house of the NSW parliament created difficulties for both Labor and Coalition governments in passing legislation. The Iemma Labor government in 2008, as we can see from Table 5.3, did not have a majority in the Legislative Council.

Queensland, the Northern Territory and the Australian Capital Territory do not experience this difficulty, as they do not have upper houses.

TABLE 5.3
Members of the NSW Legislative Council, January 2008

Party	Members
Australian Labor Party (ALP)	19
Liberal/Nationals	15
Minor parties/independents	8

(*Source*: NSW Parliament 2008, 'Legislative Council Members (by Party)', http://www.parliament.nsw.gov.au)

THE AUSTRALIAN PARLIAMENT

The Australian parliament has two houses: a House of Representatives and a Senate (that is, it is a *bicameral* legislature). Both houses are elected by universal suffrage and the minimum voting age is 18. The House of Representatives represents the people of the states in proportion to their population. The Senate represents the people of the states equally. The purpose of this design, adapted from the United States, was to ensure that laws had the support of representatives of a majority of states as well as a majority of the people. The House of Representatives is the house where government is formed by the party holding the majority of seats. The size of the houses and the distribution of their seats are determined as follows.

The Senate

All original states must have an equal number of senators:

1901–49	6 each	total 36
1949–84	10 each	total 60
From 1985	12 each	total 72

In addition, since 1975 the Northern Territory and the Australian Capital Territory have been allowed to elect two senators each.

> Total membership of the Senate in 2008 was 76.

The House of Representatives

- Section 24 of the Constitution provides that the House of Representatives must be 'as nearly as practicable' twice the size of the Senate (the *nexus* provision).
- It also provides that original states must have a minimum number of five members; Tasmania and Western Australia are the only states to have been affected by this provision, and Tasmania still is.

The Constitution set the numbers for the first House of Representatives at 75. Representation has since increased to reflect population growth, within the constraints of the nexus, and the house now also includes two members from the Northern Territory and two from the Australian Capital Territory.

> Total membership of the House of Representatives in 2008 was 150.

Seats in the House of Representatives are distributed according to the populations of the states, with the fastest growing states, Western Australia and Queensland, slowly increasing their numbers (see Table 5.4).

Women in parliament

In 1902 the Australian parliament passed the *Commonwealth Franchise Act* which gave women the right to vote and the right to stand for parliament. Despite many attempts, it was not until 1943 that the first woman was elected to the federal parliament. That position has gradually improved (see Table 5.5), particularly in the House of Representatives, but women are still very much in the minority in both houses of parliament, despite the fact that in June 2007 they made up 50.55 per cent of the population (see ABS 2007, 'Population by Age and Sex, Australian States and Territories', Cat no. 3201.0, June 2007, ABS, Canberra).

TABLE 5.4

Composition of the House of Representatives, 1901–2008, by state and territory

State/territory	1901	1949	2008
New South Wales	26	47	49
Victoria	23	33	37
Queensland	9	18	29
South Australia	7	10	11
Western Australia	5	8	15
Tasmania	5	5	5
Australian Capital Territory	—	1	2
Northern Territory	—	1	2

TABLE 5.5

Numbers of women in parliament, 1943–2008

Election year	House of Representatives	Senate
1943	1	1
1975	1	6
1996	23	22
2007	39	28*

(* From 1 July 2008, after senators who were elected at the November 2007 election had taken their seats.)

PARLIAMENT HOUSE

Until 1927 the federal parliament met in Melbourne, but in that year it moved to its own building in Canberra in the Australian Capital Territory, which had been established specifically as the seat of national government. The original Parliament House in Canberra was intended only as a temporary structure, and it proved less and less suitable as the number of its parliamentarians almost doubled, and as staff numbers (particularly for ministers) also grew.

In 1974, after many years of indecision, it was resolved that a new Parliament House would be constructed on Capital Hill, behind the existing building. A design competition was held, and early in 1979 work began on the building. The new Parliament House was opened in Australia's bicentenary celebrations by Queen Elizabeth II in May 1988, and the first sitting took place in August 1988.

Structure

Within Parliament House the two parliamentary chambers are situated on either side of the Members' Hall; the Senate chamber, decorated in red after the style of the House of Lords, is to the right-hand side on entering, and the House of Representatives, in green on the pattern of the House of Commons, is to the left. In each case, the shading of the colours is now distinctively Australian. The layout is shown in Figure 5.1.

FIGURE 5.1
Parliament House, Canberra

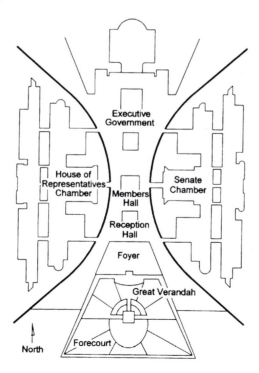

(*Source*: The Resource Centre, Parliament of Australia, 1996. Copyright Commonwealth of Australia, reproduced by permission)

Seating arrangements

A simplified sketch of the floor plan of the chamber of the House of Representatives shows something of its workings and the close relationship of the political executive to that house (see Figure 5.2).

FIGURE 5.2
Floor plan of the House of Representatives, Canberra

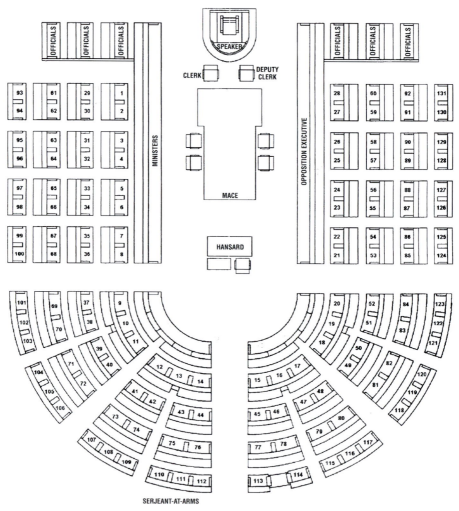

(*Source*: Seating plan of the House of Representatives, chamber, 39th parliament, No. 5, 2 December 1998. Copyright Commonwealth of Australia, reproduced by permission)

THE REPRESENTATIVE FUNCTION OF MEMBERS OF THE AUSTRALIAN PARLIAMENT

Members of parliament divide their time between attending the parliament in Canberra and looking after their constituencies. Constituency work involves assisting people with their problems. Often the MP is the last resort for people who have not been able to get a favourable outcome from the relevant government department. The MP can make representations on behalf of the person to the department and also to the minister.

The representative role also involves attending many functions around the electorate and reporting to party meetings on what they have been doing. Both of these activities are important in helping to get the member re-elected. Members have to show the constituency that they are doing their job in an active way and are concerned about what is going on in the electorate.

At the same time, they have to keep the party happy, because party members will determine whether or not the member is selected to stand for the seat at the next election. This creates difficulties for members when party policy may not be appropriate to the particular electorate they represent. Examples might be a party policy to locate an airport in a particular district that is opposed by the residents, or the Howard Coalition government's decision on the guns issue which caused difficulties for National Party MHRs in their rural constituencies. Cases like this present MPs with a no-win situation. They are criticised by the electorate for not responding to the wishes of their electorate. On the other hand, if they oppose party policy, they risk losing their party pre-selection.

Party discipline makes it difficult for MPs to vote against the policy of their party in the parliament. Those who do are marked as renegades and risk their parliamentary futures: even if they do retain their endorsement, they are unlikely to progress to the ministry. Members who resign from their party because of differences with their parties over policy sit on the cross benches as independents but are unlikely to get re-elected, as the preferential electoral system favours the major parties in the House of Representatives. There have been exceptions. Graeme Campbell, for example, who was disendorsed by the ALP because of his association with a right-wing group and his criticism of the prime minister, was re-elected in 1996 as an independent, but failed to retain his seat in 1998. Bob Katter resigned from the Nationals and successfully contested his seat as an independent at the 2001 federal election. He was re-elected in 2004 and again in 2007.

As the following figures show, MPs spend relatively little of their time in Canberra.

Number of sitting days scheduled for 2008	
House of Representatives	69
Senate	52

There is a mass exodus of parliamentarians from Canberra after a parliamentary sitting week, when members fly out to return to their electorates.

There have been arguments that the parliament should meet more often, particularly when bills are rushed through by the government at the end of a sitting using the guillotine (or time limit, as explained below) to curtail lengthy debate. When this happens, the representative function of considered debate on pieces of legislation becomes problematic.

PROCEDURES IN THE HOUSE OF REPRESENTATIVES

The speaker

The speaker supervises the business of the House of Representatives and presides over most of its discussions. Much of the tradition and dignity of the house centres on the role of the speaker. This includes an expectation that the duties of the office will be carried out in an impartial way.

> 'I think a Speaker needs a balance of strength and wisdom, and a recognition that you not only are there to see that the Government governs, but also that you give the Opposition a reasonable go. That's the job of the Speaker.'
> (Source: Prime Minister John Howard 2004, 'Interview: John Howard', Sunday, 14 November 2004)

This impartiality is sometimes difficult to achieve. The position of speaker is affected by party politics, as he or she:

- is chosen from among the governing party;
- is opposed at elections; and
- loses his or her office with a change of government.

As a consequence, the speaker continues to be involved in party matters, attends meetings and occasionally discusses issues in the media.

The Australian speaker is not seen as an absolutely impartial figure who has reached the high point of a parliamentary career, but rather as an arbiter who may favour his or her own government party in the last resort. The Opposition often feels it is disadvantaged by this process, particularly when the speaker rules against it.

> 'Despite all the calls for an independent speaker, both sides know that's only a remote possibility; but a wounded Opposition forced to retreat to the House will be looking for a fair go—and so will the electorate.'
> (Source: Shanahan, D. 2004, 'ALP's only choice is to be positive', The Australian, 29 October 2004)

In Australia, moreover, a speaker can go on to ministerial office. For example, Gordon Scholes, who served as speaker during the Whitlam years, became a minister in the Hawke government. This does not necessarily make the Australian system less effective, as the speaker retains control of the house, with Opposition acceptance of his or her rulings. It does mean, however, that the speaker's office, and to some extent the role of parliament itself, can be hard to distinguish from the continuing party contest.

There have been several attempts to deal with these problems. Sir Billy Snedden, speaker during the Fraser government, for example, proposed that the speaker should sever all links to a political party and be unopposed by the major parties at elections. A ballot of Coalition government MHRs in 1980 showed that they favoured these proposals, but there are major problems, and the government of whatever party feels better able to control parliament when the speaker is drawn from within its ranks. It would probably require an initiative of cabinet to change the present system, and that is unlikely.

Standing orders

The House of Representatives Practice provides a detailed account of the rules and context in which the house operates (see http://www.aph.gov.au/house/pubs/practice). The business of the house is conducted according to *Standing Orders* adapted from the House of Commons by way of the colonial legislatures. They govern such things as the time allowed for debate, the manner of asking a question and the behaviour of members. On a functional level, they:

- allow the speaker little discretion, further weakening his or her role as a parliamentary figure;
- provide fewer opportunities for the business of *private members* (backbench members who do not belong to the party executives) than most would like; and
- give the government power to limit debate, to compel the hasty passage of legislation, and to restrict or avoid criticism.

The clerk of the house

The clerk is the senior administrative officer of the house, responsible to the speaker, with a staff of officials to ensure that business proceeds smoothly. The clerk is usually appointed after long service in the house and is the main source of advice on its procedures. Other employees who sit at the centre table when the house is in session include the *Hansard* reporters, who take a record of all proceedings. Parliamentary debates are printed very rapidly for distribution and are later collected in large volumes. They are also available on the Internet at http://www.aph.gov.au/hansard.

> *Hansard* reports take their name from a British House of Commons reporter of the early 19th century.

Seating arrangements

The seating arrangement in the House of Representatives follows that of the House of Commons, except that the benches facing the speaker are curved, rather than the rectangle form of Westminster.

Since the formation of the main parties in Australia, a few independents have sat on the cross benches in the House of Representatives. Historically it was rare for independents to get elected, but two independents were elected in 1993, five in 1996, one in 1998, three in 2001 and 2004, and two in 2007.

> The party leaders are on the **front benches** and the private members sit with their party colleagues on the **back benches**: hence the terms that are sometimes applied to these respective groups. Independents and members of minor parties sit on what are called the **cross benches** facing the speaker (even though that term does not fit the house's seating arrangements).

The importance of the party executives is accentuated by the positioning of the prime minister and the leader of the Opposition at the centre table. This arrangement, together with the rows of opposing party members facing each other across the floor of the house, emphasises the fact that parliament contains the alternative government as well as the government of the day.

The Opposition

The Opposition has a special role, not only as the alternative government but as a constant check on government actions. The leader of the Opposition is recognised through a special salary, additional staff, and certain privileges in the house, such as being given precedence at question time, if required. The Opposition, through parliamentary procedures such as question time, Matters of Public Importance or Censure motions, enhances the role of the House of Representatives in the scrutiny of government actions. The fact that the government of the day has the majority in the House of Representatives means that such initiatives will not succeed in a formal sense. The Opposition's effectiveness relies on how much embarrassment it can cause the government through media exposure of its actions in the parliament. This depends on the quality of its leadership, its morale, issues to provide it with avenues of attack, and the qualities of the party in power.

Procedures in the Senate

The Senate also has its 'bible'—*Odgers' Australian Senate Practice* (see http://www.aph.gov.au/Senate/pubs/odgers). The Senate differs somewhat from the House of Representatives:

- It elects a president rather than a speaker. Both perform similar functions; however, the president exercises a deliberative vote but not a casting vote, while the speaker has a casting vote but not a deliberative vote.

> - The **president of the Senate**'s vote is counted with those of other senators whenever there is a division.
> - The **speaker of the House of Representatives** does not vote with members, but has a casting vote only if the numbers are equal.

In such cases, the speaker by convention votes with the government. The president has no such casting vote.

> If votes are equal in the Senate, the question is decided in the negative.

- Senate Standing Orders are slightly fewer than the Representatives, and its Procedure Committee has a majority of backbenchers, not members of the party executives.

The Senate has seen more independents and representatives of minor parties elected than the House of Representatives, particularly during the past 20 years. This is a result of the proportional voting system used for Senate elections.

Apart from its smaller size, the Senate has much the same seating arrangement as the House of Representatives. Senate party leaders sit in the chamber, as do a small number of ministers, but if the government of the day does not have a majority in the Senate, the executive is not as dominant in that house as it is in the House of Representatives.

> **Ministers in the Senate**
> In 2008, seven ministers and two parliamentary secretaries were senators and sat in the Senate.

Apart from answering for their own portfolios in that chamber, ministers in the Senate are responsible for representing those ministers who sit in the House of Representatives. The party contest is somewhat different in the Senate, for the following reasons:

- Most of the senior party leaders are in the House of Representatives.
- Minor parties and independents have a significant role to play when they hold the balance of power, because the government needs to negotiate with them to obtain their votes to pass its legislation. Alternatively, the Opposition, minor parties and independents voting together can block government legislation.
- Senators' statements and attitudes may be influenced by the knowledge that their chamber was intended to guard states' interests and to act as a 'house of review'. For example, Queensland Nationals' senators abstained from voting with their Liberal Coalition partner on an issue related to the sugar industry in Queensland and, more recently under the Howard government, Queensland Nationals senator Barnaby Joyce crossed the floor to oppose Coalition bills. But, generally, party discipline prevails when it comes to voting.

Senators are elected for a six-year term, with half retiring every three years—except territory senators, who are elected for the life of the House of Representatives. Members of the House of Representatives must face election at least every three years (ss. 7, 13 and 28 of the Constitution). The electoral systems for the House of Representatives and the Senate are explained in Chapter 8.

FIGURE 5.3
The hung Senate

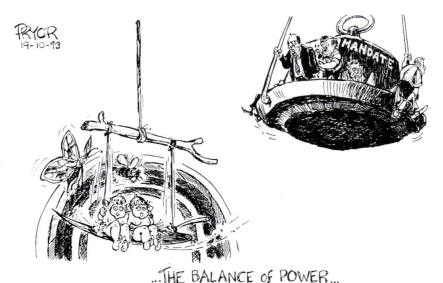

In a hung Senate, a minor party can easily frustrate the intentions of a popularly elected government. (*Source*: Geoff Pryor, 19 October 1993, copyright Geoff Pryor)

THE LEGISLATING FUNCTION

Parliament spends a good deal of its time considering and passing laws. The number of bills passed by the parliament varies from year to year, depending on the government's agenda (see Table 5.6).

Most bills become Acts of parliament, but not all. Many of these bills amend existing legislation, some making only minor adjustments requiring little debate. Nevertheless, each piece of legislation is necessary to validate government action (such as establishing an authority to oversee construction of the new Parliament House) or to allow the government to alter existing arrangements (such as increasing welfare benefits or varying the rates of personal income tax). In each case, the necessary provisions, which may be set out in a few lines or require several hundred printed pages, are drawn up by lawyers (under the direction of parliamentary counsel) employed especially for that purpose. This is an obvious point at which the government of the day, rather than parliament as a whole, has the initiative.

TABLE 5.6
Number of bills passed by both houses of parliament

Year	Bills passed by both houses
1997/98	183
2003/04	191
2006/07	207

(*Source*: The data in this table is sourced from various annual reports of the Department of the Senate and is reproduced by permission of the Department.)

All but a very small minority of bills are put forward by the government. In 2004, for example, eight private senator's bills were introduced into the Senate, and eight private member's bills were introduced into the House of Representatives. Scarcely any of these private member's bills become law.

Bills to be introduced are listed, along with other business, on the Notice Paper of the House, which serves much as an agenda does for any meeting, and it is desirable that the proposed legislation be distributed to members well in advance, particularly in the case of important bills. Members sometimes complain that they are given too little time to absorb the often complex provisions they must consider.

The progress of an Act of parliament through the House of Representatives and the Senate

1. *Giving notice*: A minister wishing to introduce a bill gives written notice to the clerk of the house.
2. *First reading*: The bill is introduced by reading out its title; there is no debate at this stage. After a first reading, it is customary that the bill proceeds immediately to the second reading stage.
3. *Second reading*: At this stage the minister moves the second reading and makes a speech explaining the bill. Debate is then adjourned to allow members time to study the bill before speaking and voting on it. Alternatively, following the minister's second reading speech, a bill may be referred to either a standing committee or to the Main Committee for further consideration.
4. *Report stage*: Bills that have been referred to a standing committee or to the Main Committee are reported back to the House of Representatives, where they are considered and voted on.
5. *Third reading*: This is mainly a formal stage, at which the house is asked to agree to the bill as a whole; there is rarely debate.

(*Source*: See the following document for more information: Parliament of Australia 2008, 'Making Laws', Infosheet No. 7, http://www.aph.gov.au/house/info/infosheets)

The Main Committee

In 1994 the House of Representatives made a significant change to its procedures with the creation of the Main Committee. This is essentially a debating committee, which operates as an extension of the chamber to allow two streams of business to be debated concurrently. The intention of establishing the committee was to give members extra opportunities to speak on non-controversial and unopposed bills or reports, which are referred on agreement between government and non-government members, and to free the chamber for debate on other matters.

All members of the House of Representatives are members of the Main Committee and eligible to participate in its proceedings. The chair of the committee is the deputy speaker. The Main Committee undertakes a more limited range of business, specifically the second reading and consideration of detailed stages of bills, the debate of committee and delegation reports, and the debate of papers presented to the house. The committee can debate and resolve motions and process bills through the relevant stages, including making amendments, but any decision it makes has to be confirmed by the house.

(*Source*: See the following document for more information: Parliament of Australia 2008, 'The Main Committee', Infosheet No. 16, http://www.aph.gov.au/house/info/infosheets)

The bill does not become law following the third reading stage. Further steps are necessary:

- The bill must be sent to the Senate for consideration. Most bills, including all money bills, are introduced in the House of Representatives, and so the flow of legislation is more often from the house to the Senate than in the other direction.
- The Senate may debate and pass the bill, according to the steps outlined above, without amendments, in which case the bill may then go from the originating house to the governor-general for assent. In the Senate many bills are examined thoroughly in the committee stage for detailed consideration and may be extensively amended, particularly if the government of the day does not have a majority in the Senate. The Workplace Relations Bill 1996, for example, was passed with 180 amendments.
- The Senate may propose amendments to the bill. (Note that the Senate cannot amend certain kinds of money bills, under s. 53 of the Constitution, but it can request amendments and refuse to pass them, as it did in 1975.) In that case, messages are exchanged between the houses until agreement has been reached; or, if agreement is not possible, the bill may be 'laid aside'.

If the government wants to proceed with a bill following repeated disagreement between the two houses, the double dissolution provisions of s. 57 of the Constitution may be brought into effect (see Chapter 3).

Once a bill has passed both houses, it is forwarded to the governor-general for royal assent. Its commencement as law is notified in the *Government Gazette*.

All regulations and bills that go before parliament are scrutinised to make sure they conform with principles of civil liberties by:

- the Senate Scrutiny of Bills Committee, which examines proposed laws before they are debated in the Senate; and
- the Senate Standing Committee on Regulations and Ordinances, which checks all delegated legislation.

Problems in legislating

As we saw above, the business of making laws is complicated by tensions between parliament and the executive, and by party rivalries. These are particularly apparent at the second reading and committee stages, and in the total time allowed for the passage of a bill.

The minister (or his or her representative in the other house) outlines the merits of the bill, and is answered by the shadow minister from the Opposition (or his or her representative in the other house). They are followed by government and Opposition members alternately. The order of speakers is usually arranged in advance and each has a limited time, determined by Standing Orders, in which to deliver a speech. This process need not be particularly illuminating, however, for the reasons set out below:

- The minister is not compelled to set out all the provisions of the bill, nor even to state a detailed case in support of it.
- Both government and Opposition speakers are inclined to overstatement in an effort to secure party political advantage, and their exchanges can develop into a ritual during which neither side takes the other's arguments seriously (although debate on issues that have bipartisan support is likely to be more useful in examining the detail and implications of the policy).

- Some speakers are relatively uninformed and tend to repeat the substance of the earlier speeches.
- Modern legislation sometimes contains complexities that cannot be dealt with in a 20-minute speech; consequently, some statements may be relatively superficial while others may concentrate on certain details, ignoring other important aspects of a bill.
- Bills may be introduced and then rushed through by the government so that Members and Senators are not given much time to consider or debate the legislation before it is passed through the parliament.

Limiting debate

In ensuring that its business is dealt with, the government of the day has power under Standing Orders to limit debate. Two main tactics can be used:

1. the '*gag*', under which debate is cut short by the passage of a motion that 'the question now be put'; the house then moves on to the next item of business; and
2. the '*guillotine*', when a time limit is imposed on parliamentary debate at the outset of each stage of a bill (for example, that the second reading stage be completed by a certain time, and so on).

These devices are usually employed when the government and Opposition are contesting a matter more strongly than usual, or when there is a rush to clear legislation before parliament goes into recess. As the government 'has the numbers' in the House of Representatives and the motions themselves cannot be debated, both tactics bring a speedy end to debate and usually lead to accusations that the government is ignoring or dictating to parliament. This is simply the most obvious procedural example of the continuing tension between parliament's 'discussing' and 'acting' functions in the House of Representatives.

The same thing happens in state parliaments.

> 'The Tasmanian Greens condemned the arrogant, undemocratic and high-handed tactics of the Bacon Labor government who used their numbers to impose the gag on debate of their controversial pokies deal with Federal Hotels.'
> (Source: *Tasmanian Greenweek*, no. 199, 20 June 2003)
>
> 'I strongly oppose the undemocratic fashion in which this important legislation—which will affect the livelihood and wellbeing of millions of NSW workers—is being rammed through this House.'
> (Source: Clover Moore, NSW MLC, second reading speech, Workers Compensation Legislation Amendment Bill, 21 June 2001, http://www.clovermoore.com)

This situation does not always apply in the Senate. If the government does not have a majority, the Opposition senators can vote together to extend or limit debate, even if the government does not agree. This occurred in 1992, when time limits were imposed on questions without notice to prevent questioners and ministers from speaking too long on a particular matter. The aim was to allow time for more questions to be put to ministers. The government and Opposition senators can also combine to gag debate to prevent the minor parties and independents from speaking.

Supporting the legislative function

For parliamentarians to take part adequately in the legislative function they need support staff to provide information about the matters under discussion. Some of this information may be provided by each MP's research assistant (one of the staff members provided for each parliamentarian), but much of it is provided by parliamentary staff. The Department of Parliamentary Services provides members with access to a specialised library, as well as providing information and specialist advice on request to individual parliamentarians.

The budget

One of the main reasons that parliament was first summoned by the British monarchs was to raise money for the business of government, especially for war. As parliament gained power, the Crown's ministers, rather than the Crown, secured the initiative in determining the amount of money to be raised through taxes and loans and the manner in which it was to be spent. From the early 18th century, additional steps were taken to ensure closer control of finance: money was supplied by parliament annually, rather than being levied on behalf of the government for years at a time; estimates setting out proposed needs and expenditure had to be presented; the government was required to account annually for the money granted to it; money could be used only for specified purposes, and not transferred to whichever project the government wished to undertake; and committees of parliament could examine the government's accounts and investigate its efficiency in using the resources supplied to it. Three other developments were involved:

1. The House of Lords lost virtually all power over financial matters in 1911.
2. As the national economy grew more complex, and as government came to take a larger share in managing it, so the annual budget exercised increasing influence over economic activity.
3. Consequently, the annual budget embraces a number of steps that occupy several weeks of parliament's time, and usually attracts more public attention than any other item of business.

Senate Estimates committees

The Australian parliament adopted the budgetary process, like so much else, from the Commons by way of the colonial legislatures, but there are important differences. For many years the Australian legislature lacked the Estimates committees, through which the Commons examines the details of the government's spending proposals. Ironically it was the Senate, which lacks the power to originate money bills, which established Senate Estimates committees in 1970. Each was responsible for checking the budgets of several departments of the Australian Public Service, although it should be remembered that the departments are responsible for less than half of the government's spending. In 1994 the functions of the Estimates committees were taken over by Senate Legislation committees. These committees have been effective in probing the details of government expenditure. This means that the Senate, when not controlled by the party in government, can be effective in maintaining scrutiny of the executive by the parliament.

House of Representatives Estimates committees

After a good deal of pressure from its backbench members, the Fraser government in 1979 agreed reluctantly to set up two Estimates committees for the House of Representatives, increasing the number to six in 1981. The Estimates committees had only limited powers, but opposition to them from within the executive remained strong, and in 1982 the estimates were not referred to the committees. The Hawke government, after its election in 1983, did not re-establish house Estimates committees.

Limitations on the financial powers of the House of Representatives

The House of Representatives' financial powers are limited in other respects:

- The Senate retains the power to request amendments to any financial measures that it cannot itself amend and to reject the whole of the money bill (s. 53 of the Constitution).
- A proportion of Commonwealth money, such as GST revenue, is paid to the states where it is disposed of according to the wishes of state governments, rather than of the federal authorities. This is related to the Commonwealth's gaining exclusive control over income tax (see Chapter 3).
- The raising and allocating of loan moneys is determined by the Loan Council. The Commonwealth has usually dominated this body, but through its senior ministers (the executive) and not through parliament.

Nevertheless, the financial initiative rests with the Commonwealth; and with its cabinet, rather than with parliament as a whole.

The budget process

The financial year in Australia is from 1 July to 30 June. The budget is usually introduced into parliament in May, but it can also be delivered at other times if it is necessary to do so.

Stages in the budgetary process for a May budget

1 July	Start of the financial year.
October/ November	**Additional or supplementary estimates** — inevitably some departments will need more funds than those appropriated by the main appropriation bills. **Appropriation Bill (No. 3)** (ordinary annual government services — see below), **Appropriation Bill (No. 4)** (other expenditure) and **Appropriation (Parliamentary Departments) Bill (No. 2)** (expenditure for the parliament) provide additional funds for the current financial year.
May	**The budget** — introduction of the main appropriation bills which appropriate money for expenditure by the government and the parliament for the next financial year. **Appropriation Bill (No. 1)** covers expenditure for ordinary annual government services (continuing expenditure by government agencies on services for existing policies), **Appropriation Bill (No. 2)** covers new policies, new capital expenditure, and payments to the states, and the **Appropriation (Parliamentary Departments) Bill** covers expenditure for the parliament.
30 June	End of the financial year.

(*Source*: Parliament of Australia 2008, 'The Budget and Financial Legislation', Infosheet no. 10, http://www.aph.gov.au/house/info/infosheets. Copyright Commonwealth of Australia, reproduced by permission)

The budget itself comprises a statement by the treasurer (the budget statement and papers can be found at http://www.budget.gov.au) concerning the national accounts and economy and several bills to give effect to the year's financial program; bills to alter taxes and charges if the government so decides; schedules of payments to the states and to local government; measures for raising loans; reports on the previous year's performance; and a series of statistics and calculations setting out the state of the economy (as seen by the government and its advisers) and likely changes in it. (It was the Senate's deferral of the appropriation bills which threatened to leave the government without money that led to the withdrawal of Gough Whitlam's commission as prime minister in November 1975.)

In addition to the budget, many other items of legislation involving the raising and spending of money are required—changes in subsidies, grants, salaries, welfare provisions, tariffs, and many other matters that are best dealt with separately or which have to be adjusted in a manner not foreseen at the time the budget was introduced. Indeed, when the budget has produced unanticipated results—loss of 'business confidence' or higher than expected rates of inflation and unemployment—supplementary adjustments are needed later in the financial year. Such additional changes, if required, are called a 'mini-budget', with the more formal title of 'economic statement'.

All money bills are introduced by ministers. (The constitutional possibility that a private member might present a money bill has been effectively ruled out by Standing Orders and convention.) Private members are further restricted in that they cannot introduce amendments that would increase the financial provisions of a money bill. Moreover, the public accounts and estimates have grown increasingly complex, and few backbenchers have the expertise or resources to unravel them completely. Debate on financial matters is consequently directed much more at the motives underlying government spending than at the money allocations themselves. Speeches of the former kind are usually predictable in party terms, and so at the second reading stage financial measures are rarely subjected to the detailed, disinterested examination that is essential in ensuring that money is being used carefully and effectively.

Debate on most money bills, as on ordinary legislation, should be 'relevant'; that is, it may touch on related matters, propose alternative measures and so on, but should not stray from the central concern of the bill. It can be hard to determine whether debate meets these conditions, although the field that a speech may cover will vary according to the breadth of the provisions in the bill under discussion. There is, however, a major exception to the rule of relevancy in financial debates. The budget debate, following the treasurer's introductory speech, can cover a very wide field indeed, acting much as a review and critique of the government's performance. (Other exceptions to the rule of relevancy are discussed later in this chapter.)

At the committee stage of money bills (including the budget legislation), Opposition motions can be moved to reduce the amounts allocated for specific purposes. In the House of Representatives this is not usually successful, because the fact that the government has the majority ensures that the initiative remains with the political executive.

THE SENATE AND MONEY BILLS

The situation in the Senate is different. Section 53 of the Constitution prevents the Senate from moving amendments to 'proposed laws imposing taxation, or proposed laws appropriating revenue or moneys for the ordinary annual services of the Government', commonly called 'supply'. The Senate may request the House of Representatives to make an amendment to such bills. It may also defer voting or vote against 'supply'. This happened, most famously, in 1975 and led ultimately to the dismissal of the Whitlam government.

> **Money bills and supply**
> - 'The term "**supply**" may be loosely applied to all of the annual appropriation bills . . . that provide the funds necessary for government to operate.
> - "**Money bills**": may be used to refer to all bills which appropriate money.'
> (*Source*: Evans, H. (ed.) 2001, *Odgers' Australian Senate Practice*, 10th ed., Department of the Senate, Canberra, pp. 295–96)

This provision does not prevent the Senate from defeating money bills. In 1995, for example, the Opposition, the Australian Democrats, The Greens (WA) and independent Brian Harradine combined in the Senate to defeat a government bill to impose sales tax on building supplies.

INVESTIGATING EXPENDITURE FUNCTION

Detailed examination of government spending by the Australian parliament commenced at Federation with the appointment of the *auditor-general* in 1901, and that officer has reported to parliament annually on the government's accounts. Initially these examinations covered only the accuracy and probity of those accounts, but since 1975 the Australian National Audit Office has also examined departments and certain government agencies in terms of their economy, efficiency and effectiveness in implementing government policy and expending public funds (for further information about these activities, see the Australian National Audit Office, http://www.anao.gov.au).

Direct parliamentary scrutiny of government expenditure commenced in 1913 with the establishment of two joint parliamentary committees—for public works and government accounts—each comprising a small number of both members of the House of Representatives and senators.

The *Public Works Committee*, a joint committee administered by the House of Representatives, examines proposals for expenditure on major works and reports to parliament on the expediency of carrying out each proposal, in terms of criteria such as its purpose, suitability, necessity, and the effectiveness of the proposed method of construction (for further information about its membership and activities, see the Parliamentary Standing Committee on Public Works, http://www.aph.gov.au/house/committee/pwc).

The *Public Accounts and Audit Committee*, a joint committee administered by the House of Representatives, examines departmental administration and management in terms of efficiency, effectiveness and economy, and has played a valuable role in achieving and sustaining higher standards of public administration. (For further information about the membership and activities of this committee, see the Joint Committee of Public Accounts and Audit, http://www.aph.gov.au/house/committee/jpaa).

THE 'SCRUTINY' FUNCTION OF PARLIAMENT

Parliament has several ways of scrutinising government actions that fall into two groups:

1 *Procedures on the floor of the house—questions, replies to government statements and speeches, special debates and expression of grievances.* These are usually affected by party considerations, but can still be seen as part of parliament's effort to make the government answerable to the electorate; and
2 *Investigations by various committees appointed by parliament from among its members.* These can be less partisan, more detailed and therefore less publicised than house proceedings, but they can subject governments to considerable pressure if conducted properly.

Procedures in the house

Question time

Question time is one of the first items of each day's business, and is broadcast from both houses daily. The duration of question time in the House of Representatives is up to the prime minister, but it has usually occupied at least 45 minutes. The duration of question time in the Senate is controlled by the leader of the house (a government minister), but it usually occupies about 60 minutes. Attempts by the government of the day to cut short question time have attracted a lot of public criticism.

Question time has two useful functions:

1 Media coverage of the proceedings provides the Opposition with the opportunity to attract public attention to particular issues and to expose deficiencies in the policies and activities of government. In recent years, government ministers have resigned from the ministry following sustained questioning in both houses and resultant media coverage of their 'indiscretions' and mistakes.
2 It allows the Opposition and backbenchers to elicit information from the executive, and in the process to make it answerable for its actions. In that respect, the procedure has been less than successful.

Questions without notice

The most noteworthy questions in the parliament are usually those presented without notice for a minister's oral answer (as compared with those put on notice in writing, which appear, with their answers, only in *Hansard* and consequently attract less attention).

Questions without notice are asked alternately from each side of the house, although the leader of the Opposition may, but rarely does, ask a follow-up question. The Senate has a practice of allowing supplementary questions, directly related to the previous question, at the discretion of the chair, and senators take full advantage of this to probe the government on a particular issue. The same prerogative is allowed the speaker of the House of Representatives, but is rarely exercised.

Each question must meet several requirements set out in Standing Orders; for example, it must refer to a matter with which the minister is officially involved, and must not put forward arguments or suggest hypothetical circumstances. Even so, the minister is not obliged to answer a question.

The prime minister receives about a quarter of all questions asked in the House of Representatives. The leader and deputy leader of the Opposition ask many more questions than any other MP.

Limits to the effectiveness of question time

- Ministers may attempt to evade a question, plead ignorance, or use the occasion to launch an attack on the Opposition; this is good party politics, but it subverts the supposed purpose of question time.
- In the absence of regular supplementary questions in the House of Representatives, it is difficult for the Opposition to coordinate its efforts if it wishes to exploit what it sees as a government weakness. This can prove difficult also because members may want to pursue different issues or ask questions relating to their own electorates rather than national affairs. Alternate questions from government members can relieve the pressure on the minister. Supplementary questions in the Senate provide more scope for the Opposition, minor parties and independents to probe a weakness.
- 'Dorothy Dix' questions, where government backbenchers ask pre-arranged questions that allow the minister to praise the government or exploit a weakness in the Opposition, are in effect occasions for ministerial speeches rather than for parliamentary criticism and scrutiny of the executive (see Figure 5.4).

> 'Government Members generally ask "**Dorothy Dixers**" i.e., questions prepared by the Government, which invite answers favourable to the Government.'
> (*Source*: Coghill, K. 2002, 'Question Time: Questionable Questioning with Few Answers', Democratic Audit of Australia, Canberra, http://democratic.audit.anu.edu.au/Coghillpaper.rtf)
>
> 'Outrageous behaviour leading to "sin-binning", accusatory statements masquerading as questions, replies that do not answer attacks on political opponents claiming to be answers to questions . . . Is it any wonder that Question Time is questioned as an accountability mechanism?'
> (*Source*: Coghill, K. 2002, 'Question Time: Questionable Questioning with Few Answers', Democratic Audit of Australia, Canberra, http://democratic.audit.anu.edu.au/Coghillpaper.rtf)

The questioning procedures in the Australian parliament provide fewer opportunities for scrutiny, criticism and putting pressure on the executive than might be supposed.

Debates on statements and reports

One of the means for making the executive responsible to parliament is to have ministers report on accomplishments, policies and future problems to their house. A *ministerial statement* is usually accorded high priority, being delivered just after question time and followed then, or on a later occasion, by speeches from Opposition and government members setting out their views on what the minister has said.

The government may also present a *Green Paper* to parliament, which reviews policies or discusses alternatives in detail. The responsible minister speaks about the paper, and a

FIGURE 5.4

Parliamentary standards — Dorothy Dix by the dozen

(*Source*: Cartoon by Nicholson from *The Australian*. www.nicholsoncartoons.com.au)

full debate on it follows at an appropriate time. Following the debate and consultation, the government issues a *White Paper*, which outlines the government's final choice of policies.

> - A **Green Paper** is a discussion document, setting out 'the government's thinking' on a particular issue.
> - Following consultation and consideration of written submissions on the Green Paper, a formal statement of government policy is issued in the form of a **White Paper**.

This process does not necessarily indicate a government's willingness to submit itself to examination and criticism by parliament, because:

- ministerial statements and government papers are fairly rare in the Australian parliament; certainly, they are a good deal less common in Canberra than at Westminster;
- the government is in no way obliged to change policies or take action in response to parliamentary debate on statements and papers; and
- the debate in the community at large is more important than the debate in parliament in determining the outcome.

Information that is presented in this way is more likely to be a government self-advertisement than an invitation to open debate; and so it often attracts a purely partisan response, which may deal with the substantive issues only incidentally.

'Open' debate

There are several ways in which members may speak on matters reflecting on the government, or of special interest to them or their constituents, without having to observe the more stringent rules of relevance applicable to debates on legislation. These include:

- *Debate on the Address in Reply*: Each new parliament is opened by the governor-general, who reads a speech that sets out the government's program. This is followed by an address expressing loyalty to the Crown, and the debate on the motion that this be agreed to is the occasion for wide-ranging speeches that usually occupy several sitting days.
- *Budget debate*: There is an annual debate on the government's budget, discussed in depth earlier in this chapter, which provides backbenchers with the opportunity to speak on matters of their own choice.
- *Adjournment debate*: This procedure allows backbenchers in both the House of Representatives and the Senate to make short speeches on almost any matter before the house adjourns for the day. Opposition and government members, who speak alternately, use this opportunity to raise individual or constituency issues. These speeches are often delivered to only a few members in the chamber and generally attract little attention.
- *Private Members' Mondays*: A period of time on Mondays is set aside in the House of Representatives to allow backbenchers to move private member's motions and bills, to make statements about a wide range of issues, to present petitions, and to participate in the Grievance Debate, where members have 10 minutes to raise any matter of interest or complaints from constituents.

> Information about the procedures of the House of Representatives can be found in Parliament of Australia 2008, 'House of Representatives—Chamber: Order of Business', http://www.aph.gov.au/house/work/order_of_business.pdf.

As with most aspects of the functioning of parliament, opinions about the usefulness of 'open' debates will vary according to notions of what they should accomplish. They act as a safety valve and a means for backbenchers to gain mention in the local newspapers, but they are rarely successful in subjecting the government to notable or sustained pressure on its policies and actions.

Debate on special motions

There are two ways in which parliament (in effect, the Opposition) can subject the government to pressure on a particular issue:

1. *Matters of public importance*: Sometimes called an urgency motion, this concerns a current issue that is potentially embarrassing to the government, and the motion amounts to a challenge which is usually accepted, lest the government be thought to lack strength and confidence.
2. *'No-confidence' motion*: This is considered the most serious motion that can be moved against a government, although it always produces no more than a debate of a predictably partisan nature. It is often moved against an individual minister. Such a motion, if carried in the House of Representatives, would lead to the resignation of the minister concerned. This is not likely to happen, because the government has the majority in the lower house.

Censure motions, on the other hand, may be carried in the Senate should the government not have the majority. However, because governments are formed in the House of Representatives, there is no obligation on the part of the government to take any notice of a Senate censure. The government would respond only if the issue caused political embarrassment and was likely to affect its standing with the electorate.

> **Australian PM censured over Iraq**
> In October 2003 the Australian Senate passed a no-confidence motion against the prime minister over his handling of the crisis in Iraq. The vote reflected the majority opinion of the Opposition and minor parties in the Senate, but could be ignored by the prime minister because he sits in the House of Representatives.

Both of these motions may be moved by the government against the Opposition, although that happens infrequently. In either case, the initiative comes from party leaders rather than backbenchers.

Questions, debates on statements and papers, 'open' debates and special motions all seem to promise ample scope for parliament to gain information, express grievances and criticise governments. However, the procedures used in the Australian parliament leave governments with by far the greatest share of power.

The greatest potential for scrutiny and challenge lies with the Senate, but even here the executive is dominant. The Westminster principle that government is formed in the lower house, and is responsible to that house, means the government who sits in the House of Representatives does not have to respond to any initiatives or directives emanating from the Senate. As we have seen with censure motions, whether it chooses to respond or not is determined usually by the political sensitivity of the matter and the potential for electoral damage should the Senate be ignored. Those who would like to see a more even contest between parliament and the executive have tended to look to parliamentary committees to strike a more even balance.

Committees of the parliament

The Australian parliament has established different kinds of committees, within which there are various sub-groups (see Table 5.7). The first distinction to be made is between:

- House of Representatives committees;
- Senate committees; and
- joint committees, comprising members from both the House of Representatives and the Senate.

A further distinction can be made between:

- standing committees (House of Representatives, Senate and joint committees), which are appointed at the beginning of each parliament to perform a particular function during the life of that parliament. These can be divided into two sub-groups: committees set up under Standing Orders or by a resolution of a house; and committees set up by law (statutory committees); and
- select committees (House of Representatives, Senate and joint committees), which are appointed to investigate and report on a specific matter, whereupon they disband.

TABLE 5.7
Committees of the Australian parliament, April 2008

Joint standing committees	House of Representatives standing committees	Senate standing committees	Senate select committees
• Australian Commission for Law Enforcement Integrity • Australian Crime Commission • Broadcasting of Parliamentary Proceedings • Corporations and Financial Services • Electoral Matters • Foreign Affairs, Defence and Trade • Intelligence and Security • Migration • National Capital and External Territories • Public Accounts and Audit • Public Works • Treaties	• Main Committee* • Aboriginal and Torres Strait Islander Affairs • Climate Change, Water, Environment and the Arts • Communications • Economics • Education and Training • Employment and Workplace Relations • Family, Community, Housing and Youth • Health and Ageing • Industry, Science and Innovation • Infrastructure, Transport, Regional Development and Local Government • Legal and Constitutional Affairs • Petitions • Primary Industry and Resources • Privileges and Members' Interests • Procedure • Publications	• Appropriations and Staffing • Community Affairs • Economics • Education, Employment and Workplace Relations • Environment, Communications and the Arts • Finance and Public Administration • Foreign Affairs, Defence and Trade • Legal and Constitutional Affairs • Privileges • Procedure • Publications • Regulations and Ordinances • Rural and Regional Affairs and Transport • Scrutiny of Bills • Selection of Bills • Senators' Interests	• Agricultural and Related Industries • Housing Affordability in Australia • Regional and Remote Indigenous Communities • State Government Financial Management

(* Information about the Main Committee can be found earlier in the chapter. Information about all committees can be found at 'Parliament of Australia: Committees', http://www.aph.gov.au/committee)

Parliamentary committees have the same powers as the parliament: to conduct inquiries; to call witnesses to give evidence; and to punish anyone who misleads or lies to a committee. Committees also have the right of parliamentary privilege, which guarantees freedom of speech in committee proceedings because members or witnesses cannot be prosecuted for what they say at a committee hearing.

Each of the political parties also has a number of party committees organised within the parliament. These committees have an impact on the passage of legislation. They form an effective link between ministers or shadow ministers and those in their respective parties who are interested in particular policy fields.

Standing committees

The basic group of standing committees was set up by each house to deal with its internal matters—procedure, privileges, publications, and so on. These are usually termed 'domestic' standing committees. Most have interests in common with the counterpart committee in the other house, with which they confer regularly.

The House of Representatives' standing committees are based around the major areas of government activity. Their function is to inquire into and report on any matters referred to them by the house or a minister, such as bills, motions, petitions or reports, including annual reports of departments and statutory authorities.

In September 2006 the Howard government restructured the Senate committee system by combining what had been separate legislation and reference committees. Each of the new standing committees has eight members: four nominated by the leader of the government in the Senate, three nominated by the leader of the Opposition in the Senate, and one nominated by minority groups and independent senators. The chair of each committee is a government senator. The Howard government instituted these changes because, it argued, it was more efficient and would avoid duplication.

Joint committees

These comprise members from both the House of Representatives and the Senate and are established to examine issues where there is considered to be a commonality of interest between the houses. They may be statutory, select or standing committees. Joint committees are chaired by a government member or senator and have government majorities. The Joint Committee on Public Accounts and Audit, because of its scrutiny of government finance, is potentially the most influential.

Select committees

Examples of Senate select committees include an inquiry into the 'children overboard' incident and the issue of drugs in sport, while House of Representatives select committees have examined specific learning difficulties and tourism. Senate committees were more widely used when the Opposition and minor parties and/or independents used their combined Senate majority to establish inquiries in a number of areas with the potential to expose government weakness and poor performance. After 1 July 2005, when senators elected at the October 2004 election took their seats, the Howard government used its majority in the Senate to prevent the establishment of select committees. The Rudd government cannot do this because, since 1 July 2008, the balance of power in the Senate has been held by minor parties and an independent senator.

The problems of committees

There are major problems associated with effective parliamentary committee work:

- Chairing a committee may not be an avenue for promotion into the ministry and may even be a disadvantage, because effective committees may need to be critical of the government of the day—that is, the chair's own party.
- There are too few parliamentarians for the many committee places that must now be filled. Most senators sit on about three committees, while MHRs sit on one.
- Committee reports are tabled in parliament, but are not binding on the government.

The committee details set out above disclose another problem—duplication of effort. The Joint Committee on Public Accounts and Audit and the various Senate committees overlap to a degree, as do the Joint and Senate committees on Foreign Affairs, Defence and Trade.

This reflects other difficulties: the reluctance of governments to make use of committees according to a comprehensive plan, the continuous party rivalry, and the tension between the Senate and the government. As governments are wary of possible challenges to their control of parliament, committees have been established as much as a result of agitation by groups of senators and MHRs as of government actions—particularly, as noted above, on those occasions in the Senate when the government did not command a majority.

> In 1998, the Opposition, minor parties and independents in the Senate voted together to establish a committee to examine the Goods and Services Tax proposed by the Howard government.

The committee system in Canberra has evolved from political factors, as well as from the desire to secure more effective parliamentary scrutiny of the executive, and this has led to uncertainty about the objectives of the system itself.

It is often assumed that parliamentary committees can provide effective checks on government. There is a strong body of opinion among backbenchers and students of parliament that committees should be stronger and more comprehensive in their concerns (extending to the committee stage of legislation, for example). This seems sensible: if one of parliament's main functions is to counterbalance the power of governments, and this proves difficult through debates, questions and similar procedures, then an extended committee system may appear essential. However, the Senate already has a wide range of committees and in both houses there is a problem of members finding sufficient time for committee work. The answer probably lies in rationalising the committee system and extending their powers, rather than in establishing more of them.

This has implications for a more general consideration: the notion developed within the Westminster system which suggests that parliament should not usurp the authority of the executive. An effective committee system, under this premise, would have to maintain a fine distinction between scrutinising the details of government actions and dictating them. This need not be the case. It depends on how the particular parliamentary committee system is structured and how much power it is given, as the following discussion on the activities of the Senate as a house of review reveals.

THE SENATE AS A HOUSE OF REVIEW

If the House of Representatives provides relatively ineffectual checks on government because its party is in the majority, then it may seem appropriate for the second chamber to act as a 'house of review'.

The review process

The Senate can act as a 'house of review' by:

- *delaying legislation*—this can provide greater opportunity for detailed consideration of a particular issue;

- *representing minority interests*—the Senate does this better than the House of Representatives because the proportional system of voting provides minor parties and independents with more opportunity to gain representation;
- *providing a forum for wide-ranging debate*—the Senate has occasionally engaged in longer debates than the Representatives, but that does not necessarily mean that it has discussed questions in greater depth;
- *the Senate committee system*—this provides an opportunity for greater examination and wide-ranging debate of issues that are the subject of inquiry;
- *producing better legislation through rigorous examination of bills*—this function could be performed equally well in the Representatives through a comprehensive and effective committee system; and
- *the continuing scrutiny of government*—when a government lacks a Senate majority, the Opposition, minor parties and independent senators can use the Senate as a forum to highlight weaknesses in the government.

As was pointed out in Chapter 3, the Senate, as the 'states' house', was intended to perform this function by acting to protect the interests of the states against encroachment or domination by the Commonwealth. As we have seen, however, the party system has become the dominant factor, and senators respond more to party loyalty than to loyalty to their respective states.

Vestiges of the original idea of the Senate as a states' house are more likely to surface within the party rooms than in the Senate itself. The equal representation of states in the Senate means that in the party rooms the smaller states have a larger representation than they would have if based strictly on population. This does not mean that they can persuade their party to take any notice of the concerns of a state if the majority of the party disagrees, nor are they likely to put aside party policy if it is at variance with the attitude of the state government. For example, Tasmanian Labor senators voted with the government to support Commonwealth action to protect gay rights in Tasmania against the wishes of the Tasmanian government.

Occasions when senators depart from the 'party line' to defend the interests of their particular state are rare, although not unknown. Queensland Nationals' senators abstained from voting with their party on an issue that they considered would have an adverse effect on the Queensland sugar industry, and Queensland Nationals senator Barnaby Joyce voted against Coalition legislation in the Senate several times during the Howard government's fourth term.

Party considerations also affect the Senate's capacity to act as a house of review on a scale wider than mere state loyalties. When the party or coalition in government possesses a Senate majority, it tries to ensure that the Senate does little more than endorse measures passed by the Representatives. Under these circumstances there are accusations that rather than acting as a house of review, the Senate is a mere 'rubber stamp' for the executive.

The situation is different when the government lacks a majority in the Senate. A hostile majority can use the Senate's considerable powers under the Constitution to block government measures, or delay legislation by referring it to a Senate committee. When this happens, there are accusations from the government of the day that the Senate is acting as a house of obstruction rather than review.

FIGURE 5.5

Rudd wants Senate to pass IR laws

(*Source*: Cartoon by Nicholson from *The Australian*. www.nicholsoncartoons.com.au)

> 'Repeated obstruction of important legislation, particularly by representatives of a small minority of voters, often serves to compromise the effectiveness of the policies and platforms of the Government of the day.'
>
> (*Source*: Hugh Morgan, President of the Business Council of Australia 2004, 'Take Senate Reform Further says BCA Submission', Business Council of Australia, 11 January 2004, http://www.bca.com.au/Content/93734.aspx)

Some people, on the other hand, regard this to be healthy—a democratic check on what might otherwise be an overbearing executive.

> 'The role of a second chamber like the Senate is crucial, and its relationship with the executive must, if it can, compensate for the ministerial dominance of the lower house.'
>
> (*Source*: Evans, H. (ed.) 2001, *Odgers' Australian Senate Practice*, 10th ed., Department of the Senate, Canberra, p. 469)

The government often controlled the Senate until the method of election was changed to proportional representation in 1949. This is a system designed to allocate seats in proportion to shares of votes. (For a detailed discussion of this system of voting, see Chapter 8.) This factor, combined with the development of significant minor parties since the mid-1950s, has seen occasions where independents and minor party members have held the balance of power in the Senate. When this happens, the government is forced to negotiate the passage of contentious legislation, often compromising and accepting amendments to the bill in the process.

The first occasion on which this occurred was between 1967 and 1972, when the balance of power was held by independent and Democratic Labor Party (DLP) senators. The same was true between 1972 and 1974, for the first Whitlam government, when the hostile majority saw the defeat of a considerable amount of government legislation. After the May 1974 elections the DLP lost all of its Senate seats, but the Coalition retained sufficient votes to block many of the government's bills.

> 'In the first 71 years of the Senate's existence, it had rejected a total of only 68 government bills. During our three years alone, it rejected 93.'
> (Source: Whitlam, E.G. 1985, *The Whitlam Government, 1972–1975*, Viking, Ringwood, Victoria, p. 737, reproduced with permission)

The Coalition senators used their numbers to defer the appropriation bills in late 1975, and so provided the main grounds for the dismissal of the Whitlam government by the governor-general.

> 'The decision was taken (by the Opposition shadow cabinet) that the Senate would seek to delay the passing of the two Appropriation Bills until the Government agreed to an election.'
> (Source: The Hon. J. Killen, shadow cabinet minister at the time, cited in Killen, J. 1985, *Killen: Inside Politics*, Methuen Haynes, Sydney, p. 240)

From 1975 until 1981 the Fraser Coalition government held a comfortable Senate majority, which proved almost as amenable to the government's wishes as did the Coalition's supporters in the House of Representatives.

For 24 years, between 1 July 1981 and 30 June 2005, successive Australian governments operated under the constraints of not having a Senate majority. This meant they had to gain the support of the minor parties and/or independents who held the balance of power in order to get their legislation passed by the Senate. This changed after 1 July 2005 when the Howard Coalition government held a majority in both houses, which meant it could pass its legislation unimpeded through the parliament.

> 'That will mean no inquiry can be set up that the Government doesn't like, and no amendment can be passed, no amendment to any legislation, unless the Government agrees in the Senate. That will make it much harder to hold the Government to account to reveal some of its misbehaviour, some of its flaws.'
> (Source: Andrew Bartlett, then leader of the Australian Democrats 2004, 'Interview: Senator Andrew Bartlett', *Sunday*, 10 October 2004, http://sunday.ninemsn.com.au/sunday/political_transcripts/article_1664.asp)

The Howard government used its Senate majority to restrict the capacity of the Opposition and minor parties to question and challenge the government; that is, to limit parliamentary scrutiny of the executive, in the following ways:

- It changed the allocation of questions without notice to give Coalition senators extra questions at the expense of the Opposition and minor parties.

- The number of questions on notice that remained unanswered at the end of a parliamentary session increased.
- The government used the gag and the guillotine to cut off debate and force its legislation through the parliament, thus reducing the time available for comment and scrutiny from the Opposition.
- It used its majority to block motions for Senate select committees that might have caused it political embarrassment.

From 1 July 2008, political control of the balance of power in the Senate returned to the minor parties and an independent senator, which means that the Rudd government, elected in November 2007, has to negotiate, and possibly compromise on its legislation, with these senators in order to get contested bills through the Senate.

With a government majority, there is little reason to expect that the Senate will play a distinctively constructive role in the Australian parliamentary system. When the government does not have a majority, the potential is there for constructive criticism of government actions, provided the balance of power is exercised in a responsible manner and not merely for the sake of party political advantage. Without that element of responsibility, if the government lacks a majority in the Senate, the prospect remains for continuing clashes between the Senate and the House of Representatives, including the threat to supply of the government, engendering what some would regard as unstable government.

> 'I was determined to assert the equally fundamental principle that a government having the confidence of the House of Representatives cannot be forced to dissolve at the whim or behest of senators who themselves need not face the electors.'
> (Source: Gough Whitlam, discussing the Senate's action in blocking supply in 1975, in Whitlam, E.G. 1979, *The Truth of the Matter*, Penguin, Ringwood, Victoria, p. 74, reproduced with permission)

Defenders of the Senate would see this as the Senate exercising its rights and duties under the Constitution.

> 'A government with this power would soon turn its attention to legislation to perpetuate itself in office and reduce its accountability.'
> (Source: Harry Evans, clerk of the Senate 2003, in Evans, H. 2003, '"Reform" of the Senate', Democratic Audit of Australia, Canberra, http://democratic.audit.anu.edu.au/papers/20030709_evans_senate.pdf)

The fact that the Senate functions as a party house, however, leads to criticisms that it is blocking government legislation for reasons related to party politics, rather than reviewing legislation on its merits. This has implications for the effective working of majority party government formed in the House of Representatives, which is the basis of the Australian system of government. A majority made up of votes from the Opposition, minor parties and independents in the Senate, which can block or amend legislation, creates frustration for governments that argue they have a 'mandate' to implement their election promises through the legislative processes of the parliament. Some would argue that the government, with the majority of seats in the House of Representatives, should be able to govern without that impediment. Others maintain that the parties and independents in the Senate also have their own mandate to review legislation and can provide a useful check on the excesses of the executive, in keeping with the principles of checks and balances characteristic of a liberal democracy.

> **Mandate**: 'a term used to describe the legitimacy of individual members of parliament, validated by popular support, expressed during elections'.
> (*Source*: Young, L. 1996, 'Competing Mandates in Australian Politics', Research Note No. 49, 1995–96, Parliamentary Library, Canberra, http://www.aph.gov.au/library/pubs/rn/1995-96/96rn49.htm)

This tension between the conventions of the Westminster system of cabinet government and the powers given to the Senate under the provisions of the Australian Constitution is one of the legacies of the founding fathers that some would like to see remedied. Others consider it to be a healthy check on the executive that should be retained.

QUESTIONS FOR DISCUSSION

1. Why do people have such a poor opinion of parliament and parliamentarians?
2. What are the impediments to the scrutiny function of the House of Representatives, and how can this function be improved?
3. Can the Senate be effective as a house of review?
4. Should the Senate be able to block government legislation and, in particular, supply?
5. Parliamentary committees are useful 'watchdogs' of the executive. Discuss.
6. Does it hinder or enhance Australian democracy when minor parties and/or independents in the Senate hold the balance of power?
7. Ethnic groups and women are not well represented in the Australian parliament. What can be done to improve the 'representativeness' of the parliament?

FURTHER READING

Australasian Parliamentary Review (formerly called *Legislative Studies*), Journal of the Australasian Study of Parliament Group, Canberra, http://www.aspg.org.au. Series of articles on parliament.

Bach, S. 2003, *Platypus and Parliament: The Australian Senate in Theory and Practice*, Department of the Senate, Canberra.

Bach, S. 2004, 'The Australian and American Senates: A Comparison', Research Paper No. 5, 2003–04, Parliamentary Library, Canberra, http://www.aph.gov.au/library/pubs/rp/.

Barlin, L.M. (ed.) 1997, *House of Representatives Practice*, 3rd ed., AGPS, Canberra. Authoritative guide to the function and procedures of the Australian House of Representatives.

Bennett, S. 2004, 'The Australian Senate', Research Paper No. 6, 2003–04, Parliamentary Library, Canberra, http://www.aph.gov.au/library/pubs/rp/.

Evans, H. (ed.) 2004, *Odgers' Australian Senate Practice*, 11th ed., AGPS, Canberra. Authoritative guide to the functions, and procedures of the Australian Senate.

Forman, F.N. & Baldwin, N.D.J. 2007, *Mastering British Politics*, 7th ed., Palgrave Macmillan, Basingstoke, UK.

Galligan, B. & Roberts, W. (eds) 2007, *The Oxford Companion to Australian Politics*, Oxford University Press, Melbourne. See the entries on 'Parliament' and 'Parliamentary Committees', pp. 386–90.

Millar, A. 1993, *Trust the Women: Women in Federal Parliament*, Department of the Senate, Canberra. An account of the struggle by women to get the vote and sit in parliament, and of the 59 women who had sat in parliament up until 1993.

Miskin, S. & Lumb, M. 2006, 'The 41st Parliament: Middle-Aged, Well-Educated and (Mostly) Male', Research Note No. 24, 2005–06, Parliamentary Library, Canberra, http://www.aph.gov.au/library/pubs/rn/.

Norton, P. 1993, *Does Parliament Matter?*, Harvester/Wheatsheaf, London. An introduction to the history, role and organisation of the British parliament. Useful to compare with the Australian system.

Singleton, G. 2008, 'The Senate a Paper Tiger?', in Aulich, C. & Wettenhall, R., *Howard's Fourth Government: Australian Commonwealth Administration 2004–2007*, UNSW Press, Sydney. This article examines the impact of the Howard government's majority in the Senate.

Solomon, D. 1986, *The People's Palace: Parliament in Modern Australia*, Melbourne University Press, Melbourne. Explains in clear language how parliament works; the people, symbols and procedures; and the legislative process.

Summers, J. 2006, 'Parliament and Responsible Government', in Parkin, A., Summers, J. & Woodward, D. (eds), *Government, Politics, Power and Policy in Australia*, 8th ed., Pearson Education, Sydney. A good discussion of the role of parliament in Australia's system of responsible government.

Uhr, J. & Wanna, J. 2000, 'The Future Role of Parliament', in Keating, M., Wanna, J. & Weller, P., *Institutions on the Edge?*, Allen & Unwin, Sydney.

Vile, M.J.C. 2007, *Politics in the USA*, 6th ed., Routledge, Oxford.

USEFUL WEBSITES

The Australian parliament

http://www.aph.gov.au/senate
The Senate
The Annual Report of the Department of the Senate and Senate Briefs are useful sources of information, e.g. Senate Brief No. 4, 'Senate Committees'.

http://www.aph.gov.au/house
The House of Representatives

House of Representatives factsheets are a useful source of information, e.g. Factsheet No. 6, 'Opportunities for Private Members', and Factsheet No. 10, 'The Budget and Financial Legislation'.

- http://www.aph.gov.au/library/pubs
  Parliamentary Library: Publications
  See Parliamentary Library Research Notes, Research Papers and Current Issue Briefs.

- http://www.parliament.uk
  UK Parliament

- http://www.parlimen.gov.my
  Parlimen Malaysia

- http://www.bundestag.de; http://www.bundesrat.de
  German Bundestag/Bundesrat

- http://www.house.gov; http://www.senate.gov
  United States House of Representatives/Senate

EXECUTIVE GOVERNMENT: CABINET AND PRIME MINISTER

THIS CHAPTER EXPLAINS:

- the executive and its role in government;
- the function of cabinet;
- the role of the prime minister;
- the workings of government in Australia, including the executive, cabinet and outer ministry;
- the selection of ministers and cabinet;
- ministerial career paths and the duties of ministerial office;
- the relationship between ministers, cabinet and Westminster conventions;
- the power of the prime minister; and
- desirable qualities of a prime minister.

previous chapter it was pointed out that the executive has come to dominate the parliament because of the central role it plays in the development and administration of policy and the laws. It is important, therefore, that we understand what is meant by the executive and the way it operates. Cabinet plays a central role in the executive in developing and administering policy. The prime minister has become a significant political figure in the parliamentary system, accruing strength from the position of head of government. Some argue that because of this, the prime minister dominates the executive and the government. This chapter will examine how executive government operates in the context of these significant factors.

THE EXECUTIVE

What is the executive?
- The **executive** is the branch of government that implements, or *executes*, the law.
- The executive may be referred to as the *administration* in presidential systems, or simply as the *government* in parliamentary systems.

What does the executive do?
The executive branch is made up of the core institutions of government: the head of state, government ministers and the public service. It is the responsibility of the executive to:
- propose new laws or make changes to existing laws;
- implement and enforce the laws once they have been passed by parliament;
- issue regulations and ordinances to support the legislation;
- administer the government departments that support the executive in carrying out its functions; and
- conduct the foreign relations of the state, and command and direct the military forces.

'The essence of government is to choose, and the executive is responsible for how those choices are defined and made.'
(*Source*: Keating, M. & Weller, P. 2000, 'Cabinet Government: An Institution under Pressure', in Keating, M., Wanna, J. & Weller, P., *Institutions on the Edge? Capacity for Governance*, Allen & Unwin, Sydney, p. 45)

The way the executive operates in the political system varies according to the constitutional arrangements of the particular country (see Table 6.1). We examine the Australian system in detail later in the chapter.

The core executive

The coordinating function of the executive is carried out by institutions that have become known as the *core executive*.

TABLE 6.1

Executive government compared

Britain	United States	Federal Republic of Germany	Federation of Malaysia
The executive operates by convention within the system of parliamentary government. It comprises the prime minister and cabinet (acting as a committee established by the majority party in the parliament that forms the government), the prime minister's private office, ministers and government departments (known as ministries). Cabinet is responsible for the armed forces.	Executive power, according to the Constitution, is vested in the president and is separate from the Congress (legislature). The president is commander-in-chief of the armed forces, and oversees the administrative branch of the executive, made up of federal departments of state and departmental heads, known as Secretaries of State.	Under Article 62 of the Basic Law (constitution), executive power is vested in the federal chancellor and federal ministers. Article 65a vests command of the armed forces with the federal Minister for Defence. Government departments and public servants are responsible to the ministry and therefore form part of the executive.	Under s 39 of the Constitution, executive power is vested in the Yang di-Pertuan Agong (king), who is also supreme commander of the armed forces (s 41). Section 40a of the Constitution limits the Yang di-Pertuan Agong to acting only on the advice of the cabinet or a minister acting under the general authority of cabinet (in practice, this means the prime minister), except on issues designated by the Constitution. This means that executive power effectively lies with the cabinet and, in particular, with the prime minister. Section 132 of the Constitution sets out the various public services of the Federation. The government departments that administer these services are responsible to the minister and therefore form part of the executive.

The **core executive** 'refers to all those organizations and procedures which coordinate central government parties, and act as final arbiters of conflict between different parts of the government machine'.

(*Source*: Rod Rhodes, cited in Keating, M. & Weller, P. 2000, 'Cabinet Government: An Institution under Pressure', in Keating, M., Wanna, J. & Weller, P. (eds), *Institutions on the Edge?: Capacity for Governance*, Allen & Unwin, Sydney, p. 48)

The core executive comprises the government departments and other organisations that coordinate the implementation of government policy across the relevant departments and organisations of government. In Britain, for example, the core executive includes the Prime Minister's Office, the Cabinet Office, inter-departmental committees

...'s role in managing government spending). The Blair
... Policy and Government Unit with the responsibility of
... into the Prime Minister's Office from various departments
...ing the prime minister's views and decisions to those who
...em.

Baldwin, N.D.J. 2007, *Mastering British Politics*, 7th ed., Palgrave Macmillan,
89–91)

CABINET

... is at the very centre of political power, the crucial link between parliament and the ...istrative arm of government.

...e executive function is carried out by a cabinet made up of the prime minister and ministers in charge of departments, supported by a group of public service officials.

> 'Cabinet is the board of directors for government, the forum in which political and policy judgements are made for the nation. Few challenge its right to govern, though that right is no more than custom and practice deriving strength and legitimacy from control of numbers in parliament.'
>
> (Source: Davis, G. 2002, 'Executive Government: Cabinet and the Prime Minister', in Summers, J., Woodward, D. & Parkin, A. 2002, *Government, Politics, Power and Policy in Australia*, 7th ed., Longman, Sydney, p. 52)

In some systems, all ministers sit in the cabinet. In other systems the ministry is divided between a cabinet, made up of the prime minister and senior ministers, and an outer ministry. Other systems, such as Australia, may also have parliamentary secretaries to assist ministers with their portfolios. The situation in the United States is different because the president establishes a cabinet comprising the secretaries of state of major departments who are not members of Congress. The different ways in which a cabinet system can be formulated can be seen in Table 6.2.

Cabinet in the Westminster system

From the earliest times the British sovereigns were assisted by groups of advisers, who came to be known as ministers (from the Latin, meaning 'servant'). On occasion, advisers had to meet with the sovereign away from the bustle of the royal palace, using for the purpose the private royal suite (in French, the 'cabinet'). As the powers of parliament grew, ministers had to gain its support—and not merely the approval of the Crown—to pass laws, ratify treaties and raise money. Nevertheless, the sovereign continued to appoint certain ministers (provided, or sometimes because, they could obtain the support of parliament), and it was well into the 19th century before it became fully accepted that ministers were responsible to parliament and had to gain its confidence, regardless of the attitude of

TABLE 6.2

Cabinet arrangements compared

Britain	United States	Federal Republic of Germany	Federation of Malaysia
Cabinet comprises the prime minister, the chancellor of the exchequer (treasurer), the home secretary and the foreign secretary, plus other senior ministers as determined from time to time by the prime minister.	Cabinet comprises the president, vice-president, White House chief of staff and the secretaries of state of significant government departments as determined by the president.	Under Article 64 of the Basic Law (constitution), the federal president appoints federal ministers, upon the advice of the federal chancellor. Cabinet is made up of the federal chancellor and the federal ministers.	Under s 43(2b) of the Constitution, the Yang di-Pertuan Agong appoints ministers on the advice of the prime minister. The composition of cabinet is determined by the prime minister. Deputy ministers are appointed for each portfolio but are not members of cabinet.
There is also an outer ministry. These ministers may attend cabinet at the invitation of the prime minister as required.	Secretaries of State of other departments do not sit in cabinet but will be consulted by the president and cabinet when required.	There is no outer ministry.	

(Source: Forman, F.N. & Baldwin, N.D.J. 2007, *Mastering British Politics*, 7th ed., Palgrave Macmillan, Basingstoke, UK, pp. 280–1; Vile, M.J.C. 2007, *Politics in the USA*, 6th ed., Routledge, Oxford, p. 158; Press and Information office of the Federal Government (Germany) 2008, 'Cabinet', http://www.bundesregierung.de/Webs/Breg/EN/Federal-Government/Cabinet/cabinet.html; *Constitution of Malaysia*, Part IV: The Federation, Chapter 3: The Executive, http://www.helplinelaw.com/law/constitution/malaysia/malaysia04b.php)

the Crown, in order to achieve office. Since then the sovereign has come to have a purely ceremonial role in the United Kingdom, and the decisive factor in forming a government is the possession of a majority in the House of Commons.

> 'The peculiar contribution of the British Constitution is . . . responsible government . . . it means that government is carried on by persons who are responsible to the representative House of the legislature, the House of Commons.'
> (Source: Jennings, W.I. 1971, *The British Constitution*, 5th ed., Cambridge University Press, Cambridge, p. 148)

Members of parliament are elected to exercise the power of government. In today's system dominated by political parties, the party with the majority in the House of Commons forms the government. It selects an executive, a group of ministers called the cabinet. Cabinet is responsible for the government of the country. Its functions are: to initiate and decide on policy, which is then presented to the parliament to be enacted as legislation; and, as we saw above, to oversee the implementation and administration of that policy.

Cabinet ministers are representatives of the governing party, but they are representatives also of the parliament and are collectively responsible to the parliament as a whole, not just to the members of their own party, for the exercise of executive power.

> In a parliamentary system of government under the convention of **collective responsibility**, cabinet is collectively responsible to the parliament for the policies of the government.

This convention of *collective responsibility* underpins the working relationship between cabinet and parliament. Collective responsibility works on the basis that once cabinet has discussed the policy options and taken a decision, it is the responsibility of all ministers to support that policy in the parliament and to the public. If a cabinet minister cannot, for any reason, support government policy, he or she is expected to resign or can be dismissed. The significance of collective responsibility in relation to the conventions of the Westminster system of parliamentary government will be discussed later in the chapter when we examine the relationship between the Australian cabinet and parliament.

Cabinet, as an integral part of parliament, must retain the confidence of the parliament in order to function.

> It is a convention of the Westminster parliamentary system that a cabinet that loses the confidence of the parliament resigns.

In the modern British system, where the party with the majority of members forms the government, this is less likely to occur as the Opposition does not have the numbers to carry a vote of no confidence. It may happen more frequently in parliaments where government is formed by a combination of parties, if some members of the coalition group decide not to support government policy. Italy is an extreme example of the instability this situation can cause.

> Italy has experienced 62 governments in the 63 years since the Second World War. The former government of Prime Minister Romano Prodi, which needed the support of nine parties to form a coalition majority government, collapsed in January 2008 after just 20 months in office, resulting in elections for a new government.

Cabinet is at the centre of public attention because it deals with the major problems of the nation and makes far-reaching decisions. Cabinet's role has taken on added significance since:

- government has increased its involvement in the affairs of the community; and
- parliament has found difficulty in closely checking government action (see Chapter 5).

An important feature of the Westminster system is that all cabinet members, including the prime minister, sit in parliament. Ministers, and the prime minister in particular, wield considerable power as decision-makers and party leaders, so their presence in parliament has important political effects. These will become clearer if we compare the Westminster system to the different pattern of government in the United States.

Responsible cabinet government in the US congressional system

The congressional system of the United States is the best-known alternative to the Westminster system. The head of government, the president, is elected by a national vote for a fixed term of four years in office. The president is not a member of Congress, and neither are the secretaries of state that administer the government departments. They are appointed by the president, subject to the approval of the Senate.

The congressional system separates the executive and legislative branches of government, and this affects political relationships in several ways:

- The president attains office through the direct vote of the people, not of Congress.
- Cabinet members rely for office on the will of the president.
- Cabinet can be drawn from a wide range of skilled and experienced people in all walks of life.
- Congress alone decides how it will conduct its business.

In the United States, the separation of powers between the presidential and congressional branches of government means that the president is responsible for the decisions of his or her administration. Because secretaries of state are appointed by the president. They are more likely to support presidential policy once a decision has been made. (See Vile, M.J.C. 2007, *Politics in the USA*, 6th ed., Routledge, Oxford, p. 160).

Relationships in the Westminster system

The Westminster system produces relationships between prime minister, cabinet and parliament different from those that emerge in the congressional system.

- The prime minister depends directly on the support of party colleagues to gain and retain office, which can leave her or him with political debts.
- The government must retain majority support in the lower house in order to hold office (that is, it is not necessarily elected for a fixed term). This makes the maintenance of party loyalty and discipline extremely important.
- Ministers tend to gain their appointments after a lengthy political career in their party and in parliament. As a result, many politicians fail to attain high office, and those who do last the distance tend to build their own base of support within the party and in parliament. The prime minister must take these factors into account when exercising power.
- The presence of a large number of influential people within the parliament gives them added strength over their party colleagues and contributes to the executive's dominance of parliament.

Party support and loyalty are such important factors in determining leadership in the Westminster system that these are more often characteristic of ministers than are qualities such as the ability to analyse policy. There are, of course, ministers who are expert in the field they come to direct (lawyers as attorneys-general being the most common example). Yet it is seen as acceptable, and probably desirable, that ministers be 'informed amateurs', rather than experts in the professional sense. We can see how broadly spread a minister's career can be from the range of portfolios held by Kim Beazley during the 13 years of the Hawke and Keating Labor governments:

- Minister for Aviation;
- Special Minister of State;
- Minister Assisting the Minister for Defence;
- Minister for Defence;
- Minister for Transport and Communications;
- Minister for Finance; and
- Minister for Employment, Education and Training.

The main arguments in favour of this situation are as follows:

- An expert may take a narrow view of his or her speciality or try to dominate his or her colleagues and advisers.
- Conversely, an intelligent 'outsider' should be able to view proposals from the viewpoint of the community.
- The government can call on many experts, whose views in any case often conflict. What is most needed in a minister is the capacity to evaluate these views.
- The minister's main function is to manage a department, rather than to be expert in policy.
- There is often no alternative anyway, as there will not be enough experts to go around.

Against this, it can be argued that not all ministers are necessarily disinterested and knowledgeable, and that party demands are likely to discount such qualities and absorb too much of a minister's time. As a consequence, the critics of the Westminster system maintain that ministers are too often dominated by the very experts and professional administrators in the public service they are supposed to control.

THE PRIME MINISTER

> The leader of the majority party in government is commonly called the **prime minister**.

With the shift of power from the Crown to parliament in Britain, and with ministers assuming greater responsibility, there was a tendency for attention, support and criticism to focus on a particular person, the most likely candidate being the minister in the Commons responsible for finance (the Exchequer). However, ministers were jealous of their influence and their role as advisers to the sovereign, so that the notion of a 'first minister' seemed appropriate for the time. Indeed, the term *prime minister* was first used, in the mid-17th century, to suggest in a derogatory way that the sovereign's closest adviser was doing too much. In succeeding years the power of the office varied according to the individuals who held it, but as the sovereign withdrew from an active part in government and the party system took on clearer form, the prime minister assumed an essential role of leadership.

> 'In the Cabinet and, still more out of it, the most important person is the Prime Minister. It is he (or she) who is primarily concerned with the formation of a Cabinet, with the subjects which the Cabinet discusses, with the relations between the King and the Cabinet and between the Cabinet and Parliament, and with the coordination of the machinery of government subject to the control of the Cabinet.'
> (Source: Jennings, W.I. 1936, *Cabinet Government*, Cambridge University Press, Cambridge, p. 1)

The term *prime minister* has now become commonplace in many modern states, such as Britain, Australia, Malaysia and New Zealand. In the Federal Republic of Germany, the leader of the majority party in the parliament is designated the *federal chancellor* by the Basic Law (constitution), but carries out the same functions as prime ministers in other countries.

Prime ministerial power

Even though a prime minister is a member of cabinet along with other ministers, and shares the collective responsibility for its decisions, the position of prime minister has gained so much political significance that it is now asked whether there has been a shift towards a presidential style of government in parliamentary systems, such as Britain and Australia. The authority exercised by the German federal chancellor in determining the number of ministries and their responsibilities has led to similar suggestions. Mahathir Mohamed, prime minister of Malaysia between 1981 and 2003, was a very powerful leader and had a great deal of influence over government policy, particularly planning initiatives such as the New Economic Policy and Malaysia 2020 that set the framework for Malaysia's economic development.

The significance of the prime minister is exemplified by the way in which governments are identified by their leaders, such as the Blair and Brown governments in Britain and the Howard and Rudd governments in Australia.

The system in the US is quite different, because the holder of executive power is the president, and a particular political regime is identified by the name of the president in power: for example, the Clinton regime or the Bush regime. The leaders of the majority parties in the House of Representatives and the Senate are senior politicians, but do not have the powers or the responsibilities accorded to a prime minister in a parliamentary system.

Nevertheless, uncertainty remains over the amount of power that should be wielded by just one person in a parliamentary system of government. This is reflected in the continuing debate about the prime minister's role as the clearly dominant figure or as merely 'first among equals' in cabinet (a matter discussed later in this chapter when we look at the power of the Australian prime minister and the limitations on that power).

FIGURE 6.1

How to become Prime Minister

(*Source*: Geoff Pryor, 19 July 1991, copyright Geoff Pryor)

GOVERNMENT IN AUSTRALIA

The executive

As with parliament, Australia adopted its form of executive government from Britain, where the functions of cabinet and the prime minister had evolved to their modern form by the time the first Australian colonies gained self-government in the 1850s. The main differences were that the colonial cabinet was small and the head of government was often termed *premier* (from the French, meaning 'first') and this term is still used today for the leaders of state governments. Apart from relatively minor changes, including increases in the numbers of ministers, practices in the Australian states have varied little from the pattern established before Federation.

It was noted in Chapter 3 that the drafters of the Australian Constitution saw no need to record the various conventions that prevailed at Westminster and which, for the most part, they had adopted in their own legislatures. The same type of conventional code (discussed later in this chapter) forms the basis for responsible government in the Australian system of cabinet government; that is, the practice that informs the process is not written into the Constitution itself but rests on conventions drawn from the Westminster system.

Executive authority

In our parliamentary system the executive authority is exercised by the governor-general, acting on the advice of the Federal Executive Council (ss. 61, 62, 63 of the Constitution). However, in practical political terms, under the conventions that underpin the Australian political system, executive power is exercised by the *cabinet*, a committee of government ministers who not only implement or execute the law, but decide government policy and present those policies to the parliament in the form of bills. Once passed by the parliament, these bills become Acts, or laws, and the executive is responsible for their implementation and administration.

> Neither cabinet nor the prime minister is mentioned in the Australian Constitution, which makes specific provision only for the essential framework needed to ratify government decisions, the Federal Executive Council.

The Federal Executive Council

Under s. 62 of the Constitution, the Federal Executive Council has the task of advising the governor-general 'in the government of the Commonwealth'. The council members are chosen by the governor-general 'and shall hold office during his pleasure'. However, in practice, the Federal Executive Council is made up of government ministers and, as we saw in Chapter 3, the governor-general is rarely called on to make decisions about government. As 'president' of the Federal Executive Council, he or she merely presides at regular meetings over the formal processes that give those decisions legal force.

The main decisions do not emerge from the Federal Executive Council, which is rarely attended by more than two or three ministers at one time, but from various meetings of cabinet members. Only rarely do the actions of the Federal Executive Council attract attention, as in the case of its role in the infamous Loans Affair of the Whitlam government in 1974–75.

The Federal Executive Council meets generally every two weeks, but can meet more often if necessary. Meetings are usually held at Government House in Canberra, but can be held in other places, such as Admiralty House, the governor-general's residence in Sydney.

Appointment and function of ministers

Section 64 of the Constitution provides for the appointment by the governor-general of 'the Queen's Ministers of State for the Commonwealth', who are also members of the Federal Executive Council. Ministers have the further duty under s. 64 to 'administer ... departments of state': that is, they are political heads of government departments—minister for foreign affairs and trade, the treasurer, and so on.

The institutional arrangements for executive government, however, operate within a system of cabinet government that is not defined or mentioned in the Constitution, but is a functional institution that has been adopted by Australia as a working model for government practice.

Cabinet

> Because of the nature of its activities, federal cabinet is usually considered to be the main focus of political power in Australia.

Cabinet comprises the leading ministers of the governing party or parties. Its meetings are usually held in the cabinet room at Parliament House, with the prime minister in the chair. Some meetings are also held away from Canberra in state capitals and regional centres. After Prime Minister Kevin Rudd took office in November 2007, he instituted a system of regular *community cabinet meetings* to be held in different regional centres around the country to provide members of the public with the opportunity to meet cabinet ministers in person and ask questions. The program for the meetings usually includes a one-hour public forum to be addressed by the prime minister, with a question-and-answer session from members of the audience, followed by pre-arranged meetings with cabinet ministers. (*Source*: Department of the Prime Minister and Cabinet 2008, 'Community Cabinet', http://www.pmc.gov.au/community_cabinet)

Cabinet meets at least once a week when parliament is sitting, and at other times as needed. The cabinet is the most significant policy-making institution of Australian government, but it is not mentioned in the constitution—nor is the fact that the ministry can be divided into a cabinet and an outer ministry (see below).

From these meetings flow the main political decisions affecting the nation, including proposals for new legislation and appointments to senior posts that are then sent to the Federal Executive Council to be ratified. The methods used by the two major parties in selecting cabinet ministers are explained below.

Cabinet procedures

For a powerful body dealing with major national questions, cabinet for many years organised itself in a surprisingly haphazard fashion. For some 40 years after Federation, outsiders were barred from cabinet meetings and records were kept, as well as they could be, by a junior minister. It was not until the Second World War that a cabinet secretariat, staffed by a small number of senior and trusted public servants, was set up in an effort to bring more order to cabinet business. This is now part of the Department of Prime Minister and Cabinet, with the difficult task of coordinating information and recording decisions while ensuring that such things remain absolutely confidential until cabinet approves their release.

The proceedings in cabinet have similarly become more formal as its number has grown from a mere 9 members in 1901 to 20 today, and as more and more submissions are presented to it from an increasing number of departments. From being a relatively informal body that once could discuss matters at some length and afford the time to try to reach genuine consensus, cabinet has come to resemble any other executive body in business or the public service which must consider a variety of questions in a limited time. Cabinet procedures are set out in the *Cabinet Handbook* (see Department of Prime Minister and Cabinet (DPMC) 2004, *Cabinet Handbook*, 5th ed., DPMC, Canberra, http://www.pmc.gov.au/guidelines/docs/cabinet_handbook.rtf).

The agenda, which is under the control of the prime minister, must be carefully arranged for full cabinet meetings. Submissions are kept to a prescribed length, and there is an elaborate system of consultation between officials before many matters are even put to cabinet. Most of this is essential under modern conditions, but it makes a clear distinction between two of the roles that cabinet must play: it is a national manager, as well as a body for balancing political demands and deciding major policy.

> 'Cabinet is a blender. It must try and reach rational, practical decisions from a most unpromising mixture of ingredients: political calculation and political hunch; a sometimes wide range of choices . . . judgement about the knock-on effect . . . reconciliation of short-term requirements with medium-term needs and long-term strategy; and a balancing of . . . administrative requirements and political imperatives.'
> (*Source*: Hennessy, P. 1986, *Cabinet*, Basil Blackwell, Oxford, p. 7)

Relationships in cabinet

Although cabinet functions at the highest level of political power, there is no reason why its members should behave very differently from any group making decisions under pressure. Some will be well prepared and argue strongly, and some will allow personal animosities or biases to outweigh their judgement of what others are saying. At all times, a great deal will depend on the skill and attitude of the chair (in cabinet, the prime minister).

The prime minister normally controls the agenda, and that is important: items can be ranked high for detailed discussion or perhaps left until last, when members of cabinet may be ready to agree in order to end the meeting. The conduct of the chair is vital to any meeting. Strong pressure in an effort to reach speedy decisions is likely to create resentment and even turn the meeting against the chair; a lenient attitude can lead to a lack of control and feelings of frustration when too little is accomplished.

A skilled chair is at a considerable advantage, particularly if supported by the status, authority and resources of the prime minister. Debate can be allowed to proceed until a trend appears, and if that accords with the prime minister's views, then the appropriate comment can usually secure a favourable decision. If there are difficulties, the prime minister can adjourn discussion or set up sub-committees in order to retain the initiative. Cabinet is traditionally supposed to engage in consensus decision making, but there is little doubt that it leaves a reasonably adroit prime minister in by far the most powerful position.

The individual personality of a prime minister can determine how cabinet will be run. Malcolm Fraser and John Howard, for example, dominated their cabinets, while Bob Hawke adopted a more consensual approach.

> 'A number of major decisions made by the government have been made by Fraser, or Fraser and cabinet, against the views of the responsible minister and his department.'
> (Source: Edwards, J. 1977, Life Wasn't Meant to be Easy: A Political Profile of Malcolm Fraser, Mayhem, Sydney, p. 99)

Cabinet decisions and management

The pressures of cabinet business and the demands of ministers in managing their departments have caused various governments to seek greater efficiency. Two particular problems have been encountered, and each has produced an attempted solution that has affected the form of cabinet government itself:

1. *Pressure of business*: As in parliament itself, general discussion of issues is time-consuming, and *cabinet committees* have been established to try to relieve the situation.
2. *Demands on ministers*: If departmental management occupies too much of their time, ministers are unable to give sufficient attention to long-term issues and policies. Assistant ministers and parliamentary secretaries (see below) have increasingly been appointed to perform the more routine duties of senior ministers, including the prime minister.

Cabinet committees

Various committee systems have been employed by Australian cabinets, particularly since the Second World War, when the Commonwealth's role started to become very much more complex. Most commonly, about five standing committees were established to deal with a broad area of government business, with additional ad hoc committees as required. Potential problems arising from this system include:

- If there are too many committees, their work can become very time-consuming, particularly for the most senior cabinet ministers, and their efforts can be hard to coordinate.
- If there are one or two powerful committees on major areas such as economic policy, they can usurp some of the functions of cabinet itself.
- Ad hoc committees may serve to delay decisions, rather than hasten them.

The usual practice has been for cabinet to endorse committee recommendations without further debate, unless there is a specific objection to them. This is another development that has tended to strengthen the position of the prime minister, who is thereby able to deal with a smaller group of ministers and so have greater chances of success than in the less easily controlled full cabinet. Prime Minister Howard, in his second term of office, decided to make more use of the committee process for general discussion of matters that did not need to come to the full cabinet other than for final endorsement. He formed a General Administrative Committee in order to free up full cabinet meetings for major policy decisions. Additional committees may be established to look at particular issues as and when required.

The 'outer' ministry

Not all ministers need be members of cabinet. In 1956, Prime Minister Robert Menzies divided his ministry into cabinet, comprising 12 senior ministers, and an outer ministry that then numbered 10. Under the Whitlam Labor government (1972–75), all 27 ministers were members of cabinet, but there was criticism that this was unwieldy. The division into two groups was reintroduced in the Fraser government and has been maintained since then. In addition, the movement to mega-departments in the late 1980s saw the appointment of non-cabinet ministers to assist the ministers responsible for those departments, with portfolios such as Minister Assisting the Prime Minister for Science, or Assistant Minister for Industrial Relations.

> The Rudd Labor government, elected in November 2007, has a cabinet of 20, an outer ministry of 11, and 12 parliamentary secretaries.

Assistant ministers

There is no provision in the Constitution for assistant ministers—that is, those in charge of a department who also assist a more senior minister, and those who are not responsible for their own department. Despite this, there has been a long, untroubled history of ministers assisting senior ministers such as the prime minister or the treasurer.

For a long time it was thought that assistant ministers without their own departments could be appointed but could not receive extra salary. Therefore, governments that wanted such assistant ministers, either to relieve senior ministers of more tedious duties or as a form of on-the-job training for future ministers, shied away from doing so. Only Robert Menzies in the early 1950s and William McMahon in the early 1970s appointed such ministers. This changed in 1987 when the Hawke government created super-departments in the charge of a cabinet minister, assisted by one or more junior ministers. The government's legal advice appears to have resolved the constitutional issue regarding these appointments.

Parliamentary secretaries

Parliamentary secretaries are sometimes appointed to assist ministers in the performance of their duties. This has become common practice since the establishment of the super-departments mentioned above. Parliamentary secretaries are able to perform the functions of ministers, but they are not permitted to be asked or to answer questions put to ministers, nor are they permitted to represent a minister before a committee examining the estimates.

Ministers in the House of Representatives and the Senate

> 'Clearly conformity with the doctrine of responsible government requires the Governor-General to appoint a Prime Minister who is likely to command the confidence of the majority of members of the House of Representatives as the more popularly elected House of the Australian Parliament.'
> (Source: Lindell, G. 2004, 'Responsible Government and the Australian Constitution: Conventions transformed into Law', Law and Policy Paper 24, The Federation Press/Centre for International and Public Law, Canberra, p. 10)

Most of the ministry is usually drawn from the House of Representatives, but there are also ministers who sit in the Senate. In the Rudd government, six cabinet ministers, one member of the outer ministry and two parliamentary secretaries are senators. The prime minister is, by convention, a member of the lower house, the House of Representatives.

SELECTION OF MINISTERS AND CABINET

The method of selecting ministers used to vary between the major political parties in Australia, but in November 2007 the newly elected Rudd government changed its procedures; both parties now leave the selection to the leader.

> John Gorton was elected leader of the Liberal Party on 9 January 1968 to replace Harold Holt who had gone missing while swimming, presumed drowned. He was sworn in as prime minister by the governor-general on 10 January 1968.
>
> Gorton was a senator and was expected to move from the Senate to lead the government in the House of Representatives. He became a member of the House of Representatives after winning the by-election for the seat of Higgins.

The Liberal–National Party Coalition

The Coalition follows the practice of allowing the prime minister (who is the elected leader of the majority Liberal Party) to choose ministers and allocate portfolios. There are, however, some constraints on a Coalition prime minister in this matter:

- It is necessary to maintain a balance between the Coalition parties. The Liberal Party has a majority of places, but the Nationals usually gain a higher proportion of portfolios than its numbers in parliament would indicate, particularly when its support is essential to keeping the government in office. The leader of the Nationals traditionally has also been appointed deputy prime minister.
- The prime minister must allocate portfolios to both the Senate and the House of Representatives. The majority of places go to the Representatives, as do the most senior and most sensitive portfolios, such as Treasury, but the Senate at times also has gained some important positions.

- Portfolios are usually allocated with an eye to the numbers of members from the various states. In the past, Victorians dominated the top Liberal Party positions, but the last four leaders of the Liberal Party have come from other states—Alexander Downer (SA), John Howard (NSW), Brendan Nelson (NSW) and Malcolm Turnbull (NSW). It is politically desirable to have the smaller states represented by at least one minister, although perhaps in a junior office.
- Certain leading figures must be given senior portfolios, lest they become resentful and use their power bases within the party and the parliament to challenge the prime minister.
- The Nationals simply notify the Liberal prime minister of their choices for the number of portfolios already agreed on between the Coalition leaders. The prime minister then allocates the portfolios accordingly. There may be some haggling about a particular individual.
- Some leading party figures will have almost automatic claim to a particular portfolio. This is particularly the case with the Nationals, whose ministers usually deal with matters of particular concern to the rural community, such as primary industry and transport.

These constraints determine the composition of perhaps half the ministry, but there are still several choices for the prime minister to make, particularly as the ministry has grown in size—from 19 in 1941 to 31 in 2008. Competition to enter the ministry remains keen, and the Coalition prime minister still has considerable power and freedom in making appointments to it. It should be remembered also that, although the most senior ministers must gain a place in cabinet, the Coalition prime minister can decide in marginal cases whether a portfolio should remain in the junior ranks or whether the minister should sit at the very centre of power—the cabinet room.

The Australian Labor Party

According to the National Platform and Rules of the ALP, the parliamentary leadership of a Labor federal government and the ministry shall be elected by the Federal Parliamentary Labor Party, usually termed the *caucus*.

> The Labor **caucus** is the name given to the Federal Parliamentary Labor Party, which comprises all Labor members of the House of Representatives and Labor senators.

The *factions* within the Federal Parliamentary Labor Party were very influential in the process of determining who would be elected to these positions. This meant that those Labor parliamentarians who did not align themselves with a faction found it very difficult to become ministers.

> 'A major innovation was the three-faction system delivered during Hawke's first term—right, centre-left and left. This became a mechanism for settling differences over policy, power and ministry appointments . . . The faction alliance between the right under Hawke and Keating, and the centre-left under Hayden delivered an ongoing majority within the party for Cabinet positions.'
> (Source: Kelly, P. *The End of Certainty*, Allen & Unwin, Sydney, 1992, p. 30)

This changed after the November 2007 election, when incoming Labor prime minister Kevin Rudd, for the first time since Federation, personally chose the ministry, even though the platform and rules of the party have not changed. The fact that Rudd was successful in leading the party to a significant electoral victory over the incumbent Howard government was a major factor in this decision, and further testament to the pre-eminence of the prime minister in the party system. The prime minister, however, does have to take into account the factional make-up of the party and state representation when making these choices.

Women in the ministry

The election of a number of women to the parliament has provided the opportunity for more women to become ministers, but the Rudd ministry remains dominated by men (see Table 6.3). However, Julia Gillard is the first woman to hold the position of deputy prime minister in an Australian government.

TABLE 6.3
Women in the Rudd ministry as at May 2008

Cabinet	Outer ministry	Parliamentary secretaries
4	3	3

MINISTERS' CAREERS

In practice, ministerial office is usually achieved only after a political apprenticeship, first in the extra-parliamentary party (as a rank-and-file member of the party outside parliament) and then as a backbencher. This will involve, in the first instance, some time spent in assisting and campaigning for party officials and candidates, perhaps a term as a party official, and even candidature for seats that the party cannot hope to win in an effort to establish a reputation for hard work and reliability. The relatively few aspiring parliamentarians who finally gain a seat then begin a new apprenticeship. Most usually wait some years before entering the ministry, in the meantime staving off challenges to their own position in the electorate and in the house, and hoping that their party will win office at the time they have established their claim to a portfolio. More recently, high-profile candidates elected to parliament have been appointed to the ministry straightaway. The Rudd ministry, for example, includes former ACTU secretary Greg Combet, and prominent union official Bill Shorten, who were both elected for the first time in November 2007 and appointed as parliamentary secretaries.

For the truly ambitious, a new process then begins, as the most desirable senior portfolios are few in number and the contest for them is keen. Attaining such a position will involve supporting the winning candidate in leadership contests, while at the same time building support among party colleagues. The next contest may be the office of prime minister. Some people, however, have had a more rapid rise to office.

The majority of ministers are, above all else, skilled politicians. Cabinet not only exercises power, but is the scene of continual contests for power between its members. This means that no minister is an automatic choice for a particular office, least of all for the office of prime minister, and none is automatically ruled out of contention. The continual competition means that ministerial power can be quite fragile. Cabinet as a body maintains its dominance of parliament, but its individual members are never

> - Bob Hawke rose from Labor backbencher to shadow minister to leader of the Opposition and then prime minister in three years. His former career as leader of the Australian trade union movement had given him the status and experience for his accelerated rise to the top.
> - Malcolm Turnbull became leader of the Opposition just four years after he entered parliament. His rapid promotion within the ranks of the parliamentary Liberal Party was aided by his former career as a prominent lawyer and high-profile business leader.

entirely free from challenge. This is one of the distinctive features of the Westminster system. It also means that cabinet is likely to be the scene of tension just as often as it is of calm, rational planning and policy formation. Much of the same can be said of other organisations—business, the public service, universities—and there is no reason to expect anything different from cabinet, particularly as its members are so directly involved in gaining and using power.

> **Career path to the ministry**
> The following personal histories of two Labor ministers and two Liberal shadow ministers indicate the types of career paths that some have taken to ministerial or shadow ministerial office.
>
> ### Australian Labor Party
> **The Hon. Kevin Rudd**
> **Prime Minister**
> - Born 1957
> - Bachelor of Arts (Hons)
> - Diplomat
> - Chief of Staff to the Queensland leader of the Opposition and premier Wayne Goss
> - Director-General, Cabinet Office, Queensland
> - Senior China Consultant, KPMG Australia
>
> **Parliamentary career**
>
> | | |
> |---|---|
> | 1998 | Elected to the House of Representatives for Griffith, Queensland |
> | 1998–2001 | Member, House of Representatives Standing Committee for Publications |
> | 1998–2002 | Member, Joint Statutory Corporations and Securities Committee |
> | 2003–2005 | Shadow Minister for Foreign Affairs and International Security |
> | 2005–2006 | Shadow Minister for Foreign Affairs and Trade and International Security |
> | 2006–2007 | Leader of the Opposition |
> | 2007– | Prime Minister |
>
> **The Hon. Julia Gillard**
> **Deputy Prime Minister**
> - Born 1961
> - Bachelor of Arts, Law
> - Solicitor, Partner
> - Chief of Staff to the Victorian Leader of the Opposition, John Brumby

Parliamentary career

1998	Elected to the House of Representatives for Lalor, Victoria
1998–2001	Member, House of Representatives Standing Committee on Employment, Education and Workplace Relations
1998–2002	Member, Joint Statutory Public Accounts and Audit Committee
2001–2003	Shadow Minister for Population and Immigration
2003	Shadow Minister for Reconciliation and Indigenous Affairs
2003	Deputy Manager of Opposition Business
2003–2006	Manager of Opposition Business
2003–2006	Shadow Minister for Health
2006–2007	Shadow Minister for Employment and Industrial Relations, and Social Inclusion
2006–2007	Deputy Leader of the Opposition
2007–	Deputy Prime Minister
	Minister for Employment and Workplace Relations
	Minister for Education
	Minister for Social Inclusion

Liberal Party
The Hon. Malcolm Turnbull
Leader of the Opposition

- Born 1954
- Bachelor of Arts, Law; BCL (Hons) (Oxon)
- Rhodes Scholar (NSW, 1978)
- Journalist
- Barrister and Solicitor
- Grazier
- General Counsel and Secretary, Consolidated Press Holdings Group
- Managing Director, Turnbull Partners Ltd
- Chairman, OzEmail Ltd
- Director, FTR Holdings Ltd
- Chairman and Managing Director, Goldman Sachs Australia
- Partner, Goldman Sachs and Co.
- Honorary Federal Treasurer of the Liberal Party
- Director, Menzies Research Centre

Parliamentary career

2004	Elected to the House of Representatives for Wentworth, New South Wales
2004–2006	Member of a number of House of Representatives Standing Committees
2004–2006	Member Joint Standing Committees on Treaties and Foreign Affairs, Defence and Trade
2006–2007	Parliamentary Secretary to the Prime Minister
2007	Minister for Environment and Water Resources
2007–2008	Shadow Treasurer
2008	Leader of the Opposition

> **The Hon. Julie Bishop**
> **Deputy Leader of the Opposition**
> - Born 1956
> - Bachelor of Law
> - Advanced Management Program (Senior Managers) (Harvard Business School)
> - Barrister and solicitor
> - Managing Partner, Clayton Utz, Perth
> - Chair, Town Planning Appeal Tribunal of Western Australia
> - Senate Member, Murdoch University
> - Director, Special Broadcasting Services (SBS) Television
> - Director and Fellow, Australian Institute of Management
>
> **Parliamentary career**
>
> | | |
> |---|---|
> | **1998** | Elected to the House of Representatives for Curtin, Western Australia |
> | **1998–2002** | Member, Joint Statutory Corporations and Securities Committee |
> | **1998–2003** | Member, House of Representatives Standing Committee on Legal and Constitutional Affairs |
> | **1999** | Member, Joint Select Committee on Republic Referendum |
> | **2001–2003** | Member, House of Representatives Privileges Committee |
> | **2002–2003** | Member, Joint Standing Treaties Committee |
> | **2003–2006** | Minister for Ageing |
> | **2006–2007** | Minister for Education, Science and Training |
> | | Minister Assisting the Prime Minister for Women's Issues |
> | **2007–** | Deputy Leader of the Opposition and Shadow Treasurer |
>
> (Source: Members' home pages and biographies can be accessed via Parliament of Australia 2008, '42nd Parliament: Alphabetical List of Members', http://www.aph.gov.au/house/members/mi-alpha.asp, reproduced with permission from Australian Parliament House)

MINISTERIAL OFFICE

It may seem strange that anyone would willingly seek a ministerial position in view of the hard work, uncertainty and probable bitterness involved in attaining it. Ministers are subjected to public abuse from the Opposition party, criticism from the media, unflattering caricatures by cartoonists, and inquiries into their private lives. There can be many different motives for entering politics: a desire to be at the centre of things, a wish to help others, the need for status and recognition, the hope of material rewards. Few are content to stay as backbenchers, however, as:

- the 'centre' is the cabinet and the top levels of the bureaucracy, not a seat in the house;
- an ordinary backbench member can do little directly to assist constituents; rather, he or she passes on requests to ministers, who have the power to direct their departments to give help;
- the backbencher's importance in the electorate diminishes rapidly on arrival at Parliament House, where it is more than ever clear that the greatest attention is paid to those with the greatest influence; and
- the backbencher in Australia is paid no more than a middle-level executive in business or the public service.

Much of this changes when a member is appointed to the ministry. A minister is paid about half as much again as a backbencher (though still less than top public servants and much less than top private-sector executives), and has a much larger personal staff, a bigger office in Parliament House as well as a suite in the Canberra headquarters of his or her department and in its offices in the major state capitals, the use of an official car at all times, flights in the RAAF 'VIP' aircraft, invitations to address prestigious gatherings, and continuous attention from the media.

The point is that the minister not only has prestige and power, but is *seen* to have it. There is a sudden transition if the politician is displaced from the ministry or the government loses power. This is not simply a loss of money and creature comforts, but of status and influence: opinions are no longer sought, and names no longer appear in the newspapers or faces on television programs.

> 'As the working year gets underway, John Howard's former team is making an uneasy adjustment to life without wall-to-wall personal staff and fat ministerial salaries.'
> (*Source*: Karvelas, P. & Walker, J. 2008, 'Ex-ministers feel the pinch', *The Australian*, 30 January 2008)

This helps to explain why ministerial office is so eagerly sought and so fiercely defended. The transition process when a government loses office is brutal and rapid, as the following newspaper comment—written three days after the Howard government lost office on 24 November 2007—indicates:

> 'Outgoing Coalition ministers have been busy packing up their parliamentary offices and will be out of the building in Canberra by tomorrow night. Ministerial staffers, the vast majority of whom will be jobless within a few weeks, began descending on Canberra on Sunday night in preparation for what is proving to be a prompt and orderly transition of power. Hundreds of wheelie bins were strewn throughout the building yesterday, with most clustered around the ministerial wing of the building. Staffers have been told to have the job completed by close of business on Wednesday [28 November].'
> (*Source*: Maley, P. 2007, 'Wheelie bin fleet ready for ex-ministers' exodus', *The Australian*, 27 November 2007)

The loss of status and trappings of office also applies to former prime ministers, although they do retain some benefits, such as an office provided by the government.

> 'Paul (Keating) had vanished from public view after the election . . . He had a backbencher's office in Parliament House and, as a former Prime Minister, would have an office in Sydney, but the whole apparatus of being Prime Minister had vanished.'
> (*Source*: Edwards, J. 1996, *Keating: The Inside Story*, Viking, Ringwood, Victoria, p. 540)

Ministers' duties

The authority of ministers derives:

- *formally*, from the commission issued by the governor-general under s. 64 of the Constitution, which also makes them executive councillors; and
- by *convention*, from the prime minister's advice to the governor-general.

The commission gives a minister responsibility for a department and an assistant minister responsibility for part of a department. Ministers assume political responsibility for their department. The senior public servant in each department, usually known as the secretary, is the minister's chief adviser in the bureaucracy. The minister usually appoints several personal staff to provide additional advice and pay special attention to political factors.

Ministerial advisers

A minister's personal staff includes policy advisers who, as we shall see in Chapter 7, play a key role as 'gatekeepers' for the minister. They can determine who has access to the minister. They filter the information that is put before the minister and can influence a minister's decision by arguing in favour of or against a particular submission or policy preference. They examine policy options to make sure they fit into the party's political agenda.

A minister also employs media advisers who manage the relations between the minister and the media. Their role includes informing the press about what is happening and putting 'spin' on that information to the benefit of the government. Because of this they are often called 'spin doctors' (see Chapter 13).

Questions have been raised about the accountability of ministerial staff in the context of ministerial responsibility.

> 'By convention, ministerial staff are exempt from the established accountability arrangements that apply to politicians and public servants. They are not required to appear before Parliamentary committees, their actions are not reported in departmental annual reports and they are not subject to auditing or other forms of scrutiny. Yet their positions are publicly funded, and their impact and influence is significant.'
> (Source: Tiernan, A. & Weller, P. 2003, *Ministerial Staff: A Need for Transparency and Accountability?*, Submission to Senate Finance & Public Administration References Committee, Inquiry Into Members of Parliament Staff, p. 10)

The issue of accountability comes to the fore when a ministerial staffer makes a mistake. Should the minister take responsibility for the error, or can it be explained away on the basis that the minister was not aware of what was going on and disclaim any responsibility? So long as the political embarrassment and fall-out of any mistake can be contained, the latter is more likely to be the case. The adviser may be asked to resign, but the minister will survive.

Managing a Commonwealth department

Each department comprises several divisions, which may be varied in size or transferred from one department to another according to executive orders issued by the governor-general, again on the advice of the prime minister (see Chapter 7). The department administers various Acts of parliament, and these give ministers more specific powers:

- by allowing them to make payments, decide entitlements or effect appointments, and a host of other things; and
- more practically, by permitting ministers to delegate certain specified powers to officials, who perform those duties on their behalf.

Ministers also have rather limited control over a number of statutory agencies. These are discussed further in Chapter 7, but it should be noted for the present that ministers do not have complete authority over those bodies, which are granted a degree of autonomy by the legislation establishing them. Nevertheless, ministers have a good deal of power placed in their hands. This is another reason why a portfolio, as it is known, is the goal of any normally ambitious politician.

MINISTERS, CABINET AND WESTMINSTER CONVENTIONS

It has been noted so far that ministers' roles are affected by two main factors:
- official appointments and duties under the Constitution and other legal provisions; and
- their situation in the party and their reliance on its members and its leader for their tenure of office.

The conduct of ministers is further influenced by the rules, conventions and expectations of the Westminster system of government that have come to operate in Australia.

Westminster conventions

Geoffrey Sawer, in his book *Federation under Strain* (p. 175), explains how in the British system a conventional code—that is, principles based on 'non-legal practices' and a 'system of political morality'—underpins the relationship between the legislature and the executive, or the cabinet, in the delivery of responsible government.

> The Westminster conventions evolved over several centuries to take account of the needs of responsible government—for all ministers to give public support to cabinet decisions.

These conventions, as they affect Australian government, are outlined in the next few pages. It has been pointed out, however, that party considerations are particularly strong in Australia, as is geography, and so the application of the Westminster conventions to the Australian system must be considered in its own context. The way in which needs have modified conventions is thus the underlying theme of the sections that follow.

> The Australian practice in these matters is sufficiently different from that of Westminster to have caused one knowledgeable British observer, David Butler, to refer to it as 'the Canberra model'.
> (Source: Butler, D. 1973, *The Canberra Model*, Cheshire, Melbourne)

These conventions of cabinet government in the Westminster system can be discussed in two groups, according to their effect on:
- the minister as an individual; or
- the minister as a member of cabinet.

There are two main conventions concerning the individual conduct of ministers:
- the expectation of integrity, sometimes referred to as 'probity'; and
- individual ministerial responsibility for executive and administrative actions in matters under the minister's control.

> Under the convention of **individual ministerial responsibility**, ministers are responsible for their actions and those of their departments to the parliament.

The two interrelated main conventions relating the conduct of ministers to the needs of the whole cabinet are:

- secrecy; and
- collective responsibility,

which were introduced earlier in this chapter.

Ministerial integrity and ethics

This broadly means that ministers should not take advantage of the power of their office in order to gain any kind of personal benefit. Ideally, ministers should not only deal even-handedly with all groups and issues that come before them, but should be *seen* to do so. Such a completely open approach to ministerial power would require the disclosure of all personal and family interests, whether in company shareholdings, directorships or professional partnerships. The motive is not so much to guard against actual ministerial corruption, but to avoid political embarrassment to the government by removing even the possibility of accusations of a conflict of interest or wrongdoing against ministers.

Attitudes towards the disclosure of ministers' interests in the past depended on the views of the prime minister or premier. Sir Robert Menzies required ministers to resign any directorships, and he himself passed over the control of his shares and other investments to a trustee. On the other hand, former Victorian premier Henry Bolte and former Queensland premier Joh Bjelke-Petersen strongly defended the rights of ministers to continue with their business activities, and Bjelke-Petersen and his family maintained close involvement with public companies.

This is an area where the attitudes of parties and leaders overrode adherence to Westminster principles. The few exceptions in recent years only serve to prove the rule. Andrew Peacock, when a junior minister in the Gorton government, offered his resignation because his then wife had appeared, unpaid, in an advertisement for bedsheets, but this was so ludicrous as to make nonsense of any convention. The treasurer in the Fraser government, Phillip Lynch, was forced into resigning shortly before the 1977 election over the involvement of a family trust in land investments. In a letter accepting Lynch's resignation, however, the prime minister referred to a 'quieter non-election atmosphere' in which matters might be 'properly resolved' and expressed the hope that Lynch might return to the ministry, which he subsequently did after the election.

The Lynch affair led to the setting up of a committee of inquiry to consider the matter of the pecuniary interests of ministers and MPs (the Bowen Committee), which reported in 1979. The government accepted one of its recommendations—that ministers had a duty to inform the prime minister in writing of their interests and to outline the nature of the business in which their companies were engaged. The Labor Party objected that this was not going far enough, and called both for full public disclosure and for the extension of this principle to senior public servants. This involved something more than a concern for Westminster; there was also a political motive. Labor presumably hoped that disclosure would reveal much greater business involvement among Coalition politicians than among its own members, which might give added weight to its claim that a Liberal–Nationals Coalition government is likely to favour those who have property. The contest for party advantage can often be rationalised by appeals to principle.

The Hawke government in 1983 introduced a new set of rules requiring ministers to make full declarations of their private interests. When the details were published, Labor ministers proved to have relatively modest assets, mostly in the form of houses. As they had objected to the values of these assets being listed, it was not possible to say whether Labor ministers were in general wealthier than might have been expected.

> The Opposition took political advantage of the disclosure provisions by criticising Prime Minister Keating for his acquisition of a new home in Sydney and his interests in a commercial piggery. As a result, the prime minister divested himself of his interest in the piggery.

When Prime Minister Howard took office, he continued the expectation of probity by disclosure of assets. This was not without some political difficulties along the way, when a minister's shareholdings came under scrutiny from the Opposition on the issue of conflict of interest and the minister in question was not required to resign by the prime minister. Following public criticism of a potential conflict of interest if Labor won government, the wife of Opposition leader Kevin Rudd sold her companies that had had dealings with the federal government.

> On 6 December 2007, Prime Minister Kevin Rudd announced the introduction of a new ministerial code of conduct, *Standards of Ministerial Ethics*. The main elements of the code are:
> - Lobbyists will be required to register their details publicly on a Register of Lobbyists, before seeking access to a minister or ministerial office.
> - Ministers are to undertake not to have business dealings with members of the government, public service or defence force on any matters they had dealt with in their official capacity as minister in the preceding 18 months.
> - Electoral fundraising at the Lodge or Kirribilli House is prohibited.
> - Ministers are required to divest themselves of all shareholdings other than through investment vehicles, such as broadly diversified superannuation funds or publicly listed managed or trust arrangements.
>
> (*Source*: Department of Prime Minister and Cabinet (DPMC) 2007, *Standards of Ministerial Ethics*, DPMC, Canberra, http://www.pmc.gov.au/guidelines/docs/ministerial_ethics.pdf, copyright Commonwealth of Australia, reproduced by permission)

Individual ministerial responsibility

According to this convention, ministers are answerable to parliament for all actions taken by the department(s) under their control.

> When parliament 'wrested power from the Crown', the balance was shifted, 'making the Crown's ministers responsible to the people's representatives . . . If ministers lost the confidence of Parliament they had to go.'
> (*Source*: Wright, T. 1994, *Citizens and Subjects*, Routledge, London, pp. 43–4)

It is a convention also that ministers who mislead parliament by tendering incorrect information should resign.

The main purpose of the *convention of individual ministerial responsibility* is to ensure that parliament retains its ultimate authority over the executive, even if in a remote way. Ministers' knowledge of their duty to answer to parliament might also lead them to check departmental actions with more than ordinary care; and public servants perhaps to strive for greater efficiency in order to protect their ministers from criticism. However, such considerations could affect only the smallest minority of senior officials, and this raises problems about the true significance of this convention.

The point is that ministers are said to be 'responsible' for all administrative actions within their field, even if these were carried out without their specific direction or even without their knowledge. This might lead to some apparently ridiculous situations—for example, parliamentary questions attacking ministers for discourtesy by counter staff at government offices. In practice, such minor matters are treated more sensibly: if they happen to come before parliament, ministers simply promise to investigate them and apply remedies where necessary.

A more difficult situation arises in issues of widespread public concern and controversy, and particularly in those involving complex organisations or technologies. Ministers face three main problems in observing 'responsibility' in modern industrial society:

1 *The scale of government activity*: A great number of matters must be dealt with, and many employees deal with them. (The larger Australian departments employ tens of thousands of public servants.)
2 *Complex relationships between organisations and ministers*: Australian governments have set up large numbers of semi-autonomous bodies for which ministers' 'responsibility' is unclear. (This and related matters are discussed in Chapter 7.)
3 *Technology and expertise*: Governments are now so closely involved with industry, science, and general economic and social development that no minister (nor any other person, for that matter) could be expert in all matters dealt with by even a single department.

Clearly, ministers must rely heavily on the advice and opinions of their personal staff, officials and experts. It therefore seems unrealistic, and perhaps unjust, to expect ministers to answer for advice that is incorrect or misleading, and doubly unfair if, under those circumstances, a minister has to resign for a serious executive error. A prime minister may also be reluctant to sack a minister for political reasons, because the taint of the scandal might affect the government's standing with the electorate. Former British minister, Richard Crossman, explains:

> In Bagehot's time . . . the House could censure and ultimately sack Ministers for failings in their Departments. This has long since disappeared. I mean, it is still there as a legend. But now, very often, the worse a Minister manages his Ministry, the more difficult it is to get him removed because it would be an injury to the prestige of the Government. So the more the House of Commons bellows against the Minister, the stronger usually is

the Prime Minister's determination to protect him in order to strengthen the hold of the Government on the House of Commons.
(*Source*: Crossman, R. 1972, *Myths of Cabinet Government,* Harvard University Press, Cambridge, Mass., pp. 45–6)

Calls for the resignation of government ministers have been made quite often and have placed the government of the day under severe pressure. Even though a prime minister may not want to sack a minister, the political heat from the Opposition and the media may be so intense that it becomes necessary to do so to save the government further embarrassment and political damage. The case of Graham Richardson, a minister in the Keating government, illustrates how this can happen. The pressure from the Opposition and the media over Richardson's alleged misleading of parliament became so politically damaging that, even though Prime Minister Keating did not sack him, the minister resigned.

> 'The day Richardson was due to report to the Prime Minister, he arrived at Keating's office with his letter of resignation. He had decided to voluntarily stand down as Minister for Transport and Communications. Richardson would later claim that Keating urged him not to resign that morning, to stay and fight. But in reality Richardson knew he was gone.'
> (*Source*: Wilkinson, M. 1996, *The Fixer*, Heinemann, Melbourne, p. 358)

> 'By now the Canberra press gallery also smelt blood and not only Richardson's. Keating was stumbling under the pressure . . .'
> 'As the crisis grew, key members of Paul Keating's staff and the ALP's National Secretary . . . decided that Richardson had to go. He was seriously damaging the new Prime Minister and the election was less than twelve months away . . .'
> 'Richardson "decided to quit" . . . for the good of the Labor government.'
> (*Source*: Wilkinson, M. 1996, *The Fixer*, Heinemann, Melbourne, pp. 356–7)

A number of other ministers have resigned or were stood down for a period of time while under investigation. Generally, these were instances of personal misjudgement or misleading the parliament. No ministers have been forced to resign in cases in which they could claim truthfully either that they had been misled by their department or that they could not possibly have known of the activities in question.

The fate of two ministers in the Hawke government illustrates the distinction between directly and indirectly misleading the parliament.

- John Brown came under attack for his role in the issuing of a theatre contract to a participant in Expo '88. He appeared to have misled the parliament over a question (the decision as to which applicant should get the contract) about which he had direct personal knowledge. He was forced to resign.
- Neal Blewett passed on to parliament, in answer to a question, information that had been supplied by the Health Insurance Commission. Later, he asked his own staff to check the accuracy of his answer, found that it was incorrect, and quickly reported his mistake to the parliament. He did not resign.

FIGURE 6.2
Ministerial resignation?

Richo resigns from the Social Security Portfolio *with a little help from Keating* . . .

. . . After some intense pressure from the Senate

(*Source*: Geoff Pryor, 8 May 1992, copyright Geoff Pryor)

> Elaine Thompson and Greg Tillotsen have pointed out that ministerial resignations usually occur under the following circumstances:
> 1. When a minister cannot support government policy: that is, cannot stand by cabinet solidarity.
> 2. Smoking gun type 1: when a minister is caught out having done something unethical either personally or financially.
> 3. Smoking gun type 2: when a minister is demonstrably directly responsible for a major error, is found out and misleads parliament. Even here, prime ministers and ministers attempt to tough it out and sometimes succeed.
>
> (*Source*: Thompson, E. & Tillotsen, G. 1999, 'Caught in the Act: The Smoking Gun View of Ministerial Responsibility', *Australian Journal of Public Administration*, vol. 58, no. 1, p. 51)

The main issue is not whether a rather vague convention is being observed. The problem is: if ministers cannot, or will not, accept total 'responsibility', then to whom can parliament and people turn? The problem is compounded by the fact that:

- outside the context of the legislation, the Australian parliament has no control over executive actions before they are taken, and rarely provides effective scrutiny after the event (see Chapter 5); and

- numerous functions have been delegated to semi-autonomous administrative bodies (see Chapter 7).

Question time as a function of ministerial accountability

A significant factor in keeping the principle of individual ministerial responsibility to parliament alive is the opportunity afforded the Opposition to probe and question ministers about their actions in question time in both houses. This is especially so in the Senate on those occasions when the Opposition, minor parties and independents are in the majority and can therefore subject the government to more intense scrutiny.

Senate committees as a function of ministerial accountability

As we saw in Chapter 5, the Senate committee system has provided the means for examining the performance of governments. Again, when the government is in the minority, the Opposition, minor parties and independents have used their majority in the Senate to establish select committees to inquire into issues that might embarrass the government.

Some governments, however, have elected not to permit ministers or their staff to give evidence before Senate committees on issues relating to ministerial responsibility, such as the matter of who was responsible for erroneous public announcements that children were thrown overboard from an asylum seekers' boat.

Whether ministers take issues that are raised in the parliament seriously enough to consider resignation is likely to depend on how much public (electoral) embarrassment is caused the government through media appraisal of any allegations raised and the minister's response.

Ministers and cabinet: collective responsibility

In addition to their individual responsibility to parliament, the electorate and their departments, ministers have obligations as members of the group that comprises cabinet.

Secrecy

The convention is that proceedings within cabinet should remain secret, apart from any authorised statements announcing decisions and setting out the reasons for them.

> 'The principle of Cabinet secrecy is closely linked to that of Cabinet solidarity and is generally thought to be necessary to secure free and candid discussion in Cabinet.'
> (*Source:* Lindell, G. 2004, 'Responsible Government and the Australian Constitution: Conventions Transformed into Law', *Law and Policy Paper 24*, The Federation Press/Centre for International and Public Law, Canberra, p. 15)

There are two main reasons for this:

- Certain matters, particularly those relating to defence, commercial transactions and major financial adjustments, should not be revealed, in order *to protect the national interest*. The case of defence appears obvious, and if such matters as increased charges in the budget were known in advance, certain interests might be able to take advantage of that knowledge.

- *Ministers should be able to speak freely in cabinet*, which might be more difficult if their views became public. Furthermore, ministers who may be opposed to the eventual decision of cabinet are then required, under the convention of collective responsibility, to defend that decision in public. Cabinet solidarity, enhanced by the code of secrecy, strengthens the ability of a government to defend its position. Public airing of differences of opinion by cabinet members would be construed as a sign of weakness in the government, with probable negative electoral repercussions.

Once again, the convention is far less clear than it seems to be. There are two main problems concerning its observance in Australia:

- tensions within parliamentary parties or between coalition partners; and
- attempts to conceal maladministration or politically embarrassing matters from the public.

Labor cabinet ministers have on occasion voiced their disagreements with each other in public. During both the Whitlam and Hawke governments, ministers sometimes differed openly on matters—such as relations with the United States, or uranium policy—that should conventionally have been confined to policy discussions in cabinet.

> Prime Minister Hawke adapted the convention to take account of the division between cabinet and the outer ministry, whereby junior ministers were bound by the code of secrecy in relation to their attendance at cabinet meetings. They were free to debate other matters within caucus, but not in public.

The Coalition has seen similar disputes, many of them amounting to campaigns by the Nationals seeking support in the electorate for proposals it has put to cabinet. These tend to arouse less comment than do disputes within a Labor government, perhaps because the media and the public expect the two Coalition partners to differ on certain questions. In such instances, the content of cabinet debate is merely implied, but detailed newspaper reports have at times suggested that ministers have provided lengthy and specific accounts of cabinet proceedings to the media either to improve their public standing or to denigrate a rival, or both.

> The degree of cabinet solidarity is a test of the leadership's strength. Leaking of cabinet or shadow cabinet proceedings becomes endemic when the leadership is under threat.

There are other powerful motives for government secrecy. It is politically desirable to conceal both differences of opinion, which could be exploited by the Opposition, and administrative errors, which could create an impression of government incompetence. This can sometimes be accomplished by invoking cabinet conventions, but secrecy extends far into the political party structures and into the bureaucracy. The need for so much confidential dealing is increasingly questioned: governments have such an impact on the community that people need to know more about their intentions, while politicians and public servants are no longer considered so expert that their actions can go unquestioned. Much cabinet business could be revealed publicly without harm; so much information is 'leaked' to the media, including budget details before they are officially released, that the leaks themselves create issues out of what might otherwise be trivial matters. On the other hand, governments themselves may leak details of a proposed policy to test public reaction, in what has been called 'kite flying'.

Freedom of information laws as a function of accountability

After some years of debate, a freedom of information (FOI) bill was put through parliament in 1982 by the Fraser government. The Labor Party argued that it did not go far enough, and promised to extend its reach when it obtained power, but in fact the new Labor government elected in 1983 left the Act much as it was.

Public servants, politicians and citizens are all getting used to the notion that it is permissible for the ordinary person to find out what has gone on behind the closed doors of government. The charges associated with accessing information through FOI may be a deterrent for extensive use of this facility by individuals (see Chapter 7), but media organisations have the financial capacity to make greater use of the facility. FOI is a useful tool in getting information about government performance on the public record, and also to place issues on the political agenda to initiate a government response. Consequently, many newspapers employ staff with a specialist role in seeking information through FOI.

The Rudd government entered office in November 2007 with a commitment to reform FOI. Whether this results in any improvement to the freedom of information process remains to be seen.

> 'The Government will also be enhancing the culture of transparency in government through reforms to Freedom of Information laws, including the abolition of conclusive certificates and the creation of a Freedom of Information Commissioner.'
> (*Source*: Prime Minister Kevin Rudd 2008, 'Address to Heads of Agencies and Members of Senior Executive Service', 30 April 2008, Canberra, http://www.pm.gov.au/media/Speech/2008/speech_0226.cfm, copyright Commonwealth of Australia, reproduced by permission)

The operation of FOI suggests that the secrecy attached to cabinet proceedings has been little touched by such legislation. Cabinet documents are kept secret for 30 years. After this passage of time, the government of the day has long gone, and their contents are more interesting and useful as an historical archive.

The convention of cabinet secrecy works imperfectly where it would seem to be most important, and too well where there is a genuine need for public knowledge. As with other cabinet conventions, it has been considerably modified in practice by party considerations.

Collective cabinet responsibility

The conventions listed so far all relate to the one that is most characteristic of the Westminster system, sometimes termed cabinet 'solidarity'. It essentially means that cabinet must appear united, but it has more than merely party-political significance. One of its main outcomes, if it is properly observed, is to ensure that no minister, including the prime minister, can achieve a position of overwhelming executive authority. Checks that can be applied to the executive in the congressional system, but which are weaker in the Westminster-style parliament, are virtually built into the cabinet itself by the solidarity convention. The convention is really a series of related conventions:

- Ministers should seek cabinet approval for policy before it is announced.
- Ministers must publicly support cabinet decisions.
- If unable to do so, they should resign.
- Ministers should not publicly criticise a colleague's actions.
- Ministers should not express opinions on policy other than in an official manner—that is, ministers do not have 'private' opinions on such matters.

> These conventions are adopted as working principles for the Australian government and are incorporated in the *Cabinet Handbook*. (See Department of Prime Minister and Cabinet (DPMC) 2004, *Cabinet Handbook*, 5th ed., DPMC, Canberra, http://www.pmc.gov.au/guidelines/docs/cabinet_handbook.rtf)

There are certain decisions, such as negotiations with a foreign country, which cabinet usually leaves to the prime minister and, say, the treasurer or Minister for Foreign Affairs. In these instances, cabinet is kept informed rather than being directly involved. Otherwise, decisions should be taken collectively. There is even a tradition that decisions should be arrived at by consensus to emphasise the principle of solidarity, although all cabinets sometimes take votes.

Australian cabinets have not distinguished themselves in observing the convention of collective responsibility, partly for reasons that have led to breaches of secrecy discussed above. Labor leaders and the Coalition partners have differed just as much after decisions have been taken as they have over the initial proposals. However, these events have prompted more questions about electoral consequences or relationships between the Coalition parties than about ministers apparently ignoring cabinet conventions.

> The dismissal of the Liberal Minister for Air, Leslie Bury, in 1962 for breaking cabinet solidarity illustrates that the convention is not highly valued always for its own sake. 'Bury had contended that Britain's entry to the Common Market would be of minor importance'—that is, it would have less serious effects on the Australian economy than the government had claimed.
> This dismissal illustrated the strength of the prime minister as much as of Westminster convention.
> (*Source*: Killen, J. 1985, *Killen: Inside Australian Politics*, Methuen Haynes, Sydney, p. 59)

On the other hand, in 1977 the Liberal attorney-general, Bob Ellicott, observed convention in an almost classic manner. He resigned after disagreeing with cabinet that a private prosecution for conspiracy against Gough Whitlam and three former Labor ministers should be assumed by the Crown and terminated.

> In 1989, Labor minister Gary Punch accepted the force of the convention when he resigned from the Hawke ministry because of his disagreement with government policy to build a third runway at Sydney airport.
> (*Sources*: 'I quit to fight runway: Punch', *Daily Telegraph*, 29 March 1989; Williams, P. 2002, 'Second Sydney Airport—A Chronology', Parliamentary Library, Canberra, http://www.aph.gov.au/library/pubs/chron/2001-02/02chr02.htm)

Stewart West, a cabinet minister in the Hawke government, was permitted a halfway measure by being allowed to resign from cabinet but remain in the outer ministry because he could not accept the government's uranium policy.

> '"I understand Cabinet arrangements regarding solidarity", he wrote to me. "Under the terms of that Cabinet arrangement I understand that I can no longer serve in the Cabinet. I, of course, remain ready and willing and expect to continue to serve the Labor Government as a member of the ministry."'
> (Source: Letter from West to Prime Minister Hawke, cited in Hawke, R.J.L. 1994, *The Hawke Memoirs*, Heinemann, Melbourne, p. 251, copyright Hon. Bob Hawke A.C.)

> A list of ministerial resignations and dismissals since 1901 can be found at: australianpolitics.com 2007, 'Ministerial Resignations and Dismissals Since 1901', http://australianpolitics.com/executive/ministry/resignations.shtml.

The solidarity convention raises wider questions for a Labor cabinet. Under Labor Party rules, the decisive role in parliamentary matters should be played by caucus, which must approve the policies and actions of the leadership. At first sight, this seems to contravene the principles of both collective and individual responsibility, as well as posing problems in maintaining security. Certainly, Labor's opponents have maintained that caucus control obscures lines of responsibility and weakens control.

In fact, there is a point at which the views of any parliamentary party must be heeded by its leaders, who ultimately depend on it for their offices. The Fraser government proposed to reintroduce television licence fees, but desisted owing to objections in the party room that the move would be electorally damaging. Indeed, the government established a series of backbench committees to examine a wide range of questions. It was suggested at the time that Fraser saw the committees mainly as a device for keeping his record parliamentary majority occupied, but several of the committees made policy proposals.

The essential difference in the parliamentary party–cabinet relationship between the Labor and Coalition parties is that the role of caucus is established formally within party rules, whereas the influence of Coalition members depends on several variable factors, such as the attitude of the party leaders and the electoral climate. The failure by the Liberals to win the 1993 election, for example, saw the Liberal parliamentary leadership promise to consult more fully with the backbench and the extra-parliamentary party on future policy proposals.

Following the election of the Whitlam Labor government, caucus approved the establishment of 10 caucus committees to be consulted on matters of policy. This was viewed with alarm by Westminster purists, but if examined from the viewpoints of either practice or principle it posed little danger and probably had a good deal to commend it. The Hawke government continued this practice in a more formal sense:

- *Practically*, the caucus committees did not obtrude on matters that were usually considered highly sensitive, and did not harass ministers or officials.

- *In principle*, the notion that the executive should not be asked to report formally to its own supporters suggests an elitist, even authoritarian, view of government. It can also be argued that committee examinations could be unsettling to the community by revealing divisions within the government, but that view could commend itself only to those who do not wish to be reminded that problems are often complex and can lead to genuine differences of opinion on particular issues, rather than be symptomatic of deeper problems of division within a government.

The debate over the role of caucus reveals a tension between Westminster conventions, such as individual and collective responsibility, and the needs of modern industrial society. The community looks for united and reassuring leadership but would also prefer a more 'open' government, whose actions can be readily assessed. Under these circumstances, the main criticism to be made of caucus action is that it should not be considered as any sort of substitute for effective parliamentary scrutiny of government.

THE POWER OF THE PRIME MINISTER

There has been much debate on whether the high profile and dominance of the prime minister within government is changing the Westminster model of cabinet government into a more presidential style of system.

> 'In many Westminster systems it is often argued that cabinet government based on collective responsibility has been undermined, in part by the increased complexity of modern decision-making, but also by a conscious effort to centralize prime ministerial authority. Moreover, in majoritarian systems such as that of Australia and Britain the prime minister now exercises unprecedented power in shaping ministerial careers, a tool in ensuring compliance and centralizing authority.'
> (Source: McAllister, I. 2004, 'Political Leaders in Westminster Systems', Australian Policy Online, 18 May 2004, http://www.apo.org.au)

The prime minister enjoys advantages over ministers through:

- public attention as head of government;
- the position of chair of cabinet;
- the exercise of patronage;
- the prerogative of setting election dates; and
- the services of an important department.

> 'The building [Parliament House] is the triumph of executive power, grander than the White House. Howard arrives and leaves by car from his executive courtyard and has the instruments of his power in proximity—the Parliament, his ministers, his staff, the Cabinet Policy Unit, 300 journalists and, at the foot of the Hill, the main policy departments whose public service chiefs trek up the Hill to advise and to listen.'
> (Source: Kelly, P. 2006, 'Re-thinking Australian Governance: The Howard Legacy', Australian Journal of Public Administration, vol. 65, no. 1, p. 9)

But there are a number of political factors within the Australian political system that suggest that the prime minister is not 'all-powerful' and without constraint. Patrick Weller explains the basis of the arguments for and against prime ministerial power.

> 'Those who argue that prime ministers are now pre-eminent point to the great powers they can wield. They have the right to select or dismiss ministers. They control the structure and proceedings of cabinet. They allocate extensive patronage. They are protected in parliament by the support of a disciplined party. They choose the date of elections. They are the focus of media attention and are able to manipulate the media. They determine the distribution of functions to departments in the public service and have developed a capacity for co-ordination that gives them access to extensive information. They speak on behalf of the country in international forums . . .
>
> Those who maintain that cabinet government is still a reality emphasise the limitations on prime ministers. They demonstrate that ministers have independence and political strength. They explain that cabinet still makes all the important decisions. They show how powerful departments have the capacity to limit the exercise of the prime minister's prerogatives. Parliament is seen as a real force. Parties do not merely give unquestioning support. The emphasis is on the dispersion of power and the collectivity of the process.'
>
> (Source: Weller, P. 1989, *Malcolm Fraser PM: A Study in Prime Ministerial Power in Australia*, Penguin, Ringwood, Victoria, pp. 1–2)

Public attention and party reliance

The prime minister is at the very centre of public attention, particularly with the heavy media concentration on personalities (rather than on underlying issues and complex policies). Almost anything that the prime minister says or does is news, so that any reasonably competent performance is bound to attract favourable notice—far more, in any event, than that accorded ministers or mere private members.

There is a cost: faults and foibles are likely to be magnified, so that the prime minister's personal deficiencies can sometimes obscure skills in planning and administration. Yet much the same problem faces any national leader in the media age. The Westminster system, on balance, provides a prime minister with certain advantages that are denied a president elected directly by the people:

- The prime minister is chosen by his or her supporters, most of whom face re-election at the same time as he or she does. Parties support candidates for the leaders whom they consider to be the best person to lead the party in winning elections. This means they have a vital interest in the success of the prime minister, because their own re-election could depend on how well he or she performs. An aspiring leader in the Labor Party also has to gain support of the dominant faction. The withdrawal of Kevin Rudd and Julia Gillard from the Labor leadership ballot in January 2005, which left the field open for Kim Beazley to take the position uncontested, is a good example.

> - **Kevin Rudd withdraws**: 'In the end, he bowed to the demands of Right factional warlords . . . They wanted Beazley as the uncontested Right candidate, arguing that factional unity was more important than the personal ambition of one of Labor's most able frontbenchers.'
>
> (Source: Lewis, S. 2005, 'Kevin was in Right place at wrong time', *The Australian*, 25 January 2005)

> - **Julia Gillard withdraws**: 'One of Ms Gillard's staunchest allies, left-wing NSW MP Laurie Ferguson, said . . . "The most disappointing thing is that a number of powerbrokers of the Left wouldn't support a Left candidate—and they made it impossible for her to win".'
> (Source: Karvelas, P. 2005, 'Gillard left with not enough to go on', The Australian, 27 January 2005)
> - **Kim Beazley** was then replaced as Leader of the Opposition by **Kevin Rudd** on 4 December 2006 because many within the parliamentary Labor Party did not think Beazley could win the next election. Rudd led Labor to victory on 24 November 2007.

◎ Public lack of support for the prime minister causes electoral problems. This discourages dissent with the prime minister by government members. An inept or unpopular prime minister may be replaced by the party before he or she can create further electoral problems. John Gorton, for example, chose to resign when a vote of no-confidence against his leadership was tied. Such a move in itself may be electorally damaging to the government, and thus it is rarely taken. However, the prospects for damage have to be balanced against the prospect that a new leader might be more appealing to the electorate.

> Successful change of a prime minister prior to an election includes the replacement in 1991 of Labor Prime Minister, Bob Hawke, with Paul Keating, who went on to win the 'unwinnable' election in 1993.

◎ Many voters scarcely think beyond the prime minister when thinking of politics and government, and a competent leader can usually take advantage of this fact to maintain his or her authority over government members. The pre-eminence of the leader is evident in the fact that governments are referred to using the name of the prime minister of the day (for example, the Rudd government).

Patronage

Patronage is usually thought of as the power to make appointments, thereby creating obligations among those appointed. In that sense, a prime minister is at a disadvantage when compared with the president of the United States, where large numbers of public service positions are filled by the president directly. Prime ministers appear to have only ministries, positions for retiring members, and some diplomatic and statutory authority appointments with which to reward their supporters. There are constraints also on the exercise of this patronage because, as we have seen above, prime ministers have to take account of a range of factors when making such appointments, such as possible political damage from charges of favouritism.

Chair of cabinet

The prime minister, as head of the government, is chair of cabinet and derives political power from the capacity to determine who will sit in the cabinet, what cabinet committees shall be established, and the membership of those committees. The prime minister also determines the issues that appear on the cabinet agenda.

> 'Say that I think something is terribly important: I must get it through and I've had a row in a Cabinet committee. I register my dissent and ask for it to go to Cabinet. Somehow it does not occur on the agenda week after week. I fume—but the PM has the last word.'
> (Source: Richard Crossman, former minister in the British House of Commons, in Crossman, R. 1972, *The Myths of Cabinet Government*, Harvard University Press, Cambridge, Mass., p. 51)

There is no doubt that the prime minister holds the pre-eminent position within cabinet, but there are factors that modify or constrain the power that a prime minister can wield. The prime minister does have some discretion over what appears on the cabinet agenda, but there are issues important to the running of government that have to be discussed and deliberated in that forum. The prime minister also has to get the support of cabinet colleagues to support his or her policy preference. This could mean a Liberal prime minister having to take into account the interests of the coalition partner, the Nationals. A Labor Party prime minister may have to gain support of the dominant faction within caucus.

> 'Since cabinet is made up of powerful and ambitious individuals, they need to be managed and handled with care.'
> (Source: Weller, P. 1989, *Malcolm Fraser PM: A Study in Prime Ministerial Power in Australia*, Penguin, Ringwood, Victoria, p. 108)

Different prime ministers go about it in different ways. Some may bully their colleagues into submission, while others work to achieve a consensus.

> 'Whatever his (or her) temperament or abilities, a Prime Minister's achievements during his (or her) term of office will largely depend on the capacity to work through the people who make up the Cabinet . . . and on the ability to conciliate, compromise, cajole or coerce.'
> (Source: W.G. Smith, former permanent head of various Commonwealth departments, in Smith, W.G. 1986, 'Superstar?: What Makes a Prime Minister?', *Quadrant*, vol. 30, no. 10, p. 41)

There are other powerful ministers within cabinet who have to be accommodated or persuaded. A good example is the relationship that existed between Prime Minister Bob Hawke and his treasurer, Paul Keating.

> 'In a Cabinet government of the kind that Australia has, a Prime Minister cannot lead a strong, intelligent Treasurer for very long. Key decisions need to be made or at least endorsed by Cabinet as a whole, which means that the Prime Minister cannot simply tell the Treasurer what to do.'
> (Source: Edwards, J. 1996, *Keating: The Inside Story*, Viking, Ringwood, Victoria, p. 250)

Some prime ministers use the device of an 'inner cabinet' sometimes called a 'kitchen cabinet'—that is, a meeting of a small group of influential ministers—to develop support for their policies.

> Whitlam's use of this strategy was called 'the Kirribilli Cabinet' because the group met at the prime minister's Sydney residence, Kirribilli House.

The main constraint on prime ministerial power is the need to maintain the support of powerful cabinet colleagues and their supporters within the parliamentary party. A prime minister who loses that support faces the political danger of being replaced. This is what happened to John Gorton and Bob Hawke. Electoral popularity and success is a critical factor in maintaining party support. A prime minister who is doing well in the polls is less likely to be challenged than one whose popularity is falling. Electoral unpopularity can also prove fatal for a leader of the Opposition, because parties want leaders who are likely to lead them to victory. Recent examples of this include the Labor Party's removal of Simon Crean, Mark Latham and Kim Beazley from the party leadership.

Election dates

Elections for the Commonwealth government can be called before the parliament has served its full term. The final decision in such instances rests with the prime minister, though he or she may consult with colleagues. There are two reasons for suggesting that this adds to the power of the office:

1. It is possible to call an election at the moment most favourable to the government, and a good result will add to the prime minister's stature and control of the party.
2. The prime minister can use the threat of an early election to quieten dissidents in the party, particularly those who do not enjoy a comfortable majority in their electorates.

This view of prime ministerial power can be qualified, partly because of Australian constitutional provisions and partly because of the importance of party support:

- Events in 1974 and 1975 have shown that a government can be forced to the polls by an Opposition that controls the Senate.
- Governors-general usually prefer that a government should have a reason, other than sheer electoral advantage, before an early election is granted. Sir Ninian Stephen insisted that his prime minister, Malcolm Fraser, place on paper his belief that the deadlocked bills were vital to his government's program before he would grant a double dissolution (and therefore an early election) in February 1983. However, prime ministers are ultimately likely to have their way.
- The prime minister cannot make a capricious decision, as an election campaign needs the support not only of ministers and backbenchers but of the party organisation and its supporting groups as well—and, of course, the electoral climate must be such that the government is likely to be re-elected. Sometimes a prime minister can make an error of judgement in going to the polls early, and lose seats instead of gaining from the initiative.

Despite these constraints, the initiative generally remains with the prime minister, and initiative is one of the most powerful of political forces.

> In 1984, Bob Hawke was persuaded by political pundits within the Labor Party to hold an election 18 months early. 'As the votes were counted on election night, Labor's federal politicians . . . watched in stunned disbelief as the landslide they expected evaporated . . . Hawke's majority was cut back to sixteen seats.'
> (*Source*: Wilkinson, M. 1996, *The Fixer*, Heinemann, Melbourne, p. 243)

The prime minister and the bureaucracy

For the first decade after Federation the prime minister also held a departmental portfolio, such as external affairs, and that department provided assistance in administration and liaison with other departments and governments. The Prime Minister's Department was established in 1911, but for many years it remained little more than a coordinating body, responsible among other things for the cabinet secretariat but having no specific policy functions or expertise. This meant that ministers could exert considerable influence if they made proper use of the special skills and knowledge of their departmental officers. There were two areas in which the prime minister could retain an obvious advantage:

- through responsibility for the Public Service Board (now abolished), which controlled many aspects of the staffing of departments; and
- through the resources of other departments, in cases where the prime minister held an additional portfolio. In more recent times, for example, Menzies and Whitlam briefly took responsibility for foreign affairs, while Chifley placed himself in the most central position of all by serving as his own treasurer. (He had been treasurer under the previous prime minister, Curtin.)

There have been three main motives for giving the prime minister's own department a wider policy role:

1. As government functions and the number of departments have grown, there has been a need for knowledge of the wide variety of programs being undertaken.
2. A second source of policy advice has made it easier to assess departmental proposals and set priorities, as well as adding to the prime minister's influence over cabinet.
3. Important initiatives, such as women's affairs, can be fostered by the prime minister.

A major step in enlarging the department's policy role was taken under Prime Minister Gorton, and that trend has continued. The Department of Prime Minister and Cabinet remains relatively small in staff numbers, but it contains a high proportion of senior officials able to assess the proposals of their counterparts in other departments. The department's encompassing role has altered relationships within both the ministry and the public service; this has led to criticism that it gives the prime minister powers that are not compatible with the Westminster system convention of collective responsibility.

> Prime Minister Kevin Rudd in 2008 expanded the Prime Minister's Department by setting up new specialist units: the Office of National Security, headed by a National Security Adviser; a Social Inclusion Unit; and an Office of Work and Family, to provide policy coordination and advise him on these issues.
> (*Source*: Norington, B. 2008, 'PM baulks at job cuts, expands staff', *The Australian*, 14 May 2008)

Personal staff

In addition to departmental officials, personal staff are attached to the prime minister's office. Until recent years these were relatively few in number and were usually seconded from the public service. Developments in media technology and rapid jet transport, which made the prime minister more immediately visible and accessible, increased the need for staff to advise on political developments, prepare press releases and arrange timetables. It became common practice to appoint people to carry out these tasks from outside the public service, usually with a party political background. The biggest single expansion of personal staff occurred following the election of the Whitlam government in 1972, and although there is no comparison between the staff numbers of an Australian prime minister and the hundreds who work for the US president, this was an obvious break with the past.

Typically, a prime minister's office includes:

- personal staff performing the role of private secretaries;
- a number of advisers and senior advisers responsible for significant policy areas such as international affairs, government, the economy, social policy and resources;
- a number of staff to deal with media issues, including a press secretary, media advisers and media assistants;
- program coordinators; and
- administrative staff, including an office manager and a number of personal secretaries.

Prime Minister John Howard strengthened his oversight of his cabinet by moving the Cabinet Policy Unit from the Department of Prime Minister and Cabinet to the prime minister's office. However, when he was leader of the Opposition, Kevin Rudd signalled his intention to move the unit back to the Department because of his belief, according to Paul Kelly, that there should be a delineation between the ministerial office and the public service (see Kelly, P. 2007, 'Rudd's mantra: service public, not political interests', *The Australian*, 3 October 2007).

There have been criticisms that the increase in the personal staff of the prime minister implies a move towards a 'presidential' style of government, particularly relating to those appointments which are made on the basis of political attachment. In 1981, Malcolm Fraser made it even clearer that the prime minister's office was to be set apart from the normal public service structure by appointing several academics as his personal advisers. One of these, political scientist Professor David Kemp, was apparently intended to emphasise the ideological content of the Liberal government's policy in a way that other advisers could not.

There could be political advantages in this strategy, but there are also costs:

- The line that distinguishes advisers employed by a political party from those paid by the government becomes increasingly hard to distinguish.

- Public servants and the party faithful may resent the apparent dominance of people whom they view as outsiders; they are believed to have undue influence because of their closeness to the prime minister.

DESIRABLE QUALITIES OF A PRIME MINISTER

The qualities thought desirable in a prime minister are likely to vary considerably with partisan loyalties and also with perceptions of the time in which each served. Sir Robert Menzies' reputation overcame the collapse of his first government in 1941, and rests on the prosperity that Australia experienced after his government came to office in 1949, during most of the 1950s and 1960s.

It is impossible to categorise Australian prime ministers in any useful way:

- Some were strong and clever, but ultimately had little success.
- Some were modest of background and manner, but are remembered as skilled and creative.
- Some served long political apprenticeships and yet seemed unfit for the office.
- Others built their success on public popularity and success with the media.

Nor is there a sensible catalogue of prime ministerial virtues:

- strong, but not dictatorial;
- patient, but not weak;
- someone looked up to, but not aloof; and
- a person the voter can identify with, but not just like the neighbours.

Attempts to list desirable qualities often end with these sorts of contradictions. This can lead to the unsatisfying conclusion that everything depends on the individual and the circumstances of the time.

> It is interesting to compare the recipe for success in maintaining political power in Machiavelli's classic treatise of 1513, The Prince, with political practice today. It is from this work that we get the term 'Machiavellian' to describe the political cunning and strategic concern with acquiring political power of modern political leaders. Consider this statement from Judith Brett and think about how it might fit with the Machiavellian 'model': 'For me one of the standout characteristics of the Howard period of government is Howard's understanding of political power and his determination to use it, and where possible to consolidate it.'
> (Source: Brett, J. 2006, 'Three Legacies of John Howard', address to the NSW Fabian Forum: John Howard: 10 Years On, 22 March 2006, http://www.fabian.org.au/1054.asp)

The *personal 'style'* that different prime ministers bring to the job can have an effect on the way particular governments operate.

- Gough Whitlam's mantra of 'the leader', as he was called by his staff, is indicative of the dominance of the Whitlam persona on the management of the Labor government between 1972 and 1975.
- Malcolm Fraser also dominated his government but in a more forceful way, controlling cabinet through his oversight of government policy as a whole and his skill in getting the numbers in cabinet to support him.

> 'He [Fraser] had not the slightest idea in the world of listening to an argument and then drawing the various points of view together. Not infrequently he would adjourn an issue on which he could not get his way to "enable us to get further advice" . . . On this occasion he took a vote. It was 8–6 against a ban. "Well," said the Prime Minister, "there is to be a ban . . . Yes, Prime Ministers do know how to count".'
>
> (*Source*: Former Fraser cabinet minister Jim Killen, in Killen, J. 1985, *Killen, Inside Australian Politics*, Methuen Haynes, Sydney, pp. 256–7)

- Bob Hawke favoured a consensus approach to decision-making and managed cabinet business in a more collegial manner.

> 'A Labor government is a rare breed of horse. You don't ride it by cracking the whip and jabbing your spurs into its flanks. You coax it, soothe it, talk to it, ease it along and point the way ahead.'
>
> (*Source*: Hawke, R.J.L. 1994, *The Hawke Memoirs*, Heinemann, Melbourne, p. 251, copyright Hon. Bob Hawke A.C.)

- Paul Keating was characterised as arrogant and forceful in driving cabinet in his preferred direction.

> 'Over the last year he [Keating] had had to drive the government from the Prime Minister's Office . . . Now he wanted to encourage ministers to do their own thing, so long as they had reached agreement with him and Cabinet on what "their own thing" was.'
>
> (*Source*: Edwards, J. 1996, *Keating: The Inside Story*, Penguin, Ringwood, Victoria, p. 514)

- John Howard, a less charismatic leader, nevertheless dominated his cabinet.

> Howard used the cabinet 'as an instrument of his authority, of ministerial consultation, obedience and unity'.
>
> (*Source*: Kelly, P. 2006, 'Re-thinking Australian Governance: The Howard Legacy', in *Australian Journal of Public Administration*, vol. 65, no. 1, p. 10)

The common factor associated with all these prime ministers is the fact that their leadership, and their influence on the direction of their governments, was accepted by their respective parties only so long as they were 'winners' or potential winners in the electoral stakes. The same is true of all party leaders, as we can see from the way in which the Labor Party has changed leaders in recent years.

- Whitlam lost the 1975 election, but stayed as leader. However, he was replaced by Bill Hayden after Labor failed to win in 1977.
- Hayden was replaced by Bob Hawke only one month before the 1983 election, because Hawke was considered more likely to win.

- Hawke, as prime minister, was dumped by Labor in 1991 in favour of Paul Keating, who went on to win the 1993 'unwinnable' election.
- Labor lost in 1996 and Keating resigned the Labor leadership. He was replaced by Kim Beazley, whose success in winning back 18 seats for Labor in 1998 secured his position as leader of the Opposition for a further term; however, he resigned following his failure to win in 2001.
- Beazley was replaced by Simon Crean, but he was seen to be electorally unpopular and was replaced by Mark Latham.
- Latham did not win the 2004 election and was replaced by Beazley as leader in January 2005.
- Under Beazley's leadership Labor performed poorly in the polls, so in December 2006 he was replaced by Kevin Rudd.

Liberal leaders have had similar experiences. Fraser's resignation after he lost government in 1983 was followed by a revolving-door Liberal leadership of the Opposition between Andrew Peacock and John Howard as their electoral popularity waxed and waned. After John Hewson lost the Liberals the 'unlosable' election of 1993, he was replaced by Alexander Downer and then John Howard, whose victory in 1996 secured him the prime ministership. The loss of a number of seats in 1998 fuelled speculation about his future, but his wins in 2001 and 2004 reaffirmed his tenure as prime minister. Howard's run of success came to an abrupt end in November 2007 when the Coalition lost the election. Howard lost his seat in parliament—the first prime minister to lose his seat at an election since Stanley Bruce in 1929.

It is clear from these experiences that prime ministerial power is tenuous, and the performance of the prime minister is consistently under scrutiny from the media, the electorate and his/her parliamentary colleagues. There is a saying that 'a week is a long time in politics'. Ex-prime ministers on the outside of parliament would agree.

Strong leadership and an ability to manage government to the best advantage of the party would be categorised as essential characteristics for any successful prime minister. In this sense, a Machiavellian approach could be regarded as central to the acquisition and maintenance of power.

The debate on desirable qualities may have approached the question from the wrong direction. Perhaps it is not so much what a person makes of the prime minister's office, but rather what the office makes of the incumbent. It can be argued that the prime minister is so powerful, yet so vulnerable, that the position is like no other in the land and so is not one that a person can learn or be trained to fill. No prime minister wishes to train successors lest they turn into usurpers. The status, authority and resources of the office are there for each prime minister to use afresh. Attempts to emulate predecessors or to avoid their mistakes may be misguided, as conditions change and may render precedents worthless. That is one of the reasons why the prime minister will attract increasing attention—that, and the fact that every person in the country, certainly every politician, at one time or another believes that he or she could do a better job.

QUESTIONS FOR DISCUSSION

1. How significant are the conventions of the Constitution to the operations of executive government in Australia?
2. It has been argued that the prime minister in Australia is becoming increasingly presidential. What are the reasons for this? What are the constraints on prime ministerial power?
3. Personality and 'style' are significant factors in determining how successful a particular prime minister will be. Is this a valid statement?
4. How well do you think the operations of the cabinet and the role of the prime minister fit with principles of representative and responsible democracy?
5. Why are the Westminster conventions of individual ministerial responsibility and collective responsibility still significant to the operations of government in Australia?
6. The conventions of cabinet and prime ministerial government are not to be found in the constitution. Should they be?

FURTHER READING

Anderson, G. 2006, 'Executive Government', in Parkin, A., Summers, J. & Woodward, D. (eds), *Government, Politics, Power and Policy in Australia*, 8th ed., Pearson Education, Sydney. This chapter provides an introductory discussion of executive government in Australia.

Keating, M. & Weller, P. 2000, 'Cabinet Government: An Institution under Pressure', in Keating, M., Wanna, J. & Weller, P. (eds), *Institutions on the Edge? Capacity for Governance*, Allen & Unwin, Sydney. This is a particularly good discussion of the operation of cabinet and the role of the prime minister.

Kelly, P. 2006, 'Re-thinking Australian Governance: The Howard Legacy, *Australian Journal of Public Administration*, vol. 65, no. 1, pp. 7–24. This article provides an extensive discussion of the relationships between the former prime minister, his cabinet and the bureaucracy.

Machiavelli, N. 1513, *The Prince*, any edition.

Singleton, G. 2005, 'Issues and Agendas: Howard in Control', in Aulich, C. & Wetterhall, R. (eds), *Howard's Second and Third Government: Australian Commonwealth Administration, 1998–2004*, UNSW Press, Sydney. This chapter examines the way Prime Minister Howard dominated his government.

Solomon, D. 2007, *Pillars of Power*, The Federation Press, Sydney. See Chapter 1, 'Government and Parliament', for a discussion of the power of the prime minister and the relationship between the prime minister and cabinet.

Uhr, J. 2002, 'Political Leadership and Rhetoric', in Brennan, H.G. & Castles, F.G. (eds), *Australia Reshaped*, Cambridge University Press, Melbourne. This chapter includes an interesting examination of prime ministerial power from the perspective of 'speechcraft' and conventions of political leadership associated with the Australian Constitution.

Walter, J. 2006, 'Ministerial Staff and the "Lattice of Leadership"', Discussion Paper 13/06 (April 2006), Democratic Audit of Australia, Canberra, http://arts.anu.edu.au/democraticaudit/papers/20060424_walter_min_staff.pdf.

Weller, P. 1989, *Malcolm Fraser PM: A Study in Prime Ministerial Power*, Penguin, Ringwood, Victoria. An insightful examination of the role of the prime minister and constraints of prime ministerial power written in the context of Prime Minister Fraser's approach to government.

Weller, P. 2007, *Cabinet Government in Australia, 1901–2006*, UNSW Press, Sydney. An authoritative discussion of the development of cabinet government.

Weller, P. (ed.) 1992, *From Menzies to Keating: The Development of the Australian Prime Ministership*, Melbourne University Press, Melbourne. A collection of essays that examines the prime minister's role by exploring the relationship of former prime ministers with cabinet, the party, parliament, the bureaucracy, the electorate and the media, and in the international setting.

USEFUL WEBSITES

http://www.pmc.gov.au
Department of Prime Minister and Cabinet
You can find information about the operations of the department on this site, as well as the procedures and guidelines relating to cabinet and the Federal Executive Council.

http://www.pm.gov.au
Prime Minister of Australia
The prime minister's website.

7

THE PUBLIC SERVICE

THIS CHAPTER EXPLAINS:

- public administration and bureaucracy;
- the origins of modern bureaucracy;
- different systems of bureaucracy in modern states;
- the development of bureaucracy in Australia;
- the structure and organisation of the Australian Public Service;
- staffing and financing the Australian Public Service;
- policy and administration;
- the policy process;
- accountability and administrative review; and
- non-departmental organisations.

PUBLIC ADMINISTRATION AND BUREAUCRACY

> 'Whether the public service consists of civilian, police, or military bureaucrats their task is to assist in the development and implementation of the country's public policies. In composite these individuals are called the **public administration** of their country, and they constitute what is often referred to as the bureaucracy.'
> (*Source:* Jackson R.J. & Jackson, D. 1997, *Comparative Government: An Introduction to Political Science*, 2nd ed., Prentice Hall/Allyn & Bacon, Toronto, p. 295)

As citizens we often complain about the irritations associated with dealing with the bureaucracy, whether having to fill out forms or trying to make sense of the complex rules that have to be complied with to obtain a government-provided benefit. Some of you will work in the business sector and find yourselves having to deal with the bureaucracy in some way on a regular basis, such as finding your way through the intricacies and mysteries of the industrial relations and tax systems, or seeking assistance to market a product overseas. Some students will find employment with an interest group whose function is to lobby government departments and ministers for some form of direct government benefit. Others may make a career working within the bureaucracy as a public servant administering government laws and regulations, or providing policy advice through the department to a minister. In any of these situations, you will need to be aware of the role of the bureaucracy and its significance to our system of government.

> 'Bureaucracy thus represents a dilemma for democracy. There is on the one hand the threat of a powerful bureaucracy that will exempt itself from political control and thereby from democratic accountability. There is on the other hand the necessity for a powerful bureaucracy that will exempt itself from political control in order to prevent the disruption of the political process itself.'
> (*Source:* Etzioni-Halevy, E. 1983, *Bureaucracy and Democracy: A Political Dilemma*, Routledge & Kegan Paul, London, p. 87)

To citizens or employees, the bureaucracy is often seen to be a powerful institution and, as the above quote from Etzioni-Halevy suggests, this can create a dilemma for a democratic system. Who has the political power? Who is pulling the strings in the policy-making process—the minister, or the public servants who provide the advice and implement the policies? A bureaucracy that develops a power base independent of the political executive and parliament does not sit comfortably with the principles that underpin Australia's system of liberal democracy.

> 'Politically bureaucracy is rule by officials and stands in direct opposition to rule by the people through their elected representatives.'
> (*Source:* Smith, B.C. 1988, *Bureaucracy and Political Power*, Wheatsheaf Books, Brighton, UK, p. 25)

How does the Australian system of government deal with this democratic dilemma? As we saw in the previous chapter, the Australian bureaucratic system functions within a framework that is consistent with the conventions of the Westminster system of responsible government: departments are responsible to ministers, who are in turn responsible to parliament. In this chapter, we will look at how this works in practice by examining the meaning of bureaucracy and bureaucratic procedures, and compare how they operate in a number of countries. We will then look at the operations of the Australian Public Service.

Why we need a bureaucracy

A society that establishes institutions intended to represent its people and decide on issues affecting them also requires machinery for putting those decisions into effect: to collect taxes, regulate conduct and provide services. This administrative machinery is known in Australia as the *public service*. (In the United Kingdom, the United States, Germany and Malaysia, it is called the *civil service*.) Two important distinctions, however, must be made:

1. Just as Australia has six state and two territory governments, and one at the federal level, so it has nine sets of administrative machinery, whose functions are determined ultimately by the same kinds of constitutional provisions that apply to their respective governments (see Chapter 3). The functions of the administrative machinery of local government are determined by state governments.
2. Each of the nine sets of public administrations comprises departments that are responsible directly to ministers, and a range of statutory bodies with varying degrees of autonomy.

> The term **public service** applies to ministerial departments and agencies and their employees funded through the budget.

> The term **public sector** is employed in a wider sense to describe all government agencies and activities, as distinct from the private sector, which—as the term implies—relates to privately owned business and activities.

Owing partly to the complexity of the administrative machinery, it is common to link the various agencies together and describe them as the '*bureaucracy*', although that practice raises difficulties that are discussed below.

The meaning of 'bureaucracy'

The term *bureaucracy* can be used in a variety of ways. The word itself comes most recently from the French *bureau*—a desk, usually containing drawers, for writing and dealing with papers. It also includes the notion of 'rule' from the Greek *kratos*.

> **Bureaucracy**: an organisation; a method of doing things; or even a style of life.

Some people think it would be preferable not to have a bureaucracy at all, believing that it is better to have a decentralised society in which authority is exercised exclusively by small groups, each of which decides its own affairs and its attitudes towards its neighbours. Such an arrangement is not possible in a modern industrialised society, despite the trend by many governments around the world to reduce the role of bureaucracy by moving functions previously performed by the public sector into the private sector. Even those governments employ a core bureaucracy to assist with policy advice and implementation of those policy functions retained by governments, such as defence, social welfare services, and management of the national economy. The regulation of private-sector activity in the public interest, such as environmental or safety issues, is another aspect of government policy that requires a bureaucracy for its implementation.

The fact is that bureaucracy characterises almost every attempt at large-scale public- or private-sector organisation. When it becomes necessary to deal with a number of people, or to make plans involving several factors, there is usually a desire to do things systematically, to establish order and routine in whatever is being organised.

> '**Bureaucracy** is defined as a hierarchical organization of officials appointed to carry out certain public objectives.'
> (*Source*: Etzioni-Halevy, E. 1983, *Bureaucracy and Democracy: A Political Dilemma*, Routledge & Kegan Paul, London, p. 85)

It can be argued:

- that such efforts reflect the wish of certain people to exercise authority over others, or to interfere in their affairs; or
- that systematic organisation can also involve a concern for the public: an attempt to ensure equity by establishing priorities, entitlements and obligations that apply to everyone.

The main requirement of an effective government bureaucracy is that it should strike a balance between concern and interference. There are different ideas about how this can be done. There are arguments that government bureaucracies become impersonal, unresponsive, rule-bound, and inefficient in delivering the benefits and services they are required to provide.

> 'On the one hand, bureaucracy is characterized as a leviathan, a monolithic and virtually uncontrollable force eating away at personal liberties and economic resources. On the other hand, bureaucracy is a fool: a fragmented set of individuals so bound with red tape and rule books that they don't know what they are about at any one time, sending television sets to people who lack electricity and doing research on the optimal shape of toilet seats.'
> (*Source*: Peters, B.G. 1989, *The Politics of Bureaucracy*, 3rd ed., Longman, New York, p. 251)

It is also thought that much of what government does can be delivered more efficiently and more cheaply by the private sector. Those governments that support this view, including recent Australian federal governments, have contracted out to the private sector the services and functions previously supplied by the public service.

Privatisation and contracting out

> Unemployment placement services previously supplied by the Commonwealth Employment Service have been **contracted out** to private agencies.

Privatisation has been another method of transferring services previously provided by the government to the private sector.

> '**Privatisation** refers to an array of ways in which there are substitutions for government-owned, -funded and -provided services by non-government agencies and private funding mechanisms.'
> (*Source*: Aulich, C. 2005, 'Privatisation and Outsourcing', in Aulich, C. & Wettenhall, R. (eds), *Howard's Second and Third Governments*, UNSW Press, Sydney, p. 60)

Privatisation has been undertaken in most of the countries in our study.

Britain
A major program of privatisation was begun by the Thatcher government in the 1980s and continued with the Blair government. The sell-off included government shares in British Petroleum (BP), British Aerospace, National Freight Company, Cable & Wireless, Amersham International (radiochemicals), Britoil, Associated British Ports, Enterprise Oil, Jaguar cars, British Telecom, British Gas, British Airways, Rolls-Royce, British Airports Authority (BAA), British Steel, regional water companies, British Rail, electricity distribution companies, and National Air Traffic Services (NATS).

Australia
Since the 1990s successive federal governments have privatised a number of Commonwealth-owned entities, such as Aerospace Technologies of Australia, the Australian Industry Development Corporation (AIDC), AUSSAT (satellites), Australian Airlines, Australian National (railway), Australian National Line (shipping), airports, the Commonwealth Serum Laboratories, the Commonwealth Bank and Qantas, and made progressive sell-offs of Telstra (telecommunications).

United States
There has not been the same emphasis on privatisation in the United States because there has not been the same extent of public ownership, with most services historically being provided by private enterprise. The telecommunications industry, for example, which has been the focus of privatisation in many other countries, has been historically under private ownership. Amtrak, the federally-owned rail corporation, remains a government corporation.

Federal Republic of Germany
Privatisation in Germany, like the other countries in our study, has been government policy since the 1980s, particularly under the conservative–liberal alliance government. Since then the federal government has sold off its shares in Volkswagen, VEBA (energy and chemicals), Lufthansa (airline), the postal service and Deutsche Telekom AG. The partial privatisation of the national railway system, German Rail (the largest state-owned enterprise in Germany), is

under consideration. The federal government also engaged in a massive sell-off of enterprises owned by the former communist East German government following the re-unification of Germany in 1990.

Federation of Malaysia

Since 1983, the federal government of Malaysia has undertaken a significant sell-off of state-owned enterprises. The Malaysian Privatisation Master Plan, produced by former prime minister Mahathir in 1991, set out the objectives and guidelines under which privatisation was to take place. By 2003, the number of federal and state government-owned enterprises had fallen from around 1,100 to 474 across many sectors of government activity and included Malaysian Airlines, postal and telecommunications services, highways, and passenger railway services (see Economic Planning Unit, Prime Minister's Department, Malaysia 2008, 'History of Privatization Programme', http://www.epu.jpm.my).

The opponents of privatisation argue that services provided solely on the basis of profit and price competition cannot meet the equity needs of the community. Governments make their own judgements about what is an appropriate balance between the two. The electorate will let them know at the ballot box if they get it wrong.

Bureaucracy in the public sector

Bureaucratic procedures are adopted not only in government but also in all forms of large-scale organisation in modern society. This will be apparent to anyone who has been employed in a private corporation, or has applied for credit from a bank or finance company. Yet it is the public, rather than the private bureaucracy, that is most often accused of an overemphasis on files and organisational procedures, commonly known as 'red tape'.

> **'Red tape'** is a term used to describe bureaucratic procedures that are considered to be onerous and a burden to citizens in their dealings with government agencies. The term derives from the practice whereby the public service tied its paper files together with red tape.

There has been a long debate, which cannot be resolved completely, about the differences and similarities between public and private organisations. However, there are four main factors that affect the community's attitude towards public bureaucracy, as follows.

Monopoly position

Someone who wants to have a tap repaired engages a plumber, and can engage another if the first proves unsatisfactory. A poor job will not cause a person to condemn all plumbers, far less all tradespeople. By contrast, public services tend to provide a service for which there is no alternative source of supply. Many clients cannot go elsewhere.

Conflicting demands

People who buy home appliances all expect much the same functions from them. However, certain groups will expect a Department of Planning to aid industrial development, while others will demand virtually the opposite—that the department has environmental protection as its first priority.

Defining objectives

It is relatively easy to measure the success of a private corporation based on increases in sales and profits. Assessing the effectiveness of the Department of Prime Minister and Cabinet is a very different matter. Even so, as we shall see later in this chapter, Australian Public Service agencies from the 1990s adopted a private-sector approach to defining their objectives through a mission statement, corporate plan and performance indicators related to outcomes, against which they measure their achievements.

Accountability

The private sector has been increasingly regulated over the years, and corporations are accountable in certain senses to their shareholders and to stock exchanges. Public service accountability extends further, mainly because the government as a whole is ultimately answerable to the whole electorate. Two main aspects affect the public's perception of their bureaucracy:

1. There should be a record of every action taken and every dollar that is spent, so that the minister can answer to parliament if necessary. Consequently, there is an accumulation of a vast amount of records on computer or on paper—files, forms, minutes of meetings, email correspondence, computer printouts—all of which contribute to the 'red tape' image.
2. Every part of the public service is responsible to, or must coordinate with, some other part. It often takes time to ensure that an agreed course can be justified to the public, and this tends to give an impression of 'buck-passing'.

The public service, being answerable both to the ministry and to the community at large, is in a complex and difficult position. For example, government pressure to perform according to market principles, and cuts in government funding for the public sector, resulted in reductions of staff and closure of some regional offices. This caused citizens to complain about difficulties in accessing government services, particularly in rural areas. It must be remembered, however, that the public service, in moving in this direction, has been acting in accordance with government policy. Therefore, the responsibility for determining the manner in which the public service responds to these conflicting pressures lies with the government of the day. That is where 'the buck stops', according to the principles of ministerial responsibility.

It is fair to say that community attitudes towards the public service are not always negative, because some citizens have positive experiences in dealing with individual agencies.

THE ORIGINS OF MODERN BUREAUCRACY

Public bureaucracy on the 'British' pattern has evolved to its present form over something longer than a century, to some degree in parallel with the development of popularly elected government. When political power was shared among just a few powerful people, administrative responsibilities were allotted to people whose loyalty was assured, because they:

- shared the values of the ruling elite; and
- depended on the ruling elite for their jobs.

This has been termed the *patronage system*: administrative appointments were based on networks of influence and produced reciprocal favours. One aspect of this arrangement was *nepotism*, in which various offices were distributed among the families of those in power. The positions were not necessarily gifts: some were sold, with the purchaser securing the profit on the charges made for the services of the office, such as the issue of licences to the public.

The ancient patronage system need not be condemned out of hand, if only because:

- it could make officials highly sensitive to the wishes of the government of the day; and
- few people outside a small, privileged circle possessed the knowledge and experience required for government service.

However, the system had some major and obvious failings, in addition to its being wholly inequitable:

- Powerful connections were no guarantee of wisdom and skill, so that many officials were incompetent; and even when they used their profits to engage educated agents, the employees often cheated both their masters and the public.
- When governments changed, so did most senior officials, and such expertise as they might have gained was lost to the incoming ministers.
- Regular changes of administrative control led to discontinuity and confusion on policy.
- Sale of offices meant that those who could pay most received the greatest attention. Owing to resultant inequitable dealing, the people resented governments; additionally, the financial returns to government were much smaller than they could have been.

Reforming the patronage system

British governments introduced minor administrative changes, but by the middle of the 19th century it was obvious, from such experiences as corruption in India and the disasters of the Crimean War, that totally new principles involved almost a complete reversal of the practices that had governed both domestic and colonial administration up to that time: and they are best understood in that light. The main reforms involved the following principles.

Open entry

Civil servants would be recruited following public examinations to determine ability. In essence, this meant that entry would depend on the amount a candidate knew, rather than on whom the candidate knew. It was intended to end patronage appointments.

Promotion on merit

This was related to the first reform's attack on patronage, but it also meant that a civil servant should earn a higher appointment through demonstrated ability rather than by spending many years in a job. This change was meant to preclude promotion on seniority alone.

Tenure

Open entry and promotion on merit would do little to end patronage and promote efficiency if civil servants could still be dismissed with a change of government, or if they displeased an incumbent politician. Appointments would therefore have to be for the whole of the civil servant's career, to be terminated only after manifest misconduct or incompetence.

Neutrality

In return for tenured appointment, the civil servant would have to be politically neutral, in the sense of serving all governments with equal dedication, regardless of their political complexion.

Anonymity

In return for the civil servant's neutrality, the government of the day would have to accept the public's criticism (or possible praise) of actions, no matter what the involvement of the civil service in recommending or opposing them. (Consider this convention in relation to individual ministerial responsibility—see Chapter 6.)

Classification

As a further barrier to patronage, and to promote equal standards of service to the public, civil servants would be graded according to their levels of responsibility and paid accordingly. That is, all officials performing similar work were to be paid the same salary; there were to be no bonus payments or perquisites for favoured employees, and paid work outside the service was generally prohibited.

By the time the public bureaucracies began their great expansion in the early decades of the 20th century, the reform principles had become the orthodoxy of all services based on the British pattern, including those of the Australian Commonwealth and states.

BUREAUCRACY IN THE MODERN STATE

The examples below indicate the extent to which these elements still inform the practices of modern public service employment arrangements. There are, however, significant departures from these principles: for example, the introduction of performance-based pay rewards for individual public servants, based on productivity and good performance, rather than each person at a particular classification level being paid at the same rate. Permanency has also been replaced in some jurisdictions by fixed-contract employment, and some government departments have the capacity to dismiss employees when their positions become redundant.

There is an argument that the use of contract positions, particularly at senior levels, has re-introduced an element of politicisation into public service employment. While not as invidious as the old patronage system, it still weakens the principle of a neutral public service giving free and fearless advice to all governments regardless of their political persuasion. Of course, the concept of politicisation is entrenched in the United States federal public service by the system of presidential appointments, even though they have to be confirmed by the Senate. Most public servants also operate within the framework of a code of ethics, or something similar.

Britain

The British civil service operates with a policy of open-entry recruitment based on merit, although some appointments can be made on other grounds. (For details, see the Civil Service Commissioners' Recruitment Code, http://www.civilservicecommissioners.org/Recruitment.) There is an accelerated development program for graduates designed to prepare them for senior managerial positions called the 'Fast Stream' (see http://www.faststream.gov.uk). Departments are responsible for their own recruitment according to their employment needs.

Although the civil service still operates notionally as a career service, permanence of tenure has been weakened by the fact that senior civil service posts (the *senior executive service*) and agency heads are now contract positions with appointment for a limited term. The concept of a career public service with promotion based on seniority within the system has also been challenged by open competition for positions from inside and outside the service. The potential for politicisation, or patronage, in contract positions is constrained by the oversight of the Commissioner for Public Appointments and the Civil Service Commission, who ensure that appointees are properly qualified for their positions. However, ministerial advisers are political appointments made to serve a particular minister.

Performance-based pay has modified the traditional classification basis of employment, where all employees at a certain grade were paid the same salary.

Under the Civil Service Code, public servants are required to owe their allegiance to the government of the day, and carry out their duties impartially, with honesty and according to the law (see Forman, F.N. & Baldwin, N.D.J. 2007, *Mastering British Politics*, 5th ed., Palgrave Macmillan, Basingstoke, UK, p. 332).

> 'The Civil Service has strengths that are priceless. The greatest is indeed its integrity. That comprises not just its impartiality, but an ingrained pervasive streak of honesty. It knows the difference between obeying legitimate political orders and impropriety. It knows it by instinct and it executes it without fear or favour. It sees its role as serving the Government of the day to the best of its ability, whatever colour the Government's politics. The transition to New Labour after 18 years of Conservative Government was achieved with remarkable ease.'
>
> 'Promotion in the Civil Service increasingly needs to reward delivering results on the ground. Already this is beginning to happen. The challenge now is to apply this approach at every level of the service, with results and outcomes paramount.'
>
> (Source: Former British prime minister Tony Blair, keynote speech on reforming the civil service, 24 February 2004, http://www.number10.gov.uk/output/Page5399.asp)

United States

The civil service of the United States federal administration has three different elements: the competitive service, the excepted service and the senior executive service.

The *competitive service* covers most civil service positions. It is a career service that operates on the basis of merit-based, open-entry recruitment with permanent tenure and performance-based payments. It has an across-the-service classification structure with a number of salary grades, and is overseen by the Office of Personnel Management, within which appointments are made.

The *excepted service* comprises appointments made on the basis of agency-specific requirements and procedures. They are not subject to the pay and conditions prescribed for the competitive service, and are not career positions. These positions occur mostly in the legislative and judicial branches of the federal administration, and within agencies such as the FBI.

The *senior executive service* includes executive and managerial positions which do not require appointment by the president and Senate confirmation. These positions can be filled by permanent career and non-career officers, or non-renewable, limited-term appointees. The senior executive service also operates under a performance-based pay system. Other senior management positions and agency heads are appointed by the president, with confirmation required by the Senate.

> 'An employee's career (and pay) potential should recognize achievement and not be determined by the passage of time or obsolete job classifications . . . enhancements to the personnel system must be made within the context of the core values, [merit] principles, and protections of the American civil service.'
>
> (*Source*: Linda M. Springer, director of the Office of Personnel Management, statement before the Subcommittee on the Federal Workforce and Agency Organisation Committee on Government Reform, 5 October 2005, http://www.opm.gov/News_events/Congress/Testimony/109thCongress/10_05_2005.asp)

The Office of Government Ethics oversees the ethical standards of government employees relating to issues of conflict of interest (http://ww.usoge.gov), and Title 5 of the United States Code sets out the core principles for civil service employees.

Federal Republic of Germany

Employment in the career civil service of Germany (*Beamte*) is permanent, with lifelong tenure. Each department is responsible for its own recruitment, and appointment is merit-based, with open competitive entry linked to formal qualifications. Article 33(2) of the Basic Law provides that 'Every German shall be equally eligible for any public office according to his aptitude, qualifications and professional achievements'. Some civil servants are employed for a limited time to perform a particular function. There are also a small number of political appointments, including permanent state secretaries, under-secretaries of state, and senior civil servants in the Foreign Office and the security services.

The service has four classification levels. Advancement no longer depends on seniority, but on individual performance rewarded through a performance-based pay system (see United Nations Department of Economic and Social Affairs (DESA) 2006, 'Federal Republic of Germany: Public Administration Country Profile', United Nations, Geneva, http://unpan1.un.org/intradoc/groups/public/documents/un/unpan023309.pdf). There is no senior executive service such as those used in Britain, the United States or Australia. According to Article 33(5) of the Basic Law, 'The law governing the public service shall be regulated with due regard to the traditional principles of the professional civil service.' (Follow the links to 'Basic Law' from http://www.bundestag.de/htdocs_e/parliament/function/legal to see the full text.) These 'traditional principles' are not spelled out in the Basic Law and there is no separate code of ethics for Germany's career civil servants. However, the general principles that civil service employees must follow are set out by statute and include:

- to exercise their office impartially and justly, not seeking their own advantage, in line with the common good and loyalty;
- to serve unreservedly and at any time;
- to not go on strike;
- to advise and obey;
- to be employed in a lifetime tenure;
- to have their employer fulfil the duty to take care of its civil servants and their families; and
- to receive suitable payment and pension provision according to rank.

(*Source*: United Nations Department of Economic and Social Affairs (DESA) 2006, 'Federal Republic of Germany: Public Administration Country Profile', United Nations, Geneva, http://unpan1.un.org/intradoc/groups/public/documents/un/unpan023309.pdf)

Federation of Malaysia

Appointment to the federal public service of Malaysia is by merit-based, open-entry recruitment. It is significant to note, however, the ethnic basis to recruitment, in which preferment is given to the Malay population. As at June 2005, 77.03 per cent of the Malaysian Civil Service was made up of ethnic Malays (see Centre for Public Policy Studies (CPPS) n.d., 'Towards a More Representative and World-Class Civil Service in Malaysia', CPPS, Kuala Lumpur, http://www.cpps.org.my/downloads/(CC)_Malaysian_Civil_Service1.pdf).

Civil servants have security of tenure. Their employment is defined by a classification system, and annual progression is determined on performance. The senior public service (the *administrative and diplomatic service*) is staffed by career civil servants who advance to this level by promotion and hold all the top positions in most departments. It has been standard practice that selection to this elite level is by merit and that appointments to senior positions are made on the basis of recommendations by the Public Service Commission to the minister. Ministers now have the option to decide whether they want a certain person to be head of their department, and these appointments are confirmed only with their agreement (see Hai, L.H., Haidar, A. & Pullin, L. 2004, 'Employment Relationship and Politicisation: View of Malaysian Civil Servants Working in Penang', *Employment Relations Record*, 1 January 2004, http://findarticles.com/ p/articles/mi_m5AZS/ is_1_4/ai _ n25102459).

The civil service operates under a code of conduct underpinned by a set of values that include the value of time, the success of perseverance, the pleasure of working, the dignity of simplicity, the worth of character, the power of kindness, the influence of examples, the obligation of duty, the wisdom of economy, the virtue of patience and the improvement of talent. Emphasis is also placed on Islamic values such as trustworthiness, responsibility, sincerity, dedication, moderation, diligence, cleanliness, discipline and cooperation.

(*Source*: Siddiquee, N.A. 2007, 'Public Service Innovations, Policy Transfer and Governance in the Asia-Pacific Region: The Malaysian Experience', *Journal of Administration & Governance*, vol. 2, no. 1, p. 85)

All civil servants are required to sign a 'letter of undertaking' with the following commitments:

1. not to subordinate their public duties to their private interest;
2. not to conduct themselves in a manner likely to bring their private interests into conflict with their public duties;
3. not to conduct themselves in a manner likely to bring the public service into disrepute or to bring it discredit; and
4. not to be insubordinate or conduct themselves in such a manner as is likely to be construed as being subordinate.

(*Source*: OECD Anti-Corruption Division 2004, 'Anti-Corruption Action Plan for Asia and the Pacific, Implementation Projects 2002–2003: Malaysia', OECD, Paris, http:// www1.oecd.org/ daf/ ASIAcom/AP/Malaysia.htm).

Violations of this code include:

- abetting the country's enemies;
- leaking government secrets;
- belittling government policies and actions;
- misusing government vehicles;
- doing personal/family business during working hours;
- going on leave when services are badly needed;
- not reporting offences committed by subordinates;
- getting into heavy debt;
- deliberately delaying the issuance of licences; and
- verbally abusing those seeking counter services.

These examples highlight the similar elements of public administration in modern states, as well as the differences that have developed based on constitutional arrangements (such as in the United States and Germany), the culture of the Westminster tradition (that informs Britain and Malaysia), and local cultural influences (such as those that inform the practices of the public service in Malaysia). The Westminster tradition is also a defining element of the Australian system, as we shall see below.

THE DEVELOPMENT OF PUBLIC ADMINISTRATION AND BUREAUCRACY IN AUSTRALIA

It was only in the last years of the 19th century that the Australian colonies moved successfully to abolish patronage in their public services, and by that time their social circumstances and political demands differed from those in England. Two features were of particular significance—the kinds of administrative staff employed in each country, and the tasks that the different services undertook.

Sources of administrative staff

England

It was accepted that the country was best governed by those of broad education, who were thought to have the capacity to adapt themselves to a wide range of duties. For many years they were drawn from privileged backgrounds, via the ancient universities of Oxford and Cambridge. They filled senior offices, which required them to deal with other people of influence and 'culture', at the same time showing a concern for the general welfare. This was an obviously elitist system, with roots deep in English history and upper-class society; indeed, senior civil servants were recruited to the administrative class.

Australia

There was no group obviously ready to form an administrative elite and no network of universities to produce one. Moreover, the country had been developing an egalitarian ethos, and it was in keeping with that ethos that public servants should be required to join at an early age and gain experience as they worked their way to senior positions.

Tasks of bureaucracy

England

The British civil service evolved during a period when the country, and its empire, seemed paramount in the world. Civil servants worked equally well with liberal and conservative governments in overseeing what appeared to be a dynamic, effective system. In doing so they established a reputation as neutral agents capable of administering almost anything. It was only later, when the inequalities of English society proved difficult to remedy, that there was a searching reassessment of the assumptions on which the elitist civil service was based.

Australia

Modern Australia began as a gaol and for more than 60 years was controlled by officials appointed by the British government under the directorship of a governor. Much of the early exploration, settlement and building was carried out on official initiative, and although there was often tension between settlers and government, most people came to rely on authority for guidance, particularly in difficult circumstances. The factors that accounted for this situation included:

- a harsh environment, long distances and sparse population, which meant that services had to be spread over a very wide area;
- a shortage of private capital to undertake projects, many of which involved considerable risk; and
- the concentration of population in a few widely separated cities, which attracted a disproportionate share of available resources and made coordination difficult.

There was from the outset a feeling that one of the main purposes of government was to assist industry and commerce to 'develop' the country. This included the provision of basic works and services, such as roads and harbours, the establishment of medical and social welfare services, and assistance with the growing and marketing of produce.

There were many problems and disputes over priorities, and these helped to produce in the community a deep cynicism about both politicians and bureaucrats. There were two main consequences:

1. Public services tended to be controlled by specialists in their fields of development, and not by 'general' administrators on the British pattern.
2. Even then, governments found it easier to settle contentious matters by establishing semi-autonomous bodies that represented producers and other groups. This procedure removed disputes from the parliamentary arena and reduced political pressure on governments.

Australian public services reflected the environment and needs of the country. Administration was not regarded as a profession but as something that involved the techniques of economic development and the provision of basic services. Until the 1940s the state bureaucracies were dominated, at least in numbers, by teachers and health workers, while some three-quarters of the Commonwealth service comprised employees of the Postmaster-General's Department, responsible for posts and telegraphs.

Crises during this period affected the public services without changing their framework: the First World War saw the Commonwealth service begin its first major expansion, but the Depression of the 1930s brought some reductions in staff levels and even in salaries under the provisions of the Premiers' Plan, which aimed to cut government spending. Innovation during the inter-war years was further limited because the public services accepted many returned servicemen with less than the usual educational qualifications. They did not necessarily make inferior public servants, but there were scarcely any provisions for training them effectively and for many years they reduced the opportunities for younger employees.

Public service expansion

Despite the significant development of government activity in the provision of services, the public services remained relatively small.

- In 1904 the NSW Public Service employed some 13,000 people in seven departments, but almost half that number worked in schools.
- In the same year, the infant Commonwealth public service possessed seven departments, but 10,000 of its 12,000 employees worked in the postal service. The Commonwealth Treasury, by contrast, had a staff of 41 permanent officers.

The extent of public service expansion since then is evident when we compare these figures with today's public service employment:

- In June 2006 the NSW Public Service had approximately 300,000 full-time staff.
- In June 2007 there were 143,525 ongoing employees in the Australian Public Service.

The most dramatic expansion of the Australian bureaucracy, particularly at the Commonwealth level, occurred during and after the Second World War. It was caused partly by the size of the war effort and the national mobilisation involved, and partly by a set of closely related factors:

- The shock of Australia's vulnerability led to the feeling that the country would have to do more for itself in defence, foreign relations, trade and manufacturing.
- The assumptions of Keynesian economics and of the importance of full employment became widely accepted by politicians and public servants.
- The Labor government of the period wanted to improve social services.
- There was a need to plan and to provide for postwar reconstruction.
- The war caused the recruitment, usually on a temporary basis, of numerous experts from universities, industry and the professions. These people not only drafted new policies, but brought with them a willingness to innovate and to challenge accepted practices. Their influence waned as orthodox bureaucrats reasserted themselves in the postwar period, but the wartime experience ensured that future governments would recognise the need for higher levels of education, in-service training, planning and coordination within the public service.

The result was an emphasis on professionalism in administration, through the introduction of new techniques, the recruitment of university graduates—especially after the report of the Boyer Committee on Public Service Recruitment in the mid-1950s—and much greater encouragement for serving officers to improve their education and skills.

By the 1960s the public services of the Commonwealth and some of the states had taken on a new style, in keeping with the growing image of Australia as a rich, rapidly developing nation in touch with the latest technology. From the end of the Second World War until 1970, public employment virtually doubled—a higher rate of increase than for the population as a whole. In that period:

- public employment increased from about one in six of the workforce to one in five; and
- the administrative agencies of the public service proper (apart from the many statutory bodies, railways, and so on) grew at by far the greatest rate of all.

This created a situation where governments not only provided a comparatively large proportion of community services, but also appeared to be involving themselves more deeply in the planning and regulation of many aspects of economic development and social conduct. The process was seen by many people to reach its peak during the period of the first Whitlam government (December 1972–May 1974), when a variety of new departments, agencies and functions appeared.

Pressures for change

From the mid-1970s, the thinking about the appropriate tasks, internal management and size of the public service began to change. The Royal Commission into Public Administration (the Coombs Report), which reported in 1976, recommended improvements to accountable management within the public service, including more freedom for heads of department to organise resources, delegation within departments and performance measurement criteria. This type of thinking has continued to influence the type of public service reforms that have been implemented in recent years at both state and federal levels of government.

These reforms have been guided by two broad objectives:

- to achieve economic and efficiency gains; and
- to redirect resources from the public to the private sector.

The first of these had its basis in arguments for improvements in managerial efficiency, sometimes called 'managerialism', and internal budgetary constraints.

Another significant imperative has been globalisation and Australia's need to become internationally competitive, which has encouraged the public service to operate under market-based conditions, benchmarking its productivity and efficiency against private-sector best practice.

> 'We will know that we have achieved our goals against the key result areas by measuring our business performance against the indicators set out in our Portfolio Budget Statements and our business plans. Our achievements are reported in our Annual Report.'
> (Source: Department of Education, Science and Training (DEST) 2002, Corporate Plan 2002, DEST, Canberra, http://www.dest.gov.au)

The second factor has its basis in the philosophical principles advocated by Liberal and Coalition state and federal governments that many functions performed by the public sector are best done by individuals or the private sector—in other words, the philosophy that 'small government is good government'.

Both of these factors became embedded in the concept of 'economic rationalism' associated with public-sector reform implemented by Coalition and Labor governments in the 1980s and 1990s, which included significant reductions in the size of state and Commonwealth public services and a market-based approach to the financial management of the public service.

> Michael Pusey, in his book *Economic Rationalism in Canberra* (Cambridge University Press, Cambridge, 1991), provides an interesting analysis of the role of Canberra bureaucrats in the development and implementation of economic rationalism as the basis for public-sector reform in Australia.

The downsizing of the public service across Australia that accompanied these reforms was facilitated by changes to the terms and conditions of public service employment. The concept of public service employment as a 'permanent' lifelong career within the Commonwealth public service, for example, changed with the introduction in 1979 by the Fraser government of the *Commonwealth Employees Redeployment and Retirement (CER) Act*, which facilitated the retrenchment of public servants surplus to requirements.

Today, public service employment conditions under the *Public Service Act 1999* include provisions for the retrenchment of staff excess to the requirements of an agency. Greater flexibility of public service employment has also occurred with changes to the employment conditions of public servants, including employment on contract.

Nevertheless, despite the great changes that both state and Commonwealth governments have initiated in recent years, the Australian public services have retained the basic structures that were established around the time of Federation. In order to carry out their functions, the public services are divided in two different ways:

- by departments and, within those departments, by divisions, branches, sections and so on, each with a certain function or area of responsibility; and
- by grades, or classification, of occupation.

> State and territory jurisdictions maintain their own public service systems, and you can find information about these from their government websites.

The following description concerns the Commonwealth service, known as the Australian Public Service.

THE AUSTRALIAN PUBLIC SERVICE (APS)

> 'The APS is fundamental to the health and smooth operations of the Australian state. If the public face of government can be found among the elected representatives, the public servants provide the sinews and muscle that make the body politic work.'
> (Source: Weller, P. 2001, *Australia's Mandarins: The Frank and the Fearless?*, Allen & Unwin, Sydney, p. 3)

Structure

The Australian Public Service, since the introduction of the *Public Service Act 1999*, has been divided into a number of agencies whose role is to provide advice and support to government and ministers and to implement government decisions and programs.

Departments

The APS has departments of defence, foreign affairs and trade, and so on, which relate to the specific functions allotted to the Commonwealth government under s. 51 of the Constitution. As we saw in Chapter 4, however, many Commonwealth and state functions overlap, with the result that both jurisdictions now have their own departments to deal with issues such as education, health, environment and transport.

> **APS agencies**
> - *Category A*: Departments
> - *Category B*: Statutory agencies with all staff employed under the *Public Service Act 1999* (the PS Act)
> - *Category C*: Statutory agencies which have the capacity to employ staff under the PS Act as well as their own enabling legislation (dual staffing bodies)
> - *Category D*: Executive agencies
> - *Category E*: Includes bodies that employ staff under the PS Act and operate with some degree of independence. These bodies are parts of APS agencies, rather than separate APS agencies as defined in the PS Act (that is, they are part of a department). For example, AusAID (http://www.ausaid.gov.au) is part of the Department of Foreign Affairs and Trade.
>
> Each agency has specific functions that are set out in legislation and by executive arrangements.
> (*Source*: Australian Public Service Commission, 'Australian Public Service Agencies', http://www.apsc.gov.au/apsprofile/agencies.htm. This document also lists the Commonwealth agencies that fall within each APS category. Copyright Commonwealth of Australia, reproduced with permission)

Statutory agencies

A statutory agency is an organisation established by an Act of Parliament in accordance with the *Public Service Act 1999* that has some independence from ministerial control. The actual degree of autonomy is prescribed by the Act that establishes a particular agency, but most are responsible for managing their own day-to-day activities. The *Australian Crime Commission Act 2000*, for example, specifies that the chief executive officer of the Australian Crime Commission (ACC) is responsible 'for the management and administration of the ACC' (ACC 2007, *Annual Report 2006–07*, ACC, Canberra, p. 74, http://www.crimecommission.gov.au). *The Human Rights and Equal Opportunity Commission Act 1986* (s. 13) prescribes that the commission 'has power to do all things that are necessary or convenient to be done for or in connection with the performance of its functions'. Agencies are required to provide an annual report of their activities to the relevant minister.

As we can see above, there are two categories of statutory agencies. The first category includes statutory agencies whose staff are wholly employed under the *Public Service Act 1999*. An example of this type of statutory agency is the Productivity Commission (http://www.pc.gov.au).

The second category includes statutory agencies that have the power to employ staff under their own terms and conditions, as well as staff who are engaged under the *Public Service Act*. Screen Australia (http://www.screenaustralia.gov.au) is an example of this type of organisation.

Statutory authorities

Included within the 'statutory agency' category are a number of organisations that have been established by Commonwealth government legislation as independent statutory authorities with prescribed functions. There are also a number of statutory authorities, as you will see below, that are not statutory agencies.

> 'The characteristics of statutory authorities, of which there are over 160, are not common to all. Differences include the extent to which powers are conferred on Ministers, governance structures, whether the authority is established as a legal entity separate to the Commonwealth and the financial management legislation that is applicable.'
> (Source: Uhrig, J. 2003, *Review of the Corporate Governance of Statutory Authorities of Office Holders* (the Uhrig Report), AGPS, Canberra, p. 16)

Roger Wettenhall, an expert on statutory authorities, provides a more detailed explanation:

1. If these bodies are created by statutes which serve as their charters, and are headed by non-ministerial executives (either boards or single executives such as the Commissioner of Taxation), they are statutory authorities.
2. If the creating Act incorporates a statutory authority (makes it a body corporate or a corporation sole), then it is also a statutory corporation—a sub-group within the statutory authority category.
3. If a body is staffed under the *Public Service Act*, then it is a statutory agency as well as a statutory authority.
4. Statutory authorities not staffed under the *Public Service Act* are not statutory agencies.

(*Source*: Personal email from Roger Wettenhall to G. Singleton, 21 April 2005)

> **Example of a statutory agency that is also a statutory authority**
> The Australian Institute of Health and Welfare (http://www.aihw.gov.au) was established under the *Australian Institute of Health and Welfare Act 1987* as an Australian government statutory authority within the Department of Health and Ageing, and reports direct to the minister. The Act provides that staff may be employed under the *Public Service Act 1999* or be appointed under terms and conditions determined by the institute.

> **Example of a Commonwealth statutory authority that is not also a statutory agency**
> The Australia Council (http://www.ozco.gov.au) was created under the *Australia Council Act 1975* as the government's arts funding and advisory body. The council provides advice on cultural matters to the Minister for the Arts. Staff are appointed under the *Australia Council Act*.

> **Example of a statutory corporation**
> The Australia Postal Corporation (Australia Post) (http://www.auspost.com.au) was established under the *Australia Postal Corporation Act 1989* as a body corporate. The corporation is subject to the reporting and accountability provisions of the *Commonwealth Authorities and Companies Act 1997* (the CAC Act).

A relevant source for further detailed study of statutory authorities is a collection of papers from a symposium edited by Thynne, I. & Wettenhall, R. 2003, 'Organizations in Public Management', *Public Organization Review*, vol. 3, no. 3. A useful article on companies that are owned by the government and not subject to the *Public Service Act* is Wettenhall, R. 2003, 'Kaleidoscope', *Canberra Bulletin of Public Administration*, December.

The subject of non-departmental organisations is discussed further at the end of this chapter.

Executive agencies

Executive agencies are non-statutory bodies that are headed by a person appointed by the minister responsible for the agency. The head of the agency is responsible for its management and is accountable to the minister, in the same manner as a departmental secretary.

> **Example of an executive agency**
> The Bureau of Meteorology reports to the Minister for the Environment and Heritage (http://www.bom.gov.au).

Coordination between agencies

Because government is a complex matter, there has to be coordination between agencies. There are processes within the public service to facilitate this—for example, *inter-departmental committees* and regular meetings between agency heads.

> **Asbestos-Related Diseases Inter-Departmental Committee**
> This committee was responsible for devising a management strategy for addressing asbestos-related disease personal injury claims made against the Australian government. Agencies involved included:
> - Department of Finance and Administrative Services
> - Department of Defence
> - Department of Transport and Regional Services
> - Department of Employment and Workplace Relations
> - Department of Veterans' Affairs
> - Attorney-General's Department
> - Comcare.
>
> (*Source*: Department of Finance and Administration (DFA) 2004, *Annual Report 2003–04*, Chapter 4, Outcome 2, DFA, Canberra, http://www.finance.gov.au/publications/annual-reports)

The significant role of the Department of Prime Minister and Cabinet (referred to as 'PM&C' below) in coordinating the development and implementation of government policy has been explained by Prime Minister Kevin Rudd.

> 'PM&C's role is to support the development and delivery of policy across all of government. In doing so, I expect it to work collaboratively with the entire APS so that genuinely we deliver "joined up" government.
>
> As Prime Minister most of my interactions with the APS occur through my Department. My expectations of PM&C are:
> - timely, well-argued, robust and forward looking policy advice;
> - a coordination role, particularly through the Cabinet process, and
> - supporting the implementation of key government programs.'
>
> (*Source*: Prime Minister Kevin Rudd 2008, 'Address to Heads of Agencies and Members of Senior Executive Service', 30 April 2008, Canberra, http://www.pm.gov.au/media/Speech/2008/speech_0226.cfm)

In 2003, the Howard government established a Cabinet Implementation Unit within the Department of Prime Minister and Cabinet to work with agencies and divisions of departments to improve the implementation of its whole-of-government policy initiatives. This unit has been maintained by the Rudd government.

Changes to the size of the APS

The number of Commonwealth departments grew steadily from Federation until 1987. This reflected the growing role and complexity of government in general, the expanding functions of the Commonwealth as it entered areas once controlled mainly by the states (such as education) or established new fields of interest (such as consumer affairs), and the growth of the federal ministry. Between 1945 and 1972, most new departments were set up to deal with the traditionally Australian areas of services and development, such as repatriation of ex-service personnel, and trade and industry.

In 1973 the Whitlam government entered some new fields, such as media and the conservation of the environment. It also reorganised many existing functions: a separate Department of Aboriginal Affairs was established, while the departments of Army, Navy, Air and Supply were absorbed within the Department of Defence.

> 'No Australian Government has achieved and none has attempted such great administrative reforms as mine . . . the amalgamation of the five defence departments and the two transport departments, the creation of departments with functions which the Federal Government was accepting and the abolition of departments with functions which the Federal Government was abandoning.'
>
> (*Source*: Whitlam, E.G. 1985, *The Whitlam Government, 1972–1975*, Viking, Ringwood, Victoria, pp. 696, reproduced with permission)

Change on that scale was unprecedented in peacetime. It caused a good deal of tension and uncertainty within the public service, which in turn contributed to Labor's difficulties in putting its programs into effect.

The Fraser government (1972–83) made more administrative changes, the early ones flowing from its policy interests and its proclaimed goal of a reduction—or at least a less rapid expansion—in government spending. Some Labor innovations, such as the Department of the Media and the Department of Urban and Regional Development, were eliminated. The government split the Treasury to produce a new Department of Finance, which was to be responsible for the government's financial housekeeping, with the Treasury to act as the government's economic adviser. This continued the practice of the public service having to adapt to relatively frequent changes in its structure.

The Hawke government initially made few changes to the administrative arrangements, apart from some name changing. Then, in 1987, it amalgamated a number of departments, including a number of very large super-departments, such as Education, Employment and Training, and Foreign Affairs and Trade. The intention of this radical restructuring was to increase political control and administrative efficiency.

> 'Just three days after the election, on 14th July 1987, I announced sweeping changes to the structure of the Commonwealth administration . . . the purpose of the reforms was to achieve better policy-coordination, administrative efficiencies and improved budget processes.'
> (Source: Hawke, R.J.L. 1994, *The Hawke Memoirs*, Heinemann, Melbourne, p. 416, copyright Hon. Bob Hawke A.C.)

The Howard government, when it came to office in 1996, did not alter this structure. Instead, it engaged in some reshuffling of functions and changes of departmental names that reflected its particular policy interests and priorities—for example:

- The Economic Planning Advisory Council (EPAC) was amalgamated with the Bureau of Industry Economics and the Industry Commission into a new body called the Productivity Commission.
- The Department of Industrial Relations became the Department of Workplace Relations and Small Business, and later the Department of Employment and Workplace Relations.

The actions of these governments and the resultant changes to the number of government departments (see Table 7.1) demonstrate clearly the power of governments to reshape a public service to reflect their own interests and political priorities.

Staffing levels of the APS

Three general points should be made about staffing levels in public services before we look at the size of the Australian Public Service since the Second World War:

- Since the mid-1970s, the size of the public service has been a very public political issue. There have been many attacks on 'big government' and discussion on the need for '*privatisation*'. In practical terms, that meant selling off agencies to private investors. As a consequence, all governments became defensive about any increase in the number of public servants and public opinion was inclined to favour a cut in public service numbers, except for those areas, as mentioned earlier, where services were cut.
- There are many superficial ways in which governments can alter the numbers of public servants, such as *the creation of statutory authorities* or handing a responsibility to

TABLE 7.1
Commonwealth government departments, 1904–2007

Year/government		No. of departments
1904	Reid	7
1938	Lyons	11
1945	Curtin	20
1956	Menzies	25
1972	Whitlam	27
1979	Fraser	27
1984	Hawke	27
1987	Hawke	18
1995	Keating	20
1999	Howard	16
2005	Howard	18
2007	Rudd	16

another level of government—for example, in 1994 a total of 829 staff were transferred from coverage of the *Public Service Act* to other agencies.
◉ *Redundancies and contracting out* to the private sector had a direct impact on public service numbers. In 1996–97, for example, the number of retrenchments was 9,893, the highest number in any financial year for the previous 10 years. Almost 50 per cent of retrenched employees were aged 30–44 years.

After the Second World War the Commonwealth public service grew steadily. It more than doubled in size between 1945 and 1970 (see Table 7.2), and grew even more rapidly—at the rate of 11,000 per year—under the Whitlam government.

Concern about the growth of the public service began to emerge during this period. In 1974 the Whitlam government fixed an annual limit on growth of 2 per cent. In 1975 the establishment of the Postal and Telecommunications Commission in place of the Department of the Postmaster-General removed 100,000 people from the coverage of the *Public Service Act*.

The Fraser government imposed strict ceilings on staffing and the number of full-time staff under the *Public Service Act* actually fell between 1976 and 1982, but this was largely accounted for by transfers to the newly established Northern Territory Public Service.

As Table 7.2 illustrates, between 1985 and 2001 there was a substantial decline in the number of public servants. However, the Howard government subsequently reversed that trend considerably in order to meet its requirements for a range of new policy initiatives. The Rudd government indicated in 2008 that it would be looking to make budgetary savings by cutting public service numbers, but it remains to be seen whether this will have a substantial impact on public service employment.

STAFFING THE APS

The terms and conditions of employment in the Australian Public Service can be found in the *Public Service Act 1999*.

Open entry and promotion on merit

Recruitment in the Australian Public Service is based on open entry and merit, with the proviso that applicants must be Australian citizens. Promotion is also based on merit.

> 'To build a first class, independent public service, promotion must be based on merit, not politics. That is why the Government has strengthened merit-based standards for appointments to many senior government appointments such as statutory office holders.'
> (*Source*: Prime Minister Kevin Rudd 2008, 'Address to Heads of Agencies and Members of Senior Executive Service', 30 April 2008, Canberra, http://www.pm.gov.au/media/Speech/2008/speech_0226.cfm)

TABLE 7.2

Numbers of ongoing (full-time) paid staff under the *Public Service Act*, 1945–2007

Year	Number of public servants
1945	99,484
1960	162,898
1970	230,927
1975	277,455*
1980	150,743
1985	169,930
1990	159,559
1994	141,690
1997	118,750
2000	102,703
2001	108,005
2005	122,102
2007	143,525

*The Postmaster-General's Department was disbanded on 1 July 1975.

(*Sources*: Australian Public Service (APS), Public Service Board, 1986; APS 1986, *Statistical Yearbook 1985–86*, AGPS, Canberra, p. 148; APS Staffing Statistics Report 1994, Department of Finance, Canberra, p. 3; Public Service and Merit Protection Commission (PSMPC) 1997, *Staffing Statistics Report 1996–97*, PSMPC, Canberra, p. 3; PSMPC 2001, *Australian Public Service Statistical Bulletin 2000–01*, PSMPC, Canberra; APS Commission 2004, *State of the Service Report 2003–04*, 'Ongoing and Non-Ongoing Staff', APS Commission, Canberra, http://www.apsc.gov.au/stateoftheservice/0304/chapter2c.htm; APS Commission 2007, *State of the Service Report 2006–07*, 'Workforce Profile', APS Commission, Canberra, http://www.apsc.gov.au/stateoftheservice/0607/parttwoongoingemployees.htm)

FIGURE 7.1
Farewell Max the Axe

(*Source:* Cartoon by Nicholson from *The Australian*. www.nicholsoncartoons.com.au)

An agency head must provide details of the selection process for appointments to the senior executive service (SES) to the Public Service Commissioner.

Tenure

There are two types of positions in the Australian Public Service: *ongoing positions* and *non-ongoing employment for a fixed term*. Members of the SES can be engaged either on an ongoing basis or on contract for up to five years. In accordance with the *Public Service Act 1999*, agency heads are employed by the prime minister on contract for a term of up to five years. Some have argued that this process has introduced an element of politicisation into the employment process of the public service. Each prime minister exercises his or her own discretion in dealing with this. When the Coalition government took office in 1996, for example, Prime Minister Howard sacked five departmental secretaries. Prime Minister Rudd, however, did not replace any existing senior departmental heads when he came into office. The only change was a new departmental secretary for the Prime Minister's Department caused by the retirement of the incumbent.

> 'We made a commitment last year that there'd be no "night of the long knives" when we came to office.'
> (*Source*: Prime Minister Kevin Rudd 2008, 'Address to Heads of Agencies and Members of Senior Executive Service', 30 April 2008, Canberra, http://www.pm.gov.au/media/Speech/2008/speech_0226.cfm)

Classification

The Australian Public Service uses a number of employment classifications, each corresponding in a general way to the skill, responsibility and salary level attaching to the positions within the service.

- The most senior public servants are called *agency heads*—that is, secretaries of departments, heads of executive agencies and heads of statutory agencies—who advise the minister on policy and are responsible to their respective ministers for the management of their departments, and other senior managers.
- The *senior executive service* the level below agency head, is made up of senior managers in the APS.
- In 1998, the Howard government introduced a new set of arrangements for officers *below the SES level*. The objective was to introduce more flexibility into the system while maintaining the concept of a cohesive public service. These classifications are made up of *APS levels* 1 to 6 and *executive levels* 1 and 2 positions. There are also a number of specified training classifications, including *Graduate APS* (or what is known as 'graduate entry'). Each agency is responsible for its own advertising and recruitment of graduate APS positions.

> Information about employment in the APS, including applying for jobs, can be found in the 'My Career' section of the Australian Government fedinfo site at http://www.fedinfo.gov.au.

Flexibility has been introduced by devolving to Commonwealth agencies the responsibility to develop a remuneration policy appropriate to their own requirements, preferably in the form of a total package, taking into account pay, allowances, conditions (for example, flexible working hours), and *performance* against corporate objective (*performance-based pay*).

Unlike the old system, where each level contained specified steps through which an officer could move, there are no specified increments within a classification; instead, agencies are required to develop their own basis for movement through the salary range of a specified level. The new flexibility in setting remuneration levels means that salaries for a particular classification may differ between agencies.

Agencies are free to label jobs to reflect qualification needs or to demonstrate the nature of the job—but within the framework of the formal APS classification level, so that service-wide cohesion is maintained and to facilitate the transfer of staff between departments and agencies.

Unlike the old system, which prescribed formal qualifications for each classification, it is the responsibility of the agency to determine the appropriate qualifications for a particular job.

In an effort to safeguard the *principle of public service neutrality* and to guard against nepotism, promotions at APS levels 1 to 6 are subject to appeal. This means that an officer who feels unjustly treated can contest the promotion of a colleague before an appeals committee.

Officers used to enter the public service at the base level to embark on a career path. In recent years, however, because most APS vacancies are open to all eligible Australians, there has been more lateral recruitment of staff, including senior positions, from outside the public service.

Ethos

The public service work ethic has special features relating to the conventions of the Westminster system: that is, public servants should serve their ministers and the government loyally and impartially, and provide frank, honest and comprehensive advice, regardless of which party is in government.

> **Apolitical, impartial and professional**
> 'The role of the APS is to serve the Government of the day: to provide the same high standard of policy advice, implementation and professional support irrespective of which political party is in power. This is at the core of the professionalism of the APS.'
> (*Source*: Australian Public Service Commission 2003, 'APS Values and Code of Conduct in Practice', http://www.apsc.gov.au/values/conductguidelines4.htm. Copyright Commonwealth of Australia, reproduced by permission)

The Howard government for the first time instituted a set of values and a code of conduct for the Australian Public Service in the *Public Service Act 1999* that embody those principles. The *set of values* confirms that the APS:

- is apolitical, performing its functions in an impartial and professional manner;
- is a public service in which employment decisions are based on merit;
- provides a workplace that is free from discrimination and recognises and utilises the diversity of the community it serves;
- has the highest ethical standards;
- is openly accountable for its actions, within the framework of ministerial responsibility, to the government, the parliament and the Australian public;
- is responsive to the government in providing frank, honest, comprehensive, accurate and timely advice, and in implementing the government's policies and programs;
- delivers services fairly, effectively, impartially and courteously to the Australian public, and is sensitive to the diversity of the Australian public;
- has leadership of the highest quality;
- establishes workplace relations that value communication, consultation, co-operation and input from employees on matters that affect their workplace;
- provides a fair, flexible, safe and rewarding workplace;
- focuses on achieving results and managing performance;
- promotes equity in employment;
- provides reasonable opportunity to all eligible members of the community to apply for APS employment;
- is a career-based service to enhance the effectiveness and cohesion of Australia's democratic system of government; and
- provides a fair system of review of decisions taken in respect of employees.

(*Source*: Australian Public Service Commission n.d., 'The APS Values', http://www.apsc.gov.au/values/index.html. Copyright Commonwealth of Australia, reproduced by permission)

These values provide the basis for the code of conduct, which requires public servants to:

- behave honestly and with integrity;
- act with care and diligence in the course of APS employment;
- treat everyone with respect and courtesy and without harassment;
- comply with all applicable Australian laws;

- comply with any lawful and reasonable direction given by someone in their department or agency who has authority to give direction;
- maintain appropriate confidentiality about dealings with any minister or the minister's member of staff;
- disclose, and take reasonable steps to avoid, any conflict of interest (real or apparent);
- use Commonwealth resources in a proper manner;
- not provide false or misleading information in response to a request for information that is made for official purposes in connection with their employment;
- not make improper use of inside information or their duties, status, power or authority in order to gain, or seek to gain, a benefit or advantage for themselves or other persons;
- at all times behave in a way that upholds the APS values and the integrity and good reputation of the APS;
- while on duty overseas at all times behave in a way that upholds the good reputation of Australia; and
- comply with any other conduct requirement that is prescribed in the regulations.

(*Source*: Australian Public Service Commission n.d., 'APS Code of Conduct', http://www.apsc.gov.au/conduct/index.html. Copyright Commonwealth of Australia, reproduced by permission)

Note that there are many similarities in these lists of values and conduct to the Malaysian example given earlier in this chapter.

Regulations were also introduced by the Howard government to give protection against victimisation of or discrimination against *whistleblowers*—that is, public servants who report, in the public interest, information which alleges a breach of the code of conduct by a public servant.

The culture of the public service has been influenced by *market-based principles* directed at delivering outstanding service to the general public. Symptomatic of these principles is the adoption by the APS of the private-sector term *customer* for those citizens in receipt of government services and benefits.

Customers and the public service
Centrelink operates 'one-stop shop' Customer Service Centres throughout Australia.

In 1997 the Howard government required all Commonwealth agencies to develop a *service charter* in consultation with 'customers' and staff, to set out the key standards of service those customers can expect to receive, as well as customers' rights and responsibilities.

Department of Agriculture, Fisheries and Forestry Client Service Charter
'This Client Service Charter expresses our commitment to providing you with quality service. It provides information on our service responsibilities and the standard of service you can expect from us.'
(*Source*: Department of Agriculture, Fisheries and Forestry 2007, 'Client Service Charter', http://www.daff.gov.au/about/publications/client-service-charter)

The APS as an equal opportunity employer

Women

Women are very much under-represented at the higher levels of the public service, despite the commitment of the APS to equal employment opportunity principles. However, as Table 7.3 shows, there has been a considerable improvement in the number of women in the upper levels of the APS in recent years.

TABLE 7.3
Classification of APS employees, by gender,* 1997–2007 (per cent)

	June 1997	June 2001	June 2007
Senior executive service	19.7	27.4	36.1
Senior officer (now executive level)	30.1	35.0	43.5
Administrative service officer (now APS levels 1–6)	58.7	56.0	61.3

*It is interesting that in 2004, 50.5 per cent of trainees and graduate trainees were women.

(Sources: Public Service and Merit Protection Commission (PSMPC) 1997, *Australian Public Service Statistical Bulletin 1996–97*, PSMPC, Canberra; PSMPC 2001, *Australian Public Service Statistical Bulletin 2000–01*, Table B, 'Ongoing Staff Classification Grouped by Gender', PSMPC, Canberra; APS Commission 2004, *State of the Service Report 2003–04*, 'Women in the APS', APS Commission, Canberra, http://www.apsc.gov.au/stateoftheservice/0304/chapter8e.htm; APS Commission 2007, *State of the Service Report 2006–07*, 'Section 3—Ongoing Staff', APS Commission, Canberra, http://www.apsc.gov.au/stateoftheservice/0607/statistics/table8.htm; copyright Commonwealth of Australia, reproduced by permission)

Workplace diversity

The Howard government introduced a workplace diversity program into the APS to give recognition to the diverse skills and cultural values and backgrounds of employees and to ensure that workplace structures, systems and procedures assist employees to balance work and family responsibilities. Table 7.4, however, shows that the number of employees designated as those with an 'employment-related disadvantage' employed in the APS, excluding women, who were discussed in the previous section, remains at a very low level.

TABLE 7.4
Diversity of APS staff (ongoing), as at June 2007 (per cent)

People with a disability	3.3
Non-English-speaking background	5.8
Indigenous Australians	2.1

(Source: APS Commission 2007, *State of the Service Report 2006–07*, 'Diversity Trends', APS Commission, Canberra, http://www.apsc.gov.au/stateoftheservice/0607/partfivetrends.htm; copyright Commonwealth of Australia, reproduced by permission)

Unionism in the APS

Employment conditions within the APS allow for staff involvement in all stages of agreement making in relation to classification and salary arrangements.

Public servants, like many other workers, have formed associations to protect and improve their conditions of employment. The main public-sector union is the Community and Public Sector Union (CPSU) (http://www.cpsu.org.au). The CPSU acts on behalf of its members as a bargaining agent, providing advocacy services as required, and represents public service officers more generally on industrial matters.

FINANCING THE APS

When a government assigns functions, or establishes a new agency, it has to allocate money to pay for the running of the agency and to keep account of how that money is spent. This role is performed by the Department of Finance and Administration, acting in consultation with agencies.

The Department of Finance and Administration, in consultation with other agencies, is responsible for producing a system of rolling forward estimates of expenditure. This enhances the government's focus on restraining government expenditure by identifying projected financial expenditure over the longer term, and allows planning for future needs (see below).

TREASURY AND ECONOMIC MANAGEMENT

A description of the budget process was outlined in Chapter 5. Once estimates of expenditure and revenue are compiled, they are examined by the Cabinet Expenditure Review Committee, where final adjustments are made before the treasurer presents the completed budget to parliament. By that time, the budget documents and the treasurer's budget speech give much more than a statement of departmental receipts and expenditure.

> **Expenditure Review Committee**: A cabinet committee, comprising the prime minister as chair, the treasurer, and other selected portfolio ministers. It is responsible for examining all expense proposals in light of the government's overall fiscal strategy, advising cabinet on budget spending priorities, and initiating reviews of individual ongoing program expenses.

The budget presents not only a list of government undertakings but also a scheme for managing the economy for the next year, which is determined by cabinet with the advice of Treasury. The expertise and specialist knowledge of Treasury with regard to economic policy issues tends to give the department a great deal of influence in the formulation of the budget strategy.

The budget contains measures designed to help the government achieve its economic objectives, and so might include reductions in taxes, meant to encourage people to spend more, or increases in taxes to restrain demand or help make up a shortfall in government revenue. Money is required also for the armed forces and for maintaining services such as health, education, housing and social welfare.

In addition, the budget makes allowances for the states' share of the taxes collected by the Commonwealth, some further amounts for special projects, and an agreed share of loans to be raised throughout the year. (See Chapter 4 for further details of these arrangements.)

All of this involves the raising and spending of thousands of millions of dollars, which can affect every person in Australia. The government's discretion in how that money is spent, however, is limited by the fact that much government spending is committed in advance—for example, to social service payments and defence spending. Nevertheless, there is scope for a government to redirect government spending according to its political priorities and changing economic conditions. The Howard government, for example, made many spending commitments in the period leading up to the November 2007 election. The Rudd government reassessed those commitments to make budget savings when it came into office.

> 'The former government made many spending decisions at the last minute before the election campaign and we will obviously be scrutinising these decisions very closely.'
> (*Source*: Lindsay Tanner, Minister for Finance 2008, cited in 'Rudd to axe Lib pledges', *The Australian*, 7 January 2008)

> 'Our nation also faces longer term challenges and opportunities, in the form of an ageing population, the economic effects of the rise of China and India, and the consequences of climate change. With careful, responsible economic management, we are confident we can meet these challenges.'
> (*Source*: Wayne Swan, Treasurer 2008, 'Budget Speech 2008–09', 13 May 2008, http://www.budget.gov.au/2008-09/content/speech/html/speech-02.htm)

The government's capacity to manage the economy is constrained also by factors such as:

- the international economic situation: for example, the 2008 global financial crisis;
- the fact that much of Australian industry is owned by overseas companies who make their own decisions about investment and activity independent of the needs of the Australian economy; and
- the constitutional limitations to the 'economic powers' of the federal government.

Because of these factors, economic management through the budget can take place only 'at the margins', through adjustments to taxes or programs.

Governments may want to make further economic adjustments throughout the year to deal with any special circumstances that might arise, and on those occasions a *'mini-budget'* may be introduced part-way through the financial year. In each of these circumstances, governments rely on the advice of Treasury, among others, so that its influence can affect many areas of policy.

POLICY AND ADMINISTRATION

Treasury's role in economic management is one example of the way in which the public service is constantly involved in forming policy and not merely carrying out directions handed down from cabinet. This is only to be expected, as ministers cannot possibly know all that needs to be done in the areas under their control, far less draw up the specific instructions for detailed action. In any case, 'policy' may often be no more than a minor change to existing arrangements with which the public servants are clearly the most familiar.

Yet the close involvement of bureaucrats in forming policy raises a number of issues for the parliamentary system and for the community generally, including the dilemma of democracy discussed at the beginning of this chapter:

- In the Westminster system of government, a minister is supposed to be responsible to parliament for all actions that are carried out in the department. Unless the minister is actually directing those actions, it is somewhat optimistic to expect the minister to accept the traditional role. It is unrealistic if the department's activities are planned in detail by the public servants themselves.
- Public servants might resist the government's policy initiatives either overtly or unconsciously, because they are likely to disturb the even tenor of life in the service or challenge the established interests of certain agencies. This gives rise to the bureaucracy's own form of 'politics', sometimes called the 'departmental line', which was the basis for the British television series *Yes, Minister*.
- The administration of policies by public servants necessarily involves the exercise of judgement and discretion, whether it is in the assessment of a tax return or the placement of unemployed people in jobs. Such administration may effectively alter, even if slightly, the intention of government in formulating policy.

Outside advice

> 'Advice from the departmental secretary will be just one opinion among many . . . they will now never be the only source. Advice has become contested.'
> (Source: Weller, P. 2001, *Australia's Mandarins: The Frank and the Fearless?*, Allen & Unwin, Sydney, p. 99)

Not all policies are determined within the bureaucracy. Parties that form governments have broad aims and philosophical objectives, which cabinet communicates in more specific form to the public service. Governments often respond also to advice and pressure from political supporters and other community and business interest groups. Outside consultants and government advisory bodies also provide an alternative source of advice to a minister. Certain ministers, and prime ministers, have very strong views on policy, as well as the will to ensure that they are heeded.

Ministerial advisers

Ministerial staff who work in the minister's office and are employed directly by the minister under the *Members of Parliament (Staff) Act 1984* are an important and significant source of alternative policy advice. They often include members of the minister's political party and specialists, such as academics, with particular knowledge of the minister's portfolio. Part of their role is to ensure that departmental submissions are in keeping with the political agenda of the government, or to put the 'political spin' on policy.

> In a reference to Kevin Rudd's advisers, Alister Jordan and Lachlan Harris, *The Weekend Australian* reported that: 'They are the two most powerful 28-year-olds in Australia. The fate of the country and certainly the fate of the Prime Minister is to a large extent in their hands.'
> (*Source*: Lyons, J. 2008, 'Inner circle', *The Weekend Australian*, 21 June 2008)

Ministerial advisers, sometimes called 'minders', act as policy 'gatekeepers' because they have regular and ready access to the minister and the capacity to argue the pros and cons of a policy put forward by the department.

> 'The minders are always on the spot, just outside the ministers' offices, on the plane, around the electorate. Proximity provides the immediate capacity to exercise influence.'
> (*Source*: Weller, P. 2001, *Australia's Mandarins: The Frank and the Fearless?*, Allen & Unwin, Sydney, p. 102)

Departmental secretaries

As we saw above, ministers are able to appoint departmental secretaries with whom they prefer to work. The fact that they are employed on a contract basis increases the likelihood that departmental policy advice will be framed to take into account the minister's priorities and interests. There is an argument that this process could lead to politicisation of the public service, with departmental secretaries being less willing to give 'frank and fearless advice' that might not be well received by the minister.

Constraints on ministerial independence from the public service

Several factors have made it impossible for ministers to initiate and carry through policies without substantial assistance and intervention from the public service. These include:

- the magnitude and complexity of the problems governments are being asked to confront: this means that the minister relies heavily on the expertise and specialist knowledge of the department for advice on relevant and workable policy options;
- the fact that ministers tend to stay in any one portfolio for a relatively short space of time, which means they rely on the 'corporate' memory of the department (the files) to provide background information and the history of a particular issue;
- the momentum of existing programs and the strength of interests that have grown up around them; and
- the complexity of the government machinery itself.

At the end of the day, however, it is the government and the minister who set policy goals and are responsible to the parliament and the people for their success or failure. Paul Keating, for example, came into government in 1983 as a 'rookie' treasurer, but by 1986 he was on top of his portfolio.

> 'More than most ministers at this stage, [Keating] was overwhelmingly reliant on experts—his own staff and Treasury officials—a reliance largely dictated by the breadth and complexity of the Treasurer's job . . . That is not to say that he did not have ideas of his own—he did. But the forceful expression of his own ideas came later. Just now, he was learning to swim.'
> (Source: Hawke, R.J.L. 1994, *The Hawke Memoirs*, Heinemann, Melbourne, p. 239, copyright Hon. Bob Hawke A.C.)

> 'Keating now fluent in the language, numbers and concepts of economic policy, the Treasurer's office became more important, the Department of Treasury less.'
> (Source: Edwards, J. 1996, *Keating: The Inside Story*, Viking, Ringwood, Victoria, p. 287)

THE POLICY PROCESS: COORDINATION AND CONTROL

Governments announce policies in a manner designed to appeal to the electorate, usually claiming maximum credit by suggesting that something entirely new is being proposed. However, few measures are truly original, as even those which appear new, such as changes in the laws relating to drug use or the regulation of atmospheric pollution, are responses to demands made over long periods of time by interested community groups. This means there is certain to be something about the matter in the files of the public service arising from past complaints and reports, or from special studies requested by ministers or senior officials. Much of this material may never produce action. It may be overlooked for years and few people outside government will be aware of it. It becomes important and relevant only if the matter that once concerned just a few people requires government action. At this point it becomes an 'issue' or, to use a fashionable term, it is placed on the 'political agenda'. It then becomes a subject for policy consideration.

The next stage may begin with a minute from cabinet or a minister requesting further proposals on the matter in question, but the request will rarely require a plan for immediate action from a single department, for the following reasons:

- Any proposal for spending money—and that includes most matters of substance—must involve several central agencies. Correspondence and discussion with those agencies will ensue.
- The Department of Prime Minister and Cabinet may need to be involved to ensure that the proposal is consistent with government policy and to assess its effects on other government activities.
- There must be consultations with legal experts if legislation is required and with other departments with an interest in the proposal.

By this time an apparently straightforward scheme can seem very complex; for example, an attempt to reduce youth unemployment may involve, in addition to the obvious agencies, authorities concerned with education, immigration, social security, employment relations and public works. Coordination is clearly necessary, and an inter-departmental committee is often set up to do this. The committee may produce an amended proposal that takes account of any factors or departmental interests that were overlooked initially. This can be submitted to the responsible minister and on to cabinet, which in turn might refer the matter to a committee of ministers for further consideration. This process illustrates that there is rarely a clear division between 'policy' and 'administration'.

The more involved this process becomes, the harder it is to answer several questions that should be fundamental to any system of responsible government:

- What are the aims of the policy?
- Have the aims been changed during the process of consultation and coordination?
- Does the policy conform to the wishes of the community, or does it now reflect the interests of the departments involved in its formulation?
- Who should be held accountable for the final policy (or, in some cases, for the fact that the policy has not been put into effect)?
- Is the public service carrying out the policy in the manner that was originally intended?

Some of these questions are related to the concept of ministerial responsibility discussed in Chapter 6; in this instance they are considered from the bureaucratic, rather than the political, viewpoint.

It was pointed out in Chapters 5 and 6 that the 'political' and parliamentary remedies, such as the system of parliamentary committees, have met with limited success in Australia. Indeed, it has been suggested that the roles of parliament, minister and public service have been so changed by the needs of modern government that a completely new system of accountability is required. An alternative approach has been to propose measures that would supplement rather than replace existing conventions of responsibility. The measures include two kinds of controls designed to complement each other:

- from the policy viewpoint, clearer indications of government intentions through the preparation of long-term plans; and
- from the administrative viewpoint, closer checks on the public service through such techniques as 'performance management' and by the various aspects of the new administrative law, such as the ombudsman and freedom of information legislation discussed below.

For many years, concern for greater accountability was confined mainly to a few academics, although an examination of letters to newspapers or complaints to members of parliament would have shown that many people were critical of the cost, inefficiency and secrecy of public services and governments in general. There had been occasional Royal Commissions on the public services of some states and the Commonwealth, but they had been held many years previously and had mostly been confined to matters of internal organisation. Since the 1970s, public interest has been sustained by several factors:

- a concern that 'big government' was becoming less effective, even while it was encroaching on individual freedom;
- a succession of inquiries into and reports on the federal public service, beginning with the Royal Commission into Australian Government Administration (RCAGA) released in 1976;
- similar investigations into most state public services which led to major reforms; and
- the Howard government's 1999 reforms, with an emphasis on customer service, business planning and organisational performance.

ACCOUNTABILITY AND ADMINISTRATIVE REVIEW

One of the useful functions of the public service inquiries of the 1970s was that they provided a wealth of information never previously available in Australia. When the Hawke government produced its 1983 White Paper, *Reforming the Australian Public Service*, it acknowledged its debt not only to RCAGA but also to the Review of Commonwealth Administration (the Reid Report of 1982) and the report of the Joint Committee of Public Accounts on senior public service managers.

Another significant report related to reforms undertaken by the Hawke government was the 1984 White Paper, *Budget Reform*, which recommended improvements to budgetary decision-making and scrutiny processes and financial management within agencies.

The 1999 reforms introduced by the Howard government included the premise that the APS would benchmark its performance against private-sector best practice. New financial arrangements introduced by the government to emphasise propriety and accountability for financial management performance included:

- portfolio budgeting;
- program management and budgeting;
- performance indicators;
- accrual budgeting and accounting to identify the full costs of departmental and agency activities;
- an integrated fiscal framework to enhance fiscal discipline and public scrutiny by requiring the secretaries of the Treasury and the Department of Finance and Administration to release an independent fiscal and economic report prior to all elections, called the Charter of Budget Honesty;
- a performance improvement cycle involving the systematic review of all activities to ensure that they are focused on the primary responsibilities of the government; and
- competitive tendering and contracting out to improve accountability, quality and cost-effectiveness.

> Detailed information about the changes to Commonwealth agency budgetary and financial management processes can be found in Chapter 6 of the Australian Public Service Commission's 2003 document, *The Australian experience of public sector reform*, APS Commission, Canberra, http://www.apsc.gov.au/about/exppsreform.htm.

One of the main difficulties in evaluating government programs and in assessing the responsibilities of ministers and public servants for carrying them out is that their objectives may not be able to be stated in quantifiable terms:

- People who have a traditional view of government maintain that vagueness or a lack of explicit objectives is inevitable, owing to the political factors that must be taken into account when forming and implementing public policy. Some would even say that vague objectives are often desired by politicians, who have no wish to alienate sections of the community by stating a clear position.

- Opponents of this view argue that it is the public service's duty to clarify the aims of its political masters. This should be accomplished by effective planning, and by testing the efficiency of the public service, as well as the responsibilities of the relevant ministers, according to whether the objectives set out in the plans are achieved using 'strategic planning' and 'performance indicators'. This, it is argued, is the technique applied by corporate management: why should it not be employed in the public sector?

Policy and planning

The purpose of planning is to achieve goals in the most efficient way, but a question still remains: who is to set the goals—the community, cabinet, public servants, or professional experts? For example, it might be decided, as part of a long-term energy program, that more dams should be constructed for producing hydroelectric power. Engineers may calculate the spots at which this can be done most efficiently, but residents whose towns will be flooded will raise objections, as will conservationists wanting to preserve wildlife in the area. Cabinet might then request alternative proposals, which public servants prepare as an attempted compromise. The experts might immediately object that the amended scheme, on a different site, is more costly and less suitable. Is this any longer a 'rational' plan? Is it planning at all, or merely arriving at a position by a series of decisions designed to meet changing circumstances (that is, a kind of incremental process)? How important should 'political' considerations be?

One way of improving this situation involves planning through the budgetary process. The Commonwealth government's introduction of the *outcomes/outputs framework* as a reporting mechanism, discussed below, requires all agencies to specify and cost their outputs against planned outcomes. *Performance indicators* are also used to specify targets for future performance. The fact that Commonwealth agencies are required to produce 'forward estimates' of their costs for a three-year period means they have to plan their future activities and associated expenditure.

This process has been successful in that it has required departments to better manage their expenditure in the context of policy goals. The need to anticipate future expenditure has also encouraged departments to focus more on medium-term planning. *Corporate and strategic plans* are another planning tool through which agencies identify their goals.

A major difficulty with the implementation of any system of medium- or long-term planning, however, is that governments tend to make policy as a reaction to their more immediate political needs. For that reason, long-term planning is difficult in any democracy. Possible reasons for its lack of success in Australia include the following:

- Economic difficulties, together with major differences in the priorities supported by different parties in government, create uncertainty about national goals.
- The Commonwealth government lacks the constitutional power to introduce authoritative plans in major issues of economic planning, such as incomes policy.
- The Liberal Party (and, to a lesser extent, the Nationals) tends to see planning as a restriction on 'free enterprise', rather than as complementing it.
- Long-term economic planning requires some kind of political consensus with vested interests if it is to work.

The failure of the Hawke government's Economic Planning Advisory Council (EPAC) to fulfil its long-term economic planning function is a good example. The government's imperative to meet more immediate political needs, such as deteriorating economic circumstances and its incomes Accord with the trade union movement, took precedence when policy was being made. EPAC was eventually abolished by Prime Minister Keating, and the research secretariat was incorporated into the Productivity Commission by the Howard government.

Making bureaucracies more accountable

There is some provision for analysing the performance of Commonwealth agencies within parliament: for example, parliamentary committees investigate certain aspects of the work of the public service, although with limited success. Individual cases of apparent unfairness can also be taken up by MPs during question time or through letters to ministers. Nevertheless, these parliamentary remedies go only part of the way towards meeting two obvious needs:

- checking the performance of public service organisations; and
- investigating and, where necessary, redressing individual grievances.

In recent years, checks and remedies have been sought more and more often outside parliament.

Performance management

Techniques of performance management rely on the ability of those conducting investigations to assess whether administrators have achieved their aims. The intention of the Howard government's 1999 reforms was to improve performance management within the public service by requiring agencies to focus on their customers, both within and outside the service, and on quality and productivity to be achieved by continual benchmarking of their performance against best practice.

Commonwealth agencies set out their objectives in broad terms within the context of their *mission statement*.

> **Department of Defence**
> *Our Mission*
> 'The Defence mission is to defend Australia and its national interests. In fulfilling this mission, we:
> - Serve all Australians, and
> - Are accountable to the Commonwealth Parliament, on behalf of the Australian people, for the efficiency and effectiveness with which we carry out the Government's defence policy.'
>
> (Source: Department of Defence 2008, 'Defence Service Charter', http://www.defence.gov.au/charters, copyright Commonwealth of Australia, reproduced by permission)

Performance indicators are used to evaluate the effectiveness of an agency. All Commonwealth agencies are required to report using the Department of Finance and Deregulation Outcomes and Outputs Framework:

> The framework works as follows:
> - government (through its ministers and with the assistance of relevant agencies) specifies the Outcomes it is seeking to achieve in a given area
> - these Outcomes are specified in terms of the impact government is aiming to have on some aspect of society (e.g., education), the economy (e.g., exports) or the national interest (e.g., defence)

- Parliament appropriates funds to allow the government to achieve these Outcomes through administered items and departmental activities
- items such as grants, transfers and benefit payments are administered on the Government's behalf by agencies, with a view to maximising their contribution to the specified Outcomes
- agencies specify and manage their activities to maximise their contribution to the achievement of the Government's desired Outcomes
- performance indicators are developed to allow scrutiny of effectiveness (i.e., the impact of Programs and departmental activities on Outcomes) and efficiency in contributing to the achievement of the Outcome. Indicators will also enable the system to be further developed to improve performance and accountability for results.

(*Source*: Department of Finance and Deregulation 2008, 'Outcomes Arrangements' http://www.finance.gov.au, copyright Commonwealth of Australia, reproduced by permission)

Public scrutiny of the performance of Commonwealth agencies is facilitated by the fact that they are required to report annually to parliament through their minister on their activities and performance in relation to their designated outcomes.

> The annual reports of Commonwealth agencies include descriptions of designated outcomes and an explanation of how the department has performed in meeting those objectives.

Performance management within the APS is maintained also by the functions of the Audit Office, an independent agency headed by the auditor-general that reports to parliament on the activities of departments. Its work includes performance audits, financial statement audits and better practice guides.

Agency Internet websites supply details of their activities, including annual reports and a feedback facility for the public to make comments or request information. This provides a readily available opportunity for scrutiny by the general public. This process is associated with what has become known as e-government. (This is discussed in Chapter 13.)

There is always the possibility, however, that when objectives, strategies and performance are defined too broadly, or couched in terms that are too general, quantifiable measurement of performance may become extremely difficult.

Review of administrative action

It is possible for individuals to seek redress against public service actions through the law courts. However, the process is complex and may be costly, as well as involving difficulties over the role of the Crown (that is, government) and such questions as executive privilege. At the same time, legislation has given ministers the right to delegate to public servants increasing authority (or 'discretion') to make decisions that can have serious consequences for citizens and can, in effect, amount to judgements on a particular question, such as a person's eligibility to receive certain social service payments. In some areas, tribunals were established to hear complaints against such decisions, but there remained many matters for which no simple remedies existed. For that reason, systems of general administrative review have been set up in most states and for the Commonwealth.

People who are affected by a government decision, or consumers who are concerned about government services, have access to a range of administrative law remedies. At the federal level, these include the following:

- *Administrative Appeals Tribunal* (http://www.aat.gov.au): The tribunal hears appeals on a wide range of matters, calling on evidence and files from the public service in order to review the merits of cases that have been decided by other bodies.
- *Federal Court* (http://fedcourt.gov.au): The *Administrative Decisions (Judicial Review) Act 1977* gives the Federal Court the power to review public employees' actions, in addition to its other function of hearing appeals against the decisions of the Administrative Appeals Tribunal. The tribunal reviews the facts of cases, while the Federal Court concerns itself mainly with questions of law (that is, whether satisfactory procedures were followed in reaching decisions about the facts or merits of cases).
- *Commonwealth Ombudsman* (http://www.comb.gov.au): The Ombudsman responds to complaints from citizens, and is able to investigate a wider range of matters than the Administrative Appeals Tribunal, but can recommend to the relevant department or authority only that a decision be reviewed. If this request is denied, the ombudsman may raise the issue in an annual report to parliament.
- *Administrative Review Council* (http://www.ag.gov.au/arc): The ARC provides policy advice on administrative law matters.
- *Freedom of information (FOI) legislation*: This is discussed at greater length below.

Administrative review has spread far within the federal government in a surprisingly short time. Administrative review also affects the executive in ways that were not anticipated. In particular, the courts have ruled that the Administrative Appeals Tribunal should not be restricted in its decisions by considerations of government policy; for example, the tribunal has refused to endorse the deportation of certain aliens convicted of drug offences, even though it has quite clearly been the ministerial intention to deport aliens in all such cases. The tribunal has been meticulous in all matters relating to policy, but a confrontation between the administrative review authorities and the government could still occur. Australians might then have to decide whether they wish to have increasing incursions by judges and quasi-judicial bodies into the work of the executive, or whether they would prefer to see some of the traditional powers of parliament restored.

Contracting out of government services may create difficulties for people seeking redress against a contractor, because members of the public have no general right to seek access to information held by private-sector bodies. There are also commercial-in-confidence issues associated with running a private business. Governments will have to address these issues if accountability is to be maintained.

Secrecy and freedom of information

One of the main difficulties a community faces in making politicians and bureaucrats accountable is finding out what they have been doing, and why. This becomes even harder as governments grow bigger, and so in recent years there have been increasing demands that governments be made to disclose information. In a number of countries, notably Sweden and the United States but also Australia, this pressure led to the passage of laws that require the bureaucracy to open its files to citizens, unless it can show that there is a compelling reason (for example, national security) to maintain secrecy. Australian public services have long had a reputation for being secretive, although it should also be pointed out that the community itself made few concerted demands for information until recently.

The *Freedom of Information Act 1982* (the FOI Act) was introduced after 10 years of political and parliamentary debate to allow individual citizens to request information from government. It was first mooted in 1972, when the Australian Labor Party promised to introduce 'open government'. The final bill was the result of extensive discussion within the public service and the parliament, and insistence by the Senate on greater openness than the government and the public service initially were inclined to allow. In 1983 the ALP promised amendments that would allow for wider disclosure and fewer exemptions from provisions of the Act, but the eventual amendments were weaker than those originally promised. Additional amendments were made in 1986 in an attempt to reduce the cost to government by raising charges for applications and the processing of requests.

> **How to apply for information under the FOI Act**
> Requests for information under the *Freedom of Information Act* are made to the Commonwealth agency that has the information required. Application fees and processing charges apply, although in certain circumstances these may not be required.

Despite the FOI Act, there are still extensive limits to citizen access to the inner workings of government. Exemptions include documents relating to the workings of cabinet and to security matters. Many people have been disappointed, and the Act is referred to by some as the 'Freedom *from* Information Act'. Most of these requests come from individuals seeking information on their own records in the fields of veterans' affairs, taxation and social security. Some departments and agencies receive no requests at all, and it is doubtful whether the higher reaches of policy making within the public service and the executive government have become much more open than they were.

NON-DEPARTMENTAL ORGANISATIONS

Governments in Australia over more than a century have established large numbers of bodies outside the public services to meet community demands and, on occasion, to reduce political pressures on themselves. These bodies have been used for a wide range of activities.

Some are essentially commercial operations. It should be noted, however, that in recent years many of these organisations, commonly known as *government business enterprises* (GBEs), have been privatised, with their functions and ownership transferred to the private sector. GBEs are prescribed under the *Commonwealth Authorities and Companies Act 1997* (the CAC Act), and the government has established a process for the oversight of these bodies. Examples of GBEs include the Defence Housing Authority (http://www.dha.gov.au) and Medibank Private Limited (http://www.medibank.com.au).

Non-departmental bodies are also used for:

- communication, education and research work, where freedom from immediate political interference was considered desirable, such as the Australian Broadcasting Corporation (http://www.abc.net.au), universities and the CSIRO (http://www.csiro.au); and

- regulating services and occupations such as hospitals, dentists, skilled tradespeople and nursing homes, such as the Aged Care Standards and Accreditation Agency (http://www.accreditation.org.au).

As we saw above in our discussion of statutory authorities, the individual statutes creating these bodies vary almost as much as the organisations themselves, but they are characterised generally by autonomy in handling the implementation of policy and management of the organisation.

Some former primary producer statutory authorities now operate as public companies with the capacity to receive government funding.

> **Dairy Australia** (http://www.dairyaustralia.com.au) is a public company limited by guarantee that operates within rules and laws set out by its constitution, the *Corporations Act 2001* and a Statutory Funding Deed with the Australian government. It has a board of nine directors and its head office is in Melbourne.

Scrutiny of financial management of non-departmental organisations

Financial management is subject to monitoring and scrutiny by the Minister for Finance under the *Commonwealth Authorities and Companies Act 1997* (CAC Act).

The CAC Act regulates:

- the corporate governance, financial management and reporting of Commonwealth authorities, which are in addition to the requirements of their enabling legislation; and
- the corporate governance and reporting of Commonwealth companies which are in addition to the requirements of the Corporations Law.

(*Source*: Department of Finance and Deregulation n.d., 'CAC Legislation', http://www.finance.gov.au/financial-framework/cac-legislation/, copyright Commonwealth of Australia, reproduced by permission)

It is clear that there have been many changes in the organisation and role of the public service in the 1990s. The challenges of globalisation and an emphasis on managerialism have caused the departments and agencies of the public service to adopt private-sector practice, with a focus on flexibility, competition and market forces, in place of what critics argued was a preoccupation with process and rules. At the same time, the framework of the Westminster tradition of accountability and ministerial responsibility that is characteristic of our system of government provides continuity in requiring the public service to maintain a set of values based on the highest ethical standards and to operate in an apolitical and impartial manner.

QUESTIONS FOR DISCUSSION

1. Why should the public service be answerable and accountable to the parliament and the community?
2. Is the concept of public service in a system of responsible parliamentary government compatible with private-sector best practice? Give your reasons.
3. There is a suggestion that the public service is where policy is really made. What is the basis of this assumption?
4. What reasons would you give for suggesting that ministers are in control of the policy process?
5. What was the basis of the concept of 'permanency' of employment in the public service? Do you think the erosion of this practice is a good thing for responsible government?
6. People with an 'employment-related disadvantage' continue to be under-represented in the public service. What measures do you think are needed to overcome this problem?
7. How relevant is the 'dilemma of democracy' to the relationship between the Commonwealth government and the Australian Public Service?

FURTHER READING

Aulich, C. 2005, 'Privatisation and Outsourcing', in Aulich, C. & Wettenhall, R. (eds), *Howard's Second and Third Governments*, UNSW Press, Sydney. This chapter provides an analysis of developments in privatisation and outsourcing under the Howard government, 1998–2004.

2008, 'Continuing Howard's Privatization Agenda', in Aulich, C. & Wettenhall, R. (eds), *Howard's Fourth Government: Australian Commonwealth Administration 2004–2007*, UNSW Press, Sydney. This chapter maps the further development of Howard's privatisation agenda and considers its impact after a decade of implementation.

Aulich, C., Halligan, J. & Nutley, S. (eds) 2001, *Australian Handbook of Public Sector Management*, Allen & Unwin, Sydney. This is a useful overview of public-sector management in Australia.

Australian Public Service Commission 2003, 'The Australian Experience of Public Sector Reform', Australian Public Service Commission, Canberra, http://www.apsc.gov.au/about/exppsreform.htm. A comprehensive explanation of Commonwealth government public-sector reform.

Colley, L. 2001, 'The Changing Face of Public Sector Employment', *Australian Journal of Public Administration*, vol. 60, no. 1, pp. 9–20. This article discusses how the emphasis on private-sector techniques, including the pursuit of greater efficiency, flexibility and responsiveness, has changed the nature of public service employment.

Davis, G. & Weller, P. (eds) 2001, *Are You Being Served?: State, Citizens and Governance*, Allen & Unwin, Sydney. Includes discussion on the role and operations of government, reshaping service delivery, accountability, and expectations and perceptions of governance.

Halligan, J. 2005, 'Public Sector Reform', in Aulich, C. & Wettenhall, R. (eds), *Howard's Second and Third Governments*, UNSW Press, Sydney. An analysis of public service reform under the Howard government, 1998–2004.

Halligan, J. 2008, 'The Search for Balance and Effectiveness in the Australian Public Service', in Aulich, C. & Wettenhall, R. (eds), *Howard's Fourth Government: Australian Commonwealth Administration 2004–2007*, UNSW Press, Sydney. An analysis of changes in public service management reform under the last term of the Howard government, with discussion of integrated governance.

Keating, M. 1999, 'The Public Service: Independence, Responsibility and Responsiveness', *Australian Journal of Public Administration*, vol. 58, no. 1, pp. 39–47. This article discusses the respective responsibilities of ministers and their public service officials, as well as politicisation, public service values and the public interest.

Malone, P. 2006, *Australian Department Heads under Howard: Career Paths and Practice. Collected Articles from the* Canberra Times, ANU EPress/*The Canberra Times*, Canberra, http://epress.anu.edu.au/anzsog/dept_heads/pdf/prelims.pdf.

Stewart, J. 2006, 'The Public Sector and its Management', in Parkin, A., Summers, J. & Woodward, D. (eds), *Government, Politics, Power and Policy in Australia*, 8th ed., Pearson Education, Sydney. This chapter discusses the problems and prospects of public-sector management related to accountability.

Weller, P. 2001, *Australia's Mandarins: The Frank and the Fearless?*, Allen & Unwin, Sydney. A comprehensive and authoritative examination of the role of departmental secretaries and their relationship to the minister.

Wettenhall, R. 2008, 'Non-Departmental Public Bodies as a Focus for Machinery-of-Government Change', in Aulich, C. & Wettenhall R. (eds), *Howard's Fourth Governments Australian Commonwealth Administration 2004–2007*, UNSW Press, Sydney.

Whitwell, G. 1986, *The Treasury Line*, Allen & Unwin, Sydney. This work suggests that the Treasury has its own interests in the development of government policy.

USEFUL WEBSITES

http://www.apsc.gov.au
Australian Public Service Commission
Find information about recent public service reforms, the classification structure and statistical data. See, for example, publications such as *State of the Service* reports, the *Statistical Bulletin* series and annual reports.

http://www.finance.gov.au
Department of Finance and Deregulation
Find information about financial reporting requirements for Commonwealth agencies, including the outputs and outcomes framework, performance management and performance indicators.

http://www.treasury.gov.au
Australian Government: The Treasury

- **http://www.australia.gov.au**
  Australian Government
  Provides an entry point for information about the Australian government.

- **http://www.fedcourt.gov.au**
  Federal Court of Australia

- **http://www.ag.gov.au/arc**
  Administrative Review Council

- **http://www.ag.gov.au/www/agd/agd.nsf/Page/Freedom_of_Information**
  Attorney-General's Department: Freedom of Information

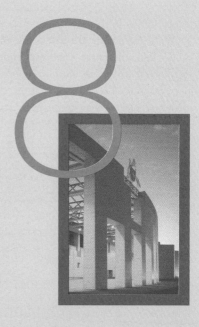

8

ELECTIONS AND VOTING BEHAVIOUR

THIS CHAPTER EXPLAINS:

- the importance of elections in a democracy;
- different types of electoral systems in modern states;
- the Australian electoral system;
- the development of the Commonwealth electoral system;
- how electoral boundaries are redistributed;
- public funding and disclosure;
- electronic voting (e-voting);
- voting behaviour; and
- how different voting methods work in practice.

THE IMPORTANCE OF ELECTIONS

Elections are an essential element of our democratic system. Elections determine who will represent us in the parliament and who will form the government. The act of voting is one of the most important decisions you will make as a citizen in our liberal democracy. It is important, therefore, that you understand the function of elections and the types of electoral systems that operate in our political system.

As we shall see in this chapter, there are different types of electoral systems. The choice of which electoral system to use is an important one, because it can influence the structure of party representation in a particular parliament.

> 'During the 1990s, debate about the electoral system moved from margin to mainstream on the political agenda. This shift produced growing awareness that electoral rules are not neutral: the way votes translate into seats means that some groups, parties and representatives are ruled into the policy-making process and some are ruled out. The core debate concerns whether countries should adopt majoritarian systems which prioritize government effectiveness and accountability, or proportional systems which promote greater fairness to minor parties and more diversity in social representation.'
> (Source: Norris, P. 1997, 'Choosing Electoral Systems: Proportional Majoritarian and Mixed Systems', *International Political Science Review*, vol. 18, no. 3, p. 298)

We can see the effect of this in the Australian parliament, where the different electoral systems used for elections for the House of Representatives and the Senate produced different outcomes in terms of party representation in each chamber.

Elections and democracy

An essential criterion for a democracy is the notion of sovereignty of the people—or, in simple terms, the concept of 'government of the people, by the people'. Direct democracy, where all citizens vote on every issue, is impossible to achieve in our modern industrialised societies, where government is complex and comprehensive. For that reason, representative institutions, made up of citizens chosen by the people to make political decisions on their behalf, have become an integral part of modern liberal democracies. The concept of liberal democracy was explained in Chapter 1.

A freely elected legislature, such as the Australian parliament, is the mechanism by which society can determine who will form the government, and gives society the capacity to control the activities of that government through frequent elections. In other words, a government that does not meet the expectations of the people can be removed through the electoral process.

> A good voting system:
> - provides for frequent elections;
> - is based on procedures that are user-friendly;
> - allows for all adults to vote, without prejudice against individuals or groups;
> - has clear and accepted laws about voting;

> - is based upon a secret ballot;
> - has a clear and accepted process for counting votes and deciding on a winning candidate;
> - incorporates 'one vote, one value';
> - has results based on majority rule;
> - provides freedom from false, misleading or unfair influence on voters; and
> - ensures elections are administered in an impartial way.
>
> (*Source*: ACT Electoral Commission 2007, 'Voting Systems', http://www.elections.act.gov.au/elections/votingsystems.html, reproduced with the permission of the ACT Electoral Commission)

Free elections and universal suffrage are necessary if this concept of democracy is to work effectively. Voting in elections is the principal instance, and for some the only occasion, when citizens participate actively and openly in the political process.

> **Elements of liberal democracy relevant to elections**
> - Representative institutions made up of citizens chosen by the people.
> - Rotation of office, so that ruling elites do not gain control of the system.
> - The right of every citizen to participate in the political system.
> - Fair and frequent elections.

Politicians and elections

Frequent elections are a positive incentive for politicians to take note of what the citizens want. It is important to them that the system is accepted by the citizens as fair, because it is elections that give governments their legitimacy.

> The result of the 1975 Australian federal election, after the contentious dismissal of the Whitlam government by the governor-general, was accepted without question on all sides of politics, even by those who felt passionately that the election ought not to have been held at all. Once the people had spoken, and so clearly in favour of the Coalition parties led by Malcolm Fraser, there was no doubt as to who should govern.

However tempted those in power may be to change the electoral system in their own favour so as to procure an indefinite stay in office, two things operate to stay their hand:

1 *Politics is always uncertain, and the manipulation of the system by one side is a change in the rules that will unquestionably be repeated by the other side when it finally returns to power.* In 1949 the Labor government of Queensland, fearing defeat in 1950, changed the system from one-man, one-vote, which had been in place since 1910. It acted to serve its own interest by varying the number of votes in each electorate to take advantage of the party's voting strength in country areas. Several years later it fell apart because of factional disputes, and the Liberal and National parties came to office. In 1958 they changed the system to benefit themselves.

In 1971, the Country Party premier, Joh Bjelke-Petersen, introduced a zonal system that gave different weighting to votes in different parts of the state and, again, favoured his party's voting strength in country areas.

> **The Bjelkemander**
> In 1977—'faced with an election—Bjelke-Petersen again used the zonal system to eliminate some Liberal party seats and lessen their challenge to coalition leadership.'
> (*Source*: Lunn, H. 1978, *Joh*, University of Queensland Press, Brisbane, pp. 120–1)

The Country Party retained office until they had lost so much support that even the electoral system could not save them—they lost the 1992 election. The new Labor government then modified the system to make it easier for them to retain office. Labor subsequently was successful in the 1995 election, albeit in a very close result.

New South Wales introduced a system of four-year fixed-term parliaments in 1991 in order to attract the support of the independents who held the balance of power in the New South Wales Legislative Assembly at that time.

> New South Wales premier, Nick Greiner, 'tried to accommodate the independents. His first concession was to guarantee that the administration would legislate to require governments to serve their full four-year term; a government would only go to an early poll if it was defeated in a confidence motion.'
> (*Source*: Dodkin, M. 2003, *Bob Carr: The Reluctant Leader*, UNSW Press, Sydney, p. 66)

The fixed four-year term was subsequently agreed to by the NSW electorate at a referendum in 1993.

Such sequences are unusual: by tacit consent the political parties leave the electoral system alone if it is generally considered a fair one.

2   *Most of those who take part in politics share a belief that electoral systems ought to be fair*—or at least as fair as possible since, as we shall see, fairness is only one of the desired qualities of an electoral system.

Occasionally, the power of these shared values is demonstrated dramatically. Senator Steele Hall, Liberal premier of South Australia in the late 1960s, brought about a change in that state's electoral system that was bound to disadvantage his own party because he felt that its current term of office was not legitimate.

So intense is the scrutiny with which changes in the electoral system are greeted, and so likely to attract charges of unfairness or bias, that few politicians will think it worth the effort unless the disadvantage their party suffers is substantial. Nevertheless, there is a strong element of self-interest in perceptions of electoral systems, and what seems fair to some people seems unfair to others. The longest running argument has been over the principle of 'one vote, one value' and the relative representation of rural and urban electors in Australia.

The debates that occurred during Labor's term of office between 1973 and 1975 about its proposals to alter the Commonwealth electoral system illustrate these points. Most of the proposed changes were minor ones, unlikely to benefit one party at the expense of another. However, one proposal involved reducing the extent to which electorates could vary in size (that is, in the numbers of electors enrolled in each seat). Here there was great disagreement, with Labor spokespersons claiming that the change would mean a fairer system, while those from the Opposition, especially the National Country Party, arguing that it would be unfair to country citizens because they would lose representation they already enjoyed. Clearly, there was disagreement about what was to count as fair.

Many of the same issues arose in 1988 around one of the Hawke government's unsuccessful referendum proposals, which attempted to enshrine 'fair and democratic elections' (one vote, one value) in the Constitution.

> **The 1988 'fair elections' referendum question**
> 'A Proposed Law: To alter the Constitution to provide for fair and democratic parliamentary elections throughout Australia. Do you approve this proposed alteration?'

The referendum was opposed by the Liberal and National parties. It did not achieve a majority of votes, nor was it approved by a majority of states, so it was not carried.

TYPES OF ELECTORAL SYSTEMS

> 'Depending on how the system is designed it may be easier or harder for particular parties to gain representation in parliament; it may be more or less likely that one party can form a government on its own.'
> (*Source*: Farrell, D.M. 2001, *Electoral Systems: A Comparative Introduction*, Palgrave Macmillan, Basingstoke, UK, p. 3)

There are different types of electoral systems used around the world to elect a government. The electoral system is complemented by electoral laws that prescribe such things as who can vote, whether voting is compulsory or not, and rules about campaign finances and public funding. Some of these laws may be derived from a country's constitution or they may be enacted as statutes by the parliament. We can see the effect of this in Table 8.1, which sets out the different ways the countries in our study have organised their elections.

Electoral systems fall within four general categories. Each has its advantages and disadvantages:

- single-member plurality, commonly known as 'first past the post';
- single-member majoritarian or 'alternative vote', commonly known as 'preferential' voting in Australia;
- proportional representation; and
- mixed plurality.

The type of electoral system a country selects may have its basis in political culture or history and the nature of the party system. We will now explain how these systems work, with examples drawn from the countries we have used for our study.

TABLE 8.1
Electoral systems and terms of office compared

Country	Type of electoral system	Term of office
Britain: House of Commons	Single-member plurality ('first past the post')	Five years
Australia: House of Representatives	Single-member majoritarian (alternative vote or preferential system)	Constitution requires election be held no later than three years after the previous election
US: House of Representatives	Single-member plurality ('first past the post')	Constitution requires elections to be held every two years; this is a fixed term. Elections held the first Tuesday in November
Malaysia: House of Representatives	Single-member plurality ('first past the post')	Constitution requires election to be held at least once every five years
Germany: Bundestag	Mixed-member proportional	Basic Law (constitution) requires elections to be held every four years

Single-member plurality

This is a simple system based on single-member constituencies, where voters are required to indicate on the ballot paper only the candidate they prefer. The candidate with the most votes, or a plurality of the votes, wins the seat. Of the countries included in our study, this system is used in Britain, the House of Representatives and the Senate in the United States, and Malaysia.

> **The Electoral College system in the United States**
>
> House of Representatives and Senate elections in the United States use the single-member plurality system, but the election of the president is conducted using an indirect electoral college system. The president is not elected by direct vote of the people but by members of the Electoral College of each state. Electors in each state cast a vote for a presidential candidate and the members of the Electoral College for that state then cast their votes accordingly. A winner-takes-all system operates, so that the candidate with the most number of popular votes in a state gets the support of the total number of delegates for that state.
>
> A candidate needs at least 270 Electoral College votes to win. Not all states have an equal number of delegates to the Electoral College, so this makes it important for a presidential candidate to win the majority of votes in the states with the greatest number of Electoral College votes. It is possible for a president to be elected who has not achieved a majority of the popular vote, but gains a majority of Electoral College votes. Electoral College electors are not legally obliged to support the candidate with the majority of the popular vote, and some occasionally fail to do so. (*Source*: For discussion of the operations of the Electoral College system, see Vile, M.J.C. 2007, *Politics in the USA*, 6th ed., Routledge, Oxford, pp. 87–92)

You will find an illustration of how the votes are counted using the single-member plurality system in the 'Notes on voting methods' section at the end of this chapter.

One advantage of this system is that it can produce stable government because it is more likely that one party, or a coalition of parties (such as the Barisan Nasional (National Front) in Malaysia), will win the majority of seats. Of course, this is less likely if minor parties and/or independents hold the balance of power, and a major party then has to rely on their support to form a government.

However, in those countries where there are two strong major parties (commonly known as a two-party system—see Chapter 9), the 'first past the post' system makes it difficult for minor parties or independents to get elected. This is evident from Tables 8.2 to 8.4, which show some election results in Britain, Malaysia and the United States.

TABLE 8.2
Britain, general election 2005 (House of Commons)

Party	Percentage of votes	Number of seats won
Labour Party	35.3	356
Conservative Party	32.3	198
Liberal Democrat	22.1	62
Scottish National Party	1.5	6
Democratic Unionist Party	0.9	9
Plaid Cymru	0.6	3
Sinn Fein	0.6	5
Ulster Unionist	0.5	1
Social Democratic and Labour	0.5	3
Independent	0.5	1
Respect	0.3	1

(*Source*: See The Electoral Commission (UK) 2006, 'UK General Election 2005', http://www.electoralcommission.org.uk/elections/results/general_elections/uk-general-election-2006 for more information.)

TABLE 8.3
Federation of Malaysia, general election 2008 (House of Representatives)

Party	Percentage of votes won	Number of seats won
Barisan Nasional (National Front coalition)	50.6	140
Opposition coalition	49.4	82

(*Source*: See Election Commission of Malaysia at http://www.spr.gov.my for more information.)

TABLE 8.4
United States, House of Representatives election 2006

Party	Percentage of votes won	Number of seats won
Democrats	52.0	233
Republicans	44.1	202

(*Source*: See Office of the Clerk, US House of Representatives, Election Statistics at http://clerk.house.gov/member_info/electionInfo/ and the Federal Election Commission at http://www.fec.gov/pubrec/fe2006/2006tables.pdf for detailed results of the 2006 election.)

Minor parties and independents did win some seats, but between them the Labour and Conservative parties secured 67.6 per cent of the votes, which delivered them 85.9 per cent of the total number of seats.

Barisan Nasional (BN) (see Chapter 9) is a coalition of parties that has won the majority of seats and formed the government of Malaysia since independence in 1955. The 2008 election was notable because it produced a marked weakening of support for the BN from the previous election in 2004, when it held 198 seats in the 222-seat parliament.

The two major parties overwhelmingly dominate elections for the US House of Representatives. In 2006, minor parties and independents between them were able to attract only 3.9 per cent of the vote.

Because the single-member plurality system favours the major parties, it is hard for minorities to win seats in the parliament, a factor which diminishes the democratic principles of equal participation and representation. It also means the votes of people who vote for minor parties can be wasted because they have little chance of seeing their candidate elected.

Another problem is the fact that when a number of candidates stand for a single constituency it is possible for one person to get elected with a minority of the total votes cast. In other words, the person with the highest number of votes gets elected, but the majority of electors did not vote for that candidate. The single-member majoritarian system was developed to overcome this problem.

Single-member majoritarian (second ballot) system

Under this system, candidates who win an absolute majority of votes are declared elected. If no candidate wins a majority, then a second ballot is conducted. In this ballot, candidates who did not get a specified proportion of votes are excluded. It is usual for only the two leading candidates to stand for the second ballot, so the winner is elected by majority vote. This system is used for the presidential election in France.

Single-member majoritarian (alternative vote) system

This system requires voters to rank the candidates on the ballot paper in their order of preference. Candidates that secure a majority of first-preference votes at the first count—that is, 50 per cent plus 1 vote—are declared elected. In seats where no candidate achieves a majority of first-preference votes, the candidate with the least number of votes is excluded and his or her second preferences are distributed. This process continues until one of the candidates obtains a majority. Very few countries have adopted this system, but it is used for elections for the Australian House of Representatives and is discussed later in this chapter.

The advantage of this system is that it gives voters the opportunity to vote for a minor party or independent candidate and still have a say in who is to be elected through the distribution of their second preferences. You will find an illustration of the method for counting votes under this system in the 'Notes on voting methods' section at the end of the chapter.

Optional preferential

This variant of the single-member majoritarian system allows voters to indicate a preference on the ballot paper for one candidate only, and is used for elections for the New South Wales Legislative Assembly. If most of the voters take this option, it will weaken the preferential character of the voting system so that it becomes more like a 'first past the post' election.

Multi-member proportional representation (PR) system

> 'Proportional systems must employ multi-seat districts, usually with party lists and typically produce parliamentary representation that largely mirrors the vote shares of multiple parties.'
> (*Source*: Shugart, M.S. & Wattenberg, M.P. 2005, 'Mixed Member Electoral Systems: A Definition and Typology', in Shugart, M.S. & Wattenberg, M.P. (eds), *Mixed-Member Electoral Systems: The Best of Both Worlds?*, Oxford University Press, Oxford, p. 9)

Proportional systems are widely used in countries around the world. Candidates stand for election in multi-member seats, either singly or as members of a party list, and become elected by gaining a 'quota'—that is, a set fraction of the total vote. Because seats are apportioned according to the percentage of the vote received, there is a greater opportunity for minor parties and/or independents to get elected.

There are two variants: the first is a *party list* system where each party draws up a list of candidates for each electorate, and electors vote for the party of their choice. The proportion of votes each party receives determines how many seats it wins, and the successful candidates are elected in the order of priority listed by the party on the ballot paper. The disadvantage of this system is that it focuses on parties at the expense of individual candidates. The electors are given no say in the candidates the party selects.

There is also a *single transferable vote* (STV) option where electors vote for individual candidates by order of preference. This system allows parties to put forward a list of candidates, and for individuals to stand as well. You will find an illustration of how votes are counted using the STV system in the 'Note on voting methods' section at the end of the chapter.

The STV system is used for the Australian Senate, although it does give voters the option of voting 'above the line' for a party list, which will be explained later in the chapter.

Because it is harder for one party to gain an overall majority, proportional representation systems can deliver unstable governments. Governments may be formed by a coalition of parties and while this arrangement may last the full term, coalitions can collapse because it may be difficult to achieve cohesion and overall agreement on the broad range of issues that a government has to deal with.

Mixed-member proportional (MMP)

Other countries have established a mixed electoral system combining a single-member plurality vote with a party list vote. This system gives electors two votes: one for an individual candidate to represent his or her constituency and another for the party it would like to govern.

> MMP systems are 'seen as providing an ideal solution because of their hybrid nature in offering both SMP (single-member plurality) and PR (proportional representation) elections in the one system.'
> (Source: Farrell, D.M. 2001, *Electoral Systems: A Comparative Introduction*, Palgrave Macmillan, Basingstoke, UK, p. 97)

MMP was adopted in New Zealand to replace the 'first past the post' system, which had resulted in the parliament being dominated by the two major parties, the New Zealand Labour Party and the National Party. The change to MMP was an attempt to gain better representation for minorities.

Federal Republic of Germany

MMP is used for elections for the German Bundestag. Each elector gets two votes: a single-member plurality vote and a party list vote. Each state (Lander) is divided into constituencies. Half the seats in the Bundestag are allotted to these constituencies, where electors vote for the candidate of their choice, and the results are decided on a single-member plurality basis ('first past the post'). The other half of the seats are allotted to the winners of the party list vote.

This is a proportional system—the successful parties are determined based on their quota of the total vote—and it is designed to ensure that seats are allocated in proportion to the votes cast for a particular party. (For an excellent discussion of this system see Farrell, D.M. 2001, *Electoral Systems: A Comparative Introduction*, Palgrave Macmillan, Basingstoke, UK, Chapter 5.)

THE AUSTRALIAN ELECTORAL SYSTEM

Origins

Arguments about fairness are a 20th-century contribution to the debate about electoral systems, but the debate is much older. Indeed, the debate about who should have the right to vote was the central episode in constitutional reform in 19th-century Britain. For the most part it hardly touched the Australian colonies, where manhood suffrage was introduced for elections to the Legislative Assembly of New South Wales in 1858, soon after responsible government began.

FIGURE 8.1

End of campaign party

In reality, some campaigns turn voters off in droves.

Along with a universal right to vote for adult men came the secret ballot, so unusual in its time that it was referred to elsewhere for a long time as the 'Australian ballot'.

> 'The effect of the ballot being taken up in the Australian colonies was immediate. The Australian precedent proved instructive in the debates which preceded the introduction of the ballot in Britain in 1872, and was also influential in the discussions surrounding the adoption of the ballot in the various State legislatures of the United States in the nineteenth century.'
> (Source: McKenna, M. 2001, 'Building a "Closet of Prayer" in the New World: The Story of the "Australian Ballot"', in Sawer, M. (ed.), *Elections Full, Free and Fair*, The Federation Press, Sydney, p. 46)

In 1893 the number of votes exercised by a NSW voter was reduced to one; previously a man could vote both where he lived and in electorates where he held property.

> The proposal to abolish plural voting in New South Wales had its supporters:
> - 'Under the present law, one man may have a vote for his residence, and give six or seven votes for his properties. There are a number of persons who contend that this is an abuse of the Constitution . . . There is no inherent right for one man to be represented more than another.'
>
> There were also those who opposed the idea:
> - 'We pass many laws which affect a man's rights, life and liberty; but we also pass a great many laws—by far the larger part of those that are passed with respect to the preservation or otherwise of the rights of property . . . It is sometimes argued that every man has a right to be represented; but that is a very different thing from arguing that every man should have an equal voice in the representation of the country.'
>
> (Source: *New South Wales Parliamentary Debates, 1892–1893*, vol. LXI, pp. 2234–5, 2463–4, 2467, cited in Crowley, F. 1980, *A Documentary History of Australia, Volume 3: Colonial Australia 1875–1900*, Nelson, Melbourne, pp. 397–9)

The colonies produced democratic electoral systems partly because of the absence of a powerful entrenched conservative class. A large proportion of the colonial populations (except in South Australia) was of convict origin or were poor immigrants or their descendants, and some of them had become wealthy. If a property qualification were to be used, it would enfranchise some former convicts but exclude some free men. The simplest solution, and one accepted by most politicians of the day, was to give all men the right to vote in elections for the lower houses of the colonial parliaments, but to guard against the feared 'excesses' of 'untrammelled democracy' through a Legislative Council which could block 'hasty' or 'ill-considered' legislation, and in which the propertied interests of the colonies were disproportionately represented.

Women generally did not have the right to vote in the 19th century. This was first granted in New Zealand in 1893. South Australia followed suit in 1894. However, voting rights for women and the right to stand for parliament were not adopted uniformly throughout Australia at the state and Commonwealth levels for some time, as Table 8.5 shows.

TABLE 8.5
Women and the right to vote in Australia

	Voting rights	Right to stand for parliament
South Australia	1895	1895
Western Australia	1899	1920
Australia (Commonwealth)	1902	1902
New South Wales	1902	1918
Tasmania	1903	1921
Queensland	1905	1915
Victoria	1908	1923

Note: Aboriginal women gained the right to vote in federal elections, along with Aboriginal men, in 1962.

(*Source*: Australian Electoral Commission 2007, 'Electoral Milestones for Women', http://www.aec.gov.au/elections/australian_electoral_history/wright.htm)

The Commonwealth electoral system in 1902

When the colonies federated, there was a need for a new national electoral system. This did not produce a sustained debate about democracy, because the general lines on which the new system would operate were those then operating in the colonies. These were agreed to be democratic under the standards operating at the time, at least insofar as they related to elections for the lower houses of parliament. The basic principles were:

- Every white man, and from 1902 every white woman, should have one vote and only one vote. Aboriginal people were not able to vote.
- Voting should be secret.
- Each state should have a share of the numbers of the federal House of Representatives on the basis of population, except that no state should have fewer than five seats.

- Within the states, the numbers of voters in the various electorates (or divisions) was to be more or less equal.
- Elections were to be held at least once every three years.
- Each member of parliament in the lower house was to represent a group of citizens in terms of where they lived.

All this was set out in the Constitution or in the first *Commonwealth Franchise Act* and *Electoral Act* of 1902, and the result has proved to be a remarkably robust and stable system. It survives to the present, unaltered except for the fact that the voting age has been reduced from 21 to 18, and Aboriginal people have had the right to vote since 1962.

AN ACT
To provide for an Uniform Federal Franchise
(Assented to 12th June 1902)

s. 3 (persons entitled to vote)
Subject to the disqualifications hereafter set out, all persons not under twenty-one years of age whether male or female married or unmarried—
(a) Who have lived in Australia for six months continuously, and
(b) Who are natural born or naturalized subjects of the King, and
(c) Whose names are on the Electoral Roll for any Electoral Division, shall be entitled to vote at the election of Members of the Senate and the House of Representatives.

s. 4 (disqualifications)
No person who is of unsound mind and no person attainted of treason, or who has been convicted and is under sentence or subject to be sentenced for any offence punishable under the law of any part of the King's dominions by imprisonment for one year or longer, shall be entitled to vote at any election of Members of the Senate or House of Representatives.

s. 5 (disqualification of coloured races)
No aboriginal native of Australia Asia Africa or the Islands of the Pacific except New Zealand shall be entitled to have his name placed on an Electoral Roll unless so entitled under section forty-one of the Constitution.

(Source: Commonwealth Franchise Act 1902)

Counting the votes

The changes that have occurred in the electoral system have mostly affected the counting of votes.

'First past the post' (single-member plurality)

In the 19th century, voters placed a cross against the name of the candidate for whom they were voting; when the votes were counted, whoever received the largest number of crosses was declared elected, even if that number was much less than an absolute majority (50 per cent plus 1). This procedure, discussed above, made good sense where the number of electors was small and the issues restricted. As the century progressed, the electorate grew large and politics more complex, and theorists pointed out that the simple majority system was less than perfect. It could, for example, result in the election of someone who had won only a tiny proportion of the total vote.

The second ballot

Several remedies were proposed. One was the 'second ballot': if no candidate won an absolute majority, then a second election was to be held between the two most successful candidates only. This system had some support then and now. As we saw above, it is used today for the election of the French president, and it was used in New South Wales between 1910 and 1920 in elections for the Legislative Assembly. The second ballot undoubtedly produced majorities, but at considerable expense and with some delay. In closely contested seats, it provided two quite different contests: the first a race or struggle to be one of the two candidates left in the second ballot; the second the ballot between those two candidates. In practice, most of the virtues of the second ballot procedure are provided also by preferential voting, and with less confusion and cost.

Elections at large

A second remedy was that there should be no individual electorates at all, and that the whole state should choose MPs from among the full range of candidates offering. This was provided in the Constitution as a possible means of electing the first House of Representatives, and two states, South Australia and Tasmania, used it for that purpose. This system was never popular, for two reasons:

1. It paid no regard to the social fact that people live in communities, and that these communities have, or are seen to have, different and competing interests. Many citizens were and are attached to the notion that 'their' local member exists to promote their interests and look after them generally. Although local communities have become less important in Australian life since the Second World War and the subsequent growth of suburbia (which submerges them), these sentiments alone are probably still strong enough to prevent the adoption of a list system for lower house elections.
2. MPs themselves are apprehensive about any system that does not give them a base in a given area. Although party endorsement is the crucial factor in determining whether or not a candidate is likely to win, he or she will win more votes if they are well and favourably known, and this is most likely to happen in local communities.

Preferential voting (single-member majoritarian—alternative vote)

> **Preferential voting** is used for elections for the House of Representatives.

This solution was first proposed in the 19th century. Voters would rank the candidates in numerical order. If no candidate won an absolute majority, the least popular candidates would in turn be excluded, and their votes distributed to the other candidates according to the preference of the voter, until one candidate finally did possess an absolute majority. In theory an attractive device, because it is simple, fair and cheap, preferential voting has not been much adopted outside Australia, probably because existing systems in other countries have broad acceptance in their own communities. This system also enhances the power of minor parties, because even though they are unlikely to win a seat in their own right, they may be able to bargain their preferences in return for concessions with the major parties. This is particularly the case where an election is likely to be decided by the allocation of second preference votes in a number of key seats. For example, the preferential system has enabled the Coalition partners—the Liberal and National parties—to stand candidates against one another and to exchange preferences without risking the seat being lost to Labor. The Greens took advantage of the system to try to gain the support of the Hawke–Keating Labor government for their preferred policies, with some success. In the 1998 election the major parties, by putting Pauline Hanson's One Nation party last on their how-to-vote cards, were able to prevent that party gaining a seat in the House of Representatives. This method of voting was used for Senate elections until 1949. It is still used for elections for the House of Representatives.

Proportional representation (mixed-member proportional representation)

> Proportional voting is used for the **Senate**.

Yet another remedy, more popular both in theory and practice, was proportional representation (PR). Advocates of PR had a particular passion for 'fairness', which PR was designed to achieve. Candidates would stand for election in multi-member seats, either singly or as members of a party list, and become elected by gaining a 'quota'—that is, a set fraction of the total vote.

Proportional representation tends to represent parties and groups in parliament very much in proportion to the shares of the vote they secured in the election, and for that reason it is desired by smaller parties, especially when their strength is spread thinly across many seats. For example, the Australian Democrats were unable to win a seat in the House of Representatives in 1990 under the preferential system, although they achieved 11.3 per cent of first-preference votes. Minor parties have been more successful with the proportional system used for Senate elections.

> Although their percentage share of first-preference votes has been small, the Australian Democrats, the Greens and Family First have been able to secure Senate seats in some states after the distribution of preferences provided them with a quota.

Proportional voting has been used in Australia for a long time. It was employed first in Tasmania in 1907, then in New South Wales in 1920–27, in elections for the Australian Senate since 1949, and more recently in elections for the Legislative Councils in South Australia and New South Wales. ACT electors voted by referendum for its introduction for elections for the ACT Legislative Assembly. Yet, proportional representation is not without its critics:

- It can divorce the MP from his or her constituents. (Members of the Legislative Assembly in New South Wales were happy to see it go in 1927, after several years of experience.)
- It tends to add to the power of state executives at the expense of local party organisations, because the selection of party teams is normally conducted by the central organisation.

For the Australian Senate, the rule is that the party executives decide who is to be allowed to win seats, both by approving candidates and by deciding the order of the party team. From 1949 to 1983, each state elected 10 senators, five at a time. The major party groups—the ALP, and the Liberal and National parties—could each normally rely on winning 40 per cent of the vote, which was a good deal more than the number of votes required to win two seats each. The real interest in a Senate election was thus the fate of the fifth seat. Much of the same has been true in 'double dissolution' elections (see Chapter 3), when all 10 senators went to the polls. Both major party groups could count on winning at least four seats each. The real contest was for the ninth and tenth seats, and candidates placed in low positions in their party's Senate team would have a low chance of success.

Since 1983 each state has returned 12 senators. The quota is determined on a state-by-state basis, so it varies between states. The quota is worked out by dividing the total number of formal ballot papers by one more than the number of vacancies to be filled and by adding one to the result. For example, for a half-Senate election with six senators to be elected for each state, this would be done as follows:

$$\frac{\textit{Formal ballot papers}}{(6 + 1)} = (\quad) + 1 = \text{Quota}$$

The smaller the quota—that is, in a double dissolution where there are 12 to be elected for each state—the easier it is for minor party candidates and independents to get elected.

Proportional representation has increased the power of the party machines, which was by no means the intention of its supporters. Furthermore, in voting for the Senate, since 1984 political parties have been allowed to register a ticket that allocates preferences according to the party's wishes.

> Prime Minister Bob Hawke explained the reasons for the change: 'Formerly ballot papers could only be validly marked by placing a number in the square beside each candidate. But in recent times Senate ballot papers carried a multitude of names and had grown unwieldy. The complexity and requirements of the ballot paper meant that the informal vote had rocketed. Under our reforms, all that was necessary now was a single mark to indicate the party preference.'
> (Source: Hawke, R.J.L. 1994, The Hawke Memoirs, Heinemann, Melbourne, p. 275, copyright Hon. Bob Hawke A.C.)

Voters may now support the party ticket by registering a single preference; that is, by placing a single number 1 for the party of their choice in a box above the line on the ballot paper. At the 1996 half-Senate election, 94.4 per cent of voters chose to allocate their vote in this manner.

This variation has further increased the power of the party machines, but it is vulnerable to another charge as well. Parliaments elected under PR often contain no party with a majority of seats, and a coalition of two or more parties is necessary to determine responsibility. If a coalition government governs badly, which party is responsible, and how should electors vote at the next elections? Questions like these are directed against PR, and it is commonly held to be associated with weak and indecisive governments. PR does not automatically produce coalitions, but it cannot be denied that PR tends to reproduce in parliament party strength in proportion to their support in the elections. Why this should be so is discussed later.

THE DEVELOPMENT OF THE COMMONWEALTH ELECTORAL SYSTEM

The methods for counting the votes in the electoral systems important to Australia—simple majority, preferential and proportional representation—are described in detail at the end of this chapter. The *Electoral Act 1902* provided for simple majority voting for both houses of Australian parliament. Preferential voting was introduced for the House of Representatives in 1918, and for the Senate in 1919. The Senate's electoral system was changed again in 1948 to provide for proportional representation. Compulsory enrolment, introduced in 1911, was seen as a means of ensuring 'clean' electoral rolls: if everyone was on the electoral roll, then there was little potential for the sudden 'stacking' of a roll just prior to an election in the interests of one or other candidate.

Compulsory voting

Compulsory voting had a different rationale. Compulsory enrolment was introduced in 1911. Compulsory voting passed quickly and quietly through parliament as a private member's bill in 1924, which has led to arguments that it was prearranged in the interests of all parties. Certainly, by reducing greatly the demands on parties at election time for cars and canvassers, compulsory voting reduces parties' costs (and the size of the parties: in Britain, where voting is not compulsory, up to 12 per cent of the electorate has belonged to one or other of the parties; in Australia the figure is 4 per cent). However, the ostensible reasons had to do with the low turnout in recent elections. Turnout at federal elections had ranged between 50 and 57 per cent between 1901 and 1906, but in the next decade it rose to around 75 per cent. In 1922, however, turnout dropped again and it was argued that Australia might be in for another period of governments elected by minorities:

- If only half of the electorate turned out to vote, and only half of them supported the winning party, then the government would be the choice of only a quarter of the citizens. This was seen to be a bad thing, as it might encourage irresponsibility on the part of governments and citizens alike.
- If everyone turned out to vote, on the other hand, then whatever the result (especially now that preferential voting produced results that were in some sense real majorities), the government had some claim to be considered the national choice; its laws and decisions would thus truly be binding on the whole community.

This is not a wholly persuasive argument, and quite heavy guns can be produced against it:

- Citizens have a right *not* to vote, so if they consider the choice offered to them to be a deplorable one they should not be forced to do so.
- An election result determined in part by the votes of those with no knowledge or interest in the matter is surely a worrying one.

The major parties have never shown any intention of revoking compulsory voting, partly because of the obvious advantages to them in terms of money and energy, and partly because no party has been relatively disadvantaged by it. The electorate seems

Arguments in favour of compulsory voting
- Voting is a civic duty comparable to other duties citizens perform, such as taxation, compulsory education and jury duty.
- There are educative benefits to political participation.
- Parliament reflects more accurately 'the will of the electorate'.
- Governments must consider the total electorate in policy formulation and management.
- Candidates can concentrate their campaigning energies on issues, rather than encouraging voters to attend the poll.
- The voter is not actually compelled to vote for anyone, because voting is by secret ballot.

Arguments against compulsory voting
- It is undemocratic to force people to vote—an infringement of liberty.
- The 'ignorant' and those with little interest in politics are forced to the polls.
- It may increase the number of 'donkey votes'.
- It may increase the number of informal votes.
- It increases the number of safe, single-member electorates—political parties can then concentrate on the more marginal electorates.
- Resources must be allocated to determine whether those who failed to vote have 'valid and sufficient' reasons.

(*Source*: Australian Electoral Commission 2007, 'Compulsory Voting', http://www.aec.gov.au/Voting/Compulsory_Voting.htm)

content: public opinion polls and other survey evidence have shown substantial support for compulsory voting and suggest that electors believe it is important that everyone turn out on election day no matter how little he or she knows about the issues, the candidates or the leaders.

'A further, less tangible benefit of compulsory voting is its function as an agent of social cohesion and a preservative of political community . . . In the lead-up to, and on election day itself, politics in Australia is, literally, everybody's business . . . Voting Saturday is a social occasion. Pamphleteers and party volunteers jostle at the entrances to polling booths, exchanging competitive but good-natured banter as incoming voters pause to join the conversational festivities on their way to the booths. Local residents congregate nearby at communal garage sales, while parents and friends of the schools which temporarily serve as polling stations hold fetes and cake stalls. The carnival atmosphere is overlaid with a more serious sense that something important is happening; that for one day we are *all* contributing to the democratic process, each of us with equal clout, regardless of our contingent status.'
(*Source*: Hill, L. 2001, '"A Great Leveller": Compulsory Voting', in Sawer, M. (ed.), *Elections Full, Free and Fair*, The Federation Press, Sydney, pp. 135–6)

The fact that Australia has compulsory voting does not mean that every person eligible to vote does so. Some people, for a variety of reasons, are not enrolled to vote where they currently reside. Some may have moved and not changed their registration.

Young people who reach the voting age of 18 years, and others, may not think of enrolling to vote until an election occurs. The Howard government made it more difficult for these people to enrol to vote: it cut the period for enrolment once the writs have been issued for an election from seven days to 8 pm on the same day. The only exceptions are young people aged 17 who will turn 18 between the day the writs are issued and the day of the election, and people who will become Australian citizens over the same period. Both of these groups have until 8 pm three working days after the writ is issued to enrol.

> Full details of the requirements for enrolling to vote can be found on the Australian Electoral Commission website at http://www.aec.gov.au. See also Brent, P. & Costar, B. 2007, 'Election 2007: Missing Voters', Australian Policy Online, 2 November 2007, http://apo.org.au.

REDISTRIBUTIONS

The 19th-century electoral reforms had one great goal: equality and universality of the franchise. When all men (later all men and women) had the vote, they argued, citizens would come into their inheritance and good laws would be made. The reformers were opposed, therefore, to plural voting and to the property franchise, but they were less concerned about equality of the sizes of electorates, for two reasons:

- Until enrolment was compulsory, the size of an electorate depended in part on the willingness of people to enrol, and could vary over time.
- Country districts were hard to get around (roads were bad, and transport slow and difficult) and country communities competitive and antagonistic: each town fought with its neighbour for the railway, for new public works, for government offices, and so on. Rural electorates therefore had to be relatively small in numbers of voters.

Once the modern party system began, however, the inequality in the sizes of electorates became an issue in the party battle, because country electorates tended to return non-Labor members of parliament. For the most part, the 20th-century wrangle about 'fairness' has gone on in the states rather than at the federal level, for from the very beginning the Australian electoral system put a limit on the extent to which one electorate could be smaller than another. In this it followed the New South Wales *Electoral Act 1893*. This limit now allows only a 10 per cent variation from the size of an average electorate.

The means whereby Australia is divided into electorates (strictly speaking, 'divisions') is known as a redistribution. It is a complex process that has been summarised by the Australian Electoral Commission as follows:

- Redistributions are one of the responsibilities of the Australian Electoral Commission. The redistribution is undertaken by a committee consisting of the Electoral Commissioner, the Australian Electoral Officer of the state concerned, and the state's Surveyor-General and Auditor-General.

- A redistribution takes place when:
  - the number of parliamentary representatives to which a state or territory is entitled has changed because of changes to the population quota;
  - the number of electors in more than one-third of the divisions in a state, or one of the divisions in the Australian Capital Territory or Northern Territory, deviates from the average divisional enrolment by over 10 per cent for more than two months; or
  - a period of seven years has elapsed since the previous redistribution.

(*Source*: Australian Electoral Commission 2007, 'Past Redistributions—Frequently Asked Questions', http://www.aec.gov.au/FAQs/Redistributions.htm)

> **The redistribution process**
> - The number of members of the House of Representatives is fixed ('as nearly as practicable') at twice the number of senators (Constitution, s. 24). This relationship is called the nexus.
> - The electoral commissioner invites public suggestions on the redistribution, which must be lodged within 30 days. A further period of 14 days is then allowed for comments on the suggestions lodged.
> - A 'quota' is calculated by dividing the number of electors in the state or territory by the number of members of the House of Representatives to be chosen for that state or territory. The Redistribution Committee then divides the state or territory into a division according to the quota.
> - A period of 28 days is then allowed after publication of the proposed redistribution for written objections. A further period of 14 days is provided for comments on the objections lodged. These objections are heard by an augmented Electoral Commission consisting of the four members of the Redistribution Committee and the two part-time members of the Electoral Commission.
> - At the time of the redistribution, the number of electors in the divisions may vary up to 10 per cent from the 'quota' or average divisional figure, but within 3.5 years the figures should not vary from the average by more or less than 3.5 per cent. Thus, the most rapidly growing divisions are started with enrolments well below the quota, while those that are losing population are started well above the quota.
> - The parliament has no power to reject or amend the final determination of the augmented Electoral Commission.
>
> (*Source*: Australian Electoral Commission 2007, 'Past Redistributions—Frequently Asked Questions', http://www.aec.gov.au/FAQs/Redistributions.htm)

This complex procedure exists because parties and MPs regard redistribution with the greatest apprehension. A change in these rules can affect a party's entitlement to seats far more powerfully than an election result. Nonetheless, the straightforwardness of the rules has reduced the debate on redistributions to a minimum, while the scrupulous conduct of the commissioners has meant that no redistribution has ever been challenged on grounds of the bias or dishonesty of the officials. This has not always been the case in the various states, where the procedures have been often both less fair and less open.

Some federal redistributions have been rejected. In 1962 the Country Party and the Labor Party combined to prevent the Liberal prime minister introducing a redistribution that would have cost these two parties seats. During the period of the Whitlam government a redistribution failed when the Opposition-controlled Senate rejected it (1975). In both cases, the objections were wholly partisan and reflected anxieties about impending losses. The first case did involve a continuing argument of principle, for the Country Party (now called the Nationals) claimed that a redistribution that abolished rural divisions while creating new urban divisions was obviously 'unfair'. Country people, the party argued, needed *more* political representation, not less, because of the difficulties under which country MPs operated.

'FAIRNESS'

On this question, the law is unclear:

- It seems obvious that the combined message of the Constitution and the *Electoral Act* is that electorates should be of approximately equal size across Australia (save for Tasmania, which is guaranteed at least five seats under the Constitution).
- On the other hand, the implication of the margins is that some seats can be smaller than others (though not a lot smaller), and the instructions suggest that country seats should be smaller.

There have been several attempts by the Nationals to have the *Electoral Act* emphasise this latter consideration, and thereby to have the notion of 'one vote, one value' moderated by its own notion of 'equality of effective representation'. The simplest way of achieving the latter would be the establishment of separate country and city regions with different quotas, as is done in all states except Tasmania and New South Wales, but the Nationals have been unable to achieve this goal in federal politics because of the opposition of the Liberals. The result is that the federal electoral system has usually been 'fairer' in terms of equality of voting than any of the state systems, save Tasmania. The unsuccessful 1988 referendum proposal 'to alter the Constitution to provide for fair and democratic parliamentary elections throughout Australia' was an attempt to extend to the states the principles that apply at the Commonwealth level.

'Fairness' remains a debating point, however, because every election seems to provide anomalies, which are used by the defeated or the otherwise disgruntled to suggest that there is something wrong with the system. Most of this debate centres about the relationship between the votes won by a party and the seats it secured as a result. An interesting example was the candidature of Pauline Hanson in the seat of Blair in 1998.

Blair
Candidates

Candidates	Party	% of first preference votes
McKenzie, Neal	DEM	3.64
White, Brett Ian	NP	10.25
Bassingthwaighte, Owen	CEC	0.29
Clarke, Virginia	ALP	25.29
Connors, Libby	GRN	1.80
Hanson, Pauline	HAN	35.97
Thompson, Cameron	LP	21.69

| Roberts, Lee | IND | 0.82 |
| Sloan, Mark | ACS | 0.25 |

The result after the distribution of preferences was:

| HANSON | 46.60 |
| THOMPSON | 53.40 |

(*Source*: Australian Electoral Commission 2007, '1998 Federal Election', http://www.aec.gov.au/Elections/federal_elections/1998)

You can see how the flow of preferences disadvantaged Pauline Hanson so that she did not win the seat, even though she had gained the greatest number of first-preference votes.

The results of the 2007 election for the House of Representatives (outlined in Table 8.6) illustrate how the distribution of votes and seats favours the major parties.

TABLE 8.6

The 2007 election: percentage of votes and seats won by party

	ALP	Liberal	Nationals	Greens	Family First	Independent
% of first-preference votes won	43.38	36.28	5.49	7.79	1.99	2.22
% of seats won	55.33	52.38	6.6	—	—	1.33

(*Source*: Australian Electoral Commission, '2007 Federal Election', http://www.aec.gov.au/Elections/federal_elections/2007, copyright Commonwealth of Australia, reproduced by permission)

PUBLIC FUNDING AND DISCLOSURE

The *Commonwealth Electoral Legislation Amendment Act 1983*, which took up most of the recommendations of a parliamentary Joint Select Committee on Electoral Reform, made a number of changes to the electoral system, some of which have already been mentioned in passing. Perhaps the most important new developments are to do with the public funding of election campaigns and the disclosure by candidates and political parties of campaign donations and electoral expenditure.

> 'We introduced public funding of election campaigns and political parties had now to disclose the source of campaign donations.'
> (*Source*: Hawke, R.J.L. 1994, *The Hawke Memoirs*, Heinemann, Melbourne, p. 275, copyright Hon. Bob Hawke A.C.)

The first election to be held under these provisions was the general election of December 1984.

Every registered political party, each state/territory branch of a registered political party, and associated organisations and trust funds are required to furnish an annual return to the commission detailing all amounts received, payments and debts for the financial year. Gifts totalling $1,500 or more made to a political party must be disclosed by the donor. Candidates and registered political parties are required also to disclose their election expenditure. This scheme is not watertight, however, as parties are able to take advantage of loopholes in the legislation to disguise the source of funding.

> 'Campaign costs continue to skyrocket and, with them the suspicion that corporate interests are buying political influence and hiding this influence behind political foundations and trusts.'
> (*Source*: Jupp, J. & Sawer, M. 2001, 'Political Parties, Partisanship and Electoral Governance', in Sawer, M. (ed.), *Elections Full, Free and Fair*, The Federation Press, Sydney, p. 229)

Public funding was introduced to alleviate possible problems, such as the potential for corruption, associated with parties having to seek large amounts of money from private sources to run their campaigns. Registered political parties, independents and Senate groups whose endorsed candidates receive at least 4 per cent of the total formal first-preference votes are entitled to election funding. This relieves some of the fund-raising pressure from these parties and groups, but tends to advantage existing parties and groups, particularly the major parties. It does not assist smaller parties or candidates who are struggling to become established and need funding to enhance their public recognition. An exception was Pauline Hanson's One Nation party, which polled sufficient first-preference votes at its first entry into a federal election in 1998 to qualify for public election funding. The Pauline Hanson Senate group qualified for public funding after the 2004 election.

> **Public funding**
> Funding is calculated by multiplying the number of formal first-preference votes received by the rate of payment applicable at the time. This amount is adjusted every six months in line with movements in the Consumer Price Index.
> - The current rate for public funding can be found at the Australian Electoral Commission's 'Current Funding Rate' web page, http://www.aec.gov.au/Parties_and_Representatives/Political_Disclosures/Current_Funding_Rate.htm.
> - A list of who was paid public funding after the 2007 election can be found on the Australian Electoral Commission's '2007 Federal Election Funding Payments' web page at http://www.aec.gov.au/Elections/federal_elections/2007/election_funding_payment.htm.

ELECTRONIC VOTING (E-VOTING)

Electronic voting is a term used to describe the range of technologies that can replace the paper ballot and pencil used by citizens to vote. This may take the form of computer touch screens, or Internet or telephone voting. Some of these systems are used in the United States and Brazil. The advantages of computer-based voting technology include the capacity for multilingual presentation of voting and, in the case of Internet or telephone voting, the convenience of not having to attend a polling station to cast a vote. It also facilitates the faster counting of votes, particularly with regard to the distribution of preferences.

There are, however, significant potential problems associated with the adoption of an e-voting system. The cost of supplying computer touch screen facilities to each polling station may be a disincentive for governments to move to e-voting. But, more significant is the issue of the security of computer systems. As we know, the secret ballot is a valued and central component of our electoral system and there are concerns whether a computer-based system, whether at a polling station or, more significantly, through the Internet, can be secured sufficiently to protect the secrecy of the vote. How do you prevent someone coercing or bullying a person voting on the Internet if they are not in a prescribed polling station? Is it possible to maintain the integrity of an electronic voting system to prevent the manipulation of voting results?

> A comprehensive discussion of e-voting can be found at:
> - Barry, C. et al 2001, 'Electronic Voting and Electronic Counting of Votes: A Status Report', Electoral Council of Australia, www.eca.gov.au/reports/electronic_voting.pdf.
> - ACT Electoral Commission 2008, 'Frequently Asked Questions—Electronic Voting and Counting', http://www.elections.act.gov.au/faqsvoting.html.

To date there has been no move at the federal level to introduce electronic voting systems for the House of Representatives or Senate elections. However, in Victoria, voters who are interstate or overseas can vote using an electronic system where provided at an early voting centre (s. 100 of the Victorian *Electoral Act 2002*).

The ACT Electoral Commission used e-voting for the 2001 and 2004 ACT Legislative Assembly elections. Voters at the pre-poll centres were given the option of a paper vote, or using the computer. Voters who chose the computer option had their names marked off the roll and were then issued a card with a barcode. An audio attachment allowed people with a visual impairment to vote independently for the first time.

> 'It's all very simple—swipe a barcode, tap on the keyboard, swipe again, and your vote is cast.'
> (Source: *The Canberra Times*, 4 October 2001)

All votes cast at the election were counted electronically, with voter preferences being entered electronically, counted, and preferences then distributed. This meant the result was known much sooner than with the previous time-consuming counting of paper ballots.

VOTING BEHAVIOUR

Analysing voter preferences

It is clearly of interest to political parties to analyse how people are likely to vote so they can target their policies accordingly. For that reason, parties regularly conduct surveys of electors, particularly in marginal seats. Newspapers and other organisations also conduct sample polls of voters in the period leading up to an election to gauge the level of support for the different parties, and to determine the issues that are of greatest concern to people. Many academic studies, based on survey techniques and quantification, also try to determine why people have voted a particular way at a particular election. See, for example:

- the Australian Election Study (http://aussa.anu.edu.au/ausElectionStudy.html), a national survey of voters taken after a number of recent elections to try and identify the main reasons why people voted the way they did;

- the British Election Study (http://www.essex.ac.uk/bes);
- American National Election Studies (http://www.electionstudies.org); see, for example, McConochie, W.A. & Dunn, K. 'Ten Values for Predicting Political Voting and Behaviour: ANES 2008 Pilot Study/2004 Study' (http://www.electionstudies.org/resources/papers/Pilot2006/nes012030.pdf); and
- German Election Studies Series (http://webapp.icpsr.umich.edu/cocoon/ICPSR-SERIES/00118.xml).

These surveys help to explain the result of a particular election. They also provide political parties with an analysis of voter choice that they can use to build their electoral support.

Long-term and short-term influences on voter preference

The results of academic analyses indicate there are both long- and short-term influences on voter preferences.

- Long-term factors that develop a person's support for a particular party, known as *partisanship*, include socioeconomic status and social class, religious beliefs, ethnicity, age, gender, region (such as living in a rural or urban area), and family preference for a particular party. Party loyalty is one of the many orientations towards life that children pick up from their parents, but this influence is not absolute. Both parents do not always have the same loyalty, and children can reject parental models as well as adopt them. The children of wealthy parents may become left-wing radicals, while labourers' children may become conservative in their views. Nevertheless, long-term factors do take effect over a person's lifetime and for this reason there are many people who maintain lifetime support for the party of their choice.

> **Partisanship** is support for a particular party; it is not the same as party membership.

- Short-term factors, including the election campaign, the performance of the parties in government and opposition, and, more significantly, the performance of their leaders are also relevant because they may influence some voters to change their vote. These people are known as 'swinging voters' and are significant in deciding what party will govern. As a result, parties spend a lot of time and money trying to identify the issues that are important to swinging voters, and what policies will attract their votes.

> In the short term, the *performance of governments* and the *relative appeal of leaders* are factors that affect party loyalty.

The significance of partisanship in the Australian party system

In the 20th century and into the 21st, the great majority of Australia's electors have been linked to politics and government as partisans of one or other of the major parties. Party identification is powerful, but it is not everything: even very loyal partisans will vote for the other side if the cause is pressing. Fluctuations in voting support are evident from the electoral results for the Australian Labor Party, shown in Table 8.7.

TABLE 8.7
Rise and fall in Labor's first-preference electoral results 1974–2007 (per cent)

Year	Electoral support (per cent)
1974	49.3
1975	42.8
1977	39.6
2004	37.6
2007	43.3

(*Sources*: McAllister, I., Mackerras, M., Ascui, A. & Moss, S. 1990, *Australian Political Facts*, Longman Cheshire, Melbourne, p. 69; Australian Electoral Commission 2004, 'Election 2004: House of Representatives: First Preferences by Party', http://results.aec.gov.au/12246/results/HouseStateFirstPrefsByParty-12246-NAT; Australian Electoral Commission 2007, 'Election 2007: House of Representatives: First Preferences by Party', http://results.aec.gov.au/13745/Website/HouseStateFirstByParty-13745-NAT.htm)

A study by Jaensch and Mathieson (see 'Further reading' at the end of this chapter) indicates that identification with the major parties weakened significantly in the 1990s, with the Liberal and National parties suffering most. Jaensch and Mathieson also identified an increasing number of uncommitted or 'floating' voters, creating some dealignment of the system, which they suggest enhanced the potential for minor parties to attract support. The rapid development of support for Pauline Hanson's One Nation party in 1997, drawn from previously partisan Liberal and Nationals voters, is an example of this. However, the first-preference vote for One Nation fell dramatically from 8.43 per cent at the 1998 election to 0.26 per cent in 2007, highlighting the difficulty that minor parties have in sustaining support in a system that remains dominated by the major parties.

> At the 2007 federal election for the House of Representatives, the two major parties between them secured 79.66 per cent of first-preference votes.

If we are to understand the forces associated with partisanship, we need to look at some of the factors that encourage people to vote the way they do.

Factors that influence the way people vote

Age

Young people entering the electorate in the 1930s and 1940s were more likely to vote Labor than non-Labor, and this trend has persisted (see Table 8.8).

Polling undertaken by *Newspoll/The Australian* on 9–11 November and 16–18 November, before the 2007 election, found that 51 per cent of voters aged 18–34 intended to vote Labor, while 44 per cent of voters over 50 intended to vote for the Coalition (see Newspoll, http://www.newspoll.com.au/cgti-bin/polling/display_poll_data.pl). This data indicates that the tendency for younger voters to prefer Labor persists, but it appears that at this election there was less support for the Coalition among older voters, a reflection no doubt of the swing

TABLE 8.8
Voter intention by age (per cent)

	2001 election Under 25	2004 election Under 25	2001 election 45–64	2004 election 45 plus
Labor	46	34	34	38
Coalition	33	45	51	50

(*Sources*: Bean, C. & McAllister, I. 2002, 'From Impossibility to Certainty: Explaining the Coalition's Victory in 2001', in Warhurst, J. & Simms, M. (eds), *2001: The Centenary Election*, University of Queensland Press, Brisbane, p. 275; Bean, C. & McAllister, I. 2005, 'Not an Election of Interest (Rates): Voting Behaviour in the Australian Federal Election of 2004', in Simms, M. & Warhurst, J. (eds), *Mortgage Nation: The 2004 Australian Election*, API Network, Perth)

to Labor that took it to government. Whether this movement away from the Coalition on the part of older voters persists will be determined by future election results.

The electorate, nevertheless, can be thought of as a set of age-defined groups displaying different patterns of party support. As they pass in, through and out of the system, the odds of a given party winning an election may change. The ageing of the population is a factor that both major parties will have to address in the future.

Party image

Parties exist principally as images in people's minds—as groups of men and women (still predominantly men) who possess a kind of corporate existence. The traditional images of the major parties have changed very little.

The notion that the Australian Labor Party is a working-class party remains, even though the Keating Labor government lost a lot of support from its traditional voters in the 1996 election to the Liberal Party, which keenly sought the vote of the Aussie 'battler'. The reason for this was the Hawke and Keating Labor governments' embrace of economic rationalism as a pathway to growth, including industry restructuring that cost many blue-collar workers their jobs, and the introduction of enterprise bargaining for wages and conditions that reduced union involvement in wage fixing. The Rudd Labor government's abolition of Work Choices continues the party's tradition of appealing to Australian workers, if not to the working class of old (see below).

The Liberal Party's traditional image of being a party for big business interests may have faded since the 1980s as Labor has built its ties with the business community, but both big business and small business would prefer to see a Liberal government in Canberra.

Party leaders need to maintain the set of notions that sustains their party's image, as too great a change risks losing the support of those who make up their core constituency. This is evidenced by the Labor Party's reiteration of its traditional principles to distinguish itself from its major opponent, even though the basic thrust of its economic policy is very similar. Hence, former Prime Minister Keating made references to his government's support for the 'true believers', while Kevin Rudd directed many campaign policies at 'working families'.

One of the difficulties for both parties is a perception that there is insufficient difference between them to give voters a real, ideology-based choice. For example, both parties have similar approaches to economic policy, although they may differ on the means and at the margin. One of the reasons for this relative lack of cleavage within the party system is the fact that Australian society remains relatively homogeneous, even though postwar immigration has brought to Australia many people of different cultural and ethnic backgrounds. There are not, as in some other countries, longstanding rivalries or enmities between parts of the nation. The society is a relatively young one, and the dimensions that do exist are not encrusted with symbols and traditions, such as those in evidence in Northern Ireland, for example. Social effects often work in different directions: for example, children of working-class homes may grow up with attitudes to work and personal ambition that make them unsympathetic to Labor's ethic of collective social responsibility.

Social class

Social class (or SES—socioeconomic status) is usually measured either 'subjectively' (by asking a person what class he or she belongs to) or 'objectively' (by classifying people according to their occupations, incomes or like attributes).

It is evident from Table 8.9 that the notion of the Australian Labor Party as a 'working-class' party that gains most of its support from manual blue-collar workers is no longer accurate. One reason is the changing nature of work resulting from economic restructuring. New jobs are more likely to be in what we might loosely term 'white-collar' occupations related to the service, hospitality, retail and finance industries than in blue-collar work of the type more closely associated with heavy industry and manual labour. As a result, the Labor Party has attempted to remodel itself as the champion of low-income earners, or 'the battlers', rather than of the working class. The fact that the Liberal Party also targeted 'the battlers' in its successful 1998, 2001 and 2004 election campaigns indicates how difficult it is to associate class with any particular political party.

> Former Liberal Party campaign director Andrew Robb replies to a question from reporter Barrie Cassidy on the 2001 election result at the National Press Club:
> CASSIDY: 'And in the end you got a big swag of the blue-collar workers . . . except you would probably call them the Howard battlers of Australia.'
> ROBB: 'I think that's where the election's been won in such a comprehensive way. We got an 8.5 per cent lead over Labor with blue-collar workers on Saturday. Now, that is an enormous shift. I think over the last 13 years they've [Labor] sought to widen their base by appealing to the Chardonnay set and in the process they've run into a conflict and they've lost their own people.'
> (*Source*: Cited in Brent, P. 2004, '"Howard's Battlers": The Electoral Evidence?', paper presented to the Australasian Political Studies Association Conference, Adelaide, 29 September 2004, p. 7)

TABLE 8.9
Party identification by occupational grade, 2004 (per cent)

Occupation	Labor	Coalition	Greens	Other
Manual	42	47	7	4
Non-manual	33	53	9	4

(*Source*: Bean, C. & McAllister, I. 2005, 'Not an Election of Interest (Rates): Voting Behaviour in the Australian Federal Election of 2004', in Simms, M. & Warhurst, J. (eds), *Mortgage Nation: The 2004 Australian Election*, API Network, Perth, reproduced with permission from the Australian Research Institute)

One interesting question is whether 'the battlers' should be identified entirely with 'blue-collar workers', in the context of social class. Rick Kuhn points out that Pauline Hanson and John Howard may have claimed to speak for the 'battlers', but he argues that these classes are 'defined in terms of the characteristics of individuals', rather than social relationships (Kuhn, R. 2005, 'The History of Class Analysis in Australia', http://www.anu.edu.au/polsci/marx/interventions/clan.htm). A significant proportion of 'battlers' may be low-income earners, but they also include within their ranks those who have become known as 'aspirational voters'—that is, middle-income earners struggling to pay off the large mortgages that come with home ownership in a city like Sydney, in constituencies identified as 'the mortgage belt'.

Former Labor leader Mark Latham examined the significance of the 'aspirational voter' for Labor's electoral prospects:

> I see them in my electorate all the time. People I grew up with in Liverpool's public housing estates are now the contractors, small business owners and information workers of the new economy, living in double-storey suburbs on Sydney's fringe.
>
> These people represent a new class of voters—aspirational voters. Anyone who denies the importance of this phenomenon is denying reality. The workers have had a taste of economic ownership and, not surprisingly, they want more.

(*Source*: Latham, M. 2003, *From the Suburbs*, Pluto Press, Sydney, p. 67)

More significant for the major parties than class is the demographic make-up of the marginal seats they need to win to secure government. This factor encourages the type of convergence that we have seen, as both parties seek the 'battler' vote in recent elections.

> For comment on social class as a factor in the large swing to Labor at the 2007 federal election, see Burchell, D. 2007, 'Voters: The Kath and Kim Twist', Australian Policy Online, 11 December 2007, http://www.apo.org.au.

FIGURE 8.2

Aspirational voter, perspirational, class gone

(*Source*: Cartoon by Nicholson from *The Australian*. http://www.nicholsoncartoons.com.au)

Region

There are some important differences between the states, especially with respect to support for minor parties and to issues and outcomes in state elections. State differences in federal party loyalty, however, are relatively small, and it is sensible to see the six states more or less as microcosms of the whole nation. Differences between city and country are important and exist in every state. Country residents are less likely to identify with Labor than people who live in cities, and this is true even of people in equivalent occupations (see Table 8.10). Farmers and graziers are notably anti-Labor.

TABLE 8.10
Party identification by region, 2004 (per cent)

	ALP	Coalition
Rural	31	57
Urban	39	48

(*Source*: Bean, C. & McAllister, I. 2005, 'Not an Election of Interest (Rates): Voting Behaviour in the Australian Federal Election of 2004', in Simms, M. & Warhurst, J. (eds), *Mortgage Nation: The 2004 Australian Election*, API Network, Perth, reproduced with permission from the Australian Research Institute)

A majority of rural voters support the Coalition, but a minority of country people support the Nationals, and the party does not hold all the country seats.

> According to David Charnock, 'a significant "countrymindedness" or rurality effect (favouring the Coalition) was found only during periods of ALP government and, moreover, at times when those governments were headed by Prime Ministers with strong centralist tendencies'.
> (*Source*: Charnock, D. 2004, 'Contextual Effects and Other Influences: Using Multilevel Modelling to Study the Extent and Causes of Spatial Variations in Post-War Australian Federal Voting', paper presented to Australasian Political Studies Association Conference, Adelaide, 1 October 2004, p. 26)

Religion

Religious denomination varies markedly in importance from person to person, even though most people accept a denominational label. Catholics tended from the beginning to support the Labor Party, and relatively few in the past achieved prominence in the Liberal Party or the Nationals, although this is changing. Two former non-Labor state premiers, Nick Greiner (New South Wales) and Mike Ahern (Queensland), were Catholics, as was Tony Abbott, Minister for Health in the Howard government.

It is interesting to note from Table 8.11 that the majority of self-identifying Catholic and Protestant voters favoured the Coalition parties at the 2004 election. Whether this indicates a trend of Catholics away from Labor or was a function of a particularly low vote for the Labor Party at this election remains to be seen.

The religious Right

The emergence of Family First at the 2004 federal election as a Christian-based party with associations with the Assembly of God church gave rise to speculation that the Christian

TABLE 8.11
Party identification and religion, 2004 (per cent)

	ALP	Coalition	Greens	Others
Catholic	41	50	5	3
Anglican	30	60	6	3
Uniting	33	59	4	4
Other	36	49	7	7

(*Source*: Bean C. & McAllister, I. 2005, 'Not an Election of Interest (Rates): Voting Behaviour in the Australian Federal Election of 2004', in Simms, M. & Warhurst, J. (eds), *Mortgage Nation: The 2004 Australian Election*, API Network, Perth, reproduced with permission from the Australian Research Institute)

Right and religious conservatism may be developing as a significant factor in Australian politics. Family First preferences assisted several Coalition Christian candidates to win seats for the House of Representatives, and the party was successful in winning a Senate seat in Victoria. The identification of a Christian vote more closely associated with the conservative side of Australian politics encouraged the Labor Party to reflect on the emergence of religion as an electoral factor.

> 'I'd hate to think people thought the Labor Party was bereft of faith and that we weren't interested in religion at all', Labor MP Maria Vamvakinou said. 'I don't think the Liberal Party should be seen to have a monopoly on God.'
> (*Source*: Cited in Price, M. 2004, 'New deity dawns for faithful Labor', *The Australian*, 27 November 2004)

There were concerns also within the ranks of Australia's liberals.

> 'Secular liberals are painting ever more apocalyptic visions of a muscular Christian right using its electoral clout . . . religion is enjoying an influence in Australian politics not seen since the Democratic Labor Party's heyday in the 1960s.'
> (*Source*: Stewart, C. 2004, 'Old-time religion is good enough for some', *The Australian*, 20 November)

In electoral terms, Family First had a minor impact, achieving only 2.1 per cent of the primary vote for the House of Representatives and 1.88 per cent for the Senate in Victoria, where it won a Senate seat as the recipient of preferences from other parties and groups. The party did not win a Senate seat at the 2007 federal election. Family First senator, Steven Fielding, had little opportunity to influence government policy while the Coalition had a majority in the Senate, but since 1 July 2008 his vote has been significant among the group of minor parties and independents who hold the balance of power.

The impact of the religious Right on Australian politics that many predicted might occur after 2004 has failed to materialise. Religious-based parties Family First and the Christian Democratic Party (CDP) between them attracted only 2.83 per cent of first-preference votes for the House of Representatives election and 2.56 per cent for the half-Senate election in 2007.

It would seem from these figures that religion remains at the fringes of Australian politics as a determinant of how people vote.

> 'Both parties were established as broad-based, secular parties designed to operate in a democratic and secular state—a state containing within it a large number of belief systems both religious and non-religious.'
> (Source: Kevin Rudd, then Shadow Minister for Foreign Affairs and International Security 2005, 'The Religious Right Cannot Hijack Values', On Line Opinion, 18 January 2005, http://www.onlineopinion.com.au)

However, according to research and marketing group Australian Development Strategies, religious affiliation was a significant factor in Labor's win at the 2007 election. According to the group's spokesman, John Black, 'the strongest correlate of the swing to Kevin Rudd's new Labor Party was Pentecostal churchgoers, alongside Baptists, Jehovah's Witnesses, Mormons, Lutherans, Salvos, Seventh-Day Adventists and the Uniting Church'. The same report showed no swing to Labor among Anglicans, and a slight swing to Labor by Catholics (cited in Pearson, C. 2008, 'On a swing and a prayer', *The Australian*, 9 March 2008). If these voting patterns have been correctly identified and recur at the next election, it may be the political issues that concern these churches will become a factor that the major parties have to consider when framing their election policies.

Ethnicity

The waves of immigration that followed the Second World War did not lead to a realignment of the party system. On the whole, the immigrants who have been absorbed into the electorate (several hundred thousand are not yet electors) have resembled native-born Australians in the relative distribution of their partisanship to the major parties.

Postwar immigration has not had a great effect on party membership generally, although some branches of the ALP in Sydney and Melbourne have strong migrant membership. The effect on the party system is likely to be felt more forcefully in the future as migrants and their children play a more obvious and confident role in Australian politics. The change over the past 20 years is already marked, with the increasing number of voters born in Asia showing a preference for Labor, along with a strong attachment for Labor on the part of immigrants from Southern and Eastern Europe.

> 'The tendency of foreign-born voters to support Labor increased from 1966 to 2001 . . . Labor's advantage among those born outside Australia rose by 13 per cent over this period.'
> (Source: Leigh, A. 2004, 'Economic Voting and Electoral Behaviour: How do Individual, Local and National Factors Affect the Partisan Choice?', paper presented to the Australasian Political Studies Association Conference, Adelaide, 1 October 2004)

The issue of race that accompanied the emergence of Pauline Hanson's One Nation party and other like-minded groups, and the establishment of the Unity Party as a multicultural alternative, injected ethnicity as a factor into Australian elections, but this has not changed the substantive shape of the Australian party system, as these parties are minor players when it comes to voter preference.

Gender

An influential 1977 study by Don Aitkin (*Stability and Change in Australian Politics*, Australian National University, Canberra) found that men were more likely to identify with Labor than women across all age groups. A further study in 1979 by Aitkin, examining party identification by sex for the years 1967 and 1979, indicated that the gender gap was closing because of what he described as 'the politicisation of women', reflected in an increasing awareness among women that politics was important to their interests.

Table 8.12 indicates that this trend continued in 2004. The same percentage of women and men indicated a preference for Labor, while a slight majority of men favoured the Coalition.

Marian Sawer (see 'Further reading') has commented on the emergence of parties such as the Abolish Child Support/Family Court Party as a function of what she calls 'the politics of "angry white men"'. In 1998, a Bean and McAllister survey found that 9 per cent of

TABLE 8.12
Party identification by gender, 2004 (per cent)

	Labor	Coalition
Male	37	52
Female	37	49

(*Source*: Bean, C. & McAllister, I. 2005, 'Not an Election of Interest (Rates): Voting Behaviour in the Australian Federal Election of 2004', in Simms, M. & Warhurst, J. (eds), *Mortgage Nation: The 2004 Australian Election*, API Network, Perth, reproduced with permission from the Australian Research Institute)

FIGURE 8.3
The search for talent

Gender has always been the Cinderella in the balancing process when ministerial vacancies are to be filled.

(*Source*: Geoff Pryor, 31 March 1990, copyright Geoff Pryor)

male voters versus 4 per cent of women voters supported Pauline Hanson's One Nation party. The slump in support for Pauline Hanson's One Nation in 2001 and 2004, however, indicates that many of those voters have returned to the major parties. The parties of the 'angry white men' also have had little impact on the party system, with the percentage of votes for 'other' parties remaining stable.

All of the long-term factors discussed above are important because they contribute to the way people think about society, the political issues that are important to them, and their attachment or loyalty to a particular party. Nevertheless, short-term factors such as the performance of the incumbent government—including the issues that are on the political agenda at the time—and political leadership can be influential in determining how people vote and in their decision to change their party allegiance. If they didn't, we would not see the movements in support between the major parties and a change in government from time to time.

In the next chapter we will look at Australia's political parties and the party system in which they operate.

A NOTE ON VOTING METHODS: COUNTING THE VOTES

1 Simple majority voting ('first past the post')

The voter can vote for only one candidate, as follows:

Brown ☐
Jones ☒
Smith ☐
Thompson ☐

The votes are counted, and the candidate with the greatest number of them is elected:

Brown	142
Jones	88
Smith	413
Thompson	357
	1000

Smith wins, but note that she received only 41.3 per cent of the votes: in other words, more people preferred candidates other than Smith. Can Smith then claim that she is the popular choice? Well, it all depends on how she makes the claim and what she means by it. The ambiguity of results like this led to suggestions for improvements, the most successful of which has been preferential voting.

2 Preferential voting (the alternative vote)

In this system the voter places a number against the name of each candidate. (Note that crosses are not permitted on ballots for the House of Representatives.) Ballot papers must be numbered to show all preferences or they will not be counted. The numbers must be ordered 1, 2, 3 and so on. If a candidate receives at least 50 per cent + 1 of the '1' votes (the 'first preferences'), then he or she is declared elected.

If not, then the votes are reallocated—those of the least successful candidate first—until one of the candidates does have a clear majority of the votes. In this process of reallocation the first-preference votes are ignored, and the counters distribute the second preferences (or the third, if the second has already been used).

Let us use the candidates and totals from the example above:

Brown	142
Jones	88
Smith	413
Thompson	357
	1000

Jones is eliminated from the count. His preferences are then distributed, as though they were first preferences, as follows:

	1st preferences		From Jones		Total
Brown	142	+	11	=	153
Smith	413	+	45	=	458
Thompson	357	+	32	=	389
	912		88		1000

There is still no candidate with a clear majority (Smith has only 45.8 per cent of the total), so now Brown is eliminated and his votes are distributed. As it happens, the great majority of those who voted for Brown preferred Thompson to Smith, and Thompson has a narrow victory, with 52 per cent of the votes:

	After distribution of Jones's votes		From Brown		Total
Smith	458	+	22	=	480
Thompson	389	+	131	=	520
	847		153		1000

This imagined example is in fact rather like many real results in Australian politics, in which Smith is the Labor candidate and Thompson the Liberal, with Brown from the Nationals and Jones a non-party or independent candidate. Labor supporters are understandably nettled by a victory for Thompson; Smith received more first-preference votes than anyone else and nearly won anyway. It is unfair, they argue, that these second- and third-preference votes that won the seat for Thompson should now have the same value as a *first*-preference vote.

Is it unfair? Well, again, it all depends on what you think these preferences indicate. They are given the same value because the voter is assumed to be saying something like this: 'I think Jones is the best, but if I can't have Jones I think Brown is better than the other two, and if it's a choice between Smith and Thompson, I'll have Thompson'. The voter is assumed to care equally about all these choices. In short, we are thought to be learning a lot about the voters' opinions, and using these opinions meaningfully. Yet, it is clear that many of these preferences have no meaning for voters (if there are 12 candidates, do the ninth and tenth preferences mean much?), and for this reason the support for optional preferential voting grew.

Under optional preferential voting, the result in the example used above might be altered because some of those voters who supported Jones and Brown will not wish to support another candidate. Therefore, they will not have indicated preferences that can be distributed. For example, once Jones is eliminated from the count, his optional preferences are then distributed as if they were first preferences, as follows:

	1st preferences		From Jones		Total
Brown	142	+	6	=	148
Smith	413	+	42	=	455
Thompson	357	+	20	=	377
	912		68		980
	No 2nd preference		20		
			88		

There is still no candidate with a clear majority, so now Brown is eliminated, and those of his votes that indicated a second preference are distributed. As with full preferential voting, the majority of those who voted for Brown preferred Thompson to Smith, but enough voters gave no second preference for the narrow victory to go this time, under optional preferential voting to Smith, not Thompson.

	After distribution of Jones's votes		From Brown		Total
Smith	455	+	20	=	475
Thompson	377	+	90	=	467
	832		110		942
	No 2nd preference		38		
			148		

There is yet another alternative: that the second preference has only half the value of a first preference, a third preference only one-third and so on. The problem is that these 'weights' are quite arbitrary, and have less justification than the assumption that the voter cares equally about all his or her choices. What is more, there are other arithmetical weights that could be used (for example, 1/2, 1/4, 1/8, 1/16, or 3/4, 1/2, 1/4, 1).

FIGURE 8.4
Major party votes after distribution of preference

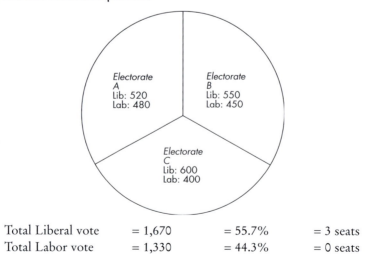

| Total Liberal vote | = 1,670 | = 55.7% | = 3 seats |
| Total Labor vote | = 1,330 | = 44.3% | = 0 seats |

While Thompson's victory can be seen as fair and just under full preferential, Smith's victory in the earlier example fair and just under first past the post, there is obviously something worrying if these results are repeated systematically in a number of electorates. Imagine a set of three contiguous electorates of much the same social and economic character. Under simple majority voting the Labor Party might win them all if a number of candidates were to stand, and under preferential voting the Liberal Party might win them all. In either case, there would be a substantial group of voters in the three seats 'unrepresented', though they would together have elected a candidate had they all been resident in the one electorate. Consider this simple example in Figure 8.4, after all preferences have been distributed.

The 'unfairness' of such a general result, no matter how fair the result in the separate seats, is one source of support for the third major electoral system.

3 Proportional representation (PR)

In this system, the MP is one of several elected to represent a large area; the single-member seat is abandoned. A candidate is elected when he or she gains a quota, and a quota is a fraction of the votes:

$$\frac{1}{(\text{number of candidates to be elected} + 1)} + 1$$

If there are three MPs to be elected, then the quota is $1/4 + 1$, if four, then $1/5 + 1$, and so on. The quota is the smallest number of votes needed to gain election that can be shown quickly by some multiplication: if, in a seat where three are to be elected, the three successful candidates each gain the quota and no more, they will together have won three-quarters of the vote plus three votes, while the remainder, 1/4 less 3 votes, is too small to elect any of the others. Note that in a single-member seat the quota is $1/2 + 1$. In practice, elections carried out under preferential voting in single-member constituencies are following a special case of the rules for proportional representation.

In practice, candidates tend to group themselves and campaign together; the elector votes preferentially. Let us adapt our earlier examples to PR. In the new three-member seat the Labor team is headed by Smith, and they win the draw for the left-hand position on the ballot paper. Then comes the non-Labor coalition team—Thompson, Brown and Deakin—then Jones and another independent, Kay. Because the teams urged their supporters to 'vote the ticket'—that is, to number the candidates from top to bottom—the results look quite lopsided:

Group A (Labor)		Group B (L-Nats)		Ungrouped	
Smith	1100	*Thompson*	1400	*Jones*	280
Cook	70	*Brown*	60	*Kay*	20
Fisher	30	*Deakin*	40		
	1200		1500		300

Total number of electors voting = 3000
Quota = $1/4 \times 3000 + 1 = 751$

In counting the votes under PR, notice is taken of the 'surplus'—the extra votes gained by a successful candidate over and above the necessary quota. In this case, it will be easy to count all preferences and distribute the surplus proportionately.

Now to the count. Thompson and Smith have far in excess of the quotas they need. Thompson is first elected, and his votes are sorted according to the second preferences shown on them. They prove to be as follows:

Smith	Cook	Fisher	Brown	Deakin	Jones	Kay
....	10	....	1250	100	....	40

As only Thompson's *surplus* is to be distributed, each of these piles of votes must be reduced to its 'transfer value'. This is obtained by multiplying the number of votes in the pile by Thompson's surplus (1,400 − 751 = 649), and dividing this product by the number of Thompson's first preferences (1,400). This procedure gives the following additions to the candidate's scores:

$$Cook \quad 10 \times \frac{649}{1400} = 5$$

$$Brown \quad 1250 \times \frac{649}{1400} = 579$$

$$Deakin \quad 100 \times \frac{649}{1400} = 46$$

$$Kay \quad \frac{40}{100} \times \frac{649}{1400} = \frac{19}{649}$$

These increases total 649, the value of Thompson's surplus.

Smith's surplus is dealt with in the same way. Most of her supporters put Cook second, just as most of Thompson's voters put Brown second, but every candidate received at least a few extra votes. Half a dozen even go to Thompson: these second preferences are ignored, and the six votes are sorted according to the *third* preferences shown.

Cook	Fisher	Brown	Deakin	Jones	Kay
995	15	30	20	32	8

The transfer of values of these votes is as follows:

$$Cook \quad 995 \times \frac{349}{1100} = 316$$

$$Fisher \quad 15 \times \frac{349}{1100} = 5$$

$$Brown \quad 30 \times \frac{349}{1100} = 9$$

$$Deakin \quad 20 \times \frac{349}{1100} = 6$$

$$Jones \quad 32 \times \frac{349}{1100} = 10$$

$$Kay \quad \frac{8}{1100} \times \frac{349}{1100} = \frac{3}{349}$$

The tally sheet shows the following progress scores:

	Smith	Cook	Fisher	Thompson	Brown	Deakin	Jones	Kay	(Total)
1st-preference votes	1100	70	30	1400	60	40	280	20	(3000)
Thompson's second surplus		5		first	579	46		19	
Smith's surplus	elected	316	5	elected	9	6	10	3	
		391	35		648	92	290	42	

None of the remaining candidates has a quota (751) so Fisher, who has the fewest votes, is excluded and his 35 votes are reallocated to the candidate next preferred by each voter:

	Cook	Fisher	Brown	Deakin	Jones	Kay
From Fisher	30	(excluded)	1	1	1	2
Progress Total	421		649	93	291	44

Still no candidate has a quota, so Kay is now excluded:

	Cook	Fisher	Brown	Deakin	Jones	Kay
From Kay	19	(excluded)	21	3	1	(excluded)
Progress Total	440		670	96	292	

Deakin is now excluded, and virtually all of his votes go to Brown, giving him the quota he needs with a few to spare:

	Cook	Fisher	Brown	Deakin	Jones	Kay
From Deakin	6	(excluded)	87	(excluded)	3	(excluded)
Progress Total	446 Third elected		757		295	

Note that the remaining votes—Cook's 446, Jones's 295, and Brown's surplus of 6—total 747, less than a quota and therefore not enough to elect either of those remaining even if he gained them all.

This all seems very complicated, and on first acquaintance it *is* complicated. However, the complications flow from the number of candidates involved: each of the steps in determining the successful candidates is in itself simple, and electoral officials have no difficulty in carrying out a count.

QUESTIONS FOR DISCUSSION

1. Which of the electoral systems described above do you consider achieves the fairest result? Discuss what is meant by 'fairness' and give the reasons for your answer.
2. Compare and contrast the electoral systems for the House of Representatives and the Senate. Which do you consider to be the most democratic? It would be useful to define first what you mean by 'democratic', before you attempt to answer this question. (See, for example, Arblaster, A. 1987, *Democracy*, Open University Press, Milton Keynes, UK.)
3. What arguments are there for and against changing the voting system for the House of Representatives from a preferential to a proportional system, or MMP like the system used in Germany?
4. The German states (Land) provide the members of the Bundesrat (Senate). Would this be a good model to adopt for the Australian Senate?
5. What are the benefits and disadvantages of the current system for the public funding of elections?
6. How well do the voting systems discussed in this chapter meet the needs of a representative democracy?
7. Is compulsory voting fair?
8. If you voted at the last federal election, identify which of the long- and short-term factors outlined in this chapter influenced your vote. Which do you think was the most important in defining your choice?

FURTHER READING

Australian Electoral Commission, *Annual Reports*, AGPS, Canberra. Each annual report lists a range of pamphlets, films and videos that have been produced to help voters understand the electoral system.

Bean, C. 1999, 'The Forgotten Cleavage? Religion and Politics in Australia', *Canadian Journal of Political Science*, vol. 32, no. 3, pp. 551–68.

Bennett, S. & Lundie, R. 2007, 'Australian Electoral Systems', Research Paper No. 5, 2007–08, Parliamentary Library, Canberra, http://www.aph.gov.au/library/pubs/rp/.

Costar, B. 2006, 'The electoral system', in Parkin, A., Summers, J. & Woodward, D. (eds), *Government, Politics, Power and Policy in Australia*, 8th ed., Pearson Education, Sydney. Discussion of elections and the electoral system, including compulsory voting.

Curtin, J. 1998, 'The Gender Gap in Australian Elections', Research Paper No. 3, 1997–98, Parliamentary Library, Canberra, http://www.aph.gov.au/library/pubs/rp/.

Jaensch, D. 1997, *The Politics of Australia*, 2nd ed., Macmillan, Melbourne. Chapters 15 and 16 contain a comprehensive discussion of the politics of electoral systems, including arguments for and against compulsory voting, the various systems of voting in Australia, and issues relating to representative democracy.

Jaensch, D. & Mathieson, D. 1998, *A Plague on Both Your Houses: Minor Parties in Australia*, Allen & Unwin, Sydney.

Leigh, A. 2005, 'Economic Voting and Electoral Behaviour: How do Individual, Local and National Factors Affect the Partisan Choice?', *Economics and Politics*, vol. 17, no. 2, pp. 265–96.

Leithner, C. 1997, 'A Gender Gap in Australia? Commonwealth Elections 1910–96', *Australian Journal of Political Science*, vol. 32, no. 1, pp. 29–48.

Manning H. 2006, 'Voting Behaviour', in Parkin, A., Summers, J. & Woodward, D. (eds), *Government, Politics, Power and Policy in Australia*, 8th ed., Pearson Education, Sydney.

Painter, M. 1997, 'Elections', in Smith, R. (ed.), *Politics in Australia*, 3rd ed., Allen & Unwin, Sydney. Discusses key variables, problems and paradoxes in Australian electoral systems.

Sawer, M. (ed.) 2001, *Elections Full, Free and Fair*, The Federation Press, Sydney. A wide-ranging study in which the authors discuss the fairness of Australian elections from a number of perspectives.

Simms, M. & Warhurst, J. (eds) 2005, *Mortgage Nation: The 2004 Australian Election*, API Network, Perth. This book, one in a series of studies of Australian federal elections, provides comprehensive discussion and analysis of the 2004 Australian federal election. See in particular the chapter by Clive Bean and Ian McAllister for discussion about leadership, issues and partisanship as factors in voter choice.

Warhurst, J. 2006, 'Religion in 21st Century Australian National Politics', Australian Senate Occasional Lecture Series, 5 May 2006, http://www.aph.gov.au/Senate/pubs/occa_lect/transcripts/2006.htm.

USEFUL WEBSITES

http://www.aec.gov.au
Australian Electoral Commission
Contains a series of fact sheets on Australia's federal electoral system and results of recent federal elections.

http://www.apo.org.au
Australian Policy Online
This is a useful source of academic comment on current political events, such as the 2007 federal election.

Discussion of the advantages and disadvantages of different types of electoral systems can be found at the following websites:

http://www.idea.int
International IDEA (Institute for Democracy and Electoral Assistance)
This publication, *Electoral System Design: The New IDEA Handbook*, includes some useful information.

http://www.elections.act.gov.au/elections/votingsystems.html
Elections ACT: Voting Systems

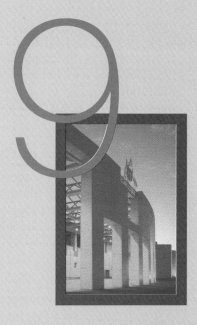

POLITICAL PARTIES AND PARTY SYSTEMS

THIS CHAPTER EXPLAINS:

- the nature of political parties;
- party ideology;
- party organisation;
- the policy process;
- party discipline;
- types of party systems;
- the party system in Australia;
- the development and ongoing functioning of Australia's two-party system; and
- changes to the Australian party system.

THE NATURE OF POLITICAL PARTIES

Because political parties are the principal actors in the political system, it is important to understand what they are and how they work. For many people, parties are almost flesh-and-blood entities to which they develop an attachment over their voting lifetime. The Australian Labor Party (ALP), for example, is a traditional character in the theatre of Australian politics, but there is no such thing as 'the ALP'. It is a label for an organisation that is made up of its members, for whom it may not be the only (or necessarily the most important) activity of their lives. Even for professional politicians, politics is only a part of life, and political parties are only a part of the lives of those who belong to or work for them.

What is a political party?

It is commonly understood that a political party is a group of people with similar ideas about what they want government to do who come together to try to secure power in a democratic system of government through the process of elections. In other words, political parties are groups of like-minded people organised to gain office in government through the electoral process.

> **Political party**: a group of citizens organised to try to secure power through elections.

This description distinguishes political parties from two other important kinds of grouping:

- interest groups, which are organisations formed to promote particular issues and interests, such as environmentalists, farmers, unionists or businesspeople (see Chapter 12); and
- people who find that the parties generally are unresponsive to a policy issue that is very important to them, and register as a 'political party' to contest elections. In this case, however, their intention is not to gain office so much as to get public attention for the issue and to persuade the major parties to take it more seriously. Examples would be the Abolish Child Support/Family Court Party, which stood candidates at the 1998 federal election but was unsuccessful in gaining a seat; and the 'no pokies' candidate, Nick Xenophon, who won a seat in the South Australian upper house election on a platform of banning poker machines in hotels. He secured a seat in the Australian Senate at the 2007 federal election as an independent.

The function of political parties

There are a number of functions that political parties perform in the political system. Most significantly, they are the principal vehicle through which citizens gain representation in a modern parliament.

> 'Political parties are one of the major developments of the nineteenth and twentieth centuries. . . . Political parties are fundamental to modern society because they are the main institution by which conflicts are dealt with . . . they help legitimise conflict and give it, so to speak, a voice in the public debate, but they are also instrumental in reducing and indeed in extreme cases repressing conflict.'
> (Source: Blondel, J. 1990, *Comparative Government: An Introduction*, Philip Allan, London, p. 111)

Parties draw together the policy interests of different groups within the community; that is, they *aggregate and articulate* those demands into a coherent set of policies. It is the same whether they are large, mass-based parties with broad constituencies, or minor parties representing a special group of interests. The acceptance of members and supporters that the party has a legitimate right to represent these views helps to underpin the foundations and stability of the democratic processes of modern party government.

Parties play an important role in the *political socialisation* of the community through their recruitment and selection processes. Through these processes, party members develop political experience and expertise that can be useful when the party gets into government; in other words, parties are a training ground for political leaders.

Candidate selection is also an important function of party membership. The majority of electors who vote for parties have no say in the candidates put forward by the parties, and in fact may know very little about them.

Classification of parties

A number of categorisations have been developed to explain different types of political parties. Maurice Duverger's classic party classification is derived from the structure of party organisation (see Duverger, M. 1954, *Political Parties: Their Organization and Activity in the Modern State*, Methuen, London). He identified what he described as:

- *cadre* parties, which are dominated by an elite group of MPs; they have little party organisation (such as branches), and do not have a broad-based membership;
- *mass-based* parties, which have broad, open membership and a well-organised local branch structure; and
- *devotee* parties, which are led by a charismatic leader and are supported by a ruling elite.

Cadre parties have no membership base and develop when a group of influential people select a person to stand as a candidate, provide the necessary financial backing and run the election campaign.

Mass-based parties are very common in modern democratic states, such as Britain, the United States and Australia, where two major parties between them vie for political power. These major parties have a broad-based membership, and a national organisation with a local branch structure. They achieve the support of a sufficient proportion of the voting electorate to have the opportunity to obtain majorities in parliament and to form governments. They aggregate the interests of their membership and supporters, and articulate those interests into party policy. One difficulty they face is accommodating the different interests and broad ideological sets of ideas that are encompassed by their membership. There is also the need to adapt their ideology to attract the broad spectrum of voters they require to obtain majority representation and form a government. This makes them behave as *catch-all* parties.

> A **catch-all** party develops when the desire to 'catch' the largest number of votes dictates party policy and political strategy at the expense of the party's ideological principles, which are compromised to achieve this objective. For a classic discussion of catch-all parties, see Kirchheimer, O. 1966, 'The Transformation of the Western European Party Systems', in LaPalombara, J. & Weiner, M. (eds), *Political Parties and Political Development*, Princeton University Press, Princeton.

FIGURE 9.1

'It's a how-to-vote card'

(*Source*: Cartoon by Nicholson from *The Australian*. http://nicholsoncartoons.com.au)

This focus on *pragmatic electoralism* in the pursuit of political power causes the central party hierarchy to develop policy that will be electorally appealing, rather than accepting policy decisions from the rank-and-file membership. Katz and Mair have argued that this dominance of the parliamentary wing of the party over its membership on policy development, and the reliance on public funding to help run the expensive media campaigns that are an integral part of the modern election process, will lead to the development of *cartel* parties (Katz, R. & Mair, P. 1995, 'Changing Models of Party Organization and Party Democracy: The Emergence of the Cartel Party', *Party Politics*, vol. 1, no. 1, pp. 5–28).

> A **cartel** develops when political parties who have experienced a declining membership base look to the state for funding. They use these resources and the state patronage that flows to the party to maintain their political dominance at the expense of rival parties who are locked out from this form of assistance, hence the formation of a 'cartel'.

German political parties are often cited in this context because of their reliance on public funding as the primary source of their income, and their manipulation of party rules to reap financial benefits, which has made it difficult for smaller parties to break into the existing party system (Ashton, M.B. 2006, 'The Cartel Theory and the Funding of German Political Parties', Nottingham Trent University, Nottingham, http://www.psa.ac.uk/journals/pdf/5/2007/Ashton.pdf).

- For a discussion of German political parties and cartel theory, see Detterbeck, K. 2008, 'Party Cartel and Cartel Parties in Germany', *German Politics*, vol. 17, no. 1, pp. 27–40.
- For a comprehensive analysis of mass-based parties, catch-all parties and cartel parties, see Katz, R. & Mair, P. 1995, 'Changing Models of Party Organization and Party Democracy: The Emergence of the Cartel Party', *Party Politics*, vol. 1, no. 1, pp. 5–28.

The following discussion examines three other significant characteristics of political parties—ideology, organisation and discipline—as well as the decision-making process relating to policy, the principal 'product' of any political party.

IDEOLOGY

> **Ideology**: a set of interrelated and relatively coherent ideas and beliefs.

In brief, ideology is the 'view of the world' that is characteristic of each party.

- It is important because it is the context in which a party's policies are shaped, the emotional link that binds the party and its supporters, and the principal cause of any change to a political party's programs and policies.
- An ideology is objectively neither right nor wrong; rather, it is more or less plausible according to one's own values, reading, knowledge and experience of the world.
- All ideologies involve an explanation of present society and an account of how it might be improved. These explanations and accounts can be simple or complicated, but they all contain propositions about people and society that are commonly accepted to be true.
- Because these 'truths' do not all point in the same direction, and because they can be given different weights, different ideologies usually clash rather than coexist peacefully.
- Most of us have an ideological layer in our consciousness but it is usually buried, and we become consciously ideological only on rare occasions (for example, if capital punishment, or some similar subject that stirs us, is mentioned).

There is no single repository of a party's ideology, nor a high priest whose role it is to enunciate it. However, a party's published program and its policy documents have a basis in the party's ideology, and its parliamentary leader and senior colleagues are given to ideological pronouncements, especially in parliament or during election campaigns.

> 'We in the Liberal Party stand for enterprise. We stand for competition. We believe in free markets. We know the way consumers get the best price is through effective competition, a free market and ensuring there is a competitive petrol market—which there is.'
> (Source: Malcolm Turnbull, then Shadow Treasurer, *House of Representatives Debates*, 27 May 2008, p. 19)

The ideologies of the parties are essentially summaries, but they do give guidance as to what the parties claim to stand for. The ideology of communist parties, for example, is based on ideas about a classless society and common ownership of the means of production promulgated by Karl Marx. The ideology of other parties may have a basis in conservatism, liberalism or democratic socialism, and there are parties who have a more specific focus—such as the Greens, whose principal focus is the environment and associated issues. Today, in Britain, Australia, the United States and Germany, democratic socialist parties compete for political power against conservative parties on economic policy, rather than radical social change. In Malaysia, racial and religious ideas are the foundation of party ideologies.

Britain

The two major parties in Britain are the Conservative Party and the Labour Party. Traditionally, conservatives believe in strong government and opposition to radical change. However, the policies of the Conservative Party (http://www.conservatives.com) are articulated today in a form to meet the needs of governing a modern democratic state, and the interests of an electorate whose support it needs to win government. The party sees government as a 'force for good to support aspirations', one which can assist the disadvantaged in society by empowering people and communities, and encourage more local democracy to achieve social justice and equal opportunity.

The foundation of the Labour Party (http://www.labour.org.uk) is democratic socialism. This ideology aims to reform capitalism to achieve greater equality within society using legitimate parliamentary processes; historically, the party also sought the socialisation of the means of production. The policies of modern Labour, however, are strongly focused on efficient economic management; the Blair government's privatisation of many government enterprises demonstrates the extent of this. The party has become more moderate and pragmatic in its social policies.

For more detailed discussion on the ideological principles of the Conservative and Labour parties, see Forman, N.J. & Baldwin, N.D.J. 2007, *Mastering British Politics*, 5th ed., Palgrave Macmillan, Basingstoke, UK, pp. 104–7 and 112–13.

United States

The ideological divide between the two major parties, the conservative Republican Party (http://www.gop.com) and the more liberal Democratic Party (http://www.democrats.org) is evident from their attitudes to policy issues. The policies of the Republican Party are conservative in the sense that they oppose government regulation of business and any increase in social spending; aim to cut taxes, and lower or eliminate the minimum wage; provide maximum punishment for criminal offenders; support religion in schools; and believe that people should be responsible for their own actions. The Democrats are more liberal in their attitudes in their support for government regulation of business and worker protection, increases in taxes to fund social spending, a minimum wage, government-controlled health care, and the maintenance of the separation of church and state in schools.

> The differences between the Republican and Democratic parties are articulated during presidential election campaigns. Searching the Internet for websites discussing the 2008 presidential election campaign will enable you to identify what these differences are.

Federal Republic of Germany

The two main German political parties are also divided by conservative and social democratic principles. The Social Democratic Party, or SPD (http://www.spd.de), as with other social democratic parties, seeks to achieve economic and social justice through parliamentary government. In recent years, there have been differences within the party on social policy—whether priority should be given to egalitarianism, or to economic management and fiscal responsibility. The Christian Democratic Union, or CDU (http://www.cdu.de), is a party with conservative principles and a basis in non-denominational Christian democracy. It embodies policies developed in the context of social conscience designed to enhance the wellbeing of the community as a whole.

The differences have not prevented these two parties from successfully governing in power-sharing coalitions. Since 2005, the CDU, the CSU (Christian Social Union) and the SPD have governed in coalition, with the parliamentary leader of the CDU, Angela Merkel, as prime minister.

Federation of Malaysia

The objectives of the main political parties in Malaysia are based on issues of race and religion. The dominant governing party, the United Malays National Organisation (UMNO), strongly supports Malay nationalism and the rights and interests of Malay citizens. The party's objectives to achieve these outcomes are set out in the UMNO constitution (http://www.irc-malaysia.com/webserver/umnoonline/PDF/UMNO.pdf). Other parties within the governing Barisan Nasional coalition are also racially based and their objectives reflect these interests. The Malaysian Indian Congress (MIC) aims 'to safeguard and promote political, economic, educational, cultural and social interests of Indians in Malaysia' and 'to represent, express and give effect to the legitimate aspirations of Indians in Malaysia' (http://www.mic.org.my). The Malaysian Chinese Association aims 'to ensure the recognition of and the safeguarding of the legitimate rights and interests of Malaysians of Chinese descent and the legitimate rights and interests of all other communities as provided under the Malaysian Constitution' (http://www.mca.org.my). The racial differences are managed politically by the parties joining together under the umbrella of the Barisan Nasional (National Front) coalition government.

The ideology of the Pan Malaysian Islamic Party, or PAS (http://www.pas.org.my), has a religious base with a commitment to Islamic political philosophy.

Electoral pragmatism

Parties that seek to win government need to attract broad-based support, which may result in the party making pragmatic election promises that depart from its ideological principles. This focus on those voters who are not firmly committed to the ideology of either of the major parties sometimes results in the ideological division between them becoming blurred, at least in terms of their election campaign policies. We see this in the Australian context when the major parties focus their campaign on who is better at economic management, rather than the ideological principles set out in their official party platforms.

A party that moves too far from its ideological base in pursuit of electoral gain, however, risks losing the support of its core constituency. On the other hand, if it adheres unrelentingly to that ideology it may fail to win the broad-based support it needs within the constituency. Striking the right balance between maintaining the party's ideology and electoral pragmatism can be challenging and difficult to achieve.

ORGANISATION

If ideology is the heart of a political party, then organisation is its body. No set of ideas gets much attention merely through its existence, at least in a short period, but political ideas and beliefs are held firmly and are seen as important and urgent. So a party's leaders feel a great need to spread ideas (this is the literal meaning of the word 'propaganda'), rally their supporters, and fight and win elections. These activities require people, and the organisation of their work in a rational way. The organisation itself makes other recurring demands for skills, money and time, and these demands tend to ensure that the organisation of a party takes on a particular shape.

Political parties tend to resemble one another in structure—with local branches and central organisations—whether they operate in a unitary system of government like Britain, or in a federal system. There are differences, however, in the political management of the parties and the power relationships between the various elements.

Britain

The Conservative and Labour parties each have branches in local constituencies but party policy-making is centralised. The Conservative Party has a central board that is responsible for party policy, fund-raising, membership and candidate selection. The Labour Party is different in that trade unions are also formally affiliated to the party, but they no longer have a block vote in the policy-making process. The party's national policy-making body is the Annual Conference made up of party delegates, but in recent years the political leadership has had significant influence on policy direction; hence the use of the term 'Blair government' to describe Labour's policies when Tony Blair was prime minister.

Australia

Australia's political parties are structured on a federal basis, with the principal point of organisation occurring at the state level. Local branches formed within an electorate represent the party in the local community and are the point at which individuals join. In each state and federal electorate there is an electorate council or conference which organises the selection of candidates, the raising of money, and the planning of local election campaigns. The Liberal Party (http://www.liberal.org.au) and the Australian Labor Party (http://www.alp.org.au) (see Chapter 10) also have state councils and executives that meet in the state capital to develop policy for the state-based parties and state elections. National party conferences and party executives are responsible for policy, campaign funding and strategy at the federal level.

United States

The decentralised organisational structure of the two major parties in the United States, the Democratic Party and the Republican Party, is a function of the federal political system. Party members join within the state in which they reside. Each party has a committee structure that operates within each layer of government activity—in local government wards, precincts, towns, cities, counties and the states. These committees are responsible for candidate selection at the state and local level. Each state determines its own rules about how the party is organised within its jurisdiction.

Both parties have national committees that are responsible for running their presidential campaigns. Presidential candidates are determined by a series of state primaries for each party that select a slate of delegates committed to one of the candidates. The candidate with the majority of pledged votes at the National Convention is selected as the party's nominee for the presidential race (see Vile, M.J.C. 2007, *Politics in the USA*, 6th ed., Routledge, New York, pp. 62–4).

Federal Republic of Germany

Germany's two major political parties have federal structures, with local and state branches and a national congress, but unlike Australia and the United States, political control is centralised. The Executive Committee of the Social Democratic Party (SPD), elected by the party congress, manages the affairs of the party. The Christian Democratic Union (CDU) operates in a similar way, with the Presidium, a sub-committee of the Federal Executive, setting party policy and making administrative decisions.

Federation of Malaysia

The organisation of political parties in the federal system of Malaysia is different. Their organisational structures reflect the federal nature of the political system, with local branches at the constituency level, state liaison committees and a national policy-making congress, but power and control of the parties and their policies is centralised with the national body. In the case of UMNO, the party president, who historically has been prime minister of Malaysia because of the predominance of UMNO within the Barisan Nasional coalition government, has had a great deal of influence over the party.

POLICY MAKING

While a party's *platform* is a statement of its beliefs and assumptions (a summary of its ideology, if you like), its *policy* consists of reasonably detailed proposals about how it would implement its platform if it became the government. Because society is constantly changing, there is constant pressure on parties to develop new policies and to modify old ones. Each party has its own distinctive way of going about this. However, all the parties are affected by some general conditions:

- The ambit of government has grown very wide. This has increased the range of policies that need to be prepared, and also increased the range of expertise that must be called upon. No party is likely to have all these resources within its membership, nor be able to mobilise them effectively.
- The resources of government are, on the other hand, very large indeed. Governments employ thousands of experts covering almost every conceivable field. A party in government will therefore have more resources available to it for policy making than its rival in opposition.
- Major political parties are set up as electoral organisations whose principal purpose is the winning of elections. The policy campaign speech and the party platform have this goal firmly in mind.
- Because each party is a coalition of interests encompassing shades of ideological opinion, clear and unequivocal statements of policy may be difficult to arrive at on contentious issues. Parties, as discussed below, deal with this problem in different ways.

All four factors tend to diminish the significance of the policy-making process within the parties once a party is in government.

PARTY DISCIPLINE

For political parties to be effective, they must be—or appear to be—united. The parliamentarians must act together if they are to be taken seriously, the party workers must cheerfully take up the common cause, and workers and MPs together must seem to be working in concert. When all this is true, the party can be effective in the community, and attract new members, money and other assistance. When it is not true, the party can be almost an embarrassment to its own members.

Unity is not something that grows on trees. Party ideologies have to be general enough to attract the widest possible support, but in their generality lies the seeds of disagreement and strife. One consequence of this is the existence of factions or groups within parties. The existence of three factions within the ALP, for example, is public knowledge and features in most media discussion of the party. Likewise, the Liberal Party includes groups of 'liberals' and 'conservatives'. While they are less formal than factions, intra-party debates over policy show that they are no less real.

The need for discipline

Parties must be prepared to endure debates within themselves, but they also need some way of ending them and compelling general agreement, at least for the short term. That is provided, in some parties, by discipline, which operates in two principal areas.

First, in all parties with parliamentary members, the *control of party endorsement* is a means by which the parliamentary party is kept in line. As the great majority of citizens now vote for parties rather than for the individuals standing for election or for policies, a member of parliament who loses his or her party's endorsement is unlikely to survive the next election. This sanction can be used by a parliamentary leader exercising influence in the executive to discipline a recalcitrant backbencher, or by those controlling the extra-parliamentary organisation to compel parliamentarians to publicly follow a policy that they find objectionable. For the most part, the threat of loss of endorsement is enough to obtain obedience. Actual withdrawals are quite rare, although in 1995 the ALP's National Executive withdrew the preselection of Graeme Campbell, who subsequently won the seat as an independent; Pauline Hanson had her endorsement withdrawn by the Liberal Party prior to the 1996 election.

Second, in all parties the ordinary member faces *expulsion* if he or she commits one of a number of sins, of which the worst is to stand as a candidate against another properly endorsed member, and to campaign against such a properly endorsed member. Although the parties differ in their response to such actions, expulsion—or the threat of it—works because party membership is important to those who belong. In general, those who are politically active rank politics very high on their scale of interests: to be expelled means being unable to take part in politics. Accordingly, members of all parties learn to accept defeats on matters of policy or candidature in the spirit of the democratic principles that accept majority decision making, even if the margin has been 51:49. Next time, they may be on the winning side.

Under the Westminster tradition of government used in Britain and Australia, the cabinet is collectively responsible for the policy of the government. Once a decision has been made by cabinet, it must be supported by all ministers and members in the parliament. The failure of any members to do so will result in a divided party, which could place the government at risk within the parliament and weaken its chances of re-election. For that reason, party discipline may be imposed on members of parliament by *party whips*—members of the party in the parliament who are given responsibility for ensuring that members 'toe the party line' and support cabinet decisions.

> The principle of **collective responsibility** requires strong party discipline to make it work.

The ideology and organisation of Australia's major parties are explained in Chapter 10, and in Chapter 11 we look at significant minor parties in the same context.

PARTY SYSTEMS

Political parties are now fundamental institutions of government, and party government has become the norm in most parliamentary systems, including Australia. Because of this, it is important for us to know how a party system works.

> **Party system**: a political system in which governments are formed as the result of an electoral contest between competing political parties.

For nearly 100 years the party system has been the crucial element in Australian politics. It determines the directions in which governmental policies and decisions proceed; it produces the politicians who made them; and it provides the citizens with an arena in which to observe, applaud and deride the gladiators and the political games they play, and to take part in the games themselves if they want to.

The party system is considered to be democratic mostly because we think of ourselves as a democratic society. As we have already seen, however, there is a clear division of work in politics, and some of the people do much more of the ruling than the rest. It was argued by Robert Michels as long ago as 1915 that the structure of parties as organisations with the characteristics of powerful executives and hierarchical bureaucracies means they will inevitably become elitist institutions.

> 'Organization implies the tendency to oligarchy. In every organization, whether it be a political party, a professional union, or any other association of the kind, the aristocratic tendency manifests itself very clearly . . . As a result of organization, every party or professional union becomes divided into a minority of directors and a majority of directed.'
> (*Source*: Michels, R. 1949 (1915), *Political Parties*, The Free Press, Glencoe, Illinois, p. 32)

Despite these criticisms, however, the party system has been the 20th century's most distinctive contribution to politics, and it seems in no great danger of serious decline or radical change. From time to time, those dissatisfied with the present order propose alternatives, such as:

- an end to 'party bickering'—the parties should sink their differences and 'pull together' for the good of all;
- 'a government of all the talents'—Australia's best leaders and thinkers from all walks of life should make up the government; or

- during an emergency (however defined), all the powers should be given to a strong leader who has the confidence of all.

These alternatives are not feasible at the moment because of the entrenched nature of the party system. Most citizens vote for a party candidate or a party list, and the significant majority of people elected to parliament are party members. Parties provide the focus for political debate, and they generate policy options both within and outside parliament. This is unlikely to change in the near future.

Types of party systems

The party system of government functions regardless of the number of political parties. The nature of parliamentary procedures, incorporating a Yes/No vote, and the notion of majority government versus an opposition, encourages voting in two blocs in parliament. If a number of parties are represented in the parliament, there will be a search for coalitions or alliances so that the majority grouping can form a government.

Different types of party systems have developed, each depending on the number of political parties represented in a legislature that can form a government. The method of electing representatives is a significant contributing factor in determining what type of party system will function in any particular polity.

One-party systems

A one-party system occurs in situations where only one political party can effectively hold office. One-party states operate in countries where opposition parties are legally banned and only one party nominates candidates for office—for example, the communist regime in China. They also occur where minor parties are allowed to exist, but have no real chance of gaining power because of manipulation of the electoral system or practices such as patronage, vote buying, or the oppression of opposition political figures by the dominant party.

Two-party systems

Those systems in which two major parties are the only real contenders for office have been called two-party systems. Other parties may exist, but are unable to generate sufficient support to form a government in their own right.

> 'Two-party systems are naturally installed when the voting system used for elections discriminates against third or smaller parties.'
> (Source: NationMaster Encyclopedia, 'Two Party System', http://www.nationmaster.com/encyclopedia/Two_party-system)

The advantages of a two-party system include the following:

- There is more stable government. A government can pass its legislation through the parliament because it has the majority of members (except in systems that have a second chamber where the government does not have a majority).
- There is a better reflection of mainstream views, because the parties tend to moderate their platforms, and may converge along similar policy lines, in order to attract a majority of the votes. At the same time, the parties have to remain distinctive enough to maintain their core support and to sell their policies as an alternative choice.

- It is easier for voters to choose between only two sets of policies.
- It is also easier for people to judge the elected government, since it cannot blame dissident coalition partners for failure to deliver on its promises or for bad administration.

There are also some disadvantages:

- If the opposition is weak, the governing party may stay in office too long and that is not conducive to the rotation of office desirable in a democratic system.
- If minorities are permanently excluded from government, they may not have their interests taken into consideration.
- An adversarial system may develop where the parties focus on discrediting their opponent, rather than promoting an alternative policy platform for government.
- Policies designed to attract the swinging, or median, voter may not be in the best interests of the broader public.

(*Sources*: For a more detailed explanation of these arguments, see Minch, K.J. 2003, 'Two-Party System', International Debate Education Association, http://www.idebate.org/ debatabase/ topic_details. php?topicID=231; and NationMaster Encyclopaedia, 'Two Party System', http:// www.nationmaster. com/encyclopedia/Two_party-system)

Two-party systems have emerged from 'first past the post' voting systems in most of the countries in our study, including Britain and the United States. Malaysia uses a 'first past the post' system and functions in practice like a two-party system because only Barisan Nasional (National Front) and the Opposition People's Front are viable contenders for office. Both, however, are coalitions of a number of parties; on that basis, it might be better to explain Malaysia as a multi-party system. The cooperative process of 'communally-based' cooperation within the Barisan Nasional to manage the diverse ethnic interests of the participating parties has also been described as 'consociationalism' (Funston, J. 2001, 'Malaysia', in Funston, J. (ed.), *Government and Politics in Southeast Asia*, Institute of Southeast Asian Studies, Singapore, p. 186).

The preferential voting system used for the Australian House of Representatives has resulted in only two major parties being able to form governments. For this reason, some people categorise Australia as a two-party system, but others argue it is a two-and-a-half party system because the Liberal Party has usually required the support of another party, the Nationals, to win and maintain government. (See, for example, Blondel, J. 1990, 'Types of Party System', in Mair, P. (ed.), *The West European Party System*, Oxford University Press, Oxford; and Jaensch, D. 1997, *Politics of Australia*, 2nd ed., Macmillan, Melbourne, p. 204.) Effectively, however, a two-party system has operated in the Australian House of Representatives since 1910.

Multi-party systems

Political systems in which a number of parties are represented, and two or more parties have to come together in coalition to form a majority government, are generally called multi-party systems.

> 'A multi-party system exists when no one party can govern alone and co-operation between the parties is required to form or maintain effective government.'
> (*Source*: Blondel, J. 1995, 'Consensual Politics and Multi-Party Systems', *Australian Journal of Political Science*, vol. 30, special issue, p. 9)

Multi-party systems can take the form of either:

- formal, stable coalitions of parties in government; or
- issue-based arrangements where a minority government has to secure the agreement of other parties to pass a piece of legislation.

Building a coalition requires finding sufficient common ground, or negotiating trade-offs, that will satisfy all partners. Coalitions, whether formal or issue-based, are more likely to form if the parties have common goals and shared principles. Parties with a strong ideological base may be reluctant to compromise those principles and will probably enter into a coalition only on their own terms. Parties that are ideologically opposed are less likely to enter into a coalition.

The advantages of a multi-party system include the following:

- A greater range of interests are represented in the government.
- Coalitions have to balance their interests and develop consensus for change, so the policies that emerge from this process are more likely to be acceptable to a broader section of the community.
- The policy-making process is open to greater scrutiny by minor parties whose votes are needed to pass legislation.

There are also disadvantages:

- Multi-party systems may be more volatile because allegiances can shift for a range of reasons, such as disagreement over policy or personality clashes between the leaders that might cause a coalition to collapse. Italy is a good example of a volatile, multi-party state because of the inability to maintain long-term coalitions in government. The greater the number of parties involved, the more difficult it will be to find common ground and reach a consensus.

    It is interesting to note that multi-party systems can produce stable government. Blondel has pointed out that Scandinavian countries, Germany and the Benelux countries, all of which have multi-party systems, are 'among the most stable polities of the world' (Blondel, J. 1995, 'Consensual Politics and Multi-Party Systems', *Australian Journal of Political Science*, vol. 30, special issue, p. 7).
- Parties may negotiate privately, behind closed doors, to agree on policies or trade-offs to gain the support of a coalition partner or partners.

(*Source*: For a more detailed explanation of these arguments, see Minch, K.J. 2003, 'Two-Party System', International Debate Education Association, http:// www.idebate.org/ debatabase/ topic_ details.php? topicID=231)

Germany: a multi-party system

As a rule, in the Bundestag no one party has a clear majority. For this reason a coalition—that is, an alliance of various parties—is normally required to form a government. The working methods of the coalition are set out in formal terms. For example:

'In the Bundestag and all bodies to which it sends representatives, the coalition parliamentary groups will vote unanimously. This will also apply to matters which are not the subject of agreed policy. The possibility of changing majorities is excluded.'

(*Source*: The Press and Information Office of the Federal Government [Germany] 2008, 'The Coalition Agreement', http://www.bundesregierung.de/Webs/Breg/EN/Federal-Government/CoalitionAgreement/coalition-agreement.html)

We have argued above that the Australian political system, where governments are formed in the House of Representatives, bears the hallmarks of a two-party system. However, as you know, the Australian parliament is made up of two houses and there is an argument which suggests that the way in which parties in the Senate function is more akin to a multi-party system. The proportional voting system for the Senate, as we saw in Chapter 8, has resulted in more seats being won by minor parties and independents than occurs in the House of Representatives.

The majority of Senate members represent either the ALP or the Liberal/Nationals Coalition. However, since 1 July 1981 (except for the period from 1 July 2005 to 30 June 2008 when the Howard government had a majority in both houses), the balance of power has been held by minor parties and/or independents. When this situation occurs, the government elected in the lower house cannot work with the certain knowledge that its legislation will pass the Senate. The result has been the type of negotiation and brokering with minor parties and/or independents on contested bills to facilitate their passage through the parliament that is characteristic of a multi-party system.

> 'The multi-party system that operated in the Australian Senate in 1996 was described as semi-consensual and pivotal, because the minor parties and independents move in and out of coalition only on those issues where their vote is needed to pass legislation.'
> (Source: Singleton, G. 1996, 'Independents in a Multi-Party System: The Experience of the Australian Senate', Papers on Parliament, no. 28, The Senate, Canberra, http://www.aph.gov.au/ SENATE/pubs/pops/pop28/c05.pdf)

THE PARTY SYSTEM IN AUSTRALIA

> The rules for registering a party for a federal election in Australia can be found in the Australian Electoral Commission's 'Fact Sheet on Funding and Disclosure', http://www.aec.gov.au.

Origins of the Australian party system

The notions of ideology, discipline and organisation attached to modern-day parties are very different from the conditions that operated in 19th-century Australian colonial politics. Responsible government began in the older colonies in the 1850s, and by 1858 Victoria, New South Wales and South Australia had what were then among the most democratic constitutions in the world, with universal manhood suffrage and the secret ballot applying for elections for the lower house of the two-chamber parliaments.

> 'The first colony to give women the vote was South Australia in 1894, followed by Western Australia in 1899. The Commonwealth Franchise Act 1902 established universal franchise for men and women over 21.'
> (Source: McAllister, A., Mackerras, M., Ascui, A. & Moss, S. 1990, Australian Political Facts, Longman Cheshire, Melbourne, p. 59)

People talked of 'Liberals' and 'Conservatives', because these were labels applied to politicians in England at the time, but the terms lacked meaning in the Australian colonies. In fact, until the late 1880s colonial politics was characterised by fluidity: governments rarely stayed long in power, and formed and broke up as politicians changed their allegiance from one leader to another. Political issues centred around the conditions and concerns associated with economic growth. Railways, public works generally, the sale of Crown land and land settlement were the dominant concerns, and they did not lend themselves to ideological politics.

Things changed at the time of, and partly because of, the great crash of the early 1890s. By 1890 the colonial economies had become more complex, with local manufacturing industries and a developing transport system becoming important as employers of labour. Trade unions had developed in these industries and among shearers and other pastoral workers, while the railway system and the telegraph allowed politicians to campaign from one end of the colony to the other. Easier travel also made citizens aware of the common problems faced by country communities, by miners or by factory workers. Each colony was quickly becoming a political community, and the issues began to reflect their broader interests. Debate about whether the Western Railway should go through Dry Creek or through Stony Gully was being replaced by debate about 'free trade or protection'—that is, whether or not the new colonial manufacturing industries should be protected from foreign competition by heavy customs charges (high tariffs), and whether or not the colony's rural industries should be similarly protected against products imported from another colony (for example, whether New South Wales wheat growers should be protected against the importation of cheaper South Australian wheat).

> The depth of feeling about the protection versus free trade issue is evident from these words of George Reid, who became premier of New South Wales with a commitment to free trade:
> 'I set about writing "Five Essays on Free Trade". Free trade was a subject on which I had often spoken in debating clubs. New South Wales had always based her fiscal policy upon Free Trade; Victoria had just entered upon a Protective policy. I believed in the former view with all the ardour which beginners sometimes share with experts.'
> (Source: Reid, G. 1917, *My Reminiscences*, Cassell and Company, London, p. 24)

The emergence of the Australian Labor Party and party politics

In 1890 a period of economic distress commenced, which was to transform Australian politics. Falling wool prices caused graziers to seek a reduction in shearing rates that was strongly resisted by the shearers' union in the form of strikes against employers who would not pay the union rate. An unconnected strike by ships' officers in August 1890 brought on a series of strikes in other industries, including wool, in which employers and employees, all worried by the general collapse of prosperity, took up adversarial positions. The failure of the strikes prompted the unions to look instead to the political system to achieve their goals through the election of union representatives to parliament and, through them, the formulation of laws that would protect the interests of workers, a strategy that formed the basis of Australian labourism. The first endeavours were spectacularly successful. The new Labor electoral leagues won more than a quarter of the seats in the New South Wales Legislative Assembly in mid-1891, and were correspondingly successful in the other colonies in the next few years.

In the beginning the new Labor parties did not try to take office themselves. Their members were nearly all political novices, who had little idea of how laws were made or how government actually worked. Their tactics, therefore, were to trade 'support in return for concessions'—to offer to vote for a particular bill in return for something that Labor wanted. The quick result was that Labor came to possess the balance of power, or at least an influence out of proportion to its numbers.

- The first Labor government in the world held office briefly in Queensland between 1 December and 7 December 1899 with the support of a group of dissident opposition members. It was unable to survive once that support was withdrawn.
- The first Labor government in the Commonwealth parliament held office between 27 April 1904 and 17 August 1904. Its leader was Prime Minister John Watson.

From 1891, other politicians and groups began to respond to the Labor challenge by adopting similar tactics. By 1910, when Andrew Fisher's Labor Party faced Alfred Deakin's Liberals in the federal elections of that year, the new party politics was supreme. The two parties won 95 per cent of the vote between them, and all but one seat. This pattern of representation has been a significant factor in shaping Australia's two-party system since 1901, with the principal parties retaining a large majority share of the vote (see Table 9.1).

The brief history of Australian government, discussed below, shows how the two-party system has provided the context and shaped the game of party politics played out since Federation. It persists today, despite a number of splits on both sides of politics along the way, and an increase in the percentage of votes achieved by minor parties and independents at recent House of Representatives elections.

The development of the two-party system, 1901–49

Elections are significant milestones for Australian political history, and a study of Table 9.1 will help to set current politics in perspective. The threefold division between Labor, Free

TABLE 9.1

Party shares of first-preference vote in elections for the House of Representatives, 1901–2007 (per cent)

Election	Labor	Liberal	Protection	Country Party/Nationals	Other
1901	19	36	43		2
1903	31	34	30		5
1906	37	40	21		2
1910*	50	45			5
1913*	48	49			3
1914*	51	47			2

(continued)

TABLE 9.1 (continued)
Party shares of first-preference vote in elections for the House of Representatives, 1901–2007 (per cent)

1917*	44	(National) 54		2
1919	42	45	9	4
1922	42	45	13	5
1925	45	42	11	2
1928	45	39	12	4
1929	49	34	11	6
1931	(2 groups) 38	(UAP) 42	12	8
1934	41	37	13	9
1937	43	34	16	7
1940	(3 groups) 48	30	14	8
1943	50	(var. groups) 41	12	17
1946	50	(Liberal) 33	11	6
1949	46	39	11	4
1951	48	40	10	2
1954	50	39	8	3
1955	45	40	8	7
1958	43	37	9	11
1961	48	34	8	10
1963	45	37	9	9
1966	40	40	10	10
1969	47	35	8	10
1972	50	32	9	9
1974	49	35	11	5
1975	43	42	(National/Country) 11	4
1977	40	38	10	12
1980	45	37	9	7
1983	49	34	(National) 9	7
1984	48	34	11	8
1987	46	35	11	8
1990	40	35	8	17
1993	45	37	7	11
1996	39	39	8	17
1998**	40	34	5	20#
2001**	38	37	6	20
2004**	38	40	5	16
2007	43	36	5***	15

* From 1910 to 1917, simple majority counting was in force, thereafter preferential voting. Voting has been compulsory since 1925.

** Rounding of figures gives a total that may be more or less than 100. Full details of the first-preference shares of the vote can be found on the Australian Electoral Commission's website: http://www.aec.gov.au.

*** The Nationals' share of the vote of 5.49 per cent has been rounded down.

\# Includes 8 per cent for Pauline Hanson's One Nation.

Trade and Protection that existed in most colonies reappeared in the new federal parliament in 1901 (though not always under those names—Liberals, Conservatives, Ministerialists and Oppositionists were other labels). As Labor's share of the vote increased, politicians in the other camps came to see virtues in amalgamation, and Deakin's Liberal Party, originally called 'the Fusion', was the result.

The Liberal Party was very much a coalition of forces and one of these, the farming and grazing interest, soon decided to establish separate representation in parliament. The first 'Country Party' had been formed in New South Wales in 1893, not long after the establishment of the Australian Labor Party, but this parliamentary grouping was not supported by an electoral organisation and failed to survive.

The First World War of 1914–18 delayed the rebirth of the Country Party because dissidents within the Liberal Party were urged to sink their differences during the conflict. The war also ensured that the Country Party would be reborn. Farmers and graziers had been suspicious of urban big business interests and their influence in the Liberal Party. When the Commonwealth Liberal Party merged with W.M. Hughes and his 'National Labor' followers to form the Nationalist Party after the 1916 split in the Australian Labor Party over conscription, the farmers' organisations became convinced that, like the trade unions before them, they would have to have their own representatives in parliament.

The federal Country Party was formed after the elections of 1919 and made a bigger impact on its entry to parliament than it otherwise would have, because the voting system had been altered to allow voters to register their preferences. Their first three years in parliament showed the new country politicians that they were too small in number to overturn the Labor versus non-Labor game that had become established, for there was now a majority of MPs from what were essentially metropolitan seats. After the 1922 elections, when the Country Party held the balance of power, the new party was able to force the retirement of Hughes and to form a coalition with the Nationalists. This coalition lasted until 1929, and established a convention in Australian politics of the Country Party as a non-Labor party, and usually part of a coalition government or an informal coalition Opposition that has persisted until today.

The Australian Labor Party enveloped within its ranks a broad range of interests and factions, including ardent socialists who wanted to socialise the means of production, and others, such as democratic socialists, who were more pragmatic in how they considered their goals should be achieved. At times this made it difficult for the party to maintain its cohesion.

The conscription issue during the First World War caused the first split in the ALP. The second occurred in 1931, when Labor was in government in Canberra and the party was divided as to the correct policies to end the calamitous Depression which Australia, in common with much of the rest of the world, was then experiencing. The Labor government was finally brought down by defections from its own ranks, with some of the angriest campaigns occurring during the 1931 election between candidates of rival Labor parties. Internal troubles that kept Labor preoccupied for most of the 1930s meant another period of non-Labor government. However, as the Second World War developed, Labor resolved its internal dissension just as the non-Labor parties began to experience their own problems with internal factional strife. The non-Labor Coalition government was defeated in parliament in 1941 and Labor took office. Two successful elections in 1943 and 1946 gave Labor the longest period in office it had known since it was established.

> The Labor government held a majority in the Senate from 1943 to 1949 and enjoyed a long period with real political power, with no hindrance to its legislation from the upper house.

Labor dominance in the 1940s caused a crisis of confidence in the principal non-Labor party, the United Australia Party, which had been so named in 1931 as a symbol of the need for national unity in a time of general distress. In the 1943 elections, several non-Labor parties campaigned, and independent candidates secured one vote in every six. In 1944 and 1945, under the leadership of Robert Menzies, the non-Labor factions regrouped into a single party—the Liberal Party—which was designed to be a mass party responsible to its members.

> Sir Robert Menzies explains how his leadership of the Liberal Party came about:
> 'I said that I would do so on two conditions. One was that our party, being the majority opposition party, should assert its right to the Leadership of the Opposition without which I believed we could not move forward effectively. The other was that I should have *carte blanche* to take all necessary steps towards gathering up all the existing organisations into one Australia-wide organisation, with a new name . . . and a carefully prepared platform.'
> (Source: Menzies, R. 1967, *Afternoon Light*, Cassell, Melbourne, p. 283)

The Country Party stayed out of the new organisation, preferring to retain its separate identity, but its alliance with the Liberals continued.

The non-Labor parties finally succeeded in defeating Labor in 1949. The continuation of wartime restrictions long after the war, serious industrial trouble, Labor's attempt to nationalise the private banks, and the enlargement of the House of Representatives from 75 to 120 members (which bottled up many Labor votes in safe seats) all contributed to the Labor government's defeat.

Non-Labor dominance, 1949–72: the 'Menzies era'

The Liberal and Country parties were in government for 23 years between 1949 and 1972. The explanation had a number of dimensions:

- *Luck*: In 1954 and 1961 a few hundred votes cast otherwise would have brought Labor back to power.
- *Prosperity*: Throughout the 1950s and 1960s (save for 1960–61), economic conditions were generally buoyant, seasons were favourable, and affluence was widely shared.
- *ALP 1955 split*: This occurred over the party's policies towards communism and attitudes towards the involvement of communists in unions. Many of the principal opponents of communists in the union movement were Catholic members of ALP anti-communist 'industrial groups'. The split produced a new splinter party, the Democratic Labor Party, which was unable to win seats in the House of Representatives because its supporters were spread evenly over the nation. The proportional voting system for the Senate, however, gave them representation in that house. The party quickly became a kind of auxiliary non-Labor party, helping to keep the Coalition in office with its preferences in House of Representatives elections.

Labor to power, 1972–75: the Whitlam years

The election of Gough Whitlam as leader of the Australian Labor Party in 1967 marked a new phase in Australian politics. Whitlam worked to make the party both a credible alternative government and a political organisation that would attract members from the groups that traditionally had supported the Liberal Party—white-collar workers, professionals and even businesspeople.

> 'The reverses which we suffered in the 1963 election for the House of Representatives convinced me that the Party was providing an inadequate alternative to the policies of the Menzies Government. New and attractive policy programs, meeting the aspirations of both the Party and the electorate, had to be developed if the Party was to regain government.'
> (Source: Whitlam, E.G. 1985, *The Whitlam Government, 1972–1975*, Viking, Ringwood, Victoria, p. 4, reproduced with permission)

Whitlam was aided by the decline in morale that the Liberal Party experienced after the retirement of Menzies in 1966. Menzies' successor, Harold Holt, was drowned in the surf, while Holt's successor, John Gorton, lacked the ability to hold a team together and eventually voted himself out of office after a party confidence vote in 1971 resulted in a tie. The last Liberal prime minister of this Liberal era, William McMahon, although an able and experienced minister, was promoted beyond his capabilities. Whitlam looked by far the more attractive and impressive candidate for prime minister and led Labor to victory in 1972.

> **'It's time'**
> Labor's campaign slogan for the 1972 election.

Labor's short period in office, 1972–75, was marked by political confrontation with the Coalition Opposition parties, a hostile Senate and an almost continuous atmosphere of 'crisis'. A double dissolution election in May 1974 confirmed Labor's control of the House of Representatives but failed to give it a majority in the Senate. This meant that the principal reason for the Whitlam government's problems—its inability to get its legislation passed through the Senate—remained. The government's confidence and command began to wane in 1975 as unemployment and inflation rose sharply. The disclosure that Labor ministers had sought to borrow very large sums from unusual sources eventually precipitated a major confrontation in October 1975, when the Senate declined to pass the supply bills. The government refused to resign on the grounds that it retained a majority in the House of Representatives. The deadlock was broken by the governor-general, Sir John Kerr, who dismissed the Whitlam government on 11 November 1975 and appointed a caretaker government under the new leader of the Liberal Party, Malcolm Fraser, until elections on 5 December 1975 decided who should govern.

The Coalition returns to office, 1975–83: the Fraser Government

The 1975 election returned the Fraser government with a majority so great that the Liberal Party had an absolute majority in the House of Representatives in its own right.

> **'Turn on the lights'**
> Liberal campaign slogan for the 1975 election.

Fraser decided nonetheless to continue the coalition. Economic troubles were probably the main cause of Labor's heavy defeat in 1975 and there had been no improvement of any consequence when Fraser called an early election in late 1977.

> '"Life wasn't meant to be easy"—a comment associated with Malcolm Fraser's approach to the economy.'
> (Source: Edwards, J. 1977, Life Wasn't Meant to be Easy, Mayhem, Sydney, p. 98)

Ordinarily, the government would have been expected to lose seats to the Australian Labor Party. Instead, a new party, the Australian Democrats, siphoned off some of that vote. Led by a former Liberal MP, Don Chipp, it attracted many who were dissatisfied with the government but not enthusiastic about the Labor Opposition. Chipp's new party (which had no connection with the Democratic Labor Party, which virtually died when it lost all its senators in the 1974 election) secured a respectable 9 per cent of the vote at the 1977 election, which saw Chipp and another Democrat win seats in the Senate. It was unable to win a seat in the House of Representatives, so the two-party dominance of the Coalition and ALP in the contest for government remained intact.

The Country Party during this period changed its name twice, first to the National Country Party (1975), then to the National Party (1983), the changes reflecting the party's response to the postwar decline in the power of the countryside.

The Fraser Liberal/National Party Coalition government retained power at the October 1980 elections with a reduced majority in the House of Representatives, but the Democrats made sufficient gains in the Senate to give them and an independent senator the balance of power in that chamber from 1 July 1981.

> **'Keeping the bastards honest'**
> Election theme of the Australian Democrats.

The Hawke and Keating Labor governments, 1983–96

Economic conditions worsened in 1982 because of a severe drought. Unemployment reached in excess of 10 per cent of the workforce, a level not experienced since the Depression of the 1930s. The Fraser government's poor relations with the trade union movement had deteriorated into confrontation and conflict. These factors did not provide favourable conditions under which to call an election, but the government's three-year term was coming to a close. Hoping to get in before the replacement of Labor leader Bill Hayden with the more popular Bob Hawke, Fraser decided on an early election for 5 March 1983. Unfortunately for him, the change in Labor leaders occurred on the same morning that Fraser gained the consent of the governor-general for the election.

A Labor victory had been highly likely, but the accession of Hawke to the Labor leadership made it more probable. Labor won the election and Bob Hawke became prime minister.

> **'Reconciliation, recovery, reconstruction'**
> Labor leader Bob Hawke's campaign theme for the 1983 election.

The Hawke government was re-elected in 1984, 1987 and 1990. In November 1991, Hawke's former treasurer, Paul Keating, displaced Hawke as Labor leader and prime minister. Keating subsequently led the party to an unexpected electoral victory in 1993.

> 'I was determined that the Hawke Labor Government would distinguish itself as a better economic manager than its predecessors and would establish a clear superiority in that respect over our Opposition. I intended to turn the Government's performance as an economic manager into an asset rather than a liability.'
> (Source: Hawke, R.J.L. 1994, *The Hawke Memoirs*, Heinemann, Melbourne, p. 169, copyright Hon. Bob Hawke A.C.)

The success of Labor in government for such a long period was unprecedented, particularly as the 1990 and 1993 election campaigns were fought in the context of economic recession and high unemployment. Significant factors that contributed to Labor's electoral successes included the following:

- The government's Accord with the Australian Council of Trade Unions (ACTU), an incomes agreement forged between the Federal Parliamentary Labor Party and the ACTU prior to the 1983 election, delivered a period of wage restraint on the part of the unions that assisted the government in its campaign to reduce inflation.
- Strategic targeting of low-income earners and their families offered a range of supplementary assistance benefits.
- A series of leadership changes, including a tussle between Andrew Peacock and John Howard, destabilised the Liberal Party.
- Considerable disagreement occurred within the National Party prior to the 1987 election, and between the National Party and the Liberals.
- A move towards a conservative economic policy on the part of the Liberals culminated in the 'Fightback!' policy document of 1993, which included an unpopular proposal for a Goods and Services Tax (GST).

> **'Fightback!'**
> The Liberal Party's campaign policy for the 1993 election.

- Effective election campaigning by the Labor Party—in particular, its skill in implanting sufficient doubts about the possible impact of 'Fightback!' and the GST—enabled it to win the 'unwinnable' election of 1993.

The Howard Coalition government, 1996–2007

Labor's time in government came to an end on 2 March 1996 when it was swept out of office in a landslide that delivered the Liberal/National Coalition parties 93 seats to Labor's 49. Five independents and one Country/Liberal Party member were also elected. The Liberals had enough seats to govern in their own right, but still retained the coalition partnership.

> **'Enough is enough'**
> The Liberal Party's campaign slogan for the 1996 election.

The first term of office was significant for the vigour with which the Howard government attacked the budget deficit, including a program of privatisation, and a significant reduction in the number of Commonwealth public servants (discussed in Chapter 7). There was no Accord with the trade union movement and the Coalition government adopted a more confrontationist attitude in its dealings with the unions.

In 1998, Prime Minister John Howard took the potentially risky step of campaigning for re-election on a Goods and Services Tax. The 1998 federal election was complicated for the government by the rapid emergence of Pauline Hanson's One Nation party (see Chapter 11), with the potential to take votes, and seats, from Coalition members, particularly rural seats held by the Nationals.

> **'Our own flag, our own people, our own language, our own future. Our own Nation.'**
> Pauline Hanson statement during the 1998 election campaign.
> (*Source*: Kingston, M. 1999, *Off the Rails*, Allen & Unwin, Sydney, p. 198)

The Coalition lost 14 seats but held on to power with 80 seats. One independent was elected. Pauline Hanson's One Nation party, including its leader, was unable to attract sufficient preferences to win a seat in the House of Representatives (see Chapter 8). The party did, however, win a Senate seat in Queensland.

The second Howard government implemented the GST in 2000. The arrival of illegal immigrants in boats and the government's hard-line stance in detaining these people—and its actions in turning back some of the boats—were significant issues towards the end of the Howard government's second term and during the 2001 election campaign. The Coalition won the election with 69 seats to Labor's 65.

> **'We decide who comes to this country and the circumstances in which they come.'**
> Liberal Party 2001 election campaign slogan.

National security and patriotism featured in the third Howard government. Following the events of 11 September 2001 in the United States, Australian troops were despatched to Afghanistan to support the United States' 'war on terror'. In March 2003, Australian troops joined the 'coalition of the willing' in the war against Iraq. The government maintained its hard line against asylum seekers. On the domestic front, it favoured family-oriented social policies and mutual obligation for welfare.

Labor, under the leadership of Mark Latham, was unable to convince the electorate that it was an attractive alternative and the Howard government was returned in October 2004 for a fourth consecutive term.

The government's unpopular Work Choices labour legislation became a significant electoral issue for the fourth Howard government. Despite the government's dispersal of a burgeoning budget surplus to various projects and groups, who were targeted in an effort to garner electoral support, the ALP's new leader, Kevin Rudd, attracted increasing support from the electorate as a potential prime minister, and Howard was unable to stave off Labor's challenge at the 2007 election.

Labor returns to office: the Rudd Labor government, 2007–

The Howard government was defeated convincingly at the 2007 federal election with a swing of 5.74 per cent against it. John Howard lost his seat of Bennelong, only the second time since Federation that a sitting prime minister has lost his seat at a general election. Labor's campaign policies focused on delivering an education revolution, better public hospitals and action on climate change, but the significant factor in its win was the promise to abolish Work Choices. This campaign was heavily supported by the ACTU and unions, particularly in marginal seats.

> **'Your rights at work'**
> Slogan used on campaign posters supported by the trade union movement

> **'Kevin07'**
> Kevin Rudd's leadership slogan; it was featured on campaign advertising and T-shirts.

The continuing strength and resilience of Australia's two-party system is evident from the 2007 election result. Between them the ALP and the Liberal Party gained 138 of the 150 seats in the House of Representatives. The Nationals won 10 seats, and independents won two.

AUSTRALIA'S TWO-PARTY SYSTEM IN RETROSPECT

Advantages of Australia's two-party system

The advantages of the two-party system outlined at the beginning of this chapter are evident from this historical description of Australian party government. The system has delivered stable government with political power changing hands smoothly, even after the bitterness associated with the party splits on both sides of politics, and the constitutional 'crisis' and sacking of the Whitlam government in 1975. The policies of the two major parties, which many regard as having converged as they have cast their 'catch-all' policy nets in the direction of the median voter, have meant that the interests of more electors are taken into consideration by government and opposition parties.

> Murray Goot suggests that a more cautionary approach should be taken to the convergence thesis, arguing that 'convergence or divergence is very much a matter of what policies one looks at, over what period, and what sort of balance (if any) between issues one is prepared to wear'.
> (Source: Goot, M. 2003, 'Party Convergence Reconsidered', *Australian Journal of Political Science*, vol. 39, no. 1, p. 69)

The preferential and proportional systems that underpin our 'two-party' system have provided opportunities for minority participation in the context of majority party rule, including the 'trade' in preferences, and the function of minor parties and independents as policy brokers when they hold the balance of power in the Senate.

Disadvantages of Australia's two-party system

We can also identify some disadvantages. There have been periods when one party has dominated and remained in office for a long period of time, such as the 23 years of Liberal government between 1949 and 1972, the 13 years of Labor between 1983 and 1996, and 11 years of the Howard Coalition government between 1996 and 2007. Weak opposition may have been a factor, but it can also be attributed to the difficulties that opposition parties experience in remaining distinctive in a two-party contest when the focus of both parties lies with attracting the same group of median voters. Because their policies are very similar, the result is an adversarial contest where the parties attack each other and their leaders.

The Howard government used the adversarial contest to its own advantage by drawing out the policy differences between itself and Labor in a tactic that has been called 'wedge politics'. Wedge politics is a strategy that focuses on issues with popular appeal on which the opposition is divided. This drives a 'wedge' between the parliamentary party and its supporters in the electorate, causing the party to lose votes. As an example, the Labor parliamentary party supported the government on Australia's participation in the war in Iraq and the detention of asylum seekers, but many of its supporters did not.

> **Wedge politics**: a 'calculated political tactic aimed at using divisive social issues to gain political support, weaken opponents and strengthen control over the political agenda'.
> (Source: Wilson, S. & Turnbull, N. 2001, 'Wedge Politics and Welfare Reform in Australia', *Australian Journal of Politics and History*, vol. 47, no. 3, p. 386)

It may be fashionable and trendy for political commentators to call the exploitation of differences of opinion within the opposition 'wedge politics', but it is a clever political tactic that has had common usage since party politics became part of the political system.

Australia's party system has not changed substantially since Labor and non-Labor first faced off against each other in the Australian parliament. Despite occasional splits and schisms, and increasing support for minor parties and independents, the only effective contenders for political office are Labor, and the Liberals in coalition with the Nationals.

> 'The Australian party system remains best characterised as a two and a half party system... The general picture, to which there are exceptions, remains that the Australian Labor Party competes nationwide with the Liberal and National parties in coalition.'
> (Source: Warhurst, J. 2004, 'Patterns and Directions in Australian Politics over the Past Fifty Years', Australian Journal of Politics and History, vol. 50, no. 2, p. 164)

CHANGES TO THE AUSTRALIAN PARTY SYSTEM

This brief historical summary contains some important lessons about the stability of the Australian party system:

- The major parties hold shares of the vote which change relatively little from one election to another.
- New parties find it difficult to win seats in parliament or to survive.
- Since the modern party system began, the tendency has been for parties to have long periods in government.
- On the whole, the dictum has been that 'Oppositions don't win elections—governments lose them'.

In a 1997 study, Clive Bean (see 'Further reading' at the end of this chapter) argued that institutional factors play a significant role in maintaining the relative stability of the system, including:

- compulsory voting that reinforces partisan attachment;
- the flexibility of the major parties in adapting to change; and
- the preferential electoral system.

Pressures for change on the Australian party system

There were indications in the 1990s, however, that the electorate was becoming more volatile. These included the election of independents to the House of Representatives and the relative ease with which Pauline Hanson's One Nation party was able to attract significant numbers of voters in a short space of time.

In 1987, minor parties (excluding the Nationals as Coalition partner) polled 8 per cent of first-preference votes in the election for the House of Representatives, while in 1998 their combined share was 20 per cent. This upswing proved to be short-lived. In 2004 their support fell to 16 per cent and in 2007 it dropped to 14.53 per cent. The number of independents elected to the House of Representatives fell from three to two. The independent member for the New South Wales seat of Calare did not stand again and the seat was won by the Nationals.

A number of causal factors discussed in the previous chapter relating to why people vote the way they do, including party identification, the absence of alternatives, the inheritance of party loyalty, the stability of party images, and the social and economic structure, contribute to the stability of Australia's party system.

Impact of change on the Australian party system

The discussion in Chapter 8 helps in an understanding of elections. If party loyalty is fixed, for the majority at least, then elections become occasions on which that loyalty is demonstrated, rather than the time at which citizens judge the performance of government and Opposition. The losses and gains of the parties are likely to be small, and to come disproportionately from those with weak party loyalty or none at all.

The parties, when they were first established, indicated cleavages in Australian society that fell more or less along the following lines:

- *Simple economic*: the haves versus the have-nots, which produced the Labor and Liberal parties.
- *Regional/economic*: the country versus the city, which produced the Country Party (now the Nationals).
- *Ideological/religious*: the Catholic anti-communists versus 'the left', which produced the Democratic Labor Party in the 1950s and (in part) the various communist parties from the 1920s.

The fact that there is now a section of the community that regards these traditional cleavages as much less important has brought about some changes to the nature of the minor parties that contest elections. Some voted, for example, for the Australian Democrats, because the party was perceived to represent the middle ground, or because voters were dissatisfied with both major parties. This dissatisfaction was a significant factor in the emergence of Pauline Hanson's One Nation.

> 'In societies in which people feel unsettled by seemingly unrelenting change there will always be people who feel they have been ignored by their politicians and who find populist remedies to be in accord with their own views. Populism offers an alternative to mainstream party views, and there is no doubt that, from time to time, it can influence a nation's agenda.'
> (*Source*: Bennett, S. 2002, 'Populism in Australian National Politics', Research Note No. 8, 2002–03, Parliamentary Library, Canberra, http://www.aph.gov.au/library/pubs/rn/)

Others are attracted by 'single-issue' campaigns on behalf of causes such as the environment or, as we discussed earlier, the values espoused by a Christian-based party.

Independents in the party system

A number of independents have held seats in the Australian parliament in recent years. Three were elected to the House of Representatives in 2004, and two in 2007. After 1 July 2005, when senators elected at the 2004 federal election took their seats, there were no independents in the Senate. One independent was elected to the Senate in 2007.

The proportional voting system for the Senate makes it easier for independents and minor parties to reach the quota for election, but few independents have been elected to that chamber. As we saw in Chapter 8, the preferential system used for the House of Representatives makes it more difficult for independents to get elected to that house.

However, in recent years independent candidates with strong local support have been able to displace the major parties. Others have had a former association with a political party, such as Pauline Hanson, who was elected as an independent in 1996 after she had been dis-endorsed late in the campaign as the candidate for the Liberal Party. The fact that the party identification remained on the ballot paper probably assisted her election. Bob Katter, elected for the Queensland House of Representatives seat of Kennedy in 2001, had formerly been the National Party member for that seat. Other independents, in the past, have included members of the House of Representatives or senators elected for a major party who later changed their status. (The role of independents is discussed in more detail in Chapter 11.)

Change and continuity

It might appear from the discussion above that the two-party system that has characterised Australian politics could be under pressure. More voters appear likely to change their allegiance to vote for minor parties and independents for a variety of reasons. Does this then herald a movement away from the two-party system to something more akin to a multi-party system?

The situation in the Senate, where governments between 1981 and 2005 required the votes of minor parties or independents to pass contested legislation, was an intrusion of multi-party politics into the political system. Minor parties and independents have had more success in the Senate because of the proportional system of voting.

The major parties continue to dominate the House of Representatives where governments are formed, assisted by the preferential system of voting. Minor parties have failed to pose any real threat to the dominance of the two-party system (or two-and-a-half-party system, taking into account the Liberal Party's coalition with the Nationals) that continues to function in the House of Representatives. So long as the major parties maintain such a large share of the first-preference vote (78.11 per cent in 2004, 79.66 per cent in 2007) and direct their preferences to minimise the impact of potential intruders such as One Nation, their dominance will be maintained.

The preferential system of voting and the electoral pragmatism of the major parties in adapting to sustain their share of the vote will be critical factors in maintaining a bulwark against radical change to the Australian two-party system of government.

QUESTIONS FOR DISCUSSION

1. Is ideology the most significant factor in the electoral success of a political party?
2. Is the development of mass-based parties inevitable?
3. 'Party discipline stifles the capacity of MPs to disagree with or vote against party policy, but is essential for stable government.' Discuss.
4. Some people would like to abolish political parties as a form of representation. Why do you think they have this view? What impact would the abolition of parties have on Australia's parliamentary system of cabinet government?
5. Which of the party systems discussed in this chapter best delivers a system of representative democracy?
6. How would you explain the 'closeness' of the two major parties in Australia in economic policy?

7   Is multi-party representation in the Senate a good or bad thing for the Australian political system?
8   What changes would you make to the Australian party system? Give your reasons.

FURTHER READING

Aitkin, D. 1982, *Stability and Change in Australian Politics*, 2nd ed., Australian National University Press, Canberra. This is an important work that argues that the shape of Australian politics has been largely unchanged since 1910 because of strong party loyalty. The results of national surveys are used to discuss the reasons in more depth.

Bean, C. 1997, 'Parties and Elections', in Galligan, B., McAllister, I. & Ravenhill, J. (eds), *New Developments in Australian Politics*, Macmillan Education, Melbourne. This chapter provides an examination and analysis of increasing volatility in the Australian party system.

Brett, J. 2008, 'What Stands between Australia and a One-Party State?', *The Monthly*, no. 35, June, pp. 10–13.

Cowan, P. 2002, 'The Role of Political Parties, Interest Groups and the Media', in Van Acker, E. & Curran, G. (eds), *Business, Government and Globalisation*, Longman, Sydney. Cowan discusses the impact of globalisation on the functions of political parties in the Australian political system.

Ghazarian, Z. 2007, 'State of Assistance? Political Parties and State Support in Australia', Australian Policy Online, 13 February 2007, http://www.apo.org.au.

Jaensch, D. 1994, *Power Politics: Australia's Party System*, 3rd ed., Allen & Unwin, Sydney. A comprehensive examination of the party system and Australian political parties. Essential reading for an understanding of the party system.

Jaensch, D. & Mathieson, D. 1998, *A Plague on Both Your Houses: Minor Parties in Australia*, Allen & Unwin, Sydney. A useful study of the impact of minor parties on the political system.

Marsh, I. (ed.) 2006, *Political Parties in Transition?*, Federation Press, Sydney. A critical study of the Australian party system.

Michels, R. 1962, *Political Parties*, The Free Press, New York (or any other edition). A classic text on the structure and organisation of political parties.

Sharman, C. 1994, 'Political Parties', in Brett, J., Gillespie, J. & Goot, M. (eds), *Developments in Australian Politics*, Macmillan, Melbourne. Examines the experiences of political parties in the Australian political system and concludes that they remain a major factor in structuring electoral choice and in providing the basis for majority government. Argues that questions about the role and justification, nevertheless, persist, as they can no longer be regarded as major avenues for citizenship participation in the political process.

Simms, M. (ed.) 1996, *The Paradox of Parties: Australian Political Parties in the 1990s*, Allen & Unwin, Sydney. A contemporary discussion of Australia's political parties.

Weller, P. & Young, L. 2002, 'Political Parties and the Party System: Challenges for Effective Governing', in Keating, M., Wanna, J. & Weller, P. (eds), *Institutions on the Edge?: Capacity for Governance*, Allen & Unwin, Sydney. Discusses the importance of political parties to Australia's political system, the organisational capacity of political parties, the parties and the adversarial system of government, the impact of minor parties on the party system, and whether new technology and declining interest may lead to a new type of party system.

Country studies
Ware, A. 1996, *Political Parties and Party Systems*, Oxford University Press, Oxford. Introductory study of political parties and party systems with examples from France, Germany, Britain, Japan and the United States.

Britain
Forman, F.N. & Baldwin, N.D.J. 2007, *Mastering British Politics*, 5th ed., Palgrave Macmillan, Basingstoke, UK. See Chapter 5.

Ingle, S. 2008, *The British Party System*, 4th ed., Routledge, London.

United States
Vile, M.J.C. 2007, *Politics in the USA*, 6th ed., Routledge, New York. See Chapters 2 and 3.

Germany
Padgett, S., Paterson, W.E. & Smith, E. 2003, *Developments in German Politics 3*, Palgrave Macmillan, Basingstoke, UK.

Saalfeld, T. 2002, 'The German Party System: Continuity and Change', *German Politics*, vol. 11, no. 1, pp. 99–130.

Malaysia
Funston, J. 1980, *Malay Politics in Malaysia: A Study of the United Malays National Organisation and Party Islam*, Heinemann, Kuala Lumpur. A comprehensive study that includes information about ideology and party organisation.

Funston, J. 2001, 'Malaysia', in Funston, J. (ed.), *Government and Politics in Southeast Asia*, Institute of Southeast Asian Studies, Singapore. An informative article on the Malaysian political system, including political parties.

Gomez, E.T. 2002, 'Political Business in Malaysia: Party Factionalism, Corporate Development and Economic Crisis', in Gomez, E.T., *Political Business in East Asia*, Routledge, London. An examination of the links between political parties in Malaysia and business.

USEFUL WEBSITES

http://australianpolitics.com/parties/functions/overview.shtml
australianpolitics.com: An Overview of Australian Political Parties

http://www.labour.org.uk
British Labour Party

http://www.conservatives.com
British Conservative Party

http://www.democrats.org
Democratic Party (USA)

- http://www.gop.com
  Republican Party (USA)

- http://www.germanculture.com.ua/library/facts/bl_parties.htm
  German Culture: German Political Parties
  A website with useful information about Germany's political parties.

- http://www.spd.de
  Social Democratic Party of Germany (SPD)

- http://www.cdu.de
  Christian Democratic Union Germany (CDU)

- http://www.umno-online.com
  United Malays National Organisation (UMNO)

- http://www.mca.org.my
  Malaysian Chinese Association

- http://www.mic.org.my
  Malaysian Indian Congress

10

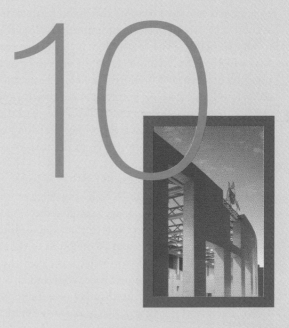

AUSTRALIA'S MAJOR PARTIES

THIS CHAPTER EXPLAINS:

- the ideology, structure, policy making and discipline of the Australian Labor Party;
- the ideology, structure, policy making and discipline of the Liberal Party of Australia; and
- policy differentiation in the 'catch-all' context.

Australia's early political development was dominated by a colonial ruling-class establishment, made up predominantly of squatters, professional gentlemen, farmers and emancipists who had become successful businessmen. This class structure of the political system came about because of limitations on political participation through restrictions to the franchise. The legislation introducing responsible government to New South Wales in 1855, for example, gave the vote only to those who owned property worth 100 pounds, or occupied premises or held a lease worth 10 pounds per annum, or paid for room and lodgings at 40 pounds per annum. It is not surprising, therefore, that the major groups that evolved from colonial politics had their basis in mercantile, rural and business interests, with the central point of division being the issues of free trade and protection; indeed, the two main parties at the turn of the century were called the Freetraders and the Protectionists.

The emergence of the Australian Labor Party from the trade union movement in 1891 and the introduction in 1902, following Federation, of universal adult franchise for men and women over 21 years of age extended the scope of party political participation to three main groups. The first elections of the federal House of Representatives returned 32 Protectionists, 27 Freetraders and 16 members of the Australian Labor Party. The anti-Labor groups coalesced in 1909, into what was called the Fusion. This marked the beginning of the two-party system that involves Labor and an anti-Labor group competing for government that has continued until today (see Table 9.1, Chapter 9). Because the Australian Labor Party and the Liberal Party of Australia play such a significant role in Australia's political system, it is important that we understand how they operate and what they claim to stand for.

THE AUSTRALIAN LABOR PARTY

The Australian Labor Party was established by the trade union movement in 1891 as its political voice.

The federal platform of the party in 1905 reflected the limited functions of the Commonwealth at the time, and the concern of the trade unions to protect the conditions of workers at the workplace and to provide for their retirement.

Australian Labor Party: the Federal Platform, 1905

General platform
1. Maintenance of a White Australia
2. Compulsory arbitration to settle industrial disputes, with provision for the exclusion of the legal profession
3. Old-age pensions
4. Nationalisation of monopolies
5. Citizen Military Force and Australian-owned Navy
6. Restriction on public borrowing
7. Navigation laws to provide
   (a) for the protection of Australian shipping against unfair competition
   (b) registration of all vessels engaged in the coastal trade
   (c) the efficient manning of vessels

(d) the proper supply of life-saving and other equipment
  (e) the regulation of hours and conditions of work
  (f) proper accommodation for passengers and seamen
  (g) proper loading gear and inspection of same
8 Commonwealth Bank of Deposit and Issue, and Life, and Fire Insurance Department, the management of each to be free of political influence
9 Federal Patent Law, providing for simplifying and cheapening the registration of patents.

(*Source*: Churchward, L. (ed.) 1983, *The Australian Labor Movement 1850–1907: Historical Documents*, selected by Noel Ebbels, Hale & Iremonger, Sydney, pp. 222–3)

Compare this with the constitution and rules of the ALP today. The ALP's platform is a large and comprehensive document that maintains the original emphasis on working people and their families, but extends its scope to reflect the complexity of modern government and society, and the breadth of interests and desires of the party's membership and its voting constituency.

FIGURE 10.1
'Freedom of Contract' — How it works

(*Source*: *The Bulletin*, 11 April 1891, reproduced by permission from *The Bulletin*, www.acpsyndication.com)

The breaking of the shearers' strike over contracts by the government was one of the factors that led to the establishment of the Australian Labor Party by the trade unions to gain political representation in the parliament.

> **ALP National Platform, 2007**
> Chapter 1 Enduring Labor Values
> Chapter 2 Building a Strong Economy for a Fair Society
> Chapter 3 Engaging with the Global Economy
> Chapter 4 Investing in Our Future: An Education Revolution
> Chapter 5 Fostering Competitive and Innovative Australian Industries
> Chapter 6 Nation Building
> Chapter 7 A New Industrial Relations System: A Fairer Future for Working Families
> Chapter 8 Fostering Participation, Security and Quality Care for all Australians
> Chapter 9 Combating Climate Change and Building a Sustainable Environment
> Chapter 10 Improving Health and Well-Being: A Health System that Delivers
> Chapter 11 Reforming Government
> Chapter 12 Ensuring Community Security and Access to Justice
> Chapter 13 Respecting Human Rights and a Fair Go for All
> Chapter 14 Strengthening Australia's Place in the World
> Chapter 15 Strengthening Regional Communities
> Chapter 16 Supporting Australia's Arts, Culture and Heritage
> (*Source:* Australian Labor Party National Constitution, adopted by the 44th ALP National Conference, April 2007. The complete text of the ALP's constitution and rules can be found on the party's website at http://www.alp.org.au)

Ideology

Labor's ideology is based on the notion that in important ways people were born equal, but that Australian society serves to create inequality. Therefore, the task of the party is to promote equality through its actions in government. Its objectives reflect this democratic socialist base to its ideology.

> **Democratic socialism**: the incremental progress and reform through parliamentary power and legislative means to achieve equality.

From this belief flows two further beliefs:

1. Equality and freedom go together.
2. Governments must have the power to deal effectively with the vested interests (private groups) that reduce both.

Groups such as the poor, the dispossessed, Aboriginal people and the unemployed cannot meaningfully be said to be 'free' while they are starving, without jobs, or without economic security generally.

This attitude underlies Labor's view of the world outside Australia as well: political freedom for Southeast Asia, for example, is next to meaningless if it is not accompanied by freedom from want. Labor is thus 'internationalist', meaning that it supports the United Nations and similar agencies founded on the same proposition, and is opposed to (or at least ideologically embarrassed by) proposals that Australia should support regimes in other countries that seem uninterested in moving quickly to promote economic equality for their people.

The ALP has never been wholeheartedly socialist, for two reasons:

- Roman Catholics are important in its ranks, and the church has a traditional antipathy to socialism.
- For the last century, Australia's working class has been affluent enough to enjoy the benefits of private property.

The party's objective, as a result, portrays an ambivalent approach towards socialism.

> 'The Australian Labor Party is a democratic socialist party and has the objective of the democratic socialisation of industry, production, distribution and exchange, to the extent necessary to eliminate exploitation and other anti-social features in these fields.'
> (Source: Australian Labor Party National Constitution, adopted by the 44th ALP National Conference, April 2007, http://www.alp.org.au)

Socialisation is the stated goal, but only where enterprises are not being run for the common good. This objective, however, has become almost meaningless since the 1990s when the Hawke and Keating Labor governments instigated a policy of privatising government business enterprises such as Qantas and the Commonwealth Bank, formerly the icon of the party's commitment to public enterprise.

The Labor Party platform, because of its relationship with its affiliated trade unions, has a labourist foundation. This adds a particular trade union element to the party's democratic socialist concept of achieving its objectives through the parliamentary process.

> **Labourism**: the idea that the 'capitalist state could be managed to the advantage of the working people by a combination of a strong trade union with a parliamentary party'.
> (Source: Hagan, J. 1981, *The History of the ACTU*, Longman, Melbourne, p. 16)

FIGURE 10.2
Prime Minister Rudd wants to rewrite ALP platform

(Source: Cartoon by Nicholson from *The Australian*. www.nicholsoncartoons.com.au)

The values articulated in Labor's platform today still embody democratic socialist ideals with their focus on fairness, justice and equal opportunity for all citizens. In practice, the party's philosophy has been moderated by a pragmatic tendency to do what is required to gain office or procure its survival in government. In this sense, it has become a 'catch-all' party (see Chapter 9).

Organisation

Members of the Australian Labor Party join a branch within their home state or territory. Members can join at age 15, and are expected to belong to the trade union appropriate to their employment, if there is one. On joining, members sign a 'pledge', which commits them to the principles and platform of the party and precludes their standing in elections and campaigning against an endorsed candidate of the party. Members of branches discuss matters relating to all levels of government. Branches can send policy resolutions forward to the State Conference and instruct their delegates in how to vote on any or all matters. At the annual general meeting, each branch elects a number of honorary officials. These include president, two vice-presidents, secretary, treasurer, fund-raising officer, returning officer, deputy returning officer, assistant secretary, two auditors, members of the credentials committee, and delegates and alternate delegates to the State Electorate Council, Federal Electorate Council, Municipal Committee and Young Labor Council. State Conferences are responsible for making policy and rules for their particular state branch. For an example of the rules under which a state branch operates, see the New South Wales branch website at http://www.nswalp.com.

The National Conference is responsible for making the national policy of the party. The National Executive administers party policy between conferences. The National Policy Committee is responsible for policy development and ongoing review of the party platform. For information about the membership of these bodies, and the rules and constitution of the national ALP, see http://www.alp.org.au.

It is difficult to estimate how many members there are, and how many branches, as party records are not publicly available.

The Australian Labor Party and the trade union movement

The Australian Labor Party is distinctive because it is one of a small group of parties specifically designated as labour parties due to their trade union affiliations. Other labour parties with ties to the trade union movement include the British Labour Party and the New Zealand Labour Party.

> 'A Labor Party must be able to maintain a special relationship with unions, or it ceases to be a Labor Party by definition.'
> (Source: Rawson, D. 1990, 'For Whom Were Labor Parties Founded?', in Easson, M. (ed.), *The Foundation of Labor*, Pluto Press, Sydney, p. 26)

Trade unions can affiliate as bodies with the Australian Labor Party in each state, though not at the federal level. The peak organisation of the trade union movement, the Australian Council of Trade Unions (ACTU), is not affiliated to the ALP, but many of its members are. Affiliation results in union representation at the State Conference; the consequence (as the conference elects the State Executive and the state's representatives to the party's National Conference) is that union delegates play a significant role in the party's organisation.

Today's National Platform reaffirms the party's historical ties to the trade union movement and its commitment to working people and their families, but from its inception, the Australian Labor Party had to attract voters outside the union movement if it was to secure enough votes to win government. This is even more relevant today when the proportion of workers who are trade union members has fallen to around 19 per cent (see ABS 2007, 'Employee Earnings, Benefits and Trade Union Membership, Australia', Cat. no. 6310.0, ABS, Canberra).

> 'Labor's traditional base of support, the working class, is shrinking and to be locked into a situation in which Labor relied heavily on support from this group would prove more and more problematic over time.'
> (*Source*: Bean, C. 2000, 'Who Now Votes Labor?', in Warhurst, J. & Parkin, A. (eds), *The Machine*, Allen & Unwin, Sydney, p. 74)

Economic policy to benefit all Australians has become a more significant issue for Labor. Many of its policies are also targeted to attract voter support from particular groups, such as families with mortgages, working mothers in need of child care, or older Australians. Even so, the party maintains its institutional links with the trade union movement, and trade unions continue to play a special role in its organisational structure and policy-making bodies. The Australian Labor Advisory Council, made up of the leader and senior members of the Federal Parliamentary Labor Party, the National President and National Secretary, and representatives of the Australian Council of Trade Unions (ACTU) is the ALP's forum for formal consultation between the party and the ACTU representing the union movement.

Candidate selection

In general, the selection and endorsement of parliamentary candidates is in the hands of electorate councils, but state executives and occasionally the National Executive have intervened to secure their own choice of candidate.

Affirmative action

The rules for preselection also state that the party 'must actively identify and encourage candidates from a wide range of occupations and life experiences' and has established a National Indigenous Labor Network to increase the involvement of Indigenous people in the party. (See the ALP National Platform and constitution at http://www.alp.org.au.)

In an effort to redress the gender imbalance of ALP members in parliament, which is predominantly male, the party has an affirmative action preselection policy that aims to ensure that 40 per cent of seats are filled by women, not less than 40 per cent by men and the remaining 20 per cent by either gender.

> After the November 2007 election, there were 27 women Labor members of the House of Representatives and 14 women Labor senators. In mid-2008, there were four women in cabinet (including the deputy prime minister), four in the outer ministry and three in parliamentary secretary positions.

Labor's factions

> 'Labor's affiliated unions are at the core of our faction system and provide the voting weight that makes our factions important determiners of issues. This often acts to ensure that union support is given to even the smallest faction groupings. In this way, factions actually dilute a major voting block throughout the party.
>
> Factions have made management of the ALP easier and effective. They increase the possibility of negotiated solutions to problems and issues. Factions make negotiations easier because they allow groups to talk to each other rather than individuals arguing.
>
> Many people describe factions as being about ideas and philosophies. The Left is often cited as being progressive while the Right is usually characterised as being pragmatic. If these characteristics were ever correct, they are less true today than ever.
>
> Today factions are often based on common interest, personalities or regional interests. Not only do factions have names, "Centre Left", "Socialist Left", "Labor Unity", etc., they often have structures, regular meetings and even their own newsletters. They may even have membership fees. Factions may elect office holders and people to be negotiators with other groups. However, frequently key faction operators hold positions of influence because of the standing they have in the broader party . . . often within factions there are subgroupings . . .
>
> At local branch level there may be local faction activity—this may be related to pre-selections or local issues. Participation in factions is a personal choice and the majority of rank-and-file members of the party choose not to participate. Factions exercise most influence on the administrative committees of state branches, the national executive and in state and federal parliamentary caucuses. This is where the most important decisions on policy and other matters tend to come to a head and it is where decisions need to be finalised through negotiation. This has been the principal advantage of Labor's factions.'
>
> (Source: Australian Labor Party, 'Factions in the ALP', http://www.alp.org.au/about/factions.html. Reproduced with permission of ALP–National Secretariat. Note: This document is no longer on the ALP's website.)

In the past, the factions would have had a significant say in determining who was elected to the ministry by the Federal Parliamentary Labor Party (caucus). The decision of Labor prime minister Kevin Rudd to choose his own ministers, even though the party's rules prescribe that the caucus should elect the ministry, changed what had been the practice since the parliamentary party was established, and is evidence of his authority within the caucus following Labor's decisive win at the 2007 election. Rudd would not have been able to ignore factional politics when selecting his ministry, but the fact that the party allowed him to select the ministry may undermine the dominance of the factions in the caucus in the longer term.

> 'I think it is incumbent upon me to put forward the best possible team for the nation. I intend to do that based on merit, based on performance.'
>
> (Source: Prime Minister Kevin Rudd, cited in Fraser, A. 2007, 'Rudd off and running new ministry by end of the week', Canberra Times, 26 November 2007)

We can see from the following the impact of the factions on the selection of leadership positions within the party organisation.

> 'The right has agreed in principle to maintain the factional balance on the Party's national executive in exchange for the left supporting right-winger Greg Sword for the Labor presidency.'
> (Source: Willacy, M. 2000, 'ALP factions set to strike a deal', ABC Radio, AM, 18 July 2000, http://www.abc.net.au/am/stories/s153177.htm)

The factions are also instrumental in determining who will be the Labor leader, such as the selection of Kim Beazley in January 2005 rather than Kevin Rudd, following the resignation of Mark Latham.

Policy making

In its rhetoric, and to a lesser degree in practice, Labor sees policy making as a principal activity of the extra-parliamentary party. The National Conference shapes and defines the party's platform and policy, which the parliamentarians must then follow. The National Executive has the responsibility to make sure that they do. It also controls the agenda for National Conference meetings.

To deal with the business of policy making in a systematic way, the National Conference established the National Policy Committee. Members of the committee need not be delegates to the conference. The committee may co-opt experts to provide advice on a particular policy. Policy resolutions come forward to the committees from State Conferences and from party branches. This process has its benefits and its costs:

- The continuing existence of the National Policy Committee means that there is no need for last-minute patchwork, and there is the potential for both the expert and the committed party member to influence the outcome.
- On the other hand, policies may be subject to the horse trading and ideological jousting between factions that is an integral factor in the Australian Labor Party at work.

The published Platform sets out the policy objectives determined by the National Conference for Labor governments to implement. When Labor won government in 1972, Gough Whitlam took the party's policy as a mandate for his government very seriously.

> 'The mandate of 1972 was the most positive and precise ever sought and ever received by an elected government in Australian history. The program was the most comprehensive, its promulgation and popularisation the most intensive and extensive in our political history. Its central elements had been developed not in the three weeks of an election campaign or even the three years preceding the campaign but over a period of half a decade and more. Three successive conferences of the Labor Party, in 1967, 1969 and 1971, had rewritten two-thirds of the Party's platform.'
> (Source: Whitlam, E.G. 1979, *The Truth of the Matter*, Penguin, Ringwood, Victoria, pp. 5–6, reproduced with permission)

Even though the Platform is the guiding force for a Labor government, the *leader's election policy speech* has become a more significant indicator of what can be expected when it is elected to office. In theory, the policy speech should be simply a restatement of what the National Conference has determined as the official policy. In practice, there are considerable differences, which arise in part because the policy speech is primarily designed to assist in winning an election. The parliamentary leaders usually have been reluctant to share the design of their speech with other parliamentarians, and speech writers are as important as experts on policy. The party's Platform continues to set the broad framework for party policy, but the detail of the election campaign policy is determined more on the basis of opinion polling and issues that are likely to win votes.

The party's rules provide Labor governments with some latitude and discretion in policy making, but they are still expected to work within the parameters of the Platform. Sometimes, a Labor government makes decisions that upset the party. The Hawke government, for example, when first elected in 1983, plotted a different course for itself from that chosen by the Whitlam government in the 1970s, and its ministers privately expressed a determination to 'avoid the mistakes of the Whitlam years'. Its cautious approach to economic matters, its preparedness to listen to the public service, and its apparent abandonment of traditional Labor emphases on an expansive public sector and new public enterprises gave it good relations with business and financial interests. However, the cost was growing tension within the party as the government, and especially the prime minister, appeared to depart from National Conference determinations on party policy. There were several notable intra-party rows on the mining and export of uranium, restructuring of the manufacturing industry, deregulation of the banking system, and privatisation of public assets, most particularly the Commonwealth Bank. In almost all cases, however, the prime minister was able either to win the support of the extra-parliamentary party or to escape with a reprimand.

> Former prime minister Bob Hawke explains how his government changed the ALP's policy on allowing foreign banks to operate in Australia at the party's 1984 National Conference:
>
> 'Throughout 1984–85 we pursued further deregulatory measures . . . Ahead of us lay the polemical exercise of persuading the Labor Party to abandon the tired certitudes of an earlier age and to prepare for the future. The party platform had to be changed . . . We were in a strong position at the conference. We had been at the crease by then for some time and had been stacking up runs at a good rate; I was able to point to the scoreboard with pride. We won the day on foreign banks.'
>
> (Source: Hawke, R.J.L. 1994, *The Hawke Memoirs*, Heinemann, Melbourne, pp. 252–3, copyright Hon. Bob Hawke A.C.)

One reason why the government was able to influence the policy agenda in this way was the necessity to maintain unity to enhance the party's chances of re-election. The extra-parliamentary party was unlikely to challenge the government to such an extent that its chances of regaining office were put at risk. Another reason was the longevity of the Labor government: the longer the party stayed in power, the more the policy process became driven by the exigencies of being in government, with policy initiatives coming from the cabinet and its departmental advisers in response to domestic, political, economic and international factors.

It could be argued that, in the process, the Hawke and Keating governments lost touch with the party platform, its principles and its constituency. Erosion in its core voting support and the desire to differentiate its policies from those of the Liberal opposition caused Labor to place more emphasis in the 1993 election campaign on its traditional values, with policies focused on child care, family assistance, health and industrial relations. A similar emphasis in 1996 was not enough. Continuing high unemployment and a sense that it was time for a change lost Labor office in a landslide win to the Coalition. The party's focus on 'the battlers' in the 1998 election—in particular, the impact of a GST on low-income earners—resulted in the winning back of a considerable amount of that lost support in terms of seats, although insufficient to achieve government.

Labor as a 'catch-all' party

The 'catch-all' nature of electoral politics has seen the policies of both major parties move closer together, as the parties vie for the votes of undecided and uncommitted electors, commonly cited as the 'middle ground'. This has put Labor in the bind of not being able to differentiate its policies sufficiently from those of its Liberal opponent.

Labor failed to win the 2001 election in part because it was unable to carve out its own policy niche on economic policy, asylum seekers and a response to the terrorist attacks on 11 September 2001. At the 2004 federal election, Labor again failed to engage with the electorate.

'Catch-all' came to the fore in the 2007 election campaign when Kevin Rudd embraced a strategy of 'me-too-ism', echoing the Coalition on a number of policy issues such as tax cuts and the federal government's intervention in Aboriginal communities in the Northern Territory. There were, however, differences on climate change, an 'education revolution', a promise to remove Australian troops from Iraq, and a promise to abandon the Howard government's Work Choices industrial relations policy, which is considered to have been a major factor in Labor's win. Labor has no intention of abandoning its links with the unions now it is in government, but, unlike the Hawke and Keating years, there is no formal Accord and the union movement will not be closely involved with the policy process.

> 'I'm sure we'll chat to them [the unions] from time to time as appropriate.'
> (Source: Prime Minister Kevin Rudd, cited in Steketee, M. 2007, 'Not just true believers', *The Australian*, 24 November 2007)

Party discipline

Labor introduced majority rule within the party processes as well as the pledge to support party policy for party members and candidates. Because ideological tension is highest in the Labor Party, questions of discipline have been most frequent there:

- The National Executive has 'disciplined' some state bodies as well as parliamentarians.
- Individual members of parliament have had their endorsements withdrawn for disciplinary reasons.
- Individual members have been expelled and reprimanded. These events usually occur as incidents in factional disputes, which are an almost continual feature of life in the party.

In parliament, members of the Labor Party always vote together; crossing the floor is unknown. A Labor MP who feels that he or she cannot, for conscience or other reasons, vote with the party on a given issue can only abstain or resign from the party to sit as an independent, and even this step is taken only rarely.

There is a class of exceptions—the non-party vote. Matters of personal morality (abortion, homosexuality, and so on) rarely come before parliament for a decision. When they do it is customary for the vote to be declared a 'non-party' or 'free' vote, which allows each MP to vote 'as his or her conscience dictates'.

THE LIBERAL PARTY OF AUSTRALIA

At the time of Federation, the non-Labor groups were divided into two factions: the Liberal Protectionist Party and the Free Trade Party; both campaigned as liberals but strongly opposed each other on the question of tariffs. The passage of the Commonwealth *Tariff Act* in 1902 introducing moderate tariffs on imported goods—the product of a truce between these groups—removed a major impediment to their cooperation. The election of Labor Party candidates to the Commonwealth parliament and the decline of liberal representation provided the catalyst for their 'fusion', because their continued division would weaken their capacity to fight against Labor. The parties agreed to unite all Liberals into one political organisation, and the fusion took place in 1909 under the leadership of Alfred Deakin and his Commonwealth Liberal Party.

Commonwealth Liberal Party Platform, 1909

Objective

The union of all Liberals, men and women, throughout the Commonwealth in one Party, to secure in the Federal Parliament, Liberal Legislation for the Development of Australia on a Democratic basis.

Platform

1. To uphold the Federal Union and to develop its National character, fostering Preferential Trade and a recognition of our Imperial responsibilities.
2. To maintain the Policy of effective Protection, and to secure its benefits alike to Producers, Workers and Consumers.
3. To amend the Electoral Laws so as to secure actual representation of majorities, and to enrol men and women voters for the Commonwealth.
4. To establish a White Australia by strenuously encouraging the Immigration of suitable settlers.
5. To develop the Australian Naval and Military Forces by means of Universal training commenced in the schools, and a Commonwealth Coastal Defence.
6. The assumption by the Commonwealth of the public debts of the States, accompanied by an equitable scheme for providing the Interest and Sinking funds.
7. To promote economy in the public expenditure, and efficiency in the public services, of the Commonwealth.
8. To assert the principle that all representatives of the people should be directly and solely responsible to the people for their votes and actions.

(*Source*: Commonwealth Liberal Party 1909, *Platform, Rules, Branch Rules, and Conference Rules*, Liberal Party, Melbourne. Courtesy Liberal Party of Australia.)

The anti-Labor groupings, however, were unstable coalitions. The Liberal Party evolved into the National Party in 1917 under Billy Hughes, a former Labor leader, and then reorganised into the United Australia Party in 1931. The party splintered into six groups in the parliament following its election defeat in 1941: UAP, Liberal Democrats, Liberal Country, Country National, Queensland Country, and Country. It re-emerged in 1944 when 18 non-Labor political organisations combined to form the Liberal Party of Australia under the leadership of Bob Menzies.

The 1948 platform of the Liberal Party was much broader than the eight simple statements of 1909, reflecting the functions of government at that time, including external affairs, defence, primary industries, industry policy, employment, social security, post-war rehabilitation, health, housing, status of women, public administration, and finance and taxation.

Ideology

The objectives of the Liberal Party established under the leadership of Bob Menzies were 'an intelligent, free and liberal Australian democracy', to be maintained by:

(a) parliament controlling the executive and the law controlling all;
(b) freedom of speech, religion and association;
(c) freedom of citizens to choose their own way of living and of life, subject to the rights of others;
(d) protecting the people against exploitation;
(e) looking primarily to the encouragement of individual initiative and enterprise as the dynamic force.

(*Source*: Liberal Party of Australia 1948, 'Liberal Platform: The Official Platform of the Liberal Party', Federal Secretariat, Sydney. Courtesy Liberal Party of Australia.)

Today the beliefs of the party are spelled out in more detail:

> **What does the Liberal Party stand for?**
>
> 'We are the party of initiative and enterprise.
>
> We believe in the inalienable rights and freedoms of all peoples; and we work towards a lean government that minimises interference in our daily lives; and maximises individual and private sector initiative.
>
> We believe in government that nurtures and encourages its citizens through incentive, rather than putting limits on people through the punishing disincentives of burdensome taxes and the stifling structures of Labor's corporate state and bureaucratic red tape.
>
> We believe in those most basic freedoms of parliamentary democracy—the freedom of thought, worship, speech and association.
>
> We believe in a just and humane society in which the importance of the family and the role of law and justice is maintained.
>
> We believe in equal opportunity for all Australians; and the encouragement and facilitation of wealth so that all may enjoy the highest possible standards of living, health, education and social justice.
>
> We believe that, wherever possible, government should not compete with an efficient private sector; and that businesses and individuals—not government—are the true creators of wealth and employment.

> We believe in preserving Australia's natural beauty and the environment for future generations.
> We believe that our nation has a constructive role to play in maintaining world peace and democracy through alliance with other free nations.
> In short, we simply believe in individual freedom and free enterprise . . .'
>
> (Source: Liberal Party of Australia 2008, 'What Does the Liberal Party Stand For?', Federal Secretariat, Canberra, http://www.liberal.org.au/about/ourbeliefs.php. Courtesy Liberal Party of Australia)

The Liberal Party's ideology is a rich mixture of 19th-century liberal and conservative assumptions and beliefs:

- Fundamental is the notion that the individual must be given pride of place: society exists to enhance the life of the individual, rather than the reverse. Society progresses because of the efforts of individuals.
- It follows that the capacities and potential of each individual ought to be allowed to develop.
- As humans are born with differing potential (because of differences in intelligence, hand–eye coordination, and so on, and the differing needs of a society at different times), there will inevitably be inequalities.
- The best society is one which harnesses these inequalities in the interests of everyone.

Even this short statement makes it clear that freedom is given more weighting than equality. A number of consequences flow from this:

- There is less need for a powerful government; indeed, a powerful government will inevitably stifle freedoms and the development of individual capacities. This is always an evil, and only rarely a necessary evil.
- It is not the business of governments to move a society in the direction of greater equality. Certainly gross inequalities are to be avoided, because they will generate envy, hatred and social disharmony (although what counts as a 'gross' inequality is likely to be a matter of opinion).
- Governments ought to encourage individuals to make the most of themselves and their talents, and this means that there must be due rewards for initiative, innovation and an understanding that society will accept them happily, knowing that all have benefited or will benefit.

Linked to this are some conservative assumptions about the nature of humanity:

- People are not really to be trusted to do the right thing, and the rules and conventions of civilised society are there to ensure that an ordered social life is possible. (Labor takes a more optimistic view: people are essentially virtuous, and it is only the problems generated by the poorly designed society they live in that make them otherwise.)
- Rules and conventions are therefore precious. Furthermore, they are easily damaged and hard to repair. Our customary ways of doing things (our political and social institutions) should therefore change only slowly and when it is beyond question that a change will be beneficial.

> 'Conservatism is the junior political tradition in the Liberal Party. There is enough conservatism there to characterise it as a liberal-conservative organisation.'
>
> (Source: Norton, A. 2000, 'Liberalism and the Liberal Party of Australia', in Boreham, P., Stokes, G. & Hall, R. (eds), *The Politics of Australian Society*, Pearson Education, Sydney, p. 26)

The liberal and conservative aspects of Liberal ideology appear not to live happily together, and are rarely espoused by the same people. There is an obvious paradox involved, for example, in being in favour of individual development where it involves economic enterprise but being opposed to it where it leads to demands for a new political order (or just to an end of censorship).

Factions

Internal divisions on the direction of economic and social policy within the Liberal Party in recent years led to factionalisation within the party into the 'wets'—those who adopted a more liberal approach to the role of government and social services—and the more conservative 'dries', who preferred a minimal approach to the role of the state. This did not, however, lead to any breakaway movement from the party.

The Liberal Party tends to adopt a winner-takes-all approach, where the dominant faction controls the agenda. In recent years this has been the 'dry' faction. But ideologies do not crumble because critics find flaws in them. We are all able to carry around in our heads flatly contradictory propositions. Partisans in politics simply play down or ignore those aspects of a party's ideology which they personally have trouble with, or work within the party to try to change it more to their own liking.

> 'Where a society's basic institutions are already substantially liberal, a conservative approach to change can readily serve liberalism, even if its intellectual justification is not liberal.'
> (*Source*: Norton, A. 2000, 'Liberalism and the Liberal Party of Australia', in Boreham, P., Stokes, G. & Hall, R. (eds), *The Politics of Australian Society*, Pearson Education, Sydney, p. 25)

Organisation

The Liberal Party developed during and after 1945 and was the fourth restructuring of the major non-Labor party since the initial 'fusion' of 1909. (As there had been virtually complete continuity at the parliamentary level, in parliament the changes meant little.) For this reason, and also because the party's ideology sees regional differences in a federation as being essential and proper, there are probably greater variations from state to state in organisational practice within the Liberal Party than is the case in the ALP:

- The Victorian party organisation (see Figure 10.3) is a good deal stronger and more centralised than that of New South Wales.
- The Liberal Party in Queensland in 2008 merged with the Nationals to form the Liberal National Party of Queensland (http://www.lnp.org.au).

The Liberal Party claims to have more than 80,000 members in more than 2,000 branches in its state divisions, which have their own constitutions.

Branches and electorate conferences have the usual functions and powers, and in New South Wales there are regional conferences as well. They all send representatives to the State Council, which in full strength has hundreds of members and is the party's governing body. The real administration of the party is in the hands of the State Executive—chosen, as are the principal office-holders, by the State Council. The New South Wales party gives women members an important place in the affairs of the party. (Party rules prescribe equal numbers of men and women in various positions.)

FIGURE 10.3
Liberal Party, Victoria division: structure and organisation

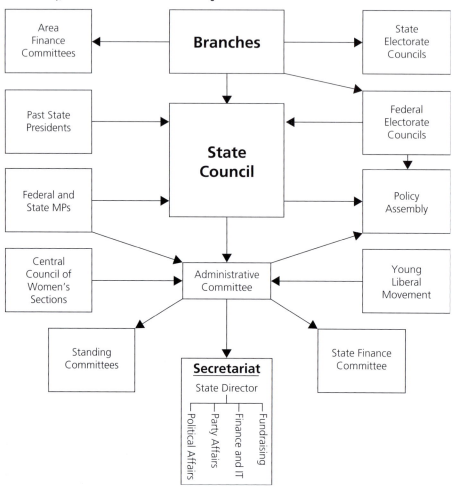

(*Source*: Courtesy Liberal Party of Australia, Victoria Division)

The Liberal Party's Federal Council is in composition not unlike the Labor Party's National Conference, with delegates from each state, but there is a special status for women members (one vice-president must be a woman and the president of each state's women's division is a member by right), and this practice is continued in the Federal Executive. The Liberal Federal Council is responsible for the party's federal constitution and platform but does not see its function lying in issuing directions to the Federal Parliamentary Liberal Party, which has the responsibility for determining the Liberal Party's policies, strategies and parliamentary priorities (see below).

Candidate selection

Liberal Party state divisions determine the rules for preselection. In Victoria, for example, candidates for preselection must have been members of the party for at least 12 months. In

Queensland, members must have 12 months' continuous membership before they can participate in a preselection ballot.

Preselection is usually carried out at the local level by selection panels. In Victoria a Preselection Convention, consisting of 60 per cent local branch and 40 per cent State Council delegates (including the state president, two vice-presidents, and the federal or state parliamentary leader), makes the choice and its decision stands. In that way, local sensibilities are protected, but there is some defence against outrageously parochial selections.

The Liberal Party does not believe in affirmative action and therefore has no quota system or targets for increasing the proportion of women candidates. However, the Liberal Women's Forum, a political network for women in parliament, encourages women to run as candidates. It runs training sessions about the party for women members and provides information about the nomination process. There are also special women's representatives within the organisational structure, such as the federal woman vice-president. The Federal Women's Committee, the peak body representing women in the Liberal Party, is represented on the Federal Executive.

The Liberal Party's record on gender imbalance in the past was as poor as Labor's. However, there have been women party presidents for the Australian Capital Territory and South Australian divisions. After the November 2007 election there were 10 Liberal women members of the House of Representatives and 11 Liberal women senators. The Liberals selected a woman to be Deputy Leader of the Opposition.

Policy making

The Liberal Party, in office for the majority of the time between 1910 and 1983, came to rely for policy development on the combined talents of its parliamentary party, and especially those of the leader and the public service.

> **Government policy making under the leadership of the Liberal prime minister, Malcolm Fraser, 1975–83**
>
> 'Fraser had the ability, the desire and the drive to dominate the machinery of government. His commitment cannot be questioned. His involvement was so extensive, his interests so broad that little or nothing was done that he actively opposed. Because of his extensive control, in the end he approved most government decisions.'
>
> (Source: Weller, P. 1989, *Malcolm Fraser PM: A Study in Prime Ministerial Power in Australia*, Penguin, Ringwood, Victoria, p. 402, reproduced with permission by Penguin Group, (Australia))

When the party is not in office, as was the case between March 1983 and March 1996, it is forced to generate its own policies. Not only is it deprived of the resources of the public service, but it is compelled to react to counter the policies of the Labor government.

The actual development of policy is always the responsibility of the parliamentary leadership, which the organisation outside parliament can only hope to influence. According to the party website, 'the Organisational wing cannot dictate policy but consults with and advises the Parliamentary wing, particularly on the development of longer-term policies' (Liberal Party of Australia 2008, 'Our Structure', http://www.liberal.org.au/about/ourstructure.php).

The federal Liberal Party has a network of committees that assist the parliamentary party with policy development. Policy is debated by the Federal Council, but its views are not binding on the parliamentary party.

Liberal policies during the Whitlam period and the early part of the Hawke government consisted in the most part of:

- analyses of what was wrong with Labor's plans and performance; and
- proposals that adapted Labor's ideas to forms with which Liberals felt more familiar.

This changed in 1993 when the party, under the leadership of John Hewson, developed a strategic economic policy document, *Fightback!*, based around a classic liberal, economic rationalist philosophy, including a proposal for a Goods and Services Tax.

> 'The Liberal and National parties waited patiently while Hewson went into the bunker for months, drawing up *Fightback!* He ultimately offered it to shadow cabinet and the parliamentary coalition parties on a "take it or leave it" basis.'
> (*Source:* Wallace, C. 1993, *Hewson*, Pan Macmillan, Sydney, p. 264)

The failure to win the 'unlosable' 1993 election left the party in a policy vacuum and a feeling among Liberal Party backbenchers and extra-parliamentary party members that they had not been consulted sufficiently by the party's parliamentary leadership. The parliamentary party restructured its policies to capture more of the mood of the electorate, and was successful in winning government in 1996. The dominance of the party leadership over policy direction is evident from the way in which John Howard brought the GST, which he had long favoured, back on to the Liberal Party's policy agenda for the 1998 election.

John Howard led the Liberal Party to four successive electoral victories. The Coalition government's policy agenda was driven by Howard and shaped by his political acumen and his determination to win elections.

> According to John Howard, the best way of governing is through 'playing out our values through practical politics'.
> (*Source:* Prime Minister John Howard 2004, doorstop interview, Canberra, 18 June 2004)

The defeat of the Howard government in November 2007 left the Liberal Party with the task of rebuilding its electoral support and differentiating its policies from Labor. This may be difficult, as both parties appear to have reached common ground on economic and welfare issues; the difference is largely in the means rather the ends. Pragmatic electoralism is the driving force in how both parties target their approaches to the electorate. For this reason, any move to the ideological right may prove difficult.

> 'If political parties simply seek to tend to . . . their own power base which in this case would be people to the Right of politics, well we'll never win an election. It's a truism of politics that if you abandon the Centre, the other political party will fill it.'
> (*Source:* Christopher Pyne, federal Liberal MHR, after the Liberal election loss in November 2007, cited in Shanahan, D. 2007, 'Liberals divided on how to get re-elected', *The Weekend Australian*, 22 December 2007)

FIGURE 10.4

Checks and balances

(*Source*: Cartoon by Nicholson from *The Australian*. www.nicholsoncartoons.com.au)

The Liberals' 'catch-all' policies

The Howard government was pragmatic on those occasions when it saw the electoral advantage of doing so (for example, the reversal of a decision to increase fees for nursing homes after concern was expressed in the community).

> 'John Howard's partial conversion to government activism . . . is consistent with the pragmatism and distinctive blend of market liberalism and social conservatism that have served him well over three terms in government.'
> (*Source*: Costar, B. & Browne, P. 2005, 'How Labor Lost', in Browne, P. & Thomas, J.P. (eds), *A Win and a Prayer*, UNSW Press, Sydney, p. 122)

The policies of the Howard government were closely associated with the views of its leader. John Howard considers himself to be 'centre-rightist' (Prime Minister John Howard 2004, press conference, Bernard Arms, London, 5 June 2004). His views of traditional family life and preservation of the monarchy, for example, reflect his conservatism, while his belief in labour deregulation is in keeping with his economic liberalism. However, the driving force of Howard to win elections at all costs was more indicative of a high level of electoral pragmatism.

> 'I frequently say to my colleagues, "It's better to be 90% pure in Government than 126% pure in Opposition". There is a fine balance. People will criticise me for that. They'll say that's being cynical and pragmatic. Well, it is being pragmatic, but it's also being sensible. Australians are very balanced people. They see the sense of that. They want reform but they don't want zealotry. When they think we're being zealous or obstinate, they send us signals. If we don't listen they start to lose interest in us.'
> (*Source*: 'John Howard reflects on highs and lows as PM', *7.30 Report*, ABC TV, 2 March 2006, http://www.abc.net.au/7.30/content/2006/s1582732.htm, copyright Commonwealth of Australia, reproduced by permission)

The 'catch-all' syndrome that drives electoral pragmatism can be associated with the fact that the Howard government used the Regional Partnerships Program to direct funds to Coalition electorates and deny them to Labor seats (O'Malley, S., Jenkins, M. & Hawthorn, M. 2007, 'PM denies vote buying after grants audit', news.com.au, 15 November 2007). However, there is no guarantee that such a spending spree to attract voters will be successful, for despite a raft of promised grants and other funds to many organisations around the country, the electorate moved away from the Howard government and voted it out of office in November 2007.

Party discipline

It is a matter of frequent celebration in Liberal Party rhetoric that in contrast to their Labor rivals, Liberal members of parliament are free men and women, able to exercise their minds and judgements as they see necessary. This is true only at the margins:

- The solidarity of the Liberal Party in parliament is hardly less marked than that of the ALP, and for much the same reasons.
- The removal of endorsement from sitting Liberals, including unsuccessful Liberal leaders, probably occurs more often than on the other side of politics. Along with comparable ideological tensions (the Liberal Party also has its left and right wings, which have clashed in preselection contests as well as in State Councils) goes a need for Liberals to be successful. Ministers or shadow ministers generally attract support and loyalty from the organisation, but a lacklustre MP in a safe seat, or one who is on the wrong side of the dominant factional fence, is likely to be in danger of a challenge from within.

Nevertheless, the Liberal Party has its rebels. There have been a number of them in the past, including senators protected to some degree by their longer parliamentary terms, or members of the 'wets' in the House of Representatives.

The locus of power in the Liberal Party is the parliamentary leader. This dominance comes from two sources:

- the power to select the ministry or shadow ministry; and
- Liberals making less of party democracy and more of party leaders.

It is true that Gough Whitlam received as much adulation from the rank-and-file members of the ALP during his heyday as did any Liberal leader from his followers. However, between 1972 and 1975 many of Whitlam's colleagues accepted his leadership grudgingly or hardly at all, and used the forms of the party against him, secure in the knowledge that caucus, not the prime minister, had put them in office. A similar caucus revolt caused changes to Prime Minister Keating's 1993 budget. Such behaviour is less easy or common in the Liberal Party because ministers owe their elevation to the prime minister alone, no matter what their power base at home. As Malcolm Fraser demonstrated, a Liberal prime minister who knows his or her own mind can dispense with a senior minister in half a day, and without much immediate cost. Yet, the supremacy of Liberal leaders is contingent on their remaining successful:

- John Gorton removed himself from office in 1971 after a tied vote of no-confidence by the parliamentary party, many of whom considered they would lose the next election if he remained prime minister.

- William McMahon accepted responsibility for the 1972 defeat and stepped down bravely, thus retaining a measure of status that would have disappeared had he sought re-election as parliamentary leader.
- His successor, Bill Snedden, could not match the Labor prime minister and was eventually manoeuvred out of office after his first election defeat in 1974—even though the result was close.
- Malcolm Fraser's dominance rested on electoral victories, but it disappeared at once when he called an early election in 1983 and lost it. Like McMahon, he accepted responsibility for defeat and stood down as leader, retiring from parliament soon afterwards.
- The period after that became a tussle as John Howard and Andrew Peacock interchanged the leadership. Peacock's failure to take the party to electoral success in 1990 saw John Hewson take on the leadership and Peacock eventually retire from parliament. Hewson departed the parliamentary scene after he failed to win the 'unlosable' election in 1993. The party turned briefly to Alexander Downer and then returned to John Howard. The Liberal Party's 2007 election loss and the defeat of John Howard in his seat of Bennelong meant a new leader had to be found. Brendan Nelson was elected leader by the parliamentary party. He was replaced by Malcolm Turnbull in September 2008 because he had failed to generate increased electoral support for the Liberals.

Sometimes, the political ambitions of rivals can undermine the leadership. Bob Hawke, for example, was displaced by Paul Keating in 1991. Howard's leadership came under pressure in mid-2005 from Peter Costello, who considered it was 'his turn' to be leader, following 10 years as a faithful treasurer. However, Costello did not have sufficient support within the Liberal Party room to mount a leadership challenge to Howard at that time.

For Liberals, party membership is not so valued a possession as it is within the Labor Party. A disappointed Liberal activist is more likely to get out of politics and devote his or her energies to local government, industrial politics or making money. For all that, the organisation treats seriously any breaches of the basic rules. In a celebrated case, Jeff Bate, MP for the New South Wales federal seat of Macarthur from 1949 to 1977, was expelled when he declared that he would contest his seat after having lost Liberal Party endorsement.

POLICY DIFFERENTIATION IN THE 'CATCH-ALL' CONTEXT

As mentioned above, one of the difficulties faced by the major parties is how to differentiate their appeal to the electorate in the context of 'catch-all' politics. In this environment, both are vying for the same constituencies to win government—the mortgage belt, and those whom Howard called the 'battlers' and Labor has termed 'working families'—and both parties have similar approaches to economic policy that aims to foster the Australian economy.

> 'The truth is that the Howard Government is not dramatically different from its Hawke and Keating predecessors. The Hawke/Keating Government (i) floated the currency, (ii) introduced financial deregulation, (iii) put the budget into surplus . . . (iv) commenced taxation reform, (v) began the privatisation process, (vi) reformed the health, education and welfare systems and

(vii) commenced compulsory employer-funded superannuation. And more besides—including the payment of generous benefits to families with young children, which has been accentuated by the Howard/Costello governments.'

(*Source*: Henderson, G. 2006, 'John Howard: 10 Years On', speech to the New South Wales Fabian Society, 22 March 2006, http://www.fabian.org.au/1048.asp)

FIGURE 10.5
Howard loses the 'battlers'

(*Source*: Cartoon by Nicholson from *The Australian*. www.nicholsoncartoons.com.au)

The difference between them lies at the margins—in the means they choose to reach their policy objectives, rather than on the ideological differences articulated in the rhetoric of their policy platforms. As a result, policy becomes a product to be marketed by the party and expressed in language constructed by party 'spin doctors' (see Table 10.1, and Chapter 13), and by advertising agencies designed to appeal to a broad spectrum of constituency interests, particularly to those in marginal seats.

TABLE 10.1

'Political speak' by the major parties

Labor Treasurer Wayne Swan's Budget Speech 2008–09	then Liberal leader Brendan Nelson's Budget Reply speech
'A Budget that strengthens Australia's economic foundations, and delivers for working families under pressure . . . A Budget that begins a new era of strategic investment in Australia's future challenges and opportunities. And a Budget that helps plan, finance and secure Australia's long-term national security and defence needs . . . Foremost in our considerations are the Australians who work hard, pay their taxes, and demand little more than a fair go . . . This government understands the stress on working families in these difficult times . . . that's why a key priority of this Budget is to deliver the Working Families Support Package . . . The Government will fully implement our promise to reduce personal income tax . . . directed to low and middle income earners—the backbone of the economy . . . We will make the Medicare Levy Surcharge fairer . . . We have decided to redirect welfare payments to where they are needed most. The Government does not believe hard earned tax dollars are best spent on cash payments to the wealthiest Australians. It is simply not defensible. We are providing new leadership in education, health, infrastructure, climate change and modernising the federation, to end the blame game . . . The Government supports the aspirations of Australian business, including small business, for a simpler tax system and less regulation . . . We promised to be a Government for all Australians. For rural and regional Australia, and for Indigenous Australia . . . We need a tax system that is fairer, that is simpler, that better rewards people for their hard work, that responds to our environmental and demographic challenges, that makes us internationally competitive, and that creates the incentives to invest in our productive capacity.' (*Source*: *House of Representatives Debates*, 13 May 2008, pp. 2600–8)	'We believe very strongly in the family as the bedrock of Australian society, while respecting and reaching out to every other Australian, whatever their economic or personal circumstances. We believe in choice. We believe Australians should be encouraged and supported in choice in health and education. Equally they should be free to join a union or not to join a union. We believe strongly in defence and security and investment in it for the protection of our nation. We believe very strongly that small family businesses are the lifeblood of our nation and its economic prosperity. We believe always in lower taxes, once our obligations to society in health, education, road infrastructure, defence and other requirements have been met. We believe ultimately in the individual. We believe that the inherent worth of every single Australian is paramount and that our task as Liberals and as Nationals is to stand against oppressive bureaucracy and governments that too often . . . appear to think that they know what is best for Australians, instead of leaving choices and freedoms in the hands of individuals who actually make this country work. We believe we will be at our best as a nation if we see ourselves and strive to be outward-looking, highly competitive and compassionate people, reconciled with our Indigenous history and imbued with fundamental values of hard work, self-sacrifice, courage, tolerance and a determination to see that we support one another, that we respect our freedoms and stand up for the rights, values and freedoms of not only all Australians but all people throughout the world.' (*Source*: *House of Representatives Debates*, 15 May 2008, p. 85)

QUESTIONS FOR DISCUSSION

1. 'The democratic socialist objectives of the Australian Labor Party have little meaning to the party today.' Discuss.
2. Is the relationship between the Australian Labor Party and the trade union movement no longer relevant to a Labor government? Discuss your views.
3. 'The values and objectives of the Liberal Party of Australia today are more closely attuned to liberalism than those of the Commonwealth Liberal Party in 1905.' Discuss.
4. Is it inevitable that the major parties will move closer together on policy issues? Explain your reasons.

FURTHER READING

Australian Labor Party

Jaensch, D. 1989, *The Hawke–Keating Hijack,* Allen & Unwin, Sydney. Examines the first six years of the Hawke Labor government and argues that every component of the ethos, structure and practice of the party had been questioned, changed, ignored or abandoned.

Kelly, P. 1992, *The End of Certainty*, Allen & Unwin, Sydney. A study of Australian politics in the 1980s. See in particular Chapter 2, which looks at what Kelly calls 'the new Labor Party', and Chapter 4, regarding the Accord.

McMullin, R. 1991, *The Light on the Hill: The Australian Labor Party 1891–1991*, Oxford University Press, Melbourne. A history of the ALP, told from the perspective of the party's leading identities and branch members. Highlights the tensions between the leaders and the rank-and-file members of the party.

Warhurst, J. & Parkin, A. (eds) 2000, *The Machine: Labor Confronts the Future*, Allen & Unwin, Sydney. An edited collection that examines the issues confronting Labor in the context of modern politics.

Liberal Party of Australia

Aulich, C. & Wettenhall, R. (eds) 2005, *Howard's Second and Third Governments: Australian Commonwealth Administration 1998–2004*, UNSW Press, Sydney. This book examines the administration and leadership style of John Howard's second and third governments.

Aulich, C. & Wettenhall, R. (eds) 2008, *Howard's Fourth Government: Australian Commonwealth Administration 2004–2007*, UNSW Press, Sydney. An examination of administration and policy in Howard's fourth term of government.

Brett, J. 2006, 'The Liberal Party', in Parkin, A., Summers, J. & Woodward, D. (eds), *Government, Politics, Power and Policy in Australia*, 8th ed., Pearson Education, Sydney. Explains the origins of the party, its revival in 1944 and political record since that time, and the challenges it faces for the future.

Brett, J. 2007, 'Exit Right: The Unravelling of John Howard', *Quarterly Essay*, no. 28, pp. 1–96.

Nethercote, J. (ed.) 2001, *Liberalism and the Australian Federation*, Federation Press, Sydney. A comprehensive reflection on over 100 years of liberalism in Australia, including the historical development of the Liberal Party, the Liberal governments of 1966–72, and prospects for the future.

Rickard, M. 2002, *Principle and Pragmatism: A Study of Competition between Australia's Major Parties at the 2004 and Other Recent Federal elections*, Australian Parliamentary Fellow Monograph, Canberra, http://www.aph.gov.au/library/pubs/monographs/rickard/.

USEFUL WEBSITES

http://www.alp.org.au
Australian Labor Party

http://www.liberal.org.au
Liberal Party of Australia

http://www.aph.gov.au
Parliament of Australia
Follow the links to the websites of the prime minister and the leader of the Opposition.

http://www.apo.org.au
Australian Policy Online
The situation after the 2007 election has been discussed in the following articles on the Australian Policy Online website:
— Brett, J. 2007, 'Defeat can be a New Dawn for the Liberals', 27 November 2007
— Chesterman, J. 2007, 'Post-Election: Putting the "liberal" back in the Liberal Party', posted 11 December 2007
— Costar, B. 2007, 'Election 2007: The Aftermath: What the Liberals Shouldn't Do', 27 November 2007.

11

MINOR PARTIES AND INDEPENDENTS IN AUSTRALIA

THIS CHAPTER EXPLAINS:

- what minor parties are and how they are classified;
- the role of minor parties in Australian politics;
- the ideology, structure and discipline of significant minor parties; and
- the role of independents in the Australian parliament.

Why is it important to study minor parties and independents when historically only the Labor Party or the Liberal Party (usually in coalition with the Nationals) have been able to form governments at the federal level in Australia? Minor parties and independents are significant to the Australian political system because:

- they have held the balance of power in the Senate and other Australian parliaments;
- their preferences may determine the result of elections; and
- they provide an alternative choice for voters who do not want to vote for either of the major parties.

> From 1 July 2008, minor parties and one independent hold the balance of power in the Senate.
>
> | Government | | Minor parties and independent | | Opposition parties | |
> |---|---|---|---|---|---|
> | ALP | 32 | The Greens | 5 | Liberal Party | 32 |
> | | | Family First | 1 | Nationals/CLP | 5 |
> | | | Independent | 1 | | |

To pass its legislation the Rudd government needs the support of the five Greens senators plus both the Family First and independent senators. If either the Family First senator or the independent senator votes with the Coalition, the vote would be tied and therefore decided in the negative.

MINOR PARTIES

What is a minor party?

Minor parties in Australia have similar characteristics to those of the major parties. They generally have a federal structure if they are nationally based, a party organisation, formal policy-making processes, and an ideology or set of principles and objectives that underpin their policies. Party discipline is a factor in maintaining cohesion among a party's elected representatives, particularly in those instances when a minor party holds the balance of power in a parliament.

> **Minor party**: a party that fields candidates for election but has insufficient voter support to win a majority of seats in a house of parliament in its own right.

Minor parties form for several reasons. They can develop from *interest groups or social movements* that desire to gain parliamentary representation. An example of an interest group that developed in this way was the No Aircraft Noise party, formed from groups opposed to building a third runway at Sydney Airport. The Australian Greens is an example of a party that developed from the environmental movement in Australia.

Other minor parties are formed by groups that *break away from a major party*. An example is the Democratic Labor Party, which split from the Australian Labor Party in the mid-1950s.

Some minor parties form around a *single issue* (for example, the Australian Shooters Party, which opposes gun laws).

Pauline Hanson's One Nation party might be identified as a *personality party*, because she was the catalyst and identity around which the party formed. However, we need to be cautious about the concept of personality as a determining factor, because there was a set of ideas that caused the party to form and which encouraged members to join. The party continued to function after Pauline Hanson left the organisation and her name was removed from its title. Pauline Hanson's One Nation could also be seen to be a party that was formed by individuals and groups who felt let down or ignored by the existing major parties.

Ideology and ideas also play a part in the formation of political parties, such as the Communist Party of Australia. There are parties that have been established by people to reflect their Christian-based principles, such as the Christian Democratic Party and Family First.

Classification of minor parties

As we can see, there are a variety of reasons why minor parties form and this has led to the development of a range of classifications to help us identify their origins and characteristics. For example:

- *Secessionist parties* form as a result of a split in the parent party.
- *Aggrieved minority parties* usually form after a group has failed in its pressure group activities.
- *Doctrinal parties* have a firm, narrow and rigid doctrine.

(*Source*: Jaensch, D. 1997, *The Politics of Australia*, 2nd ed., Macmillan Education, Melbourne, p. 331)

> For a comprehensive classification scheme of minor parties, see Jaensch, D. & Mathieson, D. 1998, *A Plague on Both Your Houses*, Allen & Unwin, Sydney, pp. 27–8.

There has been a long history of minor-party involvement with Australian politics since Federation. Looking back to Chapter 10, we saw how between 1901 and their fusion in 1909, the non-Labor side of politics comprised two parties, neither of which could win a majority in its own right. Once party representation in the House of Representatives had settled into a pattern of Labor and non-Labor groups capable of forming majorities, minor parties became inconsequential in the House of Representatives. The exception has been the Nationals, which started life as the Country Party. This party first won representation in 1919 with 11 seats, and historically has entered into coalitions with the Liberal Party of Australia to form governments.

Why do major parties dominate the Australian party system?

The major parties have dominated the party system because they have been able to maintain a high level of support among the voters. Major parties also have the membership base and resources to mount significant election campaigns, not only in terms of funding but also to provide assistance on election day at the polling booths, handing out how-to-vote cards and scrutinising the counting of the votes. They also get the benefits of public funding, which most minor parties cannot access because they do not get the required percentage of votes at an election.

Between 1934 and 1993, Labor's share of first-preference votes for House of Representatives elections did not fall below 40 per cent. The Liberal Party followed the same pattern. With 79.6 per cent of first preference votes between them in 2007, they seem reasonably secure in their domination of the House of Representatives.

Why vote for a minor party?

There are a number of reasons why voters would prefer to vote for a minor party or an independent. These include disillusionment with governments that fail to keep their promises; an impression that there is not much difference between the policies and ideas of the major parties, particularly on economic policy; and voters paying more attention to the performance of party leaders and current political issues. Voters, as a result, have become more willing to give their first-preference votes to a minor party or independent. However, predictions that there would be a surge in support for minor party and independent candidates have not been borne out. Between them they were able to achieve just 20 per cent of first-preference votes for the House of Representatives in 2007. Table 11.1 shows the levels of support for minor parties at the 2007 Senate election.

Even though the major parties have not been dislodged from their predominant position, there is more fluidity in the party system, particularly in those marginal seats where the result is determined on the distribution of the preferences of minor party and independent candidates.

The significance of this has not been lost on the minor and major parties. Some minor parties have used the situation to barter their preferences for policy outcomes — in other words, to promise support in return for concessions. They have also sought to maximise their support by reaching agreement with other parties on the way preferences are allocated, particularly in legislatures that use a proportional voting system, such as the Senate. In the 2004 Senate election, for example, the Family First party achieved only 1.88 per cent of the first-preference vote in Victoria but achieved a quota for a Senate seat for the state after they received a flow of preferences from major and minor parties.

The major parties have also managed the preferential system to help maintain their dominant position in the House of Representatives. In 1990, for example, the Labor Party asked electors who were going to vote for the Greens to give their second preference to Labor. Labor won the election, but only with the help of preferences from minor parties, including the Greens.

In 1998, as we saw in Chapter 8, both major parties directed their preferences away from Pauline Hanson in the Queensland seat of Blair and she did not win the seat, despite the fact that she topped the poll with 35.97 per cent of first-preference votes. The Liberal candidate scored only 21.69 per cent of the first-preference vote, but won the seat after the distribution of preferences, including 14,733 second-preference votes from the Labor candidate. At the 2004 House of Representatives election, some Coalition candidates were assisted by a flow of preferences from the Family First party.

Minor-party candidates, apart from the Nationals, have difficulty winning seats in the House of Representatives. An Australian Greens candidate won a by-election for

TABLE 11.1

Senate election, 2007: first preference votes for minor parties

	Total national vote	Per cent of total vote
The Greens	1,144,751	9.04
Family First	204,788	1.62
Australian Democrats	162,975	1.29
Pauline	141,268	1.12
CDP Christian Party	118,614	0.94
DLP Democratic Labor Party	115,966	0.92
Climate Change Coalition	78,763	0.62
What Women Want (Australia)	58,803	0.46
One Nation	52,708	0.42
The Fishing Party	47,379	0.37
The Australian Shooters Party/Australian Fishing and Lifestyle Party	45,932	0.36
CLP—The Territory Party	40,253	0.32
Australian Shooters Party	38,216	0.30
Australian Fishing and Lifestyle Party	24,902	0.20
Carers Alliance	24,393	0.19
The Nationals*	20,997	0.17
LDP	16,942	0.13
Conservatives for Climate and Environment	9,988	0.08
Socialist Alliance	9,525	0.08
Citizens Electoral Council	8,677	0.07
Senator On-Line	8,048	0.06
Non-Custodial Parents Party	6,385	0.05
Socialist Equality Party	4,542	0.04
Hear Our Voice	2,041	0.02
Nuclear Disarmament Party of Australia	446	0.00

* The Nationals total shown here refers to votes for the party only in WA and SA. In other states the Liberals and Nationals stood Senate candidates on a joint ticket.

(*Source*: Australian Electoral Commission 2007, 'Senate State First Preferences by Group', http://results.aec.gov.au/13745/Website/SenateStateFirstPrefsByGroup-13745-NAT.htm, copyright Commonwealth of Australia, reproduced by permission)

the seat of Cunningham in New South Wales in 2002 because of a split in the Labor vote, but he was not re-elected in 2004. Independents have been more successful in getting elected to the House of Representatives and retaining their seats, as we shall see below.

Minor parties and independents have been more successful in gaining seats in the Senate because of the system of proportional voting introduced in 1949 which, as we saw in Chapter 8, allocates seats in proportion to the number of votes won. Another reason has been the increase in the number of senators to be elected, which has lowered the quota required for election. These factors make it easier for minor-party candidates to get elected to the Senate and, consequently, it is more difficult for major parties to gain a majority in that house.

Minor parties and independents held the balance of power in the Australian Senate between 1981 and 2005. Between 2005 and 30 June 2008, the Coalition parties had a majority of 1 in the Senate, and the Howard government was able to pass its legislation without recourse to negotiation with minor parties. When senators elected at the 2007 federal election took their places in the house on 1 July 2008, however, minor parties and one independent once again controlled the balance of power in the Senate.

> **Balance of power**: the situation in a legislature where neither of the major parties has a majority and bills can be passed only with the support of minor parties and/or independents who are said to hold the balance of power.

This chapter now looks at a number of minor parties that have been significant in the Australian political system. The first group of parties was selected because they have been successful in winning seats in Australian parliaments. The second group includes parties that have historical significance, as well as parties that attract a modicum of voter support and are indicative of the breadth of ideas and issues that minor parties in Australia represent.

MINOR PARTIES WITH REPRESENTATION IN AUSTRALIAN PARLIAMENTS

Table 11.2 shows that 20 years ago there were very few representatives of minor parties in Australian parliaments. The Nationals have been excluded from the table because of their status as a Coalition partner in government, which technically removes them from the status of minor party, defined above.

The larger number of minor party candidates elected to the Senate and the Australian Capital Territory (ACT) is a function of the proportional voting systems used for those

TABLE 11.2

Minor parties, other than the Nationals, represented in Australian parliaments in the 1980s

Parliament	House	Seats
Australian parliament, 1987	Senate	9
New South Wales, 1988	MLC*	1
Western Australia, 1986	MLC	1
South Australia, 1985	MLC	1
Australian Capital Territory, 1989	MHA*	8

* MLC: Member of Legislative Council; MHA: Member of House of Assembly.

houses. Table 11.3 shows the number of representatives of minor parties in Australian parliaments in 2008, again excluding the Nationals.

The interesting result here is the fall in numbers of minor party MHAs for the ACT, where voter support in 2004 focused around the two major parties. Two reasons for this

TABLE 11.3
Minor parties, other than the Nationals, represented in Australian parliaments, 2008

Parliament	House	Seats
Australian parliament	Senate	6
New South Wales	MLC	8
Victoria	MLC	4
Queensland	MLA*	1
Western Australia	MLC	4
South Australia	MLC	4
Tasmania	MLA	4
Australian Capital Territory	MHA	4

* MLA: Member of Legislative Assembly.

included the strong level of support for the Labor Party at that election under the leadership of Jon Stanhope that secured the party majority government, and the collapse of support for the Australian Democrats.

Given the level of representation of minor parties in Australian parliaments, it is important that we know something about them and what they stand for.

The Nationals (http://www.nationalparty.org)

The Nationals in Australian parliaments, September 2008

Parliament	House	Seats
Australian parliament	House of Representatives	10
	Senate	4
New South Wales	MLC	5
	MLA	13
Victoria	MLC	2
	MLA	9
Queensland	MLA	17
South Australia	MLA	1
Western Australia	MLC	5
	MLA	4

There has been some questioning about whether the Nationals should be classified as a minor party, because they have formed a coalition government with the Liberal Party at the federal level, and a government in their own right in Queensland. Jaensch and Mathieson, for example, excluded the Nationals from their 1998 study of minor parties (*A Plague on Both Your Houses*, Allen & Unwin, Sydney) for that reason. The party has been included here, however, because of its success in gaining representation and its significance to the Australian party system.

> On 26 July 2008, the Queensland Liberal Party and the Queensland Nationals merged to form a new party, the Liberal National Party of Queensland (LNP). The purpose of the merger was to strengthen the electoral appeal of the conservative parties by providing a united front against the incumbent Labor government at the next state election. The LNP is a division of the Liberal Party of Australia (Queensland Division) and is affiliated with the National Party of Australia. State parliamentary representatives will be members of the LNP and, until it is decided otherwise, the current federal Members of the House of Representatives and senators will continue to sit with their current party, that is, as Liberals or Nationals. A copy of the constitution of the LNP can be found at http://www.lnp.org.au.

Ideology

> **The Nationals' values**
> The values of the Nationals are:
> - strong representation—members of parliament who are strong local advocates, champions for their regions and come together to act as a team;
> - security for the nation, local communities and families; and
> - individual achievement—private enterprise, a fair go and a balanced role for government.
>
> (*Source*: The Nationals n.d., 'The Nationals Values', http://www.nationals.org.au/About/values.asp)

The ideology of the Nationals is conservative, bedded in its support for the 'maximum development of private enterprise'. The ascendance of the conservative faction within the Liberal Party, with its platform of minimal government and economic rationalism, brought the Nationals' ideological program into the mainstream political agenda of the 1990s. It can be set down as a set of propositions:

- The wealth (as distinct from the existence) of Australian society comes from its primary industries—once the agricultural, pastoral and horticultural industries alone, but now the manufacturing and the extractive (mineral) industries as well.
- It is the income these industries earn from overseas which allows all Australians the high standards of living they enjoy.
- Farmers and graziers are therefore owed respect and consideration from the rest of the community; further, it is in everyone's interest to help them to be as productive as possible.
- Government intervention is quite proper, indeed laudable, where it assists to this end.
- City people outnumber and outvote those in the country, who do not get from the electoral system the degree of representation that they (and Australia) require.

The Nationals have profited immensely from this ideology, and managed to have parts of it accepted as conventional wisdom in the 1920s and 1930s, including the significant number of people who live outside the capital cities in rural areas and regional centres who have no direct contact with the land at all. The decline of rural industries in the postwar period has not resulted in the decline of the ideology. Rather, like all successful ideologies, it has adapted to changing times.

Population shift from the country to the cities encouraged the party to adopt several strategies to give it a 'national' image, to attract voters in regional and urban seats. In 1974 the party changed its name from the Country Party to the National Country Party. In 1982 it became the National Party and adopted the 'Australian' colours of green and gold for its logo. Since 2003 the party has used the title 'The Nationals'. Likewise, it has extended its policies to encompass the interests of the broader Australian population, but 'provides a vital balance, ensuring the interests of the people living beyond the capital cities have a voice in Parliament' (The Nationals n.d., 'The Nationals Values', http://www.nationals.org.au/About/values.asp).

The exigencies of being involved in a coalition partnership, where the party has to abide by the collective decision-making process of cabinet government, have created problems in sustaining support from its base constituency. This caused a significant erosion of its vote in favour of Pauline Hanson's One Nation party at the 1998 election. It was able to save the loss of several seats to One Nation only by the preferential voting system, where preferences of the major parties generally were directed away from One Nation, and by the efforts of its parliamentary leadership in reassuring rural voters that the party in future would focus its efforts within the Coalition on working for rural communities. The Nationals' vote recovered slightly in 2001 and 2004, but fell slightly in 2007. The party has lost considerable ground in the House of Representatives. In 1996 the Nationals had 18 seats, but in 2007 their representation declined to 10 seats (see Table 11.4).

TABLE 11.4

House of Representatives and Senate elections 2007: Nationals' vote and seats won

Election	House of Representatives: percentage of first-preference votes	No. of seats won	Senate: percentage of first-preference votes	No. of seats won
2007	5.49	10	n/a*	2

* Figures for Senate first-preference votes for the Nationals are not included because they are shown combined with the Liberal Party in Australian Electoral Commission figures.

(Source: Australian Electoral Commission 2007, 'The Official 2007 Federal Election Results', http://results.aec.gov.au/13745/website/default.htm)

Organisation

The Nationals' organisation is an outgrowth of farmers' organisations, and these associations and party members are inclined to see the party as the parliamentary wing of a wider country or farmers' movement and answerable to that movement. Appropriately, given its origins and ideology, the local organisation has considerable autonomy.

The state organisational structure is a simple one:

- Branch delegates make up the membership of electorate councils.
- Electorate council chairs make up the bulk of the State Council.
- The State Council chooses the State Executive and the principal office-bearers.
- Branch delegates, electorate council delegates and central councillors make up the State Conference.

Each state branch has a paid staff (most of whom recruit members and keep local organisations alive) and publishes a newspaper or journal, which is one means of overcoming the problems of distance and dispersed population.

At the federal level, a member Federal Council, which includes at least 42 branch members, is responsible for policy making. The Federal Management Committee, comprising senior officers of the party, manages day-to-day affairs. A Federal Conference, attended by delegates from each Federal Electorate Council, is convened every three years.

The Nationals, like the Liberal Party, reject gender-based quotas. The party believes that candidates should be representative of their electorates.

Party discipline

The Nationals are a 'clubby' party, because of:

- the shared backgrounds of the party's members; and
- the smaller range of its interests and its ideology.

The greater informality allows greater permissiveness. Nationals MPs who feel that they must vote against the party's agreed policy on an issue can do so provided they make their position clear to the party or, if time is short, to the leader. The extra-parliamentary organisation avoids disciplinary situations if it can (a great deal can be done informally), but, as with the other parties, a member who contests a seat against an endorsed candidate will be expelled. Infighting within the Queensland branch and events that surrounded the 'Joh for Canberra' campaign in 1987 suggests the development of much more ruthless behaviour within the party.

Being part of a Coalition government places pressure on Nationals' members of parliament who disagree with government policy not to air their criticisms publicly. Former Queensland Nationals member of the House of Representatives, Bob Katter, was an outspoken critic of some of the Coalition government's policies. He resigned from the party and successfully contested his seat as an independent at the 2001, 2004 and 2007 federal elections. Nationals Queensland Senator Barnaby Joyce voted independently from his party and against the Coalition government several times in the Senate, but has been able to maintain his party association.

The Australian Democrats (http://www.democrats.org.au)

Australian Democrats in Australian parliaments, January 2008

Parliament	House	Seats
South Australia	MLC	1

Ideology

The party was established by a group of former Australia Party and New Liberal Movement members in 1977 under the leadership of Don Chipp. He was a former Liberal Party minister in the Holt and Gorton governments and Opposition shadow minister during the Whitlam years, but was left out of the ministry by Malcolm Fraser. The party was characterised by its disillusionment with the major parties and an antipathy to party politics reflected in the party's declared non-ideological stance. In practice, however, the Australian Democrats inhabit the centre of politics.

> **The Australian Democrats' key principles**
> The Australian Democrats:
> - aim to consider the best interests of ALL Australians;
> - are committed to operating as a fully democratic party;
> - do not enter into coalitions and compromise the party's independence to secure more power;
> - believe that Australia must adopt long-term goals and objectives;
> - expect their party's politicians to follow party policy, but allow them to exercise a conscience vote;
> - believe the economy needs more local community involvement and control, jobs cannot be sacrificed for the 'needs' of the market, economic policy has to take account of social and environmental needs, and Australian industries with the ability to be sustainable in the long term must be encouraged and supported;
> - believe the survival of our planet has reached crisis point, and aim to fight vigorously for conservation issues and protection of the environment;
> - believe there is too much foreign ownership and influence of the Australian internal economy and foreign policy, and want to bring Australia back under Australian control; and
> - offer equal opportunity for women in selection of candidates and leadership positions.
>
> (*Source*: Australian Democrats 2007, 'About the Australian Democrats: Key Principles', http://www.democrats.org.au)

The greatest weakness of the party's ideology is that it does not grow out of the social experience of a relatively identifiable group of people, other than the fact that their supporters tend to be middle-class and well-educated. In this respect the Democrats' hold on political life has been tenuous. It was able to 'keep the bastards honest' and negotiate amendments to legislation when it was the major group among the minor parties and independents holding the balance of power in the Senate, but it has suffered a significant decline in electoral support in recent years and now has no members in the Senate (see Table 11.5). Its first-preference votes at the 2007 election were insufficient to make it eligible for public funding, so the party may have difficulty rebuilding from this low base.

Organisation

The Australian Democrats built on organisational innovations of the Australia Party, some of whose members formed the core of support for the new party. All members join the national party and can choose a local branch to join. Branches operate at the local level, usually based around federal electorates. Each state and territory is a division of the party. The general membership of each state division elects a Division Executive, determines the structure of the party's regional or local organisation and office-bearers, and draws up and adopts a division constitution.

The party has a National Executive, which is made up of the national president and two deputy national presidents elected by ballot of all members, the leader and deputy leader of the party in the House of Representatives (although until now there have been no Democrats elected to the lower house); the leader and deputy leader of the party in the Senate (not applicable at this time because the party has no Senate seats—see Table 11.5) and two representatives from each division, elected by division members. The party also has a non-voting Executive, comprising a national administrator, a national secretary, national treasurer, national journal editor and national campaign director, who are appointed by the National Executive. The duties of the National Executive are to organise and coordinate the policies, functions and administration of the party in accordance with its constitution.

TABLE 11.5
House of Representatives and Senate election 2007: Australian Democrats' vote and seats won

Election	House of Representatives: percentage of first-preference votes	No. of seats won	Senate: percentage of first-preference votes	No. of seats won
2007	0.72	0	1.29	0

(Source: Australian Electoral Commission 2007, 'The Official 2007 Federal Election Results', http://results.aec.gov.au/13745/website/default.htm)

The party's journal serves as an instrument of policy formulation. Members can take part in postal ballots to determine the party's stand on policy issues, using ballot papers printed in the journal. Party members also elect the parliamentary leader. Emergency policy decisions can be made by the National Executive but have to be ratified by the membership by party ballot within two months.

The Australian Democrats have a much better record than the major parties in selecting women for senior positions within the party. There were six women leaders of their Senate team.

Party discipline

Elected members of the Australian Democrats are required to adhere to the policies formulated by the party, except where they conflict with the views of the elected member. In that case, the member is entitled to exercise a conscience vote on the issue, but must justify it to the membership. Every piece of legislation is discussed in the party room and objections are raised and worked through. Any member of the party who disagrees with a policy of the party is free to express those views. Disagreements among Democrat senators that were aired publicly, however, highlighted the fact that there was disunity and animosity within the parliamentary party that no doubt contributed to its diminished voter support.

The Greens (http://www.greens.org.au)

The Greens in Australian parliaments, September 2008

Parliament	House	Seats
Australian parliament	Senate	4
New South Wales	MLC	3
South Australia	MHA	1
Western Australia	MLC	4
Tasmania	MLA	4
Australian Capital Territory	MHA	4

Ideology

The Greens developed in the 1980s from the environment movement. Environmentalism attracts support across the ideological spectrum from those with a philosophical commitment to protection of the planet. The Tasmanian Greens secured electoral success in Tasmania in 1989 with sufficient seats to hold the balance of power in the Legislative Assembly. In 1992, a national Green party, the Australian Greens, was formed, with objectives that embody the practical pursuit of environmental protection with the precepts of social democracy and a focus on direct participation.

General principles of the Greens
The general principles of the Greens are based on the following key issues:
- ecology;
- democracy;
- social justice;
- peace;
- an ecologically sustainable economy;
- meaningful work;
- culture;
- information;
- global responsibility; and
- long-range future focus.

(*Source*: The Australian Greens 2007, 'The Charter of the Australian Greens', http://greens.org.au/charter)

The Greens (WA), formed in 1990 from an amalgamation of the Jo Vallentine Peace Group, the Alternative Coalition, the Green Party and the South West Greens, remain a separate autonomous state-based party.

The Green parties have a primary concern with environmental issues, but their experience in holding the balance of power in the Tasmanian parliament and the Senate has meant they have had to extend the scope of their political attention to economic and social issues. The party is best described as left of centre in philosophical terms.

Table 11.6 shows results for the Greens in the 2007 federal election.

TABLE 11.6
House of Representatives and Senate elections 2007: the Greens' vote and seats won

Election	House of Representatives: percentage of first-preference votes	No. of seats won	Senate: percentage of first-preference votes	No. of seats won
2007	7.79	0	9.04	3

(*Source:* Australian Electoral Commission 2007, 'The Official 2007 Federal Election Results', http://results.aec.gov.au/13745/website/default.htm)

Organisation

The Greens (WA) are made up of state-based autonomous groups. Each group sends a member to a Representative Council. Councils are based on federal electorates. This means that the group's views are represented in the decision-making process, in keeping with the party's commitment to participatory democracy. The Regional Councils send representatives to a council of representatives that makes decisions for state management. They endeavour to arrive at decisions by consensus rather than a majority vote. In 1995, the Greens (WA) had two representatives in the Senate, both women. One was defeated at the 1996 half-Senate election and the other in 1998.

The Australian Greens was founded in 1992 as a confederation of autonomous Green parties in all states, except Western Australia, where it has an alliance agreement with the Greens (WA). The party has local groups based on federal electorates, who are responsible for selecting candidates for the House of Representatives. Each state and territory division of the party has a council that sends representatives to a National Council, which meets twice a year and selects the party's Senate candidates. The function of the National Council is to discuss organisational strategy, share information, and make interim policy decisions that have to be ratified by the party's National Conference. The National Conference, which is held once a year and includes four delegates from each of the territories and six delegates from each member state, is responsible for policy changes. Policy is made on the basis of consensus.

The Australian Greens has a convenor, a secretary and a treasurer to administer common issues between state parties, and coordinators for national policies, campaign issues, international contacts, constitutional review and registration issues, and interstate working groups.

The Greens achieved party status in the Senate after the 2007 election and have replaced the Australian Democrats as the significant minor party in that house.

Party discipline

Elected members are expected to support party policy, except on issues where it is against their conscience to do so.

Pauline Hanson's One Nation, 1997–2002/One Nation, 2002 (http://www.onenation.com.au)

One Nation in Australian parliaments, January 2008

Parliament	House	Seats
Queensland	MLA	1

Pauline Hanson was elected to the federal parliament for the seat of Oxley, Queensland, in 1996 as an independent. Originally selected as the Liberal Party candidate, her endorsement was removed by the party on the eve of the election because of contentious statements she had made during the campaign. Her success in winning the seat was assisted by the fact that there had been insufficient time to remove the words 'Liberal Party' from beside her name on the ballot paper.

The subsequent emergence of a political party focused around Pauline Hanson is significant for two reasons: the emphasis on Pauline Hanson as the catalyst and focus of the new party embodied in its name—Pauline Hanson's One Nation; and the party's rapid development. Because of the high profile of its leader, the party can be characterised as a personality party, but its attraction of many groups and voters disenchanted with the major parties also suggests the party might fall into the 'aggrieved minority' category.

> **Aggrieved minority**: a party formed 'on the basis of demands, aspirations or grievances of a section of society'.
> (Source: Jaensch, D. & Mathieson, D.S. 1998, *A Plague on Both Your Houses*, Allen & Unwin, Sydney, p. 24)

The party was launched in April 1997 and won 11 seats in the Queensland state parliament in June 1998, with almost a quarter of the vote.

The unprecedented success of a new party in winning so many seats at its first election outing led to suggestions that Pauline Hanson's One Nation would pose a substantial threat to the Coalition parties at the October 1998 federal election, particularly the Nationals' rural electorates. The momentum slowed when the party polled only 8.39 per cent of first-preference votes, with the leader, Pauline Hanson, failing in her quest for the Queensland seat of Blair. A combination of factors contributed to this result:

- the avoidance by the major parties during the campaign of the controversial issues related to Aboriginal reconciliation, multiculturalism and immigration raised by One Nation;
- the overriding issue of tax reform and the GST as an election issue; and
- a vigorous campaign in the bush by Nationals leader Tim Fischer.

The most significant factor, however, as discussed earlier in this chapter, was the preferential voting system. Pauline Hanson's One Nation party failed to attract sufficient second-preference votes and failed to gain a seat in the House of Representatives. One senator from Queensland was elected, but failed to get re-elected in 2004. Pauline Hanson resigned as leader of the party in January 2002 and asked that her name be removed from the party's title. The party is now called One Nation but has failed to thrive. In 1998 One Nation achieved 8.43 per cent of House of Representatives first-preference votes, but in 2007 could only manage 0.26 per cent (see Table 11.7). Pauline Hanson stood as an independent candidate for the Senate at the 2004 and 2007 elections, but was not successful.

TABLE 11.7
House of Representatives and Senate elections 2007: One Nation's vote and seats won

Election	House of Representatives: percentage of first-preference votes	No. of seats won	Senate: percentage of first-preference votes	No. of seats won
2007	0.26	0	0.42	0

(*Source*: Australian Electoral Commission 2007, 'The Official 2007 Federal Election Results', http://results.aec.gov.au/13745/website/default.htm)

Ideology
Pauline Hanson's speeches and her criticisms of the major parties, tagged the 'Laboral factions', formed the core of the party's conservative ideology. Her statements highlighted concern about continuing high levels of unemployment, levels of immigration (particularly from Asia), Aboriginal welfare, law and order, and multiculturalism, and reflected a reaction to the forces of economic and social change experienced by the Australian community in the 1980s and 1990s. Her 'practical' remedial prescriptions were indicative of a conservatism rooted in suspicion and fear of radical change, and in a desire to reactivate past experience, including the maintenance of valued institutions, customs and traditions. The party's objectives in 2008 continue to reflect those values, but also include broader objectives such as the fair and equal treatment of all Australians, freedom of expression and participation in Australia's democracy, and education to provide equal opportunity.

Organisation
The party, when it was formed in 1997, had an unusual structure. It was controlled by a company, Pauline Hanson's One Nation Ltd, which in November 1998 consisted of the party president, Pauline Hanson, a director, David Ettridge, and a senior adviser, David Oldfield. A separate entity, Pauline Hanson's One Nation Members Inc., contained the party membership. Pauline Hanson and David Ettridge faced charges related to the manner in which the party was registered. They were gaoled, but were subsequently released following a successful appeal against their conviction.

The party in 2008 is made up of five state branches. Information about the operation of these branches can be obtained from their websites:

- Queensland: http://www.onenation.com.au/qld/qld.html
- New South Wales: http://www.nsw.onenation.com.au
- Victoria: http://www.vic.onenation.com.au
- South Australia: http://www.sa.onenation.com.au
- Western Australia: http://www.onenationparty.org

Party discipline
One Nation's corporate structure gave effective control over policy to the three party executive members, as well as reported disendorsement of party candidates

deemed to be unsuitable by the party leadership. Party officials were required to submit pre-signed resignation forms, or loyalty agreements, to facilitate the removal of dissenting members. The establishment of autonomous state branches means that this is no longer the case.

CDP Christian Democratic Party (http://www.cdp.org.au)

Christian Democratic Party in Australian parliaments, January 2008

Parliament	House	Seats
New South Wales	MLC	2

Christian principles have been the basis for the establishment of two minor parties who have secured parliamentary representation. The first of these parties was the Christian Democratic Party, which had its origins in the Family Action Movement established by the New South Wales Festival of Light in 1974 to support Christian candidates for federal and state elections. In 1977 it became the Call to Australia Party. The name was changed to the Christian Democratic Party in 1997, to reflect the party's Christian principles.

> **Christian Democratic Party principles**
> The party's principles include:
> - security of our borders, streets, transport and houses;
> - improved quality of family life;
> - the protection of children from abuse;
> - the promotion of a just, honest and accountable government;
> - support for Christian schools;
> - opposition to pornography, gambling and illegal drugs;
> - legislation to guard life from all destructive forces.
>
> (*Source*: Christian Democratic Party 2002, 'About Us', http://www.cdp.org.au/fed/aboutus.asp)

These principles and objectives place the party within the 'religious, moral, Christian/humanist' category of minor parties (see Jaensch, D. & Mathieson, D. 1998, *A Plague on Both Your Houses*, Allen & Unwin, Sydney, p. 27).

The party has branches in New South Wales, Western Australia and the Australian Capital Territory. The party secured its first parliamentary seat with the election of the Reverend Fred Nile to the New South Wales Legislative Council in 1981 and continues to hold seats in that house. In 2004, the Christian Democratic Party stood candidates for the House of Representatives and the Senate. Even though the Senate ticket in New South Wales was headed by the high-profile Nile, the party failed to win a seat in either house. It failed to do so again in 2007 (see Table 11.8).

TABLE 11.8

House of Representatives and Senate elections 2007: Christian Democratic Party's vote and seats won

Election	House of Representatives: percentage of first-preference votes	No. of seats won	Senate: percentage of first-preference votes	No. of seats won
2007	0.84	0	0.94	0

(*Source*: Australian Electoral Commission 2007, 'The Official 2007 Federal Election Results', http://results.aec.gov.au/13745/website/default.htm)

Family First (http://www.familyfirst.org.au)

Family First in Australian parliaments, January 2008

Parliament	House	Seats
Australian parliament	Senate	1
South Australia	MLC	2

The other party with conservative, Christian, family-based principles to gain parliamentary representation is Family First. An association between some party members and the Assemblies of God Pentecostal church has led to suggestions that the party has a religious base.

> 'I'd characterise Family First as part of Australia's Christian Right.'
> (*Source*: Political scientist Graham Maddox, cited in Stewart, C. 2004, 'Old-time religion is good enough for some', *Weekend Australian*, 20 November 2004)

Party chairman Peter Harris has stated that the party is not formally aligned with the church (*The Age*, 4 October 2004). Even so, the nature of the party places it comfortably within the 'religious, moral, Christian/humanist' category of minor parties outlined by Jaensch and Mathieson (p. 27).

> **What does Family First stand for?**
> - We believe Australia should be the best country in the world to raise a family.
> - We are passionate about families and small businesses; two groups which do not have a strong voice in Parliament.
> - We will promote family values and campaign on the issues that really matter to families and small businesses. Issues like:
>   — Improving job security and workplace conditions
>   — Reducing unacceptably high petrol and grocery prices
>   — Helping Australians afford their own home.
> - We will lobby for sensible solutions to improve legislation and get the best outcomes for families and small businesses.
>
> (*Source*: Family First 2007, 'What Does Family First Stand For?', http://www.familyfirst.org.au/policy/policywhatffp.pdf)

Family First achieved parliamentary representation in 2002 when Andrew Evans, a former pastor with the Adelaide-based Paradise Community Assemblies of God church, won a seat in the South Australian Legislative Council. The party came to prominence federally during the 2004 election when it won a Senate seat for Victoria. There has been comment that the success of Family First at the 2004 federal election, as well as the fact that the Liberal Party's Louise Markus, who won the seat of Greenway from Labor, is a member of the Assemblies of God Hillsong Church in Sydney, heralds the emergence of the Christian Right as a force in Australian politics. This has proved not to be the case, as is evident from the results the party achieved at the 2007 election (Table 11.9).

TABLE 11.9

House of Representatives and Senate elections 2007: Family First's vote and seats won

Election	House of Representatives: percentage of first-preference votes	No. of seats won	Senate: percentage of first-preference votes	No. of seats won
2007	1.99	0	1.62	0

(*Source*: Australian Electoral Commission 2007, 'The Official 2007 Federal Election Results', http://results.aec.gov.au/13745/website/default.htm)

The Democratic Labor Party (www.dlp.org.au)

Democratic Labor Party in Australian parliaments, January 2008

Parliament	House	Seats
Victoria	MLC	1

The Democratic Labor Party (DLP) was formed as the result of a split within the Australian Labor Party in the mid-1950s. It was founded on anti-communism, with a strong Roman Catholic membership base. At the centre of all DLP policies seemed to be the view that in communism Australia faced a threat so great that all other interests and goals must take second place to the need to defeat it. The modern party's principles include support for the principles of democracy, liberty and peace (for full details see the party's website at http://www.dlp.org.au).

The party ceased to be politically effective when it lost its Senate representation at the 1974 double dissolution election. However, it continues to field candidates in federal elections and was successful in having a member elected to the Victorian Legislative Council in 2006, with the assistance of ALP preferences (see Table 11.10).

TABLE 11.10

House of Representatives and Senate elections 2007: Democratic Labor Party vote and seats won

Election	House of Representatives: percentage of first-preference votes	No. of seats won	Senate: percentage of first-preference votes	No. of seats won
2007	0.05	0	0.92	0

(*Source*: Australian Electoral Commission 2007, 'The Official 2007 Federal Election Results', http://results.aec.gov.au/13745/website/default.htm)

The Australian Shooters Party (http://www.shootersparty.org.au)

Australian Shooters Party in Australian parliaments: January 2008

Parliament	House	Seats
New South Wales	MLC	2

The Australian Shooters Party is a special issue party established in New South Wales in 1992 following the decision of the government at the time to ban self-loading firearms. The party believes it is the right of every Australian to be able to own and use a firearm for legitimate purposes, including self-defence and for recreational hunting. It supports other outdoor recreational pursuits, such as fishing and four-wheel driving, and believes that government should interfere less in people's lives. The party did not win any federal seats in the 2007 election (see Table 11.11).

> **'Reclaim freedom'**
> The motto of the Australian Shooters Party.

TABLE 11.11
House of Representatives and Senate elections 2007: Australian Shooters Party's vote

Election	House of Representatives: percentage of first-preference votes	No. of seats won	Senate: percentage of first-preference votes	No. of seats won
2007	n/a	n/a	0.30	0

(*Source*: Australian Electoral Commission 2007, 'The Official 2007 Federal Election Results', http://results.aec.gov.au/13745/website/default.htm)

SIGNIFICANT MINOR PARTIES NOT REPRESENTED IN AUSTRALIAN PARLIAMENTS

The following parties are interesting, either because they have played a significant role in the history of the Australian political system, or because they stood candidates at the 2007 election. They are examples of the breadth of philosophies and ideas that have led to the formation of minor parties in Australia.

Doctrinal parties

The Communist Party of Australia (http://www.cpa.org.au)

The Communist Party of Australia (CPA) is of interest because it has represented communist ideology in the Australian political system over a long period of time. The party was formed in 1921 and followed the line of the Communist International (Comintern) very soon after. Although never successful electorally in Australia, it built up a strong organisation in industrial unions during and after the 1930s. Its ideology was Marxist-Leninist: Australia was a capitalist society whose inequities could only be put right by a revolution, which would follow a class struggle led by the party. The details depended greatly on whatever was prescribed as orthodoxy in Moscow.

During the Second World War the ALP began to see the CPA as a threat to its own power base in the union movement, and organised against it. This was a costly battle for the ALP as it led to a split in that party in 1955, which led in turn to the formation of the Democratic Labor Party. It also caused problems for the CPA, intensified in the 'cold war' period that began in 1947 and by the changes in Russian leadership that followed the death of Stalin in 1953. The party split twice:

- The first split, in 1963, followed the breaking of the Sino-Soviet alliance, and resulted in the formation of the Communist Party of Australia (Marxist-Leninist).
- The second split, in 1971, followed dissatisfaction with the policies of the Soviet Union, especially the invasion of Czechoslovakia in 1968, and led to the takeover of the CPA by a new group and the establishment of the Socialist Party of Australia (SPA) by those who had been displaced.

While all claimed to be Marxist-Leninist parties, and to be the true or correct inheritor of that tradition:

- the CPA (Marxist-Leninist) followed the line put out from Peking (Beijing);
- the SPA followed the line put out from Moscow; and
- the CPA developed, in the manner of many other Western Communist parties, a variant which tried to be in tune with Australia's history and situation.

There were, in addition, a number of splinter groups pursuing this or that revolutionary policy, of which the best known were called 'Trotskyist' (after Leon Trotsky, exiled from the Soviet Union, who had argued unsuccessfully that the Soviet Union should export its revolution everywhere before consolidating the regime in Russia).

The CPA was dissolved in 1990 by its members. Some formed the New Left Party, which subsequently was also dissolved as it failed to develop sufficient support or to find an appropriate ideological niche. In 1996 the Socialist Party of Australia changed its name to the Communist Party of Australia.

> The CPA's objective is 'the socialist reconstruction of Australian society'. It believes Australia's economic and social problems can be overcome by replacing 'the capitalist system with a socialist one'.
> (*Source*: Communist Party of Australia 2006, 'An Introduction to the Communist Party of Australia', http://www.cpa.org.au/cpa/cpa.html)

The party has branches in all states except Tasmania. It stood candidates for the 2001 federal election, but not in 2004 or 2007.

The Socialist Alliance (http://www.socialist-alliance.org)

The revolutionary left is also represented by the Socialist Alliance, an alliance of socialist parties and individuals who support a common platform that seeks to replace capitalism with a socialist society. The Socialist Alliance stood candidates at the 2004 federal election and again in 2007 (see Table 11.12).

TABLE 11.12

House of Representatives and Senate elections 2007: Socialist Alliance's vote

Election	House of Representatives: percentage of first-preference votes	Senate: percentage of first-preference votes
2007	0.12	0.08

(*Source*: Australian Electoral Commission 2007, 'The Official 2007 Federal Election Results', http://results.aec.gov.au/13745/website/default.htm)

Socialist Alliance objectives

'The Alliance seeks to build a movement for change by developing policies, campaigns, industrial struggles and co-operation with all workers, environmental, anti-racist, and other social movements and to put forward an alternative to corporate control of society. A sustained mass campaign of total opposition to the ruling class offensive can bring together the forces to replace capitalism with a socialist society, based on co-operation, democracy and ecological sustainability.'

(*Source*: Socialist Alliance 2006, 'Constitution', http://www.socialist-alliance.org)

Socialist Equality Party (http://www.sep.org.au)

The Socialist Equality Party is the Australian section of the International Committee of the Fourth International which was established in the USSR by Leon Trotsky in 1938 in opposition to the Stalin regime. The party has branches in Sydney, Melbourne, Newcastle and Perth. It stood candidates for the Senate and the House of Representatives at the 2007 federal election with minimal results (see Table 11.13).

TABLE 11.13

House of Representatives and Senate elections 2007: Socialist Equality Party's vote

Election	House of Representatives: percentage of first-preference votes	Senate: percentage of first-preference votes
2007	0.03	0.04

(*Source*: Australian Electoral Commission 2007, 'The Official 2007 Federal Election Results', http://results.aec.gov.au/13745/website/default.htm)

Liberty and Democracy Party (http://www.ldp.org.au)

The Liberty and Democracy Party has its basis in liberal philosophy, including individual freedom and civil liberties, ethical and impartial government, individual liberty and the rule of law. Its policies also reflect the principles of economic liberalism, including support for low tax, limited public spending, minimal government regulation, the free market and free trade. The party stood candidates in the Senate election in 2007 (see Table 11.14).

TABLE 11.14

House of Representatives and Senate elections 2007: Liberty and Democracy Party vote

Election	House of Representatives: percentage of first-preference votes	Senate: percentage of first-preference votes
2007	n/a	0.13

(*Source*: Australian Electoral Commission 2007, 'The Official 2007 Federal Election Results', http://results.aec.gov.au/13745/website/default.htm)

Citizens Electoral Council (http://www.cecaust.com.au)

The Citizens Electoral Council (CEC) was established in Queensland in 1988. It is a follower of the US-based LaRouche organisation's belief that peace can be achieved through economic development. A sample of the party's policies include 'elimination of the GST', the establishment of a National Bank to provide loans at 2 per cent or less to agriculture, industry and infrastructure development, elimination of the National Competition Policy, reassertion of national control of Australia's mineral and oil and gas resources, and a 'dramatic expansion of resources to State public health facilities' (see Citizens Electoral Council 2008, 'Summary of the Fighting Platform', http://www.cecaust.com.au). The CEC stood candidates at the 2004 and 2007 federal elections (see Table 11.15).

TABLE 11.15

House of Representatives and Senate elections 2007: Citizens Electoral Council's vote

Election	House of Representatives: percentage of first-preference votes	Senate: percentage of first-preference votes
2007	0.22	0.07

(*Source*: Australian Electoral Commission 2007, 'The Official 2007 Federal Election Results', http://results.aec.gov.au/13745/website/default.htm)

CEC objectives

'A major contributing factor to the present economic collapse is the anti-human, bestial policies represented by the rock-drug-sex counterculture which took off in the 1960s. The "me first", "me only" policies championed by the counterculture, are precisely those also championed by the economic policies of globalisation, privatisation, etc.; indeed, the former has helped prepare the way for the latter. The CEC is committed, as is Mr LaRouche, to urgently re-establishing a new Golden Renaissance, based upon the Classical tradition in art and philosophy, where the creative powers of each individual are fostered, to the benefit of both the individual, and of the entire society.'

(*Source*: Citizens Electoral Council 2008, 'History and Philosophy of the Citizens Electoral Council', http://www.cecaust.com.au)

Issue parties: the environment

Climate Change Coalition (http://climatechangecoalition.com.au)

The Coalition was formed in New South Wales in 2006 to propose sustainable alternatives to the use of coal. The party believes that change can come about with the assistance of business and has a raft of objectives aimed at dealing with climate change (see Climate Change Coalition n.d., 'Climate Change Coalition Believes', http://climatechangecoalition.com.au). The party fielded candidates in the 2007 House of Representatives and Senate elections (see Table 11.16).

TABLE 11.16
House of Representatives and Senate elections 2007: Climate Change Coalition's vote

Election	House of Representatives: percentage of first-preference votes	Senate: percentage of first-preference votes
2007	0.08	0.62

(*Source*: Australian Electoral Commission 2007, 'The Official 2007 Federal Election Results', http://results.aec.gov.au/13745/website/default.htm)

Conservatives for Climate and Environment (http://www.cfce.org.au)

Conservatives for Climate and Environment is a party for conservatives with an interest in protecting the environment, addressing climate change, and taking a responsible approach to social issues while at the same time supporting a strong, enterprising economy. (See their website for detailed information on their policies.) The party stood candidates in the 2007 election for the House of Representatives and the Senate (see Table 11.17).

TABLE 11.17
House of Representatives and Senate elections 2007: Conservatives for Climate and Environment's vote

Election	House of Representatives: percentage of first-preference votes	Senate: percentage of first-preference votes
2007	0.03	0.08

(*Source*: Australian Electoral Commission 2007, 'The Official 2007 Federal Election Results', http://results.aec.gov.au/13745/website/default.htm)

Issue parties: recreation

Australian Fishing and Lifestyle Party (http://www.fishingparty.com.au)

This party was established to represent fishing enthusiasts and other recreational users to ensure that government restrictions do not impede their activities, including access to national and marine parks. At the same time, its members argue that government legislation that affects fishing and recreational activities should be fair, equitable and environmentally responsible and sustainable. (See Australian Fishing and Lifestyle Party n.d., 'Mission Statement', http://www.fishingparty.com.au/Policies.htm). The party stood candidates at the 2007 election for the House of Representatives and the Senate (see Table 11.18). In New South Wales it was grouped with the Australian Shooters Party and secured 0.36 per cent of first-preference votes in that state.

TABLE 11.18
House of Representatives and Senate elections 2007: Australian Fishing and Lifestyle Party's vote

Election	House of Representatives: percentage of first-preference votes	Senate: percentage of first-preference votes
2007	0.02	0.20

(*Source*: Australian Electoral Commission 2007, 'The Official 2007 Federal Election Results', http://results.aec.gov.au/13745/website/default.htm)

Issue parties: social policy

What Women Want (http://whatwomenwant.org.au)
This party was established to promote greater political participation of women, including greater representation in Australian parliaments, to achieve 'woman and family friendly' policies. It stood candidates in the 2007 election for the House of Representatives and the Senate (see Table 11.19).

TABLE 11.19
House of Representatives and Senate elections 2007: What Women Want's vote

Election	House of Representatives: percentage of first-preference votes	Senate: percentage of first-preference votes
2007	0.03	0.46

(*Source*: Australian Electoral Commission 2007, 'The Official 2007 Federal Election Results', http://results.aec.gov.au/13745/website/default.htm)

Carers Alliance (http://www.carers.org.au)
This party was formed to seek political recognition of the issues and problems facing family carers and people with disabilities. Its aims and objectives can be found on its website. The party stood candidates for the 2007 Senate election (see Table 11.20).

TABLE 11.20
House of Representatives and Senate elections 2007: Carers Alliance's vote

Election	House of Representatives: percentage of first-preference votes	Senate: percentage of first-preference votes
2007	n/a	0.19

(*Source*: Australian Electoral Commission 2007, 'The Official 2007 Federal Election Results', http://results.aec.gov.au/13745/website/default.htm)

Non-Custodial Parents Party (Equal Parenting) (http://ncpp.xisle.info)

Family law and child support issues were the concerns that prompted the establishment of this party in 1998. Since 2001 it has focused solely on federal elections. In 2007 it fielded candidates for two seats in the House of Representatives and for the Senate in New South Wales, Victoria, Queensland and Western Australia (see Table 11.21).

TABLE 11.21
House of Representatives and Senate elections 2007: Non-Custodial Parents Party's (Equal Parenting) vote

Election	House of Representatives: percentage of first-preference votes	Senate: percentage of first-preference votes
2007	0.01	0.05

(*Source*: Australian Electoral Commission 2007, 'The Official 2007 Federal Election Results', http://results.aec.gov.au/13745/website/default.htm)

Secessionist parties

Hear Our Voice (http://www.tonimclennan.com)

This party was founded by Toni McLennan after she failed to gain preselection for the ALP for the seat of Eden-Monaro in the 2007 federal election. The reasons for establishing the party and its objectives can be found on the website. The party stood a ticket of two candidates for the Senate, headed by Toni McLennan (see Table 11.22).

TABLE 11.22
House of Representatives and Senate elections 2007: Hear Our Voice's vote

Election	House of Representatives: percentage of first-preference votes	Senate: percentage of first-preference votes
2007	n/a	0.02

(*Source*: Australian Electoral Commission 2007, 'The Official 2007 Federal Election Results', http://results.aec.gov.au/13745/website/default.htm)

INDEPENDENTS IN THE AUSTRALIAN PARLIAMENT

What is an independent?

> **Independent**: a candidate for parliamentary election who does not represent any political party.

Given Australia's system of majority party government, why would electors vote for independents? After all, the only time that independents are likely to wield any influence over the policy process is when they hold the balance of power. Campbell Sharman has identified a set of factors that he considers facilitate the election of independent candidates to parliament:

- a strong engagement with a local community;
- a high profile, preferably associated with political activity;
- an objection to party discipline;
- a candidate selection procedure by the dominant major political party in the district that does not accommodate local preferences; and
- a dominant major party in the district becoming locked into policies that are seen to run against local interests (for example, the situation experienced by the Nationals as minority partner in a coalition government with the Liberals).

(*Source*: Sharman, C. 2002, 'Politics at the Margin: Independents and the Australian Party System', Senate Occasional Lecture, 17 May 2002, p. 14)

As we can see from Tables 11.23 and 11.24, over the past 20 years the number of independents elected to Australian parliaments has increased.

TABLE 11.23

Independents in Australian parliaments in the 1980s

Parliament	House	Seats
New South Wales, 1988	MLA	7
South Australia, 1985	MHA	3
Tasmania, 1986	MHA	2

TABLE 11.24

Independents in Australian parliaments, 2008

Parliament	House	Seats
Australian parliament	House of Representatives	2
	Senate	1
New South Wales	MLA	6
Victoria	MLA	1
Queensland	MLA	4
South Australia	MHA	3
	MLC	2
Western Australia	MLA	3
Tasmania	MLC	11
Northern Territory	MLA	2

An interesting facet of this has been the fact that, unlike minor parties, independents have held seats in the House of Representatives, and two were elected in 2007.

No independents were elected to the Senate at the 2004 federal election. This can be explained in part by the fact that Senator Brian Harradine, who was first elected in 1975 as an independent, did not seek re-election in 2004. The other two independents, Meg Lees and Shane Murphy, were elected to the Senate as party representatives and subsequently defected to sit on the cross benches. In 2004, Murphy stood as an independent and Meg Lees as a candidate for the Australian Progressive Alliance party, but neither was successful.

In 2007, independent Nick Xenophon was elected to the Senate from South Australia. He had formerly been a member of the South Australian Legislative Council as a member of the 'No Pokies' party.

Characteristics that independents have in common with political parties

In many respects, independents function in very much the same way as political parties. They:

- mediate information from the voters;
- focus attention on channelling voter opinion and evaluation of policy issues;
- shape voter preference in terms of their platform;
- recruit political personnel and present candidates to the electorate under their banner; and
- have an organisation that has taken an active part in elections, including assistance in election funding, campaigning and supporting the candidate by active propaganda.

(*Source*: Maurice Duverger, cited in Holler, M.J. 1987, 'An Introduction to the Logic of Multiparty Systems', in Holler, M.J. (ed.), *The Logic of Multiparty Systems*, Martinus Nijhoff, Dordrecht, Netherlands, p. 25)

Independents cannot rely on party identification to maintain their vote in the electorate. To enhance their prospects for re-election, it is therefore in their best interest to stay true to their ideals, support the promises and policies on which they campaigned, and look after the interests of their constituents.

The cost of mounting an election campaign can be a significant deterrent to individuals who want to stand as independent candidates.

> ### The cost of an independent campaign
> 'Independent candidates need a campaign war chest of at least $100,000 if they're to have any hope of winning a seat in federal Parliament . . . Between them, Nick Xenophon, Tony Windsor and Queensland's Bob Katter spent just under a combined $416,000 on advertising, how to vote cards, pamphlets, posters, direct mailing and opinion polling.'
> (*Source*: 'Want to run for parliament? Got $100,000?', *Brisbane Times*, 13 May 2008)

Independents and ideology

The way that party members vote in parliament is restricted by the conditions of their party membership—in particular, party discipline, which constrains them from voting in parliament against their party. It might be thought that independents, by comparison, who do not have to toe any party line, would be free to support or oppose the government's policy and legislation as they wish. This is true to some extent, but there are factors associated with the politics of getting re-elected that may constrain how they vote. These include:

- seeking to do what they perceive the constituency wants; and
- acting according to what they believe is best for the welfare of their constituents.

(*Source*: Pitkin, H.F. 1967, *The Concept of Representation*, University of California Press, Berkeley, p. 147)

Ted Mack, a former independent member of the House of Representatives, fits this profile. He was committed to meeting local community needs and cast his vote in the House of Representatives accordingly. Only where this was unclear did he make a private choice.

Ideology, or a set of principles that the independent believes in, is also an important factor in determining how his or her vote is cast. An independent may be elected for a variety of reasons. The electorate may be registering a protest vote against the party system. The independent may be a disaffected former member of a major party who has strong personal support in the electorate, or a local personality with strong links to the community. There may be particular interests or issues that have strong support within the electorate, and the independent may be a strong proponent of these issues. Regardless of why they put themselves forward for election, independents have a set of ideas, or ideology, in the sense of what they 'stand for', and a particular view of a good society and how to achieve it. That view of the world, or ideology, is presumably supported by the voters in the electorate who vote for the candidate, and they would expect him or her to vote in the parliament accordingly.

Independent Tasmanian senator Brian Harradine provides us with a good example of someone who maintained voter support at elections between 1975 and 2001 because he consistently supported a set of principles. He also delivered for his constituents by using his position, when he held the balance of power, to gain benefits for his state of Tasmania.

Some senators or members of the House of Representatives, although elected as members of a political party, have resigned from their party during their term of office and sat on the cross benches as independents. This does not necessarily mean that their votes will become more fluid, because they are likely to continue to support the principles that attracted them to the party in the first place. Members who have resigned from a political party because they have strong views on certain issues, and who successfully stand for re-election as independents, such as Bob Katter, will cast their votes on the basis of those views when particular issues arise, but are not likely to discard the general principles and philosophy of the party they have left.

> 'Bob is now free to vote in line with his conscience and the feelings and needs of the people of the electorate, without being restricted by party lines and politics.'
> (*Source*: Bob Katter 2007, 'About your MP', http://www.bobkatter.com.au/aboutbob.html)

Governments who need to obtain the votes of independents to get their legislation passed need to take these factors into consideration as a basis for negotiation.

Organisation

Like political parties, independents develop an organisation to provide support for their campaign. Independents need a group of dedicated voluntary workers to assist them during election campaigns and between elections. This may not be as formal as the organisational structure of a political party, but will perform many of the same types of functions—door knocking, fund-raising and handing out how-to-vote cards on election day.

> 'A huge thank you to all my supporters, volunteers and staff for their massive contribution to a successful campaign!'
> (Source: Nick Xenophon, independent senator 2007, 'Thank you from Nick!', http://www.xen.net.au)

Some independent candidates for the Senate have registered a slate, or group, of candidates to enhance their electoral prospects. A group is included 'above the line' so that voters can tick the box, rather than filling in a complete set of preferences below the line.

It is interesting to note from the following profiles of the two independent members of the House of Representatives that one is a former Nationals member of the House of Representatives, and one was formerly a member of the New South Wales parliament.

Robert Katter MP, Member for Kennedy (Qld)
Personal
- Born 22 May 1945 at Cloncurry, Queensland.
- Married.

Parliamentary service
- *State*: Elected to the Queensland Legislative Assembly for Flinders, 7 December 1974. Retired 25 August 1992.
- *Federal*: Elected to the House of Representatives for Kennedy, Queensland, 1993, 1996 and 1998 representing the Nationals. Elected as an independent in 2001, 2004 and 2007.

Ministerial appointments, Queensland parliament
- *State*: Minister for Northern Development and Aboriginal and Islander Affairs, 1983–87.
- Minister for Northern Development, Community Services and Ethnic Affairs, 1987–89.
- Minister for Community Services and Ethnic Affairs, January–August 1989.
- Minister for Mines and Energy, September–December 1989.
- Minister for Northern and Regional Development, September–December 1989.

Qualifications and occupation before entering federal parliament
- Labourer; insurance, small mining and cattle interests.
- Military service: Second Lieutenant, Citizen Military Forces (CMF).
- Member, Queensland Legislative Assembly, 1974–92 (see above).

(See also http://www.bobkatter.com.au)

Tony Windsor MP, Member for New England (New South Wales)
Personal
- Born 2 September 1950 at Quirindi, New South Wales.
- Married.

Parliamentary service
- *State*: Elected to the New South Wales Legislative Assembly for Tamworth, 25 May 1991. Resigned 16 October 2001.
- *Federal*: Elected to the House of Representatives for New England, New South Wales, 2001, 2004 and 2007.

Qualifications and occupation before entering federal parliament
- BEc (New England).
- Farmer.
- Member, New South Wales Legislative Assembly, 1991–2001 (see above).

(See also http://www.tonywindsor.com.au)

QUESTIONS FOR DISCUSSION

1. The history of minor parties in Australia indicates it is difficult for them to grow into a major party. What are the reasons for this? Do you think it is inevitable that this will continue?
2. Minor parties and/or independents held the balance of power in the Senate between 1981 and 2005 and have done so again from 1 July 2008. Some people think this is good for Australian democracy, while others disagree. What do you think is the basis of these arguments and which do you consider most persuasive? Give your reasons.
3. Given the problems the Nationals have had in maintaining a separate identity when in government with the Liberals, why does it stay in the coalition? What are the alternatives?
4. What makes Green parties different from environmental groups?
5. What difficulties do minor parties and independents face in having an influence on government? Under what conditions could this be overcome?
6. How independent are independents?

FURTHER READING

Minor parties

Bennett, S. 1999, 'The Decline in Support for Australian Major Parties and the Prospect of Minority Government', Research Paper No. 10, 1998–99, Parliamentary Library, Canberra, http://www.aph.gov.au/library/pubs/rp/.

Christoff, P. 1994, 'Environmental Politics', in Brett, J., Gillespie, J. & Goot, M. (eds), *Developments in Australian Politics*, Macmillan, Melbourne. A contemporary look at the impact of the environment movement on Australian politics.

Denemark, D. & Bowler, S. 2002, 'Minor Parties and Protest Votes in Australia and New Zealand: Locating Populist Politics', *Electoral Studies*, vol. 21, no. 1, pp. 47–67.

Gardiner, J. & Ferguson, C. 1996, 'Women and the National Party of Australia', in Simms, M. (ed.), *The Paradox of Parties: Australian Political Parties in the 1990s*, Allen & Unwin, Sydney. An article written by a National Party MP and the federal director of the National Party about the role of women in the party.

Jaensch, D. & Mathieson, D. 1998, *A Plague on Both Your Houses: Minor Parties in Australia*, Allen & Unwin, Sydney. An analysis of minor parties in the Australian political system, although it does not include Pauline Hanson's One Nation.

Leach, M., Stokes, G. & Ward, I. (eds) 2000, *The Rise and Fall of One Nation*, University of Queensland Press, Brisbane. This book discusses the importance of One Nation, analysing its failure at the 1998 federal election and subsequent problems within the party.

Macklin, M. 1996, 'The Australian Democrats—a Major "Minor" Party—Face the Future', in Simms, M. (ed.), *The Paradox of Parties: Australian Political Parties in the 1990s*, Allen & Unwin, Sydney. Argues that minor parties will always be with us and will form and reform in various combinations.

Marsh, I. 2000, 'Political Integration and the Outlook for the Australian Party System: Party Adaptation or System Mutation', in Boreham, P., Stokes, G. & Hall, R. (eds), *The Politics of Australian Society: Political Issues for the New Century*, Pearson Education, Sydney. Discusses reasons for weakened voter support for major parties and the political challenge of minor parties and independents.

Tilby Stock, J. 2006, 'Greens, Democrats, Minor Parties and Independents', in Parkin, A, Summers, J. & Woodward, D. (eds), *Government, Politics, Power and Policy in Australia*, 8th ed., Pearson Education, Sydney.

Warhurst, J. (ed.) 1997, *Keeping the Bastards Honest*, Allen & Unwin, Sydney. An edited collection of articles examining the history, internal party organisation, ideology and parliamentary performance of the Australian Democrats.

Woodward, D. 2006, 'National Party', in Parkin, A., Summers, J. & Woodward, D. (eds), *Government, Politics, Power and Policy in Australia*, 8th ed., Pearson Education, Sydney. Discusses the party's electoral support, its ideology and its coalition with the Liberals.

Independents

Costar, B. & Curtin, J. 2004, *Rebels with a Cause: Independents in Australian Politics*, UNSW Press, Sydney. An examination of independents in Australian politics.

Maddox, G. 1992, 'Political Stability, Independents and the Two Party System', *Current Affairs Bulletin*, vol. 69, no. 1, pp. 20–7.

USEFUL WEBSITES

http://www.apo.org.au

Australian Policy Online

See the resource guide, 'Independents in Australian Politics', accessible from http://www.apo.org.au/research_toolbox.shtml.

- **http://www.xen.net.au**
  Nick Xenophon
  Site for independent senator Nick Xenophon.

- **http://www.tonywindsor.com.au**
  Tony Windsor
  Site for independent House of Representatives MP, Tony Windsor.

- **http://www.bobkatter.com.au**
  Bob Katter
  Site for independent House of Representatives MP, Bob Katter

12

INTEREST GROUPS

THIS CHAPTER EXPLAINS:

- what interest groups are;
- why they are significant within the Australian political system;
- types of interest groups;
- the strategies used by interest groups to influence government;
- the relationship between groups and government;
- the distinction between 'insider' and 'outsider' groups;
- policy networks and policy communities;
- social movements; and
- interest groups and democracy.

WHY ARE INTEREST GROUPS IMPORTANT?

It is important to know about interest groups and how they function in the Australian political system, because they can provide citizens with an effective vehicle to make their policy demands known to government. There are benefits in joining with other people to make representations to government as a group, particularly those interest groups that are well-resourced and professional in their dealings with government. This includes individuals, employees or employers who have a particular interest they wish to pursue. If you are working in the public service or in a minister's office, you are likely to have dealings with these groups on a regular basis.

Interest groups provide an alternative means of participation in the political process to that provided by political parties. As we have seen in previous chapters, political parties that want to win government have to appeal to a broad range of citizens with many interests, so they are not likely to satisfy everyone's policy needs. The opportunity to express your policy preferences by voting for a particular party is restricted by the fact that elections are held at infrequent intervals. Membership of an interest group, by comparison, provides a more immediate and direct form of participation in the political process.

By joining a range of groups, citizens can express their views direct to government on a range of interests. This might include:

- a sporting club making representations to government for improved facilities;
- a parents' and citizens' group seeking more resources for education;
- a trade union working for better wages and conditions;
- a residents' group seeking better facilities for their suburb; and
- a group, such as Greenpeace, working to protect the environment.

The extent of participation in the political process through group participation is limited only by the number of interests of the individual concerned.

WHAT IS AN INTEREST GROUP?

> **Interest group**: a group formed to promote and protect a specific interest.

The terms *interest group* and *pressure group* are often used synonymously and interchangeably, and the distinction between them is rather fuzzy. A pressure group is said to devote its activities to the function of lobbying government, but all interest groups at some time are likely to make representations to government. We use the term *interest group* here because it gives a more clearly defined indication of the function of the group: that is, to articulate and promote the specific interests of its members, including the function of lobbying government.

> **Interest groups** are distinct from **political parties** in that they do not seek to hold office through parliamentary representation.

This difference between a political party and an interest group can sometimes seem confusing when interest groups, such as the Greens or a residents' action group, become involved in presenting candidates for election. Nevertheless, the distinction is clear when interest groups establish and register a political party in order to become involved in the electoral process. We can distinguish, therefore, between the interest group and the party that is formed for the purposes of seeking parliamentary representation. An example would be the interest groups promoting green issues, such as the Australian Wilderness Society, and the political parties that are an extension of those groups, such as the Australian Greens.

TYPES OF INTEREST GROUPS

Those who have studied interest groups and their place in politics have found it useful to categorise them according to their purpose. There are three main types:

1. *Promotional* groups promote a cause which they think everybody should favour. Charities, the Council for Civil Liberties, the RSPCA, and environmental or cultural groups are good examples. Membership is open and anyone is eligible to join.

> **RSPCA: objectives**
>
> 'The objectives of the RSPCA in Australia are:
> - To prevent cruelty to animals by ensuring the enforcement of existing laws at federal and state level.
> - To procure the passage of such amending or new legislation as is necessary for the protection of animals.
> - To develop and promote policies for the humane treatment of animals that reflect contemporary values and scientific knowledge.
> - To educate the community with regard to the humane treatment of animals.
> - To engage with relevant stakeholders to improve animal welfare.
> - To sustain an intelligent public opinion regarding animal welfare.
> - To operate facilities for the care and protection of animals.
>
> These objectives are supported by a federation of member Societies known as RSPCA Australia, a National Council and administration.'
>
> (*Source*: RSPCA 2008, 'Objectives', http://www.rspca.org.au/about/objectives.asp, reproduced with permission by RSPCA Australia)

Examples of promotional groups in other countries are:
— Britain: Friends of the Earth (http://www.foe.co.uk);
— USA: The National Organization for Women (http://www.now.org);
— Germany: Animal Peace (http://www.animal-peace.org); and
— Malaysia: Malaysian Nature Society (http://www.mns.org.my).

2. *Sectional* groups defend the interests of particular groups or sections in the community. Trade unions, employers' associations, farmers' organisations, gay liberation groups, black rights groups and similar groups all seem to fit this description. Membership is open only to those people—unionists, employers, farmers, and so on—from that particular section of the community.

> **National Farmers' Federation: mission**
> 'To influence the Commonwealth Government, Parliament and the broader community to achieve a strong, progressive and sustainable farming sector in Australia, through national and international representation and advocacy.'
> (*Source*: National Farmers' Federation 2008, 'Vision & Mission', http://www.nff.org.au/vision.html)

Sectional groups occur in most countries, for example:

— Britain: Trades Union Congress (http://www.tuc.org.uk);
— USA: Gay and Lesbian Activists Alliance (http://glaa.org);
— Germany: German Farmers' Association (http://www.bauernverband.de); and
— Malaysia: Malaysian Employers Federation (http://www.mef.org.my).

3 '*Hybrid*' groups seem to display aspects of both promotional and sectional groups. The RSL (http://www.rsl.org.au), as an example, devotes much of its energies to the care and protection of returned soldiers in need, but it also promotes a vigorous defence policy and was active in the 1999 republican debate. Church organisations, such as Churches Together in Britain and Ireland (http://www.ctbi.org.uk), could also be considered hybrid groups because they have a religious function and are also vocal on matters related to the general well-being of the community.

The German Federal Youth Ring (http://www.jugendserver.de) lobbies government on matters specifically related to youth concerns, as well as allied issues such as poverty eradication, energy policy and reform of the German federal system. In Malaysia, Sisters in Islam (http://www.sistersinislam.org.my) promotes the rights of women within the framework of Islam and addresses broader political issues of equality, justice and freedom.

Again, these distinctions break down if they are pushed too hard. All groups need to be able to argue persuasively, and that means finding a way in which the interests of one section of the community can be seen to be to everyone's advantage. Sectional groups in contemporary Australia, such as the trade unions and employer groups, speak out on just about every issue. Similarly, all groups need to find members and resources and this encourages a sectional approach, no matter how general the cause they promote. Green groups, for example, represent sections of the community concerned about the environment, as well as people who are interested in peace, social justice and direct democracy.

Peak organisations

Many interest groups join together with other groups who have a similar purpose to form an association, commonly called a 'peak' or 'umbrella' organisation. This enables them to strengthen their case to government on the basis that they can claim to speak for a broad constituency.

> Groups whose membership is made up from a number of representative interest groups are called '**umbrella**' or '**peak**' organisations.

Some examples include the Australian Chamber of Commerce and Industry, whose membership includes a number of employer groups; the Australian Council of Trade Unions, which represents nearly all of Australia's trade unions; and the Australian Council of Social Service, which includes groups from the welfare sector.

> **Australian Chamber of Commerce and Industry**
> The Australian Chamber of Commerce and Industry (ACCI) is a peak council of Australian business associations. Its membership network has over 350,000 businesses represented through Chambers of Commerce in each state and territory, and a nationwide network of industry associations. Through this network, 'each ACCI member organisation identifies the concerns of its members and plans united action. In this way business policies are developed and strategies for change are implemented. ACCI operates at a national and international level, making sure the concerns of business are represented to government at the federal level and to the community at large.'
> (*Source*: Australian Chamber of Commerce and Industry n.d., 'About Us', http://www.acci.asn.au/AboutUsMain.htm)

Other business peak bodies in Australia include:

- the National Farmers' Federation (http://www.nff.org.au);
- the Motor Trades Association of Australia (http://www.mtaa.com.au); and
- the Australian Industry Group (http://www.aigroup.asn.au), which represents 10,000 employers in manufacturing, construction, automotive, telecommunications, transport, labour hire and other industries.

In Britain, the Confederation of British Industry (CBI) (http://www.cbi.org.uk) is the peak employer representative organisation. In the United States, the US Chamber of Commerce (http://www.uschamber.com) is the peak body of hundreds of associations and thousands of local chambers representing over three million businesses, while the National Association of Manufacturers (http://www.nam.org) is the peak group for industry. In Germany, the Confederation of German Employers' Associations (BDA) (http://www.bda-online.de) represents German employers on issues relating to social policy, while the Federation of German Industries (BDI) (http://www.bdi-online.de) is the peak organisation for industrial business associations, representing 35 industry sector federations. The Malaysian Employers' Federation (http://www.mef.org.my) is the peak body for private-sector employers in Malaysia.

INTEREST GROUP STRATEGIES

> **Australian Conservation Foundation: campaign techniques**
> 'ACF's campaign techniques are as varied as the Australian environment. They include:
> - Face-to-face meetings with local farmers and pastoralists.
> - Collaborations with other environmental groups and local and Indigenous communities.
> - Using the media to get our message out to the general public.
> - Lobbying politicians at all levels of government.
> - Taking our message into the boardrooms of corporate Australia.
> - Arguing for the environment at international forums and meetings.
> - Taking part in direct actions "on the ground".'
> (*Source*: Australian Conservation Foundation 2008, 'Success Stories', http://www.acfonline.org.au)

There are a range of activities available to an interest group, and most established groups employ them all, to a greater or lesser degree. They include:

- *Meetings, advertisements, letters to the editor, interviews on television and radio current affairs programs*: Publicity activity is designed to gain attention for the group's demands from the public and the media, and therefore to acquire some status politically and give their issues priority on the government's agenda. Use of the mobile phone and the Internet enables groups to keep in touch with their members and to disseminate information about what their group is doing to the public at large.
- *Campaigning in elections in support of the group's policies*: This may include newspaper and television advertisements or issuing media releases. The focus may be negative—to defeat or help defeat an opponent or a party opposed to the group's aims—or positive, to ensure the success of the candidate preferred by the group. This is more likely to be successful when the preferences of a group's supporters could influence the results in marginal seats.
- *Negotiation with other groups and the building of alliances*: This is a perpetual activity for most groups, forever conscious of the magnitude of their task and the paucity of their resources. Groups seeking to build a broad base of support for their policy demands find it useful to create a network, or an alliance, with other groups. The National Farmers' Federation, for example, has worked closely with environmental groups over land care issues, while the Australian Chamber of Commerce and Industry has sought the support of other employer groups that are not members of their association, including small business groups, to enhance its representations to government.

> **Small Business Coalition (SBC)**
> This is an informal grouping of 27 industry associations in Australia with an interest in small business issues. Members are drawn from a wide range of trade, commerce, professional and industry associations. The SBC acts as a conduit to government on the views of the small business sector and plays an educative role with the small business community.
> The Australian Chamber of Commerce and Industry (http://www.acci.asn.org.au) provides the Secretariat for the Small Business Coalition.

- *Attracting members and funds*: Few groups can operate successfully, or at least for long, if they are little more than a name, although it is of the essence of groups to claim more support and power than they really possess. Well-established and well-funded groups can hire talented and effective people, while small groups have to rely on dedicated amateurs working in their spare time. The first business of any group, as of any organism, is survival, and membership and subscription drives consume a major part of most groups' energy. Many groups include a membership application facility on their websites so that people can join and pay their subscriptions online.
- *Research and analysis*: A significant key to success is to present government with well-researched and substantiated proposals or submissions that suggest solutions to a particular problem. The latter is regarded as more likely to be successful than a continuing stream of demands. Many groups employ research officers, including economists, to do this work for them, or hire specialist advice when required. Government looks also to specialist knowledge and expertise within the group when developing policy, and many

groups maintain offices in Canberra with expert staff to develop and maintain links to ministers and the public service.

- *Lobbying the bureaucracy*: Many policy proposals start life as a policy paper or cabinet submission drafted within the bureaucracy. Those groups with the contacts and the resources keep in constant touch with middle-level public servants responsible for gathering the information that forms the basis of these policy proposals. These bureaucrats may look also to groups for information and expertise on a particular issue.
- *Lobbying ministers*: Some groups see this as a strategy of 'last resort'. If you have to go to the minister, you have not been successful in persuading the relevant department to adopt your preferred policy. Ministers are busy people, so there is a limit to the number of groups they are able to see personally, which further restricts this as an effective tool of lobbying. Nevertheless, for those groups that do gain access, putting a case direct to the minister might influence that person in favour of the group's arguments.
- *Lobbying ministerial staff*: Most groups see this as a very important strategy. As we saw in Chapter 7, ministerial advisers act as gatekeepers between departments and the minister, and between groups and the minister. They influence who the minister sees and give advice to the minister on submissions from groups and departments. If the group can persuade the adviser that its policy proposal is worthwhile, there is a good chance that the minister will also agree.

Lobbying the Rudd Labor government

The following guidelines were issued by a consulting group specialising in government relations, to assist groups to engage effectively with the new Rudd Labor government.
- Get to know your local Labor member of parliament.
- Look up, read and understand Labor's policies.
- Forget the past—the Rudd government will pursue its own course.
- Get yourself and your business 'government-ready' by understanding what a Labor government is all about.
- Meet with MPs and ministers in an informal setting, join groups such as Progressive Business, and learn the art of the two-minute brief—but don't bore them to death when they have to mingle with guests.

(*Source*: Markstone Group 2007, 'Election 07', http://www.markstone.com.au/election07/)

- *Professional lobbyists*: Groups lacking the resources to maintain the necessary staff hire professional lobbyists to make representations to government on their behalf as the need arises. This is an expensive exercise, which means it is available only to those groups that have the financial resources to fund this activity. Groups with less money have to rely on their own lobbying initiatives, which may suffer from members not knowing who to access in the government, and a lack of professionalism in their submissions.

> The Rudd government has established a Register of Lobbyists (http://www.pmc.gov.au/lobbyistsregister). Ministers and their staff, and officers of the public service, are not permitted to have contact with lobbyists unless they are registered and comply with the Lobbying Code of Conduct. The United States, Germany, Canada and the European Parliament have similar arrangements in place.

- *Court action*: Groups, or individuals within groups, are able to take action in the courts. A significant example is the successful case brought by Eddie Mabo in 1991 on the issue of land rights for his people. The fact that it can cost a lot of money in legal fees, however, limits this type of action to those groups with the funds or those who are able to gain financial sponsorship from sympathetic members of the public to support taking the case to court.

Lobbying government in Australia is a significant business activity. The situation is similar in other countries.

> **US Chamber of Commerce**
> 'From its headquarters near the White House, the Chamber maintains a professional staff of more than 300 of the nation's top policy experts, lobbyists, lawyers, and communicators.'
> (*Source*: US Chamber of Commerce 2008, 'About Us', http://www.uschamber.com/about/)
>
> **Federation of German Industry (BDI)**
> 'The BDI is regarded as a leading centre of competence for economic policy in the Federal Republic of Germany. It has a unique concentration of expertise, thanks to the knowledge of the businessmen, who work for the BDI on a voluntary basis.' The BDI has separate departments to deal with policy issues such as energy, technology and innovation, environment, tax and transport.
> (*Source*: Federation of German Industry 2008, 'The BDI', http://www.bdi-online.de/en/3812.htm)
>
> **Confederation of British Industry (CBI)**
> The CBI employs 80 policy professionals working on 'issues that directly affect business', and 'over 65 committees representing a diverse cross section of industry, which work to influence Government Policy'.
> (*Source*: Confederation of British Industry 2008, http://www.cbi.org.uk)

GROUPS AND GOVERNMENT

The symbiotic relationship that can develop between interest groups and government is a significant factor in the political process.

> 'A **symbiotic relationship** is a mutually beneficial relationship between people, things or groups.'
> (*Source*: The Cassell Dictionary and Thesaurus 1999, Cassell, London, p. 1106)

So much of social and economic life is determined by government that the goals of interest groups can usually be achieved only through government action (or inaction). This may take the form of a new law or the repeal of an old one, the exercise of ministerial or administrative discretion, the promulgation of a regulation, the making of an appointment, or simply indefinite delay in the carrying out of a policy to which the group is opposed.

In the past, groups applied much of their pressure to political parties and members of parliament, promising benefits or penalties in return for support of their cause. In some instances the groups were formally allied to the parties, as many trade unions still are to the Australian Labor Party. However, as governments have grown more powerful and public services more extensive, groups began to appeal directly to governments—either to ministers or the public servants who serve them within the bureaucracy. Well-established groups know that they need to be able to negotiate with the government regardless of which party is in power. This explains why farmers' organisations disentangled themselves from both the Liberal and the National parties after Labor gained office in 1983. Unions have not acted in a similar fashion with respect to the ALP because they have more to gain from a Labor government, although some white-collar unions have chosen deliberately not to affiliate with the party.

At the same time, interest groups provide an invaluable service to governments. Their very existence alerts governments to a source of unhappiness in the electorate, while their communications and demands supply the detail. Those groups that have developed a sound research capability find it most beneficial to present government with a solution to its problems (and those of the group, coincidentally!), rather than raise issues that require problem solving by government.

While the activities of groups allow political problems to come to the surface quickly, if there are a number of competing groups with different views, governments can avoid unpleasant decisions for a time by playing one group off against another (for example, importers against exporters, producers against consumers).

At times, governments can use groups to try out policy ideas and to act as agents for the government within the group's constituencies.

> The Hawke and Keating Labor governments used their incomes Accord (1983–96) with the trade union movement to achieve wage restraint.

Groups that have too close an association with government, however, run the risk of being made captive to the government's interests and of ceasing to represent those who sponsor or belong to them.

Politics is very much the interplay of parties, groups and governments, and indeed there have been some political scientists who have argued that there is no politics without groups.

> A.F. Bentley, acknowledged as the originator of group theory, pointed out that groups and interests are all the same—simply so many people bound together in or along the path of certain activity.
> (*Source:* Bentley, A.F. 1967 (1908), *The Process of Government*, University of Chicago Press, Chicago)

In Australia, interest groups, like political parties, are phenomena mostly of the 20th and 21st centuries. However, whereas parties serve in part to make sense of the complexity of government, groups serve to promote this or that special interest which is of great importance to their own members. Governments in democratic societies are supposed to govern for the general good, yet they are faced with a plethora of groups, each making its own demands, sometimes in conflict with the demands of other groups. Examples of this type of conflict include groups in favour of abortion versus groups opposed to abortion, or trade unions seeking a greater share of the profits of a business for the workers versus employers who want to retain those profits for the shareholders.

How, then, does government deal with this situation when making its policy choices? Some have argued that in a liberal democracy such as Australia, a pluralist system is the best way of managing group activity.

> **Pluralism**: a process where political power is dispersed and policy is the product of government mediation and adjudication between the demands of competing groups.

According to this line of argument, political power is dispersed between a wide range of groups that have access to government and are able to influence the decision-makers in government, who then make decisions based on what is best for the 'national interest'. But we do not live in an ideal world. Some groups have greater resources and are better placed to influence government, and in practice the distinction between national and sectional interests is often hazy, for several reasons:

- It can be argued that governments are simply another kind of interest group with their own perspectives and priorities. Parties in power pretty obviously make decisions from time to time that are calculated to keep them in power, whatever the national interest.
- The 'national interest' is a value-laden term and can be hard to distinguish in a particular case. Governments and groups may justify a course of action on the grounds that it is in the 'national interest' in order to garner public support for what they intend to do, when in reality it is designed to meet their own specific needs. Sections of Australia's manufacturing industry argued in the past, for example, that maintaining a high level of tariff protection was in the national interest because it would protect employment, but high tariff rates also protected those companies from overseas competitors and enabled them to remain profitable.
- If the 'national' or 'public' interest is defined strictly, it may be impossible to find any decision that is in everyone's interests. Those who have installed a septic system at their own expense, for example, will not benefit from a sewerage system; populations are not wholly united even about government policies related to defence and national security issues. Some people supported Australia's involvement with the war in Iraq, while others were opposed to it.

It follows that people and groups benefit or are disadvantaged in different degrees from every decision of government. It is impossible, when governments are making decisions about resource allocation, to satisfy everyone. Thus, even when governments believe they are acting in the national interest, they are always acting in the interests of certain individuals, classes or groups. This has led to suggestions that group politics inevitably lodges political power with powerful elites in society—that is, those who have an advantage in terms of resources or strategic location within the economy.

> **Elitism**: the concentration of political power in the hands of a privileged group.

Marxism, for example, considers it is inevitable that the state will act as the agent for employers in a society that relies for its sustenance on the capitalist class. This is a persuasive argument, especially when we see governments making decisions on economic policy that are designed to enhance the prospects for business to improve productivity and profitability.

Powerful, sectional, economic groups are often granted privileged and regular access to government, a process that has been associated with corporatism.

> **Corporatism**: the practice of giving peak representative organisations with a strategic role in the economy, such as business and trade unions, a say in the making of economic policy, in return for the compliance of their members in its implementation.

The tripartite consultative councils, including representatives from business and industry, established to advise the Hawke Labor government on industry policy could be regarded as a form of corporatism.

It should be borne in mind, however, that economic groups do not always dominate the policy agenda in Australia. The power of business is tempered by the fact that governments in a liberal democracy have to accumulate a majority of votes to gain political power. This provides other groups with the resources to gain voter support for their cause and to enhance their potential to influence government.

The fact that groups tend to produce opponents also limits the accretion of political power by the business sector—particularly in those instances where contending groups can mobilise voter support for their cause. Examples in recent years have been the successes of environmental lobby groups in persuading some state governments to extend areas of national parks at the expense of logging, despite aggressive campaigns on the part of the forestry industry. Green groups that campaigned at the 1983 election against the building of the Franklin Dam in Tasmania by asking voters to mark 'no dams' on their ballot papers, encouraged the incoming Hawke government to use its constitutional power to stop that project going ahead.

The trade union movement's influence as a sectional, economic group has been weakened in recent years by the fall in union membership and changes to wage-setting processes that have reduced the bargaining power of trade unions.

It is a fact of political life, however, that governments do give some groups privileged access and preference over others when developing policy. This has led to suggestions that the system is divided into groups that are 'inside the loop' and working with government, compared to others that are on the 'outside' and trying to get government to listen to what they have to say.

INSIDERS AND OUTSIDERS

'Insider' groups

'Insider' groups serve as sources of advice to government and are consulted on a regular basis, either informally or through membership of government advisory bodies. These groups are more likely to be able to get an appointment to meet with the minister and maintain regular contact with the public servants who are responsible for developing policy. A great deal of regulatory activity is conducted through statutory organisations of all kinds (see Chapter 7), and selected interest groups are likely to be included in the membership of these boards, committees and tribunals by government. In this way, groups become closely linked to government.

> **'Insider' groups:**
> - are recognised by government as legitimate spokespersons for particular interests or causes;
> - engage in a dialogue with government on issues of concern to them; and
> - implicitly agree to abide by certain rules of the game, or face political exclusion.
>
> (*Source*: Grant, W. 2004, 'Pressure Politics: the Changing World of Pressure Groups', *Parliamentary Affairs*, vol. 57, no. 2, p. 408)

Sectional groups that are significant to Australia's economic prosperity are most likely to be given insider status. The Rudd government established a Business Advisory Council to facilitate consultation with the business sector. The Australian Government's Hazardous Waste Policy Reference Group is a consultative forum that includes representatives from industry, trade unions, environment and overseas development groups. Meat & Livestock Australia (http://www.mla.com.au) consults with the peak councils within the industry to develop its annual operating plan. Industry bodies make up the membership of the National Wool Alliance (http://www.daff.gov.au), which is responsible for coordinating a national wool strategy.

Groups representing significant social groups are also consulted by government. The National President of the Country Women's Association of Australia is a member of an expert panel established by the Rudd government to review the social impact of drought (http://www.daff.gov.au/agriculture-food/drought). The Rudd government also aims to facilitate consultation with the Muslim community through the establishment of a Muslim Advisory Panel.

> The potential for economic-based groups to influence government successfully is enhanced by their usefulness to government.

Organisations that represent the business sector usually have 'insider' status and are involved in formal consultation with government.

- The Australian Chamber of Commerce and Industry (ACCI) has regular contact with government and is included on government advisory bodies and committees

looking at issues that are relevant to business interests, such as the National Workplace Relations Consultative Council and the Australian Safety and Compensation Council.
- The Australian Industry Group (Ai Group), whose primary focus is the manufacturing sector, has similar relations with government. For example, it is represented on the National Workplace Relations Consultative Council (as are the Master Builders Association and the National Farmers' Federation).
- The Motor Trades Association of Australia (MTAA) is represented on the Motor Vehicle Theft Reduction Council and the ACCC Small Business Advisory Group.
- British business groups, such as the CBI, are involved in giving policy advice through their membership of government advisory committees (see Forman, F.N. & Baldwin, N.D.J. 2007, *Mastering British Politics*, 5th ed., Palgrave Macmillan, Basingstoke, UK p. 135).

  — The Association of British Mining Equipment Companies (http://www.abmec.org.uk), for example, provides the chair and secretariat for meetings of the Indo British Coal Forum and is a representative on bodies responsible for equipment standards in the coal industry.
  — The CBI was co-chair of a round table with public-sector departments and agencies, discussing proposals for a structured partnership between the public and private sectors on information assurance issues. The CBI was also involved with the Trades Union Congress and the Department for Business, Enterprise and Regulatory Reform in preparing a statement about the role of modern union representatives (http://www.cbi.org.uk).

- In Germany, employer and labour associations are involved formally in government institutions responsible for administering a range of government policies, a process associated with the principles of corporatism described above. For example, employee and employer associations are members of the Board of Governors and the Executive Board of the German Federal Labour Office, which is responsible for the administration of labour market policies such as employment and training schemes, job placement, payment of unemployment benefits and vocational guidance. The Confederation of German Employers Association is an employer representative on bodies that administer the social security system. Representatives of employer and union organisations sit on the supervisory boards of employee pension and sickness funds.
- The relationship between business and government in Malaysia is different because it is characterised by government patronage and cronyism between politicians and business owners, which has created a situation commonly known as 'Malaysia Inc.' (see, for example, Funston, J. 2001, 'Malaysia', in Funston, J. (ed.), *Government and Politics in Southeast Asia*, Institute of Southeast Asia Studies, Singapore, p. 19). The result is a system of government–business relations that bears the hallmarks of 'money politics' and 'political business' (Gomez, E.T. 2002, 'Political Business in Malaysia', in Gomez, E.T. (ed.), *Political Business in East Asia*, Routledge, London) because of the links between large corporations and companies, and UMNO, the dominant party in the ruling coalition, Barisan Nasional.
- The situation in the United States is somewhat different again, principally because of the large number of diverse business groups vying for government attention. In 2004,

there were 34,000 trade associations listed at state and national level in the US (Vile, M.J.C. 2007, *Politics in the USA*, 6th ed., Routledge, New York. p. 109). Major corporations also undertake their own lobbying activities direct with the president, members of congress and departments of state. Business associations and companies fund congressional candidates they consider sympathetic to business interests through Political Action Committees (PACs), and lobby individual members of Congress to support legislation favourable to their interests. They also lobby the presidential branch and the bureaucracy.

The fact that there are thousands of interest groups who maintain offices in Washington, lobby members of congress and the bureaucracy, and fund candidates through PACs suggests a relatively open, pluralistic system of group–government activity, but some groups do develop ongoing relationships with congressional members and departments that give them substantial influence over policy. This is not organised within formal types of corporatist frameworks such as those discussed above, but the formation of stable alliances has led to suggestions about the development of 'iron triangles' or 'sub-governments' in the policy process. (See Jordan, G. 1981, 'Issue Networks, Iron Triangles and Elastic Nets: Images of the Policy Process', *Journal of Public Policy*, no. 1, pp. 95–123.)

This does not mean, however, that cause or promotional groups, or those who do not have an economic base, are always excluded. For example, governments consult regularly with environmental groups because protection of the environment is an important political issue. The Australian Conservation Foundation, for example, may be included on government advisory bodies as a peak group representing the environmental lobby. A large number of promotional groups have offices in Canberra so that they can maintain regular contact with the federal government and its agencies.

Recfish Australia

Recfish Australia is the peak national and sport fishing organisation that represents around 3.5 million Australian fishers: 'As an angler Recfish Australia is your voice at the Federal level of Government to make sure that recreational and sport fishing gets a fair hearing and our concerns and needs are addressed regarding environmental, sport, habitat, access, allocation, protection, disease, importation and a host of other issues.'

(*Source*: Recfish Australia 2008, http://www.recfish.com.au/index.html)

Having 'insider' status does not automatically mean that government will accede to a group's demands, because, as we have seen, the political process is a complex one, with government facing the demands of contending groups and having to take into account the electoral impact of a policy decision. Wyn Grant has suggested a sub-division of the 'insider' category to take account of the different types of relationships that exist 'within the loop':

- 'core' insider groups dealing with a broad range of issues;
- 'specialist' insider groups in policy niches; and
- 'peripheral' insiders with little influence.

(*Source*: Grant, W. 2004, 'Pressure Politics: the Changing World of Pressure Groups', *Parliamentary Affairs*, vol. 57, no. 2, p. 409)

Grant points out (p. 410) that an 'insider' group may also undertake the type of activities more commonly used by 'outsider' groups, such as demonstrations and gaining publicity in the media for their particular cause. He provides the example of Greenpeace, which uses 'wet suit' strategies such as protest demonstrations, as well as 'business suit' activities, to discuss its policy demands with government. The trade union movement in Australia is an 'insider' group that also uses direct industrial and political action to promote its policy demands.

'Outsider' groups

> **'Outsider' groups** can be divided into two categories:
> - those who would like to become insider groups, but lack the necessary resources or skills to gain recognition; and
> - protest groups that by choice do not want to be drawn into the embrace of government.
>
> (Source: Grant, W. 2004, 'Pressure Politics: the Changing World of Pressure Groups', *Parliamentary Affairs*, vol. 57, no. 2, p. 409)

'Outsider' groups do not have privileged access or a close relationship with government. They are at a disadvantage because they lack financial resources and personnel and rely on direct action by their members, such as protests and demonstrations, to get publicity and thus gain government attention for their policy demands. These groups are more likely to fall into the promotional or cause category, but this is not always the case. Some economic groups have difficulty maintaining a position 'inside the loop' if their interests are not shared by the government of the day or they fall out of favour for some reason.

The focus of the activities of some 'outsider' groups is often the community as much as the government. The RSPCA, for example, fosters certain values within the community about the protection of animals, and tries to persuade the government to act according to these values where that is appropriate. A group that can convince government of the broad public support for their cause is more likely to get a sympathetic hearing. By comparison, groups that espouse a view that splits community opinion, such as the Right to Life Association, will find it more difficult to get government action on their demands, because governments tend to shy away from issues where there are as many votes to be lost as won.

It is possible for a group promoting a cause to be successful in influencing government policy through direct action and lobbying strategies. The campaigns waged by the women's movement for equal opportunity and by green groups for environmental protection are good examples. The potential for success is enhanced if groups can convince a government that there are votes available to the party that supports their cause. The Greens, for example, have used the preferential voting system to bargain their second-preference votes in return for environmentally friendly policy promises. During the 2007 federal election campaign, the National Council of Churches in Australia (http://www.ncca.org.au) produced an election briefing kit, including its views on a range of policies such as Work Choices, Indigenous Australians, climate change, housing and refugees for its members to use as a reference point for lobbying parties and candidates.

POLICY NETWORKS

Networking is a significant feature of the relationship between interest groups and government. These networks can develop formally or informally. The formal process includes membership of government advisory bodies or consultative committees. The informal process includes the capacity to discuss matters with ministers or senior bureaucrats over the telephone or at personal meetings. It also includes the social round of lunches and dinners, where contacts are made and policy issues are discussed. Interest groups engaged in this type of relationship are generally those with the 'insider' status referred to above and, as a result, can have a substantial, and ongoing, impact on government policy.

This form of interaction between groups and government is often referred to as a policy network.

> **Policy network**: a relationship involving a particular set of actors, including interest groups, ministers and government agencies, that forms around a policy area or policy issue.

The term *policy network* covers a variety of group–government relationships. Policy networks can be highly integrated with stable relationships, such as the corporatist processes referred to above, where the membership is restricted to particular groups and government representatives, and other groups and the public are excluded from the policy process. Policy networks can also be organised among groups to lobby the government.

> **Australian Industry & Defence Network (AIDN)**
> 'AIDN will provide the focal point for Defence's interaction with Australia's dynamic base of smaller defence companies.'
> (*Source*: Australian Industry & Defence Network 2005, 'Our Mission', http://www.aidn.org.au)

They can also be organised by government to facilitate consultation.

> **Communicable Diseases Network Australia (CDNA)**
> The functions of the CDNA include developing policy on the control of communicable diseases, and providing policy advice in this area to the Australian government. Its membership comprises representatives from Australian, state and territory governments, key organisations in the field, and others with relevant expertise.
> (*Source*: Department of Health and Ageing 2008, 'Communicable Diseases Network Australia', http://www.health.gov.au)

In Germany, for example, the Federation of German Industry works closely with the Confederation of German Employers' Associations and other umbrella groups to decide on common policy objectives that will enhance their influence with government. The same activity occurs in the United States.

Networks can also take a more pluralistic form. This occurs when the membership of the network is fluid and open to a number of groups, and the process—rather than being stable and long-term—is more ad hoc. In this type of arrangement, a number of groups might come together to work with or lobby government on a particular policy matter and then disband when the issue has been resolved. An example would be the working arrangement between the National Farmers' Federation and the Australian Conservation Foundation on land care policy. On other issues, these two groups may be involved in opposing networks, competing for the ear of government. In the lead-up to the 2007 federal election, several business groups got together to advertise their support for the Howard government's Work Choices system.

> 'Regulatory policies which require coercion or cooption of business are likely to develop closed networks involving the relevant sector of industry or peak organisations.
>
> The contestation involved in distributive and redistributive policies is more likely to extend membership of the network to outside interests.'
> (*Source*: Guy Peters, B. 1992, 'The Policy Process: an Institutionalist Perspective', *Canadian Public Administration*, vol. 35, no. 2, p. 169)

Policy communities

Some policy analysts have also identified the group–government relationship that develops around a policy issue as a *policy community*. There is some difference of opinion about the form that a policy community might take. Some argue that they include all the groups with shared interests in a policy area that are able to have an influence over government policy.

> 'The "policy community" approach provides a framework for examining the behaviour of a whole range of actors within a particular political arena.'
> (*Source*: Grant, W. 1987, *Business and Politics in Britain*, Macmillan, Hampshire, UK, p. 13)

> 'A **policy community** can be regarded as the actors and potential actors who have an interest in a policy issue and a **policy network** describes patterns of interaction within the community.'
> (*Source*: Atkinson, W. & Coleman, M. 1992, 'Policy Networks, Policy Communities and the Problems of Governance', *Governance*, vol. 5, no. 2, p. 156)

Those who take this view suggest that policy networks emerge from a policy community to argue for a specific policy issue. Others have argued that policy communities are stable, institutionalised networks with restricted membership, and suggest they have similar characteristics to an integrated policy network, or to a corporatist approach and the 'iron triangles' associated with group–government interaction in the US (discussed above).

Regardless of what we call these institutionalised networks where groups are invited to consult with government on a stable, ongoing basis, the outcome is the same. They are an elitist form of group–government interaction and much more likely to be able to influence government policy than ad hoc arrangements involving groups that do not have this privileged access to government.

The focus has been on policy networks in the context of elite or corporatist organisations, but elements of pluralism become evident when several different networks, each with different attitudes and preferences about how the matter should be resolved, develop around a particular policy issue. An example of this would be the conflicting policy networks that developed in Australia around the issue of trade policy, where one network supported tariff protection while the other wanted free trade.

Business representation on government advisory bodies has been a feature of the Australian political system for many years—sometimes involving policy making, at other times involving the implementation of government policy. The Hawke–Keating government (1983–96) established a number of industry advisory councils with representation from government, business and unions. The Howard government (1996–2007) established similar industry consultative bodies, called Action Agendas, but these were disbanded by the Rudd government.

Governments sometimes use these types of consultative arrangements to persuade representative groups to go along with what the government wants to do—in other words, the government co-opts groups to agree to its own agenda. At other times, they are a useful tool to sort out the differences between groups or between a particular group and the government, or to get information on the policy preferences of a particular group.

SOCIAL MOVEMENTS

'Cause' groups that seek to promote individual rights and a safe environment—such as Aboriginal, women's and environmental groups—are associated with what have been called 'new social movements'. The term *new*, however, is something of a misnomer, as they have been around for some time.

> **Social movements**: groups of citizens who work to change the values and culture of society.

These social movements include the women's movement, which seeks equality for women; Aboriginal groups, which seek a fairer deal and recognition of rights for Indigenous Australians; and the green movement, which seeks to protect the environment.

In the past, these groups would have been placed in the 'outsider' category, as groups lacking resources and unable to gain regular access to government or to influence government policy. Today, we can see that some of these groups have been successful in changing their status to 'insider' groups, with formal and informal representation on government advisory bodies, and the establishment of government departments and ministers responsible for policy related to their interests. We now have ministers and departments for the environment and Aboriginal affairs at state and federal levels of government. Women's affairs also have been given attention by government, not always through the establishment of a department or ministerial portfolio, but more significantly through legislation to facilitate equal opportunity and affirmative action.

> **The Office for Women**
> The Office for Women, located within the Department of Families, Housing, Community Services and Indigenous Affairs, provides the principal focus on consultation between the women's sector and government.
> (*Source*: The Office for Women 2008, http://www.ofw.facs.gov.au)

The environmental movement has gained significant political power through its representative political parties. In Germany, the Greens governed in coalition with the SDP. Since 1 July 2008, the Greens in the Australian Senate have held the balance of power, along with Family First senator Steven Fielding and independent Nick Xenophon.

Why have these groups been able to achieve this? The answer, in part, lies in:

- the human and moral basis to their convictions—no one is likely to argue that equal rights for women and Aboriginal people, or a clean environment, are bad things;
- their continuing ability to bring their issues to the attention of government through direct action; and
- in the case of women's and environmental groups, their potential to deliver votes at the ballot box.

The electoral argument, however, does not explain the success of Aboriginal people in gaining ministerial and departmental status, because their votes are less significant in geographical and numerical terms. The 1967 constitutional referendum was an important start, but other initiatives have been more significant for recognition of Aboriginal rights: the actions of federal Labor governments, starting with Gough Whitlam; the actions of Aboriginal groups in appealing to the High Court for land rights; the Keating government's subsequent implementation of the High Court's *Mabo* judgment on native title; and the High Court's *Wik* decision. Today, Aboriginal representatives are consulted on a range of issues of particular interest to Indigenous Australians.

National Aboriginal and Torres Strait Islander Health Council (NATSIHC)

NATSIHC provides advice to the Minister for Health and Ageing on issues relating to the health of Indigenous Australians. Its membership includes representation from the Congress of Aboriginal and Torres Strait Islander Nurses.

(*Source*: Department of Health and Ageing 2008, http://www.health.gov.au)

Wet Tropics Management Authority

The Wet Tropics Management Authority maintains a database of relevant Aboriginal representative bodies, Aboriginal community organisations and Aboriginal people, to make sure the right people for the country concerned are consulted in relation to Wet Tropics permit applications.

(*Source*: Wet Tropics Management Authority 2006, http://www.wettropics.gov.au)

This does not mean, however, that these groups have been as successful as they would have wished. Women and Aboriginal groups are still fighting for government action on a range of issues related to the achievement of full equality.

> **Foundation for Australian Agricultural Women**
> The Foundation works 'to resource, empower, research, influence and partner for the benefit of rural women', aiming to improve the wellbeing and skills of rural women and to facilitate their access to education and employment.
> (*Source*: Foundation for Australian Agricultural Women 2008, http://www.faaw.org.au)

Government has given priority to the demands of powerful economic and union groups in the community to support profitability and to protect jobs. The main reason for doing so has been the fact that these were also primary concerns of intending voters at the 1998, 2001 and 2004 elections. However, a change in voter priorities was evident in the 2007 election, with health, water, education and the environment being the top four issues of concern in that order (Newspoll/*The Australian*, 12–14 October 2007, http://www.newspoll.com.au). Climate change has become such a significant issue that governments have moved to address environmental concerns through policies such as carbon trading. However, governments that perform poorly in terms of economic management are less likely to be returned to office.

A good example of the difficulty facing government in balancing economic against 'cause' or value issues is the ongoing dispute between the forestry industry and forestry unions against environmentalists over the issue of wood chipping. The government in this instance is in a no-win situation. If it meets the environmentalists' demands, it will lose votes and support from workers in the industry. If it supports the industry, it will lose Green preferences. The Keating government in 1996, trying to tread a middle ground between them, ended up satisfying neither camp and lost votes from both sides. In the lead-up to the 2004 federal election, Labor leader Mark Latham's proposal to protect old-growth forests brought the issue to the fore again, and the contending groups stated their views.

> **Australian Conservation Foundation**
> 'The forestry industry in Tasmania must embrace change . . . current practices are not consistent with the priorities and concerns expressed by the community—that is a sustainable forestry industry with sustainable jobs and the preservation of the ancient old forests.'
> (*Source*: Australian Conservation Foundation 2004, media release, 5 October 2004, http://www.acfonline.org.au)

> **National Association of Forest Industries**
> 'Old-growth logging, which provides the high-quality end of the timber resources, is a major part of the Tasmanian economy . . . Ceasing all old-growth harvesting altogether could cost 1,800 jobs.'
> (*Source*: National Association of Forest Industries 2004, 'NAFI e-News', 24 September 2004, http://www.nafi.com.au)

The issue created a no-win situation for Labor and the party lost votes in Tasmania. The Rudd government faces similar problems in balancing the interests of the environment and industry when formulating policies on carbon emissions and carbon trading schemes.

The fact that these 'new social movements' have been able to make progress indicates that group activity can be used to persuade governments, particularly where there are votes to be had in supporting their cause—in other words, utilising the tactics of a lobby group strategically to manage the party political system to their advantage.

GROUPS AND DEMOCRACY

There is nothing undemocratic or improper about the existence or activity of interest groups. To rephrase Bentley's views, groups are just people acting collectively in politics to secure goals which they think are important. They nearly always act on behalf of other people who are thought by the group to hold these goals as important too. The difficulty is that these goals often clash. The Australian Medical Association, for example, cannot be criticised for seeking to protect the interests of doctors, but these interests may not always be the same as those of their patients, or of the government, or even of doctors who do not belong to the association. The absence of wide agreement about issues such as the 'proper' level of doctors' incomes or the 'proper' minimal level of medical attention to sick people means that the competing interests of doctors, patients and governments will clash and will not be resolved easily.

> **Democracy,** as we saw in Chapter 1, means rule by the people for the people (incorporating the principles of majority rule, the protection of minority rights, equal participation, fair and frequent elections, and the rule of law).

In a democratic system of government, this type of clash can be resolved by a party putting the issue to the voters at an election as part of their policy platform and by society accepting the verdict of the majority in terms of which party is elected to office. There are problems for the democratic process, however, when the strongest and most powerful groups are able to take advantage of their privileged access to government to persuade government in private meetings to take a particular type of action. In the past, we could argue that the protection of Australia's manufacturing industry was the product of that type of arrangement.

The strength of the Australian system in terms of the democratic process lies, it can be argued, with the expansion of group activity in recent years.

> A major challenge to business group relations with the Australian government is 'the increasingly competitive and demanding nature of interest group politics and the lobbying environment'.
> (*Source*: Bell, S. 1994, 'Australian Business Associations: New Opportunities and Challenges', *Australian Journal of Management*, vol. 19, no. 2, pp. 144–5)

This means that a wide range of competing groups have the opportunity to put their points of view on the political agenda. In that sense, we could argue that the Australian democratic system is relatively pluralist, with the government having to take account of a wider range of social and political values than those espoused by big business or the trade union movement to ensure its political survival. The ongoing disagreement and competition between the key economic groups of unions and employer associations relating to central economic issues such as wages policy also contributes to a more pluralistic political system. The evidence also lies in the breadth of social and economic policies that both major political parties, as contenders for government, put before the voters at a federal election.

A significant resource in getting government to take notice of group demands, particularly those who do not have large amounts of money at their disposal and rely heavily on the direct action of their members, is the media. It is difficult for a government to ignore or overlook an issue that attracts media attention, so in Chapter 13 we look at the role of the media in the political system, not only in terms of group activity but in its potential to influence the political agenda by its coverage and reporting of political issues.

QUESTIONS FOR DISCUSSION

1. Why would citizens be more likely to join an interest group than a political party?
2. Why does government deal with interest groups?
3. Why are some interest groups more powerful than others?
4. How can we identify what are 'insider' groups and what are 'outsider' groups?
5. What strategies can an 'outsider' group use to gain the attention of government?
6. What arguments would you make that policy networks can develop into a form of 'sub-government'?
7. What constitutes a social movement? Do you think this is a relevant concept in today's political arena?
8. What factors of interest-group activity enhance or hinder the democratic process in Australia?

FURTHER READING

Bell, S. 1992, 'Business and Government: Patterns of Interaction and Policy Networks', in Bell, S. & Wanna, J. (eds), *Business–Government Relations in Australia*, Harcourt Brace Jovanovich, Sydney. This chapter discusses the characteristics of policy networks.

Bentley, A.F. 1967 (1908), *The Process of Government*, University of Chicago Press, Chicago. The originator of group theory.

Burgmann, V. 1993, *Power and Protest: Movements for Change in Australian Society*, Allen & Unwin, Sydney. An introduction to 'new social movements' and their activities in the political system.

Eccleston, R. 2002, 'The Power of Australian Business', in Van Acker, E. & Curran, G. (eds), *Business, Government and Globalisation*, Longman, Sydney. This chapter points to the fragmentation of business interests and the fluctuating fortunes of business in its dealings with government. It is useful in analysing the significance of policy networks in relation to group–government relations.

Held, D. 1987, *Models of Democracy*, Polity Press, Cambridge. Chapter 6, 'Pluralism, Corporate Capitalism and the State', contains a good discussion of pluralism and its critics.

Matthews, T. 1997, 'Interest Groups', in Smith, R. (ed.), *Politics in Australia*, 3rd ed., Allen & Unwin, Sydney. Excellent article on the nature of interest groups, the strategies they use and their influence on policy.

Papadakis, E. 1993, *Politics and the Environment*, Allen & Unwin, Sydney. An examination of 'green' politics that introduces environmental issues and their impact on the policy process.

Rhodes, R.A.W. 2007, 'Policy Networks', in Galligan, B. & Roberts, W. (eds), *The Oxford Companion to Australian Politics*, Oxford University Press, Melbourne. An informative explanation of policy networks.

Sawer, M. & Groves, A. 1994, '"The Women's Lobby": Networks, Coalition Building and the Women of Middle Australia', *Australian Journal of Political Science*, vol. 29, no. 3, pp. 435–59. Discusses the role of networks and coalitions in getting women's issues on to the political agenda.

Stokes, G. & Jull, P. 2000, 'Social Justice and Self-Determination in Indigenous Politics', in Boreham, P., Stokes, G. & Hall, R. (eds), *The Politics of Australian Society*, Pearson Education, Sydney. A review of Indigenous politics, ideas and emerging political issues.

Warhurst, J. 2006, 'Interest Groups and Political Lobbying', in Parkin, A., Summers, J. & Woodward, D. (eds), *Government, Politics, Power & Policy in Australia*, Pearson Education, Sydney.

Warhurst, J. 2007, *Behind Closed Doors: Politics, Scandals and the Lobbying Industry*, UNSW Press, Sydney. An insightful examination of the lobbying industry in Australia.

Wilson, G.K. 1990, *Interest Groups*, Basil Blackwell, Oxford. A comparative study of the role of interest groups in the political process in a range of countries, including the relationships between interest groups and the state and political parties.

USEFUL WEBSITES

http://www.acfonline.org.au
Australian Conservation Foundation

http://www.acci.asn.au
Australian Chamber of Commerce and Industry

http://www.aigroup.asn.au
Australian Industry Group

http://www.bca.com.au
Business Council of Australia

http://www.nff.org.au
National Farmers' Federation

http://www.acoss.org.au
Australian Council of Social Service

http://www.actu.asn.au
Australian Council of Trade Unions

13

POLITICAL COMMUNICATION

THIS CHAPTER EXPLAINS:

- the role of political communication in a political system;
- the function of mass media in providing information;
- media ownership and regulatory control in Australia and other countries;
- politics in the Australian media;
- the parliamentary press gallery;
- political advertising and polling;
- the role of the Internet and technology in political communication; and
- e-government and e-democracy in Australia and other countries.

What is political communication and what is its function in a political system?

> **Political communication**: 'the role of communication in political life [is] embracing the media, opinion polls, political marketing and publicity . . . any communication that has a political purpose.'
> (*Source*: Wolton, D. 1998, *Penser la Communication*, Flammarion, Paris (glossary))

Political communication facilitates the transmission of information between citizens and their government and takes place in various ways, predominantly via the media and the Internet. The mass media, as an instrument of political communication, has been called the 'fourth estate' because of its significance in the political system in scrutinising government and keeping it accountable to the people.

> The term **fourth estate** has been attributed to Edmund Burke, an 18th-century British politician, quoted by Thomas Carlyle in his book *Heroes and Hero Worship in History*, 1841: 'Burke said there were three Estates in Parliament [The Lords Spiritual and the Lords Temporal, meaning the House of Lords, and the House of Commons], but in the Reporters Gallery yonder, there sat a fourth Estate more important far than they all.'
> (*Source*: Camp Wood 2005, 'Fourth Estate', http://www.campwood.com/FourthEstate.htm)

The media plays an important role in the political process because it facilitates the flow of information between a government and its citizens, and vice versa. The Internet and technology such as mobile phones and SMS text messaging have become important tools for political communication.

Political communication is vital to a healthy democracy. It is critical to the democratic processes by making governments aware of what people want, and providing feedback to government on its policies and actions. Freedom of speech, and open and fearless reporting of what a government is doing are essential if the principles of responsible and accountable government are to be upheld.

In earlier chapters we discussed the significance of elections, political parties and interests groups as a function of citizen political participation. These institutions provide the means by which individuals are represented in government and gain access to government. We also discussed scrutiny of government action through the activities of parliament and the principles of ministerial responsibility. All of these activities rely on effective political communication for their efficiency in providing a real say for citizens. This includes:

- the functions of the media in picking up and highlighting issues that arise from time to time and that make governments sit up and take notice. An example would be the reporting of the problems experienced by charitable and sporting organisations in getting affordable public liability insurance, which spurred the Commonwealth and state governments to hold a special ministerial meeting to discuss the issue;
- the reporting of election campaigns, including party policies and issues raised by other groups in the electorate, so that citizens are provided with information that will enable them to make a considered choice between the parties and candidates. This includes daily television coverage of the campaign, journalists reporting on issues raised during the campaign, the questioning of party leaders about the viability of their policies, televised debates between the party leaders and political advertising; and

- the reporting of parliamentary debates and committee proceedings so that citizens are aware of the issues raised and can make a judgement about how well the government is performing. A good example is the reporting of the Senate Select Committee hearings which examined the way in which the Howard government dealt with allegations of children being thrown overboard by asylum seekers.

This chapter examines the operations of the principal forms of political communication in Australia, including the mass media, the Internet, and the use of information technology to facilitate e-government and e-democracy.

THE MASS MEDIA

The 'mass media'—newspapers, radio and television—plays a central role in the democratic process by assembling and disseminating information on a daily basis.

> From the media, we find out:
> - what is going on around us;
> - what leading politicians are saying, and what they look and sound like;
> - what the important issues and problems are; and
> - what is happening in our own country and abroad.

What we learn from the media is likely to affect how we look at government and political issues and engage with the political system (though one might question the extent to which the media reinforces existing attitudes and opinions, rather than shaping opinions). The content and the control of the media, therefore, are matters of political importance.

News and newsworthiness

The crucial factor in determining what constitutes the news we see and read is the selection by media organisations of what is newsworthy. The amount of 'news' that could be published or broadcast each day vastly exceeds what will be reported. Those who make the selection—the editorial staff of newspapers or news programs—choose the most 'newsworthy' items for reporting, being careful to separate factual news from comment. That is the traditional picture, but the real picture is rather different:

- 'News' ought to be what is new, but a lot of news is old, familiar and reassuring. Moreover, the great weight of attention given to the prime minister and the leader of the Opposition, particularly in an election campaign, cannot be justified on the grounds that what they have to say, or what they do, is 'new'. They get this attention because they are the leading politicians. The political parties use this fact to manage political communication during an election campaign by providing the journalists who report on the campaign with limited opportunities to question the leaders, and by stage managing 'media events' to provide photo opportunities and television coverage for the nightly news broadcasts that will show the leaders in a good light. Political news is about the powerful, not about the weak.

- The great pressure on the media to get news to air or into print forces reporters and editors to package the reporting of events, particularly television and radio news, into the '30-second grab'—a brief comment from the newsreader or the people involved. Much news, therefore, involves the presentation of opposing and confirming statements from leaders or spokespersons. Issues are presented mostly in terms of black or white, rather than the truer shades of grey. News is disproportionately about the well-organised, and those who are not well organised (such as pensioners and the unemployed) are rarely 'news'. The news focuses on the government's mistakes, on sensation and crisis, which is an effective form of scrutiny of government failure but leaves the good things that government does or achieves in its day-to-day administration mostly unreported.
- This focus on what is 'newsworthy' has a direct impact on the ability of interest groups to get their message across to government through the media. Those groups with 'insider' status have less need for media coverage to get the attention of government, but when they do, they have the resources to put forward well-researched statements and professional media staff to handle their publicity. 'Outsider' groups, which are less well-endowed with resources, have to resort to direct action, such as protests and rallies, to gain publicity. This may give them their '30 seconds' of news coverage at the time of the event, but it is difficult to sustain media interest over a longer period. The benefits for 'outsider' groups accrue when the media takes on an issue and pursues the government for answers or action, particularly during an election campaign.
- People may pride themselves on their objectivity and balance, but they operate in a cultural setting in which the emotional 'colour' of much news is already 'given'. For example, in Australian society strikes usually are portrayed in the media in a negative way, however justified their cause, because of the inconvenience to the 'innocent public'. If strikes are reported and interpreted continually with this set of values, it is likely that those who read about them will accept those values as normal and be disapproving.

The media has the potential to promote social change, but it rarely does so. This is particularly the case with the privately owned media because of the commercial imperatives of having to appeal to a mass audience. That is why we see commercial television stations focus on political stories that have a strong element of sensationalism, such as mistakes made by governments or ministers, rather than on ideas and debate about the nature of the political system. There is more scope for critical analysis and debate in the print media by the publication of articles presenting a range of views, but this has been principally limited to major newspapers such as *The Australian*, *The Age* or *The Sydney Morning Herald*. Even then, the opportunity for pushing the boundaries of political debate may be limited if media owners use their newspapers or television stations to promote their own view of politics and government. This raises an important question: how fair or unbiased is the media when reporting or commenting on political issues?

Fairness

As the media is our fundamental source of information about politics and government, it is important that this information be presented fairly. This can be difficult, for two reasons:

1 Apart from the publicly owned Australian Broadcasting Corporation (ABC) (http://www.abc.net.au) and Special Broadcasting Service (SBS) (http://www.sbs.com.au), and the independently operated and community radio stations, the forums of mass media are privately owned and therefore subject in principle to the direction of the owners, directly

or indirectly (through the operation of the 'law of anticipated reactions'). It is impossible to say how much unfairness of this kind actually occurs as it may be unstated, but it is reflected in the type of stories that are run and the way in which they are presented.

Media proprietors have been accused of exercising control or bias. The staff of *The Australian*, for example, complained about political direction by the owner, Rupert Murdoch, during the 1975 federal election. In the 1987 federal election, the Liberal Party Opposition alleged that the press was biased in favour of the Labor government because of the friendship between the prime minister, Bob Hawke, and media owners. The ABC is also accused, from time to time, of showing bias in its comment and reporting, usually from the conservative side of politics.

- A Morgan poll taken in August 2007 found that 85 per cent of those surveyed believe that newspaper journalists are often biased, 74 per cent believed that television reporters are often biased, and 69 per cent believed that talk-back radio announcers are often biased.
(*Source*: Roy Morgan Research 2007, 'Large Majority of Australians Think the Media is "Often Biased"', Finding no. 4195, http://www.roymorgan.com/news/polls/2007/4195)

- In May 2003, the Coalition government's minister for communications asked the ABC to investigate what he claimed was 'highly subjective and not factually based' coverage of the Iraq war by the AM program.
(*Source*: Richard Alston, Minister for Communications, Information Technology and the Arts 2003, media release, 78/03, 28 May 2003)

It should be borne in mind, however, that those on the losing side of politics (or a particular issue) are most likely to complain about lack of fairness. The winners clearly have less reason to do so.

2 Fairness is not only in the eye and mind of the beholder, but it can be impossible to guarantee. As in defamation or libel, damage when done cannot easily be undone. A headline criticising an action of the government is not likely to be matched by a similar one the following day praising government action. When newspapers make mistakes, any retraction or apology will usually be in a small paragraph on an inside page.

With media focus primarily on the government, and particularly the prime minister, it is less easy for the Opposition to get its message reported with the same level of intensity. The prime minister, for example, will probably get a larger audience for a nationwide speech over radio and television than the leader of the Opposition, even though the latter speaks a week later at the same time and on the same subject. Minor parties complain consistently that they are not given the same opportunity to put their point of view and that the system is biased continually in favour of the major parties. A significant feature related particularly to radio is the talk-back host. Sometimes called 'shock jocks', these radio personalities have extensive listening audiences and may impart their own views and political bias to particular issues.

Fairness remains a goal to be striven for, but it is not always attainable. There have been suggestions that an independent, publicly owned newspaper authority should be established, along the same lines as the ABC, to provide an alternative source to commercial newspapers. It is hard to object to this in principle, but it would be unwise to expect too much from it, for a number of reasons:

- The problems of news selections and cultural constraint will be even more pressing for such a newspaper: if it is too way out, few people will read it; but if it is much the same as its rivals, what would be the point of publishing it?
- A daily newspaper without advertisements would be expensive, but to have advertisements involves reducing editorial content and possibly some reduction in editorial autonomy. Moreover, advertisements are unlikely to be forthcoming unless circulation is substantial. Newspapers are often bought for their advertisements (entertainment, classifieds and so on). Indeed, it is claimed that both *The Age* and *The Sydney Morning Herald* survive because of the large and lucrative classified advertisement sections in their Saturday issues.

Some have argued for the establishment of a left-leaning newspaper as an alternative to what they see as the conservative mainstream press, but such a paper is unlikely to survive for long. As 'the Left' is not a united or coherent group in Australian politics, a newspaper that espoused an editorial perspective from the Left—that is, one critical in a systematic way of the established order—would quickly become either a prize in the continuing war between left factions or, through attempting to stay aloof from that war, a paper not unlike its rivals. Once captured by a faction, its circulation would most likely fall. (This was the fate of official Labor newspapers such as the *Labor Daily* and the *Daily News* in the faction-ridden 1930s.)

The print media has taken some steps towards dealing with the issue of unfairness with the establishment of a voluntary Australian Press Council (http://www.presscouncil.org.au). The council is a self-regulatory body that adjudicates on complaints in the print media. It is funded by newspaper and magazine industries and is headed by an independent chair. In 2007 it dealt with 35 complaints.

It is to be hoped that over a period of time a newspaper or television or radio station can be shown to be free of systematic bias. Nevertheless, bias and fairness always operate in a context: few people would argue that a program about the evils of genocide should be followed by a program about what are thought to be its benefits.

Ownership and control

Some critics consider the concentration of ownership and control in the media to be a problem. This is a valid point, because radio and television have nearly universal coverage of the whole community. Newspapers are read less widely, but still perform a significant role in political communication.

Australia

Concentration of media ownership and control of the Australian media has been criticised in the past because it had the potential to limit the variety of news and opinion available to the public. As we saw in the discussion on 'fairness', above, media proprietors have been accused of exercising control or bias over what is reported and, from time to time, using that position to support one political party over another during an election campaign.

The Keating government restricted foreign ownership and cross-ownership of Australian media through the *Broadcasting Services Act 1992*. The Howard government's *Broadcasting*

Services Amendment (Media Ownership) Act 2006 removed broadcasting-specific restrictions on foreign investment in Australian media, although all direct media and portfolio investment over 5 per cent has to be approved by the Treasurer. Foreign ownership of Australian media assets is regulated under the *Foreign Acquisitions and Takeovers Act 1975*. Cross-media mergers in radio licences are permitted if at least five separate media groups remain in mainland state capitals, and four groups in other licence areas. All mergers involving commercial radio, commercial television and associated newspapers within a regional radio licence area have to be cleared by the Australian Competition and Consumer Commission (ACCC). Rules were also introduced to provide protection for local content in regional areas, including minimum standards for a range of community and news services. The media ownership rules are administered by the Australian Communications and Media Authority (http://www.acma.gov.au).

> There have been concerns that the new media ownership rules, introduced in 2007, will be used by media proprietors to further concentrate their holdings: 'Existing local media barons will be free to exploit the removal of the cross-media ownership restrictions that have painted proprietors as "princes of print" or "queens of the screen" for more than 20 years.'
> (Source: Tabakoff, N. 2007, 'Coonan clears the way for media revolution', The Australian, 30 March 2007)

A few 'big players' dominate the ownership of Australian media, including News Corporation Ltd (Murdoch), Rural Press Ltd, and John Fairfax Holdings Ltd. However, following the introduction of the new rules, there were significant changes to the structure of PBL, the media empire owned by Kerry Packer that passed on his death to his son James Packer, but it still remains a major player in the Australian media industry.

- October 2006: PBL Media was formed as a joint venture between PBL and a private equity investment company, CVC Asia Pacific Ltd. PBL Media operates the Nine Network, Australian Consolidated Press magazines, Ticketek and Acer Arena, and has an interest in carsales.com.au, NBN TV, ninemsn, myhome.com.au, Mathletics and Sky News.
- September 2007: PBL split into two companies: Crown, to manage its casino operations, and Consolidated Media Holdings (CMH), to manage its media businesses.

> You can find details of who owns what under the new rules on the Register of Controlled Media Groups, as well as the list of current controllers of commercial radio, television and newspapers at http://www.acma.gov.au.

Ownership or market dominance does not necessarily mean political power, even though the concentration of ownership of major newspapers and television is seen by some to be dangerous and potentially a threat to democracy. Press, radio, television and magazines compete with one another, and even newspapers owned by a single person may present different perspectives on issues. Although editorial bias may be detectable, the driving force has to be market share and profitability achieved by giving readers and viewers the types of stories and programs they like to read or watch. The mass media, for that reason, should by-and-large reflect the conventional and contemporary values of the society in which it operates. Whether or not these conventional values are those of a 'ruling' class or powerful elite in society, rather than those of the broad community, may be difficult to assess with any certainty, but highly rated television programs such as *Home and Away* are more reflective of problems concerning 'ordinary' families than of the lives of the rich and famous.

Improvements in the variety and quality of the Australian mass media may be slow in coming. The drive for profits encourages rationalisation and concentration of commercial media ownership, rather than expansion and competition. Until a more competitive environment is achieved, allegations of bias and unfairness related to the concentration of media ownership will continue.

Britain

Media ownership rules in Britain are intended to strike a balance between diversity of ownership and providing media companies with the opportunity to expand. They are managed by the Office of Communications (http://www.ofcom.org.uk).

> The media ownership rules in Britain are designed to:
> - prevent/limit control of television and radio by certain bodies whose influence might cause concern (such as political parties and religious bodies);
> - decrease the likelihood that any one owner wields too much power, and ensure that there are a sufficient number of media outlet owners to increase the likelihood of sufficient viewpoint plurality; and
> - specifically arrange for the provision of national and international news to ITV1 (or Channel 3), to ensure that the news source for the largest commercial television channel is independent of the BBC, not under the control of political or religious bodies, and suitably well funded.
>
> (*Source:* Office of Communications 2008, http://www.ofcom.org.uk)

Nevertheless, there remains a considerable concentration of media ownership in Britain. Rupert Murdoch, and Daily Mail & General Trust between them own many major newspapers, and have interests in television broadcasting.

United States

The media in the US is diverse and highly decentralised, with many newspapers locally owned (Vile, M.J.C. 2007, *Politics in the USA*, 6th ed., Routledge, New York, p. 183). However, there are rules about media ownership that are designed to maintain that diversity. These are managed by an independent regulator, the Federal Communications Commission (FCC) (http://www.fcc.gov). The current rules do not permit companies to own both newspaper and television media in one television market. In 2007 the FCC introduced new rules that would have permitted newspaper/television cross-ownership in the top 20 television markets under certain conditions, but these were disallowed by US Congress after criticism that the new arrangements would lead to a dangerous concentration of media control and restrict access to a diversity of news and information (Gattuso, J.L. 2008, 'The FCC's Cross-Ownership Rule: Turning the Page on Media', *Backgrounder*, no. 2133, The Heritage Foundation, 6 May 2008).

Federal Republic of Germany

Media ownership in Germany is concentrated. Two commercial groups dominate the television market, while five groups dominate the press. There are few rules to prevent media concentration. The Federal Cartel Office, the competition authority, is in charge of approving company mergers, and the threshold for media companies is set lower than other sectors in the economy. The Commission on Media Concentration (KEK) (http://www.kek-online.de) verifies compliance with the requirement that there is plurality of opinion on nationwide television.

Federation of Malaysia

Major newspapers and television companies in Malaysia have close connections to the governing political parties within the ruling Barisan Nasional coalition. UMNO (which also has links to Media Prima, a publisher of major daily newspapers and owner of several television stations), MCA and MIC all own media companies. The government also owns a number of television and radio stations. This means there is little anti-government comment or diversity of news in the local media.

Media operations in Malaysia that are not associated with the governing parties are controlled through a range of measures that discourage criticism of the government. The *Broadcasting Act* gives the minister for information control over broadcasting licences and television programming. The *Printing Presses and Publications Act* requires all print publishers to apply for licences, which are granted at the government's discretion. The *Sedition Act* makes it a crime to incite hatred or contempt for the government and is used against media owners and journalists who are critical of the government. The *Internal Security Act* allows detention without trial.

POLITICS IN THE AUSTRALIAN MEDIA

As we stated in the introduction to this chapter, the media is a principal and significant source of political information for citizens. The reporting of politics includes stories about current events and government policies, editorials, and articles providing information and critical analysis of political issues by reporters or informed experts, coverage of election campaigns, letters to the editor and political advertising.

There is a range of media sources that people can access for political news.

Print media

A distinction is usually made between 'quality' newspapers, such as *The Age*, *The Australian*, *The Australian Financial Review* and *The Sydney Morning Herald*, and others. The quality newspapers take politics seriously, devote more space to it and are more systematic in their treatment of it. For example, they report the end of a news story when it has ceased to be 'news' or provide the full text of an important announcement, such as the budget statement, rather than a summary.

Publicly owned media

The ABC broadcasts the national parliament when in session through the parliamentary news network station, provides a large number of news services every day in which politics and government are usually prominent concerns, and broadcasts current affairs programs that allow those interested in day-to-day politics to find out what is going on. Notions of the need for fairness and balance form an important part of the ABC's approach to public affairs reporting, and have given it—at least with respect to its news services—a reputation for integrity and reliability. However, as we saw above, this does not mean that it has not been accused of bias in its approach to political issues.

SBS provides radio and television news services, and, as a multicultural broadcaster, it also broadcasts foreign-language news programs.

Independent, community-owned and operated media

4ZZZ FM, Brisbane
4ZZZ is an independent community radio station in Brisbane, 'blasting fresh local and underground music through your radio . . . you can tune in to hear all sorts of music, including indie, punk, rock, dancehall, reggae, noise, electronica, ska and drum & bass'. The station's income comes from subscriptions, promotions and events.
(*Source*: 4ZZZ n.d., '4ZZZ Profile', http://www.4zzzfm.org.au/about/index.cfm)

There is a large number of community-owned media organisations in Australia that provide an alternative source of news for citizens across the country, including Indigenous Australians and people living in remote and regional areas of Australia. Listener surveys reported in *The Australian* (23 September 2004) indicated that approximately 725,000 people listen to community radio and it is most popular with the 15–24 age group. Many volunteers are involved in providing broadcasting and support services for community media.

EAR FM, Eurobodalla
EAR FM, based in the Eurobodalla region of southern New South Wales, provides 'an alternative music mix presented by the personalities and characters of our local community . . . As a community radio station our airwaves are open to volunteers from the public to present their own programmes.'
(*Source*: Eurobodalla Access Radio (EAR) n.d., 'About Us', http://www.earfm.com/aboutus.htm)

Commercial media

Free-to-air commercial television stations cover political news stories during morning current affairs 'chat' shows, such as Channel Seven's *Sunrise* and Channel Nine's *Today* shows. Nightly news bulletins are the main vehicle for television news and a major source of news and current affairs within the community.

- Around 1.5 million viewers watch Channel Seven's news.
- Around 1.6 million viewers watch Channel Nine's *60 Minutes*.

(*Source*: *The Australian*, 26 June 2008)

There is a tendency for commercial television networks to present 'news' stories with entertainment or sensationalist value, at the expense of those that might be informative but dull. The visual nature of television encourages the use of the '30-second grab' photo opportunity, rather than extended or complex debate about an issue. 'Docudramas' could be regarded as political news programs, but the subject matter is often selected, packaged and presented for its entertainment and potential ratings value.

The news stories presented on television are often limited in scope because of the channels' orientation towards their own states and major cities. Significant national political events will be covered, but domestic news is predominantly about what has been happening in the station's home state. For example, Sydney television channels focus on what has been happening in New South Wales, and more especially in Sydney. There is some reporting of local events by regional stations, but the coverage is limited.

Setting the political agenda

The fact that television stations and newspaper editors determine what is 'news' provides the media with the opportunity to set the political agenda at any given time and to put pressure on a government to respond to their coverage. The fact that ministers employ media specialists on their staff indicates the significance of political news to the government. Political news that emanates from a minister's office will be drafted and presented to the media to place the minister and the government in a favourable light. This has been called putting a 'spin' on a story, and the ministerial staffers who produce these statements are called 'spin doctors'.

> - **Media spin**: the monitoring and manipulation of the presentation of issues by government.
> - **Spin doctors**: 'the people responsible for the media presentation of the government and for putting a media "spin" (or angle) on its policies and activities.'
> (*Source*: Fairclough, N. 2000, *New Labour, New Language*, Routledge, London, p. 1)

A symbiotic, or mutually beneficial, relationship can develop between the government and the media. The government has to forge close relationships with the media because it wants to publicise what it is doing, and the media needs to maintain a good relationship with the government to gain access to the stories that sell newspapers and generate television ratings. There is a case to be made that members of the parliamentary press gallery who report on what is happening in federal politics (see below) are particularly susceptible because they operate in close proximity to government and rely on the information that ministers and their staff supply, usually in the form of media releases or doorstop interviews with the politicians.

This problem arises particularly during elections, when journalists travel as a group with the prime minister for the duration of the campaign. Their stories of the day's events rely heavily on the prime minister's statements and media handouts (with 'spin') issued by party advisers.

> Former premier of Queensland, Sir Joh Bjelke-Petersen, referred to his briefing of journalists as 'feeding the chooks'.
> (*Source*: Lunn, H. 1978, *Joh*, University of Queensland Press, Brisbane, p. 103)

The group of journalists travelling with the leader of the Opposition is similarly reliant on media releases and the 'spin' of party advisers. It could be argued that there is some 'balance' in what is reported, because journalists file stories from both sides of politics during an election campaign. Nevertheless, the tightly structured nature of the process allows the parties to control and manipulate the information that the media receives and reports to the public. The parties organise the daily itineraries of their leaders to try to maximise their coverage on the nightly television news bulletins, and manage 'photo opportunities' with the public so the leaders are portrayed in a positive way during the campaign.

Televised election debates

There is also political control over televised election debates between the leaders. John Howard, for example, at the 2004 election agreed to only one debate and prescribed the formula it would take.

In 2007, the Opposition leader, Kevin Rudd, requested three debates but Prime Minister Howard insisted there would be only one debate at a time of his choosing. The Liberal Party insisted that there be no 'worm' along the bottom of the screen to indicate the reaction of a panel of viewers to what the leaders were saying. The debate was broadcast live on three stations: Channel Nine, the ABC and Sky. When Channel Nine included the 'worm' in its broadcast, the National Press Club, which was hosting the debate, cut off Channel Nine's feed, but Nine continued to show the debate using a link from Sky.

This issue raises the question of whether controls and conditions should be placed by one political party on a public debate that informs about party policies and the performance of party leaders. The Labor Party recognised the significance of the televised debates to its election campaign and rehearsed Labor participants in a process they called 'war gaming', a mock event replicating the National Press Club format, which was videotaped and played back to identify strengths and weaknesses (*The Weekend Australian*, 22 December 2007).

Talk-back, or interactive, radio

Talk-back radio provides listeners with opportunities to raise issues and comment on what is happening in the political sphere. The spread of mobile phone usage in the community has enabled more people to get involved in talk-back radio and enhanced citizen participation in this type of political debate. Politicians also use talk-back radio to interact directly with the public. Prime Minister John Howard, for example, was noted for the way he utilised talk-back radio as a vehicle for discussing and promoting political issues.

> 'Talk back radio is tremendously important in Australia. Enormously important. It has played a greater role in shaping and determining the outcome of elections over the last few years than perhaps has been the case with other sections of the media.'
> (*Source:* australianpolitics.com 2002, 'John Howard's Formula for Winning Elections', 10 June 2002, http://australianpolitics.com/news/2002/06/02-06-10.shtml)

The chief minister of the Australian Capital Territory uses local talk-back radio to answer residents' questions about a wide range of issues, such as grass cutting in public reserves, the placement of pedestrian crossings or traffic lights to enhance road safety, or concerns about a particular government policy. Members of political parties and interest groups try to use talk-back radio to put their point of view, but most talk-back hosts have become adept at recognising and dealing with these types of callers.

Talk-back, however, does have its limitations because of its appeal to older listeners. Labor used a different range of media to get its message out to younger people for the 2007 election.

> Kevin Rudd appeared on FM music and chat stations, and on the *Sunrise* and *Rove* television programs. John Howard, preferring talk-back radio programs with an older listener profile, had been described as a 'media dinosaur'.
> (Source: Burchell, D. 'Successful politicians turn artlessness into an art form', *The Weekend Australian*, 15 September 2007)

Pay television

Pay television provides viewers with an extended choice of political news. Some people use the service to access news channels such as CNN or BBC World News. On the other hand, those who select sports and movie channels may be viewing less news.

Can the media 'make' policy?

Investigative journalism and television programs, such as *A Current Affair*, *Four Corners* and *60 Minutes*, draw attention to political issues that may provide the stimulus for government action. It could be argued that if a government does implement a policy that the media has promoted, then the media has been influential in the development of that policy.

> **'An exciting opportunity to shape news . . .'**
> From an advertisement in *The Australian*, 16 September 2004, for a chief of staff of a regional television station.

On the other hand, governments are subject to a range of influences, including party policy, pressure from groups with competing influences, and the need to satisfy enough voters to win elections. There is no doubt, however, that the role of the media in reporting and publicising an issue will bring it to the government's attention.

THE PARLIAMENTARY PRESS GALLERY

The workings of parliament are known to the community only if they are publicised. This is done in two ways:

- The ABC provides radio broadcasts of the proceedings of parliament, as well as television broadcasts of question time. It is part of the ABC's charter that it does this.
- Parliamentary proceedings are reported by the press gallery.

The press gallery includes representatives from major newspapers and television networks and is accommodated in Parliament House. There are two galleries in the House of Representatives and one in the Senate. The journalists have mailboxes in which parliamentarians and others deposit press releases and other material. The television networks also have studios within the building for televised press conferences and interviews with parliamentarians.

The parliamentary press gallery plays a significant role in political communication. Television and newspaper journalists working in the press gallery in Parliament House are an important source of political news about the activities of the government.

But how effective is the press gallery at providing critical information and sound analysis of political issues? On the positive side, their close proximity to the politicians provides press gallery journalists with the opportunity to find out what is going on and to ask questions. They can report on the government's performance in defending its actions and policies in the parliament and issues raised by the Opposition. This includes how ministers cope with question time when responding to difficult and testing issues.

Parliament provides one of the few occasions when the prime minister and the leader of the Opposition face each other in political debate, and media reporting of how they handle that situation can have an effect on the political reputation of a particular leader. A prime minister or Opposition leader who does not perform well may be regarded by the party as a weak leader, with implications for his or her capacity to lead a party in an election. In extreme cases, this could lead to a leadership challenge.

> 'After the 1969 elections the Liberals became concerned by Gorton's style of leadership . . . In the House he was all at sea and the Party started to look for another leader.'
> (Source: Daly, F. 1977, *From Curtin to Kerr*, Sun Books, Melbourne, p. 183)

Being located in Parliament House provides journalists with the opportunity to question ministers on issues that arise outside the parliamentary process, such as departmental performance or matters that arise within the community that require a government response.

On the negative side, the physical isolation associated with the location of ministers within their own wing of Parliament House means that journalists often have to rely on what are called *doorstop interviews*, where ministers make themselves available outside the building to make a statement and possibly answer questions. We often see excerpts from a doorstop interview on the nightly news where the minister makes a statement surrounded by a group of journalists with cameras and microphones. The Rudd government has a roster of ministers and members designated to respond to these interviews.

These types of activities provide the context for the close, symbiotic relationship between gallery journalists and ministers, mentioned above, to develop, because ministers rely on the media to get their message out to the community and the media relies on ministers for the 'news' of the day. The fact that journalists rely on ministerial sources for their 'bread-and-butter' stories could discourage critical analysis and result in the 'news' appearing as a mere rehashing of a ministerial statement.

Journalists closeted within the confines of Parliament House tend to become caught up in the ambience of working there. Rumours fly around the corridors to become the focus of excited journalistic attention as the various media outlets feed on speculation frenzy. How much this influences measured, analytical reporting is speculative, but it does have an impact in setting the 'news' agenda that could see other, important stories ignored.

However, stories regularly appear that are critical of government activity and ministerial performance. This indicates that the press gallery is prepared to pursue recalcitrant ministers and a government that has made a mistake. After all, a 'scandal' or embarrassment for government makes a good news story and is likely to sell more newspapers and improve television ratings than reportage of more mundane and relatively boring government activity.

POLITICAL ADVERTISING

Political advertising in the media is a significant form of political communication, particularly at election time.

> **Political advertising**: 'the advertisements produced by political parties and individual candidates that are shown during election campaigns in order to persuade voters to vote for them.'
> (*Source*: Young, S. 2002, 'Spot On: The Role of Political Advertising in Australia', *Australian Journal of Political Science*, vol. 37, no. 1, p. 82)

The major parties spend the major proportion of their campaign funds on television advertising because of the wide audience they can reach. We have all experienced the large number of party advertisements injected into television programming on commercial networks as the election date draws near.

One advantage in terms of political communication is that this process provides the parties with the opportunity to appeal directly to voters without editorial interference. On the other hand, the cost of paid political advertising on television is such that minor parties and independents have limited opportunity to make the most of this medium. Political advertising on television relies on making a short, sharp impression on the viewer by using images and slogans, more often than not attacking the opposing parties and candidates. The focused and concentrated nature of this type of advertising does not provide sufficient policy detail or context to inform the voter adequately about the range of issues involved. In recent years, the parties have engaged in negative political advertising—in other words, advertisements that focus on the weak points of the opposition or attack the personalities of the leaders.

> 'The use of hard-hitting, negative discourse has a long history in Australia. A fiercely partisan, two-party adversarial system has made negativity a distinct feature of Australian political advertising.'
> (*Source*: Young, S. 2003, 'Scare Campaigns: Negative Political Advertising in Australia', paper presented to Australasian Political Science Association Conference, Hobart, 29 September 2003, http://www.utas.edu.au/government/APSA/SYoungfinal.pdf)

In Australia, the *Commonwealth Electoral Act* requires that electoral advertisements must be properly authorised. This means they have to include the name and address of the person who authorised the advertisement, and the name and place of the printer. It is the policy of the Australian Electoral Commission that these requirements extend to electronic publication of electoral advertising on the Internet.

It is an interesting question whether a government that advertises its policies and programs using government funds crosses the boundary into political advertising, particularly in the months leading to an election. In other words, is it designed to inform the public about what government has been doing, or is it intended to highlight and publicise the achievements of the party in government? The increasing incidence of government advertising in the period running up to an election appears to support the latter view. This suggests that parties in government increasingly are taking advantage of incumbency and the financial resources of government to advertise their achievements and in the process seek political benefit.

> Since 1993 there has been an upward trend in pre-election expenditure on government advertising.
> (*Source*: Grant, R. 2004, 'Federal Government Advertising', Research Note No. 62, 2003–04, Parliamentary Library, Canberra, http://www.aph.gov.au/library/pubs/rn/2003-04/04rn62.htm)

During the Howard government years, there were criticisms from the Opposition about the amount the government spent on political advertising. It accused the government of authorising a 'blank cheque' campaign to promote its changes to Work Choices, but the prime minister denied it was a public relations campaign, arguing that it was 'designed to provide necessary information to the Australian public' (*The Australian*, 22 May 2007). According to the Rudd Labor government's finance minister, Lindsay Tanner, in its last 16 months in office the Howard government spent $457 million on government advertising (*The Australian*, 14 February 2008). It is interesting to question the effectiveness of this strategy; despite the large amount of government money spent on promoting the Howard government's policies, the Coalition parties suffered a major swing against them and lost office at the 2007 election.

One issue to consider is whether government advertising undertaken *before* the writs for an election are issued is party political campaigning or 'government information'. The line between them can be blurred.

> - 'The misuse of public money for undeclared partisan purposes is a major concern for Australian democracy.'
> (*Source*: Young, S. 2005, 'Theories for Understanding Government Advertising in Australia', Democratic Audit of Australia, Canberra, http://democratic.audit.anu.edu.au/papers/200508_young.pdf)
>
> - 'It is a longstanding joke in the media business that the Australian Government becomes the nation's top advertiser every three years.'
> (*Source*: Sinclair, L. & Megalogenis, G. 2007, 'Propaganda overkill', *The Australian*, 24 May 2007)

The Rudd Labor government has promised to cut the level of government advertising. As part of that process, the auditor-general will be required to approve any future advertising campaign costing more than $250,000 (*The Australian*, 14 February 2008).

POLITICAL POLLING

Political polling has become a common feature of democratic countries. This includes polls undertaken by professional polling bodies and the media to find out what voters are thinking about issues, such as the leadership of the prime minister and the leader of the Opposition, the performance of the government, and voting intentions. Polls are also used to identify what issues are important to voters at any particular time. Political parties undertake private polls to gauge what voters are thinking, and tailor their policies and campaigns accordingly. Parties may change leaders if the polls are showing that a particular leader is going to disadvantage their electoral success.

Polling organisations use a range of methods:

- The most common is *telephone sampling or personal visits* to ask questions of the householder. The sample may be taken from a random selection from the electoral roll or census-based data. The sample will be nationwide for a federal election. Other polls might be taken using marginal seats as the basis for the sample.
- *Focus groups* comprise a number of citizens who are brought together to discuss policy issues with party officers, to determine how popular a particular measure might be with the electorate.
- *Survey forms* are posted out to voters, such as the Australian Election Study conducted by academic researchers after each federal election.

Opinion polls give political parties and the public an indication of how a particular party or leader is faring in the lead-up to an election.

FIGURE 13.1

Polls unreliable—or are they?

(*Source*: Cartoon by Nicholson from *The Australian*. www.nicholsoncartoons.com.au)

> 'Between elections, opinion polls are used to assess party leadership and policy proposals. Parties may remove leaders who are unpopular in the polls, even if the leaders are popular with their party colleagues.'
> (Source: Miskin, S. 2004, 'Interpreting Opinion Polls: Some Essential Details', Research Note No. 52, 2003–04, Parliamentary Library, Canberra, http://www.aph.gov.au/library/pubs/rn/2003-04/04rn52.htm)

On the other hand, polls can be misleading if they have failed to capture a last-minute swing or the pollsters have not asked the right questions.

> 'Many senior journalists and some news editors vow after each election that they will never again chase opinion polls or treat polls as news in their own right or allow the polls to affect their judgment—never ever!'
> (Source: Morris, G. 2004, 'Why poll position is no more than a matter of opinion', The Australian, 27 May 2004)

It is possible that voters will be influenced by the results of the poll to support the party in front because that seems to reflect the majority of public opinion, or else it may merely serve to reinforce their voting intention. There is always the difficulty of assessing the accuracy of the poll in determining whether people are telling the truth when they answer the questions. People may indicate to a pollster that they are going to vote in a particular way and then change their mind when they actually get to the voting booth to cast the ballot.

Television and radio stations occasionally conduct opinion polls on particular issues. These allow citizens to express their opinion, either online, by telephone, or by SMS text messaging. The results of these polls should be viewed with caution, however, as they may be skewed by people making multiple votes. There is the potential for bias, also, when members and supporters of political parties and interest groups organise to vote in large numbers for or against a particular proposition.

Political polling and the 2007 federal election

> 'Political pollsters have assumed something of a celebrity status as many people who favour a Labor election victory now use ubiquitous opinion poll results to celebrate a triumph they do not yet have.'
> (Source: 'Politics by numbers', The Australian, 26 September 2007)

Do polls drive change? The founder of Newspoll, Sol Lebovic, argued that polls are not necessarily predictive of an election result because there are a number of factors that may cause a voter to change his or her mind right up to the day of the election. However, polls are indicative of the mood of an electorate (*The Weekend Australian*, 29 September 2007). Polls leading up to the 2007 federal election consistently showed the Coalition trailing

Labor after Kevin Rudd assumed the leadership of the party, and the voters' choice at the election reflected the swing against the Coalition that the polls had been predicting.

Rodney Tiffin was critical that the polls did not show satisfactorily *why* voters changed to Labor (Tiffin, R. 2007, 'Election 2007: Pollsters off the Pace', Australian Policy Online, 12 November 2007, http://www.apo.org.au). Companies such as Media Monitors, however, analysed and reported on topics under discussion in the media in the pre-election period, which identified the issues that were concerning the electorate.

TECHNOLOGY AND POLITICAL COMMUNICATION

The Internet

The rapid growth of Internet use has significant implications for political communication. The traditional forms of communication, such as newspapers and, more particularly, television, provide limited and selective information. The Internet, on the other hand, makes a wealth of information available to individuals in their homes to inform their political views, particularly in Australia where computer ownership and Internet access is becoming more widespread.

> Between 1996 and 2006, the number of Australian households with access to the Internet at home grew from 4 per cent to 60 per cent.
> (*Source:* ABS 2007, 'Australian Social Trends, 2007', Cat. no. 4102.0, ABS, Canberra)

The Internet, as a form of 'new media' or 'citizens' media', permits practically anybody with access to a computer to participate in political debate and improves political communication in a variety of ways.

The Internet as a source of political information

The Internet offsets the concentration of media ownership of Australian newspapers and television by providing an alternative to the commercial media as the source of news in the written and visual form, with the advantage of easy and immediate access through the home computer.

Users can obtain a broad range of information and opinion from Australian-based and international websites. US President Clinton's four-hour videotaped evidence before the Grand Jury in the Monica Lewinsky case, for example, could be viewed in its entirety by accessing the website. Information about Australian government activities and policy, including government reports, can be accessed from parliamentary, ministerial and departmental websites.

Australian political parties, including the ALP, the Liberal Party and the Australian Greens, have established websites to provide information about the objectives of their parties and their policies, as well as media releases on political issues that can be read unedited, thus eliminating any bias that the media may impart with their reporting.

Groups with limited resources can set up their own websites more cheaply than establishing a newspaper or radio station. This provides them with the opportunity to get their message across to Internet browsers and to enrol new members online with an email application, including credit card payment of membership fees.

Political news and analysis can be obtained from websites such as:

- PoliticsOnline (http://www.politicsonline.com);
- australianpolitics.com (http://australianpolitics.com);
- Crikey (http://www.crikey.com.au), an Australian website that provides an independent, alternative, online news service and political analysis, and daily email updates for paying subscribers;
- Vibewire (http://www.vibewire.net), a non-profit 'online community created by young people for young people' that has the facility for putting a point of view on issues;
- TheVine (http://www.thevine.com.au), created by media company Fairfax as a news, entertainment and social networking website, targeted at 18–29-year-olds;
- PublicTechnology.net (http://www.PublicTechnology.net), which specialises in e-government and public-sector IT news, and provides online access to information such as government reports, and the minutes and agenda of local government meetings; and
- Australian Policy Online (http://www.apo.org.au), which provides access to academic research articles and conference papers.

There are also thousands of personal websites on the Internet where individuals make their views known about political issues.

> Not all countries welcome the 'new media' and its capacity to inform citizens. The Malaysian government, for example, encourages new media technologies and does not censor the content of the Internet, but it does monitor what is being said. Bloggers and citizens making their views about the government known via the Internet, including posts on personal websites, allegedly have been harassed and threatened with prosecution under the *Sedition Act* or detention without trial under the *Internal Security Act*.
> (*Sources*: OpenNet Initiative 2007, 'Malaysia', 10 May 2007, http://opennet.net/research/profiles/malaysia; Centre for Independent Journalism, Malaysia 2005, 'Media and Information in Malaysia 2004–05', 12 May 2005, http://www.cijmalaysia.org)

The Internet as a facility for interactive political communication

> 'Interactivity makes the Internet a formidable medium for politics. Disseminating information, mobilizing, and citizen interaction lie at the heart of politics. The Internet is, therefore, well suited for political use.'
> (*Source*: Klotz, R.J. 2004, *The Politics of Internet Communication*, Rowman & Littlefield, Lanham, Maryland, p. 5)

Email as a tool for political communication

Email permits citizens to contact politicians and government departments to seek information or make their views known about a particular issue. The websites of ministers, backbench members and government departments have an email link as a contact point for this purpose. Interest groups and political parties can use email to contact their members quickly and more economically than using the postal service. Email can also be used to mobilise members for campaign purposes.

> 'The day that the war starts my office will send out a message to the thousands of people to let them know where to rally to show their opposition to a war in Iraq.'
> (*Source*: Kerry Nettle, Greens senator 2003, cited in 'Greens MPs E-Brief no. 83', 28 March 2003, http://lee.greens.org.au/index.php)

> **'Dear John'**
> This was a website established to encourage young Australians to email their views to John Howard in the lead-up to the 2004 federal election. It included a range of letters that could be clicked on and sent, such as: 'Dear John, I have some bad news. I've decided to end our relationship.'
> (*Source*: Dear John 2004, http://www.dearjohn.org/site/dearjohn_letters.html. Note that this site is no longer active.)

Newspapers, radio and television stations have interactive online links to enable the public to comment or have an online 'chat' about political issues and news items.

Blogs, Internet chat rooms and news groups

These Internet facilities provide individuals with forums for political information and discussion.

> **Blog**: short for 'weblog'; an internet-based diary.

A blog is a web diary, where people (bloggers) write what they think and interact with others about political issues. It may include links to other articles and sites on the web. Access to software through service providers such as UserLand Weblogs or Blogger makes it easy for people to set up their own blogs, and the blog has become a potent tool for sourcing and disseminating political information and opinion. Blogs are also used by politicians to communicate with citizens, and by the media as an adjunct to their traditional publishing activity.

The number of blogs has proliferated, leading to the establishment of sites that categorise and list blogs that they consider relevant to their users. The *Guardian* newspaper in the United Kingdom (http://www.guardian.co.uk), for example, provides online news about blogs and their authors, a 'link log' to a selection of stories and interesting websites, and a list of blogs established by the newspaper's readers.

Using websites as a source of information

The Australian Parliament House website (http://www.aph.gov.au) includes biographical information about ministers, members of the House of Representatives and senators with links to their personal home pages that include an email facility that citizens can use to contact an MP or senator with their concerns.

The websites for government departments provide information about departmental activities, including annual reports, and a feedback facility for seeking information about a particular subject.

The Australian Electoral Commission (http://www.aec.gov.au) provides information on its website about the electoral system, including requirements for the registration of political parties, the rules for voting, and election results. This is a valuable source of information on political participation.

Information about membership and how to join can usually be found on the websites of political parties.

> ### The 'new media' and the 2007 federal election
> The Internet was a significant element of the election campaign for the 2007 federal election. The Greens, for example, provided access to a downloadable podcast of a speech by leader Bob Brown. Political parties and their leaders used Internet video platforms such as YouTube (http://www.youtube.com) and MySpace (http://www.myspace.com) to get their message across, particularly to voters in younger age groups who commonly interact with these sites.
>
> The Labor Party created a KEVIN07 website (http://www.kevin07.com.au) with several options for interactive communication:
> - **KEVIN07**—Get involved.
> - **Have your say**—A blog site for comments.
> - **Sign up to Kmail**—When you receive your email forward it on to your friends and family, remember to include anyone you know overseas.
> - **Send videos**—There is a huge amount of video content on your YouTube site. Pick your favourites and send the link to people who may not have seen them.
> - **Downloads**—Download our wallpaper or email signature and forward it on.
> - **MySpace**—Become a friend of Kevin Rudd's on MySpace.
> - **Mobilise**—Get Kevin07 on your mobile at kevin07.mobi
> - **Facebook**—Join the official Kevin Rudd Facebook group.
>
> (*Source:* Australian Labor Party 2007, Kevin07, http://www.kevin07.com.au)
>
> The Liberal Party's website (http://www.liberal.org.au) did not have the same type of links, instead offering information about policy via email. (The website now has links to video messages from the leader of the Opposition, and the party uses YouTube to inform users about its policies.)
>
> The media also used the Internet for its election coverage, with chat room and blog sites and the facility for people to get news stories and updates about the election sent directly to their mobile phones using RSS Feed (Really Simple Syndication).

A cautionary note about the Internet as a research tool

Students of politics and government use the Internet widely to research essay topics, but they need to be cautious about how this material is used, bearing in mind that it has been placed on the Internet by people who want to provide certain information to promote their own view of the world. The information may be useful, but it should be used in the context of information and critical analysis based on a broad range of sources, including academic literature.

Mobile phones and SMS text messaging as a form of political communication

During election campaigns the political parties have approached voters through their mobile phones with personal calls and text messaging. The Liberal Party used this technique during the 2004 election campaign when people received a pre-recorded, automatically generated phone message from John Howard outlining why that person should vote for the Liberal candidate in their electorate. Text messaging was used for the same purpose. In 2007, voters in marginal seats received recorded messages on their home phones (*The Weekend Australian*, 15 September 2007).

> 'I am too young to vote (come on . . . I'm 13!!!!) but I got a text message on my mobile phone from John Howard.'
> (*Source*: ABC Online Forum 2004, http://www2b.abc.net.au/news/forum/newsonline2/archives/archives38/newposts/70/topic70179.shtm, 9 October 2004. Reproduced by permission of the Australian Broadcasting Corporation and ABC Online. Copyright 2004 ABC. All rights reserved)

Political parties use text messages to keep journalists informed about what is happening during the campaign, including where the leaders are going to be that day, policy announcements, and criticism of the other parties' policies.

> 'Well, it's seven o'clock in the morning, and that annoying beep signals the start of the day. It's a text message from the Prime Minister's press office telling the media contingent shadowing John Howard what's in store—things like visiting a battery factory in Perth.'
> (*Source*: Willacy, M. 2001, 'The Art of Spin', AM, 27 October 2001, http://www.abc.net.au/am/stories/s401913.htm. Reproduced by permission of the Australian Broadcasting Corporation and ABC Online. Copyright 2001 ABC. All rights reserved)

> 'During the leaders' debate, reporters received messages on matters such as Beazley's dress sense or why the "worm" was reacting as it did to some of Howard's statements.'
> (*Source*: Bennett, S. & Newman, G. 2002, 'Commonwealth Election 2001', Research Paper No. 11, 2001–02, Parliamentary Library, Canberra, Appendix 1)

People can also use their mobile phone to find out what is happening in the campaign. The ABC, for example, provided SMS news services during the 2004 election.

> **ABC on your phone**
> The ABC election SMS alert service 'Campaign Companion' provided one wrap-up message per day throughout the 2004 election campaign, plus seven messages direct from the newsroom on election night as the count progressed and the winners and losers emerged.
> (*Source*: ABC 2004, 'SMS News Services for the Federal Election', http://www.abc.net.au/phone. Reproduced by permission of the Australian Broadcasting Corporation and ABC Online. Copyright 2004 ABC. All rights reserved)

Text messaging, like email, can be used by individuals to make politicians aware of their views, and also by political groups as a tool for organising protests and keeping their supporters informed about what is happening.

The use of technology by political parties, including party voter databases, the Internet, mobile phone calls and SMS text messaging, does not have to be restricted to election campaigns. The technology can be used on a continuing basis by all parties to find out what people think about its leader and policies and to keep citizens informed about what they are doing. Some would regard this type of political communication to be 'spam', and intrusive on an individual's right to privacy. The *Spam Act 2003* prohibits unsolicited *commercial electronic messages* being sent by email, instant messaging, SMS and MMS messaging. However, it does not cover faxes, Internet pop-ups or voice telemarketing, and messages from political parties are exempt, although they must carry accurate identifying information about the sender.
(*Source*: Australian Communications and Media Authority 2007, 'Spam & e-Security', http://www.acma.gov.au)

E-GOVERNMENT

The ability of citizens to use the Internet to interface with government has given rise to the concept of e-government. This means that:

◉ government agencies individually, or working together, can provide individuals and businesses with information on their websites about the activities of government, including details of policies and services; and
◉ individuals can transact business direct with government by filling out forms online, such as applications to register a birth, for social welfare benefits, or for paying tax and other bills. They can also provide feedback to government on its services and policy through direct contact email facilities.

> **E-government** is:
> - 'the use of technology to enhance the access to and delivery of government services to benefit citizens, business partners and employees';
>
> (*Source*: Silcock, R. 2001, 'What is e-Government?', *Parliamentary Affairs*, vol. 54, p. 88)
> - 'the use of information and communication technologies and particularly the Internet as a tool to achieve better government'.
>
> (*Source*: Organisation for Economic Co-operation and Development (OECD) 2003, *The E-government Imperative*, OECD, Paris)

Examples of e-government

Australia

The entry portal to information about the Australian government, including services and directories, is http://www.australia.gov.au. Individual departments and agencies have their own sites:

◉ The Centrelink website (http://www.centrelink.gov.au) enables students to get information about payments that may be available to them to assist with their study and training.

- The Australian Taxation Office (http://www.ato.gov.au) offers a personal email inquiry service for a range of services, such as capital gains tax or change of name and address. Personal taxpayers can lodge a tax return and business owners can complete a Business Activity Statement online.
- The Defence Materiel Organisation at the Department of Defence website (http://www.defence.gov.au) provides information on the department's contracting policy and current tendering opportunities that is of great assistance to manufacturers of defence equipment.
- The Department of Education, Employment and Workplace Relations (http://www.deewr.gov.au) website enables citizens to find out about employment, government assistance, jobs, careers, training and working conditions.
- Business Consultation (https://consultation.business.gov.au) is an Australian government website that provides business and individuals with the opportunity to be consulted about government policies and regulations that affect them.

E-government provides citizens with 24-hour, seven-day-a-week access to government from a home computer, and the facility of having government agencies post copies of documents, such as government reports and regulations, on their website. Information posted by government agencies can also be sent automatically to interested individuals or businesses, including updates when changes are made.

Britain

Directgov (http://www.direct.gov.uk) is the official government access point for citizen information. The Government Gateway website (http://www.gateway.gov.uk) provides citizens with the facility to register to use online government services.

United States

- USA.gov ('Government Made Easy') (http://www.usa.gov) is the portal for citizen access to information about government services and government agencies.
- E-Gov (http://www.whitehouse.gov/omb/egov) is the official site of the US President's e-government entry point. The site was established 'to make it easier for citizens and businesses to interact with government, save taxpayer dollars, and streamline citizen-to-government communication'.

Federal Republic of Germany

BundOnline (http://www.bund.de) is the German federal government's access point for citizens and business to access government services and information. Deutschland-Online (http://www.deutschland-online.de) is a fully integrated e-government site including federal, state and local government services.

Federation of Malaysia

Malaysia's development of a Multimedia Super Corridor in 1996 included an application for e-government to facilitate access by citizens and business to government services. This includes an e-transaction centre for online services and a government directory site (http://www.gov.my).

Advantages of e-government

There are advantages in e-government. These include the fact that people with disabilities do not have to queue to get served at a government departmental office, and people living in remote areas can have direct and immediate access as well. E-government avoids the long delays people experience in trying to get through to someone in a government department on the telephone. (We have all experienced the frustrations of going through a sequence of numbers to find the right section to help us, and then listening to music as we are placed in a queue to which there seems to be no end!)

Problems with e-government

There are, however, potential problems with e-government. Some people might have difficulties using e-government because they do not have access to a computer at home, particularly those on low incomes who may be in greatest need of government assistance. As we saw earlier in this chapter, 60 per cent of Australian households in 2006 were connected to the Internet, but this means that 40 per cent did not have that facility. This problem could be overcome, however, with the placement of computer terminals providing access to e-government sites in public areas, such as local libraries or government shopfronts, together with free education programs on how to access and use the Internet.

Citizens in remote areas may lack the technical services that support access to the Internet. The format of the online application may not take into account the complexities of an individual's personal circumstances. Interfacing with a computer is sometimes no substitute for explaining your situation to someone who can listen sympathetically and deal with the problem appropriately.

The facility of email may raise expectations of an immediate response, but people seeking information from a minister or government department may find that does not happen.

Overall, however, e-government does have the capacity to improve the delivery of government services to citizens (e-services). It promotes information sharing between government and citizens and has the potential to produce more open government, and, in doing so, to enhance democracy.

E-DEMOCRACY

E-government has the potential to create the conditions for a form of e-democracy — that is, to enhance citizen participation in the political process using the Internet from their homes.

> **e-democracy**: The use of the Internet as a tool for public participation in the political process.
> (*Source*: Sampford, K. 2001, 'E-Democracy and Election Campaigns: Recent Case Studies from USA and Developments in Australia', Research Brief 2/01, Queensland Parliamentary Library, Brisbane, p. 1)

Citizen participation is a fundamental element of any democratic political system. We have seen how citizens can use the Internet to enhance their access to government services and information, political information and a broad range of political opinion. They can also have their say to government through email, and engage in political debate with other citizens using online forums and blogs.

The Internet can also be used by large and small political parties alike to encourage citizen participation in party activity by making it easy to enrol, and as a facility for mobilising the party membership to take action over a particular issue or for campaign purposes.

The email feedback facility on the websites of members of parliament enhances representative democracy because it enables constituents to ascertain and make judgements about what their local members have been doing, and to let them know how they feel about it. The fact that ministers and government departments have established websites to provide details of government policy and their activities makes it easier for interest groups to access information, with the potential for reducing the information-'rich' advantage held by 'insider' groups over their 'outsider' counterparts.

There is the prospect also, as we saw in Chapter 8, of citizens being able to vote from home, which will make it easier for people to exercise their democratic right to vote.

There are some limitations to e-democracy at the present time, however. Parties and government could use the Internet to find out what people are thinking through direct political polling or with 'citizen-initiated referendums', but these functions cannot be used as a comprehensive and effective facility for e-democracy when some people do not have access to a computer or lack the expertise to use one.

There is always the danger that groups who have the money could use their funds to try to dominate the political debate or influence the political agenda at the expense of other groups and individuals that do not have the same resources. However, this danger is offset by the low cost of participating through the Internet, so that individuals, as well as groups, can make their opinions known.

There is no doubt that political communication is enhanced by the Internet. This can only benefit democracy in the long run, as open portals to government and the wide dissemination of political information and debate provide the opportunity for citizens to find out what is going on, to have their say, and make government more responsive and accountable for its actions.

QUESTIONS FOR DISCUSSION

1. Assess the arguments for and against the media as a useful tool of political communication. Which do you think is the most persuasive? Give your reasons.
2. What measures could the media adopt to prevent ministerial and party 'spin doctors' from controlling the flow of political information during an election campaign?
3. Does political bias or the concentration of ownership of the media matter?
4. 'The Internet offers great potential for enhancing political communication and political awareness.' Discuss.
5. 'The use of mobile phone and SMS text messaging by individuals, groups and political parties to mobilise support and distribute political information will be beneficial tools for Australian democracy.' Discuss.
6. 'E-government will enhance Australia's system of liberal democracy.' Discuss.

FURTHER READING

Argy, F. 2005, 'What is Happening to Australian Democracy?', Democratic Audit of Australia, Canberra, http://democratic.audit.anu.edu.au/papers/20050701_argy_oz_democracy.pdf.

Barns, G. 2005, *Selling the Australian Government: Politics and Propaganda from Whitlam to Howard*, UNSW Press, Sydney.

Chen, P. 2007, 'Electronic Engagement: a Guide for Public Sector Managers', ANU E Press, Canberra, http://epress.anu.edu.au/engage_citation.html.

Gibson, R., Rommele, A. & Ward, S. (eds) 2004, *Electronic Democracy*, Routledge, London. Analyses the impact of new information and communication technologies on representative democracy.

Gibson, R.K. & Ward, S. 2002, 'Virtual Campaigning: Australian Parties and the Impact of the Internet', *Australian Journal of Political Science*, vol. 37, no. 1, pp. 99–129. This paper examines the impact of the Internet and email on Australian parties — in particular, how parties use their websites and the impact on the way smaller parties communicate.

Goot, M. 2000, 'The Performance of the Polls', in Simms, M. & Warhurst, J. (eds), *Howard's Agenda*, University of Queensland Press, Brisbane. A discussion of opinion polls related to the 1998 election.

Kingston, M. 1999, *Off the Rails: The Pauline Hanson Trip*, Allen & Unwin, Sydney. An interesting insight into the relationship between the media and political parties during an election campaign.

McEwen, M. 2007, 'Media Ownership: Rules, Regulations and Practices in Selected Countries and their Potential Relevance to Canada', Canadian Radio-television and Telecommunications Commission, Gatineau, Canada, http://www.crtc.gc.ca/eng/publications/reports/mcewen07.htm. Provides information on the media ownership rules of the United States, Germany, France and Australia.

McNair, B. 2003, *An Introduction to Political Communication*, Routledge, London. Explores the relationship between politics, the media and democracy.

Mancini, P. 1999, 'New Frontiers in Political Professionalism', *Political Communication*, vol. 16, no. 3, pp. 231–45. Explains how developments in telecommunications, including the Internet, have altered the character of political parties and government.

Miskin, S. 2005, 'Campaigning in the 2004 Federal Election: Innovations and Traditions', Research Note No. 30, 2004–05, Parliamentary Library, Canberra, http://www.aph.gov.au/library/pubs/rn/.

Peisley, M. & Ward, I. 2001, 'Parties, Governments and Pollsters: a New Form of Patronage?', *Australian Journal of Political Science*, vol. 36, no. 3, pp. 553–65. Discusses the relationship between political parties and commercial polling companies.

Simons, M. 1999, *Fit to Print: Inside the Canberra Press Gallery*, UNSW Press, Sydney. An interesting study of the press gallery in Parliament House.

Tiffen, R. 2000, 'The News Media and Australian Politics: Contemporary Challenges for Australian Democracy in the Information Age', in Boreham, P., Stokes, G. & Hall, R. (eds), *The Politics of Australian Society*, Longman, Sydney. A critical analysis of media concentration, and the processes of news making, media manipulation and opinion formation.

Ward, I. 1995, *Politics of the Media*, Macmillan Education, Melbourne. A comprehensive study of the operations and impact of the media.

Warhurst, J. 2007, 'Political opinion polls matter', *Eureka Street*, vol. 17, no. 14, 25 July 2007, http://www.eurekastreet.com.au/article.aspx?aeid=3173.

Wilson, S. 2004, 'Election 2004: Barely Registered: Is Public Opinion Good Enough for Democracy?', *Australian Review of Public Affairs*, 1 October 2004, http://www.australianreview.net/digest/2004/10/wilson.html.

Young, S. 2002, 'Spot On: the Role of Political Advertising in Australia', *Australian Journal of Political Science*, vol. 37, no. 1, pp. 81–97. Discusses the role of political advertising in the political process.

Young, S. 2004, *The Persuaders: Inside the Hidden Machine of Political Advertising*, Pluto Press, Melbourne. This book charts how political advertising has changed over time and assesses the impact on the nature of Australian democracy.

USEFUL WEBSITES

- http://www.australia.gov.au
  australia.gov.au
  Commonwealth government entry point.

- http://www.e.govt.nz
  E-government in New Zealand
  A useful discussion of what e-government is and how it operates in New Zealand.

The Australian Constitution

[63 & 64 VICT.] COMMONWEALTH OF AUSTRALIA [CH.12] CONSTITUTION ACT

CHAPTER 12
An Act to constitute the Commonwealth of Australia

[9th July 1900]

Whereas the people of New South Wales, Victoria, South Australia, Queensland, and Tasmania, humbly relying on the blessing of Almighty God, have agreed to unite in one indissoluble Federal Commonwealth under the Crown of the United Kingdom of Great Britain and Ireland, and under the Constitution hereby established:

And whereas it is expedient to provide for the admission into the Commonwealth of other Australasian Colonies and possessions of the Queen:

Be it therefore enacted by the Queen's most Excellent Majesty, by and with the advice and consent of the Lords Spiritual and Temporal, and Commons, in this present Parliament assembled, and by the authority of the same, as follows:—

Short title.	1 This Act may be cited as the Commonwealth of Australia Constitution Act.
Act to extend to the Queen's successors.	2 The provisions of this Act referring to the Queen shall extend to Her Majesty's heirs and successors in the sovereignty of the United Kingdom.
Proclamation of Commonwealth.	3 It shall be lawful for the Queen, with the advice of the Privy Council, to declare by proclamation that, on and after a day therein appointed, not being later than one year after the passing of this Act, the people of New South Wales, Victoria, South Australia, Queensland, and Tasmania, and also, if Her Majesty is satisfied that the people of Western Australia have agreed thereto, of Western Australia, shall be united in a Federal Commonwealth under the name of the Commonwealth of Australia. But the Queen may, at any time after the proclamation, appoint a Governor-General for the Commonwealth.
Commencement of Act.	4 The Commonwealth shall be established, and the Constitution of the Commonwealth shall take effect, on and after the day so appointed. But the Parliaments of the several colonies may at any time after the passing of this Act make any such laws, to come into operation on the day so appointed, as they might have made if the Constitution had taken effect at the passing of this Act.
Operation of the constitution and laws.	5 This Act, and all laws made by the Parliament of the Commonwealth under the Constitution, shall be binding on the courts, judges, and people of every State and of every part of the Commonwealth, not withstanding anything in the laws of any State; and the laws of the Commonwealth shall be in force on all British ships, the Queen's ships of war excepted, whose first port of clearance and whose port of destination are in the Commonwealth.
Definitions	6 'The Commonwealth' shall mean the Commonwealth of Australia as established under this Act. 'The States' shall mean such of the colonies of New South Wales, New Zealand, Queensland, Tasmania, Victoria, Western Australia, and South Australia, including the northern territory of South Australia, as for the time being are parts of the Commonwealth, and such colonies or territories as may be admitted into or established by the Commonwealth as States; and each of such parts of the Commonwealth shall be called 'a State.' 'Original States' shall mean such States as are parts of the Commonwealth at its establishment.
Repeal of Federal Council Act. 48 & 49 Vict. c. 60.	7 The Federal Council of Australasia Act, 1885, is hereby repealed, but so as not to affect any laws passed by the Federal Council of Australasia and in force at the establishment of the Commonwealth. Any such law may be repealed as to any State by the Parliament of the Commonwealth, or as to any colony not being a State by the Parliament thereof.
Application of Colonial Boundaries Act. 58 & 59 Vict. c. 34.	8 After the passing of this Act the Colonial Boundaries Act, 1895, shall not apply to any colony which becomes a State of the Commonwealth; but the Commonwealth shall be taken to be a self-governing colony for the purposes of that Act.
Constitution.	9 The Constitution of the Commonwealth shall be as follows:—

The Constitution

This Constitution is divided as follows:—

Chapter I.—The Parliament:

Part I.—General:

Part II.—The Senate:

Part III.—The House of Representatives:

Part IV.—Both Houses of the Parliament:

Part V.—Powers of the Parliament:

Chapter II.—The Executive Government:

Chapter III.—The Judicature:

Chapter IV.—Finance and Trade:

Chapter V.—The States:

Chapter VI.—New States:

Chapter VII.—Miscellaneous:

Chapter VIII.—Alteration of the Constitution.

The Schedule.

Chapter I

The Parliament

Part I—General

Chap 1.

The Parliament.

Part I. General.

1 The legislative power of the Commonwealth shall be vested in a Federal Parliament, which shall consist of the Queen, a Senate, and a House of Representatives, and which is herein-after called 'The Parliament,' or 'The Parliament of the Commonwealth.'

Legislative power.

2 A Governor-General appointed by the Queen shall be Her Majesty's representative in the Commonwealth, and shall have and may exercise in the Commonwealth during the Queen's pleasure, but subject to this Constitution, such powers and functions of the Queen as Her Majesty may be pleased to assign to him.

Governor-General.

3 There shall be payable to the Queen out of the Consolidated Revenue fund of the Commonwealth, for the salary of the Governor-General, an annual sum which, until the Parliament otherwise provides, shall be ten thousand pounds.

Salary of Governor-General.

The salary of a Governor-General shall not be altered during his continuance in office.

4 The provisions of this Constitution relating to the Governor-General extend and apply to the Governor-General for the time being, or such person as the Queen may appoint to administer the Government of the Commonwealth; but no such person shall be entitled to receive any salary from the Commonwealth in respect of any other office during his administration of the Government of the Commonwealth.

Provisions relating to Governor-General.

5 The Governor-General may appoint such times for holding the sessions of the Parliament as he thinks fit, and may also from time to time, by Proclamation or otherwise, prorogue the Parliament, and may in like manner dissolve the House of Representatives.

Sessions of Parliament. Prorogation and dissolution.

After any general election the Parliament shall be summoned to meet not later than thirty days after the day appointed for the return of the writs.

Summoning Parliament.

The Parliament shall be summoned to meet not later than six months after the establishment of the Commonwealth.

First Session.

6 There shall be a session of the Parliament once at least in every year, so that twelve months shall not intervene between the last sitting of the Parliament in one session and its first sitting in the next session.

Yearly session of Parliament.

Part II—The Senate

Part II. The Senate.

The Senate.

7 The Senate shall be composed of senators for each State, directly chosen by the people of the State, voting, until the Parliament otherwise provides, as one electorate.

But until the Parliament of the Commonwealth otherwise provides, the Parliament of the State of Queensland, if that State be an Original State, may make laws dividing the State into divisions and determining the number of senators to be chosen for each division, and in the absence of such provision the State shall be one electorate.

Until the Parliament otherwise provides there shall be six senators for each Original State. The Parliament may make laws increasing or diminishing the number of senators for each State, but so that equal representation of the several Original States shall be maintained and that no Original State shall have less than six senators.

The senators shall be chosen for a term of six years, and the names of the senators chosen for each State shall be certified by the Governor to the Governor-General.

Qualification of electors.

8 The qualification of electors of senators shall be in each State that which is prescribed by this Constitution, or by the Parliament, as the qualification for electors of members of the House of Representatives; but in the choosing of senators each elector shall vote only once.

Method of election of senators.

9 The Parliament of the Commonwealth may make laws prescribing the method of choosing senators, but so that the method shall be uniform for all the States. Subject to any such law, the Parliament of each State may make laws prescribing the method of choosing the senators for that State.

Times and places.

The Parliament of a State may make laws for determining the times and places of elections of senators for the State.

Application of State laws.

10 Until the Parliament otherwise provides, but subject to this Constitution, the laws in force in each State, for the time being, relating to elections for the more numerous House of the Parliament of the State shall, as nearly as practicable, apply to elections of senators for the State.

Failure to choose senators.

11 The Senate may proceed to the despatch of business, notwithstanding the failure of any State to provide for its representation in the Senate.

Issue of writs.

12 The Governor of any State may cause writs to be issued for elections of senators for the State. In case of the dissolution of the Senate the writs shall be issued within ten days from the proclamation of such dissolution.

Rotation of senators.
Altered by No. 1, 1907, s. 2.

13 As soon as may be after the Senate first meets, and after each first meeting of the Senate following a dissolution thereof, the Senate shall divide the senators chosen for each State into two classes, as, nearly equal in number as practicable; and the places of the senators of the first class shall become vacant at the expiration of ~~the third year~~ three years, and the places of those of the second class at the expiration of ~~the sixth year~~ six years, from the beginning of their term of service; and afterwards the places of senators shall become vacant at the expiration of six years from the beginning of their term of service.

The election to fill vacant places shall be made ~~in the year at the expiration of which~~ within one year before the places are to become vacant.

For the purposes of this section the term of service of a senator shall be taken to begin on the first day of ~~January~~ July following the day of his election, except in the cases of the first election and of the election next after any dissolution of the

Senate, when it shall be taken to begin on the first day of ~~January~~ **July** preceding the day of his election.

14 Whenever the number of senators for a State is increased or diminished, the Parliament of the Commonwealth may make such provision for the vacating of the places of senators for the State as it deems necessary to maintain regularity in the rotation.

15 If the place of a senator becomes vacant before the expiration of his term of service, the Houses of Parliament of the State for which he was chosen, sitting and voting together, or, if there is only one House of that Parliament, that House, shall choose a person to hold the place until the expiration of the term. But if the Parliament of the State is not in session when the vacancy is notified, the Governor of the State, with the advice of the Executive Council thereof, may appoint a person to hold the place until the expiration of fourteen days from the beginning of the next session of the Parliament of the State or the expiration of the term, whichever first happens.

Casual vacancies. Substituted by No. 82, 1977, s. 2.

Where a vacancy has at any time occurred in the place of a senator chosen by the people of a State and, at the time when he was so chosen, he was publicly recognized by a particular political party as being an endorsed candidate of that party and publicly represented himself to be such a candidate, a person chosen or appointed under this section in consequence of that vacancy, or in consequence of that vacancy and a subsequent vacancy or vacancies, shall, unless there is no member of that party available to be chosen or appointed, be a member of that party.

Where—

(a) in accordance with the last preceding paragraph, a member of a particular political party is chosen or appointed to hold the place of a senator whose place had become vacant; and

(b) before taking his seat he ceases to be a member of that party (otherwise than by reason of the party having ceased to exist),

he shall be deemed not to have been so chosen or appointed and the vacancy shall be again notified in accordance with section twenty-one of this Constitution.

The name of any senator chosen or appointed under this section shall be certified by the Governor of the State to the Governor-General.

If the place of a senator chosen by the people of a State at the election of senators last held before the commencement of the *Constitution Alteration (Senate Casual Vacancies)* 1977 became vacant before that commencement and, at that commencement, no person chosen by the House or Houses of Parliament of the State, or appointed by the Governor of the State, in consequence of that vacancy, or in consequence of that vacancy and a subsequent vacancy or vacancies, held office, this section applies as if the place of the senator chosen by the people of the State had become vacant after that commencement.

A senator holding office at the commencement of the *Constitution Alteration (Senate Casual Vacancies)* 1977, being a senator appointed by the Governor of a State in consequence of a vacancy that had at any time occurred in the place of a senator chosen by the people of the State, shall be deemed to have been appointed to hold the place until the expiration of fourteen days after the beginning of the next session of the Parliament of the State that commenced or commences after he was appointed and further action under this section shall be taken as if the vacancy in the place of the senator chosen by the people of the State had occurred after that commencement.

Subject to the next succeeding paragraph, a senator holding office at the commencement of the *Constitution Alteration (Senate Casual Vacancies) 1977* who was chosen by the House or Houses of Parliament of a State in consequence of a vacancy that had at any time occurred in the place of a senator chosen by the people of the State shall be deemed to have been chosen to hold office until the expiration of the term of service of the senator elected by the people of the State.

If, at or before the commencement of the *Constitution Alteration (Senate Casual Vacancies) 1977*, a law to alter the Constitution entitled 'Constitution Alteration (Simultaneous Elections) 1977' came into operation, a senator holding office at the commencement of that law who was chosen by the House or Houses of Parliament of a State in consequence of a vacancy that had at any time occurred in the place of a Senator chosen by the people of the State shall be deemed to have been chosen to hold office—

(a) if the senator elected by the people of the State had a term of service expiring on the thirtieth day of June, One thousand nine hundred and seventy-eight—until the expiration or dissolution of the first House of Representatives to expire or be dissolved after that law came into operation; or

(b) if the senator elected by the people of the State had a term of service expiring on the thirtieth day of June, One thousand nine hundred and eighty-one—until the expiration or dissolution of the second House of Representatives to expire or be dissolved after that law came into operation or, if there is an earlier dissolution of the Senate, until that dissolution.

Qualifications of senator.	**16** The qualifications of a senator shall be the same as those of a member of the House of Representatives.
Election of President.	**17** The Senate shall, before proceeding to the despatch of any other business, choose a senator to be the President of the Senate; and as often as the office of President becomes vacant the Senate shall again choose a senator to be the President. The President shall cease to hold his office if he ceases to be a senator. He may be removed from office by a vote of the Senate, or he may resign his office or his seat by writing addressed to the Governor-General.
Absence of President.	**18** Before or during any absence of the President, the Senate may choose a senator to perform his duties in his absence.
Resignation of senator.	**19** A senator may, by writing addressed to the President, or to the Governor-General if there is no President or if the President is absent from the Commonwealth, resign his place, which thereupon shall become vacant.
Vacancy by absence.	**20** The place of a senator shall become vacant if for two consecutive months of any session of the Parliament he, without the permission of the Senate, fails to attend the Senate.
Vacancy to be notified.	**21** Whenever a vacancy happens in the Senate, the President, or if there is no President or if the President is absent from the Commonwealth the Governor-General, shall notify the same to the Governor of the State in the representation of which the vacancy has happened.
Quorum.	**22** Until the Parliament otherwise provides, the presence of at least one-third of the whole number of the senators shall be necessary to constitute a meeting of the Senate for the exercise of its powers.
Voting in the Senate.	**23** Questions arising in the Senate shall be determined by a majority of votes, and each senator shall have one vote. The President shall in all cases be entitled to a vote; and when the votes are equal the question shall pass in the negative.

Part III—The House of Representatives

24 The House of Representatives shall be composed of members directly chosen by the people of the Commonwealth, and the number of such members shall be, as nearly as practicable, twice the number of the senators.

The number of members chosen in the several States shall be in proportion to the respective numbers of their people, and shall, until the Parliament otherwise provides, be determined, whenever necessary, in the following manner:—

(i) A quota shall be ascertained by dividing the number of the people of the Commonwealth, as shown by the latest statistics of the Commonwealth, by twice the number of the senators:

(ii) The number of members to be chosen in each State shall be determined by dividing the number of the people of the State, as shown by the latest statistics of the Commonwealth, by the quota; and if on such division there is a remainder greater than one-half of the quota, one more member shall be chosen in the State.

But notwithstanding anything in this section, five members at least shall be chosen in each Original State.

25 For the purposes of the last section, if by the law of any State all persons of any race are disqualified from voting at elections for the more numerous House of the Parliament of the State, then, in reckoning the number of the people of the State or of the Commonwealth, persons of that race resident in that State shall not be counted.

26 Notwithstanding anything in section twenty-four, the number of members to be chosen in each State at the first election shall be as follows:—

> New South Wales ....twenty-three;
> Victoria ....twenty;
> Queensland ....eight;
> South Australia ....six;
> Tasmania...five;

Provided that if Western Australia is an Original State, the number shall be as follows:—

> New South Wales ....twenty-six;
> Victoria ....twenty-three;
> Queensland ....nine;
> South Australia ....seven;
> Western Australia ....five;
> Tasmania...five.

27 Subject to this Constitution, the Parliament may make laws for increasing or diminishing the number of the members of the House of Representatives.

28 Every House of Representatives shall continue for three years from the first meeting of the House, and no longer, but may be sooner dissolved by the Governor-General.

29 Until the Parliament of the Commonwealth otherwise provides, the Parliament of any State may make laws for determining the divisions in each State for which members of the House of Representatives may be chosen, and the number of members to be chosen for each division. A division shall not be formed out of parts of different States.

In the absence of other provision, each State shall be one electorate.

Qualification of electors.

30 Until the Parliament otherwise provides, the qualification of electors of members of the House of Representatives shall be in each State that which is prescribed by the law of the State as the qualification of electors of the more numerous House of Parliament of the State; but in the choosing of members each elector shall vote only once.

Application of state laws.

31 Until the Parliament otherwise provides, but subject to this Constitution, the laws in force in each State for the time being relating to elections for the more numerous House of the Parliament of the State shall, as nearly as practicable, apply to elections in the State of members of the House of Representatives.

Writs for general election.

32 The Governor-General in Council may cause writs to be issued for general elections of members of the House of Representatives.

After the first general election, the writs shall be issued within ten days from the expiry of a House of Representatives or from the proclamation of a dissolution thereof.

Writs for vacancies.

33 Whenever a vacancy happens in the House of Representatives, the Speaker shall issue his writ for the election of a new member, or if there is no Speaker or if he is absent from the Commonwealth the Governor-General in Council may issue the writ.

Qualifications of members.

34 Until the Parliament otherwise provides, the qualifications of a member of the House of Representatives shall be as follows:—

(i) He must be *of* the full age of twenty-one years, and must be an elector entitled to vote at the election of members of the House of Representatives, or a person qualified to become such elector, and must have been for three years at the least a resident within the limits of the Commonwealth as existing at the time when he is chosen:

(ii) He must be a subject of the Queen, either natural-born or for at least five years naturalized under a law of the United Kingdom, or of a Colony which has become or becomes a State, or of the Commonwealth, or of a State.

Election of Speaker.

35 The House of Representatives shall, before proceeding to the despatch of any other business, choose a member to be the Speaker of the House, and as often as the office of Speaker becomes vacant the House shall again choose a member to be the Speaker.

The Speaker shall cease to hold his office if he ceases to be a member. He may be removed from office by a vote of the House, or he may resign his office or his seat by writing addressed to the Governor-General.

Absence of Speaker.

36 Before or during any absence of the Speaker, the House of Representatives may choose a member to perform his duties in his absence.

Resignation of member.

37 A member may by writing addressed to the Speaker, or to the Governor-General if there is no Speaker or if the Speaker is absent from the Commonwealth, resign his place, which thereupon shall become vacant.

Vacancy by absence.

38 The place of a member shall become vacant if for two consecutive months of any session of the Parliament he, without the permission of the House, fails to attend the House.

39 Until the Parliament otherwise provides, the presence of at least one-third of the whole number of the members of the House of Representatives shall be necessary to constitute a meeting of the House for the exercise of its powers.

Quorum.

40 Questions arising in the House of Representatives shall be determined by a majority of votes other than that of the Speaker. The Speaker shall not vote unless the numbers are equal, and then he shall have a casting vote.

Voting in House of Representatives.

Part IV—Both Houses of the Parliament

Part IV. Both Houses of Parliament.

41 No adult person who has or acquires a right to vote at elections for the more numerous House of the Parliament of a State shall, while the right continues, be prevented by any law of the Commonwealth from voting at elections for either House of the Parliament of the Commonwealth.

Right of electors of States.

42 Every senator and every member of the House of Representatives shall before taking his seat make and subscribe before the Governor-General, or some person authorised by him, an oath or affirmation of allegiance in the form set forth in the schedule to this Constitution.

Oath or affirmation of allegiance.

43 A member of either House of the Parliament shall be incapable of being chosen or of sitting as a member of the other House.

Member of one house ineligible for other.

44 Any person who—

Disqualification.

(i) Is under any acknowledgment of allegiance, obedience, or adherence to a foreign power, or is a subject or a citizen or entitled to the rights or privileges of a subject or a citizen of a foreign power: or

(ii) Is attainted of treason, or has been convicted and is under sentence, or subject to be sentenced, for any offence punishable under the law of the Commonwealth or of a State by imprisonment for one year or longer: or

(iii) Is an undischarged bankrupt or insolvent: or

(iv) Holds any office of profit under the Crown, or any pension payable during the pleasure of the Crown out of any of the revenues of the Commonwealth: or

(v) Has any direct or indirect pecuniary interest in any agreement with the Public Service of the Commonwealth otherwise than as a member and in common with the other members of an incorporated company consisting of more than twenty-five persons:

shall be incapable of being chosen or of sitting as a senator or a member of the House of Representatives.

But sub-section iv. does not apply to the office of any of the Queen's Ministers of State for the Commonwealth, or of any of the Queen's Ministers for a State, or to the receipt of pay, half pay, or a pension, by any person as an officer or member of the Queen's navy or army, or to the receipt of pay as an officer or member of the naval or military forces of the Commonwealth by any person whose services are not wholly employed by the Commonwealth.

45 If a senator or member of the House of Representatives—

Vacancy on happening of disqualification.

(i) Becomes subject to any of the disabilities mentioned in the last preceding section: or

(ii) Takes the benefit, whether by assignment, composition, or otherwise, of any law relating to bankrupt or insolvent debtors: or

(iii) Directly or indirectly takes or agrees to take any fee or honorarium for services rendered to the Commonwealth, or for services rendered in the Parliament to any person or State:

his place shall thereupon become vacant.

Penalty for sitting when disqualified.

46 Until the Parliament otherwise provides, any person declared by this Constitution to be incapable of sitting as a senator or as a member of the House of Representatives shall, for every day on which he so sits, be liable to pay the sum of one hundred pounds to any person who sues for it in any court of competent jurisdiction.

Disputed elections.

47 Until the Parliament otherwise provides, any question respecting the qualification of a senator or of a member of the House of Representatives, or respecting a vacancy in either House of the Parliament, and any question of a disputed election to either House, shall be determined by the House in which the question arises.

Allowance to members.

48 Until the Parliament otherwise provides, each senator and each member of the House of Representatives shall receive an allowance of four hundred pounds a year, to be reckoned from the day on which he takes his seat.

Privileges, &c. of Houses.

49 The powers, privileges, and immunities of the Senate and of the House of Representatives, and of the members and the committees of each House, shall be such as are declared by the Parliament, and until declared shall be those of the Commons House of Parliament of the United Kingdom, and of its members and committees, at the establishment of the Commonwealth.

Rules and orders.

50 Each House of the Parliament may make rules and orders with respect to—

(i) The mode in which its powers, privileges, and immunities may be exercised and upheld:

(ii) The order and conduct of its business and proceedings either separately or jointly with the other House.

Part V. Powers of the Parliament.

Part V—Powers of the Parliament

Legislative powers of Parliament.

51 The Parliament shall, subject to this Constitution, have power to make laws for the peace, order, and good government of the Commonwealth with respect to:—

(i) Trade and commerce with other countries, and among the States:

(ii) Taxation; but so as not to discriminate between States or parts of States:

(iii) Bounties on the production or export of goods, but so that such bounties shall be uniform throughout the Commonwealth:

(iv) Borrowing money on the public credit of the Commonwealth:

(v) Postal, telegraphic, telephonic, and other like services:

(vi) The naval and military defence of the Commonwealth and of the several States, and the control of the forces to execute and maintain the laws of the Commonwealth:

(vii) Lighthouses, lightships, beacons and buoys:

(viii) Astronomical and meteorological observations:

(ix) Quarantine:

(x) Fisheries in Australian waters beyond territorial limits:

(xi)	Census and statistics:	
(xii)	Currency, coinage, and legal tender:	
(xiii)	Banking, other than State banking; also State banking extending beyond the limits of the State concerned, the incorporation of banks, and the issue of paper money:	
(xiv)	Insurance, other than State insurance; also State insurance extending beyond the limits of the State concerned:	
(xv)	Weights and measures:	
(xvi)	Bills of exchange and promissory notes:	
(xvii)	Bankruptcy and insolvency:	
(xviii)	Copyrights, patents of inventions and designs, and trade marks:	
(xix)	Naturalization and aliens:	
(xx)	Foreign corporations, and trading or financial corporations formed within the limits of the Commonwealth:	
(xxi)	Marriage:	
(xxii)	Divorce and matrimonial causes; and in relation thereto, parental rights, and the custody and guardianship of infants:	
(xxiii)	Invalid and old-age pensions:	
(xxiiia)	The provision of maternity allowances, widows' pensions, child endowment, unemployment, pharmaceutical, sickness and hospital benefits, medical and dental services (but not so as to authorize any form of civil conscription), benefits to students and family allowances:	Inserted by No. 81, 1946, s. 2.
(xxiv)	The service and execution throughout the Commonwealth of the civil and criminal process and the judgments of the courts of the States:	
(xxv)	The recognition throughout the Commonwealth of the laws, the public Acts and records, and the judicial proceedings of the States:	
(xxvi)	The people of any race, ~~other than the aboriginal race in any State~~, for whom it is deemed necessary to make special laws:	Altered by No. 55, 1967, s. 2.
(xxvii)	Immigration and emigration:	
(xxviii)	The influx of criminals:	
(xxix)	External affairs:	
(xxx)	The relations of the Commonwealth with the islands of the Pacific:	
(xxxi)	The acquisition of property on just terms from any State or person for any purpose in respect of which the Parliament has power to make laws:	
(xxxii)	The control of railways with respect to transport for the naval and military purposes of the Commonwealth:	
(xxxiii)	The acquisition, with the consent of a State, of any railways of the State on terms arranged between the Commonwealth and the State:	
(xxxiv)	Railway construction and extension in any State with the consent of that State:	
(xxxv)	Conciliation and arbitration for the prevention and settlement of industrial disputes extending beyond the limits of any one State:	
(xxxvi)	Matters in respect of which this Constitution makes provision until the Parliament otherwise provides:	

(xxxvii) Matters referred to the Parliament of the Commonwealth by the Parliament or Parliaments of any State or States, but so that the law shall extend only to States by whose Parliaments the matter is referred, or which afterwards adopt the law:

(xxxviii) The exercise within the Commonwealth, at the request or with the concurrence of the Parliaments of all the States directly concerned, of any power which can at the establishment of this Constitution be exercised only by the Parliament of the United Kingdom or by the Federal Council of Australasia:

(xxxix) Matters incidental to the execution of any power vested by this Constitution in the Parliament or in either House thereof, or in the Government of the Commonwealth, or in the Federal Judicature, or in any department or officer of the Commonwealth.

Exclusive powers of Parliament.

52 The Parliament shall, subject to this Constitution, have exclusive power to make laws for the peace, order, and good government of the Commonwealth with respect to—

(i) The seat of government of the Commonwealth, and all places acquired by the Commonwealth for public purposes:

(ii) Matters relating to any department of the public service the control of which is by this Constitution transferred to the Executive Government of the Commonwealth:

(iii) Other matters declared by this Constitution to be within the exclusive power of the Parliament.

Powers of the Houses in respect of legislation.

53 Proposed laws appropriating revenue or moneys, or imposing taxation, shall not originate in the Senate. But a proposed law shall not be taken to appropriate revenue or moneys, or to impose taxation, by reason only of its containing provisions for the imposition or appropriation of fines or other pecuniary penalties, or for the demand or payment or appropriation of fees for licences, or fees for services under the proposed law.

The Senate may not amend proposed laws imposing taxation, or proposed laws appropriating revenue or moneys for the ordinary annual services of the Government.

The Senate may not amend any proposed law so as to increase any proposed charge or burden on the people.

The Senate may at any stage return to the House of Representatives any proposed law which the Senate may not amend, requesting, by message, the omission or amendment of any items or provisions therein. And the House of Representatives may, if it thinks fit, make any of such omissions or amendments, with or without modifications.

Except as provided in this section, the Senate shall have equal power with the House of Representatives in respect of all proposed laws.

Appropriation Bills.

54 The proposed law which appropriates revenue or moneys for the ordinary annual services of the Government shall deal only with such appropriation.

Tax Bill.

55 Laws imposing taxation shall deal only with the imposition of taxation, and any provision therein dealing with any other matter shall be of no effect.

Laws imposing taxation, except laws imposing duties of customs or of excise, shall deal with one subject of taxation only; but laws imposing duties of customs shall deal with duties of customs only, and laws imposing duties of excise shall deal with duties of excise only.

56 A vote, resolution, or proposed law for the appropriation of revenue or moneys shall not be passed unless the purpose of the appropriation has in the same session been recommended by message of the Governor-General to the House in which the proposal originated.

Recommendation of money votes.

57 If the House of Representatives passes any proposed law, and the Senate rejects or fails to pass it, or passes it with amendments to which the House of Representatives will not agree, and if after an interval of three months the House of Representatives, in the same or the next session, again passes the proposed law with or without any amendments which have been made, suggested, or agreed to by the Senate, and the Senate rejects or fails to pass it, or passes it with amendments to which the House of Representatives will not agree, the Governor-General may dissolve the Senate and the House of Representatives simultaneously. But such dissolution shall not take place within six months before the date of the expiry of the House of Representatives by effluxion of time.

Disagreement between the Houses.

If after such dissolution the House of Representatives again passes the proposed law, with or without any amendments which have been made, suggested, or agreed to by the Senate, and the Senate rejects or fails to pass it, or passes it with amendments to which the House of Representatives will not agree, the Governor-General may convene a joint sitting of the members of the Senate and of the House of Representatives.

The members present at the joint sitting may deliberate and shall vote together upon the proposed law as last proposed by the House of Representatives, and upon amendments, if any, which have been made therein by one House and not agreed to by the other, and any such amendments which are affirmed by an absolute majority of the total number of the members of the Senate and House of Representatives shall be taken to have been carried, and if the proposed law, with the amendments, if any, so carried is affirmed by an absolute majority of the total number of the members of the Senate and House of Representatives, it shall be taken to have been duly passed by both Houses of the Parliament, and shall be presented to the Governor-General for the Queen's assent.

58 When a proposed law passed by both Houses of the Parliament is presented to the Governor-General for the Queen's assent, he shall declare, according to his discretion, but subject to this Constitution, that he assents in the Queen's name, or that he withholds assent, or that he reserves the law for the Queen's pleasure.

Royal assent to Bills.

The Governor-General may return to the house in which it originated any proposed law so presented to him, and may transmit therewith any amendments which he may recommend, and the Houses may deal with the recommendation.

Recommendations by Governor-General.

59 The Queen may disallow any law within one year from the Governor-General's assent, and such disallowance on being made known by the Governor-General by speech or message to each of the Houses of the Parliament, or by Proclamation, shall annul the law from the day when the disallowance is so made known.

Disallowance by the Queen.

60 A proposed law reserved for the Queen's pleasure shall not have any force unless and until within two years from the day on which it was presented to the Governor-General for the Queen's assent the Governor-General makes known, by speech or message to each of the Houses of the Parliament, or by Proclamation, that it has received the Queen's assent.

Signification of Queen's pleasure on Bills reserved.

Chapter II
The Executive Government

Executive power.

61 The executive power of the Commonwealth is vested in the Queen and is exercisable by the Governor-General as the Queen's representative, and extends to the execution and maintenance of this Constitution, and of the laws of the Commonwealth.

Federal Executive Council.

62 There shall be a Federal Executive Council to advise the Governor-General in the government of the Commonwealth, and the members of the Council shall be chosen and summoned by the Governor-General and sworn as Executive Councillors, and shall hold office during his pleasure.

Provisions referring to Governor-General.

63 The provisions of this Constitution referring to the Governor-General in Council shall be construed as referring to the Governor-General acting with the advice of the Federal Executive Council.

Ministers of State.

64 The Governor-General may appoint officers to administer such departments of State of the Commonwealth as the Governor-General in Council may establish.

Such officers shall hold office during the pleasure of the Governor-General. They shall be members of the Federal Executive Council, and shall be the Queen's Ministers of State for the Commonwealth.

Ministers to sit in Parliament.

After the first general election no Minister of State shall hold office for a longer period than three months unless he is or becomes a senator or a member of the House of Representatives.

Number of Ministers.

65 Until the Parliament otherwise provides, the Ministers of State shall not exceed seven in number, and shall hold such offices as the Parliament prescribes, or, in the absence of provision, as the Governor-General directs.

Salaries of Ministers.

66 There shall be payable to the Queen, out of the Consolidated Revenue Fund of the Commonwealth, for the salaries of the Ministers of State, an annual sum which, until the Parliament otherwise provides, shall not exceed twelve thousand pounds a year.

Appointment of civil servants.

67 Until the Parliament otherwise provides, the appointment and removal of all other officers of the Executive Government of the Commonwealth shall be vested in the Governor-General in Council, unless the appointment is delegated by the Governor-General in Council or by a law of the Commonwealth to some other authority.

Command of naval and military forces.

68 The command in chief of the naval and military forces of the Commonwealth is vested in the Governor-General as the Queen's representative.

Transfer of certain departments.

69 On a date or dates to be proclaimed by the Governor-General after the establishment of the Commonwealth the following departments of the public service in each State shall become transferred to the Commonwealth:—

Posts, telegraphs, and telephones:

Naval and military defence:

Lighthouses, lightships, beacons, and buoys:

Quarantine.

But the departments of customs and of excise in each State shall become transferred to the Commonwealth on its establishment.

Certain powers of Governors to vest in Governor-General.

70 In respect of matters which, under this Constitution, pass to the Executive Government of the Commonwealth, all powers and functions which at the establishment of the Commonwealth are vested in the Governor of a Colony, or in the

Governor of a Colony with the advice of his Executive Council, or in any authority of a Colony, shall vest in the Governor-General, or in the Governor-General in Council, or in the authority exercising similar powers under the Commonwealth, as the case requires.

Chapter III

The Judicature

71 The judicial power of the Commonwealth shall be vested in a Federal Supreme Court, to be called the High Court of Australia, and in such other federal courts as the Parliament creates, and in such other courts as it invests with federal jurisdiction. The High Court shall consist of a Chief Justice, and so many other Justices, not less than two, as the Parliament prescribes.

72 The Justices of the High Court and of the other courts created by the Parliament—

  (i) Shall be appointed by the Governor-General in Council:

  (ii) Shall not be removed except by the Governor-General in Council, on an address from both Houses of the Parliament in the same session, praying for such removal on the ground of proved misbehaviour or incapacity:

  (iii) Shall receive such remuneration as the Parliament may fix; but the remuneration shall not be diminished during their continuance in office.

The appointment of a Justice of the High Court shall be for a term expiring upon his attaining the age of seventy years, and a person shall not be appointed as a Justice of the High Court if he has attained that age.

The appointment of a Justice of a court created by the Parliament shall be for a term expiring upon his attaining the age that is, at the time of his appointment, the maximum age for Justices of that court and a person shall not be appointed as a Justice of such a court if he has attained the age that is for the time being the maximum age for Justices of that court.

Subject to this section, the maximum age for Justices of any court created by the Parliament is seventy years.

The Parliament may make a law fixing an age that is less than seventy years as the maximum age for Justices of a court created by the Parliament and may at any time repeal or amend such a law, but any such repeal or amendment does not affect the term of office of a Justice under an appointment made before the repeal or amendment.

A Justice of the High Court or of a court created by the Parliament may resign his office by writing under his hand delivered to the Governor-General.

Nothing in the provisions added to this section by the *Constitution Alteration (Retirement of Judges)* 1977 affects the continuance of a person in office as a Justice of a court under an appointment made before the commencement of those provisions.

A reference in this section to the appointment of a Justice of the High Court or of a court created by the Parliament shall be read as including a reference to the appointment of a person who holds office as a Justice of the High Court or of a court created by the Parliament to another office of Justice of the same court having a different status or designation.

73 The High Court shall have jurisdiction, with such exceptions and subject to such regulations as the Parliament prescribes, to hear and determine appeals from all judgments, decrees, orders, and sentences—

(i) Of any Justice or Justices exercising the original jurisdiction of the High Court:

(ii) Of any other federal court, or court exercising federal jurisdiction; or of the Supreme Court of any State, or of any other court of any State from which at the establishment of the Commonwealth an appeal lies to the Queen in Council:

(iii) Of the Inter-State Commission, but as to questions of law only:

and the judgment of the High Court in all such cases shall be final and conclusive.

But no exception or regulation prescribed by the Parliament shall prevent the High Court from hearing and determining any appeal from the Supreme Court of a State in any matter in which at the establishment of the Commonwealth an appeal lies from such Supreme Court to the Queen in Council.

Until the Parliament otherwise provides, the conditions of and restrictions on appeals to the Queen in Council from the Supreme Courts of the several States shall be applicable to appeals from them to the High Court.

Appeal to Queen in Council.

74 No appeal shall be permitted to the Queen in Council from a decision of the High Court upon any question, howsoever arising, as to the limits inter se of the Constitutional powers of the Commonwealth and those of any State or States, or as to the limits inter se of the Constitutional powers of any two or more States, unless the High Court shall certify that the question is one which ought to be determined by Her Majesty in Council.

The High Court may so certify if satisfied that for any special reason the certificate should be granted, and thereupon an appeal shall lie to Her Majesty in Council on the question without further leave.

Except as provided in this section, this Constitution shall not impair any right which the Queen may be pleased to exercise by virtue of Her Royal prerogative to grant special leave of appeal from the High Court to Her Majesty in Council. The Parliament may make laws limiting the matters in which such leave may be asked, but proposed laws containing any such limitation shall be reserved by the Governor-General for Her Majesty's pleasure.

Original jurisdiction of High Court.

75 In all matters—

(i) Arising under any treaty:

(ii) Affecting consuls or other representatives of other countries:

(iii) In which the Commonwealth, or a person suing or being sued on behalf of the Commonwealth, is a party:

(iv) Between States, or between residents of different States, or between a State and a resident of another State:

(v) In which a writ of Mandamus or prohibition or an injunction is sought against an officer of the Commonwealth:

the High Court shall have original jurisdiction.

Additional original jurisdiction.

76 The Parliament may make laws conferring original jurisdiction on the High Court in any matter—

(i) Arising under this Constitution, or involving its interpretation:

(ii) Arising under any laws made by the Parliament:

(iii) Of Admiralty and maritime jurisdiction:

(iv) Relating to the same subject-matter claimed under the laws of different States.

77 With respect to any of the matters mentioned in the last two sections the Parliament may make laws—

> (i) Defining the jurisdiction of any federal court other than the High Court:
>
> (ii) Defining the extent to which the jurisdiction of any federal court shall be exclusive of that which belongs to or is invested in the courts of the States:
>
> (iii) Investing any court of a State with federal jurisdiction.

Power to define jurisdiction.

78 The Parliament may make laws conferring rights to proceed against the Commonwealth or a State in respect of matters within the limits of the judicial power.

Proceedings against Commonwealth or State.

79 The federal jurisdiction of any court may be exercised by such number of judges as the Parliament prescribes.

Number of judges.

80 The trial on indictment of any offence against any law of the Commonwealth shall be by jury, and every such trial shall be held in the State where the offence was committed, and if the offence was not committed within any State the trial shall be held at such place or places as the Parliament prescribes.

Trial by jury.

Chapter IV
Finance and Trade

Chap. IV.

Finance and Trade.

81 All revenues or moneys raised or received by the Executive Government of the Commonwealth shall form one Consolidated Revenue Fund, to be appropriated for the purposes of the Commonwealth in the manner and subject to the charges and liabilities imposed by this Constitution.

Consolidated Revenue Fund.

82 The costs, charges, and expenses incident to the collection, management, and receipt of the Consolidated Revenue Fund shall form the first charge thereon; and the revenue of the Commonwealth shall in the first instance be applied to the payment of the expenditure of the Commonwealth.

Expenditure charged thereon.

83 No money shall be drawn from the Treasury of the Commonwealth except under appropriation made by law.

Money to be appropriated by law.

But until the expiration of one month after the first meeting of the Parliament the Governor-General in Council may draw from the Treasury and expend such moneys as may be necessary for the maintenance of any department transferred to the Commonwealth and for the holding of the first elections for the Parliament.

84 When any department of the public service of a State becomes transferred to the Commonwealth, all officers of the department shall become subject to the control of the Executive Government of the Commonwealth.

Transfer of offices.

Any such officer who is not retained in the service of the Commonwealth shall, unless he is appointed to some other office of equal emolument in the public service of the State, be entitled to receive from the State any pension, gratuity, or other compensation, payable under the law of the State on the abolition of his office.

Any such officer who is retained in the service of the Commonwealth shall preserve all his existing and accruing rights, and shall be entitled to retire from office at the time, and on the pension or retiring allowance, which would be permitted by the law of the State if his service with the Commonwealth were a continuation of his service with the State. Such pension or retiring allowance shall be paid to him by the Commonwealth; but the State shall pay to the Commonwealth a part thereof, to be calculated on the proportion which his term of service with the State bears to his whole term of service, and for the purpose of the calculation his salary shall be taken to be that paid to him by the State at the time of the transfer.

Any officer who is, at the establishment of the Commonwealth, in the public service of a State, and who is, by consent of the Governor of the State with the advice of the Executive Council thereof, transferred to the public service of the Commonwealth, shall have the same rights as if he had been an officer of a department transferred to the Commonwealth and were retained in the service of the Commonwealth.

85 When any department of the public service of a State is transferred to the Commonwealth—

Transfer of property of state.

(i) All property of the State of any kind, used exclusively in connexion with the department shall become vested in the Commonwealth; but, in the case of the departments controlling customs and excise and bounties, for such time only as the Governor-General in Council may declare to be necessary:

(ii) The Commonwealth may acquire any property of the State, of any kind used, but not exclusively used in connexion with the department; the value thereof shall, if no agreement can be made, be ascertained in, as nearly as may be, the manner in which the value of land, or of an interest in land, taken by the State for public purposes is ascertained under the law of the State in force at the establishment of the Commonwealth:

(iii) The Commonwealth shall compensate the State for the value of any property passing to the Commonwealth under this section; if no agreement can be made as to the mode of compensation, it shall be determined under laws to be made by the Parliament:

(iv) The Commonwealth shall, at the date of the transfer, assume the current obligations of the State in respect of the department transferred.

86 On the establishment of the Commonwealth, the collection and control of duties of customs and of excise, and the control of the payment of bounties, shall pass to the Executive Government of the Commonwealth.

87 During a period of ten years after the establishment of the Commonwealth and thereafter until the Parliament otherwise provides, of the net revenue of the Commonwealth from duties of customs and of excise not more than one-fourth shall be applied annually by the Commonwealth towards its expenditure.

The balance shall, in accordance with this Constitution, be paid to the several States, or applied towards the payment of interest on debts of the several States taken over by the Commonwealth.

Uniform duties of customs.

88 Uniform duties of customs shall be imposed within two years after the establishment of the Commonwealth.

Payment to States before uniform duties.

89 Until the imposition of uniform duties of customs—

(i) The Commonwealth shall credit to each State the revenues collected therein by the Commonwealth.

(ii) The Commonwealth shall debit to each State—

(a) The expenditure therein of the Commonwealth incurred solely for the maintenance or continuance, as at the time of transfer, of any department transferred from the State to the Commonwealth;

(b) The proportion of the State, according to the number of its people, in the other expenditure of the Commonwealth.

(iii) The Commonwealth shall pay to each State month by month the balance (if any) in favour of the State.

90 On the imposition of uniform duties of customs the power of the Parliament to impose duties of customs and of excise, and to grant bounties on the production or export of goods, shall become exclusive. *Exclusive power over customs, excise and bounties.*

On the imposition of uniform duties of customs all laws of the several States imposing duties of customs or of excise, or offering bounties on the production or export of goods, shall cease to have effect, but any grant of or agreement for any such bounty lawfully made by or under the authority of the Government of any State shall be taken to be good if made before the thirtieth day of June, one thousand eight hundred and ninety-eight, and not otherwise.

91 Nothing in this Constitution prohibits a State from granting any aid to or bounty on mining for gold, silver, or other metals, nor from granting, with the consent of both Houses of the Parliament of the Commonwealth expressed by resolution, any aid to or bounty on the production or export of goods. *Exceptions as to bounties.*

92 On the imposition of uniform duties of customs, trade, commerce, and intercourse among the States, whether by means of internal carriage or ocean navigation, shall be absolutely free. *Trade within the Commonwealth to be free.*

But notwithstanding anything in this Constitution, goods imported before the imposition of uniform duties of customs into any State, or into any Colony which, whilst the goods remain therein, becomes a State, shall, on thence passing into another State within two years after the imposition of such duties, be liable to any duty chargeable on the importation of such goods into the Commonwealth, less any duty paid in respect of the goods on their importation.

93 During the first five years after the imposition of uniform duties of customs, and thereafter until the Parliament otherwise provides— *Payment to States for five years after uniform tariffs.*

(i) The duties of customs chargeable on goods imported into a State and afterwards passing into another State for consumption, and the duties of excise paid on goods produced or manufactured in a State and afterwards passing into another State for consumption, shall be taken to have been collected not in the former but in the latter State:

(ii) Subject to the last subsection, the Commonwealth shall credit revenue, debit expenditure, and pay balances to the several States as prescribed for the period preceding the imposition of uniform duties of customs.

94 After five years from the imposition of uniform duties of customs, the Parliament may provide, on such basis as it deems fair, for the monthly payment to the several States of all surplus revenue of the Commonwealth. *Distribution of surplus.*

95 Notwithstanding anything in this Constitution, the Parliament of the State of Western Australia, if that State be an Original State, may, during the first five years after the imposition of uniform duties of customs, impose duties of customs on goods passing into that State and not originally imported from beyond the limits of the Commonwealth; and such duties shall be collected by the Commonwealth. *Customs duties of Western Australia.*

But any duty so imposed on any goods shall not exceed during the first of such years the duty chargeable on the goods under the law of Western Australia in force at the imposition of uniform duties, and shall not exceed during the second, third, fourth, and fifth of such years respectively, four-fifths, three-fifths, two-fifths, and one-fifth of such latter duty, and all duties imposed under this section shall cease at the expiration of the fifth year after the imposition of uniform duties.

If at any time during the five years the duty on any goods under this section is higher than the duty imposed by the Commonwealth on the importation of the like goods, then such higher duty shall be collected on the goods when imported into Western Australia from beyond the limits of the Commonwealth.

Financial assistance to States.

96 During a period of ten years after the establishment of the Commonwealth and thereafter until the Parliament otherwise provides, the Parliament may grant financial assistance to any State on such terms and conditions as the Parliament thinks fit.

Audit.

97 Until the Parliament otherwise provides, the laws in force in any Colony which has become or becomes a State with respect to the receipt of revenue and the expenditure of money on account of the Government of the Colony, and the review and audit of such receipt and expenditure, shall apply to the receipt of revenue and the expenditure of money on account of the Commonwealth in the State in the same manner as if the Commonwealth, or the Government or an officer of the Commonwealth, were mentioned whenever the Colony, or the Government or an officer of the Colony, is mentioned.

Trade and commerce includes navigation and State railways. Commonwealth not to give preference.

98 The power of the Parliament to make laws with respect to trade and commerce extends to navigation and shipping, and to railways the property of any State.

99 The Commonwealth shall not, by any law or regulation of trade, commerce, or revenue, give preference to one State or any part thereof over another State or any part thereof.

Nor abridge right to use water.

100 The Commonwealth shall not, by any law or regulation of trade or commerce, abridge the right of a State or of the residents therein to the reasonable use of the waters of rivers for conservation or irrigation.

Inter-State Commission.

101 There shall be an Inter-State Commission, with such powers of adjudication and administration as the Parliament deems necessary for the execution and maintenance, within the Commonwealth, of the provisions of this Constitution relating to trade and commerce, and of all laws made thereunder.

Parliament may forbid preferences by State.

102 The Parliament may by any law with respect to trade or commerce forbid, as to railways, any preference or discrimination by any State, or by any authority constituted under a State, if such preference or discrimination is undue and unreasonable, or unjust to any State; due regard being had to the financial responsibilities incurred by any State in connexion with the construction and maintenance of its railways. But no preference or discrimination shall, within the meaning of this section, be taken to be undue and unreasonable, or unjust to any State, unless so adjudged by the Inter-State Commission.

Commissioners' appointment, tenure, and remuneration.

103 The members of the Inter-State Commission—

(i) Shall be appointed by the Governor-General in Council:

(ii) Shall hold office for seven years, but may be removed within that time by the Governor-General in Council, on an address from both Houses of the Parliament in the same session praying for such removal on the ground of proved misbehaviour or incapacity:

(iii) Shall receive such remuneration as the Parliament may fix; but such remuneration shall not be diminished during their continuance in office.

Saving of certain rates.

104 Nothing in this Constitution shall render unlawful any rate for the carriage of goods upon a railway, the property of a State, if the rate is deemed by the Inter-State Commission to be necessary for the development of the territory of the State, and if the rate applies equally to goods within the State and to goods passing into the State from other States.

105 The Parliament may take over from the States their public debts ~~as existing at the establishment of the Commonwealth~~, or a proportion thereof according to the respective numbers of their people as shown by the latest statistics of the Commonwealth, and may convert, renew, or consolidate such debts, or any part thereof; and the States shall indemnify the Commonwealth in respect of the debts taken over, and thereafter the interest payable in respect of the debts shall be deducted and retained from the portions of the surplus revenue of the Commonwealth payable to the several States, or if such surplus is insufficient, or if there is no surplus, then the deficiency or the whole amount shall be paid by the several States. *[Taking over public debts of States. Altered by No. 3, 1910, s. 2.]*

105A—(1) The Commonwealth may make agreements with the States with respect to the public debts of the States, including— *[Agreements with respect to State debts. Inserted by No. 1, 1929, s. 2.]*

(a) the taking over of such debts by the Commonwealth;

(b) the management of such debts;

(c) the payment of interest and the provision and management of sinking funds in respect of such debts;

(d) the consolidation, renewal, conversion, and redemption of such debts;

(e) the indemnification of the Commonwealth by the States in respect of debts taken over by the Commonwealth; and

(f) the borrowing of money by the States or by the Commonwealth, or by the Commonwealth for the States.

(2) The Parliament may make laws for validating any such agreement made before the commencement of this section.

(3) The Parliament may make laws for the carrying out by the parties thereto of any such agreement.

(4) Any such agreement may be varied or rescinded by the parties thereto.

(5) Every such agreement and any such variation thereof shall be binding upon the Commonwealth and the States parties thereto notwithstanding anything contained in this Constitution or the Constitution of the several States or in any law of the Parliament of the Commonwealth or of any State.

(6) The powers conferred by this section shall not be construed as being limited in any way by the provisions of section one hundred and five of this Constitution.

Chapter V

The States

[Chap. V. The States.]

106 The Constitution of each State of the Commonwealth shall, subject to this Constitution, continue as at the establishment of the Commonwealth, or as at the admission or establishment of the State, as the case may be, until altered in accordance with the Constitution of the State. *[Saving of Constitutions.]*

107 Every power of the Parliament of a Colony which has become or becomes a State, shall unless it is by this Constitution exclusively vested in the Parliament of the Commonwealth or withdrawn from the Parliament of the State, continue as at the establishment of the Commonwealth, or as at the admission or establishment of the State, as the case may be. *[Saving of Power of State Parliaments.]*

108 Every law in force in a Colony which has become or becomes a State, and relating to any matter within the powers of the Parliament of the Commonwealth, *[Saving of State laws.]*

shall, subject to this Constitution, continue in force in the State; and, until provision is made in that behalf by the Parliament of the Commonwealth, the Parliament of the State shall have such powers of alteration and of repeal in respect of any such law as the Parliament of the Colony had until the Colony became a State.

Inconsistency of laws.

109 When a law of a State is inconsistent with a law of the Commonwealth, the latter shall prevail, and the former shall, to the extent of the inconsistency, be invalid.

Provisions referring to Governor.

110 The provisions of this Constitution relating to the Governor of a State extend and apply to the Governor for the time being of the State, or other chief executive officer or administrator of the government of the State.

States may surrender territory.

111 The Parliament of a State may surrender any part of the State to the Commonwealth; and upon such surrender, and the acceptance thereof by the Commonwealth, such part of the State shall become subject to the exclusive jurisdiction of the Commonwealth.

States may levy charges for inspection laws.

112 After uniform duties of customs have been imposed, a State may levy on imports or exports, or on goods passing into or out of the State, such charges as may be necessary for executing the inspection laws of the State; but the net produce of all charges so levied shall be for the use of the Commonwealth; and any such inspection laws may be annulled by the Parliament of the Commonwealth.

Intoxicating liquids.

113 All fermented, distilled, or other intoxicating liquids passing into any State or remaining therein for use, consumption, sale, or storage, shall be subject to the laws of the State as if such liquids had been produced in the State.

States may not raise forces. Taxation of property of Commonwealth or State.

114 A State shall not, without the consent of the Parliament of the Commonwealth, raise or maintain any naval or military force, or impose any tax on property of any kind belonging to the Commonwealth, nor shall the Commonwealth impose any tax on property of any kind belonging to a State.

States not to coin money.

115 A State shall not coin money, nor make anything but gold and silver coin a legal tender in payment of debts.

Commonwealth not to legislate in respect of religion.

116 The Commonwealth shall not make any law for establishing any religion, or for imposing any religious observance, or for prohibiting the free exercise of any religion, and no religious test shall be required as a qualification for any office or public trust under the Commonwealth.

Rights of residents in States.

117 A subject of the Queen, resident in any State, shall not be subject in any other State to any disability or discrimination which would not be equally applicable to him if he were a subject of the Queen resident in such other State.

Recognition of laws, &c. of States.

118 Full faith and credit shall be given, throughout the Commonwealth to the laws, the public Acts and records, and the judicial proceedings of every State.

Protection of States against invasion and violence.

119 The Commonwealth shall protect every State against invasion and, on the application of the Executive Government of the State, against domestic violence.

Custody of offenders against laws of the Commonwealth.

120 Every State shall make provision for the detention in its prisons of persons accused or convicted of offences against the laws of the Commonwealth, and for the punishment of persons convicted of such offences, and the Parliament of the Commonwealth may make laws to give effect to this provision.

Chap. VI.

New States.

Chapter VI

New States

New States may be admitted or established.

121 The Parliament may admit to the Commonwealth or establish new States, and may upon such admission or establishment make or impose such terms and

conditions, including the extent of representation in either House of the Parliament, as it thinks fit.

122 The Parliament may make laws for the government of any territory surrendered by any State to and accepted by the Commonwealth, or of any territory placed by the Queen under the authority of and accepted by the Commonwealth, or otherwise acquired by the Commonwealth, and may allow the representation of such territory in either House of the Parliament to the extent and on the terms which it thinks fit. — Government of territories.

123 The Parliament of the Commonwealth may, with the consent of the Parliament of a State, and the approval of the majority of the electors of the State voting upon the question, increase, diminish, or otherwise alter the limits of the State, upon such terms and conditions as may be agreed on, and may, with the like consent, make provision respecting the effect and operation of any increase or diminution or alteration of territory in relation to any State affected. — Alteration of limits of States.

124 A new State may be formed by separation of territory from a State, but only with the consent of the Parliament thereof, and a new State may be formed by the union of two or more States or parts of States, but only with the consent of the Parliaments of the States affected. — Formation of new States.

Chapter VII
Miscellaneous

Chap. VII.

Miscellaneous.

125 The seat of Government of the Commonwealth shall be determined by the Parliament, and shall be within territory which shall have been granted to or acquired by the Commonwealth, and shall be vested in and belong to the Commonwealth, and shall be in the State of New South Wales, and be distant not less than one hundred miles from Sydney. — Seat of Government.

Such territory shall contain an area of not less than one hundred square miles, and such portion thereof as shall consist of Crown Lands shall be granted to the Commonwealth without any payment therefor.

The Parliament shall sit at Melbourne until it meet at the seat of Government.

126 The Queen may authorise the Governor-General to appoint any person, or any persons jointly or severally, to be his deputy or deputies within any part of the Commonwealth, and in that capacity to exercise during the pleasure of the Governor-General such powers and functions of the Governor-General as he thinks fit to assign to such deputy or deputies, subject to any limitations expressed or directions given by the Queen; but the appointment of such deputy or deputies shall not affect the exercise by the Governor-General himself of any power or function. — Power to Her Majesty to authorise Governor-General to appoint deputies.

Section 127 repealed by No. 55, 1967, s. 3.

Chapter VIII
Alteration of the Constitution

Chap. VIII.

Alteration of Constitution.

128 This Constitution shall not be altered except in the following manner:— — Mode of altering the Constitution.

The proposed law for the alteration thereof must be passed by an absolute majority of each House of the Parliament, and not less than two nor more than six months after its passage through both Houses the proposed law shall be submitted in each State **and Territory** to the electors qualified to vote for the election of members of the House of Representatives.

Paragraph altered by No. 84, 1977, s. 2.

Paragraph altered by No. 84, 1977, s. 2.

But if either House passes any such proposed law by an absolute majority, and the other House rejects or fails to pass it, or passes it with any amendment to which the first-mentioned House will not agree, and if after an interval of three months the first-mentioned House in the same or the next session again passes the proposed law by an absolute majority with or without any amendment which has been made or agreed to by the other House, and such other House rejects or fails to pass it or passes it with any amendment to which the first-mentioned House will not agree, the Governor-General may submit the proposed law as last proposed by the first-mentioned House, and either with or without any amendments subsequently agreed to by both Houses, to the electors in each State and Territory qualified to vote for the election of the House of Representatives.

When a proposed law is submitted to the electors the vote shall be taken in such manner as the Parliament prescribes. But until the qualification of electors of members of the House of Representatives becomes uniform throughout the Commonwealth, only one-half the electors voting for and against the proposed law shall be counted in any State in which adult suffrage prevails.

And if in a majority of the States a majority of the electors voting approve the proposed law, and if a majority of all the electors voting also approve the proposed law, it shall be presented to the Governor-General for the Queen's assent.

No alteration diminishing the proportionate representation of any State in either House of the Parliament, or the minimum number of representatives of a State in the House of Representatives, or increasing, diminishing, or otherwise altering the limits of the State, or in any manner affecting the provisions of the Constitution in relation thereto, shall become law unless the majority of the electors voting in that State approve the proposed law.

Paragraph altered by No. 84, 1977, s. 2.

In this section, 'Territory' means any territory referred to in section one hundred and twenty-two of this Constitution in respect of which there is in force a law allowing its representation in the House of Representatives.

Schedule

Oath

I, A.B., do swear that I will be faithful and bear true allegiance to Her Majesty Queen Victoria, Her heirs and successors according to law. SO HELP ME GOD!

Affirmation

I, A.B., do solemnly and sincerely affirm and declare that I will be faithful and bear true allegiance to Her Majesty Queen Victoria, Her heirs and successors according to law.

(NOTE—*The name of the King or Queen of The United Kingdom of Great Britain and Ireland for the time being is to be substituted from time to time.*)

(*Source*: Copyright Commonwealth of Australia, reproduced by permission)

INDEX

Page numbers in italics refer to tables or figures

Aborigines *see* Indigenous people
absolute monarchy 6
Administrative Appeals Tribunal 264
Administrative Review Council 264
aggrieved minority parties 373, 385
Amalgamated Society of Engineers v Adelaide Steamship Co. Ltd 66
Antarctic *105*
Asbestos-Related Diseases Inter-Departmental Committee 244
Ashmore and Cartier Islands *105*, 106
asylum seekers 336–7, 338
Athenian system 8, 9
Audit Office 263
Aurukun 118–19
Australia Day 19
Australian Capital Television Pty Ltd v The Commonwealth (No. 2) 1992 68
Australian Capital Territory 104–5, 106, 147, 148, 294
Australian Chamber of Commerce and Industry 408, 409, 410, 416–17
Australian colonies 19–20, 94
 constitutions 46–9
 electoral system 280–2
 legislative assemblies 52
 legislative councils 52
 party systems 327–8
 responsible government 327
 self-government 19, 48
 trade unions 328
Australian Communist Party v Commonwealth 67
Australian Conservation Foundation 409, 418, 421, 424

Australian Constitution 13, 18
 Act to constitute the Commonwealth of Australia 459–82
 amendment procedures 46, 54, 72–8
 banks, power over 117
 cooperation between governments 71
 corporations power 67, 68–9, 117, 126
 drafting 50–2
 external affairs power 28–9, 30, 67, 68, 117, 121, 126–7
 finance and trade 55
 finance power 117
 formal amendment 72–8, 119
 formation 44–5
 framework 49–50
 governor-general, role of 58–63
 human rights 117
 influences on 63–4
 internal affairs power 67
 interstate trade and commerce powers 126
 judicature 54–5
 judicial interpretation 64–71, 116–17, 131
 legal challenge to 54–5
 limitations 116–17
 making of 49–54
 non-problematic chapters 54
 parliament 55–8
 preamble 83–4
 problematic chapters 55–63
 problems of drafting 51–2
 provisions 54–63
 referendums 29–30, 31, 72–8
 reform 78–80
 territories power 103
Australian Council of Social Service 408

Australian Council of Trade Unions (ACTU) 335, 337, 351, 408
Australian Crime Commission (ACC) 242
Australian Democrats 21, 285, 334, 380–2
Australian Election Study 294
Australian Electoral Commission 289, 450
Australian electoral system
 see also voting
 counting votes 283–6
 development 287–9
 fairness 291–2
 federation, following 282–3
 origins 280–2
 public funding and disclosure 292–3
 redistributions 289–91
 2007 election *292*
Australian Fishing and Lifestyle Party 394–5
Australian Greens 383, 384
 see also Greens, The
Australian Industry & Defence Network (AIDN) 420
Australian Industry Group 409, 417
Australian Labor Advisory Council 351
Australian Labor Party 21–2, 27, 93, 314
 affirmative action 351
 candidate selection 351
 'catch-all' party, as 355
 caucus 194, 211–12, 352
 constitutional amendment 119
 emergence 328–9, 346
 ethnicity and 302
 factions 194, 322, 352–3
 federal platform 1905 346–7

federalism and 119, 120–1
first-preference electoral results *296*
ideology 348–50
image 297
National Conference 350, 353, 354
national platform 348, 351
organisation 320, 350
origins 328–9
party discipline 355–6
platform 346–8, 351, 354
policy differentiation 365–7
policy making 353–5
religious vote 301, 302
selection of ministers and cabinet 194–5
solidarity convention 211
split 331, 332
trade unions, and 328–9, 346, 349, 350–1, 355, 413
women 351
Australian parliament 146–8
see also House of Representatives; Parliament House; Senate
Acts, progress through parliament 157
committees 157, 168–71
debates 153, 159, 162, 165–8
expenditure, investigating 163
legislating function 156–62
limiting debate 159
members 151–2
number of bills passed *156*
problems in legislating 158–9
representative function of members 151–2
scrutiny function 164–71, 174
sitting days 151
women 148, *148*
Australian party system 325, 327
see also political parties
changes 339–41
development of two-party system 329–32, 346
issue parties 394–6
origins 327–8
pressures for change 339–40
secessionist parties 373, 396
two-party system in retrospect 337–9
Australian political institutions 12–13, 18–26
Australian political system 11–12, 28, *39–40*
Australian Public Service (APS) 241
accountability 260–5
administration 255–8

administrative review 260–1, 263–4
agencies 242–3, 262, 263
agency heads 249, 250
classifications, employment 250
code of conduct 251–2
coordination between agencies 244–5, 258–9
customers 252
departmental secretaries 257
departments 242, *247*
economic management 254–5
employment 248–55
equal opportunity employer 253
ethos 250–2
executive agencies 244
financing 254
fixed-term employment 249
freedom of information 264–5
inter-departmental committees 244–5, 258–9
market-based principles 252
ministerial independence, constraints 257–8
neutrality 250
ongoing positions 249
open entry 248–9
performance management 262–3
planning 261–2
policy 255–9, 261–2
politicisation of employment process 249
promotion on merit 248–9
recruitment 248–55
reform 259, 260, 262
secrecy 264–5
size, changes to 245–6
staffing levels 246–7, *248*
statutory agencies 242–3
statutory authorities 243–4, 246–7
statutory corporations 244
structure 242–4
tenure 249
Treasury and economic management 254–5
unionism 253–4
values 251–2
women employees 253, *253*
work ethic 250–2
workplace diversity 253, *253*
Australian Shooters Party 373, 390
authoritarianism 6, 7, 137

back benches 154, 198–9
balance of power 64, 155, 173–4, 175, 327, 376

ballots *see* voting
banking system 117
Bate, Jeff 365
'battlers' 297, 298, 299, 355, 365
Beazley, Kim 185, 214, 216, 221, 353
bicameral legislatures 138, 147
bills 156–9, 162–3
Bishop, Julie 198
Bjelke-Peterson, Sir Joh 118, 123, 202, 274
Blewett, Neal 205
Bolte, Henry 202
Botany Case 68
Bowen Committee 202
Boyer Committee on Public Service Recruitment 239
Brisbane City Council 107
British political system 11–12, 18, 19, 35–6, *39–40*
see also Westminster system
budget 160
bureaucracy 231–4, 237–9
cabinet arrangements 182–4
colonies 47, 49
constitutional arrangements 44, 45, *46*
e-government 453
electoral system *276, 277*
executive government 181–2
interest groups 409, 417
legislative process *142*
lobbying 412
local government 106
media ownership rules 436
parliament 137, 138, 139, 140, 143
political parties 317, 318, 320
privatisation 229
seating arrangements 139
Brown, John 205
budget 160–2, 254–5
Budget Reform (1984 White Paper) 260
bureaucracy 227–8
accountability 262–5
development in Australia 237–41
liberal democracy and 226
origins 231–3
private sector 228
public administration and 226–31
public perception 230–1
public sector 230–1
Second World War, expansion during 239
tasks of 238–9
bureaucratic consultation 115

Bury, Leslie 210
Business Advisory Council 416

cabinet 146, 182–6
 chair 190, 214–16
 collective responsibility 202, 207–12, 217, 322–3
 committees 191–2
 community cabinet meetings 189
 decisions and management 191
 executive power 188
 inner cabinet 216
 leaked information 208–9
 meetings 189
 procedures 189–90
 relationships in 190–1
 secrecy 145, 202, 207–9
 selection 193–5
 solidarity 208, 209–11
Cabinet Expenditure Review Committee 254
Cabinet Handbook 190, 210
cadre parties 315
Callinan, Justice 69
Campbell, Graeme 151, 322
Canada 49, 140
Canberra 104, 113, 149, 151
capitalism 7
carbon trading schemes 424
Carers Alliance 395
cartel parties 316
'catch-all' parties 315, 355, 363–4, 365–6
Censure motions 154, 168
centralisation 121–3, 125–8
Charter of Budget Honesty 260
Chifley government 120–1, 217
China 137, 324
Chipp, Don 334, 381
Christian Democratic Party (CDP) 301, 373, 387–8
Christmas Island *105*, 106
Churchill, Winston 139
Citizens Electoral Council (CEC) 393
City of Melbourne v Commonwealth 67
civil service 227
climate change 28–9, 424
Climate Change Coalition 394
Cocos (Keeling) Islands *105*, 106
coercion 4, 5, 114, 115, 116
coercive federalism 124–8
Cole v Whitfield and another (1988) 68
collective authority 7
collective responsibility 184, 202, 207–12, 217, 322–3

Combet, Greg 195
committees 143, 157, 168–71, 259
 see also Senate
 inter-departmental committees 244–5, 258–9
Commonwealth Authorities and Companies Act 1997 (CAC Act) 265, 266
Commonwealth electoral system *see* Australian electoral system
Commonwealth Franchise Act 1902 148, 283
Commonwealth government revenues 100, *102*, 103
Commonwealth grants 97, 106, 107, 116, 122–5
Commonwealth of Australia Constitution Act 81, 459–82
Commonwealth Ombudsman 264
Commonwealth–state financial relations 97–100, 110, 122–5
Commonwealth v Tasmania 68
Communicable Diseases Network Australia (CDNA) 420
Communist Party of Australia 56, 67, 75
 ideology 317, 373, 390–1
communist regimes 7, 137
Community and Public Sector Union (CPSU) 254
comparative politics 11–12, 34–8
concurrent powers 53, 54, 89
confederation 49, 88
conservation policy 117
Conservatives for Climate and Environment 394
Constitutional Commission 1985 79–80
Constitutional Convention
 1891 49
 1897–1898 49, 50
 1973 78–9
 1998 83–5
constitutional monarchy 33–4, 35, 38, 58–9, 60, 138
constitutions 10, 13, 44–6
 see also Australian Constitution
 amendment procedures 45–6
 Australian colonies, for 46–9
 referendums 46, 50
contracting out 229–30, 247, 264
cooperation between governments 71, 114–16
cooperative federalism 71, 88, 124–5

coordinate federalism 66, 71, 88, 129–30
Coral Sea Islands *105*, 106
core executive 180–2
corporations power 67, 68–9, 117, 126
corporatism 415
cost shifting 108–9
Costello, Peter 365
Council for Aboriginal Affairs (CAA) 30
Council for Australian Federation 114
Council of Australian Governments (COAG) 114, 124, 129–30
councils *see* local government
Country Party 27, 291, 331
 name change 334, 373, 379
Crean, Simon 221
Crossman, Richard 204–5
Crown, responsible government 52
Curtin government 120–1

Deakin, Alfred 329, 331, 356
debates 141–2, 144–5, 153, 165–8
 election debates, televised 440
 limiting 159
 money bills, on 162
 open debate 167, 168
 special motions, on 167–8
 statements and reports, on 165–6
defence power 66
democracy 8–9, 425
 see also liberal democracy
 e-democracy 454–5
 interest groups and 425–6
Democratic Labor Party 21, 77, 173–4, 389, *389*
 demise 334
 origins 332, 340, 372, 389, 391
democratic socialism 348–9
Department of Finance and Deregulation Outcomes and Outputs Framework 262–3
Department of Parliamentary Services 160
Department of Prime Minister and Cabinet 190, 217, 218, 231, 245
departmental secretaries 257
devotee parties 315
dictatorship 136
direct democracy 8, 136, 272
division of powers 49, 109–10, 111, 112, 131
doctrinal parties 373, 390–3
Dorothy Dix questions 165

double dissolution 57–8, 286, 333
Downer, Alexander 221, 365
'dries' 359
dual federalism 125

e-democracy 454–5
e-government 263, 452–4
economic liberalism 28
economic management 254–5
Economic Planning Advisory Council (EPAC) 261–2
economic rationalism 241
economy 26–8, 64
   see also budget
   internationalisation 28, 64
education funding 122, 127–8, 129–30
election dates 216–17
elections 272–5, 329, 329–30, 340
elections at large 284
electoral pragmatism 316, 319, 341, 362
electoral systems 272, 273–5
   see also Australian Electoral System
   fairness 274, 291–2
   types 275–80
   zonal system 274
elitism 415
Ellicott, Bob 210
Engineers Case 1920 66, 67
environmental movement 422, 423, 424
ethnic influences 23–6, 92, 302
Ettridge, David 386
exclusive powers 53, 56
executive 13, 137, 143, 146, 172
   core executive 180–2
   definition 180
   limit to parliamentary scrutiny of 174–5
   role 180
executive authority 188
executive government 58, 188–9
executive power 137, 146
expenditure, parliamentary scrutiny 163
external affairs power 28–9, 30, 67, 68, 117, 121, 126–7

fairness in electoral systems 274, 291–2
Family Court of Australia 55
Family First 285, 300–1, 373, 374, 388–9
Federal Court of Australia 55, 264
Federal Executive Council 188–9
federal system
   see also federalism

accountability 118
Commonwealth, role of 100–3
distribution of power *89*
finance 103, 121–30
liberal democracy 18–20
local government 106–9
parliament 52
powers 53–4
reasons for choosing 90–3
states, role of 94–100
territories 103–6
federalism 18, 49, 66, 88
   see also federal system
   criticisms of 113, 114
   divided responsibilities 109–10
   efficiency, and 112–13
   establishment in Australia 91–3
   future of 130–2
   policy making 113–17
   political parties 119–21
   politics 109–12
   principles 88–90
   responsible government, and 117–19
federation 49, 50, 54, 63–4, 92
   electoral system 282–3
feral federalism 131
Fielding, Steven 301, 423
filibustering 145
finance 55
   see also Commonwealth–state financial relations
finance power 117
financial control and coercion 116, 121, 127, 129–30
Fischer, Tim 385
Fisher, Andrew 329
Foundation for Australian Agricultural Women 424
fourth estate 430
Franklin Dam 415
   see also *Tasmanian Dams Case*
Fraser government 30, 79, 116, 211, 333–4
   Estimates committees 160–1
   federalism 123–4
   income tax arrangements 123
   ministry 192
   personal staff 218
   policy making 361
   public service structure 246, 247
Fraser Island 120
Fraser, Malcolm 191, 216, 333, 364
   personal style 219–20
   resignation 221, 365
free market economy 10
free trade 27–8, 68, 328, 346

freedom of information (FOI) 209, 264–5
freedom of speech 430
front benches 154
Fusion 331, 346, 356

gag 159
Garnishee Case 1932 66
general assistance payments 116
German system of government 12, 37, *39–40*, 326
   bureaucracy 235
   constitutional arrangements 44, 45, *46*
   distribution of power *89*
   e-government 453
   electoral system *276*, 280
   executive government *181*
   federalism 90–1
   interest groups 408, 409, 417, 420
   legislative process *142*
   lobbying 412
   media ownership rules 437
   parliament 138
   political parties 316, 317, 318–19, 321
   prime ministerial power 186, 187
   privatisation 229–30
   senate 140
Gillard, Julia 195, 196–7, 213, 214
globalisation 28, 130, 240, 266
goods and services tax (GST) 110, 161, 335, 362
   distribution of revenue 97, *98*, 99, 100, 131
   Intergovernmental Agreement 127
   introduction 336, 362
Gorton, John 193, 214, 216, 217, 333
   no-confidence vote 364
government business enterprises (GBEs) 265
Government Gazette 158
governor-general 13
   appointment 59
   dismissal 62–3
   dismissal of government by 22, 58, 60, 61–2
   duties 59–60
   executive authority 188
   reserve powers 60–2
   role 58–63
Grant, Wyn 418–19
Great Barrier Reef 120
Green Paper 165–6
Greens, The 285, 372, 374, *384*, 406–7
   Australian parliaments, in *383*

balance of power 423
ideology 317, 383
organisation 384
party discipline 384
preferences 374, 419
Greens (WA), The 383, 384
growth tax 123
guillotine 159

Hansard 153
Hanson, Pauline 291–2, 322, 341, 374, 385
  see also Pauline Hanson's One Nation Party
Harradine, Brian 163, 398, 399
Hasluck, Sir Paul 61, 62
Hawke, Bob 196, 214, 215, 216, 334–5
  leadership loss 221, 335, 365
  personal style 220
Hawke government 79, 80, 203, 334–5
  Aboriginal policy 30, 120
  caucus committees 211
  early election 217
  federalism 121, 124–5
  grants 124–5
  industry advisory councils 422
  microeconomic reform 121, 124
  policy making 354
  privatisation 354
  public service reform 260
  public service structure 246
  Tasmanian government and, tension between 111
  trade unions, incomes Accord 413
  tripartite consultative councils 415
Hayden, Bill 220, 334
head of state 60, 81–2
Heard and McDonald Islands *105*, 106
Hewson, John 221, 362, 365
High Court of Australia 55
  cases 66–8
  democracy, and 70–1
  functions 70–1
  judges, appointment 70
  judicial interpretation of the Constitution 64–71, 116–17, 131
  1902–20 65–6
  1920–42 66–7
  1943–83 67–9
  1983– 67–9
  political institution, as 69–70
  role 64–5
  Work Choices decision 68–9
Hobbes, Thomas 3, 6

Hollingworth, Dr Peter 62–3
Holt, Harold 193, 333
House of Representatives 136, 138, 148–9
  Australian Constitution 52, 56
  clerk of the house 153
  composition 147–8, *148*
  financial powers, limitations on 161
  ministers 193
  numbers 148
  Opposition 154
  powers 56–8
  preferential voting 284–5, 287, 325
  private members 153
  procedures 152–4
  scrutiny procedures 164–8
  seating arrangements 153–4
  seating plan 150, *150*
  Senate and, distribution of power 56–8
  sitting days 151
  speaker 152
  standing orders 153
House of Representatives Estimates committees 160–1
House of Representatives Practice 153
Howard government 9, 28, 327, 336–7
  Aboriginal policy 30–1, 32, 33
  asylum seekers, treatment 336–7
  climate change 29
  corporations power 126
  defeat 362, 364
  direct funding 128
  education 127–8
  enrolment to vote, reduced period for 289
  external affairs power 126–7
  federalism 125–8, 132
  financial coercion 127–8
  industry consultative bodies 422
  Iraq war, support for 336
  media ownership 434–5
  ministerial ethics 203
  national competition payments 116
  party discipline 364–5
  personal staff 218
  policy making 362–3
  political advertising 444
  public service code of conduct 251–2
  public service reform 259, 260, 262, 336
  public service structure 246, 247, 249

republic referendum 83–4
select committees, prevention of 170
Senate majority 174–5, 376
wedge politics 338
Work Choices 337, 355, 421
Howard, John 63, 191, 220, 299, 363
  Bennelong, loss of seat 337, 365
  leadership struggle 221, 335, 365
Hughes, W.M. 331, 357
human rights 117
hybrid groups 408

ideology 6–7, 22–3, 317–19
immigration 24–6
income tax 100, 121–2, 123, 161
independents 340–1, 372, 396
  Australian parliaments, in 396–401
  balance of power 376
  characteristics 398
  cost of campaign 398
  ideology 398–9
  organisation 400–1
  reasons to vote for 374–6, 396–7
Indigenous people 23–4
  Australian Labor Party, policy
  constitutional recognition 29–30
  discrimination 30
  land rights 120, 423
  native title 24, 30, 68, 423
  Northern Territory intervention 33
  policy 117
  Queensland government and 118–19
  reconciliation 31–3
  referendum (1967) 118, 119, 423
  representative institutions 30–1, 423
  rights 423
  social movements 422
  stolen generations, apology 31–2
  voting rights 283
infrastructure 129
insider groups 416–19
institutions 12–13, 18–26
inter-governmental agencies 115–16
inter-governmental agreements 109, 115
interest groups 372
  court action 412
  definition 406–7

democracy and 425–6
government, relationship with 412–15
importance 406
insider groups 416–19
lobbying 411–12
outsider groups 419
peak organisations 408–9
policy networks 420–2
social movements 372, 422–5
strategies 409–12
symbiotic relationship with government 412
types 407–9
international conventions 28
internationalisation 28, 64, 130
Internet 430, 447–50, 454, 455
Iraq, war in 336, 338, 355, 414
issue parties 394–6
Italy 184

Jervis Bay Territory *105*, 106
Jo Vallentine Peace Group 383
Joint Committee on Public Accounts and Audit 171
Joyce, Barnaby 155, 172, 380
judicature 13, 54–5

Katter, Bob 151, 341, 380, 399, 400
Keating government 68, 80, 82–3, 334–5
  Aboriginal land rights 423
  external affairs power 121
  federalism 121, 124–5
  grants 124–5
  industry advisory councils 422
  media ownership 434
  trade unions, incomes Accord 413
Keating, Paul 203, 214, 215, 335, 365
  personal style 220
  resignation 221
  treasurer, as 257–8
Kemp, Professor David 218
Kerr, Sir John 62, 333
Kirby, Justice 69
'kite flying' 209
Koowarta case 67, 117
Kyoto Treaty 29

Labor Party *see* Australian Labor Party
labourism 349
Lasswell, H.D. 3, 4
Latham, Mark 221, 299, 337, 424
leaders' forums 115
Lees, Meg 398
legislation 144, 145–6, 175
Legislative Assemblies 146

Legislative Councils 146
legislature 13, 137
liberal democracy 3, 10–12, 13, 41, 176
  Australian political institutions 13, 18–20, 28, 34
  British system of government 35
  bureaucracy 226
  constitutions 44
  elections 272–3
  German system of government 37
  Malaysian system of government 38
  principles of 70
  United States system of government 37
Liberal-National Country Party government 58
Liberal-National Party Coalition 193–4, 285, 334, 373, 379
Liberal National Party of Queensland 359, 378
Liberal Party 21, 93, 119, 120
  affirmative action 361
  candidate selection 360–1
  'catch-all' policies 363–4
  conservatism 358–9
  factions 359
  Federal Council 360, 362
  federalism 119, 120
  ideology 317, 357–9
  image 297, 298
  1909 platform 356
  1948 platform 357
  organisation 320, 359–60, *360*
  origins 331, 356–7
  policy differentiation 365–7
  policy making 361–4
  religious vote 301, 302
  State Council 359
  women 359, 361
Liberty and Democracy Party 392–3
Libya 137
lobbying 411–12
local government 106–9, 113
Locke, John 7–8, 35, 36
Lynch, Phillip 202

Mabo Case 24, 30, 68, 75, 412, 423
Mack, Ted 399
Main Committee 157
major parties 341, 346–67, 373–4
Malaysian system of government 12, 38, *39–40*, 325
  bureaucracy 236–7
  cabinet arrangements *183*
  constitutional arrangements 44, *46*

distribution of power *89*
e-government 453
electoral system *276*, *277*, *277*, *278*
executive government *181*
federalism 91
interest groups 409, 417
legislative process *142*
media ownership rules 437
political parties 317, 319, 321
prime minister 187
privatisation 230
senate 140
managerialism 240, 266
mandate 175, 176
Markus, Louise 389
Marx, Karl 7, 317
Marxism 415
mass-based parties 315
mass media 92–3, 431–7
  bias 433
  commercial media 438–9
  community-owned 438
  fairness 432–4
  foreign ownership 434–5
  independent 438
  news and newsworthiness 431–2
  ownership and control 434–7
  parliamentary press gallery 441–3
  pay television 441
  policy making 441
  politics in 437–41
  print media 437
  private ownership 432–3
  publicly owned 437–8
  talk-back radio 440–1
  televised election debates 440
Matters of Public Importance motions 154, 167
McMahon, William 333, 365
media *see* mass media
Melbourne City Council 107, 108
members of parliament, representative role 151–2
Menzies, Bob 357
Menzies government 117, 120, 121, 219, 332
  ministry 192, 202
Mersey Hospital, Commonwealth takeover 128
Michels, Robert 323
ministerial councils 115, 118
ministerial portfolios 185, 193–4
ministerial responsibility 200, 201–2, 203–7, 259, 260
ministerial statements 165
ministers
  accountability 18, 200, 207

advisers 200, 256–7
appointment 189
apprenticeships 195
assistant ministers 192
cabinet responsibilities 201–2, 207–12
careers 195–8
challenges 195–6
code of conduct 203
competition 195–6
duties 199–201
function 189
House of Representatives 193
independence from public service, constraints 257–8
individual responsibility 201–2, 203–7, 259, 260
integrity and ethics 202–3
management of Commonwealth departments 200–1
misleading parliament 205
office 198–9
outer ministry 192
resignation 205
salary 198–9
selection 193–5
Senate 193
Westminster conventions 201–2
women 195, *195*
minor parties 341, 372–3
  balance of power 376
  classification 373
  preferences from 374
  reasons to vote for 374–6
  representation in Australian parliaments 376–90
  Senate, election to *375*, 376
mission statements 262
mixed-member proportional (MMP) system 280, 285–6
mobile phones 430, 451–2
mobile workforce 130
monarchy 6, 19, 34, 35, 58, 60
money bills 162–3
Mornington Island 118–19
Motor Trades Association of Australia 409, 417
multicultural society 24
multi-member proportional representation (PR) system 279–80
multi-party systems 325–7
Murdoch, Rupert 433
Murphy, Shane 398
Murray-Darling River Basin 29, 126, 129
Muslims 24, 416

National Association of Forest Industries 424

National Audit Office 163
National Competition Policy payments 97, 124
National Constitutional Convention 49
National Council of Churches in Australia 419
National Country Party 334, 379
National Farmers' Federation 408, 409, 410, 421
national identity 93, 100
national interest 414
National Partnership payments 97, 116
National Party 21, 22, 93, 334, 335, 357
  Australian parliaments, in *377*
  federalism 119, 120
  ideology 378–9
  minor party, classification as 378
  organisation 379–80
  party discipline 380
National Rail Freight Corporation 124
Nationals, The *see* National Party
native title 24, 30, 68, 423
Nelson, Brendan 365, *367*
nepotism 232
New South Wales
  fixed four-year term parliaments 274
  Legislative Council 146, *147*
  Liberal Party 359
  local government 108, 109
  ministerial portfolios 95
  plural voting 281
  responsible government 346
  state government functions *96*
New South Wales v Commonwealth 66
New Zealand 138, 186
No Aircraft Noise party 372
no confidence, vote or motion 143, 167, 168
Non-Custodial Parents Party (Equal Parenting) 396
non-departmental organisations 265–6
Norfolk Island *105*
North Korea 137
Northern Territory 103–4, 106, 147, 148

Odgers' Australian Senate Practice 154
Oldfield, David 386
oligarchy 136
One Nation 385, 386
  see also Pauline Hanson's One Nation Party

one-party systems 324
open government 212, 265, 454
opinion polls 445–7
Opposition 154
outer ministry 192
outsider groups 419

Parkes, Sir Henry 48
parliament 136
  see also Australian parliament
  appointments 140–1
  Australian Constitution 55–8
  cabinet secrecy 145
  committees 143, 259
  debates 141–2, 144–5
  dissolution 141
  elections 140
  federal system 52
  fixed four-year terms 274
  functions 141–3
  legislative power 138, 141, 145–6
  naming 138
  origins 136–7
  power relationships within 144
  powers 56
  problems with parliamentary government 143–6
  seating 139
  sitting 139, *140*
  structure 138–41
  terms 139, *140*, 141, 274
parliament-executive relations 143
Parliament House 149–50
parliamentary majority government 143
parliamentary press gallery 441–3
parliamentary secretaries 192, 195
Parliamentary Standing Committee on Public Works 163
parliamentary system of government 137–8
partisanship 22–3, 295–6
party conferences 320
party discipline 151, 322–3
party endorsement 322
party loyalty 340
party systems 323–41
  see also Australian party system
  types 324–7
party whips 322–3
Patapan, Haig 70–1
patronage 214, 232–3, 237
Pauline Hanson's One Nation Party 296, 302, 304, 339, 340, 384–7
  ideology 386

organisation 386
party discipline 386–7
personality party, as 373
preferences 285, 336, 379
Peacock, Andrew 202, 221, 335, 365
peak organisations 408–9
performance indicators 261, 262–3
personality party 373
pluralism 414
policy
administration and 255–8
coordination and control 258–9
outside advice 256
planning, and 261–2
policy communities 421–2
policy making 22, 113–17, 321
policy networks 420–2
political advertising 68, 443–4
political communication 430–55
political culture 18, 34–8
political ideology *see* ideology
political parties 21–2, 119–21
see also major parties; minor parties; party systems
branches 320
candidate selection 315
classification 315–17
committees 169
definition 314
discipline 151, 322–3
ethnicity and 302
expulsion 322
factions 322
function 314–15
gender and 303–4
ideology 317–19
image 297–8
issue parties 394–6
nature 314–17
organisation 319–21
platforms 321
policy making 321
religion and 300–2
secessionist parties 373, 396
social class and 298–9
structure 320
political polling 445–7
political power 4, 6, 414, 415
political socialisation 315
political speak 367
politicians, public perception of 23
politics 2–4
instrumental perspective 20
power, and 4
pork-barrelling 124, 127
power, distribution of
House of Representatives and Senate 56–8

state and federal governments 53–4, 56, *89*
pragmatic electoralism 316, 319, 341, 362
precedents 65
preferential voting 284–5, 287, 304–7, 325, 341
premier 188
pressure group 406
prime minister 186–7
bureaucracy 217–18
chair of cabinet, as 214–16
desirable qualities 219–221
election dates 216–17
party reliance 213–14
patronage 214
personal staff 218–19
personal style 219
power 187, 212–19
public attention 213–14
private sector, regulation 228, 231
privatisation 96, 103, 130, 229–30, 246, 349
Privy Council 65
Productivity Commission 242, 262
promotional groups 407
property tax 107
proportional representation (PR) 285–6, 287, 307–9
protection 27, 346
Public Accounts and Audit Committee 163
public administration 226–31, 237–41
see also public service
public funding of election campaigns 292–3
public sector 227, 230, 241
public service 20, 226–66
see also Australian Public Service (APS); bureaucracy
accountability 231
administrative staff 237
definition 227
departments 100
downsizing 241
employment arrangements 233, 241
expansion 239–40
pressures for change 240–1
Public Works Committee 163
Punch, Gary 210

Queen 60, 63
Queensland government 118–19, 146, 148, 273–4
Queensland Legislative Council 146
question time 136, 142, 164–5, 207

questions without notice 164–5

Recfish Australia 418
red tape 230
redistributions 289–91
redundancies 247
referendums 46, 50, 72–8, 136
compulsory voting 76
constitutional recognition of Indigenous people 29–30, 72, 118–19, 423
party disagreements 77–8
problems 76–8
republic 9, 34, 76, 83–5
successful 72–5
unsuccessful 75–6
voters' attitudes 76–7, 93
Reforming the Australian Public Service (1983 White Paper) 260
Regional Partnerships Program 127
regionalisation 130
religion, party identification and 300–2
religious right 300–2
representative democracy 7–10, 70, 71, 136, 141
republic 28, 33–4, 60, 63, 130
constitutional change, and 80–5
definition 80
referendum 34, 76, 83–5
Republic Advisory Committee 1993 80–3
Reserve Bank 117
reserve powers 60–2
residual powers 53, 56, 89
responsible government 7–10, 18, 280
bureaucracy and 227
Commonwealth–state confrontation 118–19
colonies 327
Crown 52
federalism and 117–19
New South Wales 346
US congressional system 184–5
Westminster conventions 201–2
Richardson, Graham 205
Richardson v The Forestry Commission and others (1987–88) 68
Royal Commission into Australian Government Administration (RCAGA) 259, 260
Royal Commission into Public Administration (Coombs Report) 240

RSPCA 407, 419
rubber stamp 137, 172
Rudd government 2, 28, 31, 337
  climate change 29
  community cabinet meetings 189
  cooperation with states 128–30, 132
  expansion of Prime Minister's Department 218
  federal financial arrangements 97
  federalism 128–30
  FOI reforms 209
  lobbying by interest groups 411, 412
  ministerial code of conduct 203
  ministries *101*, 192, 193, 195
  National Partnerships payments 116
  public service structure 247, 249
  republic 85
  specific purpose payments 97
  stolen generations, apology for 32
Rudd, Kevin 85, 213, 214, 352, 353
  career path 196
rule of law 10

Sawer, Geoffrey 201
Scholes, Gordon 152
secessionist parties 373, 396
sectarianism 24
sectional groups 407–8
self-government 19
Senate 136, 138, 147
  amendment of bills 158
  balance of power 155, 173–4, 175, 327, 376
  committees 168, *169*, 170, 172, 207
  financial powers 161
  House of Representatives and, distribution of power 56–8
  house of review, as 171–6
  hung Senate 156
  majority 174
  ministers 155, 193
  minor parties 376
  money bills 162–3
  powers 56–8
  preferential voting 285
  president 154–5
  procedures 154–6
  proportional representation 173, 285–6, 287, 327
  review process 171–6
  role 112
  seating arrangements 155
  sitting days 151
  standing orders 155
  terms 155
  voting 154–5
Senate Estimates committees 160
Senate Scrutiny of Bills Committee 158
Senate Standing Committee on Regulations and Ordinances 158
senior executive service (SES) 249, 250
separation of powers 70
service delivery 129
Shorten, Bill 195
single-member majoritarian (alternative) system 278–9, 284–5
single-member majoritarian (second ballot) system 278
single-member plurality system 276–8, 283
Small Business Coalition (SBC) 410
Smith, Sir David 60
SMS text messaging 430, 451–2
Sneddon, Sir Billy 153, 365
social influences 23–6
social movements 372, 422–5
socialisation 349
socialism 348–9
Socialist Alliance 391–2
Socialist Equality Party 392
Solomon, David 70
South Australia v Commonwealth 66–7
special premiers' conferences 124
specific purpose payments 97, 107, 116, 124–5
spin doctors 200, 366
sport 92–3
Stanhope, Jon 377
State Banking Case 67
state governments
  boundaries 94
  complementary legislation 115
  debt 103
  federal system, role in 94–100, 113
  finance 96–100, 110
  friction between 110, 111
  functions 95–6, *96*
  jurisdiction 28
  ministerial portfolios (NSW) 95
  party system 93
  powers 53–4
  privatisation of functions 96
  public service systems 241
  revenue 96–100, *98*
  rivalry 93
  taxes 96–7
states 5–7
Stephen, Sir Ninian 216
student unions 2
supply 163
Swan, Wayne *367*
Switzerland, system of government 49
Sydney City Council 107

Tamar Valley Pulp mill 126–7
Tanner, Lindsay 444
tariffs 27, 28, 64, 356, 414
Tasmania 147
Tasmanian Dams Case 67, 68, 117
Tasmanian Greens 383
tax revenue 100, *102*, 107, 123
  see also income tax
technological change 130
technology, political communication 447–52
territories 103–6, 241
Tiffin, Rodney 447
Toohey, Justice 79
town planning 107
trade unions 253–4, 346, 349, 350–1, 415
Treasury 254–5
treaties 28
Turnbull, Malcolm 81, 196, 197, 317, 365
2020 Summit 132
two-party systems 324–5
  advantages 337–8
  development in Australia 329–32, 346
  disadvantages 338–9

umbrella organisations 408
unicameral legislatures 138
Uniform Tax Case 1942 66–7, 96
Uniform Tax Case 1957 67, 121
unions *see* trade unions
United Australia Party 332, 357
United States, system of government 12, 36–7, *39*–40, 49, 138
  bureaucracy 234–5
  cabinet arrangements *183*
  congressional standing committees 143
  constitutional arrangements 44, 45, *46*, 52
  distribution of power *89*
  e-government 453
  electoral systems 276, *276*, 278, *278*

executive government *181*
federalism 90
fixed terms 141
immigration 24
interest groups 409, 417–18
legislative process *142*
lobbying 412
local government 106
media ownership rules 436
political parties 317, 318, 320
privatisation 229
responsible government 184–5
separation of powers 144, 185
Supreme Court 69
Unity Party 302
urban development 114, 116

vertical fiscal imbalance 113, 121
Victoria 294, 359, *360*
vote counting 283–6, 304–9
vote of no confidence 143
voting
see also Australian electoral system; electoral systems
age as influencing factor 296–7, *297*
alternative vote 304–7
analysing voter preferences 294–6
aspirational voter 299
'battler' vote 297, 298, 299, 355
behaviour 294–304
compulsory voting 76, 287–9
electronic voting 293–4
enrolment, period for 289
ethnicity as influencing factor 302
first past the post 283, 304, 325
free vote 356
gender as influencing factor 303–4
influences 295, 296–304

methods 304–9
non-party vote 356
partisanship, significance of 295–6
preferential voting 284–5, 304–7, 325, 341
proportional representation (PR) 285–6, 307–9
region as influencing factor 300, *300*
religion as influencing factor 300–2
second ballot 284
secret ballot 282
simple majority voting 283, 304
single transferable vote (STV) 279
social class as influencing factor 298–9
systems 272–3

websites 449–50, 452–3, 455
wedge politics 338
West, Stewart 211
Western Australia 147, 148
Westminster system 11–12, 19, 45, 52, 171
bureaucracy 237
cabinet 176, 182–4, 201–2, 212
conventions 58, 62
relationships 185–6
responsible government 227, 256
Wet Tropics Management Authority 423
'wets' 359, 364
Wettenhall, Roger 243, 244
whistleblowers 252
White Australia policy 24, 48
White Paper 165
Whitlam, Gough 219, 364
Whitlam government 30, 57, 75, 78–9, 333

Aboriginal rights 423
caucus committees 211
centralisation by 122–3
constitutional amendment 123
dismissal 22, 62, 163, 174, 333
federalism and 119–20, 121
finance power, use of 117
Loans Affair 188
mandate 353
ministry 192
offshore resources and mining 119–20
personal staff 218
policy making 354
prime ministerial power 212, 123
public service expansion 240, 245, 247
Queensland government and, tension between 111
redistributions 291
Wik Case 24, 30, 68, 423
Windsor, Tony 400–1
women
Australian Democrats, in 382
Australian Labor Party, in 351
Liberal Party, in 359, 361
Office for Women 422
parliament, in 148, *148*, 195, *195*
public service, in 253
voting rights 282, *282*
What Women Want party 395
Work Choices 28, 68–9, 126, 337, 355
advertising 444
support for 421
working families 365
World Heritage Properties Conservation Act 1983 68

Xenophon, Nick 398, 423